Smartphone Addiction, Phone Snubbing, and Effects on Interpersonal Relationships and Mental Health

Harish Chandra Chandan
Independent Researcher, USA

IGI Global
Scientific Publishing
Publishing Tomorrow's Research Today

Vice President of Editorial Melissa Wagner
Managing Editor of Acquisitions Mikaela Felty
Managing Editor of Book Development Jocelynn Hessler
Production Manager Mike Brehm
Cover Design Phillip Shickler

Published in the United States of America by
IGI Global Scientific Publishing
701 East Chocolate Avenue
Hershey, PA, 17033, USA
Tel: 717-533-8845
Fax: 717-533-8661
Website: https://www.igi-global.com E-mail: cust@igi-global.com

Library of Congress Cataloging-in-Publication Data

Names: Chandan, Harish C., 1947- editor
Title: Smartphone addiction, phone snubbing, and effects on interpersonal relationships and mental health / edited by Harish Chandan.
Description: Hershey, PA : IGI Global Scientific Publishing, [2025] | Includes bibliographical references and index. | Summary: "This book aims to raise awareness of the smart phone addiction and phone snubbing which take a toll on the inter-personal relationships and mental health"-- Provided by publisher.
Identifiers: LCCN 2024053549 (print) | LCCN 2024053550 (ebook) | ISBN 9798369388044 hardcover | ISBN 9798369388051 paperback | ISBN 9798369388068 ebook
Subjects: LCSH: Cell phones--Psychological aspects | Internet addiction | Cell phones--Social aspects | Internet addiction--Social aspects
Classification: LCC RC569.5.I54 S63 2025 (print) | LCC RC569.5.I54 (ebook) | DDC 616.85/84--dc23/eng/20250409
LC record available at https://lccn.loc.gov/2024053549
LC ebook record available at https://lccn.loc.gov/2024053550

British Cataloguing in Publication Data
A Cataloguing in Publication record for this book is available from the British Library.

Table of Contents

Detailed Table of Contents

Mobile addiction is a highly significant issue, especially among adolescents, that affects mental health and academic performance badly. This is a narrative review based on the association of mobile addiction, mental health, and academic outcomes across the Indian, Asia, and international settings. Relevant, peer-reviewed articles were fetched and perused via Google Scholar. It indicates that mobile addiction has a positive link with anxiety, depression, and decline in terms of academic performance. Regional factors, like the extent to which parents control and cultural considerations, are at play. Long-term effects and targeted interventions should remain the focus of future research.

The use of media devices has grown over the years, and smartphones are currently the most used media device globally. The smartphone is a practical device with its several advantages. Smartphone addiction is becoming a bigger problem, particularly among youngsters. The mental and social effects of smartphone addiction on youngster's mental health are covered in this chapter. With smartphones becoming more and more important, there is a greater chance of addiction, which can have serious psychological consequences. Long-term smartphone use has been shown to negative effects on youngster's mental health like stress, anxiety, depression, attention span, etc. In conclusion, youngster's mental health is seriously at risk from excessive use of smartphone addiction. It is essential to treat the psychological symptoms and indicators of addiction, such as phubbing, failing relationships, and mental health issues. To minimize the effects and encourage youngsters to adopt better digital habits, encouraging balanced smartphone use, early understanding is essential.

Smartphone addiction has become a significant concern in modern society, particularly due to its profound effects on mental health. Moreover, smartphone addiction can adversely affect attention and focus. The frequent switching between tasks and the rapid consumption of information can impair an individual's ability to concentrate for extended periods. This fragmentation of attention is not only detrimental to productivity but also affects cognitive development and memory retention. Research has shown that the constant need to check smartphones can lead to a reduced capacity for deep, reflective thinking and problem-solving skills. In summary, the rise of smartphone addiction presents a growing concern for mental health, driven by constant connectivity, the fear of missing out, and the impact on attention, sleep, asocial relationships. As society continues to navigate the digital age, it is crucial to develop and implement strategies to manage smartphone use effectively, ensuring that technology enhances rather than detracts from overall well-being.

This chapter examines the psychological, behavioural, and social consequences of smartphone addiction, phone snubbing, and social media addiction. It explores the machinations that drive addiction, such as variable reinforcement schedules and reward systems, and how they affect our interpersonal relationships and mental health. The chapter also identifies best practices in current research and case studies, as well as trends that suggest effective interventions to help guide psychologists and mental health professionals when dealing with such issues. The chapter underscores the importance of interdisciplinary efforts in order to address the issues of digital addiction successfully. This chapter shares the perspectives from the multi-dimensional addiction behavior scale (MABS), which includes psychological, biological, social and environmental factors, cognitive and behavioral patterns, motivation, and readiness for change.

Social media addiction is a condition that continues to demand immediate attention, interworking with various social and cultural factors. With design decisions such as infinite scrolling and algorithmic content that keep users engaged longer, the influence of tech companies cannot be understated. Social norms, the desire to be continually connected with their cohort, certainly push people into compulsive behaviors. There's a distinction across generations, especially with respect to Millennials and Gen Z, who are digital natives and know of digital media through the scope of communication and socialization. That's why one should take the multi-pronged approach involving school-based education about digital literacy to enhance awareness toward addiction, along with campaigning that will spread awareness in people about possible risks of addiction and parental monitoring that inspires better digital habits in children. These would give the society an opportunity to strike a symbiotic relation with technology and combat the social media addiction.

The chapter explores the rising phenomenon of smartphone and social media addiction, emphasizing its psychological, social, and cultural impacts. As smartphones and social media become integral to daily life, excessive use has raised concerns about mental health, including anxiety, depression, and social isolation. The chapter examines key concepts such as "phubbing," the neuroscientific basis of addiction, and diagnostic criteria, highlighting the roles of brain regions like the prefrontal cortex and reward mechanisms involving dopamine. Interventions such as cognitive-behavioral therapy (CBT), mindfulness practices, and digital detox programs are discussed, alongside the need for policy measures to promote digital well-being. Integrating these perspectives, this chapter aims to provide a comprehensive understanding of smartphone and social media addiction and its implications for individual and societal well-being. The chapter attempts to give a thorough grasp of smartphone and social media addiction and its effects on both individual and societal well-being by incorporating these viewpoints.

Preface

Smartphones have transformed how people communicate and interact socially. They have become an all-in-one device that allows one to connect with people through text or talk or social media. Modern smartphone can be used as portable media player, digital/video camera, navigation unit, high-resolution touch screen, web browsers and high-speed data access via Wi-Fi and mobile broadband. Smartphones have made the communication easier but have also created some new challenges in individual behavior and social interactions. (Meister & Dael, 2024). Smart phone addiction is the obsessive and compulsive use of a mobile phone (Kwon et al., 2013).

Panova and Carbonell (2018) suggest the smartphone behaviors observed in the literature could be better labeled as problematic or maladaptive smartphone use and their consequences do not meet the severity levels of those caused by addiction. Whether it is maladaptive use of smartphone or it is a smartphone addiction, smartphones have become a double-edged sword. They allow access to boundless information at our fingertips while silently creating an overdependence. Addiction to smartphones is highly likely to cause physical and psychosocial problems as well as Internet addiction. Smartphone addiction is conceptualized as a behavioral addiction. It has an impact on physical, mental, and neurological health outcomes (Ratan et al., 2021). The mental health outcomes include anxiety and depression. Cravings, mood tolerance, salience and withdrawal, modification, conflict and relapse have been associated with excessive smartphone use. The smart phone addiction scale measures the level of addiction. The most-cited measure of problematic smartphone use is the Smartphone Addiction Scale (SAS) (Kwon et al., 2013) along with its short version (SAS-SV) (Kwon, Kim, Cho, & Yang, 2013).

There are more mobile devices than the number of people on this planet. As of 2024, there are over 6.8 billion smartphone users in the world. The number of mobile devices is expected to reach 18.22 billion by 2025. Research suggests that about 6.3% of the people may have a smart phone addiction. (World Economic Forum, 2023). The level of addiction varies by age, gender, country, socioeconomic status and family size. Younger people are more likely to be addicted to their smartphone.

About 50-57% of the Americans are addicted to their smartphones. About 50% of Americans spend 5-6 hours on their smartphone every day. The average American checks their smartphone 144 times per day. About 71% of people spend more time on their phone than with their romantic partner. Men maybe more likely addicted than women. People in large families may be more addicted to their smartphone than people in small families. A meta-analysis of 24 countries concluded that the smartphone addiction is increasing across the world. The analysis covered the years 2014-2020, had 83 samples and 33,831 participants. China and Saudi Arabia had the highest rates while Germany and France had the lowest (Olson et al., 2022).

The changes in individual behavior include spending too much time on the phone in social situations that results in less social interaction. It can lead to smart phone addiction. Research studies consistently link excessive smart phone use to reduced human social interaction, stress, anxiety, sleep deficit, loneliness, insecurity, reduced cognition, increased distraction and reduced concentration, decreased attention-span, aggravated attention deficit disorder, poor sleep quality, impaired personal relationships and poor performance in school or work settings. Excessive and obsessive smart phone use can erode our mental health, dull our professional edge, and disrupt interpersonal relationships (Meister & Dael, 2024).

Smart phone addiction is also called "nomophobia" or the "fear of no mobile phone". About 59% of the 2337 university students who participated in a study, exhibited smart phone addiction. Females who were divorced felt persistent fatigue. They felt that their mental abilities and sleep have been negatively affected by the use of smart phones (Abuhamdah & Naser, 2023).

People carry their smartphone with them where ever they go. When they are interacting with other people and are having conversations with other people, their smartphone is with them. They have a choice to engage in conversation with other people and ignore the phone. However, as the push notifications from various Apps come through, the smart phone owner tends to look at their phone screen so that they don't miss out on something. If one keeps looking at their smart phone screen, instead of looking at the person they are talking to, it is perceived as snubbing by the person who is trying to have a conversation. This is called phone snubbing or phubbing where individuals prioritize smartphones over in-person interactions and snub someone in a social setting by looking at one's phone instead of paying attention to the other person (Sbarra, et.al.,2018).

PHUBBING/PHONE SNUBBING

Phubbing refers to an individual's obsessive use of the smartphone instead of having interpersonal conversations with other individuals in a social setting. Phubbing has become normative in modern-day communication. Phubbing has roots in many intrapersonal and interpersonal issues. Phubbing is positively linked to social media addiction. There is empirical evidence that people phub more frequently those who are closely related to them than those less close to them. (Al-Saggaff & O'Donnell, 2019; (Chotpitayasunondh & Douglas, 2018; Garrido, 2021).

Phubbing is the act of snubbing someone in a social setting by paying attention to one's phone instead of talking to the person next to them. Phubbing or phone snubbing is a type of face-to-face social interaction where one person uses mobile phone instead of interacting with the person they are with. The person engaged in phubbing ignore the presence of others and focus on their mobile phone. Phubbing can lead to marital dissatisfaction, feelings of distrust and ostracism. Those who fub a lot are more likely to be phubbed themselves.

Phubbing has become commonplace. people often ignore others with whom they are physically interacting in order to use their smartphone instead. (Chotpitayasunondh & Douglas, 2018). A recent study reported that 90% of respondents used their smartphones during their most recent social activity, and also perceived that 86% of the others involved in the social interaction did the same (Ranie & Zickuhr, 2015). In another study, nearly half of adult respondents reported being phubbed by their romantic partner (Roberts & David, 2016). There are negative effects of phubbing. The act of using a mobile phone to send messages during a face-to-face conversation impacts the impression someone forms of the phone user and the perceived quality of the interaction itself.

Phubbing is the result of smart phone addiction or technology addiction. The technology addictions including smartphone, SMS and social media, boredom, fear of missing out, and lack of self-control lead to phubbing behavior. Also, the tendency to multitask and the need for immediate gratification may explain why people engage with their smartphone during face-to-face conversation with others.

The psychological factors contributing to phubbibg behavior include a lack of mindfulness, addiction to digital devices and a fear of missing out on online interactions. Phubbing affects mental health and relationships. Phubbing behavior leads to interacting with a cell phone instead of a person who is with you. It triggers feelings of exclusion and diminished self-worth. It causes interpersonal strain on relationships. In a social setting, interacting with your cell phone instead of interacting with people around you is perceived as being rude (Chotpitayasunondh & Douglas, 2016).

Phubbing is transforming the norms of human communication. Phubbing behavior has detrimental impacts on people. Phubbing heightened feelings of jealousy between romantic partners, weakened the bond between them, lowered their relationship satisfaction and increased their rates of depression. Phubbing was perceived as rude, offensive, and a violation of social norms. It undermined perceptions of empathetic concern, closeness, interpersonal trust, and conversation quality (Al-Saggaff & O'Donnell, 2019). Phubbing can trigger negative mood, feelings of ostracism, and threatens inter-personal trust (Knausenberger, Giesen-Leuchter, & Echterhoff, 2022).

Phubbing has detrimental effects on feelings of well-being, cognitive processing and relationships. Increased phone use during inter-personal interaction results in lower feelings of social connection, engagement and enjoyment. There is a blind spot to phubbing. People are aware of the harmful effects of someone else's phubbing behavior but fail to recognize the negative consequences of their own phubbing. People attribute their own phone use to positive motives and overestimate their ability to multitask compared to others, (Barrick, Barasch, & Tamir, 2022).

Women reported higher levels of phubbing behavior, emotional reactivity, and fusion with others. We conclude that fear of missing out may serve as a catalyst, triggering anxiety in individuals, which in turn drives them to adopt phubbing as a coping mechanism. Moreover, individuals with lower levels of differentiation of self appear to be at increased risk of engaging in phubbing behaviors through the mediation of fear of missing out (Peleg & Boniel-Nissim, 2024). Increased phubbing significantly and negatively affected perceived communication quality and relationship satisfaction. These effects were mediated by reduced feelings of belongingness and both positive and negative affect (Garrido, Issa, Esteban, & Delgado, 2021).

People who use their phones in social situations socialize significantly less compared to those who did not have access to their phones. People may be acting against their own best interest when they use phones in social situations. Nearly 90% of smartphone owners report having used their phones while they are physically with someone. The use of a smartphone while you are with someone can lead to phone snubbing or phubbing. Phone snubbing or Phubbing occurs when individuals pay more attention to their phones than to the people they are with. This behavior can create feelings of neglect and diminish the quality of in-person interactions. Phubbing leads to decreased face-to-face interaction. Phone Snubbing or Phubbing is commonplace and often unintentional. However, it negatively affects the social relationships and impacts mental health. Individuals in the 18-30 age range are the ones most affected in their social interactions because they use the smartphones as their main form of communication. of the reliance on smartphones (Dwyer, Zhuo, & Dunn, 2023).

INDIVIDUAL AND SOCIAL IMPLICATIONS OF SMARTPHONE ADDICTION

Smartphone addiction is a physical health and mental health issue affecting millions of users worldwide. Smartphone addiction can cause increased anxiety levels, poor sleep quality, isolation from social interactions, depression and decreased performance at school or work. Smartphone addiction can adversely affect relationships with family, friends, and partners.

Smartphone addiction can interfere with social interactions and lead to anxiety and depression. The push notifications on the phone can lead to people checking constantly one's phone even when they are having conversations with other people. When this happens in the presence of others, it can make people feel ignored and neglected. It can cause tension and conflict and can lead to decrease in closeness and intimacy in the relationships. Phubbing influences perceived interaction quality and relationship satisfaction. it threatens people's fundamental needs to belong, have control, have high self-esteem and experience meaningful existence.

Peleg and Boniel-Nissim (2024) investigated familial, interpersonal, and personal factors that could potentially contribute to the escalation of phubbing behaviors. The fear of missing out mediated the relationship between three dimensions of differentiation of self—emotional reactivity, emotional cutoff, and fusion with others and phubbing behavior. They hypothesized that differentiation of self would be associated with phubbing through the mediation of fear of missing out, romantic relationship satisfaction, and loneliness in intimate relationships. They concluded that the fear of missing out may serve as a catalyst and triggers anxiety in individuals. They use phubbing as a coping mechanism. Individuals with lower levels of differentiation of self, appeared to be at increased risk of engaging in phubbing behaviors through the mediation of fear of missing out.

The most important antecedent of the phubbing behavior is smart phone addiction (Chotpitayasunondh & Douglas, 2018; Chi, Tang, & Tang, 2024). Smartphone addiction is a kind of social media, internet and technology addiction. The Internet addiction, fear of missing out, and lack of self-control have been found to predict smartphone addiction, which in turn predicts phubbing behavior. Phubbing can create negative, resentful reactions such that people perceive their interaction to be of poorer quality (Ranie & Zickuhr, 2015), are less satisfied with their interpersonal interactions (Abeele, Antheunis, & Schouten, 2016; Abeele, Hendrickson, Pollmann, & Ling, 2019).

People form and maintain close social relationships by social interaction and indulging in self-disclosure and responsiveness which promotes trust, co-operation, intimacy, attachment bonds and close relationships. The use of Smartphones in the presence of others reduces social interactions between couples and family members and comes in the way of developing close relationships (Baym, 2015)

ORGANIZATION OF THE BOOK

Chapter 1: The Effect of Smartphone Addiction and Phubbing on Relationship Quality and Mental Health: Mixed-Methods Research

This chapter deals with the effects of "phubbing" or phone snubbing and smartphone addiction on relationship satisfaction and psychological well-being. The findings from this mixed methods research suggest that the excessive smartphone use and phubbing result in relationship dissatisfaction and increased conflict with partners, family, and friends. This research shows how smartphone overuse strained relationships through a positive relationship between the engagement level and anxiety, depression, and stress levels-increasing anxiety, depression, and stress.

Chapter 2: Mental Health and Smartphone Addiction: Understanding the Digital Impact on Well-Being

The second chapter deals with how the smartphone addiction affects mental health. It deals with how smartphone addiction fuels anxiety, depression, sleep disorders, and social isolation. It also explores how vulnerable populations, particularly adolescents and young adults, are disproportionately affected by this addiction. Solutions such as digital detox, mindfulness interventions, and cognitive-behavioral therapy are discussed to help individuals regain control of their smartphone habits and promote healthier relationships with technology.

Chapter 3: The Impact of Mobile Addiction on Mental Health and Academic Performance of School Going Adolescents: A Narrative Review

The third chapter deals with how the mobile phone addiction affects the mental health and academic performance among adolescents. This is a narrative review based on the association of mobile addiction, mental health, and academic outcomes across the Indian, Asia, and international settings. A review of the literature indicates that mobile addiction has a positive link with anxiety, depression, and decline in terms of academic performance. The extent to which parents control the children, cultural factors and cultural considerations influence the outcomes.

Chapter 4: Smartphone Addiction in Youngsters and Their Mental Health

The fourth chapter deals with how smartphone addiction in youngsters has negative effects on their mental health. It increases stress, anxiety, depression, and reduces the attention span. It is essential to treat the psychological symptoms and indicators of addiction, such as phubbing, failing relationships, and mental health issue. Youngsters should be encouraged to reduce their smartphone use.

Chapter 5: Mental Health Issues Due to Smart Phone Addiction

The fifth chapter deals with Mental Health Issues due to Smart Phone Addiction. Smartphone addiction can adversely affect attention and focus. The frequent switching between tasks and the rapid consumption of information can impair an individual's ability to concentrate for extended periods. This fragmentation of attention is not only detrimental to productivity but also affects cognitive development and memory retention. Research has shown that the constant need to check smartphones can lead to a reduced capacity for deep, reflective thinking and problem-solving skills. The smartphone addiction presents a growing concern for mental health, driven by constant connectivity, the fear of missing out, and the impact on attention, sleep, asocial relationships.

Chapter 6: Smartphone Addiction and Social Media Addiction: Prospectives From the Multi-Dimensional Addiction Behavior Scale (MABS)

This chapter shares the perspectives from the Multi-Dimensional Addiction Behavior Scale (MABS), which includes Psychological, Biological, Social and Environmental Factors, Cognitive and Behavioral Patterns, Motivation and Readiness for Change. It deals with psychological, behavioral, and social consequences of smartphone addiction, phone snubbing and social media addiction. This chapter explores the factors that drive addiction, such as variable reinforcement schedules and reward systems, and how they affect our interpersonal relationships and mental health. This chapter also identifies best practices in current research and case studies, as well as trends that suggest effective interventions to help guide psychologists and mental health professionals when dealing with such issues. The chapter underscores the importance of interdisciplinary efforts in order to address the issues of digital addiction successfully.

Chapter 7: The Digital Dilemma: Navigating Smartphone and Social Media Addiction

This chapter deals with the Digital Dilemma of navigating smartphone and social media addiction. Social media addiction is a condition that continues to demand immediate attention, interworking with various social and cultural factors. With design decisions such as infinite scrolling and algorithmic content that keep users engaged longer, the influence of tech companies cannot be understated. Social norms, the desire to be continually connected with their cohort, certainly push people into compulsive behaviors. There's a distinction across generations, especially with respect to Millennials and Gen Z, who are digital natives and know of digital media through the scope of communication and socialization. That's why one should take the multi-pronged approach involving school-based education about digital literacy to enhance awareness toward addiction, along with campaigning that will spread awareness in people about possible risks of addiction and parental monitoring that inspires better digital habits in children. These would give the society an opportunity to strike a symbiotic relation with technology and combat the social media addiction.

Chapter 8: Clicks and Cravings: The Psychology of Smartphone and Social Media Addiction

This chapter deals with the psychology of smartphone and social Media addiction. This Chapter explores the rising phenomenon of smartphone and social media addiction, emphasizing its psychological, social, and cultural impacts. As smartphones and social media become integral to daily life, excessive use has raised concerns about mental health, including anxiety, depression, and social isolation. This chapter examines key concepts such as "phubbing," the neuroscientific basis of addiction, and diagnostic criteria, highlighting the roles of brain regions like the prefrontal cortex and reward mechanisms involving dopamine. Interventions such as cognitive-behavioral therapy (CBT), mindfulness practices, and digital detox programs are discussed, alongside the need for policy measures to promote digital well-being. Integrating these perspectives, this chapter aims to provide a comprehensive understanding of smartphone and social media addiction and its implications for individual and societal well-being. Chapter attempts to give a thorough grasp of smartphone and social media addiction and its effects on both individual and societal well-being by incorporating these viewpoints.

Chapter 9: The Influence of Personality Traits on Smartphone Addiction, Phubbing, and Mental Well-Being

This chapter deals with the influence of personality traits on smartphone addiction, phubbing, and mental well-being. This chapter delves into the intricate relationship between phubbing, smartphone addiction, and social media use, emphasizing how personality traits mediate their impact on psychological well-being. Phubbing, a blend of "phone" and "snubbing," involves ignoring others in favor of mobile phone engagement and has been associated with feelings of loneliness, depression, and social exclusion. Additionally, the chapter examines how the Big Five personality traits (Extraversion, Agreeableness, Conscientiousness, Neuroticism, and Openness) influence smartphone addiction and phubbing behaviors. Individuals with high levels of Fear of Missing Out (FoMO) tend to display compulsive phone use, reinforcing these negative social behaviors. The chapter concludes by underscoring the psychological consequences of these behaviors, including reduced life satisfaction and heightened stress.

Chapter 10: Personality Traits and Smartphone Addiction: An Evolving Addictive Trend

This chapter deals with Personality Traits and Smartphone Addiction. The personality traits contribute to different forms of addiction. Addictive behaviors such as compulsion to excessively use the smartphone can be equally detrimental to human health just like any form of drug addiction. Effects of smartphone addiction can either be short term or long term based on the extent of addiction. At a personal level, the individual could experience both physical and psychological health problems ranging from mild pain, visual disturbances to severe pain, suicidal ideations and actual suicide. Interpersonally, reduced human performance and poor social network could occur. The trait theories including HEXACO and Five Factor personality trait models together with their facets will be explored to appreciate personality traits commonly associated with smartphone addiction. This chapter also discusses an approach to smartphone addiction diagnosis and management.

Chapter 11: A Study on the Relationship Between Personality Traits and Levels of Smartphone Addiction to Gain Insights into Sales Executives Behavioral Patterns

This chapter deals with the relationship between five personality traits and levels of smartphone addiction to gain insights into the behavior patterns of sales executives. The five personality traits include extraversion, agreeableness, conscientiousness, openness, and neuroticism. Data were collected from 286 sales executives using a structured questionnaire, focusing on personality traits and smartphone addiction levels. Pearson correlation and multiple regression analyses revealed that Agreeableness is the strongest predictor of smartphone addiction, suggesting that individuals who are more cooperative and empathetic are more likely to develop addictive smartphone behaviors. Conscientiousness showed a marginally significant negative association, indicating that individuals with higher self-discipline and responsibility are less prone to smartphone addiction. Extraversion, Openness, and Neuroticism did not show statistically significant relationships. These insights highlight the importance of integrating psychological factors into workplace policies to address smartphone addiction effectively.

Chapter 12: Screen to Soul: Navigating Intimacy in the Age of Digital Communication

This chapter deals with navigating Intimacy in today's digital age. The chapter examines how interpersonal relationships are shaped in the contemporary day by digital communication. With a focus on the effects on emotional closeness, relationship satisfaction, and mental health, it investigates the transition from in-person to virtual interactions. To comprehend their impact on relationships, important phenomena like as phubbing, digital intimacy, and constant partial attention are examined. The chapter covers the drawbacks, including growing loneliness, as well as the benefits, like improved social support systems. It also emphasizes the significance of cutting-edge technology like virtual reality and provides tips for striking a balance between online and offline connections. In order to promote better, more meaningful relationships in the digital age, suggestions for digital literacy and mindful technology use are given.

Chapter 13: Partner Phubbing and Relationship Satisfaction Among Romantic Partners

This chapter deals with partner Phubbing and relationship satisfaction among romantic partners. Phubbing involves neglecting someone by checking or using a smartphone during a face-to-face conversation. Phubbing is also linked to mobile addiction and feelings of deprivation when separated from one's phone. Researchers also suggest that individuals often use their phones as a coping mechanism for loneliness, anxiety, and worry. Thus, phubbing is not merely a habit; it also serves as a form of avoidance behavior. A review of prior studies indicates that romantic relationship satisfaction is closely linked to individual emotions and behaviors. Factors such as relationship commitment, perceived rewards, and the costs of investment are all significantly associated with overall satisfaction in the relationship. To foster healthier, more fulfilling relationships, it is crucial for partners to prioritize face-to-face engagement and be mindful of their phone usage in social settings. Addressing and mitigating phubbing behaviour can help strengthen emotional bonds, enhance relational satisfaction, and ultimately promote well-being for both partners.

Chapter 14: Breaking Free: Strategies for Overcoming Smartphone Addiction

This chapter explores the strategies for overcoming smartphone addiction. Through a comprehensive review of literature, the chapter investigates behavioral, technological, and societal approaches, such as self-monitoring, cognitive-behavioral therapy (CBT), and digital detox programs. Case studies and real-world examples provide insight into the practical applications of these strategies in various settings, including educational institutions and workplaces. Additionally, the chapter identifies gaps in existing research and offers recommendations for future studies and policy initiatives. By synthesizing current knowledge on smartphone addiction, the chapter offers valuable guidance for individuals, educators, and policymakers seeking to address this pervasive global issue.

Chapter 15: The Effect of Phubbing in the College Classroom

Chapter 15 deals with the effect of phubbing in the college classroom. When students use smart phones in the college classroom, it is often to their detriment as well as to the consternation of their instructors. “Phubbing,” a portmanteau of “phone snubbing,” is the term used when a person ignores activity around them while focusing intently on their phone. This behavior, which can be described as an addiction, can result in decreased learning capabilities, physical and mental health, personal relationship quality, and data security. Existing studies about phone use in the traditional classroom in addition to a new study of online live college seminars provide some insight into this issue. Fortunately, both administrative and instructor-based solutions can be found in thoughtful policy development, some changes in classroom management, and educating students, as informed by the literature and the conclusions based on this study.

Chapter 16: The Deterioration and Transformation of Personal Connection in the Digital Era: An Empirical Investigation of Social Relationships in the Technological Age

This chapter deals with the deterioration and transformation of personal connection in today's digital age. This study analyses the evolution of interpersonal relationships via digital communication platforms, focusing on the effects of social media, virtual communities, and messaging programs on emotional closeness, social intimacy, and human contact. Utilizing both quantitative and qualitative investigations. this research examines how the convenience of digital communication simultaneously promotes and weakens personal connections, although digital platforms offer unparalleled prospects for global communication, they may concurrently reduce the quality of in-person relationships and the depth of emotional engagement. This paper examines the paradox of connection in the digital era by reviewing current literature and empirical investigations. It investigates ways to cultivate meaningful personal interactions in a technology-dominated context.

CONCLUSION

Smartphones offer the opportunity to virtually socialize. Individuals in the 18-30 age range use their smartphones for social interactions. They use their smartphones for 3-5 hours a day to socialize on Instagram and Facebook (Abeele, 2016, 2019). However, virtual socialization is not the same as interacting with people. Humans are social beings and they are biologically wired to socially connect with others through self-disclosure and responsiveness. Before the technology revolution, humans relied on close relationships and face-to-face interactions with small networks of family and friends for survival. These close relationships were based on trust and co-operation that is created when people share personal information about themselves and are responsive to others. Smartphone use has reduced human social interactions.

The majority of research in the field agrees that smartphones are addictive. Phubbing behavior is a kind of technology and social media addiction. The psychosocial factors that lead to problematic use of technology including phubbing needs to be understood. Phubbing negatively affects inter-personal relationships and individual mental health. Strategies to overcome smart phone addiction need to be developed. One needs to understand the potential risk factors for pathological smartphone use. The connections between social media addiction, fear of missing out, personality traits, and phubbing behaviors for various generations need to be understood.

REFERENCES

Abeele, M. M. P. V., Antheunis, M., & Schouten, A. (2016). The effect of mobile messaging during a conversation on impression formation and interaction quality. *Computers in Human Behavior*, 62, 562–569. DOI: 10.1016/j.chb.2016.04.005

Abeele, M. P. V., Hendrickson, A. T., Pollmann, M. H., & Ling, R. (2019). Phubbing behavior in conversations and its relation to perceived conversation intimacy and distraction: An exploratory observation study. Computers in Human Behavior, 100, 35-47. DOI: 10.1002/hbe2.137

Abuhamdah, S. A., & Naser, A. Y. (2023). Smart phone addiction and its mental health risks among university students in Jordan: A cross-sectional study. *BMC Psychiatry*, 23(1), 812. DOI: 10.1186/s12888-023-05322-6 PMID: 37936164

Barrick, E. M., Barasch, A., & Tamir, D. I. (2022). The unexpected social consequences of diverting attention to our phones. Journal of Experimental Social Psychology, 101.

Chi, L. C., Tang, T. C., & Tang, E. (2022). The phubbing phenomenon: A cross-sectional study on the relationships among social media addiction, fear of missing out, personality traits, and phubbing behavior. *Current Psychology (New Brunswick, N.J.)*, 41(2), 1112–1123. DOI: 10.1007/s12144-021-02468-y

Chotpitayasunondh, Y., & Douglas, K. (2018). The Effects of Phubbing on Social Interaction. J. of Applied Social Psychology, 48(6), 304-316.

Dwyer, R.J., Zhuo, A.X., & Dunn, E.W. (2023). Why do People Turn to Smartphones during Social Interactions. J. of Experimental Social Psychology, 109. DOI: 10.1016/j.jesp.2023.104506

Garrido, E. C., Issa, T., Esteban, P. G., & Delgado, S. C. (2021). A Descriptive Literature Review of Phubbing Behaviors. DOI: 10.1016/j.heliyon.2021.e07037

Gladden, D. (2018). The Effects of Smartphones on Social Lives: How They Affect Our Social Interactions and Attitudes. OTS Master's Level Projects & Papers. 586. https://digitalcommons.odu.edu/ots_masters_projects/586

Knausenberger, J., Giesen-Leuchter, A., & Echterhoff, G. (2022). *Feeling Ostracized by Others' Smartphone Use: The Effect of Phubbing on Fundamental Needs.* Mood, and Trust.

Kwon, M., Kim, D. J., Cho, H., & Yang, S. (2013). The smartphone addiction scale: Development and validation of a short version for adolescents. *PLoS One*, 8(12), e83558. DOI: 10.1371/journal.pone.0083558 PMID: 24391787

Kwon, M., Lee, J.-Y., Won, W.-Y., Park, J.-W., Min, J.-A., Hahn, C., Gu, X., Choi, J.-H., & Kim, D.-J. (2013). Development and Validation of a Smartphone Addiction Scale (SAS). *PLoS One*, 8(2), e56936. DOI: 10.1371/journal.pone.0056936 PMID: 23468893

Meister, A., & Dael, N. (2024). Do You Have a Phone Addiction. Harvard Business Review.

Nikolic, A., Bukurov, B., Kocic, I., Vukovic, M., Ladjevic, N., Vrhovac, M., Pavlovic, Z., Grujicic, J., KIsic, D., & Sipetic, S. (2023). Smartphone addiction, sleep quality, depression, anxiety, and stress among medical students. Front. Public Health, Sec. Public Mental Health, 11. DOI: 10.3389/fpubh.2023.1252371

Olson, J. A., Sandra, D. A., Colucci, E. S., Bikaii, A. A., Chmoulevitch, J. N., Raz, A., & Veissiere, S. P. L. (2022). Smartphone addiction is increasing across the world: A meta-analysis of 24 countries. Computers in Human Behavior, 129. DOI: 10.1016/j.chb.2021.107138

Panova, T., & Carbonell, X. (2018). Is smartphone addiction really an addiction? *Journal of Behavioral Addictions*, 7(2), 252–259. DOI: 10.1556/2006.7.2018.49 PMID: 29895183

Peleg, O., & Boniel-Nissim, M. (2024). Exploring the personality and relationship factors that mediate the connection between differentiation of self and phubbing. *Scientific Reports*, 14(1), 6572. DOI: 10.1038/s41598-024-55560-1 PMID: 38504119

Ranie, L., & Zickuhr, K. (2015). Americans' views on mobile etiquette. Retrieved from http: //www.pewinternet.org/β015/08/β6/americans-views-on-mobile-etiquette/

Ratan, Z. A., Parrish, A. M., Zaman, S. B., Alotaibi, M. S., & Hosseinzadeh, H. (2021). Smartphone Addiction and Associated Health Outcomes in Adult Populations: A Systematic Review. *International Journal of Environmental Research and Public Health*, 18(22), 12257. DOI: 10.3390/ijerph182212257 PMID: 34832011

Roberts, J. A., & David, M. E. (2016). My life has become a major distraction from my cell phone: Partner phubbing and relationship satisfaction among romantic partners. Computers in Human Behavior, 54, 134-141.

Sbarra, D., Briskin, J. L., & Slatcher, R. B. (2018, November 5). Smartphones and Close Relationships: The Case for an Evolutionary Mismatch. https://doi.org/DOI: 10.31234/osf.io/rqu6f

World Economic Forum. (2023). State of the Connected World 2023 Edition. https://www3.weforum.org/docs/WEF_State_of_the_Connected_World_2023_Edition.pdf

Chapter 1
The Effect of Smartphone Addiction and Phubbing on Relationship Quality and Mental Health: Mixed-Methods Research

Manzoor Ahmad Khanday
https://orcid.org/0000-0002-0053-098X
Lovely Professional University, India

Junior Ntabanganyimana
https://orcid.org/0009-0007-8385-7446
Lovely Professional University, India

ABSTRACT

The exponential growth use of mobile devices changes the way people interact; it also brings some disadvantages to relationships and mental health. Thus, this chapter reports on the effects of "phubbing" or phone snubbing and smartphone addiction on relationship satisfaction and psychological well-being. Results reveal that excessive smartphone use and phubbing result in relationship dissatisfaction and increased conflict with partners, family, and friends. While previous research did already demonstrate that smartphone addiction was related to lower relational satisfaction, the current study furthered this evidence by showing how smartphone overuse strained relationships through a positive relationship between the engagement level and anxiety, depression, and stress levels, increasing anxiety, depression, and stress.

DOI: 10.4018/979-8-3693-8804-4.ch001

1. INTRODUCTION

In recent years, the use of smartphones has reformed the personal and social model in such a way that today's society is more linked digitally than ever. Smartphones are multifunctional devices, which derive it easy for people to right to use communication, news, social media, and entertainment; thus, they generate the convenience and productivity of new life (Andrews et al., 2015). However, over smartphone adoption comes many problems; overuse and addiction being the case in question as more studies identify the behaviors as smartphone addiction. Smartphone addiction includes oneself in extensive or obsessive use, such that an individual cannot contain his/her involvement and continue, despite having negative effects on personal relations, working efficiency, and mental well-being (Elhai, Levine, & Hall, 2017; Demirci et al., 2015).

This dependency has led to a term known as phubbing, which is a combination of the words "phone" and "snubbing." It defines snubbing people for the sake of talking on the smartphone. It has become a social and family issue that disrupts face-to-face communication and negatively affects the quality of relationships over time (Roberts & David, 2016). Other studies indicate that the targets of phubbing more frequently experience lower relationship satisfaction, fewer intimate moments, and trust in peer as well as romantic relationships than their non-targeted counterparts (Chotpitayasunondh & Douglas, 2018). This destructive nature of phubbing indicates a need to understand how addiction through smartphones and related activities is influencing interpersonal and personal mental health.

2. SOCIAL AND PSYCHOLOGICAL CONSEQUENCES OF SMARTPHONE ADDICTION

The consequences of smartphone addiction are very profound, both psychologically and socially, which is mainly based on the design and architecture of digital applications, particularly social media, which uses psychological mechanisms to keep the user engaged (Turel & Serenko, 2012). Features of social media applications include releasing dopamine in the brain, such as when one gets notifications, the personalized content feed, and variable rewards that feed into feedback loops and continue using the smartphone (Montag et al., 2019). This repeated contact habituates behaviors and turns out to be a checking compulsion, mostly found in the sense that they are interrupting everyday life. A plethora of psychological pathology, that includes depression, anxiousness, and social phobia, were associated highly in many studies with smartphone addiction. For example, Demirci et al. (2015) cited that a greater mobile phone use is compatible with more anxiety and depression among university students, especially females.

One of the factors that introduce addiction to smartphones is the feeling of missing out, described by psychologists as that feeling of anxiety over possibly missed rewarding experiences or important information.

According to Przybylski et al. (2013), one of the primary causes for compulsive smartphone use is FOMO because people cannot stop scanning their gadgets to avoid perceptions of being left out, which is a cycle that will bring about more adverse impacts on mental health. This 2017 study by Oberst et al. established that high levels of FOMO resulted in increased symptoms of anxiety and decreased life satisfaction among participants, which verified that smartphone addiction was associated with mental health problems.

3. PHUBBING AND ITS EFFECTS ON RELATIONSHIPS

Phubbing has some effects on relationship satisfaction and social cohesion. The sacrifice of face-to-face interaction for smartphone interaction makes one signal to others within his proximity that his presence and attention are not very important. According to Roberts and David (2016), phubbing negatively impacts relationships since perceptions of intimacy and responsiveness among partners become lower.

Repeated exposure to phubbing in romantic relationships may lead to jealousy, insecurity, and devaluation that eventually cause conflict and reduce the emotional intimacy of the relationship between the two partners (McDaniel & Coyne, 2016). Chotpitayasunondh and Douglas (2018) reported those salient, where subjects experienced their partner's behavior as having reduced satisfaction and increased conflict in a relationship as the negative effects of phubbing on the quality of the relationship. This even extends to affecting friendships and other family ties. Wegmann et al. (2018) have noted that social disconnection and loneliness is a state more likely to exist among frequent phubbing individuals. The vulnerable group for these digital influences will be teenagers and young adults as phubbing acts of alienation will not be effectively countered during this development phase of adolescent communication and social skills. Phubbing causes disruption in meaningful engagement by causing weaker social bonds as well as a decreased feeling of belonging within one's social circle as argued by Barry et al. (2017).

4. RESEARCH OBJECTIVES AND SIGNIFICANCE

This study is by nature a mixed-method approach; it investigates the concurrent effects of smartphone addiction and phubbing on relationship satisfaction and mental health. While quantitative analysis checks the relations between smartphone addiction and its variables, namely anxiety and depression in terms of mental health, qualitative insights recounting personal experiences and relation-based consequences of phubbing behavior are also considered for analysis.

An integrated understanding of the psychosocial dynamics involved should be provided by the combination of the methods. The findings of this study will contribute to debates about digital well-being and, indeed, responsible use of a smartphone. This would mean that some of the insights acquired can be translated into possible interventions and strategies to avoid negative results associated with the overuse of smartphones in relation to counseling programs, educational programs on digital literacy, or relationship counseling. For example, the implication of a phub is that which encourages a person to make more conscious use of smartphones, therefore enhancing healthy relations and the mental outcome of such activities (Davey et al., 2018). Thus, through the highlighting of this very need of balancing smartphone use, digital mindfulness becomes even more important to have interpersonal connections in a technologically based world.

5. LITERATURE REVIEW

Many studies on smartphone addiction and phubbing have reported in detail about the effects on interpersonal relationships and mental well-being. This review aggregates recent evidence on smartphone addiction, the psychological effects, and phubbing as a relation-disrupting factor regarding relationship satisfaction and mental well-being. Smartphone addiction refers to excessive impulses or psychological compulsion towards engaging or staying highly indulged in the usage of one's mobile at the cost of other living and vital human activities. In this regard, Andrews et al. (2015) argue that excessiveness in the smartphone may end up making one lose control over timely management of activities, and they may gradually end up neglecting face-to-face relationships and even social duties. In an analysis of cell phone use among college students, the findings of Demirci et al. (2015) indicated that high levels of use correlated with low quality sleep, more symptoms of anxiety, and symptoms of depression, as Elhai, Levine, and Hall (2017, with "non-social" uses-by which smartphone use is on games, media-with "social" uses yield a stronger relationship in terms of the mental health issues (e.g., anxiety disorders and depression).

Elhai et al. (2019) further revealed that heavy smartphone use was associated with loneliness, and most of this effect would be due to the replacement of direct social contact with virtual interaction.

As pointed out by Montag et al. (2019), the design of smartphones and more specifically, social media creates addictive features through psychological feedback loops that utilize the users' engagement to be retained.

These kinds of designs, like variable rewards and personalized feeds, activate the dopamine system of the brain and lead to compulsion. Smartphone addiction, therefore, has been associated with feelings of loneliness and psychological distress, as seen in the studies by Oberst et al. (2017) and Barry et al. (2017).

According to these researchers, FOMO (fear of missing out) is the central motivating factor behind smartphone addiction. The people who are anxiously waiting to update and catch up on social activity develop compulsive checking behavior to feed this need. As such, the dependency on the device continues with a self-perpetuating cycle that creates a never-ending negative feedback loop, enhancing anxiety and depression.

6. PHUBBING: INTER-PERSONAL AND RELATIONAL IMPLICATION

Phubbing refers to the act of snubbing someone in preference to using a smartphone; this is an effect of smartphone addiction, which brings severe impacts on relationships. Discussing phubbing as a relationship issue, some of the first people who found out that individuals who typically suffer from phubbing at the hands of their partner experience lower relationship satisfaction are Roberts and David (2016).

This behavior implicitly tells the affected partner that smartphone engagement is more important than personal contact, which might make the affected partner feel neglected and resentful. Chotpitayasunondh and Douglas (2018) also conducted a similar study because they explored the social impacts of phubbing in both romantic and friendship contexts.

Their study confirms that individuals who are often phubbed report feelings of devaluation, intimacy levels reduce, and a decrease in perceived responsiveness from their partner. In 2016, McDaniel and Coyne developed a study concerning phubbing in techno Ference-interruptions in personal conversations caused by digital stimuli. According to them, they indicated that the more chronic the interference caused by technology, for which phubbing is a part of, then the more negative emotions or irritation in any relationship will be emotionally affected regarding women.

Such disturbances typically bring relational stress, ultimately resulting in the deterioration of quality communication and intimacy between partners. Wegmann et al. (2018) looked at general social impacts of phubbing and concluded that repeatedly exposed people experience heightened social isolation and loneliness. Of course, the issue cuts sharper at the adolescent-young adult stage as in these stages, the individuals remain incomplete regarding socialization skill development and identity (Barry et al., 2017). Krasnova et al. (2017) emphasized further that phubbing behavior, especially in family or social events, negates the feelings of belonging and involvement since it interrupts meaningful interpersonal relationships. This finding shows the significant relational consequences of smartphone addiction, especially on family dynamics and social group cohesiveness. Bidirectionality between Smartphone Addiction, Phubbing, and Mental Health Consequences This relationship is bi-directional between smartphone addiction, phubbing, and consequences on mental health. These smartphone addictions not only predispose one to exhibit all the aspects of phubbing but will instead lead to further negative mental outcomes. Davey et al. (2018) emphasized how smartphone dependence, in conjunction with phubbing, increases the levels of social anxiety, especially in the younger generations who are compelled to "stay connected online". This pressure results in many mental problems, such as anxiety, depression, and low self-esteem, because affected people are under both internal and social conflict due to their dependency on smartphones. According to Chotpitayasunondh and Douglas (2018), the impact of phubbing on one's mental health is quite strongly linked to its adverse influence on interpersonal relationships, through which individuals report experiencing social exclusion and devaluation, hence heightened loneliness and depression. Similarly, the research by Oberst et al. (2017) confirms smartphone addiction and phubbing provoke this sense of social inadequacy or dissatisfaction that reinforces anxiety and depression.

7. INTERVENTIONS AND FUTURE DIRECTIONS

The consequences of smartphone addiction and phubbing are quite extensive, and there are abundant reports in the literature to this effect. Of late, however, intervention strategies are emphasized that will bring about digital mindfulness and hence relationship satisfaction. As noted by Roberts and David (2016), there is a need to make people more responsible in their use of smartphones. They can consciously draw boundaries around their digital engagement such that they will not be phubbers. Krasnova et al. (2017) suggest establishing "tech-free" zones or times in an individual and family setting to make way for uninterrupted, meaningful interaction. Turel and Serenko (2012) suggest education programs which would upgrade digital literacy, but in a way of increasing consciousness and self-regulation of phubbing through smartphone use, thus leading to fewer instances of the same. With the continued integration of digital technology in daily human life, a better understanding of smartphone addiction, phubbing, and mental health becomes relevant.

Future research should study these relationships to get the information they need to inform public health policies, relationship counseling techniques, and digital literacy programs designed to mitigate the detrimental consequences of excessive smartphone use. Better awareness of phubbing may further help improve both the quality of social interaction and depth of relationship, as well as contribute positively to overall mental health and well-being.

8. METHODS

8.1. Research design

This is an assessment through a quantitative research design that considers the effects of smartphone addiction and phubbing on relationship satisfaction and mental health. Data was obtained from a structured questionnaire of 42 participants in this study in various dimensions of use to establish the effects of smartphones on psychological and social well-being as shown in Table 1.

8.2. Measures

Questions were designed to elicit answers that would manifest the level of the participants regarding their actions toward using a smartphone, for instance, feeling uncomfortable if deprived of their smartphone, making use of their smartphones at meals or during conversations, and conducting stress-reduction exercises because of the smartphone. The respondents were presented with a Likert scale ranging from "Never" to "Always" by which to score their response to give definitive quantification for analysis.

8.3. Statistical Analysis

To make meanings out of the survey data, the following statistical methods were used:

a. Descriptive Statistics: The descriptive statistics taken on summarizing data based on responses in the five categories include means, frequencies, and standard deviations for each question on the survey. Summaries help general trends of smartphone-use behaviors, those of stress responses, and the relationship-related experiences emerge.

b. Graphical Analysis: Several bar charts were developed to understand the distribution of responses to each question. These provide a more intuitive understanding of the participant behavior patterns and thus make it easier to interpret the data as mentioned in Figure 1.
c. Analysis Of Variance (ANOVA): To determine if there was a significant variation between the response categories related to the reported behaviors, this study performed a one-way Analysis of Variance, or ANOVA. This allowed the determination of statistical significance for variations in usage behaviors across different levels of frequency.

The steps were as follows:

- Calculate the mean for each of the response categories (Never, Rarely, Sometimes, Often, Always).
- This step calculates the sum of squares between groups (SSB) which measures the amount of variation between groups.
- Sum of squares within groups (SSW), is the measure of the variance within a group.
- We have computed the mean squares between (MSB), and mean squares within (MSW), by dividing SSB and SSW with their respective degrees of freedom.
- The F-ratio was obtained by dividing MSB by MSW. Then, the F-ratio was compared with a critical value to determine statistical significance.

8.4. Data Analysis

This section describes the decomposition of analysis carried out on the data collected along with purpose and the outcome of each stage:

a. Descriptive Analysis: Frequency and intensity data about the use of smartphones from the descriptive statistics were useful. The mean scores and the frequency distributions for all the questions provide an excellent summary of participant responses to these questions. These first analyses give a foundation on which one can understand general patterns in smartphone-related behaviors and their possible impact on well-being.
b. Graphical Presentation: For presentation of the descriptive statistics, for the graphical representation of response distribution on each of the items in the survey questionnaire, bar charts and pie charts have been used in this paper. The

charts have been constructed to identify popular and not so popular behavior by showing the majority's ranking on the scale for every question.

c. ANOVA (Analysis of Variance): The table below shows the ANOVA result, demonstrating differences at the statistical level. A high F-ratio showed that there was an effect of differences in related behaviors of smartphone use and response levels. Hence, the frequency of related behaviors of smartphone use showed a significant association with impacts on mental health and satisfaction with relationships. A comparison between F-ratio and critical F-value ensured whether the differences were statistically valid as shown in Table 3.

9. RESULTS

Table 1. Data collected from 42 participants

Questions	Never	Rarely	Sometimes	Often	Always
Anxiety when no access to phone	2	2	8	18	12
Engage in stress-reducing activities	0	2	5	10	25
Symptoms of anxiety/depression	0	4	6	15	17
Urge to respond to messages	0	0	5	13	24
Check phone during meals	1	0	9	14	18
Feeling ignored due to phone use	0	2	5	13	22
Use phone during conversations	1	1	10	12	18
Stress about smartphone access	1	1	5	8	27
Urge to use phone during tasks	0	2	7	18	15
Prioritize phone over communication	2	1	8	16	15
Check phone without notifications	0	1	5	15	21
Mean	0.636364	1.454545455	6.636364	13.81818	19.45455
Standard Error	0.243935	0.340150672	0.560401	0.932428	1.422952
Median	0	1	6	14	18
Mode	0	2	5	18	18
Standard Deviation	0.80904	1.12815215	1.858641	3.092513	4.719399
Sample Variance	0.654545	1.272727273	3.454545	9.563636	22.27273
Kurtosis	-0.76389	1.657482993	-1.0609	-0.14081	-0.99484
Skewness	0.846912	0.90328917	0.651297	-0.4123	0.11889
Range	2	4	5	10	15

continued on following page

Table 1. Continued

Questions	Never	Rarely	Sometimes	Often	Always
Minimum	0	0	5	8	12
Maximum	2	4	10	18	27
Sum	7	16	73	152	214
Count	11	11	11	11	11
Confidence Level (95.0%)	0.54352	0.757902927	1.248652	2.077578	3.170535

In further interpretation of descriptive statistics, let's look across categories, "Never", "Rarely", "Sometimes", "Often", and "Always", and introduce comparisons that would be invaluable in terms of insight into how behavioral and attitudinal tendencies related to smartphones may shape mental health and social lives.

9.1. Average Comparison Across Groups

The lowest mean score is Never, at 0.64, whereas always has the highest mean at 19.45. The steady increase from "Never" to "Always" would imply that more participants said they often engage in smartphone behaviors-for instance, anxiety when they don't have their phone or urge to check it-their impact or experience becomes more intense.

There is a huge leap in the means from "Sometimes" at 6.64 to "Often" at 13.82 and to "Always" at 19.45. This shows that when the users shift from moderate to more frequently smartphone-related behaviors, very significantly increase the levels of challenges related to psychological well-being and social connectivity related to smartphone use.

9.2. Standard error and Confidence intervals

It ranges from 0.24, for Never, to 1.42, for Always, so the Standard Error goes up with frequency. Therefore, our mean estimates of the higher frequency categories have less precision, perhaps due to greater variability among persons reporting frequent smartphone use.

The Confidence Interval for every category increased from "Never" at 0.54 to "Always" at 3.17, so that the people who fall in the category of "Always" varied the most. This, therefore, would indicate the fact that the experiences and effects of frequent smartphone use were very different among people experiencing it frequently; in other words, frequent smartphone behaviors varied the effects on people in different ways.

9.3. Median and Mode

Both Median and Mode increase across categories with the "Often" group especially showing a steep increase where Median = 14 and Mode = 18; the "Always" also shows a similar rise at Median = 18, Mode = 18. This indicates that more responses are present among those participants who often or always enact these behaviors; this would imply that they either had a strong effect or most of the time went through these smartphone behaviors.

Notice that Mode for "Always" is 18, like the median, indicating that in this category, responses are always high.

9.4. Standard Deviation and Sample Variance

Standard deviations as well as sample variance increases with a change in responses from "Never" (SD = 0.81) to "Always" (SD = 4.72). It simply means that the range expands when the frequency is added in. Especially large standard deviations with "Often" and "Always" reveal that such people lead vastly different lives. It may simply be a scale to which people face anxieties, stresses, or social pressures due to mobile phones.

This trend supports the assumption of more psychological effects on mental well-being and society brought about by greater frequent smartphone use, maybe in accordance with the wide variance in smartphone use affecting personal life.

9.5. Kurtosis and Skewness

Values for Kurtosis are generally negative-mostly indicating flat distribution except for "Rarely" which has a value of 1.66-more peaked. This means most responses from the respondents within the "Rarely" category is distributed similarly; having low-moderate impact from mobile-related behaviors while variability is more obvious in other categories.

There seems to exist skewness mostly on the positive scale, indicating the fact that these responses show the tendency of right-skewness mostly. Instances, where most have evinced low scores appear, and "Often" alone has a minimum of -0.41. Therefore, this means a relatively well-balanced response shifted only slightly upward. Thus, this might imply a more sensitive point of taking such a decision wherein from the category of sometimes before coming to "often" people find impacts in consonance with the occurrence.

9.6. Range, Minimum and Maximum

The Range increases with frequency from Never to Always, where Range = 2 to Range = 15. Similarly, both minimum and maximum increase, thus showing a shift toward the higher impacts, or more frequent behaviors in the higher categories.

Huge variation in the "Always" category also reflects that though some scores close to a minimum of 12 others score as high as 27 (maximum) which present different kinds of dependence or anxiety.

For instance, increasing Mean, Consistent rise in Mean values in all the categories depicts a clear-cut positive association between the time spent on smartphone usage and the impact of smartphones on mental and social life. Such increases in sample variances, standard deviations, and wide or extended confidence intervals for frequent users are indicated by having more variance in frequent usage. Perhaps infrequent users of a mobile phone produce rather more diversified and complicated effects for some people - perhaps because of several underlying factors such as personality, way of life, or modes of coping for them. Right-skewed distribution Skewness would be positive all over the categories in general, meaning most of them would have lower-to-moderate impacts, with a significant swing toward larger impacts as frequencies go along (Agresti at al., 2012; Moore et al., 2013)

9.7. Bar Chart

Figure 1. Bar graph

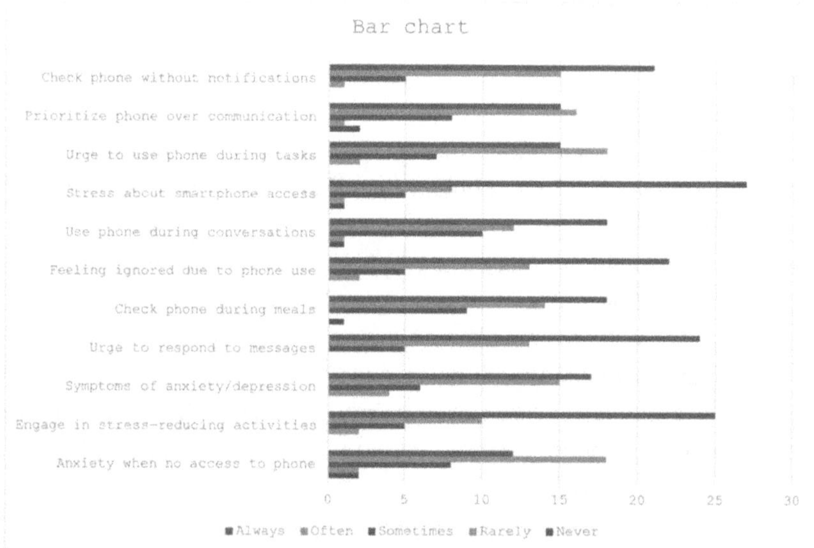

Figure 1 is a bar chart showing responses given during a survey of how addiction and phubbing related to smartphones affected relationship satisfaction and mental health. Five categories, "Never", "Rarely", "Sometimes", "Often" and "Always", represent answers for each question with regards to smartphone usage behavior, anxiety levels, and interpersonal effects. Looking at the categories provided, we find a range of patterns that relate to phone dependence symptomatology related to addiction and perhaps how it intrudes upon other relationships within life and well-being psychologically.

- **Important Observations**

Checking "Often" with Anxiety and Worry Regarding Phone Accessibility

Figure 1 shows checking one's phones even without having any notifications to feel alright most of the time is often checked or checked always. This is an impulsive need to be connected or informed, and it goes with the symptomatology of smartphone addiction. High frequencies in "Stress about smartphone access" suggest that many participants get anxious when they cannot access their phones. The urge to check the phone without notifications might indicate that participants are in the habit of using their phones for reassurance, possibly as a coping mechanism for anxiety or stress. Further, the question "Anxiety when no access to phone" has strong responses in the "Always" and "Often" categories indicating that a big portion of participants may experience symptoms of dependence or even withdrawal when separated from their smartphones.

- **Use During Social Interactions**

This implies that a user is glued to his/her cell phone all the time and gets himself/herself engaged socially, which contradicts the term phubbing, since one thinks to put cellphones first, above interpersonal engagement. A strong response to the "Use phone during conversations" and "Check phone during meals" questions reveals a norm of constantly reaching for the p9hone even when with friends or family.

Such practice may interfere very poorly with effective communication and further entice a sense of being overlooked from loved ones since participants will not seem to be paying attention or be there at social events. This trend accounts for a pattern of use that is automatic and perhaps in an increasingly ineffective sociality and satisfaction with relationships.

- **Emotional and Psychological Implication**

Another general trend that may be observed in the data set is anxiety and depression symptoms associated with smartphone usage.

Responses to the item of “Symptoms of anxiety/depression” said many respondents fell into “Often” and “Always.”. This therefore suggests that heavy usage of the smartphone is also associated with undesirable psychological outcomes because too much time spent in front of screens and continuous stimulation from the internet may lead to increased symptoms of anxiety and depression and even social isolation in some instances. The “Worried you'll miss out due to no smartphone” question also suggests that just having to worry that you might feel disconnected and need to make use of a smartphone does cause distress, which possibly represents dependency on the operation of the device to settle affect or to establish the sense of security.

- **Engagement in Activities That Relieve Stress**

Answers to the question probing into engagement with activities aimed at relieving stress are more prominent in the “Rarely” and “Never” columns.

Such responses may indicate that despite such participants' recognition of their stress related to smartphone utilization, they are not as liable to engage in activities helpful in reducing the same form of stress. It could signal a possible gap in handling the effects of over-use of smartphones. This lower engagement may be due to a lack of time and awareness, or other facilitation resources required for managing stress among these participants about using smartphones. This trend presents avenues for interventions promoting better use of digital media as well as stress-reducing techniques.

- **Cross Category Comparison**

It can be observed that the responses of the two days have significant overlaps in how checking phones with no notifications, anxiety about access, and messages often invade daily life and social activities in those individuals with smartphones.

For instance, “Always” responses were high for the activities like “Check phone without notifications” and “Stress about smartphone access,” indicating these are automatic behaviors for most of the participants. The “Always” and “Often” responses in categories relating to productive behaviors, like participating in stress-reducing activities, are few. It only further strengthens the evidence that there is a disparity between the occurrence of activities that cause and those that reduce stress.

In Conclusion, from Figure 1, one can deduce that smartphone addiction and phubbing behavior can affect one's mental health and relationships.

All behaviors, including constant checking of phones, being stressed because of lack of access, and using phones during interactions with others, have high frequencies in the "Always" and "Often" categories. This means that dependency on smartphones among participants is high. This may cause anxiety symptoms and disruption in face-to-face social interaction, thus leading to a lower relationship satisfaction. A low incidence of stress-reduction activities indicates that most of the participants are not actively reducing stress related to heavy smartphone usage. The findings raise an awareness of the need for interventions that will help break this addiction caused by the phone and encourage healthier usage behaviors and behavior in support of mental well-being and quality relationships (Elhai et al., 2016; Montag et al., 2016; Przybylski et al., 2013; Thomée et al., 2011; Wegmann et al., 2016; Roberts et al., 2016; Hawi et al., 2016; Demirci et al., 2015).

9.8. ANOVA (Analysis of Variance)

Table 2. ANOVA

Source of Variation	Sum of Squares (SS)	Degrees of Freedom (df)	Mean Square (MS)	F-Ratio
Between Groups	2895.02	4	723.75	97.23
Within Groups	372.18	50	7.44	
Total	3267.20	54		

Interpretation of ANOVA Results

The ANOVA was statistically significant, hence the general difference among groups studied is indicated. Such implies patterns for "Always" and "Often" respondents concerning frequent smartphone use and phubbing prove to follow response patterns apart from seldom occurring or happening ones concerning other categories. The strong F-Ratio (97.23), as well as the major Mean Square Between value when compared with the Mean Square Within value as shown in table 3, confirm such a conclusion that group differences occur due to chance (Keppel et al.,2004; Rutherford, A., 2001; Hinkle et al.,2002).

In relation to the research topic, these findings can be interpreted that there is probably a correlation between smartphone addiction and phubbing with varying degrees of relationship satisfaction and mental wellbeing.

Individual smartphone addiction behaviors can differ drastically for those who frequently or constantly exhibit smartphone addiction behavior from those who do rarely or never exhibit the behavior. This supports the hypothesis that smartphone addiction and phubbing are associated with a measurable effect on relationship satisfaction and mental well-being.

Analysis through ANOVA indicated presence of significant variation in the inter-group difference of smartphone addiction and phubbing behavior. The behaviors were significantly associated with negative impacts on relationship satisfaction and mental health. Therefore, such interventions to reduce dependency might help in minimizing smartphone-related negative impacts on interpersonal relations and mental health. However, future studies might observe the specific nature of impacts to inform strategies in efficiently reducing smartphone addiction and further towards healthier usage.

10. DISCUSSIONS

The intricate relationship between smartphone addiction and its consequences of phubbing behavior was given a detailed examination within this study. This paper relied on descriptive statistics as well as bar charts to be visually analyzed, along with the ANOVA test for determining the statistical significance of patterns of smartphone use across different behavioral categories: Never, Rarely, Sometimes, Often, and Always. The results are important in the sense that they describe the relationship between smartphone addiction at different levels and mental health outcomes and relational dynamics, thereby placing a necessity to deal with smartphone addiction and phubbing in the modern, digitally connected society.

10.1. Key Findings and Interpretation

The results show, without a doubt, a statistically significant relationship between the high levels of smartphone addiction and phubbing behavior with lower relationship satisfaction and worsened mental health outcomes. In fact, results indicated that those who were always and often using their phones while socializing or those who more frequently preferred their phone over in-person interaction with others tend to have higher levels of anxiety, stress, and social isolation. The outcome replicates previous literature, showing that excessive use of mobile phones can hinder sociality because attention is shifted from interpersonal interaction to the cyber environment. This behavioral drift can introduce a psychological deterrent and keep people relatively isolated in their environment, and they might have deficiencies in social and affective areas, where they could benefit from digital interactions for remediation.

Even ANOVA analysis made this a more statistically potent link in that the levels of dependence on a smartphone held significant statistical implications with regards to mental health and relational satisfaction. A high F-ratio in the ANOVA reflects that groups are highly different and tell that although smartphone use is rising in frequency, the mal-effect that is being caused to mental well-being and relationships speeds up more. Therefore, it is established that when dependency on a smartphone goes beyond habit and turns towards addiction with obvious damage inflicted upon the psyche.

10.2. Psychological Effects

This research answers an important issue that reveals insight into the mental health outcome of smartphone addiction. Evidence was obtained that those respondents categorized in the "Always" and "Often" groups claim they suffer from anxiety and stress to a greater degree when unable to access their phones. This sense of discomfort experienced away from their devices points to how smartphone addiction might also manifest in ways like other types of dependency, according to psychological lexicon. This feeling of dependence can become an anxiety-withdrawal cycle that, eventually, will contribute to the prolongation of mental illness problems.

Some people within these categories of high usage have experienced loneliness and depression more frequently, and this indicates that smartphone addiction is linked with adverse mental health consequences. This supports the argument that smartphone addiction can influence not just the user's routines but also affect their overall emotional wellbeing. Now that smartphones are a part of daily activities, there seems to be a growing line that cannot distinguish between the convenience and compulsion factors, which might be difficult for mental health. Of those, an intervention strategy may have to be devised with the help of individuals, to make people understand and limit their dependence.

10.3. Impact on Relationship Satisfaction

The findings of the present study confirm grave adverse effects of phubbing the act of using a smartphone while interacting with others-on the relationship satisfaction. The relationship built during frequent phubbing behaviors kept the participants feeling ignored and undervalued, which resulted in strained relationships and feelings of detachment from loved ones, friends, and family members. This phenomenon shows the overuse of smartphones lowers social dynamics because it decreases face-to-face interaction quality. The phenomenon creates emotional detachment among the people. If one of the counterparts feels that his or her other counterparts favor the former's smartphone above what they share, then it creates feelings of neglect which further deteriorate trust and a connection within the relationship.

Beyond its impact on psychological well-being, it can further deteriorate the social levels that go deeper. In this way, if nothing is done, the environment will degrade to unhappiness and loneliness and will reduce mutual insight and cooperation within the relationship. That leads to higher social costs from smartphone addiction, hence creating the urge for mindfulness regarding a person's usage of a smartphone to conserve the quality of interpersonal connection.

10.4. Smartphones: A New Addiction and Phubbing

Accordingly, awareness and intervention measures help reduce the negative impact on the relationship and mental wellbeing produced by smartphone addiction and phubbing. Mindful use of smartphones in relation to social settings can provide an opportunity to recover interpersonal satisfaction and better mental well-being. Behavioral interventions including the creation of specific areas or times as "photon-free" can help users decrease their dependency on using cell phones and increase more qualitative interactions in person.

Moreover, integrating well-being tools into the smartphone would help users control and manage their screen time more effectively. Therefore, it might minimize the extent of phubbing behavior and abuse of this technology. Besides, awareness through educational campaigns on the healthy usage of smart phones would be important factors for prevention from side effects of digital dependency: awareness of how the excessive use of a telephone could affect people's lives and better control to form more balanced habits between mobile and real-world interactions would be exercised.

11. LIMITATIONS AND FUTURE RESEARCH DIRECTIONS

Although this study is of great utility, several limitations must be considered. Sample size and demographic might also affect the generalization of the study. But since this is a cross-sectional study, it only established relationships and not causes. Possible future studies include longitudinal design where one may see patterns and changes within time through the influence of smartphone addiction. Another possible future study to add depth into our topic of interest is through a qualitative study of exploring the personal experience of one with phubbing towards his interpersonal relationships. Future related useful research directions can be into assessing the efficacy of given intervention strategies to reduce smartphone reliance by exploring tools of wellbeing through digital aids and behavior modification.

12. CONCLUSION

This study reveals that excessive smartphone usage and phubbing behaviors are both associated with decreased relationship satisfaction as well as increased mental health issues. Since smartphones are currently part of everyday life, the goal should be to foster responsible habits of use to both protect mental health and ensure social well-being. To that end, this work adds to the expanding literature focused on the psychological and social impacts of digital addiction in underscoring the need for tentful, mindful interaction in the digital and real worlds. With this understanding, the article will focus on revealing how the healthier use of smartphones by people, communities, and policy makers heightens digital culture with much more potential for human bonding and health promotion.

REFERENCES

Agresti, A., & Franklin, C. (2007). *The art and science of learning from data*.

Andrews, S., Ellis, D. A., Shaw, H., & Piwek, L. (2015). Beyond self-report: Tools to compare estimated and real-world smartphone use. *PLoS One*, 10(10), e0139004. DOI: 10.1371/journal.pone.0139004 PMID: 26509895

Barry, C. T., Reiter, S. R., Anderson, A. C., & Schoessler, J. M. (2017). "Let me take a selfie": Associations between self-photography, narcissism, and self-esteem. *Psychology of Popular Media Culture*, 6(1), 48–60. DOI: 10.1037/ppm0000089

Chotpitayasunondh, V., & Douglas, K. M. (2018). The effects of "phubbing" on social interaction. *Computers in Human Behavior*, 88, 176–185.

Davey, S., Davey, A., Singh, J. V., Raghav, S. K., Singh, N., & Blachnio, A. (2018). Predictors and consequences of "Phubbing" among adolescents and youth in India. *The Journal of Mental Health and Human Behavior*, 23(1), 32–38. PMID: 29386960

Demirci, K., Akgönül, M., & Akpinar, A. (2015). Relationship of smartphone use severity with sleep quality, depression, and anxiety in university students. *Journal of Behavioral Addictions*, 4(2), 85–92. DOI: 10.1556/2006.4.2015.010 PMID: 26132913

Elhai, J. D., Levine, J. C., Dvorak, R. D., & Hall, B. J. (2019). Non-social features of smartphone use are most related to depression, anxiety, and problematic smartphone use. *Computers in Human Behavior*, 93, 22–29.

Elhai, J. D., Levine, J. C., & Hall, B. J. (2017). Anxiety about electronic data hacking: Predictors and relations to mental health. *Psychiatry Research*, 256, 348–352.

Hawi, N. S., & Samaha, M. (2017). The relations among social media addiction, self-esteem, and life satisfaction in university students. *Social Science Computer Review*, 35(5), 576–586. DOI: 10.1177/0894439316660340

Hinkle, D. E., Wiersma, W., & Jurs, S. G. (2003). *Applied statistics for the behavioral sciences* (Vol. 663). Houghton Mifflin.

Keppel, G., Saufley, W. H., & Tokunaga, H. (1992). *Introduction to design and analysis: A student's handbook*. Macmillan.

Krasnova, H., Wenninger, H., Widjaja, T., & Buxmann, P. (2017). Envy on Facebook: A hidden threat to users' life satisfaction? *Information Systems Research*, 24(3), 587–605.

McDaniel, B. T., & Coyne, S. M. (2016). "Technoference": The interference of technology in couple relationships and implications for women's personal and relational well-being. *Psychology of Popular Media Culture*, 5(1), 85–98. DOI: 10.1037/ppm0000065

Montag, C., Lachmann, B., Herrlich, M., & Zweig, K. (2019). Addictive features of social media/messenger platforms and Freemium games against the background of psychological and economic theories. *International Journal of Environmental Research and Public Health*, 16(14), 2612. DOI: 10.3390/ijerph16142612 PMID: 31340426

Montag, C., Zhao, Z., Sindermann, C., Xu, L., Fu, M., Li, J., Zheng, X., Li, K., Kendrick, K. M., Dai, J., & Becker, B. (2018). Internet communication disorder and the structure of the human brain: Initial insights on WeChat addiction. *Scientific Reports*, 8(1), 2155. DOI: 10.1038/s41598-018-19904-y PMID: 29391461

Moore, D. S., & McCabe, G. P. (1989). *Introduction to the practice of statistics.* WH Freeman/Times Books/Henry Holt & Co.

Oberst, U., Wegmann, E., Stodt, B., Brand, M., & Chamarro, A. (2017). Negative consequences from heavy social networking in adolescents: The mediating role of fear of missing out. *Journal of Adolescence*, 55(1), 51–60. DOI: 10.1016/j.adolescence.2016.12.008 PMID: 28033503

Przybylski, A. K., Murayama, K., DeHaan, C. R., & Gladwell, V. (2013). Motivational, emotional, and behavioral correlates of fear of missing out. *Computers in Human Behavior*, 29(4), 1841–1848. DOI: 10.1016/j.chb.2013.02.014

Roberts, J. A., & David, M. E. (2016). My life has become a major distraction from my cell phone: Partner phubbing and relationship satisfaction among romantic partners. *Computers in Human Behavior*, 54, 134–141. DOI: 10.1016/j.chb.2015.07.058

Rutherford, A. (2011). *ANOVA and ANCOVA: A GLM approach.* John Wiley & Sons. DOI: 10.1002/9781118491683

Thomée, S., Härenstam, A., & Hagberg, M. (2011). Mobile phone use and stress, sleep disturbances, and symptoms of depression among young adults—A prospective cohort study. *BMC Public Health*, 11(1), 1–11. DOI: 10.1186/1471-2458-11-66 PMID: 21281471

Turel, O., & Serenko, A. (2012). The benefits and dangers of enjoyment with social networking websites. *European Journal of Information Systems*, 21(5), 512–528. DOI: 10.1057/ejis.2012.1

Wegmann, E., Oberst, U., Stodt, B., & Brand, M. (2017). Online-specific fear of missing out and Internet-use expectancies contribute to symptoms of Internet-communication disorder. *Addictive Behaviors Reports*, 5, 33–42. DOI: 10.1016/j.abrep.2017.04.001 PMID: 29450225

Chapter 2
Mental Health and Smartphone Addiction:
Understanding the Digital Impact on Well-Being

Ridhima Goel
https://orcid.org/0000-0002-0505-9218
Maharshi Dayanand Univesity, India

Jagdeep Singla
https://orcid.org/0000-0001-8628-9244
Maharshi Dayanand University, India

ABSTRACT

In today's hyper-connected world, smartphones are indispensable, but their excessive use is triggering a digital mental health crisis. This chapter delves into the rising phenomenon of smartphone addiction, a behavioural condition marked by compulsive usage that disrupts daily life and mental well-being. Focusing on the mental health consequences, the chapter examines how smartphone addiction fuels anxiety, depression, sleep disorders, and social isolation. It also explores how vulnerable populations, particularly adolescents and young adults, are disproportionately affected by this addiction. Solutions such as digital detox, mindfulness interventions, and cognitive-behavioural therapy are discussed to help individuals regain control of their smartphone habits and promote healthier relationships with technology. By addressing the complex link between smartphone addiction and mental health, this chapter contributes to a broader conversation on safeguarding well-being in the digital age.

DOI: 10.4018/979-8-3693-8804-4.ch002

1. INTRODUCTION: THE DIGITAL AGE AND THE RISE OF SMARTPHONE ADDICTION

1.1 Overview of Smartphone Usage

The advent of smartphones has revolutionized nearly every aspect of human life, creating a profound and lasting impact on the way people communicate, work, entertain themselves, and even relate to one another. What started as a device to facilitate basic phone calls and messages has transformed into a multi-functional tool that serves as a personal assistant, navigator, camera, entertainment hub, and social platform. The sheer ubiquity of smartphones has made them indispensable, embedding them into daily routines and activities across the globe (Dwivedi et al., 2021).

Historically, the evolution of smartphones can be traced back to the early 1990s with the introduction of IBM's Simon Personal Communicator, often considered the world's first smartphone (Collen & Kulikowski, 2015). It was a revolutionary device for its time, combining a phone, calendar, email, and fax machine into one product. However, it wasn't until the 2007 release of Apple's iPhone that smartphones began to become the cornerstone of modern life (King et al., 2016). This groundbreaking innovation offered users not only a portable telephone but also a powerful mini-computer, capable of performing tasks previously unimaginable on a handheld device. The seamless integration of internet access, touch-screen technology, and an ever-growing array of applications positioned the smartphone as a transformative tool (Vossen et al., 2017). However, as much as smartphones have enhanced convenience and connectivity, they have also introduced a host of challenges. Today, smartphone usage has transcended socio-economic and geographical boundaries, with approximately 6.2 billion people worldwide owning one (Statista, 2024). The proliferation of affordable models, increasing internet connectivity, and the rise of social media platforms have turned smartphones into an omnipresent technology that touches every corner of modern life. The constant presence of smartphones has blurred the lines between work and personal life, created new social norms, and led to a growing dependence on digital interactions (Van Zoonen et al., 2020). In many ways, the smartphone has become a double-edged sword, offering tremendous benefits while simultaneously fostering new problems—chief among them being the phenomenon of smartphone addiction.

1.2 Understanding Smartphone Addiction

While smartphone usage has become an essential part of everyday life, the question arises: at what point does frequent use turn into addiction? Smartphone addiction refers to the compulsive and uncontrollable need to use one's device, even in situations where it causes harm to personal relationships, work productivity, and mental health (Mason et al., 2022). Often classified as a form of behavioral addiction, it shares many characteristics with other types of addiction, such as gambling or substance dependence (Yang et al., 2023a). People with smartphone addiction exhibit a loss of control over their usage patterns, spending an increasing amount of time on their phones despite experiencing negative consequences (Van Zoonen et al., 2020). The rise of smartphone addiction is particularly alarming in the context of mental health (Mason et al., 2022). As individuals become more reliant on their devices for communication, entertainment, and work, they also become increasingly vulnerable to the psychological impacts of overuse (Girela-Serrano et al., 2022). This addiction is associated with a range of mental health issues, including anxiety, depression, sleep disturbances, and social isolation (Wang & Ma, 2024). A Zhang et al. (2023) examined the relationship between smartphone addiction and depression among medical graduates, revealing a significant bidirectional association, particularly in female students. For many, the smartphone becomes not just a tool, but an emotional crutch—an escape from stress, loneliness, and boredom (Li et al., 2021). However, this escape often leads to more harm than good, as excessive smartphone use can exacerbate the very issues it is meant to alleviate.

1.3 Smart Phones and Social Media

Smartphone addiction thrives on the rapid feedback loops created by notifications, messages, and social media interactions (Girela-Serrano et al., 2022). Many apps are designed with addictive features, such as endless scrolling, "likes," and push notifications, which trigger dopamine releases in the brain, reinforcing behavior through the brain's reward system (Hansen, 2022). This release of dopamine fosters a cycle of dependency, as individuals feel compelled to check their phones constantly, driven by the fear of missing out (FOMO), the desire for social validation, or the simple need to stay connected (Alabri, 2022). Over time, this habitual checking evolves into compulsive behavior, where individuals feel unable to disengage from their phones, even when it negatively impacts their personal and professional lives.

The neurobiological mechanisms behind this addiction are rooted in how the brain responds to instant gratification (Ning et al., 2024). Smartphones and social media platforms activate the mesolimbic dopamine pathway (Greenfield, 2020), the same pathway involved in behaviors like eating or gambling, which are known to be highly addictive (Kuss & Griffiths, 2017). This continuous feedback loop stimulates a sense of pleasure and reward, making it difficult for users to break the cycle of constant phone checking (Jo & Baek, 2023). Neuroplasticity further reinforces these behaviors, as the brain adapts to the constant stimuli, forming habitual pathways that make the addiction even harder to overcome (Trainor, 2011; Chen et al., 2023). While smartphone addiction affects individuals of all ages, studies show that adolescents and young adults are particularly vulnerable (Girela-Serrano et al., 2022). For these younger generations, the need to stay connected, maintain social media profiles, and engage with peers digitally can lead to stress, anxiety, and diminished self-esteem (Mason et al., 2022). The constant comparison facilitated by social media platforms can exacerbate feelings of social inadequacy and depression (Tiggemann & Slater, 2014). The World Health Organization (WHO) has recently raised concerns regarding the mental health implications of excessive smartphone use, especially among teenagers highlights that problematic social media use is linked to lower mental and social well-being, as well as higher levels of substance use (World Health Organization, 2024). As smartphones become omnipresent, serving as a constant companion for work, social life, and entertainment, their influence on mental health continues to expand, creating a growing need for awareness and intervention in managing this addiction (Ostic et al., 2021).

1.4 The Digital Mental Health Crisis

The digital age, marked by the rapid expansion of internet-based technologies, has brought about a mental health crisis that is deeply intertwined with smartphone usage. While the digital revolution has introduced incredible advancements in communication and access to information, it has also fostered environments that contribute to mental health decline. The constant exposure to curated content on social media, the pressure to stay connected, and the addictive nature of digital platforms have created a landscape where mental health issues are becoming increasingly common (Zubair et al., 2023).

One of the most concerning aspects of this crisis is the relationship between smartphone addiction and mental health disorders like anxiety and depression (Ostic et al., 2021). Social media, which is a key feature of smartphone use, often leads to feelings of inadequacy, envy, and isolation (Tandon et al., 2024). The pressure to present a perfect image online, coupled with the relentless comparison to others, can erode self-worth and contribute to depressive symptoms (Merino et al., 2024). Furthermore, the fear of missing out (FOMO) drives individuals to stay constantly engaged with their devices, leading to increased anxiety and a sense of social disconnection (Roberts & David, 2019). Sleep disorders are another critical issue linked to smartphone addiction. The blue light emitted by smartphone screens interferes with the body's natural circadian rhythms, delaying the production of melatonin and making it harder to fall asleep (Touitou & Point, 2020). Late-night smartphone use, whether for checking emails, watching videos, or scrolling through social media, disrupts sleep quality and leads to insomnia (Stevic et al., 2023). This lack of sleep, in turn, affects cognitive functioning, mood regulation, and overall mental well-being (Touitou & Point, 2020).

Social isolation is another paradoxical outcome of smartphone addiction (Wang & Ma, 2024). Although smartphones are designed to connect people, excessive use can lead to feelings of loneliness and isolation (Yang et al., 2023b). Virtual interactions often replace face-to-face communication, reducing the quality and depth of personal relationships. Individuals may find themselves physically present in social settings but emotionally disconnected, as they focus more on their digital interactions than their real-life connections (Pandya & Lodha, 2021). This phenomenon, known as "phubbing" (phone snubbing), where people prioritize their smartphones over in-person interactions, is increasingly recognized as a contributor to social isolation and weakened interpersonal relationships (Peleg & Boniel-Nissim, 2024). In addition to these individual-level impacts, the digital mental health crisis has broader societal implications. The normalization of constant smartphone use has created new social norms, where being "always online" is not only accepted but often expected (Reinecke et al., 2018). This has led to a culture of hyperconnectivity, where the boundaries between work, leisure, and personal time are increasingly blurred. The pressure to respond to messages, emails, and notifications at all hours of the day contributes to burnout, stress, and a diminished sense of well-being (Tedone, 2022). As the digital mental health crisis continues to unfold, it is becoming increasingly clear that smartphone addiction is not merely a personal issue, but a public health concern (Pandya & Lodha, 2021). The widespread nature of the problem calls for collective action to raise awareness, promote healthier digital habits, and mitigate the mental health risks associated with excessive smartphone use.

1.5 Importance of Raising Awareness

In light of the growing body of evidence linking smartphone addiction to mental health issues, raising awareness about this digital crisis is essential (Ostic et al., 2021). While smartphones have undoubtedly become an integral part of modern life, it is crucial to recognize the psychological risks associated with their overuse. Education and awareness campaigns can help individuals understand the signs of smartphone addiction and encourage them to adopt healthier digital habits (Kutluay & Karaca, 2024).

Moreover, awareness efforts should target not only individuals but also the broader societal structures that contribute to smartphone addiction. Tech companies, educators, healthcare providers, and policymakers all play a role in addressing this issue (Chen & Lyu, 2024). App developers, for example, can design platforms that prioritize user well-being over engagement metrics, while schools and workplaces can implement guidelines to promote balanced smartphone use (Nascimento et al.,

2024). By fostering a greater understanding of smartphone addiction and its mental health consequences, society can begin to address the digital mental health crisis and create a healthier, more balanced relationship with technology (Yang et al., 2023a). Raising awareness is the first step toward mitigating the harmful effects of excessive smartphone use and promoting mental well-being in the digital age (Ophir et al., 2020).

2. SMARTPHONE ADDICTION: DEFINITIONS, SYMPTOMS, AND RISK FACTORS

2.1 Defining Smartphone Addiction

Smartphone addiction, much like other forms of behavioral addiction, is characterized by compulsive engagement with smartphone usage to the point where it interferes with daily life (Chen & Lyu, 2024). Defined as a behavioural disorder, smartphone addiction involves an overwhelming reliance on smartphones to fulfill emotional and psychological needs, often at the expense of personal well-being, social relationships, and professional responsibilities (Li et al., 2021). Unlike substance addictions, where individuals become dependent on chemical substances, behavioral addictions arise from compulsive actions that trigger the brain's reward system, creating patterns of dependency and loss of control (Zubair et al., 2023). The convenience and portability of smartphones further exacerbate this addiction, making it easier for individuals to indulge in compulsive behavior anywhere and at any time (Yang et al., 2023b).

Studies have demonstrated that smartphone addiction shares many core characteristics with pathological gambling, including impulsivity, reward-seeking behavior, and difficulty in managing usage (Wegmann et al., 2021). Just as a gambling addict might chase the thrill of a win, a person addicted to their smartphone may seek the instant gratification of receiving a notification or the validation of online interactions. The behavioral patterns associated with smartphone addiction often include excessive screen time, neglect of real-world responsibilities, and increasing preoccupation with digital engagement (Stevic et al., 2023). For individuals experiencing addiction, smartphones become more than just a tool—they become a source of emotional support and fulfillment. Unfortunately, this overreliance often leads to a range of negative consequences that can impact every aspect of life, from relationships to productivity and mental health. A study in China revealed that 32% of first-year university students exhibited signs of smartphone dependency, which escalated to 52.5% by their second year. This challenge extends to healthcare trainees, who often rely on smartphones for academic resources and connectivity. Among those initially addicted, 67.1% remained reliant on their devices after 12 months, highlighting the persistent nature of this issue (Zhang et al., 2023). This growing dependence underscores the need for targeted interventions to address smart phone among multiple age groups, fostering healthier digital habits without compromising their academic and professional growth.

2.2 Symptoms of Smartphone Addiction

Recognizing the symptoms of smartphone addiction is essential to understanding the extent of the problem and its potential consequences. As with other behavioral disorders, the symptoms of smartphone addiction manifest across various domains of life, including cognitive, emotional, social, and physical health. While occasional smartphone overuse may not indicate an addiction, individuals who consistently exhibit the following symptoms may be at risk of developing a more severe dependence.

1. **Preoccupation with Smartphones**: One of the hallmark symptoms of smartphone addiction is an excessive preoccupation with one's device. Individuals may spend a disproportionate amount of time checking their phones, browsing the internet, or engaging with apps, even when it is unnecessary or inappropriate (Wilmer et al., 2017). This preoccupation often leads to neglecting other important activities, such as work, family obligations, or hobbies. Furthermore, individuals may find themselves constantly thinking about their smartphones, feeling anxious or restless if they are unable to access them.
2. **Difficulty Reducing Usage**: Individuals struggling with smartphone addiction often find it difficult to reduce or manage their usage, even when they are aware of the negative impact it has on their lives (Jameel et al., 2019). Despite setting limits or attempting to cut back, they may repeatedly return to their phones, unable to resist the temptation to check for updates, messages, or notifications. This loss of control is a defining feature of addiction, as it reflects the individual's inability to regulate their behavior, even when faced with negative consequences.
3. **Negative Effects on Personal and Professional Life**: Smartphone addiction can have far-reaching effects on personal and professional life (Hassan et al., 2024). Individuals may experience strained relationships as they prioritize their devices over face-to-face interactions with loved ones. "Phubbing" (phone snubbing), where individuals ignore those around them in favor of their phones, is a common manifestation of this behavior. In professional settings, excessive smartphone use can lead to decreased productivity, missed deadlines, and poor performance (Pandya & Lodha, 2021). The compulsion to check one's phone during work hours can disrupt focus and lead to procrastination, creating a cycle of stress and underachievement.

4. **Withdrawal Symptoms**: Similar to substance addiction, individuals with smartphone addiction may experience withdrawal symptoms when they are deprived of access to their devices (Zhang et al., 2024). These symptoms can include feelings of anxiety, irritability, restlessness, and even depression. For some, the inability to check their phone can lead to a sense of disconnection or isolation, as smartphones have become a primary means of social engagement and validation (Chan et al., 2024). This psychological dependence highlights the extent to which individuals have come to rely on their devices to regulate their emotions and cope with daily stressors.
5. **Continued Use Despite Negative Consequences**: One of the most concerning aspects of smartphone addiction is the tendency to continue using the device despite being aware of its negative impact (Prodanova & Chopdar, 2023). Whether it is damage to relationships, poor work performance, or declining mental health, individuals often feel unable to break free from their dependence on their smartphones. This persistence in the face of harm is a key indicator of addiction, as it reflects the compulsive nature of the behavior.

2.3 Risk Factors for Smartphone Addiction

Smartphone addiction is influenced by a combination of personality traits, environmental factors, and psychological motivations. While anyone can develop a dependency on their smartphone, certain individuals are more vulnerable based on their psychological makeup and external circumstances.

1. **Personality Traits**: Research has shown that certain personality traits may predispose individuals to developing smartphone addiction. Two traits that are frequently associated with behavioral addictions are impulsivity and neuroticism.
    - o *Impulsivity:* Impulsive individuals tend to act on their urges without considering the long-term consequences. This trait can lead to excessive smartphone use, as impulsive individuals may find it difficult to resist the temptation to check their devices whenever they receive a notification or experience boredom (Dadandı & Kalyon, 2024). Impulsivity is closely linked to the reward-seeking behavior that drives addiction, making individuals more susceptible to becoming hooked on the instant gratification provided by smartphones.
    - o *Neuroticism*: Neuroticism, characterized by emotional instability and a tendency to experience negative emotions such as anxiety, stress, and depression, is another risk factor for smartphone addiction (Eichenberg et al., 2024). A mixed method approach from a research by Chen (2022) highlighted that, individuals with high levels of neuroticism may turn

to their smartphones as a coping mechanism, using digital engagement to escape from uncomfortable emotions or to distract themselves from life's stressors or to fill in a void. Unfortunately, this reliance on smartphones for emotional regulation can exacerbate negative mental health outcomes over time and can lead to mobile addiction syndrome (MAS) (Chen, 2022).

- o *Other traits*: Traits like *emotional instability* and *openness to experience*, drives addiction to smartphones, which in turn nurtures materialistic tendencies. The study, Tan (2024) reveals how addictive smartphone behavior not only fuels this habit among millennials but also acts as a mediator, intensifying the connection between constant connectivity and materialism, particularly among the younger generation.

2. **Environmental and Cultural Factors**: The environment in which individuals live and work plays a significant role in shaping their relationship with technology. In a world that is increasingly interconnected, digital connectivity has become both a necessity and a social expectation. Factors such as easy access to smartphones, the prevalence of social media platforms, and the pressure to stay connected all contribute to the risk of smartphone addiction.
   - o **Digital Connectivity**: In highly connected societies, smartphones are essential tools for communication, work, and entertainment (Chen & Lyu, 2024). The expectation to be "always online" for work emails, social media interactions, or personal communication can create a culture of constant digital engagement (Caldeira et al., 2024). As a result, individuals may feel pressured to check their phones frequently, even when it is not necessary, leading to compulsive behavior.
   - o **Social Pressures**: Social norms also contribute to the risk of smartphone addiction. In many cultures, staying connected through social media and messaging apps has become a social imperative (Akhtar et al., 2024). The fear of missing out (FOMO) on social events, news, or updates can drive individuals to constantly check their phones, creating a cycle of compulsive use (Roberts & David, 2019). Additionally, the pressure to maintain an online presence, whether for social validation or professional networking, can make it difficult for individuals to disengage from their devices.
   - o **Psychological Factors**: Several psychological motivations contribute to the development of smartphone addiction, particularly escapism, the need for validation, and the avoidance of stress (Stenseng et al., 2021).
   - o **Escapism**: For many individuals, smartphones offer an easy escape from the challenges of daily life. Whether through social media, online games, or streaming services, smartphones provide a convenient

way to avoid dealing with stress, boredom, or negative emotions (Shi et al., 2022). However, this escapism can quickly turn into addiction, as individuals become increasingly reliant on their devices to cope with discomfort.

- **Seeking Validation**: Social media platforms are designed to encourage engagement by offering users instant feedback in the form of "likes," comments, and shares (Lissitsa & Kagan, 2024). For individuals who seek social validation, this feedback can be highly addictive. The desire for approval and recognition from others can drive individuals to spend excessive amounts of time curating their online personas and engaging with social media, reinforcing their dependence on their smartphones (Roberts & David, 2019).

Smartphone addiction is a complex behavioral disorder influenced by a variety of psychological, environmental, and social factors. Defined by compulsive smartphone use and characterized by symptoms such as preoccupation, withdrawal, and continued use despite negative consequences, this addiction poses significant risks to both mental and physical well-being. Personality traits like impulsivity and neuroticism, combined with environmental pressures and psychological motivations, contribute to the development of smartphone addiction in individuals. As the digital age continues to evolve, understanding the factors that contribute to smartphone addiction is crucial in addressing the mental health challenges associated with excessive smartphone use. By raising awareness of these risk factors and symptoms, individuals can begin to develop healthier relationships with technology, fostering a more balanced approach to digital engagement.

3. THE MENTAL HEALTH CONSEQUENCES OF SMARTPHONE ADDICTION

The rise of smartphone addiction has brought with it a range of mental health issues, affecting individuals' emotional, cognitive, and social well-being (Dadandı & Kalyon, 2024). The accessibility and pervasiveness of smartphones, coupled with constant digital engagement, have led to significant psychological challenges that can exacerbate pre-existing mental health conditions or create new ones. In this section, we explore the major mental health consequences of smartphone addiction, including *anxiety, depression, sleep disorders, social isolation, cognitive overload, and burnout.*

3.1 Anxiety and Depression

A growing body of research indicates a strong correlation between excessive smartphone use and heightened anxiety levels. This association is particularly evident in users who are overly reliant on social media platforms, where they are continuously exposed to curated, idealized portrayals of other people's lives. These platforms, designed to encourage constant engagement, contribute to feelings of inadequacy, stress, and a phenomenon known as *FOMO (Fear of Missing Out)* (Roberts & David, 2019). The more users compare their own lives to the seemingly perfect lives of others on social media, the more likely they are to experience heightened anxiety and dissatisfaction (Dadandı & Kalyon, 2024).

Smartphone addiction, creates a digital trap where anxiety and emotional instability thrive when individuals are separated from their devices (Yilmaz et al., 2023). This irrational fear or anxiety of being without a mobile phone or being unable to use it, often leading to stress and emotional instability particularly known as *Nomophobia* (Jahrami et al., 2023). As highlighted by Pinochet et al. (2023), this reliance on constant connectivity breeds loneliness and depression, particularly in high-stress work environments, ultimately hindering communication and productivity. This growing dependency calls for urgent attention to the balance between digital engagement and mental well-being in today's connected world.

Excessive smartphone use often creates an unhealthy cycle of comparison and validation-seeking. As individuals check their phones multiple times throughout the day for notifications, messages, and updates, they become trapped in a loop where their emotional well-being is dictated by external feedback. The "likes," comments, and shares on social media posts, or the lack thereof, can lead to heightened anxiety. This is especially true for younger users who may be more sensitive to social approval and validation, as their self-esteem and sense of identity are still developing (Lissitsa & Kagan, 2024).. Moreover, studies have linked smartphone addiction to depressive symptoms, particularly among adolescents and young adults. The constant pressure to engage in social media can lead to a decline in self-esteem and emotional resilience, as users begin to base their self-worth on online interactions rather than meaningful, real-world connections (Merino et al., 2024). For many, the need for validation through social media becomes a coping mechanism for deeper emotional issues, resulting in withdrawal, low moods, and a sense of loneliness (Caldeira et al., 2024). This is particularly concerning because depression among younger populations is already on the rise, and smartphone addiction appears to be contributing to this alarming trend.

3.2 Sleep Disorders

Smartphone addiction also has a detrimental impact on sleep quality, contributing to sleep disorders such as insomnia (Wang et al., 2019). One of the primary factors behind this issue is the exposure to blue light emitted by smartphones. Blue light, particularly when absorbed late in the day, disrupts the body's natural circadian rhythms, which regulate sleep-wake cycles (Zhang et al., 2024). Blue light exposure suppresses the production of melatonin, the hormone responsible for inducing sleep, making it more difficult for individuals to fall asleep and maintain restful sleep throughout the night (De Toledo et al., 2023).

The habit of scrolling through smartphones before bedtime has become increasingly common, particularly among younger generations. Whether it is checking social media feeds, responding to messages, or watching videos, this behavior overstimulates the brain at a time when it should be winding down for sleep. This hyperactivity, coupled with the disruption of circadian rhythms, contributes to poor sleep quality and insomnia (Van Den Eijnden et al., 2021). Studies have shown that individuals who spend more time on their smartphones before bed experience significantly shorter sleep duration, poorer sleep efficiency, and more frequent wakefulness during the night (Orzech et al., 2015). A recent research from the universities in China (Yang et al., 2023b), have unveiled the profound interplay between smartphone addiction, disrupted sleep quality, and declining psychological well-being, emphasizing the critical need for targeted interventions to mitigate these cascading effects. Moreover, the relationship between sleep disorders and mental health is reciprocal. Poor sleep quality exacerbates symptoms of anxiety, depression, and emotional dysregulation (De Oliveira et al., 2020). When individuals are sleep-deprived, they are more likely to experience heightened irritability, mood swings, and difficulty managing stress (Wang et al., 2019). This creates a vicious cycle, as those with smartphone addiction are often more prone to experiencing sleep disorders, and the resulting poor sleep further exacerbates their mental health issues. Emotional regulation, which is vital for maintaining mental health, is impaired by sleep deprivation, making individuals more vulnerable to the negative effects of smartphone addiction (Mahapatra, 2019).

3.3 Social Isolation and Loneliness

One of the most paradoxical consequences of smartphone addiction is that while smartphones provide users with virtual connectivity, they often lead to physical social isolation. As individuals become increasingly engrossed in their digital worlds, their real-life relationships may suffer, leading to feelings of loneliness and disconnection. (Squires et al., 2020) The constant engagement with smartphones often comes at the expense of meaningful face-to-face interactions, as people prioritize virtual conversations over in-person communication.

Social isolation has been shown to have a profound impact on emotional well-being. While smartphones allow individuals to stay connected with others at all times, this digital connectivity is often superficial (Wang & Ma, 2024). The lack of deep, meaningful interactions can result in emotional isolation, even when individuals are constantly in contact with others online. Over time, reliance on digital communication can reduce the quality of real-life relationships, as individuals become less adept at forming strong emotional bonds and engaging in meaningful conversations.

The rise of "phubbing" (phone snubbing), where individuals ignore those around them in favor of their phones, is a clear example of how smartphone addiction can erode real-life relationships (Peleg & Boniel-Nissim, 2024). Whether in family settings, social gatherings, or even romantic partnerships, smartphone addiction can lead to a breakdown in communication and emotional closeness (Van Zoonen et al., 2020). This can create a sense of loneliness, as individuals may feel disconnected from those around them, despite being constantly connected through their devices.

Dependence on digital communication over face-to-face interactions can also impact psychological health (Van Zoonen et al., 2020). Humans are inherently social creatures, and real-world interactions are essential for emotional fulfillment and mental well-being. When individuals replace these interactions with virtual ones, they may begin to feel isolated, misunderstood, or unsupported, contributing to feelings of loneliness and emotional distress.

3.4 Cognitive Overload and Burnout

Another significant mental health consequence of smartphone addiction is cognitive overload, which occurs when the brain is bombarded with too much information, leading to mental fatigue. Smartphones provide constant notifications, messages, and updates from various apps, creating a perpetual state of alertness and engagement (Prodanova & Chopdar, 2023). This overwhelming influx of information can contribute to cognitive fatigue, as individuals struggle to process and prioritize the multitude of digital stimuli they encounter throughout the day (Mao et al., 2022).

Cognitive overload can have a range of negative effects, including decreased attention span, impaired focus, and reduced productivity (Wilmer et al., 2017). With the constant stream of information from smartphones, individuals may find it difficult to concentrate on tasks for extended periods. The habit of switching between apps, messages, and notifications can fragment attention and make it harder to engage in deep, focused work (Shanmugasundaram & Tamilarasu, 2023). As a result, smartphone addiction is often associated with decreased work efficiency, as individuals struggle to manage their digital distractions while balancing their responsibilities (Y et al., 2023).

Additionally, cognitive overload can lead to emotional exhaustion and burnout (Wilmer et al., 2017). When the brain is constantly processing information without adequate rest, it becomes fatigued, leading to feelings of overwhelm and stress (Eichenberg et al., 2024). This is particularly true for individuals who are highly engaged with their smartphones for work-related purposes, such as checking emails or responding to messages after hours. The blurring of boundaries between work and personal life, facilitated by smartphones, can result in chronic stress and burnout (Van Zoonen et al., 2020).

Burnout is a state of emotional, physical, and mental exhaustion that occurs when individuals are unable to cope with prolonged stress (Goel et al., 2024). For smartphone addicts, the constant engagement with digital content can deplete emotional resources, leaving individuals feeling drained and incapable of managing their responsibilities. Burnout not only impacts productivity but also has significant consequences for mental health, contributing to symptoms of anxiety, depression, and emotional dysregulation (Goel & Singla, 2024).

4. SMARTPHONE ADDICTION AMONG VULNERABLE POPULATIONS

Smartphone addiction is not uniformly distributed across all age groups and demographics. Certain populations are more vulnerable due to unique psychological, social, and environmental factors. Smartphone addiction affects a wide range of populations, but certain groups are particularly vulnerable due to a combination of psychological, social, and environmental factors (Zubair et al., 2023). Adolescents, driven by social pressures and the need for validation, are highly susceptible to addiction, while gender differences reveal unique patterns of smartphone use between men and women (Bai et al., 2024). Cultural and societal influences also play a significant role in shaping addiction trends across regions (Merino et al., 2024). Furthermore, the rise of smartphone addiction among the elderly and middle-aged populations highlights that this issue is not confined to younger generations (Mason et al., 2022). As smartphones continue to become more integrated into daily life, it is essential to recognize and address the unique vulnerabilities of different populations to foster healthier relationships with digital technology (Van Zoonen et al., 2020). This section delves into how smartphone addiction affects adolescents and young adults, explores the gender differences in addiction patterns, highlights the role of cultural and societal influences, and touches upon the growing concerns regarding smartphone addiction among the elderly and other underexplored demographics.

4.1 Smartphone Addiction Among Adolescents and Young Adults

Adolescents and young adults are among the most vulnerable populations when it comes to smartphone addiction (Bai et al., 2024). Their susceptibility is driven by a combination of developmental, social, and psychological factors that make them more prone to excessive smartphone use. One of the primary reasons adolescents are particularly vulnerable is that they are still in the process of forming their identities generations (Mason et al., 2022). During this critical phase of development, they are highly sensitive to external influences, including peer pressure, social validation, and cultural trends (Mason et al., 2022). Smartphones, with their access to social media platforms, serve as tools for adolescents to seek validation and approval from their peers (Wood et al., 2023). Social media provides a curated platform where users can present idealized versions of themselves, often creating a cycle of comparison, competition, and self-doubt (Chan et al., 2024). Adolescents may feel compelled to keep up with these digital representations, leading to an unhealthy preoccupation with their online personas (Akhtar et al., 2024).

Cyberbullying is another factor that exacerbates smartphone addiction among adolescents (Xiong et al., 2023). The anonymity and reach of online platforms can lead to harassment, bullying, and negative social interactions (Chan et al., 2019). Adolescents who experience cyberbullying may turn to their phones even more as a way to cope, seek support, or retaliate, thereby reinforcing their addiction (Sengupta & Chaudhuri, 2010). The emotional toll of cyberbullying, combined with the addictive nature of smartphones, can lead to heightened levels of anxiety, depression, and emotional dependence on their devices (Sylwander, 2019). In terms of mental health risks, adolescents who are addicted to their smartphones are more likely to experience negative emotional outcomes such as anxiety and depression (Girela-Serrano et al., 2022). The constant need for validation, coupled with the negative effects of social comparison, can erode self-esteem and contribute to feelings of inadequacy. Studies have shown that adolescents with higher levels of smartphone use are more likely to report symptoms of depression, as they become emotionally dependent on their digital interactions for validation and self-worth (Edwards et al., 2022). Emerging researches have shed light on the ripple effects of parental smartphone habits, revealing that parents' own device dependency have also significantly heightened the risk of similar addictive behaviors in their adolescents. A study Mun (2024) underscores how family dynamics play a pivotal role, highlighting that managing the smartphone addiction also requires a household-wide approach to foster healthier digital habits across generations.

4.2 Gender and Smartphone Addiction

Smartphone addiction also exhibits gender-specific patterns, with research indicating notable differences between males and females in how they engage with their devices (Alhassan et al., 2018). While both genders are susceptible to addiction, the motivations and usage patterns often differ (Merino et al., 2024).

Studies suggest that women, particularly young women, tend to use smartphones more for social purposes, such as maintaining relationships, connecting with friends, and engaging on social media platforms (Thelwall & Vis, 2017). As a result, women are often more prone to developing smartphone addiction related to social media use. The need for social connection, coupled with the pressure to conform to societal expectations regarding appearance and behavior, can lead to compulsive smartphone use among women (Bai et al., 2024). Social media platforms, with their emphasis on visuals and social validation, can intensify these pressures, leading to higher rates of addiction among women who seek affirmation through likes, comments, and shares (Ochs & Sauer, 2022).

In contrast, men may be more inclined to use their smartphones for gaming, entertainment, and information-seeking purposes (Shao, 2009). While these behaviors can also lead to addiction, the underlying motivations are often different from those of women. Men may be drawn to the competitive and immersive aspects of smartphone games, which offer instant gratification and a sense of accomplishment (Li et al., 2021). This type of engagement can foster addiction, especially when gaming or entertainment apps become a primary source of stress relief or escapism. Research has highlighted that the patterns of smartphone addiction differ not only in terms of usage but also in terms of the emotional and psychological consequences (Akhtar et al., 2024). Women who are addicted to smartphones are more likely to experience negative emotional outcomes related to social comparison, body image issues, and emotional dependence on online interactions (Wang et al., 2019). Men, on the other hand, maybe more prone to addiction related to competitive or performance-driven activities, such as gaming, which can result in issues like cognitive overload and burnout (Thelwall & Vis, 2017).

4.3 Cultural and Societal Influences in Shaping Smartphone Addiction

Cultural norms, societal expectations, and the availability of digital infrastructure play a significant role in shaping smartphone addiction across different regions. The way smartphones are integrated into daily life varies greatly depending on cultural attitudes toward technology, communication, and social interactions (Merino et al., 2024). This creates an environment where excessive smartphone use is normalized, making it difficult for individuals to recognize the signs of addiction (Reinecke et al., 2018). Studies reveal variations in smartphone addiction trends across different regions. For instance, research from South Korea, a highly connected society, indicates that adolescents face significant risks of addiction due to the pervasive use of social media platforms and gaming apps (Cha & Seo, 2018). In the Indian cultural context, particularly in highly connective urban geographical regions of the country, smartphones are seen as essential tools for productivity, socialization, and entertainment. In these settings, constant connectivity is often encouraged, with smartphones being used for everything from work-related tasks to maintaining social connections (Pandya & Lodha, 2021).

Conversely, in cultures where face-to-face communication is still highly valued, smartphone addiction may be less prevalent, as social interactions are less dependent on digital communication. However, as global digital connectivity increases, even regions with traditionally low levels of smartphone use are beginning to see rising addiction rates (World Health Organization, 2015). This is particularly true in developing countries where smartphones have become more affordable and accessible. As these regions adopt digital technologies at a rapid pace, cultural norms around smartphone use are shifting, leading to a potential increase in addiction. Moreover, societal pressures can influence how individuals engage with their smartphones. In highly competitive environments, where academic or professional success is prioritized, individuals may feel compelled to stay connected at all times to keep up with work, school, or social obligations (Bai et al., 2024). This constant pressure to remain engaged can foster smartphone addiction, as individuals struggle to balance their digital and real-world responsibilities (Cohn, 2016).

4.4 Association of Smartphone Addiction With Elderly and Other Demographics

While smartphone addiction is often associated with younger generations, there is a growing concern about its impact on older populations, particularly the elderly. Traditionally, older adults have been less likely to engage with smartphones as frequently as younger individuals (Caliandro et al., 2021). However, as digital literacy among older populations increases, particularly post-retirement, there is potential for a rise in smartphone addiction among this group. For many elderly individuals, smartphones serve as a means of staying connected with family, especially when they live far from their loved ones (Beneito-Montagut et al., 2022). While this connectivity is undoubtedly beneficial for maintaining relationships and preventing isolation, it can also lead to over-reliance on smartphones. The accessibility of digital platforms for news, entertainment, and social media can create a dependency that mirrors the addiction seen in younger populations (Csibi et al., 2019).

Additionally, as older adults become more familiar with digital platforms, they may experience similar issues related to social comparison and validation, particularly through social media (Caliandro et al., 2021). This is especially true for those who use smartphones to reconnect with old friends or to stay updated on the lives of family members. While this can foster positive interactions, it can also lead to the same negative emotional consequences seen in younger individuals, such as anxiety and feelings of inadequacy (Choudrie et al., 2018). Another demographic that is increasingly at risk of smartphone addiction is the middle-aged population, particularly those who use smartphones for work-related purposes (Csibi et al., 2019). With the rise of remote work and the expectation of constant availability, many middle-aged professionals find themselves struggling to disconnect from their smartphones, leading to potential addiction. This over-reliance on smartphones for work-related communication can blur the boundaries between personal and professional life, contributing to stress, burnout, and mental health challenges (Choudrie et al., 2018).

5. MITIGATING THE IMPACT OF SMARTPHONE ADDICTION ON MENTAL HEALTH

As smartphone addiction continues to pose significant challenges to mental health, finding effective strategies to mitigate its impact has become a priority for individuals, healthcare professionals, and policymakers alike. This section explores various approaches to reducing smartphone addiction, focusing on digital detox strategies, mindfulness and behavioral interventions, cognitive-behavioural therapy (CBT), and the broader role of educators, healthcare providers, and policymakers in addressing this growing concern.

5.1 Digital Detox Strategies

One of the most straightforward approaches to mitigating the effects of smartphone addiction is the practice of a "digital detox." A digital detox involves voluntarily reducing or completely disconnecting from smartphones and other digital devices for a specified period, allowing individuals to reset their relationship with technology and improve their mental health (Radtke et al., 2021). The concept of a digital detox is rooted in the idea that constant exposure to digital devices overstimulates the brain, leading to mental fatigue, anxiety, and poor emotional regulation (Coyne & Woodruff, 2023). By taking intentional breaks from screens, individuals can regain control over their time and attention, leading to improved well-being (Nascimento et al., 2024).

Practical Steps for a Digital Detox

1. **Setting Daily Screen Time Limits**: One of the most effective ways to implement a digital detox is by setting daily screen time limits. Many smartphones now come equipped with built-in features that allow users to track and limit their screen time (Noë et al., 2019). These tools can be customized to reduce time spent on specific apps, such as social media, games, or entertainment platforms, which are often the primary contributors to addiction (Rahmillah et al., 2023). By being mindful of screen time, individuals can gradually reduce their dependence on their devices.
2. **Engaging in Offline Activities**: To successfully reduce smartphone use, it is essential to replace screen time with fulfilling offline activities. Engaging in hobbies, physical exercise, or spending quality time with family and friends can help individuals reconnect with their physical environment and strengthen real-world relationships. Activities such as reading, painting, hiking, or learning a new skill offer meaningful alternatives to the constant lure of digital engagement.
3. **Using "Do Not Disturb" Features**: Another effective strategy is utilizing the "Do Not Disturb" or "Focus" modes on smartphones. These features allow users to block incoming notifications during designated periods, reducing the impulse to check their phones frequently (Jarupreechachan et al., 2023). This can be particularly helpful during work hours, study sessions, or before bedtime to create a more distraction-free environment. By reducing the constant barrage of notifications, individuals can reduce cognitive overload and improve their focus and productivity.
4. **Designated Device-Free Zones and Times**: Establishing device-free zones, such as bedrooms, dining areas, or living rooms, can help limit smartphone use during important personal or family moments (Wasie, 2024). Similarly, setting aside specific times of the day, such as during meals or before bed, as "device-free" times can encourage healthier habits and reduce compulsive checking of phones.

Overall, digital detox strategies provide a simple yet powerful way for individuals to regain control over their smartphone use, offering tangible improvements in mental well-being and overall life satisfaction.

5.2 Mindfulness and Behavioral Interventions

In addition to digital detox strategies, mindfulness and behavioral interventions can help individuals develop healthier digital habits by increasing their awareness of how they engage with technology. These approaches aim to foster a more intentional relationship with smartphones, allowing users to break free from compulsive behaviors and regain a sense of balance (De Oliveira et al., 2020).

Mindfulness Techniques

Mindfulness involves paying attention to the present moment in a non-judgmental way. When applied to smartphone use, mindfulness can help individuals become more aware of their digital behaviors and reduce the automatic, mindless scrolling that often characterizes smartphone addiction (Baym et al., 2020).

1. **Mindful Use of Technology**: Practicing mindfulness can involve simple techniques such as pausing before using a smartphone, asking oneself whether checking the device is necessary or beneficial, and noticing how one feels before, during, and after engaging with digital content (Palalas, 2017). This practice helps individuals recognize emotional triggers for smartphone use, such as boredom, loneliness, or anxiety, and allows them to make more intentional choices about when and how to use their devices.
2. **Digital Well-Being Apps**: Several apps are designed to help users track their digital habits and practice mindfulness in their smartphone use. These apps often provide data on screen time, offer daily reminders to take breaks, and encourage users to reflect on their digital consumption patterns (Almourad et al., 2021). By using these tools, individuals can increase their awareness of how much time they spend on their phones and make conscious efforts to reduce their usage.

5.3 Self-Regulation Strategies

Self-regulation is another key component of behavioral interventions for smartphone addiction. Self-regulation involves setting personal boundaries, resisting temptations, and managing impulses to check smartphones unnecessarily.

1. **Goal Setting**: One effective self-regulation strategy is setting clear, achievable goals for reducing smartphone use (Mahapatra, 2019). For example, individuals can start by aiming to reduce their screen time by 30 minutes per day or limiting social media use to specific time blocks. Gradually increasing these goals over time can lead to sustained improvements in smartphone habits.

2. **Creating Digital Boundaries**: Establishing personal rules around smartphone use, such as not using phones during meals or avoiding phone use in bed, can help individuals create healthy boundaries between their digital and offline lives (Van Zoonen et al., 2020). Consistently enforcing these boundaries reinforces positive behavior and reduces the likelihood of addiction.

By combining mindfulness with self-regulation strategies, individuals can develop a healthier relationship with their smartphones and reduce the mental health risks associated with excessive use.

5.4 Cognitive-Behavioral Therapy (CBT) Approaches

Cognitive-behavioural therapy (CBT) has proven to be an effective intervention for addressing a wide range of behavioral addictions, including smartphone addiction (Shanmugasundaram & Tamilarasu, 2023). CBT helps individuals identify and challenge unhealthy thought patterns and modify behaviors that contribute to addiction.

Techniques to Challenge Unhealthy Thought Patterns

1. **Identifying Cognitive Distortions**: CBT involves identifying cognitive distortions, or irrational beliefs, that may drive compulsive smartphone use (Wilmer et al., 2017). For example, individuals may believe that they must respond to messages immediately or that they need constant validation from social media to feel good about themselves. These distorted beliefs can lead to excessive smartphone use as individuals seek to fulfill these perceived needs. Through CBT, individuals learn to challenge these thoughts and replace them with healthier, more rational beliefs (Shanmugasundaram & Tamilarasu, 2023).
2. **Reframing Smartphone Use**: Another key CBT technique is reframing how individuals view their smartphone use. Instead of seeing smartphones as a necessary source of constant entertainment or social interaction, individuals are encouraged to view them as tools that should be used purposefully and in moderation (Baym et al., 2020). By changing their mindset, individuals can reduce their emotional dependence on their devices.

5.5 Modifying Harmful Behaviors

CBT's structured and evidence-based approach makes it one of the most effective interventions for individuals struggling with smartphone addiction. By addressing both cognitive and behavioral aspects of the addiction, CBT helps individuals regain control over their digital habits and improve their mental health.

1. **Breaking the Cycle of Addiction**: CBT helps individuals break the cycle of addiction by developing strategies to avoid triggers that lead to compulsive smartphone use. This might involve identifying specific situations or emotions that prompt excessive use, such as stress or boredom, and finding alternative coping mechanisms, such as physical activity or relaxation techniques (Coyne & Woodruff, 2023).
2. **Building Healthier Habits**: CBT encourages individuals to replace unhealthy smartphone habits with healthier alternatives. For example, instead of using a phone as a way to unwind after a long day, individuals can be encouraged to engage in offline activities, such as reading or practicing mindfulness, as suggested by Baym et al. (2020). Over time, these healthier habits become ingrained, reducing the reliance on smartphones for emotional satisfaction.

5.6 Role of Educators, Healthcare Providers, and Policymakers

Addressing smartphone addiction and its impact on mental health requires a coordinated effort from educators, healthcare providers, and policymakers. These stakeholders play a critical role in raising awareness, providing support, and implementing policies that promote healthier digital habits.

5.6.1 Importance of Awareness Campaigns

1. **Schools and Workplaces**: Awareness campaigns in schools and workplaces are essential for educating individuals about the risks of smartphone addiction and promoting healthier digital behaviors (Kutluay & Karaca, 2024). Schools can integrate digital literacy programs that teach students how to use technology responsibly and recognize the signs of addiction. Similarly, workplaces can offer workshops and resources to help employees manage their screen time and prevent burnout (Goel & Singla, 2024).
2. **Public Health Campaigns**: Public health campaigns can also play a significant role in raising awareness about the mental health risks associated with excessive smartphone use. These campaigns can focus on promoting digital well-being, encouraging individuals to take breaks from their devices, and providing resources for those struggling with addiction (Coyne & Woodruff, 2023).

5.6.2 Recommendations for Educators and Healthcare Providers

1. **Identifying and Supporting At-Risk Individuals**: Educators and healthcare providers are often in a unique position to identify individuals at risk of smartphone addiction (Cha & Seo, 2018). Teachers, counselors, and healthcare

professionals can monitor for signs of addiction, such as decreased academic performance, social withdrawal, or mental health concerns, and provide appropriate interventions, such as counseling or referral to digital detox programs (Y et al., 2023).

2. **Integrating Digital Well-Being into Healthcare**: Healthcare providers, particularly mental health professionals, can integrate digital well-being into their treatment plans for patients struggling with smartphone addiction (Philippe et al., 2022). By addressing the underlying emotional and psychological factors contributing to addiction, healthcare providers can offer comprehensive support to help individuals improve their mental health and reduce their dependence on digital devices.

5.6.3 Policy Recommendations

Policymakers also have a critical role to play in addressing smartphone addiction on a larger scale. By implementing public health policies that promote digital well-being, governments can help mitigate the mental health impact of excessive smartphone use.

1. **Regulating Screen Time for Children and Adolescents**: Policymakers can introduce regulations to limit screen time for children and adolescents, particularly in educational settings (Blumberg et al., 2019). These regulations could include guidelines for the responsible use of smartphones in schools and recommendations for parents on how to manage their children's screen time at home (Anaby et al., 2013).
2. **Supporting Research and Intervention Programs**: Governments can allocate funding to support research on smartphone addiction and develop intervention programs aimed at reducing its impact. A systematic review analyzing over 50 studies found a pooled prevalence of smartphone addiction to be approximately 23%, with significantly higher rates among adolescents and young adults (Busch & McCarthy, 2020). These insights highlight the urgent need to address this growing behavioral health issue with targeted strategies informed by empirical data. By investing in public health initiatives that address the digital mental health crisis, policymakers can help create a healthier, more balanced digital environment for society.

Mitigating the impact of smartphone addiction on mental health requires a multifaceted approach involving digital detox strategies, mindfulness and behavioural interventions, CBT techniques, and the active involvement of educators, healthcare providers, and policymakers. Together, these strategies can help individuals break free from the grip of smartphone addiction and lead healthier, more fulfilling lives.

6. EMERGING TRENDS AND FUTURE DIRECTIONS IN RESEARCH

As smartphone usage continues to dominate modern life, understanding its long-term impact on mental health remains a growing area of concern and interest for researchers. The rapid pace of technological innovation is constantly shaping how individuals interact with their smartphones, with emerging trends in artificial intelligence (AI), digital platforms, and mental health solutions playing a pivotal role in both exacerbating and alleviating the mental health consequences of excessive smartphone use. This section delves into how these technological advancements may influence future research on smartphone addiction and mental health, as well as the potential for long-term implications. Furthermore, the section also delves into the positive aspects of smartphones, highlighting their significant contributions to society as a whole.

6.1 Technological Innovations and Mental Health

Technological advancements in smartphones show no signs of slowing down. From 5G networks and AI-driven personalized content to augmented reality (AR) and virtual reality (VR), the capabilities of smartphones are becoming more sophisticated and immersive (Rashid & Kausik, 2024). These innovations will inevitably continue to shape how people use their devices, with both positive and negative implications for mental health.

1. **AI-Driven User Experience**: Artificial intelligence is increasingly being integrated into smartphone applications, personalizing the user experience by analyzing behavior patterns and tailoring content accordingly. While this can enhance convenience and satisfaction, it may also intensify smartphone addiction. Algorithms that curate content based on user preferences can lead to extended screen time and create a feedback loop of engagement, keeping individuals hooked on their devices. This raises concerns about the deepening of addictive behaviors, particularly among vulnerable populations such as adolescents.
2. **Augmented and Virtual Reality**: AR and VR have the potential to offer new forms of engagement, transforming how individuals interact with digital content. However, the immersive nature of these technologies can also blur the lines between the virtual and real worlds, further distancing users from offline

experiences. Increased use of AR and VR features may result in heightened risks of escapism, exacerbating feelings of social isolation and contributing to addiction. Moreover, the psychological impact of these immersive technologies on cognitive load and emotional regulation is still under-researched, leaving open questions about how they may influence mental health in the long term.

3. **AI and Mental Health Solutions**: While AI may pose risks, it also offers promising solutions for addressing smartphone addiction and mental health. AI-driven mental health apps are being developed to monitor users' digital behavior, provide real-time feedback on unhealthy usage patterns, and offer support for stress management, anxiety, and depression. These innovations have the potential to bridge the gap between mental health care and technology, providing accessible resources for those struggling with smartphone addiction.

6.2 Long-Term Implications of Smartphone Addiction

While much is known about the short-term effects of smartphone addiction, such as anxiety, depression, and sleep disruption, the long-term implications remain less clear. The current body of research suggests that prolonged and excessive smartphone use could have significant, lasting effects on mental health and overall well-being (Blumberg et al., 2019).

1. **Cognitive and Emotional Impact**: Studies have shown that excessive smartphone use can lead to cognitive overload, attention deficits, and emotional dysregulation. Over time, these effects may accumulate, resulting in diminished cognitive functioning, lower emotional resilience, and an increased risk of mental health disorders such as chronic anxiety and depression. The constant need for stimulation and instant gratification that smartphones provide may also hinder the development of emotional coping skills and social resilience, particularly among younger users (Blumberg et al., 2019).
2. **Social and Relational Consequences**: The long-term social consequences of smartphone addiction are another area that warrants further research. As individuals become increasingly reliant on digital communication, the quality of face-to-face interactions may deteriorate, leading to weaker social bonds and greater feelings of loneliness (Alabri, 2022). Over time, this could contribute to a more profound sense of social isolation, undermining the foundations of community and interpersonal relationships.
3. **The Need for Longitudinal Studies**: To fully understand the long-term mental health effects of smartphone addiction, comprehensive longitudinal studies are required. Such studies would track individuals over extended periods, providing insights into how excessive smartphone use impacts mental health, cognitive

development, and social relationships across the lifespan. Currently, much of the research on smartphone addiction focuses on short-term outcomes, leaving a critical gap in knowledge about its long-term consequences.

6.3 The Future of Digital Mental Health Solutions

As the digital mental health crisis continues to unfold, the demand for innovative solutions that address smartphone addiction and its psychological toll is growing. Future developments in mental health technologies hold promise for both preventing and treating the mental health effects of smartphone addiction.

1. **Mental Health Apps**: The rise of mental health apps designed to combat smartphone addiction is already underway, with applications like Headspace, Calm, and Forest offering tools for mindfulness, meditation, and screen time management. As these apps evolve, they are likely to become even more sophisticated, incorporating AI to provide personalized interventions based on users' behaviors. These tools can help users self-regulate, offering real-time feedback and resources to reduce screen time, improve mental health, and prevent addiction.
2. **Teletherapy Platforms**: Teletherapy has emerged as an important tool for delivering mental health care, particularly in the wake of the COVID-19 pandemic. The accessibility of therapy through smartphones and digital platforms has opened up new possibilities for addressing smartphone addiction. In the future, teletherapy platforms may integrate more specialized treatments for individuals struggling with digital addiction, offering cognitive-behavioral therapy (CBT) and other evidence-based interventions remotely.
3. **Wearable Technology for Mental Health**: Another promising avenue for research is the integration of wearable technology, such as smartwatches and fitness trackers, into mental health interventions. These devices can monitor physical signs of stress, anxiety, and sleep quality, providing users with feedback that helps them recognize the impact of smartphone addiction on their overall health. In combination with smartphone apps, wearable technology may play a pivotal role in promoting digital well-being.

6.4 Positive Aspects of Smartphones: A Balanced Perspective

While smartphone addiction has undeniable implications for mental well-being of the individuals, it is important to acknowledge the significant positive contributions that these devices can offer, particularly in the realms of education, communication, and personal development. A balanced discussion must encompass not only the risks but also the opportunities that smartphones bring to contemporary life. To ensure a comprehensive understanding of smartphones' impact, it is crucial to highlight these positive aspects while addressing potential risks. Striking a balance between the two can foster a more nuanced perspective, encouraging responsible use while maximizing the benefits these devices offer.

1. **Educational Opportunities**: Smartphones have revolutionized access to learning materials, enabling users to engage with educational content from virtually anywhere (Mohtar et al., 2022). Through apps, online courses, and educational platforms, individuals can pursue lifelong learning, acquire new skills, and stay informed about the latest developments in various fields (Bonfield et al., 2020).
2. **Social Connectivity**: Smartphones facilitate instant communication, bridging geographical divides and enabling individuals to stay connected with family, friends, and colleagues (Marlowe et al., 2016). Social media platforms, video calls, and messaging apps have redefined how we interact, offering avenues for social support, networking, and collaboration (Verhoef et al., 2017).
3. **Personal Development Tools**: With the availability of mindfulness apps, fitness trackers, and mental health resources, smartphones can play a role in promoting well-being (Baym et al., 2020; Palalas, 2017). These tools empower users to track their health, manage stress, and adopt healthier lifestyles.
4. **Productivity Enhancement**: Smartphones offer a range of productivity tools that can improve time management, task organization, and professional efficiency (Carayannis et al., 2012). From calendar apps to project management platforms, these devices help individuals streamline their work and personal lives (Lund & Wiese, 2021).

7.CONCLUSION: A CALL FOR ACTION

In conclusion, smartphone addiction poses significant challenges to mental health, with its effects ranging from heightened anxiety and depression to sleep disorders, social isolation, and cognitive overload. The pervasive nature of smartphones, while offering convenience and connectivity, also drives compulsive behaviors that can negatively impact emotional well-being and interpersonal relationships. As technological advancements continue to shape the way we use smartphones, the need for comprehensive strategies to mitigate these risks becomes paramount. Public health campaigns, policy interventions, and mental health solutions, such as digital detox strategies and cognitive-behavioral therapy, offer a pathway to addressing this growing issue. It is essential to raise awareness about the dangers of excessive smartphone use and to encourage responsible digital habits, particularly among vulnerable populations like adolescents. By fostering a balanced approach to technology, society can harness the benefits of smartphones while minimizing their detrimental effects on mental health. The urgency to act is clear, and continued research and proactive interventions are necessary to ensure a healthier digital future.

REFERENCES

Akhtar, N., Islam, T., Hameed, Z., Ghaffar, A., Sharma, A., Kincl, T., & Islam, F. (2024). Unveiling mechanism of SNSs addiction on wellbeing: The moderating role of loneliness and social anxiety. *Behaviour & Information Technology*, 1–20. DOI: 10.1080/0144929X.2024.2417390

Alabri, A. (2022). Fear of Missing Out (FOMO): The Effects of the Need to Belong, Perceived Centrality, and Fear of Social Exclusion. *Human Behavior and Emerging Technologies*, 2022, 1–12. DOI: 10.1155/2022/4824256

Alhassan, A. A., Alqadhib, E. M., Taha, N. W., Alahmari, R. A., Salam, M., & Almutairi, A. F. (2018). The relationship between addiction to smartphone usage and depression among adults: A cross sectional study. *BMC Psychiatry*, 18(1), 148. Advance online publication. DOI: 10.1186/s12888-018-1745-4 PMID: 29801442

Almourad, M. B., Alrobai, A., Skinner, T., Hussain, M., & Ali, R. (2021). Digital wellbeing tools through users lens. *Technology in Society*, 67, 101778. DOI: 10.1016/j.techsoc.2021.101778

Anaby, D., Hand, C., Bradley, L., DiRezze, B., Forhan, M., DiGiacomo, A., & Law, M. (2013). The effect of the environment on participation of children and youth with disabilities: A scoping review. *Disability and Rehabilitation*, 35(19), 1589–1598. DOI: 10.3109/09638288.2012.748840 PMID: 23350759

Bai, H., Liu, J., Bai, W., & Cao, T. (2024). Social pressures and their impact on smartphone use stickiness and use habit among adolescents. *Heliyon*, 10(7), e29111. DOI: 10.1016/j.heliyon.2024.e29111 PMID: 38601604

Baym, N. K., Wagman, K. B., & Persaud, C. J. (2020). Mindfully Scrolling: Rethinking Facebook After Time Deactivated. *Social Media + Society*, 6(2), 205630512091910. DOI: 10.1177/2056305120919105

Beneito-Montagut, R., Rosales, A., & Fernández-Ardèvol, M. (2022). Emerging Digital Inequalities: A Comparative Study of Older Adults' Smartphone Use. *Social Media + Society*, 8(4), 205630512211387. DOI: 10.1177/20563051221138756

Blumberg, F. C., Deater-Deckard, K., Calvert, S. L., Flynn, R. M., Green, C. S., Arnold, D., & Brooks, P. J. (2019). Digital Games as a Context for Children's Cognitive Development: Research Recommendations and Policy Considerations. *Social Policy Report*, 32(1), 1–33. DOI: 10.1002/sop2.3

Bonfield, C. A., Salter, M., Longmuir, A., Benson, M., & Adachi, C. (2020). Transformation or evolution?: Education 4.0, teaching and learning in the digital age. *Higher Education Pedagogies*, 5(1), 223–246. DOI: 10.1080/23752696.2020.1816847

Busch, P. A., & McCarthy, S. (2020). Antecedents and consequences of problematic smartphone use: A systematic literature review of an emerging research area. *Computers in Human Behavior*, 114, 106414. DOI: 10.1016/j.chb.2020.106414

Caldeira, S. P., Jorge, A., & Kubrusly, A. (2024). "How Can You Be a Feminist if You're Always Online?" Online Activisms, Ambivalence, and Dis/Connection. *Television & New Media*, 15274764241281693. Advance online publication. DOI: 10.1177/15274764241281693

Caliandro, A., Garavaglia, E., Sturiale, V., & Di Leva, A. (2021). Older people and smartphone practices in everyday life: An inquire on digital sociality of italian older users. *Communication Review*, 24(1), 47–78. DOI: 10.1080/10714421.2021.1904771

Carayannis, E. G., Clark, S. C., & Valvi, D. E. (2012). Smartphone Affordance: Achieving Better Business Through Innovation. *Journal of the Knowledge Economy*, 4(4), 444–472. DOI: 10.1007/s13132-012-0091-x

Cha, S., & Seo, B. (2018). Smartphone use and smartphone addiction in middle school students in Korea: Prevalence, social networking service, and game use. *Health Psychology Open*, 5(1). DOI: 10.1177/2055102918755046 PMID: 29435355

Chan, C. K. Y., Burton, K., & Flower, R. L. (2024). Facilitators and barriers of technology adoption and social connectedness among rural older adults: A qualitative study. *Health Psychology and Behavioral Medicine*, 12(1), 2398167. Advance online publication. DOI: 10.1080/21642850.2024.2398167 PMID: 39234572

Chan, T. K. H., Cheung, C. M. K., & Wong, R. Y. M. (2019). Cyberbullying on Social Networking Sites: The Crime Opportunity and Affordance Perspectives. *Journal of Management Information Systems*, 36(2), 574–609. DOI: 10.1080/07421222.2019.1599500

Chen, G., & Lyu, C. (2024). The relationship between smartphone addiction and procrastination among students: A systematic review and meta-analysis. *Personality and Individual Differences*, 224, 112652. DOI: 10.1016/j.paid.2024.112652

Chen, H., Dong, G., & Li, K. (2023). Overview on brain function enhancement of Internet addicts through exercise intervention: Based on reward-execution-decision cycle. *Frontiers in Psychiatry*, 14, 1094583. Advance online publication. DOI: 10.3389/fpsyt.2023.1094583 PMID: 36816421

Chen, W. (2022). Exploring digital natives' mobile addiction syndrome in Taiwan: Psychological issues and beyond. *Information Technology & People*, 36(3), 1326–1355. DOI: 10.1108/ITP-08-2021-0633

Choudrie, J., Pheeraphuttranghkoon, S., & Davari, S. (2018). The Digital Divide and Older Adult Population Adoption, Use and Diffusion of Mobile Phones: A Quantitative Study. *Information Systems Frontiers*, 22(3), 673–695. DOI: 10.1007/s10796-018-9875-2

Cohn, J. (2016). "Devilish Smartphones" and the "Stone-Cold" Internet: Implications of the Technology Addiction Trope in College Student Digital Literacy Narratives. *Computers & Composition. Computers and Composition*, 42, 80–94. DOI: 10.1016/j.compcom.2016.08.008

Collen, M. F., & Kulikowski, C. A. (2015). The Development of Digital Computers. In *Computers in health care* (pp. 3–73). DOI: 10.1007/978-1-4471-6732-7_1

Coyne, P., & Woodruff, S. J. (2023). Taking a Break: The Effects of Partaking in a Two-Week Social Media Digital Detox on Problematic Smartphone and Social Media Use, and Other Health-Related Outcomes among Young Adults. *Behavioral Sciences (Basel, Switzerland)*, 13(12), 1004. DOI: 10.3390/bs13121004 PMID: 38131860

Csibi, S., Griffiths, M. D., Demetrovics, Z., & Szabo, A. (2019). Analysis of Problematic Smartphone Use Across Different Age Groups within the 'Components Model of Addiction.'. *International Journal of Mental Health and Addiction*, 19(3), 616–631. DOI: 10.1007/s11469-019-00095-0

Dadandı, İ., & Kalyon, A. (2024). Impulsivity and problematic smartphone use: Mediating role of self-handicapping. *Behaviour & Information Technology*, 1–17. DOI: 10.1080/0144929X.2024.2313705

De Oliveira, M. L. C., De Nogueira Holanda, F. W., Valdez, P., De Almondes, K. M., & De Azevedo, C. V. M. (2020). Impact of Electronic Device Usage Before Bedtime on Sleep and Attention in Adolescents. *Mind, Brain and Education : the Official Journal of the International Mind, Brain, and Education Society*, 14(4), 376–386. DOI: 10.1111/mbe.12260

De Toledo, L. H. S., Moraes, M. N., De Oliveira Poletini, M., Neto, J. C., Baron, J., & Mota, T. (2023). Modeling the influence of nighttime light on melatonin suppression in humans: Milestones and perspectives. *Journal of Photochemistry and Photobiology*, 16, 100199. DOI: 10.1016/j.jpap.2023.100199

Dwivedi, Y. K., Ismagilova, E., Hughes, D. L., Carlson, J., Filieri, R., Jacobson, J., Jain, V., Karjaluoto, H., Kefi, H., Krishen, A. S., Kumar, V., Rahman, M. M., Raman, R., Rauschnabel, P. A., Rowley, J., Salo, J., Tran, G. A., & Wang, Y. (2021). Setting the future of digital and social media marketing research: Perspectives and research propositions. *International Journal of Information Management*, 59, 102168. DOI: 10.1016/j.ijinfomgt.2020.102168

Edwards, E. J., Taylor, C. S., & Vaughan, R. S. (2022). Individual differences in self-esteem and social anxiety predict problem smartphone use in adolescents. *School Psychology International*, 43(5), 460–476. DOI: 10.1177/01430343221111061

Eichenberg, C., Schneider, R., & Rumpl, H. (2024). Social media addiction: Associations with attachment style, mental distress, and personality. *BMC Psychiatry*, 24(1), 278. Advance online publication. DOI: 10.1186/s12888-024-05709-z PMID: 38622677

Girela-Serrano, B. M., Spiers, A. D. V., Ruotong, L., Gangadia, S., Toledano, M. B., & Di Simplicio, M. (2022). Impact of mobile phones and wireless devices use on children and adolescents' mental health: A systematic review. *European Child & Adolescent Psychiatry*. Advance online publication. DOI: 10.1007/s00787-022-02012-8 PMID: 35705765

Goel, R., & Singla, J. (2024). Workplace Transformation. In *Advances in marketing, customer relationship management, and e-services book series* (pp. 178–207). DOI: 10.4018/979-8-3693-1314-5.ch008

Goel, R., Singla, J., Arora, M., & Mittal, A. (2024). From stress to success: Role of green atmospherics on employee well-being in the Indian hotel and tourism industry. *Journal of Human Resources in Hospitality & Tourism*, 23(3), 359–385. DOI: 10.1080/15332845.2024.2335091

Greenfield, D. N. (2020). Digital distraction: What makes the internet and smartphone so addictive? In *American Psychological Association eBooks* (pp. 27–47). DOI: 10.1037/0000208-003

Hansen, K. (2022, October 17). *Our Social Media Addiction*. Harvard Business Review. https://hbr.org/2022/11/our-social-media-addiction

Hassan, M. R., Mahmud, M. S., & Hasan, M. K. (2024). Social Media Addiction and Its Consequences Among Youth: A Developing Country Perspective. *Global Business Review*, 09721509241276720. Advance online publication. DOI: 10.1177/09721509241276720

Jahrami, H., Romdhane, F. F., & Pandi-Perumal, S. R. (2023). Global research evidence on nomophobia during 2008-2022: A bibliometric analysis and review. *Psychology Health and Medicine*, 29(5), 889–904. DOI: 10.1080/13548506.2023.2268888 PMID: 37846044

Jameel, S., Shahnawaz, M. G., & Griffiths, M. D. (2019). Smartphone addiction in students: A qualitative examination of the components model of addiction using face-to-face interviews. *Journal of Behavioral Addictions*, 8(4), 780–793. DOI: 10.1556/2006.8.2019.57 PMID: 31619046

Jarupreechachan, W., Kitchat, K., & Surasak, T. (2023). 'Do Not Disturb': An Implication Design To Be Alerted But Less Stress. In *nternational Seminar on Application for Technology of Information and Communication (iSemantic), Semarang, Indonesia, 2023* (Vol. 128). DOI: 10.1109/iSemantic59612.2023.10295289

Jo, H., & Baek, E. (2023). Exploring the dynamics of mobile app addiction: The interplay of communication, affective factors, flow, perceived enjoyment, and habit. *BMC Psychology*, 11(1), 404. Advance online publication. DOI: 10.1186/s40359-023-01440-8 PMID: 37986198

Kutluay, E., & Karaca, F. (2024). A model proposal explaining the influence of smartphone addiction related factors on high school students' academic success. *Education and Information Technologies*. Advance online publication. DOI: 10.1007/s10639-024-12947-x

Li, J., Zhan, D., Zhou, Y., & Gao, X. (2021). Loneliness and problematic mobile phone use among adolescents during the COVID-19 pandemic: The roles of escape motivation and self-control. *Addictive Behaviors*, 118, 106857. DOI: 10.1016/j.addbeh.2021.106857 PMID: 33676160

Lissitsa, S., & Kagan, M. (2024). The enduring echoes of juvenile bullying: The role of self-esteem and loneliness in the relationship between bullying and social media addiction across generations X, Y, Z. *Frontiers in Psychology*, 15, 1446000. Advance online publication. DOI: 10.3389/fpsyg.2024.1446000 PMID: 39156810

Lund, J. R., & Wiese, J. (2021). Less is More: Exploring Support for Time Management Planning. *Designing Interactive Systems Conference*, 392–405. DOI: 10.1145/3461778.3462133

Mahapatra, S. (2019). Smartphone addiction and associated consequences: Role of loneliness and self-regulation. *Behaviour & Information Technology*, 38(8), 833–844. DOI: 10.1080/0144929X.2018.1560499

Mao, B., Jia, X., & Huang, Q. (2022). How do information overload and message fatigue reduce information processing in the era of COVID-19? An ability–motivation approach. *Journal of Information Science*. Advance online publication. DOI: 10.1177/01655515221118047

Marlowe, J. M., Bartley, A., & Collins, F. (2016). Digital belongings: The intersections of social cohesion, connectivity and digital media. *Ethnicities*, 17(1), 85–102. DOI: 10.1177/1468796816654174

Mason, M. C., Zamparo, G., Marini, A., & Ameen, N. (2022). Glued to your phone? Generation Z's smartphone addiction and online compulsive buying. *Computers in Human Behavior*, 136, 107404. DOI: 10.1016/j.chb.2022.107404

Merino, M., Tornero-Aguilera, J. F., Rubio-Zarapuz, A., Villanueva-Tobaldo, C. V., Martín-Rodríguez, A., & Clemente-Suárez, V. J. (2024). Body Perceptions and Psychological Well-Being: A Review of the Impact of Social Media and Physical Measurements on Self-Esteem and Mental Health with a Focus on Body Image Satisfaction and Its Relationship with Cultural and Gender Factors. *Health Care*, 12(14), 1396. DOI: 10.3390/healthcare12141396 PMID: 39057539

Mohtar, S., Jomhari, N., Mustafa, M. B., & Yusoff, Z. M. (2022). Mobile learning: Research context, methodologies and future works towards middle-aged adults – a systematic literature review. *Multimedia Tools and Applications*, 82(7), 11117–11143. DOI: 10.1007/s11042-022-13698-y PMID: 36035325

Mun, I. B. (2024). Longitudinal relationship between parental and adolescent smartphone addiction: Serial mediating effects of adolescent self-esteem and depression. *Internet Research*, 34(6), 2031–2056. DOI: 10.1108/INTR-02-2023-0110

Nascimento, P., Oliveira, T., & Neves, J. (2024). The battle against screen time: A systematic review of hedonic information systems use reduction. *Internet Research*. Advance online publication. DOI: 10.1108/INTR-10-2023-0857

Ning, W., Turel, O., & Davis, F. D. (2024). Potential treatments of technology addiction: Insights for information systems scholars. *Internet Research*. Advance online publication. DOI: 10.1108/INTR-12-2023-1122

Noë, B., Turner, L. D., Linden, D. E., Allen, S. M., Winkens, B., & Whitaker, R. M. (2019). Identifying Indicators of Smartphone Addiction Through User-App Interaction. *Computers in Human Behavior*, 99, 56–65. DOI: 10.1016/j.chb.2019.04.023 PMID: 31582873

Ochs, C., & Sauer, J. (2022). Disturbing aspects of smartphone usage: A qualitative analysis. *Behaviour & Information Technology*, 42(14), 2504–2519. DOI: 10.1080/0144929X.2022.2129092

Ophir, Y., Rosenberg, H., Lipshits-Braziler, Y., & Amichai-Hamburger, Y. (2020). Digital adolescence. In *Routledge eBooks* (pp. 122–139). DOI: 10.4324/9780429468360-8

Orzech, K. M., Grandner, M. A., Roane, B. M., & Carskadon, M. A. (2015). Digital media use in the 2 h before bedtime is associated with sleep variables in university students. *Computers in Human Behavior*, 55, 43–50. DOI: 10.1016/j.chb.2015.08.049 PMID: 28163362

Ostic, D., Qalati, S. A., Barbosa, B., Shah, S. M. M., Vela, E. G., Herzallah, A. M., & Liu, F. (2021). Effects of Social Media Use on Psychological Well-Being: A Mediated Model. *Frontiers in Psychology*, 12, 678766. Advance online publication. DOI: 10.3389/fpsyg.2021.678766 PMID: 34234717

Palalas, A. (2017). Mindfulness in Mobile and Ubiquitous Learning: Harnessing the Power of Attention. In *Perspectives on rethinking and reforming education* (pp. 19–44). DOI: 10.1007/978-981-10-6144-8_2

Pandya, A., & Lodha, P. (2021). Social Connectedness, Excessive Screen Time During COVID-19 and Mental Health: A Review of Current Evidence. *Frontiers in Human Dynamics*, 3, 684137. Advance online publication. DOI: 10.3389/fhumd.2021.684137

Peleg, O., & Boniel-Nissim, M. (2024). Exploring the personality and relationship factors that mediate the connection between differentiation of self and phubbing. *Scientific Reports*, 14(1), 6572. Advance online publication. DOI: 10.1038/s41598-024-55560-1 PMID: 38504119

Philippe, T. J., Sikder, N., Jackson, A., Koblanski, M. E., Liow, E., Pilarinos, A., & Vasarhelyi, K. (2022). Digital Health Interventions for Delivery of Mental Health Care: Systematic and Comprehensive Meta-Review. *JMIR Mental Health*, 9(5), e35159. DOI: 10.2196/35159 PMID: 35551058

Pinochet, L. H. C., Da Silva Santos, S., Pardim, V. I., & De Souza, C. A. (2023). Watch out for nomophobia, so it does not catch you! Effects of digital dependence syndrome on mental health. *Journal of Systems and Information Technology*, 25(3), 296–318. DOI: 10.1108/JSIT-03-2022-0064

Prodanova, J., & Chopdar, P. K. (2023). The interplay of app characteristics and smartphone addiction in mobile shopping behaviour. *International Journal of Consumer Studies*, 48(1), e12992. Advance online publication. DOI: 10.1111/ijcs.12992

Radtke, T., Apel, T., Schenkel, K., Keller, J., & Von Lindern, E. (2021). Digital detox: An effective solution in the smartphone era? A systematic literature review. *Mobile Media & Communication*, 10(2), 190–215. DOI: 10.1177/20501579211028647

Rahmillah, F. I., Tariq, A., King, M., & Oviedo-Trespalacios, O. (2023). Evaluating the Effectiveness of Apps Designed to Reduce Mobile Phone Use and Prevent Maladaptive Mobile Phone Use: Multimethod Study. *Journal of Medical Internet Research*, 25, e42541. DOI: 10.2196/42541 PMID: 37643002

Rashid, A. B., & Kausik, M. K. (2024). AI Revolutionizing Industries Worldwide: A Comprehensive Overview of Its Diverse Applications. *Hybrid Advances*, 7, 100277. DOI: 10.1016/j.hybadv.2024.100277

Reinecke, L., Klimmt, C., Meier, A., Reich, S., Hefner, D., Knop-Huelss, K., Rieger, D., & Vorderer, P. (2018). Permanently online and permanently connected: Development and validation of the Online Vigilance Scale. *PLoS One*, 13(10), e0205384. DOI: 10.1371/journal.pone.0205384 PMID: 30359368

Roberts, J. A., & David, M. E. (2019). The Social Media Party: Fear of Missing Out (FoMO), Social Media Intensity, Connection, and Well-Being. *International Journal of Human-Computer Interaction*, 36(4), 386–392. DOI: 10.1080/10447318.2019.1646517

Sengupta, A., & Chaudhuri, A. (2010). Are social networking sites a source of online harassment for teens? Evidence from survey data. *Children and Youth Services Review*, 33(2), 284–290. DOI: 10.1016/j.childyouth.2010.09.011

Shanmugasundaram, M., & Tamilarasu, A. (2023). The impact of digital technology, social media, and artificial intelligence on cognitive functions: A review. *Frontiers in Cognition*, 2, 1203077. Advance online publication. DOI: 10.3389/fcogn.2023.1203077

Shao, G. (2009). Understanding the appeal of user-generated media: A uses and gratification perspective. *Internet Research*, 19(1), 7–25. DOI: 10.1108/10662240910927795

Shi, Y., Koval, P., Kostakos, V., Goncalves, J., & Wadley, G. (2022). "Instant Happiness": Smartphones as tools for everyday emotion regulation. *International Journal of Human-Computer Studies*, 170, 102958. DOI: 10.1016/j.ijhcs.2022.102958

Squires, L. R., Hollett, K. B., Hesson, J., & Harris, N. (2020). Psychological Distress, Emotion Dysregulation, and Coping Behaviour: A Theoretical Perspective of Problematic Smartphone Use. *International Journal of Mental Health and Addiction*, 19(4), 1284–1299. DOI: 10.1007/s11469-020-00224-0

Statista. (2024, August 20). *Number of smartphone users worldwide 2014-2029.* https://www.statista.com/forecasts/1143723/smartphone-users-in-the-world

Stenseng, F., Falch-Madsen, J., & Hygen, B. W. (2021). Are there two types of escapism? Exploring a dualistic model of escapism in digital gaming and online streaming. *Psychology of Popular Media*, 10(3), 319–329. DOI: 10.1037/ppm0000339

Stevic, A., Schmuck, D., Thomas, M. F., Karsay, K., & Matthes, J. (2023). Distracted Children? Nighttime Smartphone Use, Children's Attentional Problems, and School Performance Over Time. *The Journal of Early Adolescence*, 44(2), 223–249. DOI: 10.1177/02724316231164734

Sylwander, K. R. (2019). Affective Atmospheres of Sexualized Hate Among Youth Online: A Contribution to Bullying and Cyberbullying Research on Social Atmosphere. *International Journal of Bullying Prevention : an Official Publication of the International Bullying Prevention Association*, 1(4), 269–284. DOI: 10.1007/s42380-019-00044-4

Tandon, A., Laato, S., Islam, N., & Dhir, A. (2024). Social comparisons at social networking sites: How social Media-induced fear of missing out and envy drive compulsive use. *Internet Research.* Advance online publication. DOI: 10.1108/INTR-10-2022-0770

Tedone, A. M. (2022). Keeping Up With Work Email After Hours and Employee Wellbeing: Examining Relationships During and Prior to the COVID-19 Pandemic. *Occupational Health Science*, 6(1), 51–72. DOI: 10.1007/s41542-021-00107-3 PMID: 35097187

Thelwall, M., & Vis, F. (2017). Gender and image sharing on Facebook, Twitter, Instagram, Snapchat and WhatsApp in the UK. *Aslib Journal of Information Management*, 69(6), 702–720. DOI: 10.1108/AJIM-04-2017-0098

Touitou, Y., & Point, S. (2020). Effects and mechanisms of action of light-emitting diodes on the human retina and internal clock. *Environmental Research*, 190, 109942. DOI: 10.1016/j.envres.2020.109942 PMID: 32758719

Trainor, B. C. (2011). Stress responses and the mesolimbic dopamine system: Social contexts and sex differences. *Hormones and Behavior*, 60(5), 457–469. DOI: 10.1016/j.yhbeh.2011.08.013 PMID: 21907202

Van Den Eijnden, R. J., Geurts, S. M., Ter Bogt, T. F., Van Der Rijst, V. G., & Koning, I. M. (2021). Social Media Use and Adolescents' Sleep: A Longitudinal Study on the Protective Role of Parental Rules Regarding Internet Use before Sleep. *International Journal of Environmental Research and Public Health*, 18(3), 1346. DOI: 10.3390/ijerph18031346 PMID: 33540882

Van Zoonen, W., Sivunen, A., & Rice, R. E. (2020). Boundary communication: How smartphone use after hours is associated with work-life conflict and organizational identification. *Journal of Applied Communication Research*, 48(3), 372–392. DOI: 10.1080/00909882.2020.1755050

Verhoef, P. C., Stephen, A. T., Kannan, P., Luo, X., Abhishek, V., Andrews, M., Bart, Y., Datta, H., Fong, N., Hoffman, D. L., Hu, M. M., Novak, T., Rand, W., & Zhang, Y. (2017). Consumer Connectivity in a Complex, Technology-enabled, and Mobile-oriented World with Smart Products. *Journal of Interactive Marketing*, 40(1), 1–8. DOI: 10.1016/j.intmar.2017.06.001

Vossen, G., Schönthaler, F., & Dillon, S. (2017). *The Web at Graduation and Beyond: Business Impacts and Developments*. https://openlibrary.org/books/OL28222685M/The_Web_at_Graduation_and_Beyond

Wang, P., Chen, K., Yang, S., & Lin, P. (2019). Relationship of sleep quality, smartphone dependence, and health-related behaviors in female junior college students. *PLoS One*, 14(4), e0214769. DOI: 10.1371/journal.pone.0214769 PMID: 30943270

Wang, Y., & Ma, Q. (2024). The impact of social isolation on smartphone addiction among college students: The multiple mediating effects of loneliness and COVID-19 anxiety. *Frontiers in Psychology*, 15, 1391415. Advance online publication. DOI: 10.3389/fpsyg.2024.1391415 PMID: 39105145

Wasie, T. (2024). *Screen to Green: Navigating the Digital Dilemma*. Teshome Wasie.

Wegmann, E., Billieux, J., & Brand, M. (2021). Internet-use disorders: A theoretical framework for their conceptualization and diagnosis. In *Elsevier eBooks* (pp. 285–305). DOI: 10.1016/B978-0-12-822201-0.00022-8

Wilmer, H. H., Sherman, L. E., & Chein, J. M. (2017). Smartphones and Cognition: A Review of Research Exploring the Links between Mobile Technology Habits and Cognitive Functioning. *Frontiers in Psychology*, 8, 605. Advance online publication. DOI: 10.3389/fpsyg.2017.00605 PMID: 28487665

Wood, G., Goodyear, V., Adab, P., Al-Janabi, H., Fenton, S., Jones, K., Michail, M., Morrison, B., Patterson, P., Sitch, A. J., Wade, M., & Pallan, M. (2023). Smartphones, social Media and Adolescent mental well-being: The impact of school policies Restricting dayTime use—protocol for a natural experimental observational study using mixed methods at secondary schools in England (SMART Schools Study). *BMJ Open*, 13(7), e075832. DOI: 10.1136/bmjopen-2023-075832 PMID: 37407051

World Health Organization. (2015). Public Health Implications of Excessive Use of the Internet, Computers, Smartphones and Similar Electronic Devices. In *Meeting Report*. https://iris.who.int/bitstream/handle/10665/184264/9789241509367_eng.pdf

World Health Organization. (2024). *Teens, screens, and mental health*. WHO Europe. Retrieved December 21, 2024, from https://www.who.int/europe/news-room/25-09-2024-teens--screens-and-mental-health

Xiong, S., Zhang, A., Zhang, B., & Xu, Y. (2023). Patterns of smartphone addiction in adolescents and their association with multiple ecological factors: A latent profile analysis. *Children and Youth Services Review*, 155, 107223. DOI: 10.1016/j.childyouth.2023.107223

Y, P. R., Aiswarya, B., & A, J. a. S. (2023). Disruptive charms of wearable technologies: Navigating digital distractions and work performance. *Journal of Information Technology Teaching Cases*. DOI: 10.1177/20438869231203341

Yang, H., Guo, H., Zhu, Z., Yuan, G., Zhang, X., Zhang, K., Lu, X., Zhang, J., Du, J., Shi, H., Jin, G., & Zhang, Z. (2023a). Intervention of Internet Addiction and Smartphone Addiction: An Umbrella Review of Systematic Reviews and Meta-Analyses. *Current Addiction Reports*, 11(1), 125–148. DOI: 10.1007/s40429-023-00536-w

Yang, L., Guo, C., Li, G., Gan, K., & Luo, J. (2023b). Mobile phone addiction and mental health: The roles of sleep quality and perceived social support. *Frontiers in Psychology*, 14, 1265400. Advance online publication. DOI: 10.3389/fpsyg.2023.1265400 PMID: 37809316

Yilmaz, F. G. K., Ustun, A. B., Zhang, K., & Yilmaz, R. (2023). Smartphone Addiction, Nomophobia, Depression, and Social Appearance Anxiety Among College Students: A Correlational Study. *Journal of Rational-Emotive & Cognitive-Behavior Therapy*, 42(2), 305–321. DOI: 10.1007/s10942-023-00516-z

Zhang, H., Zhao, G., Meng, S., & Kong, F. (2024). The Impact of Smartphone Deprivation on Attentional Bias in Problematic Smartphone Users: Evidence from Behavioral and Physiological Perspectives. *Computers in Human Behavior*, 161, 108412. DOI: 10.1016/j.chb.2024.108412

Zhang, K., Guo, H., Wang, T., Zhang, J., Yuan, G., Ren, J., Zhang, X., Yang, H., Lu, X., Zhu, Z., Du, J., Shi, H., Jin, G., Hao, J., Sun, Y., Su, P., & Zhang, Z. (2023). A bidirectional association between smartphone addiction and depression among college students: A cross-lagged panel model. *Frontiers in Public Health*, 11, 1083856. Advance online publication. DOI: 10.3389/fpubh.2023.1083856 PMID: 36761134

Zubair, U., Khan, M. K., & Albashari, M. (2023). Link between excessive social media use and psychiatric disorders. *Annals of Medicine and Surgery (London)*, 85(4), 875–878. DOI: 10.1097/MS9.0000000000000112 PMID: 37113864

Chapter 3
The Impact of Mobile Addiction on Mental Health and Academic Performance of School Going Adolescents:
A Narrative Review

Geemol John
https://orcid.org/0000-0002-6196-9531
Lovely Professional University, India

Mohammad Amin Wani
https://orcid.org/0000-0002-4737-3731
Lovely Professional University, India

ABSTRACT

Mobile addiction is a highly significant issue, especially among adolescents, that affects mental health and academic performance badly. This is a narrative review based on the association of mobile addiction, mental health, and academic outcomes across the Indian, Asia, and international settings. Relevant, peer-reviewed articles were fetched and perused via Google Scholar. It indicates that mobile addiction has a positive link with anxiety, depression, and decline in terms of academic performance. Regional factors, like the extent to which parents control and cultural considerations, are at play. Long-term effects and targeted interventions should remain the focus of future research.

DOI: 10.4018/979-8-3693-8804-4.ch003

INTRODUCTION

The past decade may have witnessed a near revolution, almost in the light of mobile telephone technology, shifting from relatively single-purpose communication devices to multifunctional machines that nowadays hold centre stage in the daily lives of teenagers. This has made information, social networking, and entertainment available in ways impossible to date, thus dramatically enriching the relationship between youth and the world (Valkenburg & Peter, 2011).

It has then become a place of creation and learning, a platform for connection, and a medium of interaction, putting beyond limits what used to be an impossibility.

However, such advantages came with a disturbing issue that was referred to as "mobile addiction." This term refers to excessive use and an inability to control the use of mobile phones. Mobile addiction differs from a habit; it is a dependency that disturbs normal functioning and general well-being (Joel Billieux, 2012). The consequence of mobile addiction is dangerous to adolescents' cognitive development. This has consequences on their psychological and emotional well-being because there is an increased prevalence of anxiety, depression, and social isolation because of excessive smartphone use (Elhai et al., 2017; Rosen et al., 2013).

Background of the Study

Mobile technology has dramatically changed from being a simple communication tool to a multi-functional model that is frequently used by the youth. Information, social networking, and entertainment have created a much closer closeness between youth and the digital world through these means. (Valkenburg & Peter, 2011). With such advantages, though, comes another new challenge: mobile addiction described as an excessive or uncontrollable use of mobile devices such that it interferes with daily life and well-being in general (Billieux, 2012).

Mobile Addiction

Mobile addiction, or problematic mobile phone use, goes beyond mere frequent use: it is a behavioral dependence with features of addiction as characterized by other behavioral addictions. According to Billieux et al. (2015), "mobile addiction is conceptualized as patterns of excessive and repetitive mobile use that are experienced as uncontrollable, causing problematic consequences for mental health, academic performance, and social relationships". Diagnostic tools, such as the Smartphone Addiction Scale and Nomophobia Questionnaire are used to track and measure mobile addiction among adolescents. The tools help to distinguish the concepts of addiction and normal use as they focus on compulsive behaviors, emotional dependency, and the inability to control usage despite knowing its harmful effects.

Historical and Cultural Context of Mobile Addiction

The last decade has seen a drastic rise in mobile addiction among adolescents because of fast progress in the technology of smartphones and widespread access to the internet. Initially, mobile phones were only used for communication between individuals, but nowadays, following the emergence of social media, gaming applications, and instant messaging, these devices have become incredible sources of gratification and engagement for adolescents. This has highly influenced Asian, European, and North American youth; mobile addiction trends have been increasingly experienced within such countries as South Korea, China, and the United States, which have widespread availability of smartphones (Seo et al., 2016; Tsitsika et al., 2014).

Critical to mobile addiction is its cultural factor. For instance, in most Asian cultures, there is a high level of expectations for academic success; these teenagers might find themselves stressed and look for ways to alleviate this stress through mobile use, increasing their potential chances of becoming addicted (Tangmunkongvorakul et al., 2020). More importantly, the high level of individualism, combined with increased social media influence, can encourage adolescents who live in Western cultures to use mobile phones to establish their social identity and express themselves, leading them to dependency. Understanding these cultural contexts will help tailor prevention strategies for targeted populations.

Psychological Mechanisms Contributing to Mobile Addiction

Adolescents are particularly vulnerable to mobile addiction due to different psychological mechanisms that make mobile phone use more rewarding and harder to moderate.

Fear of Missing Out (FOMO): Apprehension of missing important social events, diffusion of social updates, and so on may keep adolescents perpetually connected. According to Elhai et al. (2017), FOMO leads to frequent checking of the phone and a longer stay on social media sites, increasing the chance of being an addict. Adolescents feel a need to be available and respond quickly online, perpetuating a cycle of compulsive use.

Social Comparison: The comparison among peer adolescents through social media often results in low self-esteem and lack of satisfaction. This validation urge makes them stay engaged at an activist level, continuously interacting in these social platforms, as they elicit positive reinforcement from likes, comments, and messages, upping the addiction risk (Valkenburg & Peter, 2011).

Instant Gratification: The instant feedback through notifications, likes, and rewards in mobile applications activates the dopamine release in the brain, thereby forming a reward-seeking loop that may make it challenging for adolescents to put their phones down. This mechanism is particularly strong for adolescents whose brains are developing and extremely responsive to instant gratification (Samaha & Hawi, 2016).

Escapism and Emotional Regulation: The teen seems to use his or her phone as a way to avoid unfavorable feelings, like loneliness or stress. The mobile application is an easy channel for a person to be far from reality about challenges, however, having such reliance on mobile gadgets for emotional regulation makes it one of those factors that make them develop unhealthier modes of coping mechanisms (Nasution & Daulay, 2022).

Contemporary Findings and Trends

Recent studies, especially from the last 3-5 years, have further explored the multifaceted impact of mobile addiction among adolescents across different cultural settings.

Mental Health Impacts: Such research, conducted by Buabbas et al. (2020) in Kuwait and by Elhai et al. in the United States (2017), indicates that mobile addiction has significant correlations with mental health problems of anxiety, depression, and low self-esteem in adolescents. Therefore, these studies indicate that the effects of mental health are constant across all cultures even though they may manifest differently.

Academic Performance: There have been studies from Spain that demonstrate how mobile addiction negatively impacts the academic performance of adolescents. Tsitsika et al. (2014) also conducted a study across six European countries and discovered that mobile addiction hurts the academic performances of adolescents, reducing their ability to focus and making them score low grades in school. There is an indication that this trend is worse with adolescents who extensively use their phones at night, leading to sleep disturbances and other adverse effects on cognitive functions for academic success.

Cross-cultural comparisons: The prevalence and psychological effects of smartphone addiction are different cross-culturally, and Thai and Japanese adolescents present different cases, attesting that cultural and environmental factors influence the prevalence and severity of mobile addiction. It thus implies that effective interventions must consider cultural attitudes toward technology use.

Taken together, these most recent research works vindicate the fact that mobile addiction is a grave public health concern going much beyond immediate implications in ruining the mental and academic well-being of adolescents. This updated literature shall further provide great validity to the relevance of the chapter, depicting current trends of research in most regions regarding the prevalence of smartphone usage among young people.

Objectives

- To explore the level and patterns of mobile addiction among school-going adolescents in the country, Asia, and the globe.
- To find out the impact of mobile addiction on adolescents on mental health such as anxiety, depression, and self-esteem
- To analyze the intertwining dynamics between mobile addiction and academic performance among adolescents from different cultural and educational settings.
- To outline the interventions that could reduce mobile addiction among teens, by lessons gleaned from studies in India, Asia, and the rest of the globe.

Method

Quantitative studies were included in this review. After identifying the need for the current review, the literature was selected by identifying the inclusion and exclusion criteria using different search strategies and various databases. The collected research and review papers were checked for clarity and content and then considered for review.

Inclusion Criteria

- Studies published in a peer-reviewed journal
- Research focusing on mobile phone addiction, mental health, and academic performance
- Research focusing on school-going adolescents aged 10-20 years
- Research from India, Asia, and Worldwide
- Studies are done from 2013 to 2022
- Literature published in English

Exclusion Criteria

- Studies with incomplete information on research methodology

- Studies that did not satisfy the considered variables

ELECTRONIC DATA BASE SEARCHING AND DATA EXTRACTION

For this narrative review on mobile addiction, mental health, and academic performance in adolescence, Scopus, Dimensions AI,Google Scholar were the principal sources of literature. This electronic database has a wide array of scholarly articles, and therefore it is an appropriate platform for finding relevant studies from different regions, including India, Asia, and worldwide. This database was selected to access the research on covering areas as interdisciplinary because research papers on mental health, mobile addiction, and educational outcomes are interdisciplinary fields.

Search Strategy

A systematic search in the database was applied. Related search terms like "mobile addiction," "adolescent mental health," "academic performance," "India," "Asia," "global," etc. were used as filters to narrow down recent studies of relevance. Boolean operators such as AND, and OR were used to further refine results so that no relevant study is missed. Filters by publication dates, peer-reviewed, and relevance were also applied to ensure that only the most recent relevant scientifically rigorous articles would be retrieved.

Data Extraction

With 30 relevant articles identified, 10 articles were from India; 10 were from Asia, and ten were global studies. Structured information extraction regarding the objects or aims of the study, methodology, sample size, main findings, and conclusions was systematically documented in a preset format. The focus of attention, therefore, was on extrapolating information regarding the relationship between mobile addiction and its effects on adolescent mental health and subsequent impacts on academic performances in different geographic settings. The information came together to be synthesized for a comparative regional analysis of tendencies and global perspectives.

NARRATIVE REVIEW OF THE STUDIES

Pan Indian Studies

According to a study conducted on the screen addiction of school-going adolescents (Johnson et al., 2022) it was proven that 20% felt preoccupied with screens,12% had depression and 3.9% had screen addiction. In another cross-sectional community-based study by N. Gangadharan et al., 2022 done on 264 adolescents, it was proven that mobile phone addiction was more prevalent in boys than girls. When nomophobia was studied in higher secondary schools in Kerala, (J. Elias et al., 2021) 67.81% of prevalence was noticed whereas in Uttarakhand a mobile phone dependence study, (M. S. Yadav et al., 2021) 67% had behavioral changes and had a low academic performance. When mobile phone usage pattern and dependency was studied by (B Dilip and SR Jawalkar,2018), it showed that the prevalence rate is 67.2% and it also affects their daily routine and sleep pattern, whereas another study in Agra (Vashishta & Sharma, 2017) proved that students who are addicted to Facebook, showed academic underachievement. In the Ahmedabad cross-sectional study (C. N. Pandya et al., 2021) four hours of daily smartphone use was found among adolescents. Another survey study was done on the overuse of gadgets in a government school in Bangalore (A. M. Hegde et al., 2019). it was shown that 59% reported online networking sites among school students in a cross-sectional study, the proportion of use was 87.1% and 110 out of 388 students said that their studies were affected by social networking sites. In another Mumbai-based study (C. S. Nikhita, 2015) dependent syndrome was associated with the use of a smartphone and was identified as an emerging public problem. Table 1 illustrates the pan Indian studies.

Table 1. Pan Indian studies

Author and Year of Study	Place of Study	Journal Name	Age Group of the sample	Sample Size	Variables	Study Design	Tools used	Results
(Johnson et al., 2022)	Karnataka	Journal of Indian Association for Child and Adolescent Mental Heath	10-19 years	335	Screen Addiction Physical and Mental Health	Cross-Sectional Study conducted in four schools in Karnataka	Tao Diagnostic Criteria for Internet Addiction Physical Health Questionnaire -9	Out of 335 adolescents,20% felt preoccupied with screens,8% were restless moody, and irritable,12% reported depression, and 3.9% ad screen addiction.
(Vashishta & Sharma, 2017)	Agra	MEIR Journal of Educational Studies	15-18 years	178	Facebook addiction Study Habits Academic Achievement	Random Selection of samples from four classes of a secondary school	The Bergen's Facebook Addiction Scale (BFAS,2012) Study Habit Inventory	The students who are addicted to Facebook showed poor study habits which ultimately affected their academic achievement
Hegde et al., 2019	Bangalore	Journal of Advanced Medical and Dental Sciences Researches	12-16 years	240	Overuse of electronic gadgets Effects on children's behaviour Academic performance	Survey method among students at a government high school	A closed-end questionnaire associated with the overzealous use of electronic gadgets	59% of the children reported frequent headaches in the morning after continuous use at night. 53% could not concentrate in class. 29% were found to have speech and language delays.
(N. Gangadharan et al., 2022)	Delhi	Cureus	10-19 years	264 adolescents	Mobile Phone Addiction	Community-based cross-sectional study	Interview Schedule Mobile Phone Addiction Scale (MPAS)	The mobile phone addiction prevalence was higher in boys (33.6%) than girls (32.3%) The addiction rate was higher when there were more than three siblings

continued on following page

Table 1. Continued

Author and Year of Study	Place of Study	Journal Name	Age Group of the sample	Sample Size	Variables	Study Design	Tools used	Results
(Nayak, 2018)	India	Computers and Education	Higher education adolescents	429	Mobile Phone Addiction	Cross-Sectional Study	Smart Phone Addiction Scale Smart Phone Addictive Use Scale Mobile Phone Problem Use Scale Internet Addiction Test	The utilization is higher among female students than male students, according to the results. For the male pupils, however, the impact on performance is found to be quite substantial. In contrast to male students who were observed to lose control of themselves, feel nervous, and ignore their work, female students were shown to have very little behavioral changes as a result of their smartphone addiction.
Nikhita et al., 2015	Mumbai	Journal of Clinical and Diagnostic Research	Students of 8th,9th and 10th	361	Mobile Phone Dependence	Cross-Sectional Observational study	Self-Designed Proforma and Mobile Dependant Questionnaire	Dependence was found in 31.33% of the sample Dependant Syndrome for mobile phone use was associated with the use of smartphone
(Raj, 2018)	West Bengal	Indian Journal Of Psychiatric Medicine	Students from class 9th to 12th	388	Social Networking Sites Addiction	Cross-sectional Descriptive study	Self-Designed Questionnaire	The Proportion of the use of online SNS among the study population is 87.1%. 110 students said that their academic performance was affected because of this.
(C. N. Pandya et al., 2021)	Ahmedabad	Journal of Evidence-Based Medicine and Health Care	15-24 years	239	Smart Phone Addiction	Cross-Sectional Study	Smart Phone Addiction Scale (SAS)18	The mean age of starting smartphone use was 14.51 years. On average four hours of daily smartphone use was found among teenagers.

continued on following page

Table 1. Continued

Author and Year of Study	Place of Study	Journal Name	Age Group of the sample	Sample Size	Variables	Study Design	Tools used	Results
(J. Elias et al., 2021)	Kerala	Turkish Journal of Physiotherapy and Rehabilitation	Higher Secondary Students	1068	Nomophobia	Descriptive Research design	Nomophobia Rating Scale developed by investigators	67.81% of nomophobia rate was found during the study which means that most of the students are not prevalent to nomophobia
(M. S. Yadav et al., 2021)	Uttarakhand	Journal of Education and Health Promotion	12-18 years	600	Mobile Phone Dependence Behavior Academic Performance	A descriptive Correlational Study	Socio-Demographic Profile Test of Mobile Dependence Academic Performance was assessed by the percentage of two-term exam results	Among the participants,54.70% reported low dependency .30.5%reported no dependence and 30.5% with moderate dependence 67% had mild behavioral change,29.80% had moderate and 3.20% reported severe levels of behavioral changes. 43.90% had fair academic performance,29.10% had very good scores, and .70% had excellent performance.

Pan Asian Studies

In an Indonesia study, (F. K. Nasution & Daulay, 2022) academic resilience in smartphone addiction was investigated. The results revealed that when academic resilience is good, then smartphone use is less. A study conducted in China, (Cheng et al., 2021) where smartphone addiction, parent-child relationship, loneliness, and self-efficacy was studied and it proved that self-efficacy improved with less mobile phone use and when there was a good parent-child relationship, mobile phone use also reduced. When the association between smartphone addiction and psychological distress was studied, (Jasem et al., 2021)there was a positive correlation observed. A population-based comparative study(Arunrat Tangmunkongvorakul et al., 2020) was done between Japanese and Thai school students, smartphone addiction was more found in Thai students and it was more prevalent in females than in males. There were incidences (M.-H. Kim et al., 2019) of increased conflicts with family and friends, suicidal attempts, and poor academic performance with high adolescent smartphone use. (Gökalp et al., 2022) studied the nomophobia and smartphone addiction predictors among adolescents in Turkey, there was a positive relation observed and it significantly predicted low academic performance. As mobile phone games contribute a lot to smartphone addiction, an investigation was done to prove the same in Turkey (Ekinci et al., 2017) The research proved that female students are more addicted to mobile phones than male students and students involved in sports are less addicted than others. In China, when a random sample of middle and high school students was selected (Tao et al., 2016) to see the problematic mobile phone use and psychopathological symptoms, it was noted that increased pathological symptoms like loneliness, increased alcohol and substance use poor academic performance and decreased motivation and confidence was observed among students In another Korean study (Dong Gi Seo et al., 2016) mobile phone dependency negatively predicted attention and positively predicted depression among elementary and middle school students. In Korea,(R. Kim et al., 2015) mobile phone overuse and parental attitude were considered for a study that proved that mobile phone use negatively correlated with parental attitude. Table 2 illustrates the Pan Asian Studies.

Table 2. Pan Asian studies

Author and Year of Study	Place of Study	Name of the Journal	The Age Group of the sample	Sample Size	Variables	Study Design	Tools used	Results
(Tao et al., 2016)	China	BMC Public Health	Middle School and High School students	14221	Problematic Mobile Use Psychopathological Symptoms	Random selection of samples from 32 schools	SQAPMPU MSQA	Increased psychopathological symptoms were reported with PMPU Psychopathological symptoms included loneliness, poor academic performance, increased alcohol and decreased motivation and confidence
(Gökalp et al., 2022)	Turkey	Social Science Journal	12-18	621	Smart Phone Addiction Nomophobia	Convenient Sampling	Smartphone Addiction Questionnaire Nomophobia Questionnaire	There is a positive relationship between smartphone addiction and nomophobia. The level of smartphone addiction decreases when academic performance increases and vice versa
(Buabbas 2020)	Kuwait	PLoS One	High school and secondary school students	1993	Smart Phone Use Psychological Distress	Correlational Study Design	SAS-SV DASS -21	Positive correlation between student's smartphone device use and psychological symptoms
(F. K. Nasution & Daulay, 2022)	Indonesia	Journal of Basic Education	Students of 7th,8th and 9th	198	Smart Phone Addiction Academic Resilience Student well being	Random Sampling	Academic Resilience Scale The Student Well-Being Scale Smart Phone Addiction Scale	There was a significant effect of academic resilience on
(Kim et al., 2015)	Korea	Journal od Addictions Nursing	Elementary school students	351	Mobile Phone Overuse Parental Attitude anxiety	Convenient sampling	Mobile Phone Overuse Questionnaire State-Trait Anxiety Inventory Parenteral Attitude Inventory	Mobile phone use was greater in boys It positively correlated with anxiety and negatively correlated with a parental attitude

Author and Year of Study	Place of Study	Name of the Journal	The Age Group of the sample	Sample Size	Variables	Study Design	Tools used	Results
(Dong Gi Seo et al., 2016)	Korea	Computers in Human Behavior	Elementary and middle school students	6172	Mobile Phone Dependency Social behavior Academic behavior	Longitudinal search based on a repeated survey	Individual Interviews Self-reported questionnaire on attention, depression, relationships with friends, teachers, and mobile phone dependency	Mobile phone dependency negatively predicted attention and positively predicted depression.
(Ekinci et al., 2017)	Turkey	Journal of Human Sciences	14-19 years	931	Digital Game addiction	Cross-sectional analytical method	Game Addiction Scale	Female students are more addicted than male students Students involved in sports are less addicted to mobile phones
(Cheng et al., 2021)	China	Sustainability	Mean age 16 years	2172	Smart Phone Addiction Parent-Child Relationship	Cross-sectional survey	Smart Phone Addiction Scale Parent-Child relationship Scale Russell's UCLA Loneliness scale Self-Efficacy scale	The results showed that the parent-child relationship was negatively related to
(M.-H. Kim et al., 2019)	Korea	Plos One	12-18 years	62,276	High Adolescent smartphone use Academic impairment Psychological Issues	A nationally representative Web-based survey	Self-made questionnaire	Conflicts with family and friends, suicidal attempts, poor academic performance were related to higher smartphone use
(Arunrat Tangmunkongvorakul et al., 2020)	Japan Thailand	Plos One	16-17 years	7694	Smartphone addiction	Population-based survey	Young Diagnostic questionnaire for Internet Addiction	Smart Phone addiction was more found in Thai adolescents than in Japanese and more prevalent among females than males.

Pan Global Studies

However, in another study (Kliesener et al., 2022) associations between problematic smartphone use and behavioral difficulties were studied, it was shown that with an increased number of smartphone use, there is a decreased quality of life and behavioural problems. When mobile phone use, physical fitness, and academic performance were studied in Spain (Bravo-Sánchez et al., 2021) proved that 12.8% of high school students struggled with addiction and it affected their studies and physical fitness. In 2022, (T. Gerosa et al., 2022) studied smartphone use and academic performance, and the impact of addiction positively predicted academic decline. In another study (Danilo B. Buctot et al., 2020) it was shown that nomophobia and smartphones were associated with low academic performance There was a negative correlation between the quality of life and mobile addiction according to research conducted in the Philippines(Buctot et al., 2020). According to a school survey conducted in Hungary(Bányai et al., 2017), 4.5% of the children reported low self-esteem and high depression. When a survey was conducted in six countries across the globe (A. K. Tsitsika et al., 2014) on online social networking in adolescents, it was shown that heavier use is associated with more internalizing problems and decreased academic performance. Video games have been an essential part of smartphone use. A survey conducted in Norway (Geir Scott Brunborg et al., 2013) studied video game addiction, depression, and academic achievement, it showed a positive correlation the addiction, depression, conduct problems, and low academic achievement. When studying the prevalence of internet addiction among children, (Nikolic et al., 2023) it was proven that internet addiction was found in every fifth adolescent which is adversely affecting their social activities and academic performance. In a Nigerian study (B. Obadofin et al., 2020) impact of smartphone addiction on academic performance was investigated and it showed that there is a significant impact on academic performance with smartphone overuse. Table 3 illustrates the Pan Global Studies

Table 3. Pan global studies

Author and Year of study	Place of Study	Journal Name	Age Group of the sample	Sample Size	Variables	Study Design	Tools used	Results
(A. K. Tsitsika et al., 2014)	Greece Spain Poland Netherland Romania Iceland	Journal Of Adolescent Health	14-17 years	10,930	Online Social Networking Psychosocial functioning	Survey	Online Communication Tools Youth Self Report Problem Checklist	Heavier SNS use is associated with more internalizing problems and decreased competencies in academics and other activities.
(Bravo-Sánchez et al., 2021)	Spain	International Journal of Environmental Research and Public Health	12-18 years	501	Mobile Phone Use Physical Fitness Academic Performance	Cross-Sectional Study	Mobile Related Experience Questionnaire Euro Fit Battery for PF Academic Performance was assessed by grade point average from the previous exams	12.8% of high school students struggled with an addiction. Boys were more addicted than girls in terms of conduct. The relationship between physical fitness and academic performance was relevant
(T. Gerosa et al., 2022)	Italy	Social Science Computer Review	10th-grade students	3289	Smart Phone Use Academic Performance	Extensive Survey	SPS -A SPS-SV	The impact of smartphones positively predicted academic decline
(Kliesener et al., 2022)	Germany	BMC Psychiatry	10-18 years	564	PSU QOL SP	Cohort Study	SAPS SDQ Self-Report Version of KIDSCREEN	The increased number of smartphones may cause decreased quality of life and behavioral problems
(Geir Scott Brunborg et al., 2013)	Norway	Journal of Behavioural Addiction	13-17	1928	Video Game Addiction Depression Academic achievement Conduct problems	Survey	Video Game Addiction Scale for Adolescents Hopkin's Symptom Checklist School Grades of previous exams	Video game addiction was related to depression, conduct problems, low academic achievement,
(Danilo B. Buctot et al., 2020)	Philippines	Children and Youth Services Review	16-24	1447	Smart Phone Addiction Quality of Life	Cross-sectional study	SAS-SV KIDSCREEN-27	Prevalence was 62.6% Negative correlation between smartphone addiction and QOL
Buctot et al., 2021	Philippines	International Journal of Environmental Research and Public Health	High school students	3374	Smart Addiction, Family Environment Perceived Academic performance	Cross-Sectional Study	Nomophobia scale Smartphone Addiction Scale	Nomophobia and smartphone addiction were associated with low PAP. But the frequency of use on weekends and type of internet access had a positive association with high PAP
(Boer et al., 2020)	29 countries	Journal of Adolescent Health	13.5	1549,81	Problematic Social Media Use Adolescent Well being	School Aged Children Survey		Teens expressing troublesome SMU are especially vulnerable to a decline in wellbeing. Intense SMU may be a normative teenage activity that benefits several aspects of their well-being in many different cultures.

Author and Year of study	Place of Study	Journal Name	Age Group of the sample	Sample Size	Variables	Study Design	Tools used	Results
(Nikolic et al., 2023)	Serbia	archive for the entire medicine	14-18 years	553	Internet addiction	Cross-Sectional Study	Young's Diagnostic Questionnaire for Internet Addiction	Internet Addiction is found in every fifth adolescent which is adversely affects their social activities and academic performance
(B. Obadofin et al., 2020)	Nigeria	International Journal of Advances in Multidisciplinary Research	Secondary school Students	130	Smartphone addiction Academic performance	Descriptive Survey	Addiction to smartphone inventory	There is a significant impact on academic performance Academic performance is not gender-based

DISCUSSION

Pan Indian Studies

Numerous studies across India have shown significant problems and consequences associated with smartphone addiction in adolescents, focusing on both psychological and physical effects and academic impacts. The differences between all these studies are various regional and thematic facets of mobile phone dependency; however, the present alarming trend of excessive mobile usage among Indian youth reveals the fact that these gadgets have invaded academic performance, mental health, and behavior.

In Karnataka, a study found that 3.9% of adolescents were victims of screen addiction with 20% given over to excessive use of screens. Even more revealing are figures that 8% of the youths complained of moodiness and 12% displayed symptoms of depression, showing the psychosocial effects of excess screen time in younger adolescents between the ages of 10 and 19. Another study by Hegde et al. (2019) at Bangalore evaluated the overuse of electronic devices and their effects on children's health and behavior, showing 59% of the students surveyed were afflicted with frequent headaches, and 53% complained of being unable to concentrate in class while 29% showed instances of speech and language delay, implying detrimental cognitive effects resulting from the extended exposure of screens on children's minds.

Pan Asian Studies

A meta-review of global studies on smartphone addiction and the impact of smart phones on psychological, social, and academic outcomes among adolescents shows negative implications that are as daunting at a global scale. The consistency in pointing out negative implications for mental well-being, academic performance, and social relationships is the reason that calls for targeted interventions.

Tao et al. in 2016, for China, studied the prevalence of PMPU among middle and high school students with a sample size of 14,221. The findings indicated that adolescents who suffered from PMPU had significantly more psychological symptoms such as loneliness, lower academic performance, alcohol consumption, and lesser motivation. The design of the study is robust as it includes 32 schools and random sampling; this would strengthen the external validity of the finding. Tao et al used a Self-Report Questionnaire and Multivariate Logistic Regression to prove that mobile addiction worsens mental health issues, giving way to academic pursuits and risky behaviors.

In Turkey, Durak's 2018 study established a positive correlation between smartphone addiction and nomophobia among adolescents aged 12 to 18 years that is inversely related with academic performance. Smartphone Addiction Questionnaire and Nomophobia Questionnaire usage for analysis through Linear Multiple Regression led to conclusion that factors of smartphone addiction contribute towards academic disengagement, suggesting interventions targeted at increasing the involvement of adolescents with academics could temper these factors.

A related study by Buabbas et al. in 2018 on Kuwait found a significant positive correlation between excessive smartphone use and psychological distress, specifically anxiety and depression, among 1,993 high school students. This confirms that smartphone addiction adversely affects psychobehavioral well-being in adolescents. The results of this study stress the need for focused interventions that may help mitigate these mental health risks.

Nasution et al. (2022) studied the association of smartphone addiction with academic resilience among students in Indonesia. The results indicated that the students who had a higher academic resilience were relatively lesser by the mobile addiction's negative impact. This research used multiple linear regression analysis and valid measures like the Academic Resilience Scale and Student Well-Being Scale to prove that resilience serves as a protective function against mobile use's adverse effects.

Kim et al. analyzed parental involvement in mitigating smartphone addiction in Korea and found that boys showed more frequent overuse of mobile phones, which had a corresponding increase in anxiety. The study underscored the buffering effect of supportive parental attitudes in reducing psychological consequences from mobile addiction and indicates a critical role for the family environment in managing adolescent smartphone use.

For example, Seo et al. (2016) followed a panel of Korean students over time and found that smartphone dependency was toxic to attention and positive to depression. The results present considerable concerns regarding how extreme mobile use practices can harm both academic performance and social relations and call for interventions focusing on both mental health and academic results.

Cheng et al. (2021) explored the parent-child relationship and smartphone addiction among Chinese adolescents. The level of mobile addiction was positively correlated with poor relationships between parents and their children; stronger parent-child relationships had lower levels of loneliness and greater self-efficacy, reinforcing the positive role of family support systems.

Besides those, there are studies made by Erinci et al. (2017) and Tangmunkongvorakul et al. (2020). These studies focused on gender and cultural differences on smartphone addiction. The study suggested that adolescents and cultures with a tendency to a higher rate of addiction, such as Thailand, are more vulnerable to the problems of addiction. In addition, these studies emphasize the need for taking into account gender and cultural factors in designing interventions.

Overall, this has in fact pointed out that smartphone addiction impacts academic performance, mental health of individuals, and their social behavior in a negative way. Such findings call for wholesome intervention strategies to foster resilience, parental engagement, and academic engagement to eliminate the ill effects of smartphone addiction.

Pan Global Studies

A critical review of studies from other countries on smartphone addiction has demonstrated a convoluted relationship between heavy usage and the serious consequences to adolescence. This is supported by evidence showing the impact on their level of academic success, reduction in psychosocial functioning, as well as escalating mental health problems such as anxiety and depression. This calls for quick intervention strategies to be enforced to check such a developing problem.

A critical study by Tsitsika et al. (2013) covered six European countries, focusing on the associations between heavy SNS usage and internalizing problems like anxiety, depression, and poor school performance. With 10,930 adolescents in its study population, it was determined that there was a strong association between addiction to SNS and lower competencies of students in school subjects. The study using the Youth Self Report Problem Checklist confirmed that adolescents addicted to SNSs generally value social bonding over academic work. This ends up affecting them badly psychologically. The results were statistically supported by Chi-square tests and Bonferroni correction, making the outcomes extremely powerful in confirming the malignant effects of over-exposure to mobile use.

Similarly, Bravo-Sánchez et al. 2021; Spain found that mobile phone addiction hurt academic performance particularly among male students. This cross-sectional survey of 501 adolescents, revealed a significantly higher level of problematic behaviors about the use of smartphones among boys than in girls. Another positive relationship was established with fitness based on physical training and academic performance. It entails that the promotion of physical activities may become an excellent approach to minimize smartphone addiction negativity from affecting academic results. All the results were accepted by simple linear regression and correlation analysis.

In addition, more evidence supporting such research is offered by Kliesener et al. (2022) from Germany. They find problematic smartphone use significantly contributed to decreasing QOL and increased behavioral problems through this cohort study. They have used assessment tools, such as KIDSCREEN and the Strengths and Difficulties Questionnaire, to prove that more usage of smartphones correlates with worsening psychological mental health. It suggests adolescents are exposed to a moderate number of smartphones to reduce bad psychological effects.

Similar results are found in other studies, such as Geir Scott Brunborg et al. in Norway and Buctot et al. from the Philippines, reporting negative correlations between smartphone video game addiction and school performance. Video game addiction of Brunborg is related to depression and lower academic achievement; similarly, Buctot, whose research was conducted in the Philippines, has demonstrated that smartphone addiction badly affects quality of life and academic performance. This kind of result is further reinforced by regression analysis, which pinpoints the powerful penetration that is digital media in adolescent wellness.

Buctot et al. (2021) study reveals that the relationship between smartphone usage and PAP is complex. Although weekend smartphone usage and internet access had a positive effect on academics, smartphone addiction overall was still related to lower PAP. This means that not all smartphone usage is inherently harmful, but moderation or controlled use might alleviate the negative consequences.

Other studies, such as Nikolic et al. in Serbia and Obadofin et al. in Nigeria, in 2016 and 2020, respectively, further affirm the way internet and smartphone addiction negatively impacts social life as well as academic performance. Internet addiction amongst teenagers in Serbia leads to dramatic reclusive behavior and academic backwardness. Interestingly, Obadofin's study of Nigeria had found an unidirectional relationship between smartphone addiction and poor performance at school. Both studies used statistical tests like Mann-Whitney and Kruskal-Wallis to demonstrate the significance of these correlations.

Overall, the review of these studies brings out the existence of mobile phone addiction all over the world and heaps extensive effects on mental health and degradation of academic performance in school-going adolescents. There is a need for co-intervention strategies by the school, parents, and policymakers in countering negative associations existing between excessive mobile use and poor mental health with the decline in school performance. These strategies ensure balanced digital usage, incorporate physical activity in the life of an individual, and promote the social interaction needed by such individuals. Such findings have cross-cultural generalizability, which highlights how universal this problem is, saying that there is a call for worldwide efforts to counter smartphone addiction and its effects on youth.

Suggestions and Policy Recommendations

Smartphone addiction is a global issue that is growing at an alarming rate among the youth. More and more varied studies conclude that it has negative effects on mental health, academic performance, as well as social behaviour. Based on findings from such studies, there is an urgent need for coordinated efforts at the policy level globally to respond to this issue effectively.

All regions have revealed one major issue that is associated with smartphone addiction- how smartphone addiction brings severe harm to a person's mental health. Teenagers who experience extremely high dependence on smartphones have higher chances of developing anxiety, depression, loneliness, and other mood disorders. According to Kim et al. (2019), excessive use of smartphones has psychological implications, such as conflicts between a teenager and family members and friends, suicidal tendencies, and poor performance in school.

This is the psychological implications of excessive smartphone use on young people worldwide. Similar results were documented by Sridhar et al. (2022), reporting a high prevalence of depression and mood disturbances among Indian teenage smartphone addicts. Policymakers should try to focus on mental health support for school systems through counsellors and psychologists. They should hire counsellors and psychologists to identify the problems early on in the case of smartphone-addicted students.Schools must initiate a mental health awareness program for their students so that they are able to make themselves aware of the psychological impacts of excessive smartphone usage and its way out. Another is smartphone addiction that hampers academic performance. Vashishta et al, 2017, have done research in India that shows an inverse relationship between smartphone addiction and academic performance. The study of the addicted children found that the addicted children would have poor study habits, lack concentration, and receive low grades in their classwork.

Therefore, schools need to create stronger policies about what are some limits on the use of smartphones while in school and setting up a digital detox program. The teaching community can be very useful by creating "no-phone zones" and more concentration on in-the-face friendships.

Other than this mental issue, smartphones also have physical effects as most teenagers claim to have headaches, eye strain, and sleeping problems among others. A study in Bangalore, India made by Hegde et al. (2019) demonstrates that high usage of electronic gadgets resulted in headaches and inability to focus during school hours. Another study, conducted in China by Cheng et al. (2021), also reported similar observations that indicated physical health problems such as sleep deprivation in students with higher levels of smartphone addiction. Governments and schools could motivate this to reduce those kinds of effects.

Sports and other kinds of recreational activities can be included in the daily plan of the student so that he spends ample time on the screen compared to physically sedentary states. The government could further take a "digital detox" campaign across the country by demanding families to limit their communication on the digital platform and spend time outdoors. From the international review, it is brought out that parents also have an important role in regulating the use of mobile phones by children.

Buabbas et al. (2020), Kuwait, and Gangadharan et al. (2022), Delhi reported that in general, in students who reached a higher level of mobile phone addiction, low supervisory practices prevailed among their parents. Educating parents about the potential dangers of overexposure to screens and offering them tools to track and provide boundaries for the usage of smartphones would help. Parent-targeted workshops or campaigns initiated by schools and healthcare organizations can be one efficient approach. Such governments can allow the creation of mobile applications on mobile phones that may grant parents abilities to cap the amount of time the children spend on front screens and track the amount of time spent. Internationally, research also links smartphone addiction with socio-economic factors.

For instance, research work from Kim et al. in Korea reveals that boys of larger families have a higher prevalence of mobile phone addiction as they are exposed to less parental supervision during their infant and toddler years.

In addition, research has suggested that it is not just a behavioral addiction but also about social connectivity and relationships. Teenagers may sometimes want to connect socially using mobile phones, and excessive usage in most instances proves to be symptomatic of some social or psychological needs. Seo et al. conclude in a study carried out in 2016 that dependency on mobile phones has negative effects on social behaviour and performance in school, which needs an all-rounded approach to redressing such issues. Governments, schools, and communities should then collaborate in providing more substantial opportunities for in vivo social relations to be formed, as well as in creating a setting where adolescents rely less on these types of digital connectivity to make their relationships last.

While such addiction matters in different countries have been termed the most challenging issue globally in 2019, measures aimed at reducing and mitigating the psychological, academic, and physical effects among adolescents require a multifaceted approach. Policymakers across the world need to act as one to counter this problem. Schools must limit non-essential use of smartphones, make time for physical activities, and provide access to mental health counselling services. Educating parents about the effects of screen time and providing them with tools to manage their children's smartphone use effectively is the final measure that should be taken.

Governments and international bodies shall encourage research on socio-economic and cultural factors in smartphone addiction, with interventions equitably conducted to maximize access for as many parties as possible. Recommendations will guide global players toward healthier digital habits and the protection of welfare adolescents in the digital era.

Future Research Directions

There are a few more areas that research into smartphone addiction needs to expand upon in the future so that the complications associated with it might be understood better and effective interventions implemented.

Longitudinal Studies: Most of these studies provide cross-sectional data, though longitudinal research is required to study teenagers over time. In this approach, causal relationships between smartphone use mental health outcomes, and academic performance could be detected. Understanding the trend of how addiction develops over time will give deeper insights into prevention strategies.

More Diverse Populations: Such studies should be extended to more diverse populations with a mix of different socio-economic, cultural, and geographical backgrounds. So far, most of the studies have been conducted within Asia and Europe. Different cultural setups might be compared to help researchers understand specific factors that may be peculiar to particular demographics and set up interventions differently. Further, interventional studies in the form of more experiments would be required to determine the effectiveness of interventions designed to abate smartphone addiction. This could include assessing school-based interventions and parental training workshops as well as community awareness programs. Findings will guide policy and educators in making more informed decisions.

Emerging Technologies Impact: The rapid advancement of technology leads to the emergence of new platforms and applications. With such advancements, the emerging effect of technologies such as virtual reality and augmented reality, in relevance to smartphone addiction and its influences among youths, can be identified. These dynamics will somehow be also relevant because the new trends continue to emerge. Through all these established linkages between smartphone addiction and mental health problems, further research on mechanisms may be pursued. Social media interactions, cyberbullying, online peer pressure, and other avenues would offer interesting insights into psychology.

REFERENCES

Billieux, J. (2012). Problematic use of the mobile phone: A literature review and a pathways model. *Current Psychiatry Reviews*, 8(4), 299–307. DOI: 10.2174/157340012803520522

Billieux, J., Maurage, P., Lopez-Fernandez, O., Kuss, D. J., & Griffiths, M. D. (2015). Can disordered mobile phone use be considered a behavioral addiction? An update on current evidence and a comprehensive model for future research. *Current Addiction Reports*, 2(2), 156–162. DOI: 10.1007/s40429-015-0054-y

Boer, M., van den Eijnden, R. J. J. M., Boniel-Nissim, M., Wong, S.-L., Inchley, J. C., Badura, P., Craig, W. M., Gobina, I., Kleszczewska, D., Klanšček, H. J., & Stevens, G. W. J. M. (2020). Adolescents' intense and problematic social media use and their well-being in 29 countries. *The Journal of Adolescent Health*, 66(6, 6S), S89–S99. DOI: 10.1016/j.jadohealth.2020.02.014 PMID: 32446614

Bravo-Sánchez, A., Morán-García, J., Abián, P., & Abián-Vicén, J. (2021). Association of the use of the mobile phone with physical fitness and academic performance: A cross-sectional study. *International Journal of Environmental Research and Public Health*, 18(3), 1042. DOI: 10.3390/ijerph18031042 PMID: 33503943

Brunborg, G. S. (2013). Video game addiction and its relation to depression and academic achievement. *Journal of Behavioral Addictions*, 2(2), 125–132.

Brunborg, G. S., Mentzoni, R. A., Melkevik, O. R., Torsheim, T., Samdal, O., Hetland, J., Andreassen, C. S., & Palleson, S. L. (2013). Gaming addiction, gaming engagement, and psychological health complaints among Norwegian adolescents. *Media Psychology*, 16(1), 115–128. DOI: 10.1080/15213269.2012.756374

Buabbas, A. (2020). The association between smartphone addiction and psychological distress in adolescents. *PLoS One*, 15(4).

Buctot, D. B. (2020). Smartphone addiction and its relationship with quality of life in Filipino adolescents. *Children and Youth Services Review*, 119.

Buctot, D. B., Kim, N., & Kim, J. J. (2020). Factors associated with smartphone addiction prevalence and its predictive capacity for health-related quality of life among Filipino adolescents. *Children and Youth Services Review*, 110(104758), 104758. DOI: 10.1016/j.childyouth.2020.104758

Buctot, D. B., & Nikolic, S. M. (2016). Internet addiction and academic performance in Serbian adolescents. *Archives for the Entire Medicine*, 68(1), 35–43.

Cheng, Y.-C., Yang, T.-A., & Lee, J.-C. (2021). The relationship between smartphone addiction, parent–child relationship, loneliness and self-efficacy among senior high school students in Taiwan. *Sustainability (Basel)*, 13(16), 9475. DOI: 10.3390/su13169475

Demirci, K., Akgönül, M., & Akpinar, A. (2015). Relationship of smartphone use severity with sleep quality, depression, and anxiety in university students. *Journal of Behavioral Addictions*, 4(2), 85–92. DOI: 10.1556/2006.4.2015.010 PMID: 26132913

Dilip, B., & Javalkar, S. R. (2018). Mobile phone usage pattern and dependency among school-going adolescents in Davanagere, Karnataka. *Medica (Stuttgart)*, 7(1), 35.

Dong, D., Xu, B., Shen, N., & He, Q. (2021). The adverse impact of air pollution on China's economic growth. *Sustainability (Basel)*, 13(16), 9056. DOI: 10.3390/su13169056

Durak, H. Y. (2018). Smartphone addiction, academic performance, and nomophobia among adolescents. *The Social Science Journal*, 55(1), 13–24.

Ekinci, N. E., Yalçın, İ., Özer, Ö., & Kara, T. (2017). An investigation of the digital game addiction between high school students. *International Journal of Human Sciences*, 14(4), 4989. DOI: 10.14687/jhs.v14i4.4936

Elhai, J. D., Dvorak, R. D., Levine, J. C., & Hall, B. J. (2017). Problematic smartphone use: A conceptual overview and systematic review of relations with anxiety and depression symptomatology. *Journal of Affective Disorders*, 207, 251–259. DOI: 10.1016/j.jad.2016.08.030 PMID: 27736736

Elhai, J. D., Levine, J. C., Dvorak, R. D., & Hall, B. J. (2017). Fear of missing out, need for touch, anxiety, and smartphone use: A multiple mediation model. *Computers in Human Behavior*, 68, 139–146.

Elias, J., Mirunalini, M., & Paul, I. (2021). Nomophobic rate and social media usage of higher secondary students. *International Journal of Current Research and Review*, 13(24), 132–138. DOI: 10.31782/IJCRR.2021.132423

Elias, M. (2021). Nomophobia among higher secondary students. *Turkish Journal of Physiotherapy and Rehabilitation*.

Erinci, A. (2017). Gender differences in digital game addiction among Turkish high school students. *Uluslararas Insan Bilimleri Dergisi*, 14(3), 315–325.

Fernandez-Gallardo, M., González-Ramírez, R., Sandoval, A., Felix, R., & Monjaraz, E. (2016). Adenosine stimulate proliferation and migration in triple negative breast cancer cells. *PLoS One*, 11(12), e0167445. DOI: 10.1371/journal.pone.0167445 PMID: 27911956

Gangadharan, N., Borle, A. L., & Basu, S. (2022). Mobile phone addiction as an emerging behavioral form of addiction among adolescents in India. *Cureus*, 14(4), e23798. DOI: 10.7759/cureus.23798 PMID: 35518537

Gangadharan, P. (2022). Prevalence of mobile phone addiction in Delhi adolescents. *Cureus*.

Gerosa, M. (2021). The impact of smartphones on academic performance in high school students. *Social Science Computer Review*, 39(6), 1103–1120.

Gerosa, T., Gui, M., & Büchi, M. (2022). Smartphone use and academic performance: A pervasiveness approach beyond addiction. *Social Science Computer Review*, 40(6), 1542–1561. DOI: 10.1177/08944393211018969

Gökalp, Z. Ş., Saritepeci, M., & Durak, H. Y. (2022). The relationship between self-control and procrastination among adolescent: The mediating role of multi screen addiction. *Current Psychology (New Brunswick, N.J.)*, 42(15), 1–12. DOI: 10.1007/s12144-021-02472-2 PMID: 35035199

Hegde, A. M., Suman, P., Unais, M., & Jeyakumar, C. (2019). Effect of electronic gadgets on the behaviour, academic performance and overall health of school going children-a descriptive study. *Journal of Advanced Medical and Dental Sciences Research*, 7(1), 100–103.

Hegde, S. (2019). Overuse of gadgets and its effects on children's behavior. *Journal of Advanced Medical and Dental Sciences Researches*.

Hegde, S., Bhatia, M., & Bhandarkar, A. (2019). The effects of electronic gadgets on children's behavior and academic performance: A cross-sectional study in Bangalore, India. *India.Journal of Advanced Medical and Dental Sciences Researches*, 7(4), 102–106.

Johnson, A. R., Sridhar, P. R., & Joseph, M. (2022). Is screen addiction a problem among rural school-going adolescents? A cross-sectional study in South Karnataka. *Journal of Indian Association for Child and Adolescent Mental Health*, 18(2), 137–143. DOI: 10.1177/09731342221096481

Kim, H., & Lee, Y. (2018). Socioeconomic status, perceived inequality of opportunity, and attitudes toward redistribution. *The Social Science Journal*, 55(3), 300–312. DOI: 10.1016/j.soscij.2018.01.008

Kim, J. (2015). The effect of parental attitude on mobile phone addiction and anxiety in elementary students. *Journal of Addictions Nursing*, 26(4), 204–212.

Kim, M.-H., Min, S., Ahn, J.-S., An, C., & Lee, J. (2019). Association between high adolescent smartphone use and academic impairment, conflicts with family members or friends, and suicide attempts. *PLoS One*, 14(7), e0219831. DOI: 10.1371/journal.pone.0219831 PMID: 31306455

Kliesener, T., Meigen, C., Kiess, W., & Poulain, T. (2022). Associations between problematic smartphone use and behavioural difficulties, quality of life, and school performance among children and adolescents. *BMC Psychiatry*, 22(1), 195. DOI: 10.1186/s12888-022-03815-4 PMID: 35300635

Nasution, A. (2022). Smartphone addiction and its impact on academic resilience and student well-being. *Journal of Basic Education*, 12(2), 59–72.

Nasution, F. K., & Daulay, N. (2022). The influence of academic resilience and student well-being on smartphone addiction. *Jurnal Basicedu*, 6(3), 4415–4422. DOI: 10.31004/basicedu.v6i3.2864

Nayak, J. K. (2018). Relationship among smartphone usage, addiction, academic performance and the moderating role of gender: A study of higher education students in India. *Computers & Education*, 123, 164–173. DOI: 10.1016/j.compedu.2018.05.007

Nikhita, C. (2015). Mobile phone dependence and its psychological effects. *Journal of Clinical and Diagnostic Research : JCDR*.

Nikhita, C. S. (2015). Prevalence of mobile phone dependence in secondary school adolescents. *Journal of Clinical and Diagnostic Research : JCDR*. Advance online publication. DOI: 10.7860/JCDR/2015/14396.6803 PMID: 26672469

Nikolic, A., Bukurov, B., Kocic, I., Vukovic, M., Ladjevic, N., Vrhovac, M., Pavlović, Z., Grujicic, J., Kisic, D., & Sipetic, S. (2023). Smartphone addiction, sleep quality, depression, anxiety, and stress among medical students. *Frontiers in Public Health*, 11, 1252371. DOI: 10.3389/fpubh.2023.1252371 PMID: 37744504

Obadofin, B., Onyeka, E. B., & Nchedochukwu, E. C. (2020). Impacts of Smartphone addiction on Academic Performance of students in senior secondary schools in Lagos state. *Research and Analysis Journal*, 253–260.

Obadofin, R. O. (2020). Impact of smartphone addiction on academic performance among secondary school students. *International Journal of Advances in Multidisciplinary Research*, 7(4), 21–28.

Ontoria, Y., Cuesta-Gracia, A., Ruiz, J. M., Romero, J., & Pérez, M. (2019). The negative effects of short-term extreme thermal events on the seagrass Posidonia oceanica are exacerbated by ammonium additions. *PLoS One*, 14(9), e0222798. DOI: 10.1371/journal.pone.0222798 PMID: 31536606

Pandya, C. N., Christian, D. S., & Patel, M. M. (2021). A cross-sectional study on smartphone addiction among late adolescents and young adults (aged 15 to 24 years) of Ahmedabad city, Gujarat, India. *J Evid Based Med Healthc*, 8(9), 491–496. DOI: 10.18410/jebmh/2021/96

Pandya, N. (2021). Smartphone addiction among teenagers in Ahmedabad. *Journal of Evidence-Based Medicine and Health Care.*

Philip, D. (2018). *Mobile Phone Dependence in Karnataka*. Medica Inovatica.

Rahman, A. U., Chaudary, A., & Varandani, S. (2022). A rare case of aggressive peripheral T-cell lymphoma-not otherwise specified. *Cureus*, 14(5), e24857. DOI: 10.7759/cureus.24857 PMID: 35702462

Raj, M., Bhattacherjee, S., & Mukherjee, A. (2018). Usage of online social networking sites among school students of Siliguri, West Bengal, India. *Indian Journal of Psychological Medicine*, 40(5), 452–457. DOI: 10.4103/IJPSYM.IJPSYM_70_18 PMID: 30275621

Raj, R. (2018). *Social Networking Sites addiction among adolescents*. Indian Journal Of Psychiatric Medicine.

Rosen, L. D., Lim, A. F., Carrier, L. M., & Cheever, N. A. (2013). An empirical examination of social networking addiction: The relationship between social networking and depression. *Social Networking*, 2, 1–9.

Rosen, L. D., Whaling, K., Rab, S., Carrier, L. M., & Cheever, N. A. (2013). Is Facebook creating "iDisorders"? The link between clinical symptoms of psychiatric disorders and technology use, attitudes and anxiety. *Computers in Human Behavior*, 29(3), 1243–1254. DOI: 10.1016/j.chb.2012.11.012

Samaha, M., & Hawi, N. S. (2016). Relationships among smartphone addiction, stress, and anxiety in university students. *Computers in Human Behavior*, 57, 321–325. DOI: 10.1016/j.chb.2015.12.045

Samaha, M., & Hawi, N. S. (2016). Relationships among smartphone addiction, stress, academic performance, and satisfaction with life. *Computers in Human Behavior*, 57, 321–325. DOI: 10.1016/j.chb.2015.12.045

Sanchez, Z. M. (2021). Mobile phone addiction, physical fitness, and academic performance in adolescents: A cross-sectional study. *International Journal of Environmental Research and Public Health*, 18(1), 1–15. PMID: 35010261

Screening for at-risk alcohol use in older adults: What progress have we made? (2015). *Journal of Addictions Nursing, 26*(3), 152–156. DOI: 10.1097/JAN.0000000000000089

Seo, D. G., Park, Y., Kim, M. K., & Park, J. (2016). Mobile phone dependency and its impacts on adolescents' social and academic behaviors: A longitudinal study. *Computers in Human Behavior*, 63, 282–290. DOI: 10.1016/j.chb.2016.05.026

Seo, D. G., Park, Y., Kim, M. K., & Park, J. (2016). Mobile phone dependency and its impacts on adolescents' social and academic behaviors. *Computers in Human Behavior*, 63, 282–292. DOI: 10.1016/j.chb.2016.05.026

Seo, Y. (2016). Mobile phone dependency, depression, and social behavior in adolescents. *Computers in Human Behavior*, 60, 63–69.

Sridhar, S. (2022). Screen Addiction and its impact on adolescents. *Journal of Indian Association for Child and Adolescent Mental Health.*

Sridhar, V., Swaminathan, K., & Patil, D. (2022). Prevalence of screen addiction and its effects on physical and mental health among adolescents in Karnataka, India. *India.Journal of Indian Association for Child and Adolescent Mental Health*, 18(3), 214–221.

Tangmunkongvorakul, A. (2020). Cross-cultural comparison of smartphone addiction among adolescents in Japan and Thailand. *PLoS One*, 15(9). PMID: 32898191

Tangmunkongvorakul, A., Musumari, P. M., Tsubohara, Y., Ayood, P., Srithanaviboonchai, K., Techasrivichien, T., Suguimoto, S. P., Ono-Kihara, M., & Kihara, M. (2020). Factors associated with smartphone addiction: A comparative study between Japanese and Thai high school students. *PLoS One*, 15(9), e0238459. DOI: 10.1371/journal.pone.0238459 PMID: 32898191

Tao, S., Wu, X., Wan, Y., Zhang, S., Hao, J., & Tao, F. (2016). Interactions of problematic mobile phone use and psychopathological symptoms with unintentional injuries: A school-based sample of Chinese adolescents. *BMC Public Health*, 16(1), 88. DOI: 10.1186/s12889-016-2776-8 PMID: 26821534

Tsitsika, A. (2013). Online social networking and psychosocial functioning in adolescents. *The Journal of Adolescent Health*, 54(2), 207–213. PMID: 23332486

Tsitsika, A. K., Tzavela, E. C., Janikian, M., Ólafsson, K., Iordache, A., Schoenmakers, T. M., Tzavara, C., & Richardson, C. (2014). Online social networking in adolescence: Patterns of use in six European countries and links with psychosocial functioning. *The Journal of Adolescent Health*, 55(1), 141–147. DOI: 10.1016/j.jadohealth.2013.11.010 PMID: 24618179

Valkenburg, P. M., & Peter, J. (2011). Online communication among adolescents: An integrated model of its attraction, opportunities, and risks. *The Journal of Adolescent Health*, 48(2), 121–127. DOI: 10.1016/j.jadohealth.2010.08.020 PMID: 21257109

Vashishta, R., & Sharma, A. (2017). Impact of Facebook addiction on study habits and academic achievement among adolescents in Agra, India. *India.MEIR Journal of Educational Studies*, 25(1), 66–74.

Vashishtha, S., Ahuja, S., & Sharma, M. (2021). Impact of Facebook Addiction Disorder (fad) on study habits and academic achievement of adolescents. *MIER Journal of Educational Studies Trends & Practices*, 195–207. DOI: 10.52634/mier/2017/v7/i2/1422

Yadav, M. (2021). Correlational study on mobile phone dependence and academic performance. *Journal of Education and Health Promotion.*

Yadav, M. S., Kodi, S. M., & Deol, R. (2021). Impact of mobile phone dependence on behavior and academic performance of adolescents in selected schools of Uttarakhand, India. *Journal of Education and Health Promotion*, 10(1), 327. DOI: 10.4103/jehp.jehp_915_20 PMID: 34761013

Chapter 4
Smartphone Addiction in Youngsters and Their Mental Health

Suvidha Rastogi
https://orcid.org/0000-0003-4718-8808
Banasthali Vidyapith, India

Sangeeta Yadav
Banasthali Vidyapith, India

ABSTRACT

The use of media devices has grown over the years, and smartphones are currently the most used media device globally. The smartphone is a practical device with its several advantages. Smartphone addiction is becoming a bigger problem, particularly among youngsters. The mental and social effects of smartphone addiction on youngster's mental health are covered in this chapter. With smartphones becoming more and more important, there is a greater chance of addiction, which can have serious psychological consequences. Long-term smartphone use has been shown to negative effects on youngster's mental health like stress, anxiety, depression, attention span, etc. In conclusion, youngster's mental health is seriously at risk from excessive use of smartphone addiction. It is essential to treat the psychological symptoms and indicators of addiction, such as phubbing, failing relationships, and mental health issues. To minimize the effects and encourage youngsters to adopt better digital habits, encouraging balanced smartphone use, early understanding is essential.

DOI: 10.4018/979-8-3693-8804-4.ch004

USE OF SMARTPHONE AND ITS INTEGRATION IN DAILY LIFE

In just a few decades, smartphones have completely changed the way youngsters interact, communicate, work, do chores, find information, and spend the time. With its many features, faster and larger memory, and continual internet connectivity, the smartphone has become more and more popular, increasing the amount of time spent on it and suggesting that it is used almost everywhere (Thomée, 2018).

In the majority of developed nations, nearly 50% of people use smartphones. Due to South Korea's high level of technology advancement, 84% of children owned a smartphone in 2014, and over 24 million Koreans owned a smartphone in 2013 (Alam et al., 2014 as cited in Lee et al., 2016). According to a survey, 84% of participants used smartphones for specific purposes (Bhanderi et al., 2021). Due to its capabilities, smartphones have become an essential component of everyday life in the era of technological advancement and change, impacting people's personal and professional lives (Talan et al., 2023).

Every smartphone is built with the ability to access the internet. A standard smartphone has several fundamental features that contribute to its intelligence, like as:

- Internet search or web browsing- Youngsters use smartphone to search online anything related to their study, entertainment, any news etc. Anything is possible in this period to search on internet.
- Phone calls- Youngsters uses their smartphone to talk their family, friends on any geographic location.
- Listening to music- When youngster feeling happy, joyous, sad, grief they listen to music to better up their mood.
- Using social media apps- Youngsters use smartphones to connect with peoples on social sites.
- Sharing or sending photos and videos- Youngsters use smartphones to share their moments in the form of photos or videos on social sites or on instant messaging apps.
- Playing online games- Nowadays lifestyle of youngsters increases the use of smartphone to release their pressure, anxiety to feel good by playing games online. There are many forms of games are available online. Such as Pubg, Free Fire etc.
- Watch movies- Youngsters use their smartphones to watch movies with their convenience.
- Online shopping- Most of the youngsters use online shopping instead of traditional shopping.
- Online education- Youngsters enrolled in online programs can take any course they like and finish the assignments whenever it is most convenient

for them, eliminating the need to change their schedules. Youngsters can get the knowledge they need to advance in their careers or obtain their degrees through online courses.

Finally, it can be said that smartphone is nothing without internet. The internet, or simply "net" has completely changed and revolutionized the way that people used to communicate and conduct business. The internet provides access to information on every industry, including apps, learning, recreation, business, leisure, literature, friendship, medicine, and tourism. This is the reason why people are so addicted to smartphones. Internet addiction is a manifestation of smartphone addiction.

SMARTPHONE INTEGRATION IN YOUNGSTERS LIFE IN THE FORM OF

Connections

By using smartphones to make calls, send messages, and video chat, people may stay in touch with friends and family back home, get information, and meet people all over the world (Ahmed et al., 2023). Additionally, they give people social networking sites so that they can interact with friends and family and tell them about significant events in our lives. Making the lives of their clients a little bit easier in business. Electronic mail systems and chat applications have replaced traditional letters by enabling real time online messaging as well as instant messaging (Gangwar, 2022).

Academic

The world is now in our homes because of smartphones. Smartphones are a symbol of the limitless knowledge that is available to students. The fact that a student always has easy access to all the technology and information they could possibly require makes studying considerably more efficient and successful. Accessing educational materials via a smartphone is simple, regardless of time or day or place. Personalized instruction, self-regulated learning, classroom engagement, mobile learning, and second language acquisition are some of the educational advantages of smartphone use that have been studied. This research emphasized the educational advantages of smartphone use, including closing the digital divide, finishing assignments, peer collaboration, rapid information accessibility, and vocabulary development. These advantages led to a dependence on smartphone use for tasks pertaining to education. Smartphones are also useful for managing important due dates exam schedules, and communication with teachers and classmates.

Information or Worldwide Knowledge

Youngsters use their smartphones to investigate a variety of topics and to check the weather and global news. When it comes to accessing knowledge, smartphones are the great equalizer. Never before have so many people had such easy access to so much knowledge at such a low cost. When knowledge was limited to printed materials, the expense of publication and distribution, as well as the requirement to print new information on a regular basis, made it difficult for people, communities, and nations to access the world of knowledge. Additionally, the internet made it possible to access information from websites run by government departments as well as from other sources like Wikipedia and YouTube.

Despite attempts to have information and news access restricted or outlawed, citizens living under repressive regimes continue to do so, frequently at the risk of being arrested or even put to death. Consider it to be a barrier, yet many people are nevertheless willing to take the chance of paying it because they are so eager to obtain accurate information. Because of smartphones, people are now recording revolutions, crimes, and injustice and then disseminating their film on social networking sites like Twitter and news channels like Reddit, AAJTAK, NDTV, and others. A greater degree of accountability from individuals in positions of authority has resulted from the world watching in ways that were before impossible (Abeyta, 2015).

Entertainment

In addition to being a significant source of information and knowledge, smartphones are also incredibly useful for pleasure. Smartphones provide an extensive range of entertainment alternatives. Playing games, reading books, watching videos, movies, or documentaries, listening to music on various apps like spotify and wink music, taking photos, editing them with a variety of programs, and sharing them on social media or sending them as messages. Youngsters can view films and serials whenever it's convenient for them by visiting a variety of video websites. Apps like Amazon Prime, Netflix, Hotstar, and others have even gained a lot of attention to smartphones. With membership packs, users may stream or download an infinite number of TV series and films. This is done in order to provide the greatest experience for users of these apps.

Health

Health information can be accessed via a smartphone. Every human has access to services through smartphones. Thus, they can use internet databases to access their emotional, mental, and physical problems without having to visit a doctor. If a youngster has an issue and is unable to see a doctor in person, a smartphone can be used to interact with a doctor online. Utilizing smartphones to monitor patient health data and convey health messages to modify lifestyle choices has improved patient care and health promotion initiatives.

Smartphones can improve communication between youngsters and their physicians in a number of ways. For instance, the ability to construct medical profiles makes apps like My Medical Info and others fantastic. The user can add health history, allergies, medication and dosage instructions, contact details for doctors, and appointment reminders to each profile.

Online Banking

Furthermore, these technical devices provide a variety of capabilities for a range of demands and objectives, including banking. In order to facilitate immediately apparent money transfers from one account to another accounts, banks are now offering online banking services. Paytm, Phonepe, Freecharge, Amazon, and many other applications currently offer their customers mobile wallets for bill payments, recharges, etc.

Occupation/Job

In the workplace, smartphones are also helpful for managing work calendars, checking emails, setting up appointments, connecting with clients and coworkers, and keeping track of deadlines. Youngsters can look up a variety of career alternatives with smart phones. They can compare many occupations at the same time and determine which one will be best for them in the future.

Online Shopping

Many commercial operations and e-commerce platforms utilize these new capacities to their fullest potential. Numerous apps for online purchasing have been created especially for mobile devices. These applications are mobile-friendly. They typically have quicker checkout procedures as a result, guaranteeing simple and speedy transactions. A few Indian e-commerce companies that provide its clients a wide range of possibilities for buying from the convenience of their homes are Flipkart, Amazon, and Myntra. Youngsters can shop from any location. Youngsters can also store purchase information using the payment apps. Online purchasing is convenient at any time.

Phubbing (Phone + Snubbing)

The use of smartphones is linked to the emergence of a new maladaptive behavior called "phubbing" (Bajwa et al., 2023). The terms "phone" and "snubbing" are combined to form the term "phubbing". A group of lexicographers, poets, and writers came up with the term as part of the Macquarie Dictionary campaign to describe the practice of ignoring the other person during social interactions by focusing on one's smartphone rather than the person they are speaking to (Ivanova et al., 2020). Phubbing is a contemporary type of social snubbing in which an individual ignores another person in a social setting by concentrating on their smartphone rather than starting up a conversation. Youngster's social activities are disrupted by phubbing. Youngsters prioritize their virtual social lives over in-person social interactions when they use their smartphones during interactions. Despite being physically present, a smartphone user may be mentally absent. This kind of behavior is a perfect example of how poor communication may actually damage relationships with others and one's sense of wellbeing (Bajwa et al., 2023).

Phubbing is positively connected with smartphone addiction, according to earlier research, and is utilized as a coping mechanism for loneliness, anxiety, and fear as well as for deprivation when one is separated from their phone. Phubbing, on the other hand, not only help but also makes phubbers' issues worse: Using a smartphone makes one feel more isolated from the social world. People who are phubbed also feel excluded from society, which makes them feel more pressure to be the center of attention in their significant social circles. This makes them turn to social media to feel less excluded (Ivanova et al., 2020).

Consequences of Phubbing

This phubbing phenomenon clarifies the actual harmful effects of communication breakdowns, which have a negative impact on relationships and emotions of personal wellbeing. The impact of phubbing to mental health issues is essentially unclear, however in India, where youngsters make up 21% of the population, approximately 20% of them suffer from attention deficit hyperactivity disorder and concentration issues as a result of excessive smartphone use. The prevalence of smartphone addiction and problematic internet use among youngsters in India is rising, which suggests that phubbing may be an issue among young people (Davey et al., 2018).

Most people find phubbing irritating and detrimental to the quality of their relationships and social interactions, according to studies. These ideas are supported by some research, which shows that phubbing reduces the perceived quality of social interactions and relationships, causes conflict and jealousy in partnerships, and makes co-present people feel socially rejected (Abeele, 2020).

Thus, the aim is to put light on the ways in which phubbing might have detrimental consequences when interacting with partners who are physically present. Phubbing is a social behavior that indicates a breakdown in a relationship. That serves as a foundation for comprehending the mechanisms underlying the negative effects of phubbing. The impact of phubbing on relational outcomes is explained by three socio-cognitive mechanisms, according to the literature: attentional conflict, social ostracism, and expectancy violations (Abeele, 2020).

I. Expectancy Violation

Expectancy Violation is the first socio cognitive mechanism that explains the negative effects of phubbing. Expectancy violation theory states that people have cognitive schemata about what behavior is proper in a particular circumstance. Expectations of other people's behavior are guided by these schemata. Because of the confusion of the circumstance, individuals get startled when others act in ways that differ from their expectations. Mostly youngsters anticipate receiving their full attention from their partners at the time of conversation. When a partner pays attention, they react quickly, listen intently, lean towards the partner and maintain eye contact. Negative expectations can be formed when these immediacy behaviors are not displayed, and this can have a detrimental impact on things like social attraction, relationship appraisal, impression construction, and relational message interpretation.

Phubbing is considered as disrespectful and a painful breach of expectations, especially for young people who want exclusive and undivided attention. When their interaction partner phubbs them, youngsters see phubbers as less respectful and focused than non phubbers, and they give the interaction a less favorable assessment.

II. Ostracism

Ostracism is a second sociocognitive mechanism that connects phubbing to unfavorable relational consequences. The need threat model of ostracism suggests that being left out of a social interaction might be a challenge to basic human needs including the need to feel worthwhile and to belong. Ostracism puts at risk their basic requirements for control, self-worth, belonging, and a purposeful life. This experience is influenced by immediate inputs, especially eye behavior: Individuals suffer relationship devaluation in response to averted eye gaze because they interpret it as "the silent treatment", which indicates social exclusion. According to the need-threat model, which is similar to Expectancy violations theory, people will evaluate and ascribe stress arousal during a reflective and evaluative stage in an effort to determine its motivation, significance, and relevance. Regarding self-evaluations, people who have been ignored often believe that their relationship value is lower and constantly reflect on their behavior and how others saw them throughout the contact.

III. Attentional Conflict

Mechanisms such as expectation breaches and ostracism depend on people recognizing and interpreting their interaction partner's behavior as a sign of disengagement and indifference. A person experiences attentional conflict when something in their surroundings competes for their attention with their main focus. Distraction conflict theory (Baron, 1986, as cited in Abeele, 2020) states that youngsters experience an attentional conflict that leads to cognitive overload when they are unable to decide where to focus their attention. Youngsters may activate and rely on heuristics and schemata that direct their perceptions and social judgements of the situation in response to this cognitive overload, which creates arousal. A person experiences attentional conflict when something in their surroundings competes for their attention with their main focus. In order to prime relational schemata that affect perception and judgement, smartphones may act as environmental cues. Outside of the immediate spatial context, smartphones represent a person's social network. Phubbing may be socially judged as a sign of disengagement due to the activation of such schemata, which can be regarded as a sense of expectancy violation and/or ostracism.

PERSPECTIVE ON SMARTPHONE ADDICTION

Cognitive Behavioral Models

In his approach, Caplan (2002, as cited in Gangwar, 2022) offered internet or technology addiction as a subset of behavioral addiction with a wide range of symptoms. The main traits of behavioral addiction, such as mood modulation, withdrawal, salience, conflict, tolerance, and relapse, are frequently seen in internet addiction. Additionally, Caplan added the following symptoms to the list of signs of addiction: using the internet as a distraction from unwanted emotion, raising the threshold for achieving satisfaction, experiencing withdrawal symptoms when reducing internet use, increasing arguments and conflicts in real life relationships due to virtual activity, and relapsing back to problematic internet usage.

Davis (2001, as cited in Gangwar, 2022) proposed the cognitive theory of Pathological Internet Use (PIU) because he believed that online habituation was abnormal. The causes, development, and outcomes of Pathological Internet Use are explained by the theory. In contrast to other behavioral addictions, Davis thought Pathological Internet Use was a distinct pattern of internet related thoughts and actions that led to negative life effects. Pathological Internet Use was divided into two categories by Davis: generalized and specific. Pornography, stock trading, and gambling are only a few examples of the content specific misuse or overuse of online sources that are of concern to Specific Pathological Internet Use. A variety of online sources are abused in generalized Pathological Internet Use, which can have detrimental effects on one's career and personal life. Internet related dysfunctional thoughts and behaviors are frequently identified as a sign of generalized Pathological Internet Use. When someone has generalized Pathological Internet Use, they are more attracted to and feel closer to their ideal self in virtual relationships than in interpersonal interactions or face to face interactions.

Neuropsychological Model

As per the China Youth Association for Network Development's (CYAND) report (2005, as cited in Gangwar, 2022), a person must meet three requirements in addition to one criterion in order to be diagnosed with internet addiction. The requirement is that using the internet impairs one's ability to function effectively in social and interpersonal situations. Additionally, a diagnosis can be made based on the existence of any one of the following three conditions: 1) People who are online experience a sense of self-actualization. 2) Depressive and anxious symptoms if internet access is limited. 3) Attempts to conceal internet usage from relatives.

Concern Around Excessive Use of Smartphone

Despite these advantages and other helpful functions, research shows that using a smartphone might disrupt people's daily lives. During the past few years, smartphones have become increasingly popular due to their practicality and ease of use (Yang et al., 2023). The widespread use of smartphones in culture has led to serious worldwide problems, including addiction and excessive use. Smartphones have drawbacks, including decreased productivity, decreased personal attention, social annoyance, and psychological addiction, despite its many positive aspects (Parasuraman et al., 2017). This circumstance may cause people to spend more time on their smartphones, which can have a detrimental impact on interpersonal communication and result in behavioral and physical issues. Due to this, an increasing number of people utilize smartphones to fulfil their various demands during their free time, which significantly increases the devices' user stickiness.

Specifically, people develop the habit of always carrying or using their smartphones, which raises the risk of smartphone addiction. When using smartphones, these youngsters displayed comparable signs of non-material addiction. As a result, smartphone addiction has raised concerns among researchers and the general public as a major danger factor for youngster's mental health. Researchers have looked into the drawbacks of smartphones that arise from excessive use. Overuse of smartphones can impair cognitive capacities, cause dependence, and limit thinking capacity.

According to recent studies, smartphone dependence is on the rise, which may lead to a rise in internet addiction. Psychological illnesses include dry eyes, computer vision syndrome, wrist and thumb weakness, stiffness and soreness in the neck, tactile hallucinations or hallucinations, nomophobia, insecurity, delusions, low self-esteem, and smartphone addiction disorders can result from excessive smartphone use. Addiction to smartphones can also have detrimental effects on a youngster's family relationships. Numerous studies have found that family relationships suffer as a result of smartphone addiction. Similar to this, people can use smartphones to communicate with anyone in the world while establishing friends, but studies have shown that smartphones have an impact on social life. People who are more likely to be addicted to smartphones are also more likely to have poor social relationships (Sinsomsack & Kulachai, 2018).

Not withstanding the ongoing controversy, smartphone addiction is becoming more and more common, particularly among young people, who have more opportunity to form social bonds, communicate with others more frequently, and are more adept at using contemporary technology (Ivanova et al., 2020).

UNDERSTANDING SMART PHONE ADDICTION

Psychological Factors Contributing to Smartphone Addiction

The term "smartphone addiction" has recently been suggested as a diagnostic term to describe issues associated with the sharp rise in smartphone use. Psychopathologies such as withdrawal, somatic complaints, anxiety or depression, social problems, thought problems, attention problems, aggressive behavior, delinquent behaviors, and self-destructive or identity problems were substantially more prevalent in children at high risk of smartphone addiction. Additionally, youngsters who were at a higher risk of developing a smartphone addiction had higher anxiety levels and worse self-esteem.

Results shows a correlation between aggressive behavior and self-esteem and the degree of smartphone addiction. Aggression and internet addiction are closely related, according to numerous research. It was discovered that online gambling, online gaming, online pornography, and online talking were all linked to aggressive behavior in terms of particular contents.

Other psychological factors that related to smart phone addiction:

FOMO- The psychological component of Fear of Missing Out (FOMO) has been connected to inappropriate internet use and smartphone addiction. Addiction to smartphones can lead to increased FOMO and excessive social media use, and vice versa. FOMO, smartphone addiction, and social media use are closely related. Youngsters who experience FOMO may experience detrimental effects on their mental health. People who worry about missing out on other people's or anything else's amazing experiences are said to suffer from FOMO, which is a diffuse form of anxiety. Youngsters who experience high levels of FOMO are more likely to spend time on social media, which increases their risk of becoming addicted to smartphones. Frequent social media checks brought on by FOMO might heighten anxiety and raise awareness of missed activities. Individuals with FOMO or loneliness may turn to smartphones as a way to cope with their feelings. A high amount of FOMO makes people more depressed. People who are lonely may experience hopeless and FOMO. Both loneliness and FOMO are passive feelings and depression risk factors, and they may strengthen the relationship between FOMO and sadness (Liu et al., 2024).

Instant Gratification- In a society where technology rules, the need for immediate gratification has grown to be a strong factor influencing many of our choices and actions. A basic idea in psychology, instant gratification describes the preference for short term, immediate pleasures or rewards over long term, delayed ones (Brook & Santos, 2023). The constant demand for immediate approval, enjoyment, and input from smartphones is one way that smartphone addiction presents itself. Youngster's mental health can be adversely affected by instant gratification in a number of ways, including encouraging rash decisions, impairing their capacity to establish and accomplish long-term objectives, causing emotions of discontent, and possibly exacerbating anxiety and despair.

Social Validation- People frequently evaluate their own behavior by looking at what others do, a psychological phenomena called as social validation or social evidence. Smartphones are used to record social media interactions, likes, and comments in an effort to win social acceptance. This encourages excessive mobile use and leads to the development of addictive behaviors.

Interpersonal Relationships

People are sociable creatures by nature. Their social, emotional, and physical well-being are greatly influenced by the relationships they form with others. Maintaining interpersonal ties can help youngster create a network of support that gives them the fortitude to face life's obstacles. "A social connection or affiliation between two or more people is known as an interpersonal relationship". The interactions individual have with their parents, loved ones, close friends, acquaintances, and many others who comprise their social network can be classified as many forms of interpersonal relationships (Cherry, 2023).

Youngster's physical and mental wellbeing are greatly influenced by their connections with others. The relationships youngsters have with their parents from an early age have a significant impact on their physical and emotional well-being as they grow up. Youngsters who get along well with their parents grow up to have healthy personal qualities, such being sociable and passionate and being more likely to do well in school. On the other hand, the lack of friendly relationships may raise the likelihood of mental disease and emotional disorders.

Additionally, peer pressure has a significant impact on decision-making, emotions, social relationships, and health behavior. Youngsters use their relationships with peers to develop their sense of self, self-worth, and self-efficacy. Numerous elements influence how youngsters interact with others. One major aspect is that, as a result of their inappropriate usage, smartphones have caused youngster to spend more time on screens and engage with others less in real life. According to one study, children who spend more time staring at screens also spend less time engaging in activities that aren't related to screens, like sports, religion, or in person social connections. Despite the fact that smartphones were once thought of as equipment for fostering social networks or preserving interpersonal ties, smartphone addiction can cause separation from and/or worsen existing interpersonal relationships in real life (Yang et al., 2022).

Addiction to smartphones can harm youngster's connections with others in a number of ways, including:

- **Connections in real life-** Addiction to smartphones can cause a decline in connections in real life. Regardless of distance, smartphones make it simpler to keep in touch. They enable youngsters stay in touch with friends, family, and coworkers by enabling real time communication via calls, messages, and apps. The quality of face-to-face talks may suffer from an excessive dependence on devices. People may engage in superficial conversations as a result of being more preoccupied with their smartphones than with others around them.
- **Social media-** Social media and smartphones can improve relationships between youngsters by giving them new ways to connect and communicate, but they can also make them worse. Youngsters could select friends from online communities rather than in person. Overuse of smartphones can result in fewer in person encounters, which are essential for strengthening emotional bonds. Continually using a phone in social situations might make people feel emotionally distant. People may feel ignored when you browse social media or answer notifications during a conversation, which diminishes empathy

and understanding between people. Rather than fostering lasting connections, social media frequently encourages relationships based on likes, comments, and brief conversations. Despite having a large number of virtual "friends", this can lead to weakened ties and feelings of loneliness. Unhealthy comparisons can be fostered via social media. Relationship problems or feelings of inadequacy might arise from jealously or frustration caused by viewing well maintained, images of other people's lives.

- **Communication skills-** Youngster's communication skills might be adversely affected by excessive smartphone use. Face to face interactions have decreased as a result of how simple it is to communicate via text, messaging, and social media. This hinders the growth of nonverbal communication abilities, which are crucial for successful communication and include reading tone of voice, body language, and facial emotions. Youngsters may find it increasingly difficult to empathize with others as they communicate more through devices. Text based communication's lack of emotional clues and real time answers makes it harder to completely comprehend other people's feelings. Younger generations in particular have grown so used to interacting via smartphones that they may find it difficult to communicate in person, which can cause social anxiety or awkwardness in face-to-face situations.
- **Loneliness-** In youngsters, loneliness may be an indicator of physical wellbeing. Individuals may feel disconnected from their immediate social surroundings as a result of prioritizing these virtual or distant connections above those that are physically nearby. Social media users who are constantly exposed to well chosen, idealized depictions of other people's life may experience feelings of inadequacy and loneliness, particularly if they believe they fall short of others in terms of their social or personal accomplishments. Loneliness may worsen as a result of digital communications that are frequently short and lack deeper emotional content.
- **Academic performance-** Addiction to smartphones can have a detrimental effect on academic achievement. Overuse of smartphones while studying can cause students to become distracted in class and during in person interactions with classmates. Constant smartphone connectivity can lead to more stress, especially for students who feel under constant pressure to reply to group work or academic messages. Depression and poor interpersonal connections may result from this.

Social issues or being introverted are examples of interpersonal connection challenges that might serve as a platform for compulsive or problematic smartphone use.

Signs of Smartphone Addiction

Few ways to discern if someone has signs of a smartphone addiction:

Spending more and more time on a smartphone- Smartphones make it simple and quick to communicate, obtain information, and entertain oneself. Many youngsters use their smartphones for hours every day for a variety of purposes, including social media, gaming, and video streaming. Youngsters spend more time on these platforms because they need to maintain relationships with their friends and peers.

Constantly checking people's profiles- Compulsive behavior is fueled by the fear of being excluded or of missing significant social contacts. Even when they are aware that it is negatively impacting their wellbeing, youngsters may experience an overwhelming temptation to look through other people's profiles.

Injuries or accidents- Young people who are addicted to smartphones may sustain a range of accidents and injuries. Texting or using a phone while driving is one of the most hazardous effects of smartphone addiction. Even utilizing navigation apps while operating a vehicle can cause distractions and raise the risk of accidents. People who use their smartphones while distracted walking frequently bump into doors, poles, street signs, and other obstructions.

Putting in extra time to finish things- In order to use their smartphones as much as possible, youngsters procrastinate their work.

Little or no social life- People who spend a lot of time on smartphone are at least twice as likely to feel socially isolated, according to studies. Those who spend more time on social media have less time for in person interactions.

Isolation from loved ones- Overuse of smartphones can result in diminished interpersonal interactions, feelings of loneliness, and disengagement from family activities.

Use smartphone to cover their loneliness- When youngsters feeling alone or bored, they use smartphone to entertain themself.

Angry or irritated if phone use is interrupted- If they are unable to use their smartphone, people who are addicted to it may get stressed, anxious, and confused.

Getting up at night to check a phone- Due to smartphone addiction, youngsters are waking up in the middle of the night to check their phones. The compulsive need to stay connected, which is frequently driven by social media, notifications, FOMO, gaming, and online engagement, is reflected in this attitude.

Phantom vibrations- Youngsters thinking the phone buzzes when it doesn't.

Limiting smartphone use is difficult- Young people find it difficult to limit their phone use because smartphones have become an essential part of their everyday life for socializing, entertainment, learning, and staying informed.

Craving access to a smartphone or another device- There are multiple psychological, social, and neurological reasons for this obsessive need to use a smartphone. Continually checking the phone for notifications, feeling nervous or anxious when the phone is not close by (Dahiya & Khanam, 2024), or going through withdrawal symptoms when you can't access it are just a few ways that the craving might show up.

Without any reason scroll screen again and again when bored- Scrolling a smartphone screen endlessly for no apparent purpose, especially while bored. It's commonly known as "mindless scrolling" or "doomscrolling" and occurs when people are bored, anxious, or looking for distractions.

Prioritizing phone over other activities- In order to take advantage of smartphones, young people may quit engaging in hobbies or sports that they once enjoyed.

Use mobile to feeling good- Smartphones provide quick and simple access to a variety of entertainment, social media, and information that can momentarily improve mood, so youngsters use them to feel happy.

Anxiety and Depression- Depressive thoughts may be increased by using the phone to avoid addressing social settings, emotions, or personal issues. Despite this, excessive use can cause feelings of loneliness and disengagement in the actual world. Experiencing anxiety, irritability, or upsetness when unable to use your phone or when social media participation doesn't go as planned, as well as a constant need to check your phone, even at inappropriate times.

No track of time- Smartphones completely and extremely interesting features have caused people to lose track of time. Especially applications that are meant to keep users interested, such as social media, gaming, and streaming services. With features like auto-play and unlimited scrolling, apps like YouTube, Instagram, and TikTok offer an infinite amount of content. Because there's constantly something new to be seen, it's easy to lose sight of time.

Smartphone Addiction and Health Effects

Distance is beginning to invade people's healthy relationships with friends and family as more and more people get stuck in virtual worlds. For instance, youngsters would rather play video games online or in virtual reality than go outside and play, which is bad for their social and physical growth. From little problems to big ones. Addiction to smartphones has a variety of negative impacts on a person's health. It can cause backaches, irregular eating, dry eyes, sleep difficulties, severe headaches, poor personal cleanliness, and Carpal Tunnel Syndrome, a condition marked by numbness, pain, and a burning feeling in the hands that may spread up the wrists, elbows, or shoulders.

Additionally, excessive, and continuous use of smartphones has been linked to detrimental impacts on behavior and mental health. Addiction to smartphones has been identified as a significant contributing factor to a number of behavioral and psychological adaption issues. For example, smartphone users may suffer from severe anxiety and do poorly in academics (Lepp et al., 2014, as cited in Sunday et al., 2021). In addition to being addicted to smartphones, children's excessive use of these devices was causing serious sleep and behavioral issues. As the most obvious psychological issue brought on by excessive or uncontrolled smartphone use, psychological discomfort has drawn increasing attention from researchers among these negative effects.

In addition to more sleep issues, smartphone addicts also have higher rates of attention deficit, academic procrastination, strained interpersonal connections, and poor academic achievement. It has been established that procrastination and poor sleep quality are linked to stress, worry, and depression. Smartphone addiction disorders, dry eyes, computer vision syndrome, wrist and thumb weakness, neck pain and stiffness, nomophobia, sensory hallucinations, insecurity, delusions, and hallucinations are among the psychological conditions that can result from excessive smartphone use (Parasuraman et al., 2017).

Smartphone Addiction Is Further Subcategorized as Follows

Social media addiction- The general definition of social media addiction, a subtype of behavioral addiction, is obsessive use of social media platforms that seriously impairs a user's ability to function in key areas of their lives, including relationships with others, productivity at work or school, and physical health. The components model of behavioral addiction conceptualized social media addiction as a collection of symptoms associated with six categories of problematic behavior: (1) Salience is the term used to describe how social media activities influence a person's thoughts and day to day activities; (2) Tolerance is the urge to use social media more frequently in order to experience the same level of enjoyment; (3) Mood modulation is the practice of avoiding or lessening negative feelings that are felt during real-life situations by using social media; (4) Relapse is the term used to describe the inability to stop excessive social media use following attempts at control or abstinence; (5) Withdrawal is the term for the mental distress that arises when one is unable to use social media.; and (6) conflict, which describes how inappropriate social media use might negatively affect one's career or academic performance. 'Social media addicts' or 'social media enthusiasts' are terms frequently used to describe those who are very addicted to social media. They are the ones who are committed to using social media sites like Facebook, Instagram, Snapchat, Twitter, and others extensively (Cheng et al., 2022).

Online Gaming Addiction- An inability to manage one's gaming behaviors is a hallmark of online gaming addiction, which can have detrimental effects on relationships, self-care, education, and employment, among other areas of life. An addiction to online gaming occurs when people procrastinate and/or neglect their everyday tasks in order to spend more time playing online games. People may become distracted and neglect their obligations in the real world. One of the criteria for Internet gaming disorder, as stated in the fifth edition of the Diagnostic and Statistical Manual of Mental Disorders (DSM-5) criteria, is that people continue to play online games even when they are aware of psychosocial issues (American Psychiatric Association). Here, people play online games rather than fulfilling their essential daily obligations (Kaya et al., 2023).

Texting or messaging addiction- Text messaging technologies have fundamentally altered how people interact with one another by facilitating more text-based communication than in-person meetings and by giving consumers greater access to information about their friends, family, social issues, and current events (Harrison & Gilmore, 2012, as cited in Sultan, 2014) Specifically, the advent of Internet-based mobile text messaging apps like WhatsApp and Blackberry Messenger (BBM) has made it possible for users to communicate and socialize on their smartphones for extended periods of time without having to pay for short message service (SMS) fees from network operators. People who have a message addiction react as quickly as they can out of fear of missing a conversation. They rely more on applications for instant chatting.

Information Addiction- An obsessive or problematic engagement with gathering and analyzing information is known as information addiction. This can include compulsive online research, such as product or health research, obsessive organizing or hoarding of data (via notes, lists, bookmarks, etc.), an addiction to the news, online shopping, online encyclopedias, continuously checking smartphones, e-mails or social media accounts for new activity, listening to podcasts and the radio, compulsively searching for any question one is curious about, and other similar behaviors.

Video Streaming Addiction- The obsessive and detrimental use of streaming video content is known as streaming addiction. Excessive use of video channels, such as YouTube, Netflix, TikTok, TV shows, documentaries, and other video streaming services. Addiction to video streaming, a subtype of internet and technology addiction, can cause brain alterations that eventually impair our capacity for concentration, setting priorities, mood regulation, and interpersonal relationships.

Cyber sexual Addiction- Internet sexual activity has been considered as a characteristic of Internet sex addiction, often referred to as cybersex addiction. The following are some of the behaviors associated with internet sex addiction: reading erotic stories; watching, downloading, or trading pornography online; participating in adult fantasy chat rooms online; cybersex relationships; masturbating while doing anything online that raises one's sexual arousal; and looking for offline sexual partners and information about sexual activity.

Cyber relational Addiction- An individual who becomes addicted to or dependent on Instant Messaging (IM), chat rooms, or social networking sites may become overly involved in online interactions or engage in visual adultery. Online relationships become increasingly significant, sometimes even endangering their friends' and families' in-person relationships. Consequently, there are more cases of marital disagreement and family instability.

Net Compulsions- The post-internet era has seen an increase in addiction to online gambling and gaming, among other activities. Due to instant availability and habitual use, people lose a lot of money playing interactive games, shopping online, and playing virtual casinos. It also significantly reduces people's productivity in their professional and social lives.

Online Shopping Addiction- An excessive or uncontrollable desire to purchase online is referred to as an online shopping addiction. An uncontrollable shopping and spend, either for oneself or for other people, is characterized as compulsive spending, oniomania, shopping addiction, or pathological buying. It can be explained by an inability to manage the urge to buy things online. A lot of people purchase in order to feel happy and stay away from bad emotions like despair and anxiety.

Entertainment Addiction- Overuse of media for amusement purposes is frequently referred to as an addiction associated with entertainment. Using apps that provide enjoyment, such games, music, podcasts, movies, short videos, social media, and real life tales, for the majority of the time. These applications end up serving as a way to escape from duties.

Selfie or photo addiction- Selfie addiction, sometimes referred to as selfitis, is the practice of taking numerous selfies during the day, posting them to social media, and then waiting for your friends to comment or likes on them. A person with a photo addiction takes pictures of events, locations, food, other people, or anything else they wish to save as a memory or share on social media. Selfies are a pleasant method for some people to commemorate a good hair day or to record a moment. Others wind up taking a lot of selfies during the day and developing an emotional bond with the reactions they get.

Impact on Mental Health of Youngsters

Physical issues (hypertension, sleep disturbance), psychological issues (social anxiety, sadness, and loneliness), and harmful behaviors (substance abuse, sexting) are all consequences of smartphone addiction. Gaming, Internet addiction, parental smartphone addiction, and FOMO are risk factors and predictors.

1. Anxiety and Depression

Youngsters become "smartphone addicted" when they become overly dependent on smartphones. Although they make their lives easier, smartphones also bind them. Depression is the most significant mental illness when it comes to the effects of smartphone addiction on mental health. In addition to its physical consequences, smartphone addiction also has psychological ones. In addition to being linked to internet abuse, sleep deprivation, worry, stress, and depression have all been linked to smartphone addiction (Shoukat, 2019; Nikolic et al., 2023). A person may use their smartphone excessively, be unable to reduce their usage, utilize their device as a way to pass the time when they are bored, experience anxiety or despair when their phone is out of reach, or lose their relationships. In their studies, numerous researchers discovered that depression is either directly or indirectly caused by smartphone addiction. Due to their late-night smartphone use, youngsters develop sleeplessness, which in turn leads to depression. Anxiety and depression are also strong indicators of smartphone addiction. The risk of anxiety and depression may be raised by excessive smartphone use combined with a negative outlook, worry, and a dependence on technology (Rosen et al., 2013; Thomée et al., 2011, as cited in Shoukat, 2019)

Youngsters feel as though they have missed significant events and information when they are cut off from their phones. FOMO is what causes people to get anxious. This is accompanied by the observation that the user must constantly switch between apps while the main phone is running many ones at once. It causes them to get anxious as a result of their inability to concentrate on cognitive overload.

2. Cyberbullying

Cyberbullying is similar to traditional kinds of intimidation, but it occurs online, using digital devices like computers and smartphones, as well as through social media and gaming platforms. An online setting that is meant to foster connections can degenerate into a hazardous and harmful place.

In order to cause embarrassment or humiliation, cyberbullying usually involves exposing someone else's personal information or sending or posting damaging or misleading stuff about a peer. For instance, a cyberbully may upload an inappropriate image of someone else or a post that has been taken out of context. Another form of cyberbullying is being called insulting names online. Online bullying occurs not only through the most popular social media platforms but also through text messages or instant messaging applications between youngsters. Online harassment causes serious emotional and psychological harm.

According to research, youngsters who are the targets of cyberbullying are more likely to have physical symptoms brought on by mental health conditions as well as sadness, anxiety, loneliness, and suicidal thoughts and actions. Moreover, substance abuse, aggressiveness, and deviant behaviors are more common among young individuals who engage in cyberbullying.

3. Stress

Our society has changed significantly since the invention of smartphones and social media, and these developments have had a big impact on mental health. Nowadays, the primary purposes of youngster's smartphone use are social interaction, recreational activities, and information searching. Stress in youngster is a significant proximal risk predictor of smartphone addiction behavior in addition to being linked to psychological discomfort like anxiety and depression (Zhang et al., 2024). According to research, "the behavior becomes stressful when smartphone use becomes an addiction". The way we communicate, learn, and amuse ourselves has been completely changed by smartphones. But the widespread nature of them can result in obsessive use and dependency. A sense of urgency and excessive tension might be brought on by the continuous stream of messages and updates. According to a CNN investigation, youngsters who receive constant bombardment with messages suffer detrimental consequences and the 200 11–17-year-old participants in the Common Sense Media study from 2023 checked their phones an average of 100 times per day, with many of them feeling as though they couldn't put them down (as cited in, Zwahlen et al., 2023). According to a study, the temptation to reply to notifications not just from friends and relatives, but also from notifications of tragic events occurring all over the world is closely linked to excessive smartphone use.

In the end, participants' anxiety and stress levels rose as a result of their increased phone use due to notifications. Notifications can be unpleasant because they demand constant attention, which can lead to cognitive overload and distraction. An important predictor of the onset and worsening of smartphone addiction is stress. According to research, stress not only directly but also indirectly predicts youngster smartphone addiction by impairing self-control.

4. Sleep

Getting enough good sleep is essential for both mental and physical health. Addiction to smartphones, however, may have a detrimental effect on sleep. According to studies, using screens for two or more hours in the evening can significantly interfere with the melatonin surge that is necessary for falling asleep. Youngster's sleep patterns have a variety of effects, including:

4.1. Sleep Deprivation

Young people's sleep duration and quality are shortened when they use their smartphones excessively before bed. Poor academic performance and daytime drowsiness have been linked to decreased sleep quality (Gupta et al., 2024). Poor sleep hygiene is caused by excessive smartphone use, particularly when it comes to social media, gaming platforms, or late-night movie viewing. That has an impact on how well youngsters sleep. Long term sleep deprivation brought on by poor sleep quality may raise youngster's rates of alcohol and tobacco use (Parlak et al., 2023). Mood fluctuations and irritation, which lead to worry and despair, are associated with inadequate sleep.

4.2. Exposure to Blue Light

Concerns about eye strain and vision issues are also growing. Additionally, the sun emits blue light, which helps us feel alert, rejuvenated, and prepared to tackle the day's tasks. However, blue light is also emitted by digital devices like smartphone screens, which can interfere with our ability to fall asleep. People who use their smartphones at night find it more difficult to fall asleep because the blue light they emit disrupts the creation of melatonin. Blue light from screens can interfere with circadian cycles, which may have an effect on general health. It also contributes to weight gain and psychological issues. Although there is not any solid proof that regular exposure to artificial blue light damages your eyes over time, most researchers think more research is necessary. But blue light from electronics can induce eye strain, which can lead to symptoms including dry eyes, watery eyes and tears, blurred vision, headaches, tired eyes, and stiffness and irritation.

It also contributes to weight gain and psychological issues. Although most researchers think more research is necessary, they have not discovered any solid proof that everyday exposure to artificial blue light damages your eyes over time. But blue light from electronics can induce eye strain, which can lead to symptoms including dry eyes, watery eyes and tears, blurred vision, headaches, tired eyes, and stiffness and irritation.

5. Loneliness

When interpersonal interactions fall short of expectations, loneliness is a subjective psychological state that is frequently accompanied by depressive symptoms, helplessness, boredom, and other unpleasant psychological sensations (Zhang et al., 2023). Many experts think that being constantly surrounded by technology, especially smartphones, may interfere with our ability to interact with others. Reaching for a smartphone whenever they have a moment to spare has become a habit for many youngsters, and this behavior may be exacerbating feelings of loneliness. Since it is socially unacceptable to neglect friendship and social connections, loneliness carries a significant social stigma, according to Lau & Gruen (1992, as cited in Singh & Kumari, 2021), who also noted that loneliness can be experienced by a person in a crowd, or by someone who is alone but feels socially connected. Loneliness is characterized by a lack of social connections and a lack of socially desirable attributes (Masi et al., 2011, as cited in Singh & Kumari, 2021).

A strong and positive correlation between smartphone addiction and heightened feelings of social isolation and loneliness revealed by Sarkar et al., (2018) and Wacks & Weinstein, (2021). Research has also shown that loneliness is a feeling that someone who needs some level of interaction, different from what is currently discovered experiences. The quantity of social bonds is irrelevant; what matters is their quality. However, people do not always benefit from having more social interactions in their social lives (Tan et al., 2013, as cited in Singh & Kumari, 2021).

6. Attention Span

Notifications that are sent to smartphones might cause vibrations and sounds. For people, these alerts and possible noises can be distracting. Even when participants do not reply to the messages, studies demonstrate how distracting smartphone notifications may be. According to another study, when the smartphone is actively listened to, an involuntary attention mechanism is activated. Strong effects of smartphones can be observed in specific areas, with a particular focus on how they affect working memory, attention, and inhibition. The smartphone has the potential to impair human cognition. This is not just true when it comes to media multitasking, but the simple existence of a smartphone can already have an impact on cognition (Liebherr et al., 2020, as cited in Skowronek et al., 2023).

Addiction to smartphones can impair focus and attention spans. It may lead to less in person social engagement, which could harm relationships and social skills (Gupta et al., 2024). Numerous studies show that excessive smartphone use can interfere with daily routines, safety, and overall wellbeing.

7. Memory Loss

One of the main things that affects the formation of memories is distraction. We are only partially engaged on learning a new skill when we are occupied with multitasking on our smartphones and rapidly searching through numerous applications and notifications for information. Therefore, it is improbable that the information will be retained in our long-term memory. The accuracy of memory recall was considerably impacted by the presence of the smartphone and frequent thoughts about it, indicating that they were a contributing factor to the "bandwidth effect," which is an increase in cognitive load that disrupts participants' memory processes (Tanil & Yong, 2020).

Addiction to smartphones can disrupt sleep patterns. Deep sleep is necessary for brain detoxification. The brain only does synaptic pruning the process of removing outdated information to make room for new information when people are deeply asleep. Sleep disruption prevents synaptic pruning, which affects our capacity to remember new information and create new memories. According to the University of London's Institute of Psychiatry, excessive screen time also considerably lowers our IQ in addition to sleep.

A recent study by experts at the Swiss Tropical and Public Health Institute (Swiss TPH) found that young people's figural memory is severely impacted by increased exposure to smartphones. Figural memory is found in the right hemisphere of the brain and aids in our understanding of shapes, patterns, and images. Youngsters are therefore most impacted since they hold their smartphones close to their right ears.

According to the researchers, who conducted this study on 700 children, a developing brain is more vulnerable to changes brought on by smartphone waves until the age of 15. They discovered that when a youngster's average call time is 10.6 minutes, they are exposed to 858 mJ/kg of radiation daily on average.

8. Reduced Social Interaction

People spend more and more time staring at their smartphones when they are using them. They avoid face-to-face interactions with their neighbors, friends, and family as a result. Additionally, their social life shrinks and contracts. Furthermore, a person runs the risk of losing their social skills if they rely too much on electronic gadgets like smartphones for communication. On social media, youngsters are spending more time with their friends, imitating them, creating new content and monitoring their likes and comments, viewing films and web series for amusement, and playing games primarily. As a result, people participate less in social events involving friends, family, and more in smartphone functions.

9. Low Self-Esteem or Poor Body Image

Numerous aspects of life may suffer as a result of excessive and compulsive smartphone use that leads to smartphone addiction. Youngsters in particular may have low self-esteem and body dissatisfaction as a result of constant exposure to carefully maintained social media pictures and lifestyles.

Furthermore, people's impressions of their bodies are connected to it because they may compare their appearance to idealized social media photographs, which may or may not make them feel more satisfied with their bodies. Additionally, smartphone addiction has an impact on self-esteem. Higher levels of smartphone addiction were associated with more negative body image evaluations and poorer levels of self-esteem.

CONCLUSION

Across decades, the use of media devices has increased, and smartphones are now the most used media device worldwide. The smartphone is a useful technology that offers a lot of benefits. It can be a good substitute study methods and gives youngsters access to a variety of facilities, which allow them to pursue various facilities. People check the weather from their beds, trade stocks and gossip while stuck in traffic, talk to their significant others in between appointments, shop online while standing in queue and provide real time live streaming of one other's experiences from across the globe. They can be used as gaming systems, calendars, tip calculators, internet portals, phone books, and maps, among many other things. Smartphones are useful, but they also have drawbacks, who use the internet excessively struggle to manage their daily social and academic routines. Conversely, the lives of youngsters are negatively impacted by unrestrained and excessive smartphone use. Youngsters who use the smartphone excessively are likely to exhibit social withdrawal, anxiety, and psychological and cognitive problems. Due to their indulgence in virtual world, their connection to reality may weaken and they may lose their ability to respond quickly and properly to situations in the actual world. Some of these include decreased cognitive function, stress, anxiety, sadness, lack of sleep, loneliness, and short attention span.

REFERENCES

Abeele, M. B. (2020). *The social consequences of phubbing: A framework and a research agenda. Handbook of Mobile Communication, Culture, and Information.* Oxford University Press.

Abeyta, L. (2015). *How the Smart Phone Has Equalized Access to Information.* Linkedin. https://www.linkedin.com/pulse/how-smart-phone-has-equalized-access-information-lisa-abeyta

Ahmed, A. H., Elemo, A. S., & Hamed, O. A. O. (2023). Smartphone Addiction and Phubbing in International Students in Turkey: The Moderating Role of Mindfulness. *Journal of College Student Development*, 64(1), 64–78. DOI: 10.1353/csd.2023.0002

Bajwa, R. S., Abdullah, H., Zaremohzzabein, Z., Jaafar, W. M. W., & Samah, A. A. (2023). Smartphone addiction and phubbing behavior among university students: A moderated mediation model by fear of missing out, social comparison, and loneliness. *Frontiers in Psychology*, 13, 1072551. DOI: 10.3389/fpsyg.2022.1072551 PMID: 36687837

Bhanderi, D. J., Pandya, Y. P., & Sharma, D. B. (2021). Smartphone Use and Its Addiction among Adolescents in the Age Group of 16-19 Years. *Indian journal of community medicine: Official publication of Indian Association of Preventive &. Social Medicine (Social Medicine Publication Group)*, 46(1), 88–92. DOI: 10.4103/ijcm.IJCM_263_20 PMID: 34035584

Brook, B., & Santos, T. (2023). The Temptation of Instant Gratification: A Double-Edged Sword. *Journal of Addiction Research & Therapy*, 14, 564.

Cheng, C., Ebrahimi, O. V., & Luk, J. W. (2022). Heterogeneity of Prevalence of Social Media Addiction Across Multiple Classification Schemes: Latent Profile Analysis. *Journal of Medical Internet Research*, 24(1), e27000. DOI: 10.2196/27000 PMID: 35006084

Cherry, K. (2023). *Tips to Maintain an Interpersonal Relationship*. Verywell Mind. https://www.verywellmind.com/how-to-maintain-interpersonal-relationships-5204856

Cyberbullying: The Mental Health Impact and How to Help Your Teen. (2023, January 18). Newport Academy. https://www.newportacademy.com/resources/restoring-families/teen-cyberbullying/

. Dahiya, A., & Khanam, A. (2024). Exploring the Impact of Smartphone Addiction on Body Image and Self-Esteem among Young Adults. *International Journal of Indian Psychology, 12*(2), 3242-3248. DOI:DOI: 10.25215/.286

Davey, S., Davey, A., Raghav, S. K., Singh, J. V., Singh, N., Blachnio, A., & Przepiórkaa, A. (2018). Predictors and consequences of "Phubbing" among Youngsters and youth in India: An impact evaluation study. *Journal of Family & Community Medicine*, 25(1), 35–42. DOI: 10.4103/jfcm.JFCM_71_17 PMID: 29386960

Gangwar, G. (2022). *Influence of internet use upon life style of adolescents (10603)* [Doctoral dissertation, Banasthali Vidyapith University, Rajasthan]. Shodhganga.

Gupta, A. K. S. K., Singh, P. S. B., & Krishak, A. K. S. (2024). Smartphone addiction: Impact on health and well-being. *International Journal of Community Medicine and Public Health*, 11(5), 2100–2106. DOI: 10.18203/2394-6040.ijcmph20241213

Internet and Technology Addicts Anonymous. (2024). *Signs of Internet and Technology Addiction Anonymous*. https://internetaddictsanonymous.org/internet-and-technology-addiction/

Ivanova, A., Gorbaniuk, O., Błachnio, A., Przepiórka, A., Mraka, N., Polishchuk, V., & Gorbaniuk, J. (2020). Mobile Phone Addiction, Phubbing, and Depression Among Men and Women: A Moderated Mediation Analysis. *The Psychiatric Quarterly*, 91(3), 655–668. DOI: 10.1007/s11126-020-09723-8 PMID: 32146681

Kaya, A., Türk, N., Batmaz, H., & Griffiths, M. D. (2023). Online Gaming Addiction and Basic Psychological Needs Among Youngsters: The Mediating Roles of Meaning in Life and Responsibility. *International Journal of Mental Health and Addiction*, 1–25. Advance online publication. DOI: 10.1007/s11469-022-00994 PMID: 36643385

Lee, J., Sung, M., Song, S. H., Lee, Y. M., Lee, J. J., Cho, S. M., Park, M. K., & Shin, Y. (2016). Psychological Factors Associated With Smartphone Addiction in South Korean Adolescents. *The Journal of Early Adolescence*, 38(3), 288–302. DOI: 10.1177/0272431616670751

Liu, N., Zhu, S., Zhang, W., Sun, Y., & Zhang, X. (2024). The relationship between fear of missing out and mobile phone addiction among college students: The mediating role of depression and the moderating role of loneliness. *Frontiers in Public Health*, 12, 1374522. DOI: 10.3389/fpubh.2024.1374522 PMID: 38584914

Nikolic, A., Bukurov, B., Kocic, I., Vukovic, M., Ladjevic, N., Vrhovac, M., Pavlović, Z., Grujicic, J., Kisic, D., & Sipetic, S. (2023). Smartphone addiction, sleep quality, depression, anxiety, and stress among medical students. *Frontiers in Public Health*, 11, 1252371. DOI: 10.3389/fpubh.2023.1252371 PMID: 37744504

Parasuraman, S., Sam, A. T., Yee, S. W. K., Chuon, B. L. C., & Ren, L. Y. (2017). Smartphone usage and increased risk of mobile phone addiction: A concurrent study. *International Journal of Pharmaceutical Investigation*, 7(3), 125–131. DOI: 10.4103/jphi.JPHI_56_17 PMID: 29184824

Parlak, M. E., Öz, E., Özbey, M. Y., & Kapıcı, Y. (2023). Smartphone Addiction and Sleep Quality in Youngsters. *Medical Science and Discovery*, 10(1), 35–40. DOI: 10.36472/msd.v10i1.864

Sarkar, T., Taneja, N., Jana, P., Gupta, S., Dalal, R., Dasgupta, R., Halder, R., & Adhikary, M. (2018). Effect of mobile phone overuse on health of medical students. *International Journal of Medical Science and Public Health*, 8(1), 91–94. DOI: 10.5455/ijmsph.2019.0516506122018

Shoukat, S. (2019). Cell phone addiction and psychological and physiological health in Youngsters. *EXCLI Journal*, 18, 47–50. PMID: 30956638

Singh, R., & Kumari, V. (2021). Loneliness and smartphone addiction among youths: A correlational study. *Indian Journal of Applied Research*. DOI: 10.13140/RG.2.2.25510.24647

Sinsomsack, N., & Kulachai, W. (2018). A study on the impacts of Smartphone addiction. *Proceedings of the 19th International Symposium on Management (INSYMA 2022)*. DOI: 10.2991/insyma-18.2018.61

Skowronek, J., Seifert, A., & Lindberg, S. (2023). The mere presence of a smartphone reduces basal attentional performance. *Scientific Reports*, 13(1), 9363. DOI: 10.1038/s41598-023-36256-4 PMID: 37291199

Sultan, A. J. (2014). Addiction to mobile text messaging applications is nothing to "lol" about. *The Social Science Journal*, 51(1), 57-69. DOI: 10.1016/j.soscij.2013.09.003

Sunday, O. J., Adesope, A. O., & Maarhuis, P. L. (2021). The effects of smartphone addiction on learning: A meta-analysis. *Computers in Human Behavior Reports*, 4, 100114. Advance online publication. DOI: 10.1016/j.chbr.2021.100114

Talan, T., Doğan, Y., & Kalinkara, Y. (2023). Effects of Smartphone Addiction, Social Media Addiction and Fear of Missing Out on University Students' Phubbing: A Structural Equation Model. *Deviant Behavior*. Advance online publication. DOI: 10.1080/01639625.2023.2235870

Tanil, C. T., & Yong, M. H. (2020). Mobile phones: The effect of its presence on learning and memory. *PLoS One*, 15(8), e0219233. DOI: 10.1371/journal.pone.0219233 PMID: 32790667

Thomée, S. (2018). Mobile Phone Use and Mental Health: A Review of the Research That Takes a Psychological Perspective on Exposure. *International Journal of Environmental Research and Public Health*, 15(12), 2692. DOI: 10.3390/ijerph15122692 PMID: 30501032

Wacks, Y., & Weinstein, A. M. (2021). Excessive Smartphone Use Is Associated With Health Problems in Adolescents and Young Adults. *Frontiers in Psychiatry*, 12, 669042. DOI: 10.3389/fpsyt.2021.669042 PMID: 34140904

Wikipedia contributors. (2024). *Internet sex addiction*. Wikipedia. https://en.wikipedia.org/wiki/Internet_sex_addiction

Yang, L. L., Guo, C., Li, G. Y., Gan, K. P., & Luo, J. H. (2023). Mobile phone addiction and mental health: The roles of sleep quality and perceived social support. *Frontiers in Psychology*, 14, 1265400. DOI: 10.3389/fpsyg.2023.1265400 PMID: 37809316

Yang, S. Y., Wang, Y. C., Lee, Y. C., Lin, Y. L., Hsieh, P. L., & Lin, P. H. (2022). Does Smartphone Addiction, Social Media Addiction, and/or Internet Game Addiction Affect Youngsters' Interpersonal Interactions? *Healthcare (Basel)*, 10(5), 963. DOI: 10.3390/healthcare10050963 PMID: 35628099

Zhang, Y., Han, M., Lian, S., Cao, X., & Yan, L. (2024). How and when is academic stress associated with mobile phone addiction? The roles of psychological distress, peer alienation and rumination. *PLoS One*, 19(2), e0293094. DOI: 10.1371/journal.pone.0293094 PMID: 38346023

Zhang, Y., Li, Y., Xia, M., Han, M., Yan, L., & Lian, S. (2023). The relationship between loneliness and mobile phone addiction among Chinese college students: The mediating role of anthropomorphism and moderating role of family support. *PLoS One*, 18(4), e0285189. DOI: 10.1371/journal.pone.0285189 PMID: 37115749

Zwahlen, A., Peters, Q., & Mulryan, M. (2023, November 7). *Notifications are taking over the lives of teens*. Mill Valley News. https://www.mvnews.org/notifications-are-taking-over-the-lives-of-teens/

Chapter 5
Mental Health Issues Due to Smart Phone Addiction

Jayashree Prabhakar A. A.
https://orcid.org/0000-0003-4324-5916
Vels Institute of Science, Technology, and Advanced Studies, India

Sudheer V. N.
https://orcid.org/0009-0004-8776-9409
CMR University, India

Vishnu Priya N. S.
Vellore Institute of Technology, India

P. Selvakumar
https://orcid.org/0000-0002-3650-4548
Nehru Institute of Technology, India

Ravi Kishor Agrawal
https://orcid.org/0009-0001-2768-4946
MATS University, India

Manjunath T. C.
https://orcid.org/0000-0003-2545-9160
Rajarajeswari College of Engineering, India

ABSTRACT

Smartphone addiction has become a significant concern in modern society, particularly due to its profound effects on mental health. Moreover, smartphone addiction can adversely affect attention and focus. The frequent switching between tasks and the rapid consumption of information can impair an individual's ability to concentrate for extended periods. This fragmentation of attention is not only detrimental to productivity but also affects cognitive development and memory retention. Research has shown that the constant need to check smartphones can lead to a reduced capacity for deep, reflective thinking and problem-solving skills. In summary, the rise of smartphone addiction presents a growing concern for mental health, driven by constant connectivity, the fear of missing out, and the impact on attention, sleep, asocial relationships. As society continues to navigate the digital age, it is crucial to develop and implement strategies to manage smartphone use effectively, ensuring that technology enhances rather than detracts from overall well-being.

DOI: 10.4018/979-8-3693-8804-4.ch005

INTRODUCTION TO SMART PHONE ADDICTION AND MENTAL HEALTH: A GROWING CONCERN

Smartphone addiction has become a significant concern in modern society, particularly due to its profound effects on mental health. Moreover, smartphone addiction can adversely affect attention and focus. The frequent switching between tasks and the rapid consumption of information can impair an individual's ability to concentrate for extended periods. This fragmentation of attention is not only detrimental to productivity but also affects cognitive development and memory retention. Research has shown that the constant need to check smartphones can lead to a reduced capacity for deep, reflective thinking and problem-solving skills. The phenomenon of "phubbing," where individuals ignore those around them in favor of their phones, exemplifies how smartphones can create social isolation and impact personal relationships. This detachment can contribute to feelings of loneliness and social anxiety, further exacerbating mental health problems. Addressing smartphone addiction requires a multifaceted approach. Awareness and education about the potential negative effects of excessive smartphone use are essential in fostering healthier habits. Implementing strategies such as setting specific times for phone use, engaging in digital detoxes, and prioritizing face-to-face interactions can help mitigate the adverse effects. Additionally, integrating mindfulness practices and promoting digital literacy can empower individuals to use smartphones more responsibly and consciously. In summary, the rise of smartphone addiction presents a growing concern for mental health, driven by constant connectivity, the fear of missing out, and the impact on attention, sleep, asocial relationships. As society continues to navigate the digital age, it is crucial to develop and implement strategies to manage smartphone use effectively, ensuring that technology enhances rather than detracts from overall well-being.

Anxiety and Stress: The Link between Smart Phone Use and Increased Anxiety

The link between smartphone use and increased anxiety is a growing area of concern as our reliance on these devices deepens. Smartphones, designed to keep us constantly connected, have inadvertently become a source of stress and anxiety for many users. This connection is driven by several interrelated factors: the constant influx of notifications, the pressure of social media, and the compulsion to remain engaged with digital content. One of the primary ways smartphones contribute to anxiety is through the incessant stream of notifications and alerts. These notifications create a state of perpetual alertness, as users feel compelled to respond immediately to messages, emails, or app updates (Al-Khani, A. M., et al., 2019).

This continuous engagement disrupts users' ability to relax and can lead to chronic stress. Research indicates that the anticipation of notifications and the need to constantly check one's phone can heighten anxiety levels, as individuals experience a heightened sense of urgency and pressure to stay connected. This phenomenon, known as "notification anxiety," can interfere with daily activities and contribute to an overall sense of overwhelm. Social media platforms, accessible via smartphones, further exacerbate anxiety through a range of mechanisms. Social media fosters an environment where users are constantly exposed to curated images and idealized portrayals of others' lives.

The cycle of poor sleep and increased smartphone use thus creates a detrimental feedback loop, exacerbating the impact of anxiety. Moreover, the pervasive nature of smartphones blurs the boundaries between work and personal life. Many individuals use their smartphones for work-related tasks outside of office hours, leading to a constant state of connectivity and reduced downtime. This lack of separation between work and leisure time can contribute to burnout and heightened anxiety, as individuals struggle to disconnect and unwind. The expectation of immediate responses and the pressure to stay available can intensify feelings of stress and reduce overall job satisfaction. To address the anxiety associated with smartphone use, it is crucial to adopt strategies that promote healthier usage patterns (Augner, C., et al., 2023). Setting specific times for checking notifications, utilizing features that limit screen time, and creating designated tech-free zones can help mitigate the impact of smartphones on mental well-being. Additionally, mindfulness practices, such as meditation and relaxation techniques, can aid in managing stress and improving emotional resilience. By fostering a more balanced relationship with technology, individuals can reduce the anxiety associated with smartphone use and enhance their overall quality of life (Adams, S. K., et al., 2013). In conclusion, the link between smartphone use and increased anxiety is evident through the constant barrage of notifications, the impact of social media, and disruptions to sleep and work-life balance. As smartphones continue to play a central role in our lives, it is essential to develop mindful and strategic approaches to their use, aiming to alleviate the associated stress and promote better mental health outcomes.

Depression and Smart Phone Addiction: A Complex Relationship

Smartphones, with their constant connectivity and access to digital content, have become integral to daily life, but their pervasive presence has introduced new challenges to mental health, particularly concerning depression. Smartphone addiction, characterized by excessive and compulsive use of mobile devices, is closely linked to depressive symptoms in several ways. First, the nature of smartphone use often involves extensive engagement with social media platforms, where users are exposed to a continuous stream of curated and often idealized representations of others' lives (Barnes, C. M., et al., 2011). The fear of missing out (FOMO) is another significant factor linking smartphone addiction to depression. Smartphones facilitate real-time updates and constant connectivity, which can amplify the sense of urgency to stay engaged with social networks and current events. This constant need to be in the loop can lead to heightened anxiety and stress (Bartel, K., et al., 2019), contributing to depressive feelings. The pressure to remain connected and the anxiety of missing out on social interactions or trending topics can overwhelm users, creating a sense of disconnection and dissatisfaction that exacerbates depressive symptoms. Smartphone use also impacts sleep patterns, which is closely related to depression. Poor sleep quality and sleep deprivation are well-documented risk factors for depression. Individuals who use smartphones excessively, especially before bedtime, may experience difficulties falling asleep and maintaining restful sleep, which can lead to fatigue, irritability, and mood disturbances. This disruption in sleep can create a vicious cycle, as the lack of rest impairs emotional regulation and cognitive function, further contributing to depressive symptoms.

Additionally, the constant bombardment of notifications and digital stimuli can lead to cognitive overload and reduced attention spans (Bastien, C. H., et al., 2001). The frequent interruptions and multitasking associated with smartphone use can hinder an individual's ability to engage in meaningful activities and relationships. This diminished capacity for deep, focused engagement can lead to a sense of frustration and dissatisfaction, contributing to feelings of depression. Moreover, the inability to disconnect from digital demands can result in a lack of personal fulfillment and increased emotional strain. Social isolation, paradoxically, can also be a consequence of excessive smartphone use. While smartphones facilitate virtual connections, they can sometimes undermine face-to-face interactions, leading to a decrease in the quality of personal relationships. This social detachment can result in feelings of loneliness and isolation, both of which are strongly linked to depressive disorders. The superficial nature of online interactions may not provide the emotional support and depth needed for mental well-being, leaving individuals feeling disconnected and unsupported. In conclusion, the relationship between smartphone addiction and depression is intricate and influenced by various factors, including social comparison, FOMO, disrupted sleep, cognitive overload, and social isolation. As smartphones become increasingly embedded in daily life, understanding and addressing these issues is vital for promoting mental health and well-being. By adopting mindful technology use and fostering supportive offline connections, individuals can navigate the digital landscape more effectively and reduce the risk of developing depressive symptoms related to smartphone addiction.

Sleep Disturbances and Smart Phone Use: Impact on Mental Health

The impact of smartphone use on sleep disturbances and, consequently, mental health, has emerged as a critical area of concern in the digital age (Calpbinici, P., et al., 2019). The pervasive use of smartphones has transformed the way individuals interact with technology, but this constant connectivity has introduced new challenges, particularly in relation to sleep quality and mental well-being. Understanding how smartphone use affects sleep and its subsequent impact on mental health requires examining several key factors: blue light emission, the influence of constant notifications, and the psychological effects of pre-sleep smartphone activities. One of the primary ways smartphones disrupt sleep is through the emission of blue light. Research has consistently demonstrated that using smartphones before bedtime is associated with delayed sleep onset and reduced sleep efficiency, leading to increased fatigue and daytime sleepiness. The resulting sleep disturbances can exacerbate various mental health issues, including mood disorders and cognitive impairments.

The role of smartphone notifications in disrupting sleep cannot be understated (Christian, M. S., et al., 2011). Constant alerts and updates, such as text messages, social media notifications, and email alerts, can create a sense of urgency and prevent individuals from achieving restful sleep. The intermittent interruptions from notifications can fragment sleep cycles and lead to frequent awakenings throughout the night. This disruption not only impacts sleep quality but also affects the ability to progress through the various stages of sleep necessary for cognitive and emotional restoration. The lack of restorative sleep can contribute to heightened stress, irritability, and impaired cognitive function, all of which are linked to poorer mental health outcomes. Furthermore, the content consumed on smartphones before bed can have a significant impact on sleep and mental health. The cumulative effect of such pre-sleep activities is often a compromised sleep pattern that contributes to increased feelings of anxiety, depression, and general psychological distress. The relationship between sleep disturbances caused by smartphone use and mental health is bidirectional. Poor sleep can lead to increased vulnerability to mental health issues, including anxiety and depression (Chu, X., et al., 2021). Chronic sleep deprivation affects emotional regulation, cognitive functioning, and stress resilience, making individuals more susceptible to developing mood disorders.

Cyberbullying and Online Harassment: Mental Health Consequences

Cyberbullying and online harassment have become pervasive issues in the digital age, with profound and far-reaching consequences for mental health (Clement-Carbonell, V., et al., 2021). The rise of social media platforms, messaging apps, and online forums has unfortunately also facilitated the spread of harmful behaviors, creating an environment where individuals, particularly adolescents, are increasingly vulnerable to various forms of online abuse. The mental health consequences of cyberbullying and online harassment are severe and multifaceted, affecting emotional, psychological, and social well-being. One of the most significant mental health impacts of cyberbullying is the development of anxiety and depression. Victims of cyberbullying often experience persistent fear and worry due to the nature of online harassment, which can be relentless and invasive. This constant exposure to negative interactions can lead to heightened stress and anxiety, as individuals feel perpetually threatened and vulnerable. The emotional toll of such harassment can manifest as depressive symptoms, including persistent sadness, loss of interest in previously enjoyed activities, and a general sense of hopelessness. Cyberbullying can also lead to a significant decline in self-esteem and self-worth. The anonymous and often public nature of online harassment can exacerbate feelings of inadequacy and shame (Desouky, D. E. S., et al., 2020). Negative comments, derogatory messages, and humiliating content shared online can undermine an individual's self-confidence and self-image. The effects on self-esteem are particularly pronounced in young people, who are still developing their self-concept and are highly susceptible to external validation.

Social isolation is another significant consequence of cyberbullying and online harassment. Victims often withdraw from social interactions and isolate themselves to avoid further abuse (Dowran, B. 2020). This withdrawal can result in a lack of social support and decreased opportunities for positive social engagement. The absence of a supportive network can exacerbate feelings of loneliness and depression, making it more challenging for individuals to cope with the effects of cyberbullying. The resulting isolation can perpetuate a cycle of distress and mental health issues, as individuals struggle to reconnect with others and rebuild their sense of belonging. Furthermore, the impact of cyberbullying extends beyond the immediate psychological effects, influencing broader life outcomes. Victims may experience difficulties in academic and professional settings, as the emotional toll of harassment can interfere with concentration, performance, and overall motivation. The stress associated with cyberbullying can lead to absenteeism, decreased productivity, and impaired academic achievement. In the workplace, online harassment can undermine job satisfaction, hinder career progression, and contribute to higher rates of absenteeism and turnover.

Addressing the mental health consequences of cyberbullying and online harassment requires a multifaceted approach. Prevention strategies, including educational programs that promote digital citizenship and resilience, can help mitigate the incidence of online abuse. Schools, workplaces, and communities must work collaboratively to create environments where individuals are educated about the impacts of cyberbullying and are equipped with the tools to address and report harassment (Elhai, J. D., et al., 2017). Support systems, including counseling services and mental health resources, play a crucial role in providing assistance to victims and helping them navigate the emotional challenges associated with online abuse. In conclusion, cyberbullying and online harassment have severe mental health consequences, including increased anxiety, depression, diminished self-esteem, and a heightened risk of suicidal ideation. The pervasive nature of online abuse can lead to social isolation and negatively impact academic and professional outcomes. Addressing these issues effectively requires a comprehensive approach that includes prevention, education, and support systems to safeguard individuals and promote mental well-being in the digital era.

Loneliness and Social Isolation: The Dark Side of Smart Phone Addiction

Smartphone addiction, while often lauded for its convenience and connectivity, harbors a darker side that significantly contributes to loneliness and social isolation (Friedrich, A., et al., 2018). As smartphones have become integral to modern life, they have transformed how we communicate and engage with others. However, the very tools designed to connect us can paradoxically lead to profound feelings of isolation and emotional disconnection. The mechanisms through which smartphone addiction fosters loneliness and social isolation are multifaceted, involving the nature of digital interactions, the erosion of face-to-face communication, and the psychological impact of constant connectivity. One of the key ways smartphone addiction contributes to loneliness is through the nature of digital interactions. While smartphones facilitate virtual connections via social media, messaging apps, and other platforms, these interactions often lack the depth and emotional richness of face-to-face communication. Digital conversations can be superficial and fragmented, which might not fulfill the emotional needs for meaningful, personal connections. This superficiality can lead individuals to feel disconnected and unfulfilled, despite frequent online interactions. The quality of communication is a critical factor in emotional well-being, and the reduction in meaningful, face-to-face interactions can exacerbate feelings of loneliness. The phenomenon of "phubbing," where individuals ignore those around them in favor of their smartphones, illustrates how smartphone addiction can erode personal relationships. The resulting lack of genuine social connection contributes to a growing sense of loneliness. Moreover, smartphone addiction can lead to a diminished capacity for developing and maintaining deep, meaningful relationships. The constant engagement with digital content and notifications often distracts individuals from engaging in sustained, face-to-face interactions(Gangadharan, N.,et al., 2022).

Additionally, the addictive nature of smartphones can create a cycle of escapism that exacerbates loneliness. Individuals may turn to their smartphones to escape from feelings of loneliness or dissatisfaction, seeking solace in virtual interactions or digital content (Ghrouz, A. K., et al., 2019). However, this escapism can often lead to further isolation, as individuals may avoid engaging in real-life social activities and relationships. The temporary relief provided by digital interactions may not address the underlying feelings of loneliness, leading to a cycle where the use of smartphones to cope with isolation ultimately exacerbates the problem. Addressing the loneliness and social isolation resulting from smartphone addiction requires a multifaceted approach. Promoting mindful smartphone use and encouraging individuals to prioritize face-to-face interactions can help mitigate the negative effects of excessive digital engagement. Implementing strategies such as designated technology-free times and spaces, fostering opportunities for in-person social activities, and promoting awareness about the impact of smartphone use on relationships are crucial steps in combating the isolation associated with smartphone addiction. Additionally, mental health resources and support systems can provide assistance for individuals struggling with loneliness and help them develop healthier, more fulfilling social connections. In conclusion, smartphone addiction has a significant dark side that contributes to loneliness and social isolation. The nature of digital interactions, the erosion of face-to-face communication, and the psychological effects of constant connectivity all play a role in exacerbating feelings of loneliness. Addressing these issues involves fostering mindful technology use, promoting meaningful social interactions, and providing support for those affected by isolation. By understanding and addressing the impact of smartphone addiction on social well-being, individuals can work towards creating a more balanced and connected social life.

Attention Deficit Hyperactivity Disorder (ADHD) and Smart Phone Use

Smartphone use is a burgeoning area of concern, particularly as smartphones become increasingly embedded in daily life. ADHD, characterized by persistent patterns of inattention, hyperactivity, and impulsivity, may be exacerbated by the constant stimulation and demands of smartphone technology (Hao, Z., et al., 2019).

The relationship between smartphone use and ADHD is complex, involving both the potential for exacerbation of symptoms and the challenges in managing ADHD in a digitally dominated environment. Smartphones can impact individuals with ADHD in several significant ways. The constant influx of notifications, messages, and digital content can exacerbate the symptoms of inattention and distractibility that are central to ADHD. For individuals with ADHD, the barrage of incoming alerts can create a constant state of cognitive overload, making it difficult to focus on tasks and maintain sustained attention. The tendency to switch frequently between apps and activities further fragments attention, reducing the ability to concentrate on any single task for an extended period. This fragmented attention span can undermine productivity and exacerbate the difficulties experienced by individuals with ADHD in managing their daily responsibilities. These design choices can lead to compulsive use patterns, where individuals with ADHD may find themselves repeatedly drawn to their devices, despite their intentions to focus on other tasks. This compulsive behavior can reinforce and perpetuate symptoms of inattention and impulsivity, making it challenging to establish effective strategies for managing ADHD.

The cycle of poor sleep and increased smartphone use can create additional challenges in managing ADHD and maintaining overall well-being. Furthermore, the use of smartphones for managing ADHD-related tasks, such as reminders and organizational apps, can be a double-edged sword. While these tools offer potential benefits, such as improved time management and task organization, they can also contribute to cognitive overload and distractibility if not used mindfully (Haripriya, S., et al., 2019). The constant presence of digital reminders and notifications can interrupt focus and lead to an increased sense of being overwhelmed. The effectiveness of these tools largely depends on how they are integrated into the individual's routine and whether they are used in a way that supports rather than detracts from managing ADHD symptoms. In addressing the challenges associated with smartphone use and ADHD, it is crucial to implement strategies that balance the benefits of digital tools with the need to manage attention and focus effectively. Establishing boundaries for smartphone use, such as designated times for checking notifications and setting limits on screen time, can help mitigate the impact of constant digital stimulation. Educational programs and support resources can also play a vital role in helping individuals with ADHD navigate the challenges of smartphone use. The constant stimulation, cognitive overload, and impact on sleep associated with smartphones can present significant challenges for individuals with ADHD. By implementing mindful technology use practices, setting boundaries, and utilizing supportive tools, individuals with ADHD can work towards managing their symptoms more effectively and navigating the digital landscape in a way that enhances rather than hinders their attention and overall well-being.

Obsessive-Compulsive Disorder (OCD) and Smart Phone Addiction

The interplay between Obsessive-Compulsive Disorder (OCD) and smartphone addiction is an area of increasing concern, as the pervasive nature of smartphones can significantly impact individuals with OCD (Hayes, A. F., et al., 2014). This complex relationship involves several factors, including the reinforcement of compulsive behaviors, the impact of constant digital stimuli, and the challenges of managing OCD symptoms in a hyper-connected environment. Smartphones can amplify OCD symptoms through the reinforcement of compulsive behaviors. For individuals with OCD, smartphones offer a platform for engaging in repetitive checking behaviors, such as frequently reviewing notifications, verifying information, or repeatedly engaging with certain apps. These digital compulsions can serve as a form of reassurance or a way to manage intrusive thoughts, mirroring traditional OCD behaviors such as hand washing or checking locks. The immediate feedback provided by smartphones can reinforce these compulsions, making it difficult for individuals to break the cycle of repetitive behavior and increasing overall symptom severity.

The constant digital stimuli from smartphones can also exacerbate the distress associated with obsessive thoughts (Ivanova, A., et al., 2020). Notifications, messages, and social media updates can be sources of anxiety and intrusive thoughts, especially if the content is related to personal concerns or triggers. For individuals with OCD, the need to address or respond to these digital stimuli can intensify obsessive thinking and compulsive behaviors. The incessant flow of information and alerts can lead to heightened anxiety and increased pressure to engage in compulsive checking or reassurance-seeking behaviors, further complicating the management of OCD. Moreover, smartphones can create an environment where avoidance behaviors are easily facilitated. For individuals with OCD, avoidance of certain triggers or anxiety-inducing situations is a common compulsion. Smartphones, with their access to various digital distractions, can enable avoidance by providing an alternative to confronting distressing thoughts or situations. This avoidance can prevent individuals from addressing the underlying issues related to their OCD, reinforcing maladaptive coping strategies and potentially worsening symptoms over time.

The use of smartphones late into the night can further disrupt sleep, creating a cycle where sleep deprivation exacerbates OCD symptoms, leading to increased reliance on digital behaviors as a form of reassurance or distraction. Addressing the challenges of smartphone addiction for individuals with OCD requires a multifaceted approach that integrates mindful technology use with effective OCD management strategies. Establishing boundaries for smartphone use, such as designated periods for checking notifications and limiting screen time, can help reduce the reinforcement of compulsive behaviors and minimize digital stimuli that trigger obsessive thoughts (Jun, S. 2016). Utilizing smartphone features that support mental health, such as apps designed for mindfulness and stress management, can offer beneficial tools for individuals with OCD, provided they are used in a way that does not contribute to compulsive behaviors. For example, therapists may work with individuals to develop strategies for managing digital compulsions and addressing the impact of smartphone use on OCD symptoms (Körmendi, A., et al., 2016). Education and support for individuals with OCD can also play a crucial role in helping them navigate the digital landscape and implement effective coping strategies.

Smart Phone Addiction and Trauma: A Review of the Literature

The relationship between smartphone addiction and trauma is an emerging area of research that reveals a complex interplay between technology use and psychological outcomes (Lee, K. 2020). As smartphones become ubiquitous, their impact on mental health, particularly in relation to trauma, warrants careful examination. Trauma, which can arise from experiences such as abuse, violence, or catastrophic events, often leads to symptoms such as intrusive thoughts, hyperarousal, and avoidance behaviors. The pervasive use of smartphones can interact with these trauma symptoms in several significant ways. One way smartphone addiction can intersect with trauma is through the use of digital media as a form of avoidance. For individuals with trauma-related disorders, smartphones offer a readily available escape from distressing thoughts and feelings. Engaging in excessive smartphone use, including social media browsing, gaming, or other digital distractions, can serve as a method to avoid confronting painful memories or emotions associated with trauma. While this digital avoidance may provide temporary relief, it can prevent individuals from addressing the underlying trauma and hinder effective therapeutic progress.

Furthermore, smartphone addiction can exacerbate trauma symptoms by contributing to a cycle of hyperarousal and emotional dysregulation. The constant influx of notifications, messages, and digital content can heighten anxiety and stress, which are common in trauma survivors. The need to remain perpetually connected can disrupt daily routines and sleep patterns, leading to increased emotional instability and exacerbation of trauma symptoms. The interaction between digital stimuli and trauma-related hyperarousal can create a feedback loop where increased smartphone use intensifies trauma symptoms, further compounding the individual's distress. The literature also highlights how smartphone use can impact the process of trauma recovery. On one hand, smartphones can offer valuable resources for trauma survivors, such as access to mental health apps, online support groups, and therapeutic resources (Leung, L. 2008). These digital tools can provide important support and facilitate connections with others who have experienced similar traumas. However, the potential for smartphone addiction can complicate recovery by fostering compulsive behaviors and reducing engagement in face-to-face therapeutic interventions. The challenge lies in balancing the benefits of digital resources with the need to address the potential for addictive behaviors that may undermine recovery efforts. Additionally, trauma-related symptoms can influence smartphone use patterns. For instance, individuals with post-traumatic stress disorder (PTSD) may use smartphones to seek reassurance or engage in compulsive checking behaviors related to their trauma (Lin, C. Y., et al., 2021). This can include frequently checking news updates, social media, or communication platforms for information or validation, which can perpetuate a state of hypervigilance and anxiety.

Body Image Concerns and Smart Phone Use: The Impact of Social Media

The pervasive nature of smartphones and the ubiquity of social media have reshaped how individuals perceive themselves and others, with profound implications for body image and self-esteem (Mahadev Madgule, et al., 2023). This relationship involves several key dimensions, including the impact of idealized images, social comparison, and the reinforcement of body dissatisfaction through digital media. Social media platforms, accessible through smartphones, often present highly curated and idealized images of beauty and lifestyle. Influencers, celebrities, and peers frequently share photos that highlight unattainable body standards, filtered and edited to enhance attractiveness. This constant exposure to idealized images can distort individuals' perceptions of beauty and lead to unrealistic comparisons. The phenomenon of social comparison, facilitated by social media platforms, plays a crucial role in shaping body image concerns. Social media allows users to constantly compare their appearance with that of others, often leading to feelings of inadequacy and inferiority. This comparison is not only limited to celebrities and influencers but extends to peers who may also present curated versions of their lives. Studies have shown that engaging in social comparison can exacerbate body image issues, as individuals measure their own bodies against the often unrealistic standards portrayed online (Mahmoodi, H., et al., 2018).

The normalization of diet culture, body modification, and appearance-based validation through social media can reinforce unhealthy body image ideals and contribute to disordered eating patterns or excessive exercise. This content can perpetuate a culture of body shaming and perfectionism, further compounding body image issues. Addressing the negative impacts of smartphone use and social media on body image requires a multifaceted approach. Promoting media literacy and critical thinking skills can help individuals better understand and question the authenticity of the content they encounter online. Educational initiatives that emphasize the unrealistic nature of many social media portrayals and encourage self-acceptance can empower individuals to resist harmful comparisons and unrealistic standards. Additionally, fostering a positive online environment that values diverse body types and promotes body positivity can contribute to healthier body image perceptions. Mental health professionals also play a crucial role in supporting individuals struggling with body image concerns related to smartphone use and social media (Park, S. Y.,et al., 2019).

Eating Disorders and Smart Phone Addiction: A Growing Concern

The nexus between smartphone addiction and eating disorders is an increasingly urgent area of concern, as the pervasive nature of smartphones and their integration into daily life intersect with the complexities of disordered eating. Smartphones, particularly through their capacity to connect users with social media, fitness apps, and diet-related content, can significantly influence behaviors and attitudes related to food, body image, and overall health (Paramasivam Selvakumar, et al., 2024). This relationship is multifaceted, involving the promotion of unhealthy eating behaviors, reinforcement of disordered eating patterns, and the broader psychological impacts of constant digital connectivity. Social media platforms accessed via smartphones often play a critical role in shaping attitudes towards eating and body image. These platforms frequently feature content that emphasizes dieting, weight loss, and idealized body standards. Influencers, celebrities, and peers may share posts about restrictive eating habits, fitness routines, and weight management, which can contribute to unrealistic expectations about body image and health. For individuals susceptible to eating disorders, such as anorexia nervosa, bulimia nervosa, and binge eating disorder, exposure to such content can exacerbate disordered eating behaviors and reinforce harmful attitudes towards food and body weight. The rise of fitness and diet apps, commonly used on smartphones, also presents a significant concern. While these apps can offer beneficial tools for tracking nutrition and exercise, they can also promote unhealthy behaviors. Many of these applications emphasize calorie counting, weight tracking, and body measurements, which can encourage obsessive monitoring and preoccupation with weight and body shape. For individuals with eating disorders, this obsession can perpetuate and intensify disordered eating patterns, leading to further complications and difficulties in recovery.

Moreover, the instant and often public nature of smartphone interactions can amplify the psychological impact of disordered eating behaviors (Perilli, E., et al., 2021). Social media provides a platform for seeking validation through likes, comments, and shares related to appearance, dietary choices, and exercise routines. This validation can become a form of reinforcement for unhealthy eating behaviors, as individuals may seek approval or recognition for their restrictive eating habits or weight loss. Conversely, negative feedback or lack of engagement can exacerbate feelings of inadequacy and drive further disordered eating behaviors as a coping mechanism. The constant connectivity enabled by smartphones can also disrupt the management and treatment of eating disorders. For individuals undergoing therapy or treatment, excessive smartphone use can contribute to distractions and hinder adherence to therapeutic recommendations. The constant access to diet-related content and social media can undermine efforts to develop healthier eating habits and challenge disordered eating patterns. Additionally, the pervasive nature of digital content can create a relentless environment where individuals are continuously exposed to triggers and stressors related to their eating disorders. Addressing the intersection of smartphone addiction and eating disorders requires a comprehensive approach that considers both the benefits and risks of digital tools (Reis, M., et al., 2019). Media literacy education can play a crucial role in helping individuals critically assess and navigate the content they encounter on social media and fitness apps.

Smart Phone Addiction and Relationships: Conflict, Jealousy, and Attachment Issues

Smartphone addiction has increasingly been recognized as a factor influencing personal relationships, manifesting in various forms such as conflict, jealousy, and attachment issues. As smartphones become central to daily life, their impact on interpersonal dynamics—both positively and negatively—requires careful examination (Sanusi, S. Y., et al., 2022). The pervasive presence of smartphones introduces new dimensions to relationship challenges, often exacerbating existing issues or creating new ones that affect emotional well-being and relational satisfaction. One of the primary ways smartphone addiction affects relationships is through conflict. Excessive smartphone use can lead to significant disruptions in face-to-face interactions, where individuals may become absorbed in their devices, neglecting their partners, family members, or friends. This behavior, known as "phubbing" (phone snubbing), can result in feelings of neglect and frustration among those who are being ignored. Studies have shown that phubbing is associated with increased relationship dissatisfaction and emotional distress, as the constant preoccupation with smartphones undermines the quality of direct communication and emotional connection.

Attachment issues are also a significant concern in the context of smartphone addiction. Smartphones can impact attachment patterns by altering how individuals engage with each other emotionally and socially (Reis, M., et al., 2021). For instance, individuals with anxious attachment styles may become increasingly reliant on their smartphones for reassurance and validation, seeking constant communication and feedback from their partners. This reliance on digital communication can strain relationships, as the quality of in-person interactions may suffer, leading to increased dependence on virtual affirmation (Selvakumar, P. 2023). Conversely, those with avoidant attachment styles may use smartphones to create emotional distance, avoiding direct confrontation or deep emotional engagement by engaging more in digital interactions. The impact of smartphone addiction on relationships extends to the realm of parenting and family dynamics as well. In therapeutic settings, professionals can assist individuals and couples in exploring the underlying dynamics of smartphone addiction and its effects on relationships. Cognitive-behavioral strategies may be used to address maladaptive patterns of smartphone use and promote healthier relational behaviors (Seo, D. G., et al., 2016). Therapists can work with clients to develop strategies for managing technology use, enhancing communication skills, and addressing attachment-related concerns.

Mental Health in Children and Adolescents: The Impact of Smart Phone Addiction

The impact of smartphone addiction on mental health in children and adolescents is a growing concern, reflecting the pervasive integration of digital technology into the lives of young people (Sugumaran K. M, D., et al., 2024). As smartphones become increasingly ubiquitous, their influence on psychological well-being is evident in various domains, including anxiety, depression, attention deficits, and social development. Understanding these effects is crucial for developing effective strategies to mitigate potential negative outcomes and support healthier digital habits among youth. One of the primary concerns regarding smartphone addiction in children and adolescents is its association with increased anxiety and stress. The constant exposure to digital notifications, social media updates, and online interactions can create a sense of perpetual connectivity that may contribute to heightened anxiety. Research has shown that excessive smartphone use is linked to increased feelings of worry and stress, particularly related to social media pressures. Adolescents may experience anxiety from the need to maintain a certain online persona, respond promptly to messages, and engage in social comparison, all of which can exacerbate feelings of inadequacy and stress. Depression is another significant mental health concern associated with smartphone addiction in young people. The link between excessive screen time and depressive symptoms has been well-documented, with studies indicating that high levels of smartphone use, especially through social media, are correlated with increased risk of depression. The exposure to idealized representations of life and body image on social media platforms can contribute to negative self-perception and dissatisfaction. Additionally, the lack of face-to-face interactions and the potential for cyberbullying further compound depressive symptoms, as online interactions can be less supportive and more prone to negative experiences. Excessive smartphone use can limit opportunities for in-person interactions, leading to social isolation and difficulties in forming meaningful connections

(Tao, S., et al., 2017). This can be particularly concerning during adolescence, a critical period for social development and identity formation.

Parents and guardians play a crucial role in setting boundaries for smartphone use, modeling healthy behaviors, and fostering open communication about the impact of technology on mental health. Implementing strategies such as designated phone-free times, encouraging participation in offline activities, and promoting face-to-face interactions can support healthier technology habits. Schools and community programs can also contribute by integrating digital wellness education into their curricula and providing resources for managing smartphone use. Additionally, mental health professionals can offer support by addressing smartphone addiction as part of broader therapeutic interventions for anxiety, depression, and attention-related concerns. In conclusion, smartphone addiction poses significant challenges to mental health in children and adolescents, impacting areas such as anxiety, depression, attention deficits, and social development. By adopting a multifaceted approach that includes education, parental guidance, and the promotion of healthy digital habits, it is possible to mitigate the negative effects of smartphone addiction and support the overall well-being of young people (Oits, P. A. 2011). As technology continues to evolve, ongoing research and adaptation of strategies will be essential for addressing the complex interplay between digital media and mental health in youth.

Neuroplasticity and Smart Phone Addiction: How Smart Phones Shape Our Brains

The intersection of neuroplasticity and smartphone addiction presents a compelling area of study, highlighting how smartphones can shape and potentially alter brain function and structure. Smartphone addiction, characterized by excessive and compulsive use of mobile devices, can drive significant changes in brain activity and connectivity. One key area of interest is the impact of smartphone use on attention and cognitive control (Omee, S. 2018). Smartphones often provide continuous and rapid feedback through notifications, apps, and social media, which can foster a state of constant partial attention. This frequent multitasking and switching between tasks can lead to changes in brain regions associated with attention and executive functions, such as the prefrontal cortex. Studies have suggested that excessive smartphone use may impair the ability to sustain attention and engage in deep, focused thinking, potentially affecting cognitive performance and problem-solving skills. Moreover, the constant engagement with smartphones can influence reward processing systems in the brain. Smartphones are designed to provide immediate gratification through features such as social media likes, notifications, and gaming rewards. This frequent stimulation can activate the brain's reward pathways, particularly involving the release of dopamine, a neurotransmitter associated with pleasure and reinforcement. Over time, the constant seeking of digital rewards can contribute to changes in reward sensitivity and addictive behaviors, as the brain becomes accustomed to the immediate feedback and gratification provided by smartphone interactions.

The impact of smartphone addiction on memory and learning is also an area of concern. Smartphones and digital media provide easy access to vast amounts of information, which can affect how information is encoded, stored, and retrieved. Research indicates that reliance on digital devices for information retrieval—often referred to as "Google effect" or "digital amnesia"—can impact memory retention and the ability to recall information without digital aids (Vijayakumar G, et al., 2024). Additionally, the use of smartphones for social connectivity can affect the development of social skills and empathy, as digital interactions may not fully capture the nuances of face-to-face communication. The concept of "technoference," where technology interferes with real-life interactions, also reflects how smartphone use can shape brain function. The presence of smartphones during social interactions, such as family dinners or conversations, can lead to reduced engagement and less meaningful connections (Watson, R. J.,et al., 2016). Additionally, integrating mindfulness practices and cognitive exercises that support attention and memory can contribute to maintaining healthy brain function and mitigating the effects of excessive smartphone use.

Breaking the Cycle: Strategies for Mitigating Mental Health Issues Due to Smart Phone Addiction

Addressing the mental health issues arising from smartphone addiction requires a multifaceted approach that targets both the technological and psychological aspects of this pervasive problem. As smartphones have become central to modern life, their potential for causing anxiety, depression, and other mental health issues necessitates effective strategies to break the cycle of addiction and promote well-being. Here are several key strategies for mitigating mental health issues related to smartphone addiction Establish Clear Boundaries Setting boundaries for smartphone use is crucial for managing addiction and reducing its impact on mental health. Establish specific times and places for phone use, such as designated phone-free zones during meals or before bedtime (Xu, Q., et al., 2018). Implementing digital detox periods, where phone use is limited or eliminated for certain hours, can help reduce the compulsive checking of notifications and foster healthier habits. Implement Technology-Free Zones and Times Create technology-free zones in your home, such as the dining room or bedroom, to encourage face-to-face interactions and improve sleep quality. Designate specific times for phone use, such as a set period in the morning and evening, to prevent constant engagement with digital devices. Establishing these boundaries helps in reducing screen time and promoting more balanced lifestyles. Use Smartphone Features to Manage Use Take advantage of built-in features on smartphones designed to help manage screen time. Many devices offer tools to track usage, set app limits, and enable "Do Not Disturb" modes. Utilizing these features can help monitor and control the amount of time spent on devices and mitigate the risk of overuse.

Promote Mindful and Purposeful Use

Encourage mindful smartphone use by being intentional about how and why you use your device. Instead of mindlessly scrolling through social media or checking notifications, focus on purposeful activities that provide genuine value, such as connecting with friends or accessing educational content. Developing mindfulness practices related to smartphone use can help reduce impulsive behaviors and promote healthier digital habits. Engage in Offline Activities Increase engagement in offline activities that provide fulfillment and enjoyment outside of digital interactions. Pursue hobbies, exercise, read books, and spend quality time with family and friends. Engaging in these activities not only provides a break from screens but also supports overall mental and emotional well-being. Foster Face-to-Face Communication Prioritize face-to-face communication over digital interactions whenever possible. Strengthening in-person relationships can enhance emotional connections and reduce reliance on digital platforms for social interactions (Yi, H., et al., 2006). Make an effort to have meaningful conversations and spend time with loved ones without the distraction of smartphones. Practice Digital Detox and Tech-Free Times Implement regular digital detox periods, where smartphone use is limited or eliminated for specific durations. Tech-free times, such as during meals or before bed, can help reduce screen time and promote healthier habits. Engaging in activities that do not involve screens can help reset your relationship with technology and improve mental health. For individuals struggling with severe smartphone addiction and associated mental health issues, seeking professional support from mental health professionals can be beneficial (Zhang, X., et al., 2022). Therapists and counselors can provide tailored strategies and interventions to address underlying psychological issues and help individuals develop healthier coping mechanisms. Use tracking tools or journaling to assess how smartphone use affects mental health and make necessary adjustments to improve balance and well-being. In conclusion, breaking the cycle of smartphone addiction and mitigating its impact on mental health involves a combination of setting boundaries, fostering mindful use, engaging in offline activities, and seeking professional support when needed (Zhou, H. L., et al., 2021). By implementing these strategies, individuals can develop healthier relationships with technology, reduce the risk of mental health issues, and promote overall well-being in an increasingly digital world.

CONCLUSION

Smartphone addiction has emerged as a significant factor influencing mental health, with profound implications for individuals across various age groups. The omnipresence of smartphones and their integration into daily life have introduced a host of mental health challenges, including anxiety, depression, attention deficits, and social isolation. The constant connectivity facilitated by smartphones fosters a digital environment where individuals are perpetually engaged, often leading to heightened stress and diminished psychological well-being.

The impact of smartphone addiction on mental health is multifaceted. Anxiety is frequently exacerbated by the relentless influx of notifications and the pressure to maintain a curated online presence. Social media platforms, accessed through smartphones, often present idealized images and lifestyles, contributing to unrealistic comparisons and increased feelings of inadequacy. Depression is also linked to excessive smartphone use, particularly through the reinforcement of negative self-perceptions and the potential for cyberbullying. Additionally, attention deficits and cognitive impairments arise from constant multitasking and fragmented focus, which can undermine productivity and overall cognitive function. Social development suffers as well, as excessive digital interactions can impede the development of essential face-to-face communication skills and lead to increased feelings of loneliness and social isolation. Addressing these mental health issues requires a comprehensive approach that includes both individual and systemic strategies. On an individual level, setting boundaries for smartphone use and fostering mindful engagement with technology are essential steps in mitigating negative effects. Implementing practices such as digital detox periods, technology-free zones, and prioritizing offline activities can help restore balance and improve mental health. Seeking professional support, when necessary, can provide tailored interventions to address severe cases of smartphone addiction and associated mental health concerns. From a broader perspective, raising awareness about the potential mental health impacts of smartphone addiction is crucial. Educational initiatives that highlight the importance of balanced technology use and promote digital literacy can empower individuals to make informed choices about their smartphone habits. Support systems, including family, friends, and community resources, play a vital role in encouraging healthier digital behaviors and providing support for those struggling with addiction. In conclusion, smartphone addiction poses significant challenges to mental health, impacting anxiety, depression, attention, and social development.

By adopting strategies to manage smartphone use, promoting digital literacy, and seeking appropriate support, individuals can work towards mitigating the negative effects of smartphone addiction and fostering a healthier relationship with technology. As society continues to navigate the complexities of digital life, ongoing research and adaptation of strategies will be essential in addressing the evolving landscape of mental health in the context of smartphone use. In conclusion, the link between smartphone use and increased anxiety is evident through the constant barrage of notifications, the impact of social media, and disruptions to sleep and work-life balance. As smartphones continue to play a central role in our lives, it is essential to develop mindful and strategic approaches to their use, aiming to alleviate the associated stress and promote better mental health outcomes.

REFERENCES

Adams, S. K., Daly, J. F., & Williford, D. N. (2013). Adolescent sleep and cellular phone use: Recent trends and implications for research. *Health Services Insights*, 6, 99–103. DOI: 10.4137/HSI.S11083 PMID: 25114565

Al-Khani, A. M., Sarhandi, M. I., Zaghloul, M. S., Ewid, M., & Saquib, N. (2019). A cross-sectional survey on sleep quality, mental health, and academic performance among medical students in Saudi Arabia. BMC Res. Notes, 12,665. doi: DOI: 10.1186/s13104-019-4713

Barnes, C. M., Schaubroeck, J., Huth, M., & Ghumman, S. (2011). Lack of sleep and unethical conduct. *Organizational Behavior and Human Decision Processes*, 115(2), 169–180. DOI: 10.1016/j.obhdp.2011.01.009

Bartel, K., Scheeren, R., & Gradisar, M. (2019). Altering adolescents' pre-bedtime phone use to achieve better sleep health. *Health Communication*, 34(4), 456–462. DOI: 10.1080/10410236.2017.1422099 PMID: 29313721

Bastien, C. H., Vallières, A., & Morin, C. M. (2001). Validation of the insomnia severity index as an outcome measure for insomnia research. *Sleep Medicine*, 2(4), 297–307. DOI: 10.1016/S1389-9457(00)00065-4 PMID: 11438246

Calpbinici, P., & Tas Arslan, F. (2019). Virtual behaviors a ecting adolescent mental health: The usage of internet and mobile phone and cyberbullying. *Journal of Child and Adolescent Psychiatric Nursing*, 32(3), 139–148. DOI: 10.1111/jcap.12244 PMID: 31310412

Christian, M. S., & Ellis, A. P. (2011). Examining the e ects of sleep deprivation on workplace deviance: A self-regulatory perspective. *Academy of Management Journal*, 54(5), 913–934. DOI: 10.5465/amj.2010.0179

Chu, X., Li, Y., Wang, P., Zeng, P., & Lei, L. (2021). Social support and cyberbullying for university students: The mediating role of internet addiction and the moderating role of stress. *Current Psychology (New Brunswick, N.J.)*, 42(3), 2014–2022. DOI: 10.1007/s12144-021-01607-9

Clement-Carbonell, V., Portilla-Tamarit, I., Rubio-Aparicio, M., & Madrid-Valero, J. J. (2021). Sleep quality, mental and physical health: A differential relationship. *International Journal of Environmental Research and Public Health*, 18(2), 1–8. DOI: 10.3390/ijerph18020460 PMID: 33435528

Desouky, D. E. S., & Abu-Zaid, H. (2020). Mobile phone use pattern and addiction in relation to depression and anxiety. *Eastern Mediterranean Health Journal*, 26(6), 692–699. DOI: 10.26719/emhj.20.043 PMID: 32621504

Dowran, B., Amiri, M., Salimi, H., & Zarghami, M. H. (2020). The problematic use of mobile phone and mental health: A review study in Iran. *Journal of Education and Health Promotion*, 9(1), 290. DOI: 10.4103/jehp.jehp_268_20

Elhai, J. D., Dvorak, R. D., Levine, J. C., & Hall, B. J. (2017). Problematic smartphone use: A conceptual overview and systematic review of relations with anxiety and depression psychopathology. J. A ect. *Journal of Affective Disorders*, 207, 251–259. DOI: 10.1016/j.jad.2016.08.030 PMID: 27736736

Friedrich, A., & Schlarb, A. A. (2018). Let's talk about sleep: A systematic review of psychological interventions to improve sleep in college students. *Journal of Sleep Research*, 27(1), 4–22. DOI: 10.1111/jsr.12568 PMID: 28618185

Gangadharan, N., Borle, A. L., & Basu, S. (2022). Mobile phone addiction as an emerging behavioral form of addiction among adolescents in India. *Cureus*, 14, e23798–e23799. DOI: 10.7759/cureus.23798 PMID: 35518537

Ghrouz, A. K., Noohu, M. M., Manzar, D., & Warren Spence, D. (2019). Physical activity and sleep quality in relation to mental health among college students. *Sleep and Breathing*, 23(2), 627–634. DOI: 10.1007/s11325-019-01780-z PMID: 30685851

Hao, Z., Jin, L., Li, Y., Akram, H. R., Saeed, M. F., Ma, J., Ma, H., & Huang, J. (2019). Alexithymia and mobile phone addiction in Chinese undergraduate students: The roles of mobile phone use patterns. *Computers in Human Behavior*, 97, 51–59. DOI: 10.1016/j.chb.2019.03.001

Haripriya, S., Samuel, S. E., & Megha, M. (2019). Correlation between smartphone addiction, sleep quality and physical activity among young adults. *Journal of Clinical and Diagnostic Research : JCDR*, 13, 5–9. DOI: 10.7860/JCDR/2019/42168.13212

Hayes, A. F., & Preacher, K. J. (2014). Statistical mediation analysis with a multicategorical independent variable. *British Journal of Mathematical & Statistical Psychology*, 67(3), 451–470. DOI: 10.1111/bmsp.12028 PMID: 24188158

Ivanova, A., Gorbaniuk, O., Błachnio, A., Przepiórka, A., Mraka, N., Polishchuk, V., et al. (2020). Mobile phone addiction, phubbing, and depression among men and women: a moderated mediation analysis. Psychiatry Q., 91, 655–668. doi: DOI: 10.1007/s11126-020-09723

Körmendi, A., Brutóczki, Z., Végh, B. P., & Székely, R. (2016). Smartphone use can be addictive? A case report. *Journal of Behavioral Addictions*, 5(3), 548–552. DOI: 10.1556/2006.5.2016.033 PMID: 27599674

Lee, K. (2020). Social support and self-esteem on the association between stressful life events and mental health outcomes among college students. *Social Work in Health Care*, 59(6), 387–407. DOI: 10.1080/00981389.2020.1772443 PMID: 32538324

Leung, L. (2008). Linking psychological attributes to addiction and improper use of the mobile phone among adolescents in Hong Kong. *Journal of Children and Media*, 2(2), 93–113. DOI: 10.1080/17482790802078565

Lin, C. Y., Namdar, P., Griffiths, M. D., & Pakpour, A. H. (2021). Mediated roles of generalized trust and perceived social support in the effects of problematic social media use on mental health: A cross-sectional study. *Health Expectations*, 24(1), 165–173. DOI: 10.1111/hex.13169 PMID: 33253480

Mahadev Madgule, N. (2023). Mechanical properties and microstructure of activated TIG welded similar joints of Inconel alloys by desirability approaches. *Materials Today: Proceedings*, 77, 528–533. DOI: 10.1016/j.matpr.2022.12.250

Mahmoodi, H., Nadrian, H., Shahaghi, A., Jafarabadi, M. A., Ahmadi, A., & Saqqezi, G. S. (2018). Factors associated with mental health among high school students in Iran: Does mobile phone overuse associated with poor mental health? *Journal of Child and Adolescent Psychiatric Nursing*, 31(1), 6–13. DOI: 10.1111/jcap.12202 PMID: 29974565

Oits, P. A. (2011). Mechanisms linking social ties and support to physical and mental health. J. Health Soc. Behav., 52, 145–161. DOI: 10.1177/0022146510395592

Omee, S. (2018). Mobile phone use and mental health. A review of the research that takes a psychological perspective on exposure. Int. J. Environ. Res. Public Health, 15, 1–25. DOI: 10.3390/ijerph15122692

Park, S. Y., Yang, S., Shin, C. S., Jang, H., & Park, S. Y. (2019). Long-term symptoms of mobile phone use on mobile phone addiction and depression among Korean adolescents. *International Journal of Environmental Research and Public Health*, 16(19), 35–84. DOI: 10.3390/ijerph16193584 PMID: 31557844

Perilli, E., Necozione, S., Bianchini, V., Perazzini, M., Grassi, M., & Americo, A. (2021). Mobile phone addiction and mobile phone use in dangerous circumstances: Prevalence and correlates in a sample of Italian university students. *Mediterranean Journal of Clinical Psychology*, 9, 1–16. DOI: 10.13129/2282-1619/MJCP-3014

Reis, M., Matos, M. G., & Ramiro, L. (2019). Worries, mental and emotional health di culties of Portuguese university students. *Advances in Social Sciences Research Journal*, 6, 558–569. DOI: 10.14738/assrj.67.6818

Reis, M., Ramiro, L., Paiva, T., & Gaspar-de-Matos, M. (2021). National Survey on the importance of sleep in the quality of academic life and mental health of college students in Portugal. Sleep Sci, 14, 125–132. doi: .20200090DOI: 10.5935/1984-0063

Sanusi, S. Y., Al-Batayneh, O. B., Khader, Y. S., & Saddki, N. (2022). The association of smartphone addiction, sleep quality and perceived stress amongst Jordanian dental students. *European Journal of Dental Education*, 26(1), 76–84. DOI: 10.1111/eje.12674 PMID: 33527620

Selvakumar, P. (2023). Novel Drug Target with Diverse Therapeutic Potential in Cancer Therapy. *Pharmacy Times*, 55(1), 11–14.

Selvakumar, P., Mariappan, P., Shunmugam, S., Paul, R., & Jabez, S. (2024). Removal of chemicals from effluent using photobioreactor technology to improve environmental and health impacts. *Zeitschrift für Physikalische Chemie*, 2024(7), 1295–1302. Advance online publication. DOI: 10.1515/zpch-2023-0450

Seo, D. G., Park, Y., Kim, M. K., & Park, J. (2016). Mobile phone dependency and its impacts on adolescents' social and academic behaviors. *Computers in Human Behavior*, 63, 282–292. DOI: 10.1016/j.chb.2016.05.026

Sugumaran, K. M. D., Pandiyarajan, V., Y., B. S., Selvakumar, P., & M., S. (2024). Analysis of Electromyography Signals for Control of Mechanical Prosthesis using Machine Learning Techniques. 2024 2nd International Conference on Intelligent Data Communication Technologies and Internet of Things (IDCIoT), 1059-1067. DOI: 10.1109/IDCIoT59759.2024.10467707

Tao, S., Wu, X., Zhang, Y., Zhang, S., & Tao, F. (2017). E ects of sleep quality on the association between problematic mobile phone use and mental health symptoms in Chinese college students. *International Journal of Environmental Research and Public Health*, 14(2), 1–10. DOI: 10.3390/ijerph14020185

Vijayakumar, G., Rajkumar, M., Rajiv Chandar, N., Selvakumar, P., & Duraisamy, R. (2024). Environmentally friendly TDS removal from waste water by electrochemical ion exchange batch-type recirculation (EIR) technique. *Environmental Science. Water Research & Technology*, 10(4), 826–835. DOI: 10.1039/D3EW00793F

Watson, R. J., Grossman, A. H., & Russell, S. T. (2016). Sources of social support and mental health among LGB youth. *Youth & Society*, 51(1), 30–48. DOI: 10.1177/0044118X16660110 PMID: 30636819

Xu, Q., Li, S., & Yang, L. (2018). Perceived social support and mental health for college students in mainland China: The mediating effects of self-concept. *Psychology Health and Medicine*, 24(5), 595–604. DOI: 10.1080/13548506.2018.1549744 PMID: 30451537

Yi, H., Shin, K., & Shin, C. (2006). Development of the sleep quality scale. *Journal of Sleep Research*, 15(3), 309–316. DOI: 10.1111/j.1365-2869.2006.00544.x PMID: 16911033

Zhang, X., Gao, F., Kang, Z., Zhou, H., Zhang, J., Li, J., Yan, J., Wang, J., Liu, H., Wu, Q., & Liu, B. (2022). Perceived academic stress and depression: The mediation role of Mobile phone addiction and sleep quality. *Frontiers in Public Health*, 10, 1–12. DOI: 10.3389/fpubh.2022.760387 PMID: 35145942

Zhou, H. L., Jiang, H. B., Zhang, B., & Liang, H. Y. (2021). Social anxiety, maladaptive cognition, mobile phone addiction, and perceived social support: A moderated mediation model. *Journal of Psychology in Africa*, 31(3), 248–253. DOI: 10.1080/14330237.2021.1927354

Chapter 6
Smartphone Addiction and Social Media Addiction:
Prospectives From the Multi-Dimensional Addiction Behavior Scale (MABS)

Ranjit Singha
https://orcid.org/0000-0002-3541-8752
Christ University, India

ABSTRACT

This chapter examines the psychological, behavioural, and social consequences of smartphone addiction, phone snubbing, and social media addiction. It explores the machinations that drive addiction, such as variable reinforcement schedules and reward systems, and how they affect our interpersonal relationships and mental health. The chapter also identifies best practices in current research and case studies, as well as trends that suggest effective interventions to help guide psychologists and mental health professionals when dealing with such issues. The chapter underscores the importance of interdisciplinary efforts in order to address the issues of digital addiction successfully. This chapter shares the perspectives from the multi-dimensional addiction behavior scale (MABS), which includes psychological, biological, social and environmental factors, cognitive and behavioral patterns, motivation, and readiness for change.

DOI: 10.4018/979-8-3693-8804-4.ch006

INTRODUCTION

In this day and age of omnipresent smartphones, fast wireless internet access, social media, and mobile applications that have been inundating our lives for the past few years, there is now a fine line between utility and dependency. What began as a technological revolution to bring the world together through instant-truncated communication and connectivity — has evolved into an obligatory activity for many. With more attention focused on the issue at hand, smartphone addiction (excessive and uncontrollable use of mobile devices) and social media addiction (engagement with platforms like Instagram, Twitter, and Facebook compulsively) have grown as popular terms. These behaviours, which have unfortunately been added to current technologies, have alterations in our behaviour by how we interact with people around us and build relationships that now some believe are suffering as a consequence of overuse (Pera, 2020; Wacks & Weinstein, 2021).

Therefore, the in-depth study of smartphone and social media addiction is crucial to understanding their broader implications on modern living. These addictions not only have an impact on the individual user but also impinge upon our interpersonal relationships and broader social formations. Smartphone and social media addiction have been associated with myriad malaise, from increased feelings of loneliness, anxiety and depressive symptoms to a corresponding decrease in quality face-to-face interaction. Each time someone does this too often, it could fry how they interact with people outside the device, endlessly making one realize that these issues are things to dive into as we look deeper into what causes someone to fixate on a screen and where it defects when left unchecked. In addition, the examination of these addictions increases our understanding of the psychological and social processes in behavioural dependencies that are relevant to public health challenges for researchers, practitioners and policymakers (Áfra et al., 2023; Lin et al., 2023).

This chapter will start with a brief look into the definitions and symptoms of smartphones, as well as social media addiction and follow by introducing central behavioristic aspects combined with psychological factors playing a role in these addictions when it comes to mental health and the psychological disorders or emotional upsets of these addictions. The chapter will then explore the impacts of screen addiction, including interactions between family members and in romantic partnerships or among friends. Lastly, it will conclude by outlining potential interventions and prevention strategies to target these addictive behaviours and develop some guidelines for healthier technology use.

BACKGROUND

Now, smartphones and social media have managed to fundamentally alter the way human beings communicate with one another which created a few decades ago. The advent of mobile phones started in the final years of the 20th century as essential cellular devices primarily featuring voice call services have been developed. However, the real revolution was in 2007 when Apple launched its first iPhone, where the world saw a smartphone. Unlike cell phones before, smartphones allow internet access with multimedia capabilities and run third-party applications to support modern essential functions.

That was the time when smartphones came into existence, paralleled by various social media platforms. Since its inception with the early platforms like MySpace in the 2000s, it has slowly grown from Facebook around 2004 to Twitter and Instagram, then later on TikTok, etc. Social media quickly emerged as the leading digital platform, where people now could share content and interact together online, engaging in global communities using live communication. Smartphones and social media have blended our online lives with the offline world in a way that was unimaginable two decades ago. With the rise of smartphones and social media use, concerns surrounding its addictiveness as well as how it interacts with mental health were raised, thereby spurring interest in studies looking at societal impacts.

Long-term technological advancements have contributed to the increase in smartphone and social media addiction. The advent of high-speed mobile networks, first 3G to 4G, then the soon-coming fifth-generation, have given smartphones a tremendous power boost and made them faster, with more apps requiring horsepower for smoother experience in graphics and media functions. These high-definition cameras, unlimited storage spaces and touch-friendly screens are now a central point in every personal as well as professional life.

Furthermore, critical progress has been made in the emergence of AI and ML for social media platforms to deepen customer engagement. The algorithms operating to select content have been a substantial factor in keeping users engaged and even increasing usage as they constantly present customized recommendations, notifications, etc., aimed at holding the user's attention within the platform. This is further complicated by the embedding of real-time features, such as chat messaging or video calls in-game, and sometimes, to use them constantly, you are never forced actually able to properly disengage from playing whatever the game. This repeating engagement can be unintentionally addictive.

Trends can be seen all over the world that reflect an increasing use of smartphones and social media. Smartphone usage is so common that a vast part of the world's population has access to it, as it has become one of our daily routines. The social media sphere has also grown tremendously, with millions of people investing a huge chunk of their day in various apps. Studies have shown that we are constantly looking at our smartphones, and a massive chunk of this time is spent on social interactions in the online world. Especially in the era of social media, teenagers and young adults are more likely to develop an addiction or become distressed as a result of activities online (Adorjan & Ricciardelli, 2021; Áfra et al., 2023; Pera, 2020).

Each new update to iOS, Android and even the apps themselves means there is always a differently styled app being released, all with various features which manage users from watching television like Netflix & Now TV, listening to music like Spotify, YouTube or protect us our data for social media platforms, the lines between productive tech and distractive tech are getting ever more blurred. The overall trends show that smartphones continue their rise as an addiction alongside inevitable trouble brewing behind maintaining eye gaze synergy clashes against screen greed throughout 2016. The psychologically manipulative nature of these platforms is no accident, many are literally designed to harness primary human psychological motivations such as the fear of isolation and ostracism or our innate desire for instant or baby-step gratification. This has caused several mental health problems, such as anxiety, depression, sleep disturbances, and reduced face-to-face communication and social skills in the users. The combination of the increase in their use and its psychological consequences has made smartphone addiction, mainly when it includes social media, a unique phenomenon requiring urgent attention.

THEORETICAL FRAMEWORK

The dual solution, as stated in the title, is that the initial step towards research on smartphone and social media addiction would be a multi-perspective method considering various functional dependencies from a numbering of evolutionary theories that answer why humans all end up addicted to this technology. For this reason, the nature of addiction is best represented on different levels, from behavioural through cognitive to social, in a second sense, all contributing what they can hold illumination into characteristic determinants driving driven consumption.

Two psychological models of addiction are based on classical and operant conditioning, which state that behaviours become learned habits when responses to such repeated actions lead either to rewards or avoidance of negative repercussions. This is an addiction that the example of smartphone and social media can serve to illustrate as everyone from constant device-checkers to compulsive liker-post-commentators daily get their 'hit' in response to notifications, likes or messages offering readily available dopamine (Pera, 2020; Khan & Khan, 2021).

Cognitive theories examine how thoughts, beliefs and perceptions contribute to engagement in addictive behaviours. Humans, for one thing, may develop all kinds of cognitive distortions, such as needing to always be on call and linked digitally; otherwise, we will miss out (fear of missing out or FOMO). Consequently, these cognitive biases operate in tandem with and encourage the addictive use of smartphones (Montag & Becker, 2023) and social media (Pera, 2019), where the psychological dynamics are exploited to reinforce continuous engagement.

In the popular social theories of addiction, abstinence narratives are held to be certain formulae which help society develop a better understanding and explanation for why people with an addiction do what they do. This relentless need to be associated with, update your social platforms or keep up with trends can often lead to the overuse of smartphones and social media. Social theories hypothesize that the need for acceptance, validation, and social belonging may be underlying addiction (Áfra et al., 2023; Pera, 2020). Together, these theoretical perspectives help to provide a comprehensive picture of addiction in smartphones and social media spanning individual cognition (CABS model), behaviour conditioning (desensitization theory) and social influences.

Variable Reinforcement Theory is particularly applicable to smartphone and social media addiction. Based on what the theory of operant conditioning would suggest, behaviours tend to be more addictive when reinforcement is given randomly with reduced frequency and amount. This intermittent schedule of rewards creates a vicious cycle that forces people to engage in more compulsive behaviour as they are always after the next possible giveaway.

Smartphones and social media, variable reinforcement takes place when notifications are delivered, like between likes or comments or messages, but not regularly. Users also do not know when they will be rewarded for e.g. new "likes" on the photo or a new message somewhere, and a beginner reinforcement-seeking instinct is formed, which makes us all look at our phones with little reason. That unpredictability activates your dopamine system, triggering a kind of reward cue that we usually experience during gambling. The urge to find these inconsistent rewards further cements the behaviour of using our phones often and constantly interacting with social media platforms, which in turn fuel addictive behaviours.

Another critical way to think about smartphone and social media addiction is through the lens of The Social Learning Theory. The Social Learning Theory, introduced by Albert Bandura, postulates that individuals learn specific behaviours through observing others and repeating these modelled actions, especially when demonstrated or seen in a figure whom they look up to. This theory is helpful in understanding the manners by which social interactions and observed behaviours are central to an individual's patterns of use (Adorjan & Ricciardelli, 2021; Pera, 2020) compared with smartphone addiction.

Social media users are bombarded with a barrage of daylong behaviours and interactions revolving around peers, influencers or celebrities. Social desirability, replication of trending attitudes, and observational learning in self-altering online behaviour are all factors that could be pushing compulsive smartphone usage. For example, if someone sees that all of their friends are incredibly active on social media, they may feel like they need to be equally involved in order not to become a frump and social outcast. Moreover, the platforms promote these behaviours themselves by displaying logs of responses like likes and shares as well as follower numbers (Topino et al., 2023), acts that make us perceive social validation is linked with online life.

This study, therefore, contrasts with approaches rooted in Social Learning Theory that stress mobile phone and social media addictions as problems within the overall external setting because other people's actions always influence asynchronous systems in the online community.

CONCEPTUAL FRAMEWORK

It is based on a conceptual model that addiction cannot be considered in philosophical isolation from its technological design, psychological mechanisms and behavioural outcomes. Using these pillars, the model explains how smartphones and social media are addictive when they converge serving to support compulsive use in each instance.

Central to the model is the technological architecture of smartphones and social media platforms that have been designed in a way intended to facilitate compulsive use, thereby maximizing user retention. For example, these algorithms result in a feedback loop based on personalized content fuelled by push notifications and infinite scroll, which encourages constant engagement. By basing on variety, continuality of exposure and variability in reward provision for the offering cycle topography that has been recognized to fall into place with the human senses input-neurology behaviour, this may have excited a notch beyond what we intuitively can feel if there is no involved addiction.

These technologies then go on to activate psychological mechanisms, think the release of dopamine, FOMO or fear of missing out, and the craving for social validation. These psychological responses are exploited by design features in smartphones and social media platforms, keeping users feel a needful engagement. The need for quick results and validation in the form of likes, comments, messages, etc., keeps them coming back, which, over the period, becomes a habit as well as addiction.

What emerges from this interaction are the compulsions to check devices, extended screen time and increased difficulty in disentangling themselves especially young people from their social media. Eventually, these actions become addictive behaviours whereby their smartphones and social media behemoth are now something both cognitively and emotionally reliant on. It is a vicious cycle, the more that people rely on emotional reward for validation, pleasure and meaning in their lives from technology, or you name it, the more driven they are to use their devices and platforms, feeding back into dependency.

A critical extension of this model focuses on how smartphone and social media addictions affect mental health and relational outcomes. More often than not, as people become more immersed in their digital worlds, their physical relationships start to suffer. However, addictive behaviours can extend to phone snubbing, or 'phubbing', where people prefer their smartphones over meeting other people in person. This can destroy the fabric of relationships, foster feelings of loneliness and frustration, and reduce emotional intimacy.

For example, when it is overdone in itself and becomes a routine item that consumes too much time of family members (e.g., smartphone usage with or without associating social media within the context subject), this can impair the communication process —and ultimately become an emotional distance generator between parents-daughters. Addiction can provoke tension or unhappiness within romantic partnerships, with partners reporting that they feel ignored and unappreciated. Friendships can also suffer as people concentrate on spinning their virtual selves rather than strengthening real connections (Topino et al., 2023).

This is a crucial outcome of this model, which is the effect on mental health. Smartphones and excessive use of social networking are associated with more signs of depression, anxiety and loneliness among young people in academic life — particularly women than men who aim to trade your fixing screen phone or their batteries after a while very cheap process possible so that they do not feel alone market there across the country pick up fix iPhone. The added pressure of FOMO only magnifies feelings of not being good enough or impostor syndrome, as people see idealized versions of others on social media doing things that they think are better than them. Such profound wasting of time can lead to sleep disorders, stress and attention deficit disorder in the most addicted users (Adorjan & Ricciardelli, 2021; Pera, 2020).

This model highlights both the addictive cycle instigated by technological design and perpetuated via psychological mechanisms as well as its behavioural dependencies, with ramifications for social interaction and mental health. The relationship among these factors underscores the challenge that smartphone and social media addiction pose to addressing crucial issues such as awareness or intervention strategies.

DEFINING SMARTPHONE ADDICTION AND SOCIAL MEDIA ADDICTION

Smartphone addiction is defined as a behavioural dependency on smartphones that typically involves excessive, compulsive and inappropriate use. Like other behavioural addictions, smartphone addiction is a compulsion to use the device along with an inability to control or limit the use of it in spite of any social and personal adverse consequences. Some of the critical criteria are mentioned in this section. For example, excessive time spent on the device; in this situation, an individual absorbs so much of his or her time on the smartphone that it hampers one-to-one correspondence and work or home school duties. Another example is inability to reduce usage; even after giving it many tries, one may need help to restrict or control the time spent on a smartphone.

Another example is a preoccupation with the smartphone, such as you are more or less living in the smartphone world, always thinking about it and checking for text messages and updating your status to likes, even when inappropriate. Some of the other symptoms that come are Withdrawal Symptoms like irritability, anxiety or distress when the phone cannot be used, and a reduced frequency of use can no longer be maintained. Numerous daily life activities may be impacted by addiction, for instance, interference with daily life like the addiction intrudes on work, school education, social connections or relationships and sleep, which has adverse effects. The other example is continued use. Despite negative consequences, for example, you cannot stop yourself from using the smartphone, even when it seriously affects your relationships with other people. It makes you experience a type of stress that is detrimental to health or hinders professional development. As smartphone addiction becomes a growing concern in younger populations, the immediacy that comes with constant connectivity and notifications delivered to you by these devices is likely better than human nature.

DEFINITION AND CRITERIA FOR SOCIAL MEDIA ADDICTION

Social media addiction is a term that refers to the syndrome where an individual's engagement in social networking sites becomes compulsive, cancels out offline activities with online interactions and leads to preoccupancy with maintaining high levels of Involvement throughout their network. Convergent evidence links social media addiction with standard features observed in the cycle of behavioural addictions, specifically in the neurobiological processes related to the reward system and dependence (Pellegrino et al., 2022; Ostic et al., 2021). Some of the Criteria for diagnosing social media addiction are mentioned in this section, like excessive social media use. For example, this person spends disturbing amounts of time scrolling, posting or engaging on social networking sites at the expense of real-world encounters. Another preoccupation with social media, another sign, could be their addiction to social media; they are continuously checking other people's posts or creating content for the World Wide Web so people can affirm them by giving them likes on everything and comments, etc. Inability to Limit Usage: Making repeated efforts to cut back on social media but failing or wanting (and trying) to use it less often. Emotional dependence is increased emotional reactions towards different kinds of social media activities, such as worrying about the number of likes or comments on a post. Withdrawal Symptoms include anxiety, feelings of abandonment or loneliness when you experience an extended period without being able to look at your social media feeds. Negative Impact on Daily Life This interferes with how well you do at work or school and in your relationships, and it negatively impacts the lives of others around you e.g., sleep deprivation. FOMO the full form is Fear of Missing Out is like fear of missing out the looming dread that if they disconnect from social media, they will miss important information or social life. This pervasiveness is attributed to the design of these platforms, which are designed in a way where notifications, personalized feeds, and social validation mechanisms keep us constantly hooked.

DISTINGUISHING FEATURES AND OVERLAP

Smartphone addiction and social media addiction are very closely related but do have distinctions between the two with overlapping in other aspects. The scope of addiction involves more types of behaviour, including app use, gameplay, messaging, browsing and social networking addiction. It speaks to a more extensive compliance within the device. Social media addiction It is more specific, talking only about compulsive use of social networking sites (Facebook addiction, Twitter addiction, etc).

Behavioural Drivers include people who typically become addicted to their smartphones as they rely on them for continuous connectivity and up-to-the-minute information or entertainment. Non-social activities such as gaming or video watching may also be addictive.

Social media addiction is a result of the urgent social desire for validation and socio-peer engagement. It is basically about our behaviour on the social web and how we get hooked on feedback loops of social validation such as likes, comments.

Overlap includes technological interdependency. There is a high overlap between the primary accompaniments for social media use and those devices most popularly used to access smartphones, making it such that if a person has a smartphone, they likely have all the drivers, as well. The overlap here is clearly significant, for social media addiction can be described as a subtype of smartphone addiction.

Psychological Mechanisms involve the reward system such as dopamine release; both addictions have a common mechanism involving behavioural addiction and social pressures like FOMO. The dopamine rush that comes with checking your notifications, engaging in content, or looking for likes are all the same.

Smartphone addiction ranges from gaming addiction, an over-reliance on using mobile apps or simply being dependent on the device for communication, work and productivity.

Social media addiction to social media sites has become a significant problem, primarily affecting online individual presence as well as self-esteem and relationships. It is closely related to socio-emotional aspects that can result in social comparison, cyberbullying and online social environment disorder.

PSYCHOLOGICAL AND BEHAVIORAL MECHANISMS

One of the primary psychological principles driving addiction to smartphone and social media use is variable reinforcements, which we can see as a leading component in addictive behaviours. Variable reinforcement, this is a type of reward system where something good like likes, comments or the bell icon next to your channel, which happens randomly and not on a predictable basis. This randomness generates an expectation and ambiguity, which reinforces addictive conduct.

Even in the case of our smartphones and social media, we are prepared to be bombarded with notifications from an app that has become so accustomed to a reward system, triggering your brain's dopamine associating pleasure and motivation. Because the rewards could be more consistent, sometimes they come in waves, sometimes there is only a trickle, users become obsessed with constantly checking their phones and social media to get that hit. The behaviour mirrors the variable reward schedules of gambling addiction, where theoretical opportunities are enough to keep users playing, even if rewards are not guaranteed.

This intermittent reinforcement also keeps you on your toes, always waiting to receive the next dose of dopamine from behind a digital screen. This ends up creating a compulsive loop, where people have an intense, often uncontrollable, desire to peek at their phone or social media even when it is inappropriate driving or dangerous.

IMPACT OF SMARTPHONE AND SOCIAL MEDIA INTERFACES

Smartphones and their accompanying social media platforms have design elements that actively drive addictive behaviours. You can live with any modern intelligent device, which turns out mostly to be a smartphone, where practically every social media app that calls offers features designed not just to get you the most clicking and messaging from the end of the day but also to spend a specified number of minutes in touch every 24 hours.

For example, push notifications like y ou probably know that one of the most potent ways to promote addictive behaviour here is through turn-based games. Out of these alerts' users several times a day and re-engages them with their smartphones or social media platforms. Whether it be an alert, a like on your photo/post or the latest news, those are the sort of notifications that need immediate action and make you feel compelled to check up.

Another example is infinite scroll; social networking sites have an infinite scroll, which means you can keep scrolling, and the posts will never end. This infinite cycle of information does not have a way to give users natural stopping points even when they want to because there is always more content behind it. It creates a flow that is almost impossible to break.

E.g. likes and social validation like this are made even worse by likes, shares, and comments on social media, which are designed to keep you coming back the next day in search of validation from your peers. This feedback loop plays on human psychology's wants of social validation and, in many cases, community, thus encouraging the posting of content as well as checking back to see responses. It creates a feedback loop: the more engagement one gets, the more they have to come back and post again, making it easier for them to continue their addict behaviours.

For example, personalized algorithms like social media networks heap personalized content feeds up to the sky thanks, in part at least, to algorithms designed with relevance sensors that detect who you are and what your behaviours have been. It all works to keep users stuck inside their social media bubble; these algorithms serve highly relevant and very entertaining content. The more the experience is personalized, the stickier it makes to your users.

This is not a design mistake but rather a by-design way of taking advantage of psychological weaknesses and getting more airtime. For many people, this combination of constant stimulus and occasional rewards makes smartphones and social media almost narcotic.

Cognitive and Emotional Factors

However, there are many cognitive and emotional factors which aid smartphone and social media addiction in men. All of these factors come together to determine the way people think about using their smartphones and social media, so they dictate our emotional responses when we do use platforms. Fear of Missing Out is one of the influential cognitive factors that drive us to become addicted to social media. People feel that they always need to be in the loop so as not to disappear or lose information, events and trendy news. Humans use this platform and feel disconnected from its fear, which will lead to feelings of loneliness or being left out; as a result, there will be rise-check-in uploads on every social media platform. For example, instant gratification, such as smartphones and social media, allows users to gain immediate fulfilment. Whether it be a reply to a message, the result of some like buttons on posts or instant answers from Google, users have become hooked on getting instantaneous results. The chronic expectation that apps will open immediately can weaken the tolerance for delayed gratification and make individuals more susceptible to compulsive behaviour. For example, in social comparison, we are bombarded with the perfect versions of ourselves on different social media platforms, all in a constant state of comparison. This leads to social comparison — people comparing their lives with the perceived success, beauty and happiness of others. This processing pattern usually creates a sense of inferiority, envy or insecurity in others that leads them to validate themselves by increasing their activity on social media. Emotional regulation, e.g. people use their smartphone or social media to feel better when they are experiencing negative emotions e.g. it makes you less bored and can reduce stress, loneliness. They offer some refuge from discomfort: distractions and pseudo-friendships. Unfortunately, just as with any addiction, when a user uses something as a crutch for emotional regulation tools that have been mainly available only to the lower life fields, they lose their ability to manage emotions elsewhere healthily and, in time, deepen their dependence.

Attention and Cognitive Overload: For example, users can suffer from cognitive overload, too many notifications, messages, and content, all at the same time bombarding users. This division of attention can prevent the user from focusing on their work as well as just taking away from fully engaging in face-to-face conversations, creating stress and anxiety. This decreased attention, in turn, may play a part in strengthening addictive behaviours as users look for an escape from the demands of having to be connected at all times by diving even deeper into their online surroundings.

In other words, the addiction to phones or social media is floating upon schedule reinforcement and strategically designing their interfaces, which are not only cognitive but also emotional. These work in concert to create a positive feedback loop, making it hard for users to even disengage from the devices or platform at all.

IMPACT ON INTERPERSONAL RELATIONSHIPS

Addiction to smartphones and social media plays a pivotal role in disrupting communication patterns and social interactions, thereby affecting the depth of personal relationships. With the broader adoption of interconnected people, they are focusing less on real-life conversation, which has a huge impact. Such a thing interferes with the normal rhythm of conversations, leading to less depth and emotional connection, essential factors for positive relationship building.

Smartphone and social media addiction lead to attentional fragmentation – where users stop what they are doing and flee interactions with others, whether in person or online, by receiving notifications on their devices. This hinders 'active listening' and also restricts 'touch points' with others, and the resultant effect is superficial conversations/misunderstandings. For friends, families or couples (Pera, 2020; Ratan et al., 2021; Wacks & Weinstein, 2021), these disruptions can gradually break down trust and intimacy between them.

In addition, overuse of smartphones and social media can result in isolation despite the façade that it creates a world where we are never truly alone. People may replace in-person interaction with online communication and, thus, feel alone and more isolated from others. This paradoxical slant on social connection shows that actual human connections can be inhibited with addiction reinforced by technological innovation meant to further it.

EVALUATING THE MULTIDIMENSIONAL ADDICTION BEHAVIOUR SCALE (MABS)

It is a multivariate scale created by Ranjit Singha, the Multidimensional Addiction Behaviour Scale (MABS), that measures addiction behaviour across multiple dimensions. This scale sheds light on multiple important dimensions of addiction and is critical in developing a greater understanding of how green entrepreneurship may affect recovery. More specifically, here is the rundown of how MABS assesses these dimensions:

1. **Psychological Factors**: MABS investigates the emotional drivers and mental health aspects of addiction. These factors will be considered, including psychological stressors and emotional states that are proven to have a relationship with addictive behaviours (Ferrer-Pérez et al., 2024; NIDA, 2014; Smith & Borden, 2020).
2. **Biological Factors**: The scale assesses inherited and hard-wired physiological traits implicated in substance addiction. With this, we can better understand the core biological components of addiction (Ferrer-Pérez et al., 2024; Hayes et al., 2020; NIDA, 2014; Sinha, 2011).
3. **Social and Environmental Factors**: To what extent do social interactions and environmental contexts affect addictive behaviours, according to MABS? This also includes studying how different social networks, community support systems, and environmental stressors are mechanisms that lead to addiction (NIDA, 2014; Paul et al., 2024; Winters et al., 2012).
4. **Cognitive and Behavioral Patterns**: This scale examines thought processes and behavioural routines that are directly connected to addiction. This dimension serves to unravel the cognitive distortions and behavioural patterns that support addictive cycles (Fordham et al., 2021; Heinz et al., 2019; NIDA, 2014).
5. **Motivation and Readiness for Change**: This dimension helps in determining how ready a person is to come out of addiction. One of the dimensions is motivation and Readiness to Change (Crane et al., 2024; DiClemente et al., 2004; NIDA, 2014; Opsal et al., 2019).

Case Study: AL's Struggle With Smartphone Addiction and Its Impact on Relationships

AL is a 20-year-old female college student currently enrolled in one of the colleges to obtain a professional degree. A studious individual, he has an excellent academic track record. However, within the last 12 months, AL's friends and family have noticed his smartphone use rise, particularly when it comes to interacting with social media sites. AL is having relationship problems and has started to feel restless when he cannot use his smartphone. He blows off playdates all the time to hang out online. He is glued to his phone during family dinners, adding very little to conversations. He has cut to neglect his friends, they say, and given preferential treatment to his online life over spending time with them.

Ranjit Singha from Christ (Deemed to be University) has developed a tool called the Multidimensional Addiction Behaviour Scale (MABS). This scale has been validated, and its psychometric properties have been determined to be a reliable instrument that measures different aspects of addiction behaviour.

The MABS was used to measure how much anxiety there might be in AL, which is leading to smartphone addiction. Psychological Factors, Biological Factors, Social and Environmental Factors, Cognitive and Behavioural Patterns, Motivation and Readiness for Change. The social and environmental factors of the AL scores were shown to be high, as well as psychological factors. The other thing he found out in further counselling was that many of his issues are related to FOMO (fear of missing out) and compulsion to stay connected.

From the above case study, we had seen that AL has a borderline high MABS in Psychological factor, Social and Environmental Factor, which may suggest that he is addicted to his smartphone as it compensates for the management of an underlying mental health problem with regard to his apparent level of stress. The virtual world allows him to be out of his comfort zone without feeling so vulnerable, and being procedural like that helps minimize some anxiety when dealing with strangers face-to-face. Eighth, the reliance on digital media has led to a lower quality of personal preferences due to missing out on social ≈ face evaluations.

RECOMMENDATIONS

Interventions like Cognitive-behavioural therapy (CBT) or mindfulness sessions can be used to tackle the Social and Environmental Factors along with Psychological Factors for coping strategies that may work best in her case. Digital Detox is setting times throughout the day when you cannot use your phone in order to encourage real-world interactions. Social Skills Training, like joining different social events for workshops or even group therapy sessions, helps you develop interpersonal skills and the ability to stop any unnecessary feeling of nervousness in a situation. Family and Peer Support, by not exclude friends and family from your therapy treatment; a sound support system is everything. They will understand more about what you are going through and help you in the areas of open communication. To help AL rebuild and enhance his social connections, it should work on treating the root cause of the problem that fuels high usage rates for digital use by using this approach to reduce reliance on those platforms.

ASSESSMENT IN A SCHOOL OR COLLEGE SETTING

Screening for Smartphone Addiction and Anxiety, the first step is to administer a digital wellness survey, e.g. Schools and colleges can conduct surveys or questionnaires like MABS to identify if students are at risk for smartphone addiction. And the second step is to conduct one-on-one assessments like T-risk students-identified students, especially those who likely have smartphone addiction which can trigger a more comprehensive assessment, which could take them to specialized counsellors, psychologists or mental health professionals. For AL, for example, his scores were within the range, indicating moderate anxiety regarding social and environmental factors on MABS, reflecting that he is responding with psychological factors because of these stressors, justifying the individual approach.

Identifying Triggers and Coping Mechanisms, the third step is personalized interviews, School or college counsellors could follow up with interviews to delve into the specifics related to how a student uses his/her phone, the academic and social impact of that usage, and other specific psychological triggers (e.g. FOMO). AL's core issues were an intense case of FOMO or fear of missing out, as well as needing to be connected. Integration with Educational Outcomes, and the fourth step is academic and behavioural data, which is basically using academic data, which include attendance, participation performance with behavioural attendance to try and understand how smartphones are playing a role in academics — teachers could collaborate with counsellors/ mental health. Similarly, showing up to social or extracurricular events increases, but that information is also linked to increased smartphone use, like AL.

THERAPEUTIC INTERVENTION IN A SCHOOL OR COLLEGE SETTING

Cognitive Behavioural Therapy (CBT) or Mindfulness-Based Intervention, for example, CBT Group Sessions. Schools or college counselling services are able to put on weekly CBT group sessions for students struggling with smartphone addiction and stress. Through these sessions, students such as AL have learned to pinpoint irrational thoughts (like the importance of continuous tethering) and how to replace them with more positive strategies. Regular mindfulness practices or workshops can help students to become resilient against psychological factors. Practices such as deep breathing and various body scans can provide the grounding necessary to break the cycle of compulsive smartphone use, and actually focus. These workshops can be provided in schools during potentially stressful times, such as exam periods.

Digital detox programs, for example, establish screen-free zones and periods. Schools and colleges can strategically set aside screen-free zones, such as libraries and study areas, where students should be told not to use their smartphones. School hours could also be set aside during which smartphone usage is restricted, promoting students to do non-digital activities. Another example is structured breaks from technology, which promote school activities like events, sports and club meetings as opportunities to disconnect. For AL, the blocked times to avoid using his phone would lead him to re-establish relations with his peers outside of the online world.

Social Skills Training and Group Therapy, like Peer Support Groups for Schools, can create peer support groups which involve students of the AL nature together on a common platform for sharing their psychological factors to social, environmental factors and Smartphone addiction. According to the same report, these feelings of being not alone in their struggles in three groups together increase students' empathy levels and shared experiences so that they do not look for isolation in other ways. Another example is social skills workshops. Social skills workshops can provide help for children who struggle with social factors or find it hard to interact with others in person. They have a specific workgroup on enhancing communication, body language and conflict resolution through different workshops. These exercises involve role-playing assignments and group tasks where students are required to communicate without the use of their cell phones. Another process may include the Involvement of family and peer networks, such as parental Involvement in therapy. For example, the fact that family involvement could be instrumental in decreasing smartphone addiction and helping the student overcome it will do well to stop using smartphones is crucial. One way schools can integrate parents is by providing parent-student counselling sessions, in which both sides share their experiences of smartphone addiction and come up with a list of objectives. Other examples include Peer and Mentor Support. For example, in order to assign model students within the school with healthy usage patterns, they may act as positive role models for AL. In the same way, fostering peer accountability (such as having friends ask each other about time spent on their phones) can be a supportive measure.

IMPLEMENTATION STEPS FOR SCHOOLS AND COLLEGES

School-Wide Awareness Campaigns for Initiate campaigns on smartphone addiction, how it has been changing bonds, and the need for digital balance. Run orientation week workshops for first-years on developing healthy digital habits from the get-go.

Create an On-Campus Support System to Offer specializations for trained counsellors in smartphone addiction related counselling to students. Provide students with access to anonymous support lines for those who are afraid of reaching out in person.

Track Progress and Provide Feedback like Develop a monitoring system to track student progress interventions. Regular feedback that allows students to track improvements in controlling their smartphone use regarding assessments such as MABS, digital detox measures, and therapeutic Students like AL can have a healthier relationship with technology, improved interpersonal skills, and psychological relief by using assessment tools that are embedded within the school or college environment. Implementation of these structured programs leads to the growth in holistic health, leading deeper into positive academic and social outcomes.

PHENOMENON OF "PHONE SNUBBING"

Phone snubbing or "phubbing" is a particularly toxic form of toxophiliac involving the act of using your phone while moot to another person. Phubbing has been a significant social problem, particularly in places where people should be together during face-to-face communication, such as at dinner or meetings, and mostly while having fun at a party. It is the situation where one person starts looking into his/her phone and gives a feeling to others that I am ignoring you or that it is not important enough.

Its repercussions on relationships are destructive as it erodes the emotional bonding and breaks down mutual respect. For example, if one partner is constantly phubbing their significant other in a romantic relationship, then the person being phubbed could end up feeling left out and not cared for or included, leaving them to experience loneliness like in-person but somehow emotionally distanced by what occurs on social media, frustration like a result of lacking attention from who they love and rejection like brought about due to feelings that come with FOMO. Phubbing can produce social connectivity blockages in group environments where instead of sharing an actual real-time interpersonal exchange, the people included withdraw to their gizmos(Fleming, 2024; Peleg & Boniel-Nissim, 2024).

The effects of Phubbing are profound. O'Mara added, "When someone perceived that their partner phubbed them, they were more likely to report conflict in the relationship and less satisfied overall. Phubbing can also evolve into a relational disengagement, through which people eventually feel restrained in communicating repeatedly and hence turn to become the victim of emotional distance (Yasin, 2018; Yin et al., 2024).

Over time, it can create irreparable damage to the social dynamics, causing relational conflicts and a reduced sense of intimacy as well as weakening the bonds formed between individuals. We have already been faced with the toxic combination of tech addiction and phubbing, which have strained relationships among everyone in this app-enabled age, depriving humans – a biological species that requires connection and attention to grow, what they need.

In summary, the consequences of smartphone and social media addiction severely influence interpersonal relationships, first and foremost changing communication styles, and the second is cumulative relational conflicts, and new behaviours such as phubbing, which detracts from engagement. The impact of long-term addiction requires an address for more than just personal well-being, but also because relationships play a crucial role in structuring a healthy and enriching life.

IMPACT ON MENTAL HEALTH

Smartphone and social networking addiction have been associated with a variety of adverse mental health outcomes, like various psychological factors . The compulsive checking of smartphones, the never-ending scrolling on social media feeds and the yearning for round-the-clock digital alignment with others cause more mental health issues . People constantly check what others are doing, messages and updates with the pressure to participate in everything online; imagine continuously putting that running back foot forward—no emotional balance. Moreover, a constant vigilance mode like hypervigilance, which infects from being concerned with missing out on social gatherings to lagging in online connectivity amidst this state of endurance (Pera, 2020; Yin et al., 2024).

That being said, a separate study confirms that prolonged use of smartphones can make you depressed. Specifically, the connectivity illusion of social media can simultaneously breed intense feelings of loneliness and isolation. They have an emotional low if they do not get the affirmation through likes/comments/online interactions. This shallow connection often causes emotional burnout and insufficient real social support, all of which exacerbate depression (Gao et al., 2023; Peleg & Boniel-Nissim, 2024).

Stress is one of the many widespread consequences of the overuse of smartphones and social media. The sheer amount of information that we are exposed to through notifications alone, in addition to messages and the plethora of anything else stored online, contributes to what is called our never-ending tussle with the existence of data overload. This overstimulation leads to decreased cognitive capacity and a rise in stress by making users feel enervated within their digital ecosystem. In the most severe of cases, this stress may escalate to physical signs and symptoms such as headaches, muscle tension or an inability to sleep, which only enhances the impact on one's overall well-being.

STRATEGIES AND SOLUTIONS

The effective prevention and management of smartphone and social media addiction reflect a blessing triage, such as the characteristics of individual behaviours, societal influences (macro-variables), family variables (Meso level) or technological capacity. With proper education and awareness, prevention strategies can address this problem. Promotion campaigns that educate people, especially young users, on the possible negative consequences of excessive smartphone usage and social media interaction can lead them to more conscious choices. Schools can further promote digital literacy by means of programs designed to teach students how they should balance their online and offline lives, knowledge about the signs pointing towards addiction, and tools for fostering critical thinking when it comes to consuming content.

Install Usage Policies Another preventative measure that works well is implementing usage policies. People can set limits on time on screens, "phone-free" areas (e.g., at meal times and communal gatherings), and breaks from electronic devices. In addition to this application feature, mindfulness practices such as meditation and reflection may also help people become more conscious of how often they consume media on their devices, which in turn helps them understand the impact it has had upon victim's mental health, well-being or tired further harm others relationships. Practice regular self-assessments as part of the owner, operator and ready-to-drink (RTD) supplier check-in to see how you are tracking with your management.

Practical Strategies for Individuals, Educators, and Practitioners

For those seeking to control their addiction to phones and social networking, here are some practical solutions like Digital detox. For example, people can put down their devices regularly to build new habits that reset behaviour and reliance, such as having times when everyone goes phone- and social media-free every week. Another Mindful Usage, like the use of technology, can be mindful of using the devices when appropriate and having off times. Tracking the time one spends using apps and creating targets to reduce unnecessary usage can help reclaim control over app habits. Examples include engaging in offline activities, e.g., Recruiting out typing keyboards themselves to get part in punching leisure time, as well as social consumers or free cooperative ventures. Topics such as descending jaw, games including final decision play micro-learning communities they intend read to allow them to achieve those tangible life resonances yet research.

Educators' Role Educator gums could help in curricula on how to add smartphone and social media addiction, what that looks like for our kids, the effects of this addiction, and balancing between digital life vs real into their gum where they can communicate some signs symptoms cause outcomes of having overuse on daily routine. Coping strategies and resilience skills can be taught to better prepare students for media saturation. The bottom line is teaching coping skills. Practitioners' Involvement, like Mental health providers, can help those struggling with addictive disorders by offering Cognitive Behavioural Therapy (CBT) to adjust problematic thought processes and behaviours surrounding technology use. Practitioners can also teach clients better ways to reduce stress and other psychological faxtors without the use of a digital device.

POLICY RECOMMENDATIONS AND TECHNOLOGICAL SOLUTIONS

Dealing with Smartphone and Social Media Addiction at a societal level poses strategic policy recommendations along with innovative technological solutions such as Regulatory Measures. Governments must enforce policies requiring tech companies to include wellness-promoting features like screen time loggers and usage alerts in addition to low-off notifications. These features help users to identify their habits and moderate use.

Public Health Campaigns like Governments and non-profit organizations must put public health campaigns in place to educate people about smartphone/social media addiction. For example, these campaigns can focus on different demographics and the importance of good mental health along with social interaction.

Collaboration with Tech Companies Policymakers should work together with the tech industry to create norms and standards for ethical app design. This includes assisting behaviours contrary to value exchanges predicated on time-in-app, most importantly, such as timer reminders and better user-content gatekeeping.

Research funding, such as funding more research on smartphone and social media addiction, will provide a deeper understanding of the influence/effectiveness of intervention strategies. Policymakers have opportunities to support efforts that pilot new types of interventions and determine the most effective approaches in care and prevention.

Digital Literacy Education, like Teaching the skills necessary for kids to navigate technology safely and productively, should be built into educational curricula. Schools should instead focus on the risks of addiction to digital devices, viewing content online critically and balancing between the physical environment and in front of a screen.

Smartphone and social media addiction will need to be addressed with a collective response from individuals, educators, mental health professionals, policymakers and technology developers. Implementing prevention techniques, practical strategies built from years of experience working with individuals in crisis, and policy recommendations is how we can start to lessen the impact of addiction and shift our technology use to one that fosters human potential rather than degrades it.

FUTURE RESEARCH DIRECTIONS

Although the issue of smartphone and social media addiction has been widely discussed in academic literature, some gaps still need to be filled. Longitudinal research on the lasting effects on mental health and interpersonal relationships due to smartphone addiction and social media trauma is one big gap. Most of the research that has been done to date has concentrated on short-term impacts, leaving open how sustaining such addictions might shape well-being in a more long-run sense.

A notably vast area is the absence of studies on cultural differences in smartphone and social media addiction. There have been many studies on Western populations, both for the usage patterns of phones and social media and also for how society handles addiction. Cross-cultural inputs will offer a more holistic view of the manifestations of addictions globally and also guide as to how interventions might be tailored given local differences in cultural contexts.

More research is also needed on the age-specific effects of smartphone and social media addiction. Although there is much attention paid to teens and young adults, even the elderly are using their smartphones more often than ever before. Collecting more information on the patterns of addiction among specific age groups and its correlates in terms of mental health and social behaviours will prompt better-focused intervention strategies.

RECOMMENDATIONS AND SOLUTIONS

Addressing smartphone and social media addiction necessitates a comprehensive approach that includes mindfulness, education behind usage impacts, cognitive-behavioural therapy (CBT), and peer support group environments. On a personal level, individuals can create healthy boundaries, take digital detox breaks, and have in-person conversations to minimize reliance on the educational front. Children can be introduced to digital wellness programs, and device-free classrooms should also become mandatory. Policymakers can also introduce regulations on app design and build digital well-being programs. At the same time, tech companies can adopt ethical user experience designs that put the health of users before engagement. Therapeutic interventions have to take addiction management into account, and technology agreements can be drafted where families come together and put away all devices at a particular time while in each other's company. By taking it one step further and working to increase awareness, encourage other activities as alternatives, and install the necessary support systems for us all to better deal with smartphone addiction, we create a healthier tech-life balance.

It is important to remember that smartphone and social media addiction might be managed not only via individual interventions but also through group-level interventions and support networks. Schools, employers and community organizations can remain in workgroups where participants disguise their struggles with dependency. These are collective efforts that not only hold people accountable for their behaviour but also serve as a safety net for individuals who do want help and act desperately because they are struggling with active addiction. By incorporating digital literacy programs in school curriculums, younger generations can learn to use technology responsibly. Workplace initiatives for practising digital wellness will encourage employees to take regular breaks or create work-life balance.

In addition, the importance of research and innovation in the fight against digital addiction must be addressed. Further research on the psychological and neurophysiological consequences of the extensive use of smartphones as well as social media may bring in better interventions. According to research, technology companies can use AI to create tools for self-regulation of screen time that send notifications prompting people to take a break or limit their usage. Nevertheless, family and community engagement are imperative. With offline activities like outdoor adventuring, team-building meals and collective hobbies taking precedence, online users are likely to leave their digital devices behind for less depressing real-world experiences.

DISCUSSION

In this chapter, we covered the complex dynamics of smartphone and social media addiction and outlined both the psychological, behavioural, and technological forces behind such addictive behaviour. One prominent feature of both smartphone and social media addictions is their variable reinforcement schedules, built into the infrastructure design to help maximize user engagement. This compulsive use can affect everyday stress-inducing situations in relationships, using the phone as a solution (however temporary) to problems and increase other consequences such as "phubbing", which is an increasingly stand-offish experience from our interlocutor due to digital distractions. The chapter goes on to highlight mental health concerns, such as increased many psychological factors and other mental health issues, love or stress due to prolonged use of social media, and how this can affect the sense of self by looking at the way in which online lives are lived.

Additionally, the chapter stated a conceptual framework connecting addiction theories — e.g. Social Learning Theory and Variable Reinforcement Theory used traditional addictions— with addictive behaviours, television to smartphone use and also social media consumption. There was also a cognitive and emotional component of addiction involving the need for instant approval as well the highs that came along with engaging in digital interactions. Case studies and recent research, too, seem to concur in narrating the real-life challenges for society, particularly for social systems and psychologists, when they attempt with people with an addiction.

There are some crucial takeaways that we can derive regarding managing our addiction to smartphones and social media from the findings shared in this chapter. Steam Machines also help the addiction; learning how Steam operates its variable reinforcement and reward system components can turn a very dangerous mechanism, on the one hand, into what many might see as cheesy, harmless fun. At the individual level, this could mean taking digital detoxes, using screen time monitoring and limiting apps if necessary, or just being more mindful in their interactions online. These insights may be helpful to input for educators and health practitioners in the development of digital literacy programs as well as behavioural interventions to try to change technology use practices towards healthy uses. However, in the real world, families and professionals will need to develop proactive plans like creating "no phone zones", setting time limits on screen usage, and more face-to-face conversation.

Additionally, policymakers and tech companies can work together to advance the ethical design of technology that reduces addictive behaviour. Social media and tech companies, for example, can build features like screen time alerts that limit infinite scrolling. At the same time, policymakers can establish institutional guidelines to reduce children's exposure (and potential dependency) on harmful technology use.

These results are an extension of research on behavioural addictions in a digital environment. Previous research has focused on the reinforcement learning and social modelling explanations of addictive behaviour that underlie smartphone and social media addiction, incorporating these theories into a single overarching framework. The fact that psychological mental health issues, other psychological factors including stress are up on the shelf of comparisons will fit with previous studies we have discussed, indicating adverse mental health outcomes aligned with excessive screen time. Moreover, someone examining social comparison again and its effect on self-esteem backs up this earlier information entirely as it is also good news putting inferiority together with solitude, which, unfortunately, people today usually search for curation alongside the preteens (that other than authenticity) in lifestyle.

In a dangerous age, this chapter seeks to engage with the emergent discourse by positing new assemblers of addiction in an attempt to provide case studies that can be clear enough for us all—stakeholders who scour journals and theoretically tinker —to anticipate what is happening rather than theorize about how it happened. This is the first, to our knowledge, view in which technological design elements are included in this framework and focuses on how interface designs may promote or ameliorate addictive behaviours. This chimes with a more recent conversation in the field of HCI that asks for digital design to be less evil and non-addictive.

In sum, this chapter provides an in-depth exploration of smartphone and social media addiction by combining psychological theories with technological insights to create a complete picture. The results support continued work in research, education and policy around the emerging problem of digital addiction in society today.

CONCLUSION

This chapter is an examination of smartphone and social media habits under a highlight, culminating by highlighting their critical role in mental health as well as lives with other people. So, what you will learn includes things like the psychological mechanisms driving addiction, including variable reinforcement schedules and reward systems, as well as tech design features that promote excessive use. Through this addiction, we also turned on how our communication patterns began to spiral into conflicts such as 'phubbing', and this led us down the road of many psychological issues including depression without conversing about a sense that it is. Our shared experiences drove with social comparison upped in insecurity. This also included some significant theories of addiction, such as the Social Learning and Variable Reinforcement Theory, which were designed to explain how these behaviours are learned and maintained. Real-world scenarios with case studies and research findings demonstrating the scale of an addiction challenge, both from smartphones as well as social media, underline a dire requirement for intervention.

The chapter also identified areas for future research in order to understand better the mental health, behavioural and societal impacts of addiction. We also highlight the need for a future research agenda focused on areas neglected mainly within the existing literature, such as changes in access to treatment, how addiction interacts with other socio-demographic variables (including age), longer-term psychosocial outcomes and emerging patterns of use in response to clinical evidence and practice development. These may include investigating technological advances such as artificial intelligence and machine learning to recognize addictive patterns, predict addiction before it occurs or worsens, and modernize treatments. There is also room for longitudinal studies to evaluate the long-term consequences of high smartphone and social media consumption rates on mental health outcomes, as well as relationship qualities.

The insights shared here, in practice, can inform individuals as well as educators, health professionals, and policy creators to invent methods for the prevention and control of addiction. Promising avenues for addressing these problems include digital literacy programs, the use of mindfulness-based interventions that target mechanisms underlying addictive behaviour, and ethical design in the development of distributed systems. However, separately, we also need more regulation of the tech companies themselves so that they no longer profit from encouraging addictive behaviour.

Smartphones and social media dictate aspects of a progressively digital world, so attending to addiction should be fundamental. There is nothing wrong with these tools, but they can have a negative impact on our mental health and relationships if overused. What is learned from this chapter is that they need to look for more technological segment services, integrate different schools of disciplines (behavioural sciences) and revisit or tune up the social policies being prepared in many developing countries. We must continue down a technological path but find balance with personal integrity before it gets too much.

REFERENCES

Adorjan, M., & Ricciardelli, R. (2021). Smartphone and social media addiction: Exploring the perceptions and experiences of Canadian teenagers. *Canadian Review of Sociology/Revue Canadienne De Sociologie, 58*(1), 45–64. DOI: 10.1111/cars.12319

Áfra, E., Janszky, J., Perlaki, G., Orsi, G., Nagy, S. A., Arató, Á., Szente, A., Alhour, H. M., Kis-Jakab, G., & Darnai, G. (2023). Altered functional brain networks in problematic smartphone and social media use: Resting-state fMRI study. *Brain Imaging and Behavior*, 53(4), 835. Advance online publication. DOI: 10.1007/s11682-023-00825-y PMID: 38049599

Crane, C., Hotton, M., Shelemy, L., & Knowles-Bevis, R. (2024). The Association between Individual Differences in Motivational Readiness at Entry to Treatment and Treatment Attendance and Outcomes in Cognitive Behaviour Therapy: A Systematic Review. *Cognitive Therapy and Research*, 48(1), 10504. Advance online publication. DOI: 10.1007/s10608-024-10504-x

DiClemente, C. C., Schlundt, D., & Gemmell, L. (2004). Readiness and stages of change in addiction treatment. *The American Journal on Addictions*, 13(2), 103–119. DOI: 10.1080/10550490490435777 PMID: 15204662

Ferrer-Pérez, C., Montagud-Romero, S., & Blanco-Gandía, M. C. (2024). Neurobiological Theories of Addiction: A Comprehensive Review. *Psychoactives*, 3(1), 35–47. DOI: 10.3390/psychoactives3010003

Fleming, L. (2024, May 30). *Are you phubbing your partner?* Verywell Mind. https://www.verywellmind.com/what-is-phubbing-8647390

Fordham, B., Sugavanam, T., Edwards, K., Stallard, P., Howard, R., Nair, R. D., Copsey, B., Lee, H., Howick, J., Hemming, K., & Lamb, S. E. (2021). The evidence for cognitive behavioural therapy in any condition, population or context: A meta-review of systematic reviews and panoramic meta-analysis. *Psychological Medicine*, 51(1), 21–29. DOI: 10.1017/S0033291720005292 PMID: 33455594

Gao, B., Shen, Q., Luo, G., & Xu, Y. (2023). Why does the mobile social media-related fear of missing out promote depressive symptoms? The roles of phubbing and social exclusion. *BMC Psychology*, 11(1), 231. Advance online publication. DOI: 10.1186/s40359-023-01231-1 PMID: 37568184

Hayes, A., Herlinger, K., Paterson, L., & Lingford-Hughes, A. (2020). The neurobiology of substance use and addiction: Evidence from neuroimaging and relevance to treatment. *BJPsych Advances*, 26(6), 367–378. DOI: 10.1192/bja.2020.68

Heinz, A., Beck, A., Halil, M. G., Pilhatsch, M., Smolka, M. N., & Liu, S. (2019). Addiction as learned Behavior patterns. *Journal of Clinical Medicine*, 8(8). Advance online publication. DOI: 10.3390/jcm8081086 PMID: 31344831

Khan, N. F., & Khan, M. N. (2021). A bibliometric analysis of peer-reviewed literature on smartphone addiction and future research agenda. *Asia-Pacific Journal of Business Administration*, 14(2), 199–222. DOI: 10.1108/APJBA-09-2021-0430

Lin, C., Ratan, Z. A., & Pakpour, A. H. (2023). Collection of smartphone and internet addiction. *BMC Psychiatry*, 23(1), 427. Advance online publication. DOI: 10.1186/s12888-023-04915-5 PMID: 37316810

Montag, C., & Becker, B. (2023). Neuroimaging the effects of smartphone (over-) use on brain function and structure—A review of the current state of MRI-based findings and a roadmap for future research. *Psychoradiology*, 3(1), kkad001. Advance online publication. DOI: 10.1093/psyrad/kkad001 PMID: 38666109

National Institute on Drug Abuse. (2014). *Drugs, brains, and behaviour: The science of addiction* (NIH Publication No. 14-5605). https://nida.nih.gov/sites/default/files/soa_2014.pdf

Opsal, A., Kristensen, Ø., & Clausen, T. (2019). Readiness to change among involuntarily and voluntarily admitted patients with substance use disorders. *Substance Abuse Treatment, Prevention, and Policy*, 14(1), 0237. Advance online publication. DOI: 10.1186/s13011-019-0237-y PMID: 31694664

Ostic, D., Qalati, S. A., Barbosa, B., Shah, S. M. M., Vela, E. G., Herzallah, A. M., & Liu, F. (2021). Effects of Social Media Use on Psychological Well-Being: A Mediated Model. *Frontiers in Psychology*, 12, 678766. Advance online publication. DOI: 10.3389/fpsyg.2021.678766 PMID: 34234717

Paul, F. A., Dangroo, A. A., Saikia, P., Ganie, A. U. R., Zaid, M., Das, M., & Gogoi, R. (2024). Societal and individual impacts of substance abuse. In *Springer eBooks* (pp. 1–24). DOI: 10.1007/978-3-030-68127-2_430-1

Peleg, O., & Boniel-Nissim, M. (2024). Exploring the personality and relationship factors that mediate the connection between differentiation of self and phubbing. *Scientific Reports*, 14(1), 55560. Advance online publication. DOI: 10.1038/s41598-024-55560-1 PMID: 38504119

Pellegrino, A., Stasi, A., & Bhatiasevi, V. (2022). Research trends in social media addiction and problematic social media use: A bibliometric analysis. *Frontiers in Psychiatry*, 13, 1017506. Advance online publication. DOI: 10.3389/fpsyt.2022.1017506 PMID: 36458122

Pera, A. (2020). The Psychology of addictive smartphone behaviour in young adults: Problematic use, social anxiety, and depressive stress. *Frontiers in Psychiatry*, 11, 573473. Advance online publication. DOI: 10.3389/fpsyt.2020.573473 PMID: 33101087

Ratan, Z., Parrish, A., Zaman, S., Alotaibi, M., & Hosseinzadeh, H. (2021). Smartphone Addiction and Associated Health Outcomes in Adult Populations: A Systematic Review. *International Journal of Environmental Research and Public Health*, 18(22), 12257. DOI: 10.3390/ijerph182212257 PMID: 34832011

Sinha, R. (2011). New findings on biological factors predicting addiction relapse vulnerability. *Current Psychiatry Reports*, 13(5), 398–405. DOI: 10.1007/s11920-011-0224-0 PMID: 21792580

Smith, C. H., & Borden, K. A. (2020). Introduction to the special issue on substance use disorders and addictions. *Professional Psychology, Research and Practice*, 51(1), 1–4. DOI: 10.1037/pro0000299

Topino, E., Gori, A., Jimeno, M. V., Ortega, B., & Cacioppo, M. (2023). The relationship between social media addiction, fear of missing out and family functioning: A structural equation mediation model. *BMC Psychology*, 11(1), 383. Advance online publication. DOI: 10.1186/s40359-023-01409-7 PMID: 37941011

Wacks, Y., & Weinstein, A. M. (2021). Excessive smartphone use is associated with health problems in adolescents and young adults. *Frontiers in Psychiatry*, 12(12), 669042. Advance online publication. DOI: 10.3389/fpsyt.2021.669042 PMID: 34140904

Winters, K. C., Botzet, A., Fahnhorst, T., Arria, A., Dykstra, L. G., & Oliver, J. (2012). Social factors and the addiction syndrome. In *American Psychological Association eBooks* (pp. 229–250). DOI: 10.1037/13751-012

Yasin, K. (2018, September 29). *I quit social media for 65 weeks. This is what I learned*. Healthline. https://www.healthline.com/health/my-65-week-digital-detox #I-cant-believe-you-blocked-me!

Yin, L., Feng, J., Hou, W., Wang, P., & Yin, Y. (2024). Smartphones on, humannesses off Phubbing breeds dehumanization via subjectivity uncertainty. *Computers in Human Behavior*, 160, 108378. DOI: 10.1016/j.chb.2024.108378

KEY TERMS AND DEFINITIONS

Digital Addiction: The problematic use of cell phones and multiple social media accounts results in adverse effects on daily life, a balanced state of mental well-being, and human relationships.

Interpersonal Relationships: Social and emotional bonds with others, which may be affected by communication styles, trust levels in your connection to another person or the impact of digital interactions like consequences from overuse of smartphones.

Mental Health: A sense of psychological well-being, or an absence thereof, that affects the ability to work and contribute socially. Smartphone — social media addiction has been linked with adverse mental health outcomes, including anxiety, stress, depression and low self-esteem.

Phone Snubbing (Phubbing): The act of the generation to ignore others in social environments by fixing our regard upon our smartphones instead of enchanting, including brain touching, relational conflicts, and communal isolation.

Smartphone Addiction: The habit of becoming overly passionate and obsessed with smartphones or having an uncontrollable use of them as they have a significant impact on daily life; emotional well-being can weaken too, which makes relationships broken.

Social Learning Theory: is a psychological theory that says people can learn behaviours through observation of others and the social environment. Encore. With addiction, it means to what degree smartphone and social media use is adopted due to imitation of peers or cultural expectations.

Social Media Addiction: Becoming obsessed with social media to the extent that it is excessive is playing a part in personal relationships, and it has a detrimental impact on mental health, among other things.

Variable Reinforcement Theory: Behavioural theory that unstable and intermittent rewards spur addictive behaviour. For example, in smartphone and social media addiction, users are kept going due to the expectation of unpredictable rewards such as new notifications or likes.

Chapter 7
The Digital Dilemma: Navigating Smartphone and Social Media Addiction

Saptarshi Kumar Sarkar
https://orcid.org/0009-0004-1786-8284
Brainware University, India

Piyal Roy
https://orcid.org/0009-0007-5378-2789
Brainware University, India

Amitava Podder
https://orcid.org/0009-0004-9268-3781
Brainware University, India

Shivnath Ghosh
https://orcid.org/0000-0001-7368-7139
Brainware University, India

Anupama Sen
Brainware University, India

ABSTRACT

Social media addiction is a condition that continues to demand immediate attention, interworking with various social and cultural factors. With design decisions such as infinite scrolling and algorithmic content that keep users engaged longer, the influence of tech companies cannot be understated. Social norms, the desire to be continually connected with their cohort, certainly push people into compulsive behaviors. There's a distinction across generations, especially with respect to Millennials and Gen Z, who are digital natives and know of digital media through

DOI: 10.4018/979-8-3693-8804-4.ch007

the scope of communication and socialization. That's why one should take the multi-pronged approach involving school-based education about digital literacy to enhance awareness toward addiction, along with campaigning that will spread awareness in people about possible risks of addiction and parental monitoring that inspires better digital habits in children. These would give the society an opportunity to strike a symbiotic relation with technology and combat the social media addiction.

1. INTRODUCTION

Smartphones and social media services that took over our lives have changed the paradigm of communication, collaboration and interactions. These technologies have had positive effects regardless of the numerous negative impacts they have brought in people's lives such as; communication, information access, and continuity of relationship over long distances. Nevertheless, they have also brought different concerns in particular, those that are connected with mental health issues. In the present chapter, the reader is introduced to the current epidemic of smartphone and social media dependency, its explanation, consequences, and ways to overcome it.

1.1 Opening Anecdote or Statistic

Pew Research Centre indicated that in 2023, 97% of people in the United States own a cellphone of some sort while 85% own a smartphone. This is however attributed by the use of common mobile technologies that permeate everyday life and one cannot even dream of a life without the smartphones. Consider the following scenario: A young professional wakes up with the notification on her phone, opens her emails and social media accounts on the bed and spends most of her working hours monitoring her phone and working. After spending the greater part of the day with the smartphone, she spends little or no time with her friends and family, doing other meaningful activities. This scenario is not uncommon and highlights a growing concern: The risks which arise in the account are possible signs of dependence on smartphones and social networks.

Dependence on the smartphone and on social media is common in the contemporary society, and research suggests that the use of these technologies may negatively affect a number of aspects of life for worse such as increases in anxiety, depression, and decreased sleep among others. Such knowledge is more important at the present time due to the constant evolution in technology specifically on smartphone and social media addiction. It is this paper's goal to give a clear understanding of these addictions, including the causes for them, what they result in, and possible ways through which they can be prevented.

1.2 Definition of Terms

To further appreciate the factors that relate to smartphone and social media addiction, that it is mandatory for one to define these terms. Indeed smartphone addiction differs from social media addiction although these two terms are sometimes used interchangeably.

1.2.1 Smartphone Addiction

Smartphone addiction otherwise known as nomophobia: is a compulsive behavior in relation to the use of mobile phones to an extent that it hinders normal functioning. This dependency is evident through notifications that one feels the need to keep checking, use of applications and the inability to get off the device. The use of smartphone is dependent on the multiple utilities of the device including social media, games, messaging apps and internet. These functions are easily accessible and always available and this make it hard for users to refrain from using their phones hence promoting addictive behaviors.

Smartphone addiction is similar to other behavioral addictions including gambling and that of the use of the internet. These include loss of control over usage, withdrawal symptoms whenever the device is not in sight, as well as negative impacts in personal, social and vocational arenas. For this reason, a smartphone addiction is maintained through the brain reward system; it releases dopamine, which relates to the positive stimuli resulting from the interactions with the smartphone such as notifications (Twenge, 2017).

1.2.2 Social Media Addiction

Smart phone dependency is just a kind of specially dependency on Social media apps like Facebook, Instagram, twitter, tik tok etc. Social media dependent have the irresistible urge to navigate and interact with their feeds and post episodes, always sacrificing time for other pursuits. This is because the use of the social platform necessitates that individuals require the approval of the society, acceptance and belongingness.

It has been established that there's a correlation between SNS (Social Networking Service) addiction and psychological factors including low self-esteem, social anxiety, and the necessity of social approval. Algorithms used in the design of social media platforms also make users develop addiction by continuously presenting them with engaging content. Social networking addiction is also a problem that results in the appearance of such consequences as low efficiency, sleep disturbances, and conflicts with family and friends (Carr, 2010).

1.3 Importance of the Topic

It is rather crucial to pay attention to the addictive use of smartphones as well as social media platforms. This increases the addictive possibility since the world is shifting towards the digital platform in all aspects hence having profound effects on mental health, physical health and social life as a whole. It is not just an individual ailment but a social one which negatively affects the efficiency of work, people's overall well-being and ways of communication. Among them, the stakes related to this area are considered to be the most crucial one, and these are the consequences of the addictions influencing the sphere of mental health. A study done found out that the more the individuals spend time on their smartphones and social media, the more they are likely to experience high levels of anxiety, depression and stress. These problems pale most among the young persons who appear to be most vulnerable and most involved with these technologies. Smartphone and social media addiction are particularly more harmful to adolescents and young adults since the brain is still developing and is also easily influenced by peers and social media comparisons. Consequently physical health is also comprimized. The disadvantages of gazuging a mobile phone include eye strain, neck ache, and sleeplessness among other. This may make people sit for long, which is evident with the increased use of smartphones and social media networks, which has caused obesity, and related matters. These health conditions are not individualistic in nature they have implications on the general population health and health care services.

Another very important issue is the social effect of smartphone and social media addiction. These addictions can reduce face-to-face communications over time, reduce social connectivity and breed loneliness. One of the negative effects is that as more hours are spent using the devices, they leave their face to face communication with other people. Apart from the personal and social effects, the smartphone and social media addiction has the economic impact. Cyberloafing through the use of smartphones and social media websites may cut down productivity thus economic losses among companies and global economy (Room et al., 2001). Further, cost implications that arise from management of the health complications due to these addictions fall under the healthcare sector may likewise be high. Because smartphone addiction and social media dependency are very common and can have such adverse effects on a person and society as a whole, it is imperative to create the best ways of controlling such risks. The purpose of this chapter is to explain what smartphone and social networking dependence is, how and why it occurs, and what may be done to avoid such processes.

2. UNDERSTANDING ADDICTION: THE SCIENCE BEHIND IT

Addiction, about drugs, behaviours, etc., is one of the extensively researched and discussed subject areas in psychology, neurology, sociology, and other branches of science. It is therefore important that when addressing smartphone and social media addiction how they work is well understood on the science side to formulate the right intervention and measures to be taken. This section looks at the psychological aspects of addictions, the behavioral symptoms of addictions and differences between smartphone/ social media addiction with other types of addiction.

2.1 Psychological Basis

Addiction can be traced to the psychological part of the human brain known as the reward system. This system is intended to promote activities that are necessary and critical to an organism's existence including feeding, procreation, and communication. Particularly, when we participate in such behaviors, the brain releases such chemicals as dopamine which gives positive emotions such as pleasure and satisfaction. This reward system has been found to play central role in the formation of various types of addiction such as the smartphone and social media (Neupane et al., 2017).

Dopamine and Reward System: Dopamine is central in addiction formation and can clearly be seen from the above post. The same ideas come about when one uses his or her smartphone or social networks, when receiving notifications, likes, or messages, the brain secretes dopamine making a feeling of pleasure. This reinforcement aims at ensuring that the same actions are repeated mainly because an individual wants to feel that 'tingle' once again. Gradually, it forms a pattern that the smartphone or the social media platform is useful to cause a release of the happy hormone hence resulting in the formation of a vice.

Conditioning and Habit Formation: Psychological processes of conditioning and habit formation also play the part of creating addictions. According to Pavlov's classical conditioning, these stimuli; such as the sound of a smartphone ringtone, may become linked to a reward and the child will have an involuntary response. Skinner in his work on operant conditioning also provides explanation on how behaviors that are followed by rewards (e. g. receiving likes on the social media) are most likely to recur (Turkle, 2015). This results in the process of creating habits where an action such as checking the phone, or turning to social networks happens unconsciously (Sarkar et al., 2023).

Social Validation: Self-esteem is a basic emotional determination, doing with social acceptance. Sufficient members-a-like likes, theirs commenting, or theirs sharing through the generic or social media raises self-esteem efficiently; thus it ought to be rewarded. With the creating expectation for approval not met or under threat, one experiences anxiety, stress, and the urge to be back around-that is, engage on the platform more frequently.

Fear of Missing Out: This is another psychological reason for addiction -(FOMO): The fear of missing out on some exciting or rewarding experiences that others seem to be having. It leads to a compulsive desire to stay connected and informed via social media. It involves a frequent checking of the social media accounts, causing interference with other aspects that ought to be more important since such an attitude contributes to addiction development (Neupane et al., 2017).

Escapism and Coping Mechanisms: For some people, smartphone and social media use may serve as a coping mechanism to evade stress, anxiety, or other negative feelings. The brief time spent engaging with digital content does provide a temporary distraction or escape; and that's when it becomes a habit, in cases where individuals use it as a means of avoiding, coming to terms with, or overcoming deeper issues (Newport, 2019). Such reliance on digital devices for emotional regulation can nurture a vicious cycle of addiction whereby individuals would appear to quite obstinately resort to smartphones or social media to help them cope with their troubles.

2.2 Behavioral Signs

These signs can range from mild to severe; however, controlling the urge to use devices, negative implications, and an inability to regulate or completely refrain from use are the generalized aspects from which these signs arise.

Compulsive Checking: Of these identified behavioral signals of addiction to smartphones and social media, compulsive checking stands out as among the most common. Individuals feel such a compulsion to keep on checking their phones or social media accounts almost all the time and for an insufficient or no purpose and hardly ever triggered by anything specific. The individual may engage in this compulsive checking behavior during inappropriate times, such as when there is a serious work meeting, a social gathering, or while driving, leading to significant disruption in daily life (Turkle, 2015).

Increased Tolerance: Stemming from the model of substance addiction, individuals become tolerant in nature: as a result, longer sleep hours are now needed to offer just the same level of person satisfaction. Therefore, consumption would occur for increasingly longer periods: those addicted to smartphones and social networking spend hours on their gadgets and frequent the mentioned platforms, thereby omitting earned activity to cater for work, studies, or social interaction (Walker, 2017).

Withdrawal Symptoms: When deprived of access to the phone or social media, withdrawal-reflecting symptoms in large part resemble symptoms associated with more established modes of addiction. Symptoms may include anxiety, irritability, restlessness, and a strong desire to be back on a particular social media platform or have access to their phone. This is a definite sign of dependency on technology and a reflection of some ongoing, concealed battle with addiction.

Neglecting Personal and Professional Responsibilities: Addiction to smartphones and social media may lead to the neglect of personal and professional duties, allowing the individual to prioritize electronic activities over work, school, and household responsibilities. Poor performance, missed deadlines, and hurt feelings among loved ones may arise as a result of this. Neglect can have serious consequences for both life and livelihood, including job loss and academic failure (Turkle, 2015).

Social Isolation: Ironically, although social media is an attempt to connect people, addiction to social media has also been associated with social isolation. An addicted person will withdraw from real interaction in favor of time spent on a device rather than participating in an actual social activity. This isolation may worsen loneliness and depression and create a vicious spiral that makes them even more dependent on smartphones and social media for social interaction.

Reduced Productivity: On top of that, a decrease in productivity can be another sign of addictive behaviors. From social media notifications to the urgency of constantly checking on one's phone, it can become difficult for an addict to consistently focus on tasks or finish work competently. Academic and work-related underperformance from a persistent loss in productivity may invite other factors, such as heightened stress and anxiety.

Disruption of Sleep Patterns: The excessive use of smartphones and social media, particularly when indulged just prior to bedtime, has disrupted sleep patterns. Blue light from screens interferes with melatonin production, a substance that regulates sleep from consummation with stimulancy. This, compounded by other stimulants LGBT media indulges, can keep the mind active long into the night, thus contributing to lower quality sleep.

2.3 Comparison With Other Addictions

While addiction to smartphones and social networking is very similar to other types of addiction, including substance addiction, gambling addiction, and Internet addiction, the dissimilarities in this particular case can be viewed as reflective of some other characteristics of these different addictive disorders.

Similarities with Substance Use: Smartphone and social media addiction share fundamental characteristics of substance abuse disorders, such as the compulsive nature of the behaviors, profound loss of control, and negative consequences. Both groups of behaviors hinge considerably on the reward system in the brains of their perpetrators, benefiting from the release of dopamine that reinforces them. Both types of addiction also manifest symptoms of withdrawal in the form of increased anxiety and irritability. However, unlike substance abuse, which is marked by ingestion of a tangible substance, smartphone and social media addiction entail behavioral patterns revolving around certain behaviors of a person and do not lead to dictation of physical consumption.

Comparison with Gambling Addiction: Gambling addiction, like smartphone and social media addiction, is classified as a behavioral addiction. Both types incorporate repetitive behaviors that are intermittently rewarded, where reinforcement is drawn from such winning a bet or receiving a social media like. In IED, the rewards are unpredictable, which makes the addiction even stronger, as people will continue performing these acts under the hope of getting the next forthcoming supply of reinforcement. However, while from gambling you normally lose money, in the case of smartphone and social media addiction, people primarily lose time and attention and suffer possible adverse impacts on their mental health and relationships.

Internet addiction: Smartphone and social media addiction exist within internet addiction; thus, both involve excessive uses of online platforms and services. Internet addiction is shaped in a broad spectrum of compulsive web surfing, online gaming, and shopping of behavioral training, whereas smartphone and social media addiction is relatively more definite in intention. Still, the way addiction works for all sorts of digital addiction-from the role of dopamine to conditioning to habit formation-thus far persists across these types of addictions.

Contrast with Physical Addiction: One of the essential differences between smartphone and social media addiction and the other forms of addiction-e.g., drug or alcohol addiction-is the type of substance or behavior. Physical addiction involves taking in a chemical substance that, once absorbed into the body, alters the physiological state and leads to a state of physical dependence and the presence of withdrawal symptoms following cessation of use. In contrast, smartphone and social media addiction do not involve the taking in or use of a substance but relate rather to activities that may trigger psychological dependence. Although withdrawal in the case of behavioral addiction is predominantly psychological, such withdrawal is often strong and combined with hardship to overcome.

Influence on Health: Another way in which smartphone and social media addiction differs from other forms of addiction is in health effects. Substance addictions usually have direct, severe physical health consequences, including damage to organs, disease susceptibility, or overdose. In contrast, the impact of smartphone and social media addiction on physical health is not so direct and results mainly from sedentary behaviors, disrupted sleep, and stress. That said, the psychological and social influences of smartphone and social media addiction can be just as harmful and impact mental health, relationships, and quality of life.

Social Acceptance and Stigma: Finally, stigma surrounding addictive behaviors is very disparate and always in acceptance through the exercise of social acceptance. Formerly, substance-oriented addictions like the use of illegal drugs had given rise to social isolation and discrimination; on the other hand, modern society seems to be able to accept or even support usage planning through smartphones and social sites, making it extremely difficult to somehow recognize and manage their addictive behavior forms (Pariser, 2011). The absence of this stigma can further make it easier for individuals to deny or downplay their addiction, which can inadvertently delay the acknowledgment and treatment of their problem.

3. IMPACT OF SMARTPHONE ADDICTION

Smartphones have permeated daily life; they give flexibility, connection, and access to overwhelming information and services. They have also created some controversies concerning overuse and addiction. Smartphones are bound up with addiction in the sense of excessive and habitual use and thus entail the corresponding consequences on a person's life. In this section, too much smartphone use may influence mental health problems, physical health problems, and relationships. The following discussion will give an overview of some of the harmful consequences affiliated with this phenomenon.

3.1 On Mental Health

Smartphone addiction and its influence on mental health, therefore, form a vital area of concern for researchers, health care providers, and society. Smartphone overuse has been associated with a variety of mental health challenges, including anxiety, depression, stress, and sleep disorders.

Anxiety and Depression: Several studies have established close associations between smartphone addiction and increase in generalized anxiety and depression symptoms. One often refers to this condition as "nomophobia"-the fear of being unable to use mobile phones. This tendency engenders anxiety in the subject because they have been barred from contacting their mobile phones. This culture of comparison that social media just subsidizes instigates feelings of inadequacy and low self-esteem, greatly enhancing depressive symptoms (Gupta & Sharma, 2017). Heavy smartphone usage is associated with online social comparison and self-perception that ultimately leads one to experience symptoms of depression due to self-perception (Kardefelt-Winther, 2017).

Stress and Burnout: Chronic stress and burnout, brought about by smartphone addiction, are commonly reported. The barrage of notifications, emails, and messages from diverse sources puts users in a constant state of urgency to respond; it imparts different features of stress because of the sense of perpetual connectivity (Ribble, 2015). Constant availability promotes the blurring of boundaries between work and personal life, which in turn adds towards burnout and stress, especially for those who find it difficult to unplug. The inability to switch off from the virtual world has a substantial toll on its invariably exhausting lifestyle, leading to further impacts on mental health.

Sleep Disorders: Smartphone addiction has been considered a strong signal to some sleep disorders which include insomnia and poor quality of sleep. When a smartphone screen emits bright blue light, it reduces melatonin-hormone production that regulates sleep, creating difficulty for the user in falling asleep. Besides, the habit of looking at one's phone before bed can cause mental stimulation, which can then cause a delay in falling asleep and reduce sleep time. Use of smartphones just before sleeping, mainly through social media, will disturb one's sleep patterns, since whatever is watched might have an emotional or mental engagement that will make the relaxing and sleeping process even more difficult. Poor quality of sleep may lead to several mental health problems, viz., anxiety, depression, and cognitive impairments (Kardefelt-Winther, 2017).

Attention Deficit and Cognitive Impairments: Smartphone addiction has another effect on mental health, namely, the opening out of the attention span and cognitive functions. Studies have shown that smartphone multitasking and its nature of requiring fragmented information mode of presentation negatively impact attentive capabilities and decrease the extent of concentration one can sustain on-the-go. This decline in attention span is often referred to as "digital distraction," which is a situation where a person finds it exceedingly hard to concentrate on work without any distractions from cell phone use, switching to other activities, and the like. Besides, excessive phone use may intervene with cognitive functions, such as memory retention and processing information, because the mind is used to the unending amounts of digital stimulis.

Social Anxiety and Isolation: Paradoxically, smartphones, while designed to enhance communication and social connectivity, are, more so than not, responsible for addiction, social anxiety, and isolation. Over-reliance on digital communication, instead of face-to-face communication, can eventually deteriorate their skills at interaction and increase feelings of loneliness. For younger people, social anxiety can be exacerbated by the persistent need to project a curated and ideal self-image on social media, thereby having a fear of being judged or rejected (Pariser, 2011).

This fear can lead to the avoidance of real-life social circumstances which fortify an individual's plunge into social isolation and worsens mental health issues.

Addiction and Mental Health Comorbidity: Likewise, respect must also be rendered to comorbidity per se between smartphone disease and most other mental disorders. The individual suffering from anxiety, depression, or any of the sets of psychological disorders could be more prone to getting addicted to the smartphone to somehow ease the state. Then, smartphone disease tends to augment pre-existing forms of mental malaise into a vicious relationship between one being addicted and living with that in reference to mental health. Hence, this makes individuals increasingly comfortable the more they fall into addiction, reinforcing it.

3.2 On Physical Health

Clearly, the impact of smartphone addiction on mental health has been firmly established, and similarly, the unfortunate consequences on physical health are sometime not taken seriously. A range of options from either side would be exercised, such as musculoskeletal problems, vision problems, and lifestyle-related health problems.

Musculoskeletal Problems: If on any count lesions take place on the phone debauch, musculoskeletal problems are the very first one. Perhaps it is mainly left upon the organs like the neck, shoulders, and hands. Text-neck refers to strain on another name, and it has its roots again in muscle pull or strain somewhere about the neck while one has his/ her eye directly focused down on the screen of one's smartphone. It could produce tightness and stiffness about the neck, causing pain eventually, most concisely spoken chronic conditions starting from cervical spondylosis down to minor irritation (Gupta & Sharma, 2017). To some extent, repetitive strain injuries like texting thumb or smartphone thumb are results of prolonged use of smartphones artistically done to deal with the pressure and consequence quantities of texting and scrolling that confers, in its course, all together to cause pain, inflammation, and reduced dexterity among all the affected joints within specific parameters.

Vision Problems: Referring to some considerable amount of physical health and welfare linked to smartphone addiction is an impact of the referee wretched towards that of vision-straining. The blue light that comes up from the smartphones, which could be said to produce digital eye strain-a condition marked firstly to be seen from the eyes in dry form to blurred vision and later signaled by a mild headache that contributed mostly thereafter to serious perilous conditions toward servality of the eye like macular degeneration and cataract. Because there are later frights with exposure to blue light for an extended period close to the affected eyes, one has been conducting a venture of this nature towards such conditions of light used mostly on low light, however giving rise to fantastic eye strain and sub-optimal sleep that would together kill the very health altogether.

Sedentary Lifestyle and Obesity: Smartphone addiction is constantly brought on by sedentary lifestyle; that individuals who spend inordinate time on mobile phones are unlikely to be involved in any physical activities. The answer for leisure or entertainment on mobiles or social media makes them stay in one posture for too long. With less physical exercise comes obesity, rates accordingly with the other lifestyle diseases related to sedentary life. Further, pairing the smartphone with unnatural snacks and folly beverages can increase the propensity to wear obesity and other metabolic conditions.

Sleep Disruption and Related Health Issues: As shown above, smartphone addiction leads to sleep disturbances, poor sleep quality, and other sleep disorders. Consequences of long-standing sleep deprivation could range from immune dysfunction to a great enhancement in the occurrence of chronic diseases, e.g., hypertension, diabetes, to impairment of cognitive functions. On the side of other physical health issues, an ongoing lack of sleep relates to weight gain as it disrupts the balance of hormones that regulate appetite with increased cravings for high-calorie foods.

Hearing Loss: One more concern that is coming up with smartphone addiction is hearing loss, especially for those who listen to music or video using earphones or headphones with excessive volume. The hair cells of one's inner ear can get damaged because of continuous exposure to loud sound and then, in working together, be tilted to develop noise-induced hearing loss (NIHL). Although it cannot be said that this risk is unique only to smartphones, their heavy use for content consumption has raised numerous discussions about their long-term impacts on hearing health, particularly among younger people.

Posture and Spinal Injury: Smartphone addiction can aid in the degeneration of both posture and spinal health, in addition to musculoskeletal disturbance. Looking down at the smartphone screen can contribute to poor body posture, characterized by rounded shoulders, forward head position, and curvature of the upper back. This wrong posture over time may cause spinal deformity, muscle imbalances, and chronic pain. Prolonged use of smartphones leads, therefore, to a lack of movement and can diminish the range of motion and strength of the core muscles that are essential for maintaining posture and supporting the spine.

Accidents and Injuries: In its last perspective, smartphone addiction makes users more vulnerable to accidents and injuries, especially under circumstances where people are using their phones while driving, walking, or doing anything else requiring vision and coordination. Distracted driving, which often results from the use of a smartphone, has become one of the leading causes of roadway accident and fatality in the world. Likewise, "texting while walking" is associated with put individuals in increased risk for pedestrian accidents, as people have diminished awareness of their surroundings when concentrating on their phones. Such accidents invariably lead to serious injuries or even death, thus marking another reason for raising awareness of the necessity of regulating smartphone usage in potentially threatening pursuits.

3.3 On Relationships

The impact of smartphone addiction reaches beyond the individual, affecting the interpersonal sphere and social dynamics. Excessive smartphone use puts pressure on relationships, lowers the quality of social interaction, and contributes to feelings of disconnection and loneliness.

Effects on Dating Partnerships: Among the most significant ways in which smartphone addiction affects relationships is through its effect on dating partnerships. This is where phubbing, which means 'snubbing with a phone', comes in. Phubbing can cause feelings of abandonment, jealousy, and resentment in romantic relationships, as one partner feels discriminated against and inferior to the phone. Over time, phubbing builds distance, erodes trust and intimacy, which at times results in dissatisfaction and possibly separation or divorce.

Effects on Family Relationships: Family relationships can additionally become strained due to smartphone addiction, with emphasis on parent-child relationships. Smartphone-addicted parents may be inattentive and unresponsive toward meeting their children's needs, which may create a sense of neglect and emotional insecurity. Children growing in an environment where smartphone use trumps bonded interaction may also face hurdles in social and emotional development due to missing out on essential bonding time with a parent. In addition, kids and adolescents hooked on smartphones can face conflicts with their parents, specifically regarding limits and screen time (Sagacious, 1950).

The present knowledge affects friendship: Apart from romantic relationships and family dynamics, smartphone addiction affects friendships too. Unhealthy dependence on digital communication damages quality interaction with friends face-to-face, making interactions shallow and deprived of depth. Moreover, constant pressure to have an online presence, be on social media, and run with the herd can provoke a sense of inadequacy and filing for competition with friends, creating frictions and infighting. Smartphone addiction invites isolationism into one's social life. As some sink deeper into the addiction, their own devices become more important than actual friendships, eroding social support, with implications for well-being (Hollandsworth et al., 2011).

Work Relations: Smartphone addiction does not merely include relationships and marriage; it extends itself into professional life too. Having employees addicted to their smartphones leads to decreased productivity, low levels of focus, clashes between colleagues and superiors. The constant desire to check for notifications and messages distracts them from work: a leisure act that would be reduced in quality and quantity, straining professional relationships and growing tension in a workplace, one that can be accused of earmarking a displeasurable flaw in the work relationship.

Communication skills: At the end of the day, smartphone addiction could also be well-off into, entirely exploring altogether broader communication skills- the warranted ones for establishing and keeping relationships. Excess of digital communication can affect a person's ability to have that intimate and important face-to-face interaction, thus reversing verbal and nonverbal skill development. The attention that was once going toward verbal communication, conflict resolution, and emotion expression, thereby creating huge bounds within relationships, is now cycled back to electronic mediators, thus mixing up the true meaning in-betweenwhat one means and what he intends to communicate.

4. IMPACT OF SOCIAL MEDIA ADDICTION

Social media platforms have been integrated with a part and parcel of human life; some of them, eg., Facebook, Instagram, Twitter, and TikTok, have turned into the biggest network connecting friends, family relations and the other one in pursuit of career advancement. However, increasing research has corroborated the darker aspects of the use of social media and its addictive nature. In simple terms, social media addiction is simply excessive use of social media that interferes with the normal functioning of life, interpersonal relationships, and else, possibly crucial, psychological health (Andreassen, 2015). In this chapter, as it paints a gloomy picture, the human behavior resulting from social media addiction will be outlined in respect of self-esteem, mental health, and cognitive functioning that provides a fully-fledged understanding of how social media can benefit yet disadvantage its users.

4.1 On Self-Esteem

Self-esteem refers to an individual's general assessment of self-worth or personal value. It is one of the central aspects of psychological well-being and dictates the way people perceive themselves and their abilities. Social media no longer only appeals to individual self-image, but also feeds the fire of inadequacy, envy, and low sense of self-worth.

Comparison Culture and Envy: The culture of comparison that social media inculcates is one of the major areas within which social media influences self-esteem. These include social media tools filled with curated content where users upload their highlights, such as vacations, triumphs, and party invitations. These portrayed lives can often provoke upward social comparisons, with users feeling like they are not as accomplished and glamorous as others. This downward social comparison has come to be associated with feelings of envy and lower self-esteem since users may perceive their lives as inferior to others.

The Role of "Likes" and Validation: The architecture of social media platforms, with features like likes, comment sections, followers, etc., is a further very important factor in the influence of self-esteem. Social validation through these means can become addictive as users seek external approval for their posts and materials. A study found that receiving more likes increased brain activity in the reward center, much like when drug addicts take in drugs. Fostering a dependence on social validation can have dire socio-psychological effects that spawn anxiety, insecurity, and instability in self-esteem, contingent upon their approval or disapproval by others.

Body Image and Self-Perception: Social Media also has high impact on body image, especially young women. Instagram, for example, is filled with images of idealized body types that may be unattainable, and even impossible. Exposure to such unrealistic standards can result in body dissatisfaction and low self-esteem since people start comparing their bodies to those they see online. The influence is further intensified with the use of photo-editing apps and a variety of filters (Fardouly et al., 2015).

Cyberbullying and Self-Esteem: One other way social media may damage self-esteem is through cyberbullying. Unlike traditional bullying, which can be extremely painful for the victim, cyberbullying is incessant and unrelenting because it occurs online and can reach the victim at any time. Those targeted by cyberbullying show a tremendous reduction in their self-esteem, feeling that they are degraded, threatened, subject to humiliation in public platforms, etc. Social media platforms allow anonymity, which increases the abuse of cyberbullying to a greater height, making it even tougher for the victims to seek help or defend themselves.

Positive Aspects: Whereas the influence of social media on self-esteem can be negative, some argue that the benefits should also be acknowledged. In particular, these platforms offer an opportunity for self-expression and creative development for some members of their community, providing them opportunities in community formation. They are a personhood solution with a sense of belonging, especially for those who feel they are alone in their offline world. Social media can therefore also be a tool for self-promotion, allowing people to present their talents and ordinary lives to a much larger audience.

In summary, the multidiemensionality of social media influences self-esteem positively and negatively: a culture of comparison, validation-seeking, and exposure to idealized pictures may lead to lower self-esteem and body image dissatisfaction. The other side also allows one to express oneself, connect with others, and find community. It is essential to understand this complicated relationship prior to developing strategies that reduce the risk while promoting the gain of social media.

4.2 On Mental Health

The nexus amid social media usage and mental health has received much empirical attention, with studies showing both pros and cons. Though social media may give the much-needed emotional support and foster a sense of community, there, however, lies abuse and addiction on the extreme end of the continuum with other psychological disorders like anxiety, depression, and loneliness.

Anxiety and Social Media: For many users, social media platforms can be a source of great anxiety. There is the added pressure of being on top of issues, staying up with posts, or responding to messages. This condition is referred to as social media anxiety disorder and is characterized by fear of missing out (FOMO), including stress over friend interactions, and obsessive checking behavior in times of distress. The FOMO from anxiety can cause the compulsive checking of social media platforms-a vicious circle because when one checks and realizes that others are having nice times, it aggravates their anxiety (Andreassen, 2015).

Depression and Social Media Use: Many studies have found media use correlating with depression symptoms. As previously noted, perhaps the primary reason for these associations is the culture of comparison itself. People's constant comparison of themselves to those who seem more successful or happier can lead to feelings of inadequacy and hopelessness, which serve as a backdrop for depressive symptoms. Out of these delirious scrolls emerge feelings of depression and loneliness as a result of passive consumption of social media. In comparing their seemingly non-engaged life to some other seemingly active lives, passive users certainly do not feel empathy towards them.

Loneliness and Isolation: Although social media's very development hinges upon interpersonal bonding, social media can at times lead to loneliness or feelings of isolation. Studies conducted on the subject indicate that increased use of social media correlates with heightened feelings of loneliness, especially among young adults. The paradox could lie in the very nature of interactions offered there: shallow, feeble attempts at contact that, in turn, could serve to dilute the potency of human emotions in comparison to traditional face-to-face communication. Additionally, the comparison that takes place among individuals and curatorial content on social media could leave the consumers a sense of inadequacy, leading them to feel a disconnect from others-with much fuller lives.

Sleep Disruption and Mental Health: Another considerable way that social media can have an impact on mental health association is through its effect on sleep. Many people use social media until late at night, often to the detriment of sleep. The blue light emitted by screens interferes with melatonin-a hormone that helps the body to sleep-and causes difficulties in falling and staying asleep. Poor sleep and sleep deprivation correlate concretely and statistically with various mental health issues, such as anxiety, depression, and mood disorder. Furthermore, distressing news or stimulating discussions experienced through social media could increase emotional arousal, making it more difficult to relax or fall asleep.

Addiction and Mental Health: Social media addiction in itself can have considerable mental health effects. Compulsive necessity to check social media and inability to put a damper on its usage can trigger stress, anxiety, and feelings of losing control over other areas of one's life. In some ways similar to gambling, social media addiction places the user in a cycle of craving, use, and negative consequences. Quite difficult is breaking free from dependence and addiction because of the widespread availability of social media, and because of rewards which comes in the form of likes, comments, and notifications.

Positive Mental Health Aspects: The other side is, however, of positive mental health attributes, since sometimes social media may indeed have a positive collection of influences on mental health. Social media may offer social support toward connecting friends, family, and communities of interest or experience. Such social support may be precious for isolated people in real life or even where mental health conditions are causing disruptions. Social media, apart from all this, might also serve as an information resource for mental health advocacy by allowing users access to support groups, educational resources, and contacts of health professionals (Hollandsworth et al., 2017).

Everything said above makes it quite clear that the complex nature and multifaceted nature of how social media addiction impacts mental health. If social media capable of enhancing symptoms of anxiety, depression, loneliness, and poor sleep, social media, on the other hand, also offers social support, community, and access to mental health resources. It is also vital to keep both aspects in mind as we learn how to minimize social media's negative effects while tapping into its potential strengths.

4.3 On Cognitive Functioning

Cognitive functions relate to the processes that converge through mental faculties to acquire knowledge and understanding-marked by memory, attention, perception, and decision-making. Social media addiction may lead to damaging cognitive functioning-an area of interest especially is attention, memory, and critical thinking.

Attention and Concentration: One of the most-touted effects of social media addiction on cognitive functions has to do with attention and concentration. All social media outlets are purposely designed to attract and keep users' minds on a stream of updates, notifications, and content; such a design is prone to split attention because the individual is not able to focus on any one task for a prolonged period. Switching constantly from one task to another, such as checking media when working or studying, is bound to compromise cognitive performance and decrease productivity (Yang & Brown, 2016).

Memory and Information Processing: Social media addiction also affects memory and information processing. Due to the flood of information on social media, cognitive overload can occur in which the brain cannot process and retain information. Overload like that can render the consumer with a lack of proper short-term memory and the ability to address information. In addition, given that most content accessed on social media is superficial, such as headlines and snippets-the user may not delve deep into critical reasoning about complex issues, for each content is presented without substantive guidelines propelling the user to critical reflection.

Multitasking and Cognitive Impairment: The common habit of multitasking among users of social media could cause cognitive impairment. Although multitasking looks like an efficient way to complete the tasks, studies revealed that it can be detrimental to cognitive functioning, slowing task completion, raising errors, and decreasing comprehension. Social media addiction worsens the situation because it trains users to shuffle their attention between numerous tasks-like social media surfing to message responses and task completion-at a time.

Impact on Critical Thinking: The addictiveness posed by social media may impact critical thinking. Algorithms on social media sites tend to prioritize sensational, emotionally charged, or already aligned with users' beliefs and preferences content. Thus, this "filter bubble" effect results in limiting exposure to different viewpoints and discourages critical thinking as users' chances of encountering content repugnant to their views are reduced. Moreover, the passive consumption of content through scrolling feeds without careful analysis or discussion may lead to a loss of critical thinking.

Positive Cognitive Aspects: Although the adverse effects attributed to the use of social networking sites remain rife, some positive cognitive contributions also abound. Broadly speaking, social networking sites could earn users a chance, some creativity, and mental engagement. Social networking sites can stimulate cognitive growth and motivate users to explore new volunteer perspectives by facilitating educational content, online courses, and intellectual discussions. Even the problem-solving, decision-making, or collaborative opportunities that will lead to enhanced cognitive functioning flourished through online communities and groupwork activities (Fardouly et al., 2015).

In conclusion, the explanation above broadly highlights some possible cognitive domains, including attention, memory, multitasking, and critical thinking, in which social media addiction may interfere. The distractive nature of social media, coupled with information overload, may degrade cognitive functions. At the same time, such an environment can develop cognitive growth and intellectual engagement. Therefore, balancing media usage with mindfulness and criticality thus becomes a healthy mediating point for cognitive health in the digital age.

5. CULTURAL AND SOCIETAL INFLUENCES

Social media addiction is not simply about individual choices but is deeply rooted in cultural and societal contexts. Technology companies' roles, social norms and pressures, and generational differences all shape the manner in which people interact with social media and contribute to addictive behaviors. This section examines their influences in detail.

5.1 The Role of Technology Companies

The design and programming of social media platforms heavily influence how users behave on these platforms. Features, such as endless scrolling, notifications, and algorithm-driven content suggestions, are included in the designs on most social media platforms to keep users engaged for as long as possible. Such design features may encourage addiction behaviors, wherein users remain glued to their platforms. Furthermore, in order to make money from advertising, these companies depend on the users' engagement, and hence, the design becomes increasingly addictive as time passes by (Twenge & Campbell, 2018).

5.2 Social Norms and Pressures

Social norms and pressures are big influences on social media usage. In the modern-day society, there is a big demand for constant connectivity and activity by social media platforms. Quite often, this demand may lead to compulsive behavior, as some individuals might feel the incessant need to be updated, respond to the messages at the moment, and continue having an active profile. The fear of missing out (FOMO) is what pushes this to happen: people, in fear of exclusion, spend excessive time on social media lest they miss anything out (McDaniel & Radesky, 2018).

5.3 Generational Differences

Thus, it's crucial that we understand how these generational differences inform the way people use and relate to social media. The Millennials and Gen Z tend to reflect a greater deal of use and dependence on social media than older generations, which can be attributed to the fact that they've grown up with the role of social media vis-a-vis everyday life, affecting patterns of communication, socialization, and even identity formation.

6. CASE STUDIES AND PERSONAL STORIES

Such narratives and case studies present themselves as the human perspective on smartphone addiction and social media addiction. Such examples show the hurdles suffered by individuals and their lives impacted by addiction. This section examines both ordinary users and celebrities challenged by addiction.

6.1 Real-Life Examples

This section presents first-person chronicles of rich, vibrant, real-life experiences of people experiencing an addiction to smartphones or social media. Through them, these cases should clarify the different manifestations of addiction and allows them to relate to the impact that it can have on mental wellness, relationships, and daily activities. Stories extend from teenagers overwhelmed with connection to adults whose work and personal lives are disrupted by their digital habits.

Table 1. Real-life examples of smartphone and social media addiction

Example	Age/ Gender	Addiction Type	Consequences
Sarah, High School Student	17/ Female	Social Media	Decline in grades, social anxiety, loss of real-life connections
John, Corporate Professional	34/Male	Smartphone	Work performance issues, insomnia, strained family relationships
Emma, College Student	20/ Female	Social Media	Body image issues, depression, FOMO
David, Freelance Artist	28/Male	Smartphone and Social Media	Creative block, procrastination, anxiety
Lucy, Stay-at-Home Mom	39/ Female	Social Media	Neglect of household duties, increased stress, relationship issues
Alex, Software Engineer	26/Male	Smartphone	Burnout, lack of focus, social isolation
Grace, Retiree	67/ Female	Social Media	Reduced physical activity, loneliness, dependency on virtual interactions
Michael, High School Teacher	45/Male	Smartphone	Classroom management issues, decreased engagement with students
Mia, Small Business Owner	33/ Female	Social Media	Distraction from business tasks, financial losses due to decreased productivity

6.2 Celebrity and Public Figures

The pernicious impacts of smartphone/social media addiction extend to non-professional and professional domains: several celebrities and public figures have surfaced with their life-threatening engagement into these addictions. Such sagas attract much visibility, primarily because of the raised platform that such individuals enjoy. Included below are examples of how even those living in the public eye are not shielded from the effects of digital addiction.

Table 2. Celebrity and public figures affected by social media addiction

Celebrity/Public Figure	Profession	Addiction Type	Impact on Career/Personal Life
Selena Gomez	Singer/Actress	Social Media	Took a break from social media to focus on mental health
Ed Sheeran	Musician	Smartphone	Quit social media to reduce stress and anxiety
Chrissy Teigen	Model/TV Personality	Social Media	Openly discussed social media detoxes to manage mental health
Demi Lovato	Singer/Actress	Social Media	Experienced cyberbullying, took social media breaks
Justin Bieber	Musician	Smartphone and Social Media	Cited digital detox as essential for mental well-being
Ariana Grande	Singer/Actress	Social Media	Frequently takes breaks to avoid negative online interactions
Pete Davidson	Comedian/ Actor	Social Media	Deleted social media accounts to escape negativity
Emma Stone	Actress	Smartphone	Discussed the benefits of limiting smartphone use
Prince Harry and Meghan Markle	Royals	Social Media	Advocated for mental health awareness, highlighting online pressures

In these tables, one learns lucidly how smartphone and social media addiction influences the daily person and prominent figures whom they observe, conveying that addiction is a progressive development phenomenon with no restrictions whatsoever.

7. STRATEGIES FOR MANAGING AND OVERCOMING ADDICTION

The approaches to tackling the issue of smartphone and social media addiction include self-regulatory techniques, detox, micro-minimalism, and therapeutic interventions. This section outlines those methods, complemented by real-life examples and evidence-based approaches.

7.1 Self-Regulation Techniques

Self-regulation techniques involve conscious efforts toward regulating one's behavior, emotions, and thoughts, thus making essential choices for addiction management. This basically includes usage restrictions such as installing screen time monitoring apps and mindfulness meditation to combat compulsive behaviors. Adopting these slaves may drastically cut down on time spent on Smartphones and social media, thereby staving off the addiction.

Table 3. Self-regulation techniques for managing addiction

Technique	Description	Impact on Behavior
Screen Time Monitoring	Using apps to track and limit screen time	Increased awareness and reduced usage
Setting Time Boundaries	Establishing specific times for using devices	Reduces impulsive checking and overuse
Mindfulness Practices	Engaging in activities that promote present-moment awareness	Decreases compulsive behaviors and anxiety
Goal Setting	Defining clear personal goals for social media use	Encourages purposeful and mindful usage
Avoiding Triggers	Identifying and avoiding situations that lead to overuse	Reduces temptation and increases self-control
Positive Reinforcement	Rewarding oneself for meeting usage goals	Strengthens motivation to maintain healthy habits
Digital Fasting	Implementing short-term breaks from all devices	Resets habits and reduces dependency

Whereas the table reiterates the potential of self-regulatory techniques in empowering the user to take charge of their smartphone and social media use, thus advancing healthier habits with respect to digital space.

7.2 Detox and Digital Minimalism

Digital detox and minimalism are strategies aimed to reduce dependency on technology. A digital detox refers to the complete cessation of any use of devices for a space of time, which resets the pipeline associated with addiction to devices and clears on the way to mental clarity. On the other hand, digital minimalism relates to the mindful use of technology only when that use is consistent with their personal values and as a means to fulfill their individual goals. This presents the advantage of cutting down on unnecessary virtual clutter, which, in turn, motivates relations more meaningful.

Table 4. Benefits of detox and digital minimalism

Approach	Description	Benefits
Digital Detox	Temporarily abstaining from all digital devices	Improved mental clarity, reduced stress, better sleep
Digital Minimalism	Intentional use of technology aligned with values	Increased focus, enhanced productivity, more meaningful relationships
Device-Free Zones	Designating areas in the home where devices are not allowed	Encourages face-to-face interactions and relaxation
Scheduled Breaks	Taking regular breaks from devices throughout the day	Reduces digital fatigue and promotes balance
Content Curation	Unfollowing accounts or unsubscribing from services that do not add value	Creates a more positive and intentional online experience
Single-Tasking	Focusing on one task at a time rather than multitasking with devices	Enhances concentration and efficiency
Limiting Notifications	Turning off non-essential notifications	Decreases distractions and anxiety

The table exhibits the various benefits of digital detox and minimalism in articulating the possibilities of developing a healthy relationship between individuals and technology.

7.3 Therapeutic Approaches

Therapeutic approaches are targeted at those who are heavily addicted to smartphones and social media. Such persons may benefit from cognitive-behavioral therapy, wherein treatment is targeted at changing maladaptive patterns of thought and behavior related to addiction. Other avenues might be group therapy, which would be a place of support of fellow addicts tackling the very same obstacles, and mindfulness therapies that could enhance self-awareness and emotional regulation.

Table 5. Therapeutic approaches for overcoming addiction

Therapy Type	Description	Effectiveness
Cognitive-Behavioral Therapy (CBT)	Focuses on changing negative thought patterns	Highly effective in reducing addictive behaviors
Group Therapy	Provides a supportive environment with peers	Encourages shared experiences and accountability
Mindfulness-Based Stress Reduction (MBSR)	Combines mindfulness practices with stress management	Reduces anxiety and improves self-control
Family Therapy	Involves family members in the treatment process	Strengthens family support and communication
Motivational Interviewing	Helps individuals find internal motivation to change	Effective in enhancing commitment to change
Online Support Groups	Provides virtual support and resources	Convenient access to support and guidance
Psychoeducation	Educates individuals about the effects of addiction	Increases awareness and promotes informed decision-making

The given table summarizes different treatment modalities that are quite effective against smartphone and social media addictions and point out how professional support is essential for heavy cases of addiction.

8. THE ROLE OF EDUCATION AND AWARENESS

Lack of education and awareness will never see an end to cell phone and social media addictions. This battle gives society a chance to endow their addiction victims with knowledge about the pitfalls of technology addiction and to help implement some changes to their digital habits; society could create a more balanced approach to technology. This section discusses three broad themes concerning educational programs, public awareness campaigns, and parenting support.

8.1 Educational Initiatives

Educational initiatives form a foundation of the war against digital addiction. Schools, colleges, and universities possess the ability to shape the minds of the youth and therefore become a key venue for the impartation of healthy digital behavior. These initiatives often include curricula on digital literacy, dangers from overuse, and balance between online and offline activities. Another essential ingredient to these educational programs is that courses in digital citizenship are indispensable. Digital citizenship refers to responsible use of technology, knowledge on digital rights and responsibilities, and promotion of respect for other citizens' online behavior. Although promoters of digital citizenship hold students as their audience, teaching digital citizenship may help the student develop a critical understanding of the digital footprint and the far-reaching implications of their digital use. Moreover, these educational initiatives should not be primarily directed only at students. Continuous professional development for teachers and school staff needs to ensure they stay ahead in their knowledge of trends in technology use and next-generation risks related to them. Through workshops, seminars, or online courses, educators can gain the support needed to better guide students (Nassen et al., 2023).

Example of Successful Educational Initiatives:

Finnish Schools' Approach: While digital literacy classes in Finland are not separate subjects, schools have piled them all together into a general curriculum, where students learn about cognitive effects of social networking, importance of breaks, and how to thoughtfully evaluate online content. Thus, this method anticipates an increase in a sense of awareness about the concern over digital overuse among all students (Blum-Ross et al., 2019).

Be Internet Awesome by Google: The program gives free resources for teachers and parents to engage children in lessons about online safety, digital citizenship, and responsible use of technology through interactive lessons and games, making it fun and enticing to learn (Erstad et al., 2020).

8.2 Public Awareness Campaigns

Awareness campaigns must target a larger audience that extends beyond the educational institutes. Such campaigns seek to inform society about the threats posed by smartphone and social media addiction while providing practical solutions to address these risks. Public awareness can be conducted through government, nonprofit organizations, or private entities and come in different forms, such as social media campaigns, television ads, posters, or community workshops. Effective public awareness campaigns engage audience attention and encourage thought-evoking discussions with the use of persuasive messages and visuals. Most often, it is carried out by employing relatable stories or shocking statistics so as to stress the important message. Campaigns on digital detox, mental health awareness, or the benefits of disconnection tend to be more effective in recent times (Green et al., 2021).

Example of Public Awareness Campaigns:

Scroll Free September: This campaign is sponsored by the Royal Society for Public Health in the UK to persuade people to take a month off from social media. Participants could do a complete scroll-free month or set their own parameters, like not logging into social media during the evening. The campaign has successfully brought attention to the effects of social media on mental health and has inspired many people to adopt healthier behaviors in terms of their digital habits.

Disconnect to Reconnect: This campaign to decrease smartphone engagement is run through the Center for Humane Technology, advocating relationships and mental health in this regard. It encompasses sustained efforts beyond the training of online interactions and presents materials for people desiring to reduce their screen time (Albris et al., 2024).

8.3 Parental Guidance

With this new development in technology, children and teenagers are more reliant on parent-sponsored guidance to operate efficiently in the digital realm. This allows them to establish guidelines on screen-use and practice proper behavior. Recent surveys and research studies indicate that children whose parents are involved in managing their digital media time while talking openly about the implications of excessive screen use are less likely to engage in the behaviors of addiction. One of the better ones would probably be parents structuring a well-rounded environment whereby there are set rules as to when and where devices can be used in the house; for example, no phones at the table and limiting screen time before bed. Further, parents can motivate children to lead an overtly well-rounded lifestyle by getting them involved in offline activities like sports, outdoor activities, and reading. In the life of a conversation where parents and children hate to be involved in a focus talk, facts become of great importance. Thus, it is mandatory for parents to talk to children about what they encounter while online and how it makes them feel. This active interaction can serve as a stimulus to help kids develop a sense of critical thinking as well as resilience in face of negative social media input (Barr, 2019).

Example of Parental Guidance Strategies:

Setting time limits on devices: Some parents use special applications to set daily screen time limits for their children. These apps can automatically deny access to certain apps or devices when the time limit is reached, enabling children to develop self-control and realize that moderation is wise.

Family Detox Days: Some families go all the way and schedule days during which there is no digital engagement from any household member, thereby breaking screen time and creating opportunities for face-to-face time and communication among family members.

Co-viewing and co-playing: Following what children are doing on screen, if done in a relaxed manner as a family, offers a way to get to know the kids' online lives better, making it possible to coach them more effectively (Livingstone et al., 2015).

9. FUTURE IMPLICATIONS

In light of rising smartphone and social media addiction, it becomes paramount to reflect upon the future implication of this growing trend. The fast-paced development of technology, transformation of societal norms, and thus requiring" informed consideration—by future policymakers—will all significantly affect the milieu of digital addiction and what it means for individuals along with communities.

9.1 Technological Advancements

With technological improvements, smartphone and social media addiction is likely to grow in severity. The more immersive and engaging the digital experiences provided-for instance, virtual reality and augmented reality-the harder it may become for users to disconnect. While these technologies may open up new avenues for entertainment, education, and communication, they may also aggravate addiction by designing even more attractive digital environments that are very difficult to resist. Besides, with the rapid incorporation of artificial intelligence into social media platforms, even more personalized and targeted content will be available. Algorithms powered by AI are already customizing content to users' tastes, ensuring users are glued to their screens most of the time. As these algorithms grow, they may obscure the line between healthy use and addiction further, making it even more challenging for individuals to notice and manage their digital consumption.

9.2 Societal Shifts

Changes in society would also determine in shaping future patterns of smartphone and social media addiction. As digital technology comes to be integrated into such a wide range of modern lifestyles-from vocational activities to social activities-societal norms regarding technology use will continue to evolve. This might create a normalization for constant connectivity. Being "always online" may not only be accepted but also bettered into expectation. However, there is a rising value place upon the need for balance and prioritization of digital well-being. Digital detoxes and digital minimalism movements are on the rise, implying that future societal shifts might include pushbacks toward the excessive dimension of digital technologies. This may lead to some kind of cultural evolution in which being mindful and intentional with technology is preferred over what is considered continuous engagement. Also, with greater awareness of the increase in digital addiction traits with respect to negative implications, the demand for mental health support and resources may also surge. The development of various tools, apps, and service angles to support the management of an individual's digital engagement may rise in society, thus promoting healthier contact with technology.

9.3 Policy Considerations

Policy considerations will, however, be key in dealing with challenges engulfing smartphone and social media addictions. In most cases, Governments and regulatory institutions must step up to draft statutes and regulation intended to protect users, most notably, children and adolescents. This could take the form of content bans, limits on targeted advertising, or demands on platforms to incorporate features supporting digital wellbeing-such as screen time reminders and usage analytics. There will, furthermore, be a push for educational policy to mandate adding digital literacy and digital citizenships to school curricula. Such proactive efforts equip students with the know-how and abilities required in handling issues involving responsible digital navigation; hence, preventing the onset of addiction from an early age.

Moreover, our future regarding smartphone and social media addiction will be mapped by the muddy waters of technological revolutions and evolutions, societal-based shifts, and policy considerations. As far as technology evolves differently, our managing programs for that impact ought to evolve differently, too, so that they can ultimately permit us to enjoy digital novel changes without excessive corollary entrapments.

10. CONCLUSION

In conclusion, the overwhelming evidence of smartphone and social media addiction is a growing concern with respect to mental and physical health, relationships, and societal impact. An aspect of this addiction is the psychological and behavioral pattern of addiction as any other phase of compulsive behavior that needs to be tackled by personal and social efforts. The inferiority of mental health due to this addiction ow has cast the burden of complications in interpersonal relations, particularly the rise of SNS-alienated communities. Educational initiatives, public awareness campaigns, and adequate parental training for enhancing digital literacy and healthier digital practices are crucial. Technological advances could enhance the intensity of the situation. This means societal equilibrium, where balance is provided, must be created and secured as policies to protect sherworn populations. In any case, smartphone and social media addiction must be dealt with using a systemic approach in the directions of education, regulation, and mass commitment to digital safety. It is a matter of necessity to see digitally so that individuals, educators, policymakers, and technology firms must work in concert toward ensuring a healthier digital future in which technology enriches our lives without compromising our mental health and relationships.

REFERENCES

Albris, K., Fast, K., Karlsen, F., Kaun, A., Lomborg, S., & Syvertsen, T. (2024). The Digital Backlash and the Paradoxes of Disconnection.

Andreassen, C. S. (2015). Online social network site addiction: A comprehensive review. *Current Addiction Reports*, 2(2), 175–184. DOI: 10.1007/s40429-015-0056-9

Barr, R. (2019). Parenting in the digital age. In *Handbook of parenting* (pp. 380–409). Routledge. DOI: 10.4324/9780429401695-13

Blum-Ross, A., Kumpulainen, K., & Marsh, J. (2019). *Enhancing digital literacy and creativity*. Routledge. DOI: 10.4324/9780429243264

Carr, N. (2010). *The shallows: What the Internet is doing to our brains*. W. W. Norton & Company.

Erstad, O., Flewitt, R., Kümmerling-Meibauer, B., & Pereira, Í. S. P. (Eds.). (2020). *The Routledge handbook of digital literacies in early childhood*. Routledge.

Fardouly, J., Diedrichs, P. C., Vartanian, L. R., & Halliwell, E. (2015). Social comparisons on social media: The impact of Facebook on young women's body image concerns and mood. *Body Image*, 13, 38–45. DOI: 10.1016/j.bodyim.2014.12.002 PMID: 25615425

Green, L., Holloway, D., Stevenson, K., Leaver, T., & Haddon, L. (Eds.). (2021). *The Routledge companion to digital media and children*. Routledge.

Gupta, A., & Sharma, M. (2017). Social media and its impact with special reference to Indian teenagers: A review. *International Journal of Multidisciplinary Approach and Studies*, 4(3), 27–35.

Hollandsworth, R., Donovan, J., & Welch, M. (2017). Digital citizenship: You can't go home again. *TechTrends*, 61(6), 524–530. DOI: 10.1007/s11528-017-0190-4

Hollandsworth, R., Dowdy, L., & Donovan, J. (2011). Digital citizenship in K-12: It takes a village.

Kardefelt-Winther, D. (2017). How does the time children spend using digital technology impact their mental well-being, social relationships, and physical activity? An evidence-focused literature review. *Innocenti Discussion Paper*. UNICEF Office of Research - Innocenti.

Livingstone, S., Carr, J., & Byrne, J. (2015). One in three: Internet governance and children's rights.

McDaniel, B. T., & Radesky, J. S. (2018). Technoference: Parent distraction with technology and associations with child behavior problems. *Child Development*, 89(1), 100–109. DOI: 10.1111/cdev.12822 PMID: 28493400

Nassen, L. M., Vandebosch, H., Poels, K., & Karsay, K. (2023). Opt-out, abstain, unplug. A systematic review of the voluntary digital disconnection literature. *Telematics and Informatics*, 81, 101980. DOI: 10.1016/j.tele.2023.101980

Neupane, S., Ali, U. T., & Mathew, A. (2017). Text neck syndrome-systematic review. *Imperial Journal of Interdisciplinary Research*, 3(7), 141–148.

Newport, C. (2019). *Digital minimalism: Choosing a focused life in a noisy world.* Portfolio/Penguin.

Pariser, E. (2011). *The filter bubble: What the Internet is hiding from you.* Penguin Press.

Ribble, M. (2015). *Digital citizenship in schools: Nine elements all students should know*. International Society for Technology in Education.

Room, R., Rehm, J., Trotter, R. T., Paglia, A., & Üstün, T. B. (2001). Cross-cultural views on stigma, valuation, parity, and societal values towards disability. *Disability and Culture: Universalism and Diversity*, 77, 247–291.

Sagacious, S. A. S. (1950). 475 Place Names On Scroll In Freedom Crusade Campaign Being Conducted At College.

Sarkar, S. K., Podder, A., & Roy, P. (2023). An Analysis of the Privacy and Security Related Problem with Social Networks. ESP Journal of Engineering and Technology Advancements (ESP-JETA), 3(4), 37-43.

Turkle, S. (2015). *Reclaiming conversation: The power of talk in a digital age*. Penguin Press.

Twenge, J. M. (2017). iGen: Why today's super-connected kids are growing up less rebellious, more tolerant, less happy–and completely unprepared for adulthood–and what that means for the rest of us. Atria Books.

Twenge, J. M., & Campbell, W. K. (2018). Associations between screen time and lower psychological well-being among children and adolescents: Evidence from a population-based study. *Preventive Medicine Reports*, 12, 271–283. DOI: 10.1016/j.pmedr.2018.10.003 PMID: 30406005

Walker, M. (2017). *Why we sleep: Unlocking the power of sleep and dreams*. Scribner.

Yang, C. C., & Bradford Brown, B. (2016). Online self-presentation on Facebook and self development during the college transition. *Journal of Youth and Adolescence*, 45(2), 402–416. DOI: 10.1007/s10964-015-0385-y PMID: 26534776

Chapter 8
Clicks and Cravings:
The Psychology of Smartphone and Social Media Addiction

Sowmya D. S.
https://orcid.org/0009-0005-2408-432X
PES University, India

V. Anokha
https://orcid.org/0009-0008-9286-6819
PES University, India

L. Nithya
PES University, India

ABSTRACT

The chapter explores the rising phenomenon of smartphone and social media addiction, emphasizing its psychological, social, and cultural impacts. As smartphones and social media become integral to daily life, excessive use has raised concerns about mental health, including anxiety, depression, and social isolation. The chapter examines key concepts such as "phubbing," the neuroscientific basis of addiction, and diagnostic criteria, highlighting the roles of brain regions like the prefrontal cortex and reward mechanisms involving dopamine. Interventions such as cognitive-behavioral therapy (CBT), mindfulness practices, and digital detox programs are discussed, alongside the need for policy measures to promote digital well-being. Integrating these perspectives, this chapter aims to provide a comprehensive understanding of smartphone and social media addiction and its implications for individual and societal well-being. The chapter attempts to give a thorough grasp of smartphone and social media addiction and its effects on both individual and societal well-being by incorporating these viewpoints.

DOI: 10.4018/979-8-3693-8804-4.ch008

INTRODUCTION

Social media and smartphone technology have completely changed how people connect with one another, communicate, and obtain information. More than 85% of adults in developed countries already own a smartphone, and emerging markets are showing comparable trends (Pew Research Center, 2019). Social networking sites (SNS), which are already a necessary part of everyday life, are instantly accessible through these gadgets. Millions of people use social media sites like Facebook, Instagram, and TikTok regularly, and many of them spend several hours a day on them (Twenge, 2017).

Incorporating social media and cellphones into daily life has facilitated quicker and easier communication, but it has also resulted in greater time spent online. Concerns over excessive technology use and its possible effects on wellbeing have been raised by this trend (Kuss & Griffiths, 2017). The average daily screen time has increased dramatically, according to studies, and many smartphone users find it difficult to limit their use (Elhai et al., 2017).

Smartphone and Social Media Addiction

Billieux et al. (2015), compulsive usage behaviors and an unwillingness to limit time spent on the device despite negative effects are common signs of smartphone addiction. Like other non-substance addictions, such as internet addiction, it is categorized as a behavioral addiction. A related issue called social media addiction is characterized by excessive use of social networking sites, which results in emotional dependence and obsession with online interactions (Andreassen, 2015). Both forms of addiction have traits in common, including withdrawal symptoms (such as worry or irritability when unable to use the phone), tolerance (the need to increase usage to attain satisfaction), and an inability to control usage patterns (Kardefelt-Winther, 2017). In addition to the need for social engagement, these addictive behaviors are fueled by the psychological benefits of likes, comments, and the immediate satisfaction that comes from online interactions (Montag & Walla, 2016).

Psychological, Social, and Cultural Impacts

Smartphones and social media is significant because of its wide-ranging effects on social connections, individual mental health, and wider cultural norms. Problematic smartphone use has been linked to higher levels of stress, anxiety, and depression, especially among younger users, according to research (Elhai et al., 2017). Addiction to social media has been connected to loneliness, a poor assessment of oneself, and a decline in in-person social connections (Andreassen, 2015). Particularly for teenagers, the continual exposure to idealized depictions of life on social media platforms can result in social comparison, which has a detrimental effect on body image and self-esteem (Twenge, 2017).

Both the individual user and their interpersonal interactions are impacted by these addictions. One glaring illustration of how smartphone addiction can degrade the quality of interpersonal connections is the phenomenon known as "phubbing" (phone snubbing), in which people prefer their devices over in-person encounters (Roberts & David, 2016). It has been discovered that this conduct has a detrimental impact on romantic partners' relationship satisfaction, resulting in diminished emotional intimacy and feelings of neglect (Wang et al., 2017).

Culturally speaking, the pervasive use of social media and smartphones has changed communication norms by prioritizing online connectivity above face-to-face contact. People are more connected than ever before, yet they may also feel more socially isolated and lack meaningful interactions as a result of this change (Hertlein & Ancheta, 2014).

Behavioural Addiction

A pattern of behavior that involves compulsive participation in rewarding activities in spite of negative outcomes is known as behavioral addiction. In contrast to substance addiction, which is fueled by chemical substances like drugs or alcohol, behavioral addiction is fueled by excessive use of technology, gambling, or gaming (Grant et al., 2010). Similar to the mechanisms seen in substance use disorders, these actions trigger the brain's reward system, which results in a loop of engagement, reinforcement, and yearning (Robinson & Berridge, 2008).

The defining characteristics of behavioural addiction include:

- **Preoccupation**: Constant thoughts about the activity.
- **Loss of Control**: Difficulty in limiting the time spent on the behavior.
- **Tolerance**: Increasing engagement over time to achieve the same level of satisfaction.
- **Withdrawal**: Negative emotions or distress when unable to engage in the behavior.
- **Negative Consequences**: Continued behavior despite awareness of its harmful impact on daily life, relationships, or mental health (Griffiths, 2005).

A framework for comprehending how non-substance-related activities, such as using a smartphone or social media, might develop into an addiction is provided by this view of addiction.

Other Forms of Addiction

Particular forms of behavioral addiction that entail compulsive usage of mobile devices and social networking sites are smartphone and social media addiction. They have distinctive characteristics pertaining to technology use and online social interactions, even if they share many characteristics with other behavioral addictions like gambling or gaming disorder.

- **Smartphone addiction** is the overuse of mobile devices for a variety of purposes, such as accessing the internet, playing games, and downloading apps (Billieux et al., 2015). It is typified by an obsessive need to check the phone constantly, even when doing so is improper or dangerous (e.g., while driving). The need for immediate gratification—such as notifications, messages, or new content—often motivates this behavior (Elhai et al., 2017).
- **Social Media Addiction** according to Andreassen (2015), excessive use of social media platforms such as Facebook, Instagram, and TikTok is referred to as social media addiction. It is typified by an unwillingness to set time limits for using these platforms, which results in an obsession with social comparison, online interactions, and FOMO. A reliance on online approval and reinforcement via likes, comments, and shares is frequently the result of social media addiction (Kuss & Griffiths, 2017).

Smartphones and social media, in contrast to other types of addiction, is closely linked to contemporary cultural trends and communication standards. Because these platforms are social, they are especially addictive because they offer chances for self-presentation and social interaction, both of which might encourage obsessive use (Ryan et al., 2014). This sets them apart from other addictions where the activity itself serves as the main motivator instead of social interaction.

Theoretical Models (e.g., Biopsychosocial Model)

The biopsychosocial model is frequently employed to comprehend the complex nature of addiction to social media and smartphones. According to this paradigm, biological, psychological, and social elements interact to cause addiction (Engel, 1977). It offers a thorough framework for investigating the reasons why some people are more prone to addiction than others.

- **Biological factors** - These comprise neurobiological processes and genetic predispositions. According to research, addiction to social media and smartphones may be connected to alterations in the brain areas responsible for impulse control and reward processing (Hong et al., 2013). Just as drugs engage the brain's reward pathways, dopamine release in response to social rewards (likes or comments) can perpetuate the addictive behavior (Montag & Walla, 2016).

- **Psychological Factors** - Addiction is significantly influenced by psychological factors, including personality traits, stress, and emotional regulation. Because social media platforms offer a sense of belonging and self-worth, those who suffer from high levels of social anxiety, loneliness, or low self-esteem are more likely to get addicted to them (Wang et al., 2017). Compulsive behavior can be fueled by the satisfaction of positive social interactions on the internet, making it hard to stop (Ryan et al., 2014).
- **Social Factors** - Addiction to smartphones and social media is greatly influenced by the societal and cultural context. Compulsive usage of these platforms is exacerbated by the normalizing of constant connectivity and the pressure to maintain an online presence (Twenge, 2017). The fear of missing out (FOMO) and social norms around digital communication can make addictive behaviors worse (Wolniewicz et al., 2018).

Diagnostic Criteria

The diagnostic criteria for smartphone and social media addiction draw on the broader framework used for behavioural addictions. They include:

- **Tolerance** - The requirement to gradually increase smartphone or social media use in order to get the same degree of satisfaction. Spending more time online or continuously looking for fresh notifications and material are examples of actions that indicate this (Kardefelt-Winther, 2017).
- **Withdrawal** - Adverse emotional states brought on by not being able to access social media or smartphones, such as restlessness, impatience, or anxiety. When they are unable to check their phones for updates, for instance, some people may experience anxiety (Elhai et al., 2017).
- **Loss of Control** - Consistently failing attempts to limit or manage social media and smartphone use. This can show up as constantly checking phones, even when it's not suitable, or breaching self-imposed rules about limiting screen time (Billieux et al., 2015).
- **Preoccupation** - Constantly thinking about social media or cellphones, such as scheduling future uses or considering the online world while engaging in offline activities (Andreassen, 2015). This obsession may get in the way of job, study, or everyday tasks.

- **Persistent Use Despite Adverse Effects** - Using smartphones and social media continuously even when doing so causes issues including poor sleep, decreased productivity, or damaged relationships (Griffiths, 2005). Even when people are aware of the detrimental effects, they may not be able to stop.

Although they are tailored to the particulars of smartphone and social media use, these criteria are similar to those used to diagnose other behavioral addictions, such as internet gaming disorder (American Psychiatric Association, 2013). They draw attention to how difficult it is to identify and treat these new types of addiction in clinical settings.

Prevalence and Demographics

With significant variations in usage patterns among age groups, smartphone and social media use has almost become ubiquitous. More than 95% of persons between the ages of 18 and 29 and over 88% of those between the ages of 30 and 49 own a smartphone, according to a 2019 Pew Research Center survey. Even more common is smartphone ownership among teenagers; according to polls, 95% of American teenagers have access to a smartphone (Twenge, 2017).

Young folks utilize social media at a similar rate. Teenagers and young adults are increasingly using platforms like Instagram, TikTok, and Snapchat, with a considerable percentage of users spending several hours a day on them (Vannucci et al., 2017). For example, according to data from the Pew Research Center (2022), 67% of teenagers use TikTok and 72% use Instagram on a daily basis. More than 70% of adults between the ages of 18 and 49 routinely use Facebook, making it a dominant platform among adults (Pew Research Center, 2022).

The United States is not the only country experiencing an increase in screen time. With users spending an average of 2.5 hours a day on social media, social media usage has been increasing gradually on a global scale (We Are Social & Hootsuite, 2022). This increase in use is especially noticeable in nations like Brazil, Indonesia, and India where internet access is expanding quickly and social media penetration has become a necessary component of everyday communication (Kuss & Griffiths, 2017).

Analysis of Vulnerable Populations

Teenagers and young people are especially susceptible to addiction to social media and smartphones. Because they are in a crucial phase of social and identity development, this age group is particularly vulnerable to the social benefits that these platforms provide (Twenge, 2017). Young people are more prone to suffer from compulsive use and FOMO, which fuels their use of social media, according to research (Wolniewicz et al., 2018).

According to King et al. (2013), there has been an increase in "nomophobia" (no-mobile-phone fear) among teenagers, which is typified by worry when they are unable to use their cellphones. The urge to maintain relationships with peers and the desire for social validation are frequently linked to this anxiety (Elhai et al., 2017). The extent of teens' reliance on digital connectivity is demonstrated by studies showing that about 40% of them experience anxiety when they are unable to check their smartphones (Vannucci et al., 2017).

Young adults (ages 18 to 29) are also quite active on social media and frequently use cellphones for social media, work, and study, in addition to teenagers. This group is more susceptible to the stresses of social comparison and upholding an online persona, which can result in low self-esteem and more time spent on social media (Andreassen, 2015).

Lifestyle factors like flexible work or school schedules make it simpler for young adults to access and spend a lot of time on social media, which further exacerbates these vulnerabilities (Twenge, 2017). Because of this, they frequently have greater rates of problematic use than older adults, whose use is typically more controlled and restricted (Pew Research Center, 2019).

Factors Contributing to Addiction

People can become addicted to smartphones and social media due to a variety of personal characteristics, with personality factors and mental health issues being major contributors. According to research, characteristics such as impulsivity, neuroticism, and low self-esteem are indicators of excessive smartphone use (Billieux et al., 2015). For instance, people with high neuroticism scores may develop obsessive use of social media and cellphones as coping strategies for unpleasant feelings (Elhai et al., 2017).

Another important element that may contribute to social media addiction is social anxiety. Social media may appeal to those who are anxious in face-to-face situations because it provides a means of connecting without the stress of face-to-face contact (Wang et al., 2017). Nevertheless, this might lead to a vicious cycle since more social media use may further distance users from in-person social connections, intensifying loneliness (Kuss & Griffiths, 2017).

Another important factor that contributes to addiction is the idea of FOMO. FOMO is the widespread fear that one is missing out on fulfilling experiences that others may be having (Wolniewicz et al., 2018). According to Przybylski et al. (2013), it is especially common in younger people and causes compulsive behavior and a persistent need to keep up with others' activities by causing them to check their social media feeds frequently.

Because extroverted people may utilize social media to keep up a vast network of contacts and seek out social stimulation, personality factors like extraversion can also have an impact on smartphone use (Andreassen, 2015). On the other hand, introverted people might use digital communication because they believe it to be a safer way to contact with others, which is why they use these platforms (Ryan et al., 2014).

Cross-Cultural Perspectives

Cultural circumstances can have a substantial impact on the prevalence and consequences of smartphone and social media addiction. Social media is frequently used to preserve family and social group relationships in collectivist civilizations, such those in East Asia, which can affect usage patterns and the risk of addiction (Hong et al., 2013). For example, there are greater rates of internet and smartphone addiction among teenagers in South Korea and China, where digital communication is ingrained in daily life (Choi et al., 2015).

Conversely, social media use may be more motivated by self-expression and personal branding in individualistic societies such as Western Europe and the United States (Twenge, 2017). Users in these areas tend to concentrate on platforms like Instagram and YouTube that prioritize individual content creation, which might result in various addiction patterns (Kardefelt-Winther, 2017).

How addiction is viewed and treated can be influenced by cultural perspectives on technology use and mental health. Extended screen usage is more socially acceptable in some nations, particularly among youth, which may lead to a larger tolerance for compulsive use behaviors (Kuss & Griffiths, 2017). On the other hand, nations with robust public health programs, like Scandinavia, have seen steps to prevent excessive use and promote digital well-being (Montag & Walla, 2016).

Differences in the association between social anxiety and smartphone addiction have also been brought to light by cross-cultural study. For instance, research has shown that social media is used to prevent conflict and preserve social peace in societies with high levels of social conformity, like Japan. As a result, those who are socially apprehensive use it more frequently (Takahashi et al., 2020). On the other hand, social media can serve as a forum for self-expression and the pursuit of social support in more individualistic societies (Przybylski et al., 2013).

Psychological and Social Consequences

Psychological Effects - Excessive use of smartphones and social media is strongly associated with various psychological issues, including anxiety, depression, and stress.

Anxiety - According to research, having to constantly check social media for messages, updates, and notifications can make people feel more anxious (Elhai et al., 2017). This worry is frequently linked to a condition called FOMO, which is the fear of missing out on social experiences that other people may be having (Przybylski et al., 2013). This worry feeds a vicious cycle of social media platform dependence and constant checking activities.

Depression - Numerous research have discovered a connection between depressive symptoms and poor social media use. For example, studies show that extended exposure to social media's idealized depictions of other people's lives can result in low self-esteem and feelings of inadequacy, which can exacerbate depression (Twenge, 2017). According to a meta-analysis by Keles et al. (2020), teens who use social media more frequently are more likely to experience depression symptoms because of low self-esteem and unfavorable social comparisons.

Stress - The persistent demand for interaction and the pressure to maintain an online presence are frequently the causes of the stress connected to smartphone and social media addiction (Thomée et al., 2011). Being unable to access their phones causes stress for many users, which can result in restlessness and irritation. Digital weariness can also result from users feeling overburdened by the need to manage numerous social media accounts and reply to communications quickly (Elhai et al., 2017).

Social Effects - Smartphone and social media addiction can also have profound social consequences, affecting relationships and social interaction patterns.

Impaired Relationships - Constant smartphone use frequently interferes with in-person interactions, lowering the quality of friendships, romantic connections, and family ties. “Phubbing” (phone snubbing), a prominent phenomenon associated with this, is when people focus more on their phones than on those around them (Roberts & David, 2016). Phubbing has been found to have a detrimental impact on romantic partners' relationship happiness, resulting in diminished emotional intimacy and feelings of neglect (Roberts & David, 2016).

Social Isolation - Ironically, excessive use of social media and cellphones has been linked to higher levels of social isolation and loneliness, despite the fact that these tools are meant to improve social interactions (Kuss & Griffiths, 2017). For instance, Primack et al. (2017) discovered a correlation between young adults' perceived social isolation and their increased usage of social media. According to the study, even while users may have a large number of online contacts, the quality of these exchanges is frequently shallow and lacks the depth of in-person relationships.

Reduced Face-to-Face Interactions - As people become more dependent on digital communication, there has been a correlation between the rise in smartphone and social media addiction and a decrease in in-person encounters (Twenge, 2017). Opportunities for real, in-person socialization—which is essential for fostering strong bonds and improving social skills—have decreased as a result of this change. According to Twienge (2017), adolescents in particular are spending more time online and less time participating in activities like sports, clubs, and family get-togethers that promote in-person social relationships.

Real-World Examples

Case Study 1 - Adolescent Social Media Use and Depression

Researchers in the United States tracked a group of teenagers for two years in order to investigate how social media use affected their mental health (Vannucci et al., 2017). According to the study, teenagers who used social media for more than three hours a day had a greater chance of eventually experiencing depressed symptoms. When participants saw posts about events they were not a part of, they reported feeling excluded, which added to their emotions of loneliness and despair.

Case Study 2 - Impact of Phubbing on Relationships

An Australian study looked at how phubbing affected romantic relationships. According to Roberts and David (2016), researchers conducted interviews with couples in whom one partner regularly used their phone during meals or chats. Since their partner's smartphone use made them feel inconsequential, many of the "phubbed" partners expressed feeling devalued and less content with their relationship. This study emphasizes how an addiction to smartphones can harm close relationships by obstructing real communication.

Case Study 3 - Social Isolation in College Students

According to a UK college student poll, people who used social media more frequently also said they felt more isolated and less connected to others (Primack et al., 2017). Even while they were active on social media sites like Instagram and Snapchat, many students felt that their virtual connections did not transition into in-person relationships, which made them feel even more alone. The contradiction of feeling alone offline while socially connected online is exemplified by this case.

Impact on Family Dynamics and Friendships

Family Dynamics - Parent-child disputes about screen time may result from the widespread usage of cellphones in homes. According to Hertlein and Ancheta (2014), parents frequently voice concerns about their kids' excessive smartphone use, which can lead to disputes and strained relationships. Furthermore, excessive phone use by parents themselves can result in "technoference," which is the diversion of parental attention from children and has a detrimental effect on attachment and bonding between parents and children (McDaniel & Coyne, 2016).

Impact on Friendships - When people value their online relationships more than their face-to-face contacts, friendships may suffer. According to a study by Wang et al. (2017), teens who use social media frequently may find it difficult to have meaningful, in-person conversations with their friends. A lot of teenagers said they felt their peers were "always on their phones," which made their conversations less enjoyable. Teenagers should be especially concerned about this issue because in-person contacts are crucial for the development of empathy and social skills.

Parental Influence and Role Modeling - Children's behavior can be influenced by the smartphone habits of their parents. Children are more prone to imitate parents who use cellphones during family time, which can result in similar patterns of excessive use (McDaniel & Radesky, 2018). A culture of perpetual connectivity where family members engage with their gadgets more than with one another may be sustained by this intergenerational trend.

Interpersonal Relationships and Phubbing

Phubbing is a term that combines the words "phone" and "snubbing." Ignoring someone in favor of using a smartphone or other mobile device is what it means. People who prioritize their electronics over the people in their immediate vicinity frequently engage in this behavior in social settings. Phubbing, as defined by Roberts and David (2016), is the "interpersonal neglect" that happens when one partner spends more time on their smartphone than their partner, resulting in feelings of emotional detachment and exclusion. Phubbing can occur during meals, chats, or social events, among other situations. The increasing usage of cellphones, which provide continuous access to social media and messaging apps and frequently divert people from in-person encounters, has contributed to the rise in phubbing (Hale et al., 2017). Because of this, phubbing can have a negative effect on relationships by making the people being ignored feel neglected and resentful.

Effects of Phubbing

The impact of phubbing on interpersonal relationships is profound, affecting romantic partnerships, friendships, and family dynamics.

Romantic Relationships- It has been demonstrated that phoning reduces couples' contentment with their relationships. According to a study by Roberts and David (2016), people who were often phubbed by their spouses expressed more envy and insecurity as well as decreased relationship satisfaction. The stability of the relationship may be threatened by the increasing tension and communication breakdowns brought on by the emotional neglect connected to phubbing. When a significant other prefers to use their phone rather than actively participating in conversations or activities that are shared, for instance, couples may feel undervalued or irrelevant.

Friendships- Phubbing can drive a wedge between people in friendships, causing them to feel alone and alienated. Phubbing friends may unwittingly convey that their phone conversations are more significant than their face-to-face connections (Wang et al., 2017). Friends may become resentful of this behavior since the people who are ignored may feel ignored and undervalued. Frequent phubbing might eventually cause friendships to deteriorate because people may decide to avoid social events where they feel ignored.

Family Ties - Phubbing can cause a breakdown in communication and connection within the family by upsetting interactions. Families frequently get together to eat meals or do activities, however smartphones can divert focus from deep family connections (McDaniel & Radesky, 2018). Device-obsessed parents risk missing out on valuable time with their kids, which damages family bonds and impedes emotional connections. According to research, phubbing during shared activities makes family members feel less connected to one another, which can lead to a lack of communication and trust within the family (Hertlein & Ancheta, 2014).

Empirical Research on Phubbing and Social Interaction Quality

Roberts and David (2016) conducted a survey of couples and discovered a significant link between phubbing activities and a decline in relationship satisfaction. Because of their partner's obsession with their phones, participants expressed feelings of uneasiness and jealousy, indicating that phubbing damages emotional intimacy and trust. Pilling and Edney (2017) investigated the effect of phubbing on college students' peer connections in another study. According to the results, students who thought their peers were phubbing more often expressed less happiness with their friendships. Additionally, the study found that phubbing was associated with a higher likelihood of social disengagement, suggesting that phubbing can have a negative impact on social interaction. Roberts et al. (2020) conducted a thorough meta-analysis that examined numerous studies on phubbing and its effects in a variety of relationship types. According to the investigation, phubbing was consistently linked to detrimental relationship outcomes, such as worse communication, more conflict, and a lower level of relationship satisfaction overall. The findings highlighted how widespread phubbing is and how it can threaten the core tenets of interpersonal communication.

Strategies for Mitigating the Negative Impact of Phubbing

Communication and Awareness - It's critical to spread knowledge about the negative effects of phubbing. Families, friends, and couples should have candid conversations about smartphone use and how it affects their relationships. People can promote empathy and set limits on phone use during shared time by communicating their feelings about phubbing behaviors (Wang et al., 2017).

Establishing Limits - Phubbing can be lessened by setting aside particular periods for interactions without devices. To encourage everyone to participate fully in talks and activities without interruptions, families should, for example, establish a "no phone" rule during meals or designated family time (McDaniel & Radesky, 2018). In a similar vein, couples can decide to emphasize their relationship by putting their phones aside on date evenings.

Mindfulness Techniques- Promoting mindfulness techniques can assist people in becoming more socially present. People can lessen their urge to check their devices by engaging in mindfulness practices that increase their awareness of their environment and the people they are with. Methods like guided breathing exercises or mindfulness meditation can be helpful (Hertlein & Ancheta, 2014).

Social Media Detox - People can unplug from their gadgets and reestablish connections with their loved ones by taking regular digital detoxes. People can develop stronger relationships and appreciate the importance of face-to-face encounters by taking pauses from social media and smartphone use (King et al., 2013).

Modeling Healthy Behavior- Parents and other adults can set an example for kids and teenagers by using smartphones in a healthy way. Parents can urge their children to emulate their conduct by restricting their own gadget use in social situations and highlighting the value of in-person connections (McDaniel & Radesky, 2018).

Neuroscientific Perspectives

Numerous brain areas have been found to be crucial in the neuroscientific study of social media and smartphone addiction. The following areas are especially important:

Prefrontal Cortex (PFC) - Executive functioning, impulse control, and decision-making are all influenced by the PFC. According to studies, those who are addicted to smartphones and social media may show less activity in the PFC, which can impair self-control and increase impulsivity (Lemieux et al., 2019). Limiting usage is more difficult when users are absorbed in their devices because the PFC's capacity to control and suppress impulsive behaviors is weakened.

Nucleus Accumbens (NAc) - A vital part of the brain's reward system, the NAc is essential for motivation and reward processing. According to research, the pleasurable effects of using cellphones and social media are linked to dopamine release in the NAc, which reinforces the urge to repeat these behaviors (Montag et al., 2018). As people look for the rewarding sensations connected to social connections or receiving notifications, this reinforcement may result in obsessive use.

Amygdala - Processing emotions and creating emotional memories are functions of the amygdala. Addiction to social media has been associated with increased amygdala activity, especially in reaction to social feedback like likes and comments (Wang et al., 2018). Increased connection to social media sites might result from the emotional reactions elicited by interactions on these platforms, which can further reinforce addictive behaviors.

Insula - Self-awareness, emotional control, and interoceptive awareness are all influenced by the insula. According to research, people who use social media and smartphones frequently may have changed insula activity, which may impact their awareness of their emotional states and make it more difficult for them to understand how their device use affects their general well-being (Montag et al., 2018).

Role of Dopamine and Reward Mechanisms

A neurotransmitter that affects motivation, pleasure, and reinforcement, dopamine is essential to the brain's reward system. Notable is the connection between dopamine and addictive behaviors, such as addiction to social media and smartphones:

Dopaminergic Pathways - Social media and smartphone use can cause dopamine to be released in the brain, especially in regions like the ventral tegmental area (VTA) and the NAc. The expectation of incentives, such likes on a post or notifications from social media platforms, is frequently linked to this release (Robinson & Berridge, 2008). People will seek out these stimuli repeatedly because of the pleasant quality of these interactions, which reinforces the behavior.

Incentive Sensitization Theory - This idea states that stimuli linked to positive events cause the brain's reward system to become more sensitive (Robinson & Berridge, 2008). People's brains may start to seek these interactions as they use smartphones and social media more frequently, which could result in more obsessive usage. Users may need more involvement to reach the same degree of enjoyment as a result of this sensitization, which could lead to an escalating loop of behavior.

Dopamine and FOMO - The release of dopamine is intimately related to the idea of FOMO. The expectation of possible social rewards can cause dopamine to be released when people feel as though they could be missing out on social encounters, which heightens the want to check their devices (Przybylski et al., 2013). Because people feel pressured to always be connected, this cycle may lead to unhealthy usage practices.

Neuroimaging Studies

Functional Magnetic Resonance Imaging (fMRI) - According to fMRI research, those who are heavily addicted to smartphones and social media display different brain activation patterns in response to social cues or stimuli related to smartphones. When examining social media posts, for instance, people with social media addiction showed higher activity in the NAc and amygdala than people without addiction, according to a 2018 study by Montag et al. The strong emotional and reward-related reactions brought on by social media interactions are reflected in this increased activation.

Electroencephalography (EEG) - The neurological correlates of smartphone addiction have been investigated through EEG investigations. According to research, people who use smartphones problematically exhibit variations in their brain wave patterns, especially in the alpha and beta frequency bands, which are linked to cognitive processing and attention (Lemieux et al., 2019). These variations might be the result of deficiencies in cognitive control and attention regulation, two skills essential for controlling smartphone use.

Longitudinal Studies - Excessive use of smartphones and social media can cause structural changes in the brain, according to longitudinal neuroimaging research. For instance, Hong et al. (2013) showed that teens who were addicted to the internet had a gradual reduction in gray matter volume in the insula and prefrontal cortex. These modifications could lead to the emergence of obsessive behaviors and a loss of self-control.

Implications

Compulsive Behaviors- Researchers can gain a better understanding of the neurological underpinnings of compulsive behaviors in a variety of circumstances by pinpointing the brain areas and mechanisms implicated in smartphone and social media addiction. For those battling these addictions and associated disorders, this information helps guide treatment strategies (Montag & Walla, 2016).

Targeted Interventions - Developing focused therapies to lessen problematic smartphone use can result from an understanding of the neurological correlates of addiction. For instance, the compulsive character of smartphone addiction may be best addressed by cognitive-behavioral therapies that emphasize improving self-regulation and impulse control (King et al., 2013).

Public Health Implications - The findings from neuroscientific research can help guide public health initiatives that support digital well-being as the use of smartphones and social media continues to increase. Public health campaigns can urge people to adopt healthy usage patterns and support a balanced attitude to technology by drawing attention to the neurobiological impacts of excessive use.

Future Research Directions - The neuroimaging studies' results emphasize the need for more investigation into the long-term impacts of social media and smartphone addiction on the structure and function of the brain. Longitudinal studies that look at how behavioral outcomes and brain changes interact can help explain the causes behind addiction and guide preventative measures.

Interventions and Treatment

Cognitive-Behavioral Therapy (CBT) - The goal of cognitive-behavioral therapy (CBT), a popular psychological intervention, is to recognize and change harmful thought patterns and behaviors. It works especially well for treating addictions to social media and smartphones, among other types of addiction.

Core Principles of CBT: The foundation of cognitive behavioral therapy is the idea that feelings, thoughts, and behaviors are all related. People can alter their behavior and enhance their emotional health by addressing problematic ideas and beliefs (Beck, 2011). CBT assists people in identifying the cognitive distortions that contribute to excessive gadget use, such as the idea that they must continuously check their alerts in order to stay connected, when it comes to smartphone and social media addiction.

Application in Treating Smartphone Addiction - CBT for smartphone addiction typically involves several key components:

Cognitive Restructuring - Clients learn to identify and challenge irrational beliefs related to their smartphone use, such as the fear of missing out (FOMO) or the need for immediate social validation.

- o Behavioral Interventions - Clients are encouraged to develop healthier habits around smartphone use, such as setting limits on screen time, using apps that monitor usage, or engaging in alternative activities that do not involve devices.
- o Skills Training - CBT often includes training in coping skills to manage anxiety and stress without relying on smartphones or social media as a coping mechanism (King et al., 2013).

Evidence of Effectiveness - CBT can considerably lessen the symptoms of smartphone addiction, according to studies. In comparison to a control group, participants in a CBT program reported less smartphone use and better psychological well-being, according to a randomized controlled experiment by Alavi et al. (2019). These results lend credence to the effectiveness of cognitive behavioral therapy in assisting people in regaining control over their smartphone use.

Mindfulness-Based Interventions and Digital Detox Programs - Mindfulness-based interventions and digital detox programs have emerged as effective strategies for managing smartphone and social media addiction.

Mindfulness-Based Interventions - According to Kabat-Zinn (2003), mindfulness is the practice of developing a nonjudgmental awareness of the present moment, which can aid people in becoming more emotionally resilient and self-reliant. It has been demonstrated that mindfulness-based therapies, like Mindfulness-Based Stress Reduction (MBSR) and Mindfulness-Based Cognitive Therapy (MBCT), can lessen the anxiety and depressive symptoms linked to excessive smartphone use (Goyal et al., 2014).

Techniques Used in Mindfulness Interventions

- o Meditation - Guided meditation practices help individuals focus on their breath and observe their thoughts and feelings without judgment, reducing the urge to engage with their smartphones.
- o Body Scanning - Participants learn to connect with their bodies and become more aware of physical sensations, which can promote relaxation and reduce the urge to check devices (Keng et al., 2011).
- o Mindful Awareness - Individuals are encouraged to practice being fully present in their interactions and activities, enhancing their awareness of the impact of smartphone use on their well-being.

Digital Detox Programs - Programs for digital detoxification encourage people to disconnect from their gadgets in order to re-establish a connection with their environment and with themselves. These programs, which encourage activities that create deep connections with people and the environment, frequently include planned times of total device-free time (Przybylski et al., 2013).

Evidence of Effectiveness - Studies have demonstrated the efficacy of mindfulness-based therapies in mitigating smartphone addiction. According to a study by Firth et al. (2017), mindfulness training participants reported better mental health outcomes and less problematic smartphone use. Programs for digital detoxification have also showed potential in assisting people in lessening their dependence on electronics and improving their general health (Miller, 2017).

Evaluation of the Effectiveness of Interventions

Evaluating the effectiveness of interventions for smartphone and social media addiction is crucial for understanding their impact and informing future treatment approaches.

Quantitative Assessments - Standardized assessment instruments are used in many research to gauge how well interventions work. For instance, the Problematic Use of Mobile Phones Questionnaire (PUMP) and the Smartphone Addiction Scale (SAS) are frequently used to measure addiction levels both before and after treatment (Kwon et al., 2013). Significant scores decrease after CBT, mindfulness, and digital detox therapies, according to statistical studies.

Qualitative Evaluations- Participants' experiences with interventions are revealed through qualitative research. Focus groups and interviews can provide insight into how people interpret behavioral, emotional, and interpersonal changes following treatment. Participants in a mindfulness program, for instance, might report feeling more satisfied with their offline interactions and more conscious of their smartphone usage habits (Firth et al., 2017).

Long-term Outcomes - Determining the long-term efficacy of interventions requires longitudinal research that looks at how sustainable their benefits are. Studies show that people who participate in mindfulness and cognitive behavioral therapy (CBT) frequently sustain gains in their mental health and smartphone use over time (Alavi et al., 2019). To evaluate the sustainability of these results and pinpoint potential relapse triggers, more investigation is necessary.

Role of Policy Measures and Public Health Campaigns

Addressing smartphone and social media addiction requires a multifaceted approach that includes policy measures and public health campaigns.

Policy Measures - Governments and educational institutions can implement policies to promote responsible smartphone use and raise awareness of its potential risks. For example

- Regulating Device Use in Schools - Implementing policies that limit smartphone use during school hours can reduce distractions and promote face-to-face interactions among students. Schools can encourage digital literacy programs that educate students about the healthy use of technology (Hale et al., 2017).
- Creating Public Awareness Campaigns - Governments can launch campaigns to educate the public about the risks of excessive smartphone use, similar to campaigns addressing smoking or unhealthy eating. These campaigns can provide resources and support for individuals seeking to reduce their screen time.

Public Health Campaigns - Public health organizations can promote initiatives that encourage mindful technology use and foster healthy habits. Campaigns might include:

- Promoting Digital Well-Being - Initiatives aimed at promoting balance in technology use can empower individuals to establish healthier boundaries with their devices. This could involve tips for reducing screen time, engaging in outdoor activities, or fostering social connections without technology (Miller, 2017).
- Supporting Mental Health Services - Providing access to mental health services for individuals struggling with smartphone addiction is crucial. Public health campaigns can highlight the availability of therapy options, support groups, and community resources for those seeking help.

Collaboration with Technology Companies - Policymakers, mental health specialists, and tech corporations working together can result in the creation of features and tools that encourage better usage habits. Manufacturers of smartphones, for instance, should include tools that assist consumers in tracking their screen time and establishing usage caps (Duffy, 2019). Stakeholders may foster a positive atmosphere that promotes appropriate smartphone use by cooperating.

Implications for Future Research

Longitudinal Studies- Understanding the long-term impacts of social media and smartphone addiction on mental health and interpersonal relationships requires longitudinal research. By repeatedly observing the same people over an extended period of time, these studies enable researchers to monitor changes in behavior, cognition, and emotional health.

Capturing Developmental Trajectories - Longitudinal studies can shed light on the evolution of smartphone and social media addiction over time, especially throughout crucial developmental stages like adolescence and early adulthood. According to Twienge (2017), research might look into how early smartphone use patterns affect social skills, interpersonal interactions, and mental health effects later on.

Assessing Long-term Effects - Researchers can have a better understanding of the long-term effects of excessive smartphone use by tracking individuals over a number of years. This involves looking into the possibility of social isolation, sadness, and chronic anxiety as well as how these impacts might vary by age and demographic (Keles et al., 2020).

Identifying Relapse Patterns - Relapse patterns and the factors that lead to recovery or recurrence of addictive behaviors can be clarified by longitudinal investigations. Interventions intended to support people in sustaining longer-term, healthier smartphone habits can benefit from an understanding of these dynamics (Alavi et al., 2019).

Need for Cross-Cultural Research

As smartphone and social media use transcends cultural boundaries, cross-cultural research is critical for understanding how different cultural contexts shape patterns of addiction and their effects on mental health and social behavior.

Cultural Influences on Technology Use - People's interactions with smartphones and social media can be influenced by cultural differences in views about technology. For instance, collectivist cultures may place more value on community and family involvement than on individualistic displays, which could result in distinct addiction tendencies (Montag & Walla, 2016). How cultural norms and values affect smartphone use and the danger of addiction can be determined with the use of cross-cultural research.

Vulnerability and Resilience - Cultural characteristics that either increase or decrease the likelihood of addiction can be found through research conducted in a variety of cultural contexts. For instance, in certain cultures, community involvement and social support networks may operate as protective factors, lowering the risk of addiction (Kuss & Griffiths, 2017). Culturally sensitive intervention strategies can be informed by the identification of these factors.

Generalizability of Findings - Researching smartphone addiction in diverse cultural contexts can improve the findings' generalizability. To enable more thorough conclusions and suggestions, it is essential to determine whether the psychological and social effects shown in one culture are applicable to others (Twenge, 2017).

Potential Protective Factors and Resilience Strategies

Identifying protective factors and resilience strategies can help mitigate the negative effects of smartphone and social media addiction. Research into these areas can lead to more effective prevention and intervention programs.

Social Support - It has been demonstrated that social support can mitigate the adverse impacts of technology use. Strategies that encourage healthy smartphone behaviors may benefit from an understanding of how robust social networks can lessen feelings of loneliness and offer emotional support (Wang et al., 2018).

Digital Literacy and Education - Improving people's digital literacy, especially among teenagers, could provide them the tools they need to use social media more carefully. Research can investigate educational programs that offer self-regulation techniques and inform users about the dangers of excessive smartphone use (Hale et al., 2017).

Mindfulness and Coping Strategies - A deeper comprehension of how people might safeguard themselves against addiction can result from research into mindfulness techniques and other coping mechanisms that foster resilience in the face of stressors associated with technology. Positive results may emerge from studies that concentrate on incorporating mindfulness practices into therapeutic and educational contexts (Firth et al., 2017).

Recommendations for Future Studies

Integrate Multiple Disciplines - Future studies ought to take an interdisciplinary approach, combining viewpoints from public health, psychology, neuroscience, and sociology. This can help develop comprehensive intervention techniques and offer a more comprehensive understanding of the elements impacting smartphone addiction (Montag et al., 2018).

Explore Technological Influences - Given how quickly technology is developing, studies should look at how user behavior is affected by new features and design elements in social media platforms and cellphones. Ethical design methods that put user well-being first can be informed by knowledge of how persuasive technology promotes addictive behaviors (Duffy, 2019).

Long-term Effectiveness of Interventions - The long-term efficacy of many strategies meant to lessen smartphone addiction should be the subject of more research. Practitioners and policymakers can gain important insights by assessing the long-term effects on mental health and the sustainability of behavioral changes (King et al., 2013).

Underrepresented Populations - Diverse populations, such as individuals from various age groups, ethnicities, and socioeconomic origins, should be the focus of future research. This can lead to more focused treatments by identifying particular strengths and vulnerabilities within different groups (Keles et al., 2020).

CONCLUSION

Social media and cellphones have revolutionized communication, but they have also brought up new problems, such as addiction. The intricacies of smartphone and social media addiction have been covered in this chapter, ranging from its social repercussions, like strained relationships and social isolation, to its psychological affects, like anxiety and despair. The importance of dopamine and reward systems in reinforcing behaviors is highlighted through an examination of the neuroscientific underpinnings of addiction. While public health campaigns and legislative initiatives can promote a healthy digital lifestyle, effective therapies such as cognitive behavioral therapy, mindfulness-based techniques, and digital detox programs offer promising solutions for controlling addiction. Research is still lacking, though, especially in the areas of cross-cultural variations in addiction tendencies and the long-term impacts of smartphone use. Future studies should focus on these areas to provide more tailored and effective solutions. Ultimately, fostering a deeper understanding of smartphone addiction can help individuals and society navigate the digital age with greater awareness and well-being.

REFERENCES

Alavi, N., Sadeghi, S., & Jafarian, R. (2019). The Effectiveness of Cognitive Behavioral Therapy on Smartphone Addiction in University Students. *Journal of Health Psychology*, 24(11), 1488–1498.

American Psychiatric Association. (2013). *Diagnostic and Statistical Manual of Mental Disorders* (5th ed.). American Psychiatric Publishing.

Andreassen, C. S. (2015). *Online social network site addiction: A comprehensive review. Current addiction reports, 2(2), 175-184.*

Billieux, J., Maurage, P., Lopez-Fernandez, O., Kuss, D. J., & Griffiths, M. D. (2015). Can disordered mobile phone use be considered a behavioral addiction? An update on current evidence and a comprehensive model for future research. *Current Addiction Reports*, 2(2), 156–162. DOI: 10.1007/s40429-015-0054-y

Choi, J. S., Park, S. M., Roh, M. S., Lee, J. Y., Park, C. B., Hwang, J. Y., & Lee, H. W. (2015). Dysfunctional Information Processing in Adolescents with Internet Addiction. *Psychiatry Research: Neuroimaging*, 224(3), 184–192.

Duffy, B. (2019). Tech Addiction: What Can Parents and Schools Do? *Child Trends*. Retrieved from https://www.childtrends.org/tech-addiction-what-can-parents-and-schools-do

Elhai, J. D., Dvorak, R. D., Levine, J. C., & Hall, B. J. (2017). Problematic smartphone use: A conceptual overview and systematic review of relations with anxiety and depression psychopathology. *Journal of Affective Disorders*, 207, 251–259. DOI: 10.1016/j.jad.2016.08.030 PMID: 27736736

Engel, G. L. (1977). The need for a new medical model: A challenge for biomedicine. *Science*, 196(4286), 129–136. DOI: 10.1126/science.847460 PMID: 847460

Firth, J., Torous, J., & Wykes, T. (2017). The Digital Mindfulness Project: A Randomized Controlled Trial of Mindfulness Training for Young People with Smartphone Addiction. *Psychological Medicine*, 47(1), 40–48.

Goyal, M., Singh, S., Sibinga, E. M., Gould, N. F., Rowland-Seymour, A., Sharma, R., Berger, Z., Sleicher, D., Maron, D. D., Shihab, H. M., Ranasinghe, P. D., Linn, S., Saha, S., Bass, E. B., & Haythornthwaite, J. A. (2014). Meditation programs for psychological stress and well-being: A systematic review and meta-analysis. *JAMA Internal Medicine*, 174(3), 357–368. DOI: 10.1001/jamainternmed.2013.13018 PMID: 24395196

Griffiths, M. (2005). A 'components' model of addiction within a biopsychosocial framework. *Journal of Substance Use*, 10(4), 191–197. DOI: 10.1080/14659890500114359

Hale, J. L., & Pigliuca, R. (2017). Phubbing and Relationship Satisfaction: An Exploratory Study. *International Journal of Human-Computer Interaction*, 33(11), 911–918.

Hale, L., & Guan, S. (2015). Screen time and sleep among school-aged children and adolescents: A systematic literature review. *Sleep Medicine Reviews*, 21, 50–58. DOI: 10.1016/j.smrv.2014.07.007 PMID: 25193149

Hertlein, K. M., & Ancheta, K. (2014). Advantages and disadvantages of technology in relationships: Findings from an open-ended survey. *The Qualitative Report*, 19(11), 1–11. DOI: 10.46743/2160-3715/2014.1260

Hong, S. B., Zalesky, A., Cocchi, L., Fornito, A., Choi, E. J., Kim, H. H., Suh, J.-E., Kim, C.-D., Kim, J.-W., & Yi, S. H. (2013). Decreased functional brain connectivity in adolescents with internet addiction. *PLoS One*, 8(2), e57831. DOI: 10.1371/journal.pone.0057831 PMID: 23451272

Kardefelt-Winther, D. (2017). Conceptualizing Internet Use Disorders: A Critical Perspective on Diagnostic Criteria and Causal Assumptions. *Current Addiction Reports*, 4(2), 229–235.

Keles, B., McCrae, N., & Grealish, A. (2020). A systematic review: The influence of social media on depression, anxiety and psychological distress in adolescents. *International Journal of Adolescence and Youth*, 25(1), 79–93. DOI: 10.1080/02673843.2019.1590851

Keng, S. L., Smoski, M. J., & Robins, C. J. (2011). Effects of mindfulness on psychological health: A review of empirical studies. *Clinical Psychology Review*, 31(6), 1041–1056. DOI: 10.1016/j.cpr.2011.04.006 PMID: 21802619

King, A. L. S., Valenca, A. M., Silva, A. C. O., Baczynski, T., Carvalho, M. R., & Nardi, A. E. (2013). Nomophobia: Dependency on virtual environments or social phobia? *Computers in Human Behavior*, 29(1), 140–144. DOI: 10.1016/j.chb.2012.07.025

Kuss, D. J., & Griffiths, M. D. (2017). Social networking sites and addiction: Ten lessons learned. *International Journal of Environmental Research and Public Health*, 14(3), 311. DOI: 10.3390/ijerph14030311 PMID: 28304359

Lemieux, A. J., & Wartenberg, D. (2019). The Brain on Smartphone Addiction: A Study of Brain Activity. *Computers in Human Behavior*, 101, 189–197.

McDaniel, B. T., & Coyne, S. M. (2016). “Technoference”: The interference of technology in couple relationships and implications for women’s personal and relational well-being. *Psychology of Popular Media Culture*, 5(1), 85–98. DOI: 10.1037/ppm0000065

McDaniel, B. T., & Radesky, J. S. (2018). Technoference: Parent distraction with technology and associations with child behavior problems. *Child Development*, 89(1), 100–109. DOI: 10.1111/cdev.12822 PMID: 28493400

Miller, A. (2017). The Digital Detox: A New Approach to Smartphone Addiction. *Psychology Today*. Retrieved from https://www.psychologytoday.com/us/blog/tech-support/201708/the-digital-detox

Montag, C., & Walla, P. (2016). Carpe diem instead of losing your social mind: Beyond digital addiction and why we all suffer from digital overuse. *Cogent Psychology*, 3(1), 1157281. DOI: 10.1080/23311908.2016.1157281

Montag, C., Zhao, Z., Sindermann, C., Xu, L., Fu, M., Li, J., Zheng, X., Li, K., Kendrick, K. M., Dai, J., & Becker, B. (2018). Internet communication disorder and the structure of the human brain: Initial insights on WeChat addiction. *Scientific Reports*, 8(1), 2155. DOI: 10.1038/s41598-018-19904-y PMID: 29391461

Pew Research Center. (2019). Mobile Fact Sheet. Retrieved from https://www.pewresearch.org/internet/fact-sheet/mobile/

Pew Research Center. (2022). Teens, Social Media, and Technology. Retrieved from https://www.pewresearch.org/internet/2022/teens-social-media-and-technology/

Pilling, S., & Edney, J. (2017). Phubbing and Its Effect on Social Interaction. *Computers in Human Behavior*, 70, 146–152.

Primack, B. A., Shensa, A., Sidani, J. E., Whaite, E. O., Lin, L., Rosen, D., Colditz, J. B., Radovic, A., & Miller, E. (2017). Social media use and perceived social isolation among young adults in the US. *American Journal of Preventive Medicine*, 53(1), 1–8. DOI: 10.1016/j.amepre.2017.01.010 PMID: 28279545

Przybylski, A. K., Murayama, K., DeHaan, C. R., & Gladwell, V. (2013). Motivational, emotional, and behavioral correlates of fear of missing out. *Computers in Human Behavior*, 29(4), 1841–1848. DOI: 10.1016/j.chb.2013.02.014

Roberts, J. A., & David, M. E. (2016). My life has become a major distraction from my cell phone: Partner phubbing and relationship satisfaction among romantic partners. *Computers in Human Behavior*, 54, 134–141. DOI: 10.1016/j.chb.2015.07.058

Roberts, J. A., & David, M. E. (2020). The Impact of Phubbing on Relationships: A Meta-Analytic Review. *Computers in Human Behavior*, 107, 106324.

Robinson, T. E., & Berridge, K. C. (2008). The incentive sensitization theory of addiction: Some current issues. *Philosophical Transactions of the Royal Society of London. Series B, Biological Sciences*, 363(1507), 3137–3146. DOI: 10.1098/rstb.2008.0093 PMID: 18640920

Ryan, T., Chester, A., Reece, J., & Xenos, S. (2014). The uses and abuses of Facebook: A review of Facebook addiction. *Journal of Behavioral Addictions*, 3(3), 133–148. DOI: 10.1556/JBA.3.2014.016 PMID: 25317337

Takahashi, Y., Shinohara, R., & Ikeda, M. (2020). Cultural Influences on the Relationship between Social Anxiety and SNS Usage in Japan. *Journal of Cross-Cultural Psychology*, 51(1), 56–68.

Thomée, S., Härenstam, A., & Hagberg, M. (2011). Mobile phone use and stress, sleep disturbances, and symptoms of depression among young adults-a prospective cohort study. *BMC Public Health*, 11(1), 1–11. DOI: 10.1186/1471-2458-11-66 PMID: 21281471

Twenge, J. M. (2017). *iGen: Why today's super-connected kids are growing up less rebellious, more tolerant, less happy and completely unprepared for adulthood and what that means for the rest of us*. Simon and Schuster.

Vannucci, A., Flannery, K. M., & Ohannessian, C. M. (2017). Social media use and anxiety in emerging adults. *Journal of Affective Disorders*, 207, 163–166. DOI: 10.1016/j.jad.2016.08.040 PMID: 27723539

Wang, H., Hu, J., & Li, Q. (2018). The Neural Correlates of the Relationship Between Social Media Addiction and Emotional Intelligence. *Computers in Human Behavior*, 81, 64–71.

Wang, P., Xie, X., Wang, X., Zhao, F., Chu, X., & Lei, L. (2017). The Need to Belong and Adolescent Facebook Use: The Mediating Role of Loneliness and Moderating Role of Gender. *Computers in Human Behavior*, 69, 136–141.

Wolniewicz, C. A., Tiamiyu, M. F., Weeks, J. W., & Elhai, J. D. (2018). Problematic Smartphone Use and Relations with Negative Affect, Fear of Missing Out, and Fear of Negative and Positive Evaluation. *Psychiatry Research*, 262, 618–623. DOI: 10.1016/j.psychres.2017.09.058 PMID: 28982630

Chapter 9
The Influence of Personality Traits on Smartphone Addiction, Phubbing, and Mental Well-Being

G. Kaviya
PES University, India

S. Likitha
https://orcid.org/0009-0002-2970-6042
PES University, India

ABSTRACT

This chapter delves into the intricate relationship between phubbing, smartphone addiction, and social media use, emphasizing how personality traits mediate their impact on psychological well-being. Phubbing, a blend of "phone" and "snubbing," involves ignoring others in favor of mobile phone engagement and has been associated with feelings of loneliness, depression, and social exclusion. Additionally, the chapter examines how the big five personality traits (extraversion, agreeableness, conscientiousness, neuroticism, and openness) influence smartphone addiction and phubbing behaviors. Individuals with high levels of fear of missing out (FoMO) tend to display compulsive phone use, reinforcing these negative social behaviors. The chapter concludes by underscoring the psychological consequences of these behaviors, including reduced life satisfaction and heightened stress.

DOI: 10.4018/979-8-3693-8804-4.ch009

INTRODUCTION

The term "phubbing" combines "phone" and "snubbing," and was coined during a campaign by the Macquarie Dictionary, led by a group of lexicographers, poets, and authors (Peplau, L. A., 1982; Ivanova, A., et al., 2020). It describes the action of ignoring someone in a social setting by prioritizing a mobile phone over engaging with the person present (Guazzini, A., et al., 2019). Phubbing is particularly noticeable when an individual directs their attention to their phone while conversing with someone, despite the phone's content being unrelated to the discussion. Research has revealed a positive correlation between phubbing and mobile phone addiction (Chotpitayasunondh, V., & Douglas, K. M., 2016; Garcia, M. A.,et al., 2024), with many individuals using their phones as a coping mechanism for feelings of loneliness, anxiety, and worry—especially when separated from their devices (Karadağ, E., et al., 2015).

Paradoxically, phubbing intensifies the very issues it seeks to address; the use of smartphones contributes to feelings of exclusion from social interactions. Those who experience being phubbed often feel socially isolated, prompting them to seek attention and validation on social media as a means of alleviating these feelings (Ivanova, A., et al., 2020). Research indicates that phubbing is positively correlated with loneliness (Zhan, S., et al.,2022), which is characterized as a prolonged and negatively perceived form of social exclusion (Peplau, L. A., 1982).

PSYCHOLOGICAL IMPACT OF SOCIAL MEDIA ADDICTION

Social Media and Phubbing

The excessive use of social networking sites can be considered a form of Internet addiction, which is a broad concept encompassing various types of online content. To gain a better understanding of behavioral addiction related to media use, it is important to differentiate between addictions to specific types of Internet content, such as online gambling, online sex, or social networking sites (SNSs), rather than analyzing addiction to the Internet as a whole (Andreassen, C. S., et al., 2012). With the growing number of users and the increasing time spent on platforms like Facebook, the issue of social media addiction is becoming more relevant and warrants deeper investigation.

In the literature, terms like "Facebook intrusion" and "Facebook addiction" are used interchangeably, with the former emphasizing the impact on interpersonal relationships. Facebook intrusion refers to excessive engagement with the platform, disrupting daily activities and relationships. It is characterized by withdrawal symptoms, relapse and reinstatement patterns, and feelings of euphoria (Elphinston, R. A., & Noller, P., 2011). Individuals deeply involved with Facebook experience distress when unable to stop using it, have difficulty reducing their use, and feel a strong connection with other Facebook users.

Research indicates that Facebook addiction is linked to various psychological variables, including subjective vitality, happiness, and dissatisfaction in relationships. Moreover, Internet addiction often coexists with other disorders such as depression, loneliness, sexual dysfunction, and various forms of addiction (Bozoglan, B., et al., 2013). However, there remains no consensus on whether depression is a cause or a consequence of Internet addiction. Factors such as stress and negative self-comparison are associated with depressive symptoms. Individuals with low self-esteem, fear of rejection, diminished motivation, and a heightened need for social acceptance are more prone to dysfunctional Internet usage (Young, K. S., & Rogers, R. C., 1998; Błachnio, A., et al., 2015; Alenezi, A., et al.,2023). Additionally, severe depression, anxiety, and insomnia have been identified as predictors of Facebook addiction in certain populations.

While some studies indicate a positive correlation between having a Facebook account and a lower level of depression, other research has reported no significant relationship between depression and social networking (Błachnio, A., et al., 2015). Excessive use of social media platforms can lead to problematic behaviors in some users, including obsessive-compulsive tendencies and uncontrolled usage. Research has identified addictive behaviors and social media addiction as key predictors of such patterns (Franchina et al., 2018; Balta et al., 2020). Additionally, the fear of missing out has emerged as a significant predictor of excessive social media use and phubbing behavior, both of which can adversely affect interpersonal relationships. These findings provide valuable insights into the psychological factors associated with social media addiction and phubbing (Chotpitayasunondh & Douglas, 2018).

In recent years, the surge in smartphone usage has prompted researchers to explore the factors contributing to phubbing, a behavior characterized by ignoring someone in a social setting in favor of focusing on a smartphone (McCann Paris, 2014). Research indicates that several factors can lead to phubbing. Notably, studies have identified links between smartphone addiction, texting addiction, social media addiction, Internet addiction, and, to a lesser extent, game addiction (Karadağ, E., et al., 2015; San-Martín, S., & Jiménez, N. 2023). Furthermore, other research suggests that Internet addiction, fear of missing out (FoMO), and a lack of self-control can contribute to smartphone addiction, which is subsequently associated with a higher likelihood of phubbing (Al-Saggaf, Y., et al., 2019; Chotpitayasunondh, V., & Douglas, K. M., 2016).

ROLE OF FoMO IN SOCIAL MEDIA ADDICTION

The fear of missing out (FoMO) is a prevalent emotion marked by the anxiety that others may be enjoying fulfilling experiences while one is absent, as well as the urge to remain constantly updated on the activities of others. FoMO is frequently linked to excessive smartphone use, which can result in behaviors such as "phubbing," where individuals snub those around them in favor of their devices (Chi et al., 2022). Recent research has shown that individuals with high levels of FoMO often exhibit excessive smartphone usage, engaging in phubbing as they strive to meet their need for online connectivity (Balta et al., 2020). Additionally, studies indicate that some individuals are more susceptible to experiencing FoMO than others.

Tandon et al. (2021) conducted a meta-analysis of 58 empirical studies on the Fear of Missing Out (FoMO). They recommended that future research should further investigate additional potential factors contributing to FoMO, particularly suggesting a focus on personality traits. Similarly, Reer et al. (2019) argued that individual psychological traits influence the development of FoMO. They highlighted the lack of empirical studies examining the mediating effects of FoMO and urged scholars to explore psychological factors, including the mediating influences of reasons for selecting specific social media platforms and the emotions associated with their use.

The phenomenon known as FoMO, or "fear of missing out," can be understood as a challenge stemming from an abundance of choices. Individuals often grapple with the decision of whether to engage with social media, and if they do, which platforms to focus on, given their limited time. There are three key scenarios associated with FoMO: the anxiety of missing out before making a choice, the concern of making the wrong choice due to extensive comparisons with others, and the apprehension of having missed out after a decision has been made. A study explored the underlying causes of FoMO through a model that examined maximizing tendencies, social comparison orientation, and regret tendencies. Notably, the study found a lack of similar research on this topic, as highlighted by a recent review of FoMO-related literature (Lin, S., & Jian, E., 2022).

Furthermore, the swift spread of information on social media intensifies feelings of Fear of Missing Out (FoMO), encouraging individuals to seek greater engagement with these platforms in order to remain informed and connected. This behavior can take on a compulsive nature, and if left unaddressed, may result in detrimental emotional effects, such as stress and melancholy (Matusik, S. F., & Mickel, A. E., 2011). Importantly, FoMO is marked by a strong desire to stay updated on others' activities, often resembling a form of surveillance. Social media platforms facilitate this monitoring, thereby amplifying the influence of FoMO.

Fear of Missing Out (FoMO) is considered a form of social anxiety associated with the apprehension of missing new experiences or more fulfilling situations due to content seen on social media (Dossey, L., 2014). A comprehensive study by Przybylski et al. (2013) investigated the motivational, behavioral, and happiness-related dimensions of FoMO through the lens of self-determination theory. They developed a Fear of Missing Out Scale (FoMOs) to assess FoMO, discovering that it can mediate the relationship between psychological satisfaction and engagement with social media. The findings indicated that lower levels of psychological satisfaction are linked to heightened FoMO, establishing a strong connection between FoMO and social media usage. Individuals with elevated FoMO tend to engage more intensively with social media, making it a significant motivator for online activity. Additionally, the research delved into how FoMO impacts happiness, revealing a negative correlation with emotional well-being and overall life satisfaction. Those with high FoMO often check social media before bed, upon waking, or during meals, and they are more likely to become distracted by social media in settings such as classrooms or while driving.

FoMO: MEDIATOR OF DIGITAL BEHAVIOR AND DECISION MAKING

The FoMO (Fear of Missing Out) moderated mediation model, initially proposed by Przybylski et al. (2013), was further explored by Alt, D. (2015) in a study examining the motivations for learning among college students and their engagement with social media during class sessions. The findings indicated that FoMO served as a mediating factor in the positive correlation between external influences and non-learning motivations, as well as overall social media engagement. This research builds a solid framework for understanding how FoMO affects individuals' psychological well-being.

Additionally, other studies have utilized the FoMO model to investigate various relationships. For instance, Wang et al. (2018) used the model to analyze the link between the need to belong and authentic self-presentation on social networking sites (SNSs). Their results demonstrated that FoMO mediated the relationship between the need to belong and the authentic self-presentation of adolescents on SNSs (Alutaybi et al., 2020).

In recent research, Dou et al. (2021) examined the connection between perceived social support and Fear of Missing Out (FoMO). Their findings indicated that there is an inverse relationship between these two factors, suggesting that higher levels of perceived social support are associated with lower levels of FoMO. Furthermore, they discovered that psychological needs play a partial mediating role in this relationship.

Similarly, Bodhi et al. (2023) investigated how work-related social media usage impacts psychological well-being and innovative work performance. Their study found that FoMO acts as a moderator in the indirect relationship between work-related social media use and innovative work performance, highlighting its significant role in workplace dynamics.

Additionally, Li and Ye (2022) applied a moderated mediation model focusing on FoMO to explore its influence on irrational procrastination within the context of mobile social media (Deniz M., 2021). Their results revealed that FoMO is a positive predictor of irrational procrastination, with cognitive failure fully mediating the relationship between FoMO and procrastination. These studies collectively underscore the intricate dynamics between social support, FoMO, and various forms of performance and behavior.

Schwartz et al. (2002) introduced the concepts of maximizing and satisfying. Maximizing refers to the behavior of individuals who, when faced with numerous choices, seek to gather and analyze extensive information in order to identify the optimal option. In contrast, satisfying describes the inclination to select an option that meets a predetermined level of acceptability, without dedicating excessive time to the decision-making process.

To assess individual differences in maximizing tendency, Schwartz et al. (2002) developed a set of maximizing tendency scales. They highlighted that maximizers aim to maximize their interests when faced with multiple choices, investing significant effort in information gathering and analysis. However, despite their efforts, maximizers often experience dissatisfaction with their choices due to their sensitivity to potential losses associated with their decisions. Even when their choices are satisfactory, maximizers tend to believe that better options exist. Research by Chowdhury et al. (2009) further suggested that maximizers are inclined to change their original choices when given the opportunity, and they generally exhibit dissatisfaction with their decisions (Iyengar, S. S., et al., 2006) .

In the context of the overwhelming volume of real-time information available on social media platforms, maximizers face challenges in processing and absorbing the extensive array of choices. Due to time and attention constraints, maximizers struggle to thoroughly evaluate all available information, leading to concerns about potentially missing out on better alternatives. Consequently, maximizers tend to experience negative emotions and suboptimal experiences compared to satisficers (Ding, H., & Li, A., 2018), who are more inclined to accept satisfactory outcomes.

FoMO, REGRET AND THE SOCIAL MEDIA TRAP

Regret is a negative cognitive emotion that emerges when an individual recognizes that a different decision could have produced a better outcome (Zeelenberg, M., 1999). According to Sagi and Friedland (2007), regret occurs when a person perceives that their chosen option is not the optimal one, or when there is a gap between their selection and the best alternative they did not choose. This emotion is unique in that it is felt only after a decision has been made.

Dan Ariely suggests that the fear of missing out (FoMO) is closely related to the concept of regret. Individuals may worry about making poor decisions regarding how to spend their time, which leads them to contemplate alternative scenarios of what they could have pursued (Lin, S., & Jian, E., 2022). The real-time nature of social media exacerbates this fear by consistently presenting updates about what others are doing and what is currently happening. This continuous flow of information can foster feelings of missing out on significant activities, intensifying both regret and the fear of missing out.

Individuals have an innate tendency to engage in comparisons, often doing so subconsciously when they receive information about others (Mussweiler & Bodenhausen, 2002). Research by Mussweiler et al. (2006) indicates that people frequently relate information about others' achievements to their own lives, resulting in social comparisons that permeate daily life as individuals effortlessly gather insights about others through various channels. Wood (1989) further emphasizes that social comparison is a common interactive process in everyday situations. Not everyone finds pleasure in comparing themselves to others, and the frequency and intensity of these comparisons can vary significantly. Those who are more inclined toward social comparison tend to show greater interest in the performances of others (Van der Zee et al., 1998).

Social media serves as an accessible source of vast information and is frequently utilized by individuals with high social comparison orientations to seek and evaluate the achievements of others. However, this tendency can lead to feelings of inadequacy, as individuals often encounter aspects in which they feel lacking compared to their peers.

Compulsive behavior, as defined by O'Guinn and Faber (1989), refers to the inability to regulate instinctual needs and desires, resulting in repetitive and potentially harmful actions. This behavior is commonly observed in everyday individuals who may engage in cyclical and meaningless patterns as a response to anxiety. Additionally, Fear of Missing Out (FoMO) is classified as a form of social anxiety and has been associated with various psychopathological symptoms, including anxiety, depression, decreased well-being, and social media fatigue.

Individuals with high Fear of Missing Out (FoMO) may feel compelled to remain constantly connected and pursue new experiences, which can lead to excessive use of digital technology (Coskun, S., & Karayagız Muslu, G. 2019) and a compulsive tendency to check their mobile devices. Research indicates that the immediacy and responsiveness of smartphones can enhance this compulsive phone-checking behavior (Oulasvirta, A., et al., 2012). Additionally, studies have identified a positive correlation between FoMO and "phubbing," the act of ignoring someone in favor of a mobile phone (Tandon, A., et al., 2022). Those experiencing high levels of FoMO may be driven to seek connections through social media, leading to repetitive checking behaviors.

IMPACT OF TECHNOLOGY-INDUCED STRESS ON PHUBBING BEHAVIOUR

Technostress, a modern issue arising from the struggle to adapt to new computer technology in a healthy manner, has been studied extensively (Brod, C., 1984). Tarafdar et al. (2007), identified "technostress creators," which are factors leading to technostress. Among these factors, two are particularly relevant to this study: Techno-overload occurs when employees are inundated with excessive information and communication due to the use of mobile technology and software, leading to stress (Fisher, W., & Wesolkowski, S., 1999). Techno-invasion occurs when the continuous connectivity provided by technology encroaches on employees' personal time and space, causing stress.

Research indicates that regular exposure to stressors, such as technology, can have detrimental long-term effects on psychological well-being (Charles, S. T., et al., 2013). The compulsive use of smartphones has been correlated with increased technostress, as the continuous flow of information and the pervasive nature of technology in daily life contribute to elevated stress levels. Additionally, excessive engagement with social media has been linked to technology overload and intrusion, further exacerbating stress. These findings suggest a significant positive relationship between high compulsive social media use and the experience of technostress.

Social media allows users to meticulously curate the impressions they create by utilizing various technologies to shape their self-presentation and foster desired relationships. Goffman's concept of self-presentation as a form of impression management (Goffman, E., 2023) suggests that individuals engage in behaviors aimed at "guiding" others' perceptions during interactions, much like a performer on stage who seeks to be viewed in a specific way by the audience. The information shared and gathered about others on social media is largely constructed, as individuals aim to project an appealing image. The disparity between these idealized representations and one's actual circumstances can lead to negative emotions. For example, compulsive social media users may frequently post glamorous selfies from upscale restaurants to craft a particular impression, only to feel dissatisfied when comparing these posts to their real lives. Aladwani and Almarzouq (2016) propose that such compulsive use is influenced by self-awareness factors, which may ultimately result in adverse outcomes. Excessive engagement with social media can trigger various comparison behaviors and negative effects. Consequently, this study asserts that high levels of compulsive social media use are positively correlated with negative feelings arising from social comparisons.

SOCIAL COMPARISON AND PHUBBING

Surveillance use involves the deliberate gathering of data and information about other people through electronic means (Marx, G. T., 2004). Tarafdar et al. (2007) have pointed out that technology overload can lead to pressure by providing excessive information and invading personal space through constant connectivity. The abundance of information on social media can lead to technostress, caused by both technology overload and intrusion into daily life. This can result in individuals feeling overwhelmed and experiencing negative emotions (Lee, S. Y., 2014) due to frequent surveillance and comparison behaviors.

Recent studies have highlighted two factors related to smartphone use that do not correlate with phubbing: multitasking and challenges in dividing attention. Research by Wang and Tchernev (2012) established a strong link between media multitasking and the motivation to pass the time. Given that multitasking is closely associated with phubbing, this finding suggests a potential connection between phubbing behavior and the urge to alleviate leisure boredom. Additionally, existing literature indicates that excessive smartphone usage is tied to impaired attention, with users exhibiting signs of 'divided attention' (Halpern, D., & Katz, J. E., 2017; Al-Saggaf, Y., et al., 2019). Considering that smartphone applications utilize push notifications to engage users, it is understandable that individuals often turn to their devices to satisfy their attentional needs (Leung, L., & Zhang, R., 2016). Since boredom is linked to the fulfillment of attentional requirements, a relationship between phubbing behavior and boredom seems plausible (LePera, 2011; Al-Saggaf, Y., et al., 2019).

One study indicated a potential link between phubbing and boredom. Oduor et al. (2016) conducted a qualitative analysis involving 20 participants from North America, revealing that boredom appeared to trigger phubbing. However, since boredom was not quantitatively assessed, the precise nature of the relationship between phubbing and boredom remains ambiguous. For example, it is unclear whether those participants who cited boredom during their interviews were generally prone to boredom or were simply experiencing a temporary sense of boredom (state boredom) (Damon, C.-H. P., & Louis, W.-C. L., 2010) or leisure boredom (Leung, L., & Zhang, R., 2016).

BOREDOM PRONENESS AND BEHAVIORAL OUTCOMES

Trait boredom, often referred to as boredom proneness, is defined as a chronic tendency to experience boredom (Hunter et al., 2016; Ng et al., 2015; Schroeter et al., 2015). This differs from state boredom (Gorelik, D., & Eastwood, J. D., 2024), which is a temporary feeling that occurs in specific situations. Research indicates that trait boredom is associated with various negative outcomes, including increased levels of depression and anxiety (Goldberg et al., 2011; LePera, 2011; Sommers & Vodanovich, 2000). Additionally, it can lead to behaviors such as anger, aggression (Dahlen et al., 2005; Rupp & Vodanovich, 1997), impulsivity(Watt & Vodanovich, 1992), substance abuse, risky driving(Dahlen et al., 2005), and problem gambling (Mercer & Eastwood, 2010).

The attentional theory of boredom proneness suggests that this trait arises from deficiencies in attentional processes (LePera, 2011). While there are no specific studies linking trait boredom directly to phubbing—where individuals ignore others in favor of their phones—there is a considerable body of research connecting trait boredom to various forms of addiction, including Internet use, mobile phone use, and social media engagement. These factors have all been shown to be predictive of phubbing behavior.

A study conducted among university students revealed significant positive correlations among trait boredom, impulsivity, and mobile phone addiction (Zhao et al., 2016; Al-Saggaf, Y., et al., 2019). Additionally, impulsivity was found to act as a mediator in the relationship between trait boredom and mobile phone addiction. This finding is consistent with previous research that has demonstrated a positive correlation between trait boredom and mobile phone addiction, particularly within university student populations (Yao et al., 2015; Elhai et al., 2017).

Trait boredom has been shown to positively correlate with Internet addiction. In a study by Biolcati et al. (2018), researchers explored the role of trait boredom in 'extreme' behaviors, including binge drinking and Internet addiction, among a sizable group of Italian adolescents (N = 478). The findings indicated that adolescents exhibiting high levels of boredom were more likely to engage in excessive technology use, participate in binge drinking, and develop Internet addiction compared to their peers with lower levels of boredom. This conclusion is consistent with research by Chou et al. (2018), which demonstrated that a higher score on the Boredom Proneness Scale—Short Form for 'lack of external stimulation' was significantly linked to an increased risk of Internet addiction among Taiwanese children and adolescents with ADHD.

While no specific studies have directly examined the link between trait boredom and addiction to social media apps, research has investigated leisure boredom—defined as boredom experienced during leisure time—and its relationship with social media app addiction. For instance, Zhou (2010) identified a significant positive correlation between leisure boredom and addiction to social media apps. Similarly, Huang (2014) found that leisure boredom was significantly and positively associated not only with social media addiction, but also with all four addiction symptoms: preoccupation, alleviation of negative emotions, adverse consequences, and a diminished interest in offline activities.

DEMOGRAPHICS AND PHUBBING BEHAVIOUR

Numerous studies have explored the relationship between gender and the frequency of phubbing, as well as the effects of urban versus rural living conditions on this behavior. However, research examining the association between age and phubbing frequency remains limited. Findings from Chotpitayasunondh and Douglas (2016) and Karadağ et al. (2015) indicate that females engage in phubbing more often than males. Additionally, preliminary results from an Australian study by Vernon and Uink (2017) suggest that individuals residing in metropolitan areas are more likely to exhibit phubbing behaviors compared to those in rural settings.

These observations are believed to be linked to various factors that predict phubbing behavior. For instance, females are more likely to experience mobile phone addiction, SMS addiction, and social media addiction. Conversely, research indicates that older individuals tend to use mobile phones, the Internet, social media, and SMS less frequently and are less likely to develop addictions compared to younger individuals. Therefore, it is suggested that older adults are less prone to engaging in phubbing behavior than their younger counterparts. Based on these insights, it is anticipated that demographic characteristics can effectively predict phubbing frequency (Al-Saggaf, Y., et al., 2019).

Research indicates that personality traits measured by the Ten Item Personality Inventory (TIPI), which assesses the Big Five personality dimensions, can predict social media addiction. Specifically, studies have shown that an individual's tendencies toward mobile phone addiction and excessive social media usage are associated with levels of certain personality traits, including extraversion, agreeableness, conscientiousness, emotional stability, and openness to experience (Zamani et al., 2011).

Moreover, later research has pinpointed personality traits that may serve as both protective and risk factors for problematic social media and smartphone usage. These findings suggest a potential connection between these personality traits—commonly linked to social media addiction and smartphone overuse—and phubbing behaviors. It is important to note, however, that the exploration of the relationship between personality traits and phubbing is still in its nascent stages (Chi, LC et al., 2022).

DARK TRIAD TRAITS AND PHUBBING

The impact of phubbing on individual wellbeing has been explored by Roberts and David (2016), who discovered that it correlates with feelings of depression and diminished life satisfaction. Phubbing, defined as the act of ignoring someone in favor of a mobile phone, can result in various negative outcomes, including musculoskeletal disorders, disrupted daily routines, sleep disturbances, reduced physical activity, heightened stress, communication challenges, lower academic performance, and feelings of loneliness. This behavior is often associated with addictions to mobile phones, the internet, social media, mobile gaming, and nomophobia. Additionally, it is influenced by individual characteristics and personality traits.

Recent studies have explored the relationship between phubbing (phone snubbing) and socially adverse personality traits, particularly the "Dark Triad" traits of Machiavellianism, narcissism, and psychopathy. Individuals high in these traits tend to display manipulative, grandiose, and low empathy behaviors (Paulhus & Williams, 2002). Research has shown a positive correlation between problematic smartphone use and the Dark Triad traits (Balta et al., 2019; Pearson & Hussain, 2015). Vulnerable narcissism has been specifically linked to phubbing. Politeness theory may help explain the connections between phubbing and adverse personality traits. Given that phubbing is often seen as impolite behavior, individuals with adverse personality traits may be more likely to engage in phubbing.

Alongside the Dark Triad traits, a new personality trait known as "need for drama" has emerged. This trait encompasses interpersonal manipulation, impulsive outspokenness, and a persistent sense of victimhood. Individuals exhibiting this trait tend to manipulate others impulsively while adopting a stance of perceived victimization. Unlike those with high Dark Triad traits, individuals with a need for drama are not characterized by low empathy (Frankowski et al., 2016). Previous research has highlighted a positive correlation between social media addiction and the need for drama; however, the relationship between phubbing and the need for drama remains unexplored.

Personality traits, particularly the Big Five personality dimensions, significantly influence individual behavior. Personality is characterized as the unique blend of innate temperament and attributes that differentiate one person from another, enabling us to predict future behaviors. Research has delineated five key aspects of personality, which are crucial in understanding the effects of phubbing on interpersonal relationships and overall well-being.

Data from the Indonesian Internet Service Providers Association (APJII), in collaboration with the Indonesian Polling Institute (LPI), reveals noteworthy trends. In 2017, approximately 143.26 million individuals, or around 54.68% of Indonesia's population, were internet users. This figure rose to 171.17 million by 2018, reflecting an increase to 64.8% of the total population—an impressive 10.12% growth. The trend continued into 2019 and 2020, with 196.7 million users, representing about 73.7% of the population, marking an additional 8.9% rise. The data also indicated that the demographic with the highest internet usage is aged 15-24, with 91% of 15-19-year-olds and 88.5% of 20-24-year-olds utilizing the internet. This surge in internet usage can be attributed to the array of services it offers and its rapid connectivity, facilitating remote communication and real-time information access. However, while the internet provides myriad benefits, an increasing body of literature highlights its potential negative impacts on user behavior.

PERSONALITY AND THE PERILS OF INTERNET OVERUSE

Problematic Internet Use (PIU) refers to the difficulty in managing internet usage, often driven by an impulsive urge to go online. This behavior can lead to significant distress and functional impairments in everyday life (Shapira et al., 2000). Caplan (2010) identified several components of PIU, including Preference for Online Social Interaction (POSI), Mood Regulation, and deficiencies in self-regulation, which manifest as cognitive preoccupation and compulsive internet use, among other negative outcomes. The consequences of PIU can be severe, contributing to various psychological issues such as pathological gambling, paraphilias, compulsive buying behaviors, mood disorders, low self-esteem, anxiety, reduced life satisfaction, increased depression, and fear of missing out (FoMO) (Stead & Bibby, 2017; Islam, M. A., & Hossin, M. Z., 2016).

Research conducted by Stead and Bibby in 2017 highlights the influence of personality traits on problematic internet use (PIU). Various studies, including those by Angesti and Oriza in 2018, suggest that certain personality characteristics can predict the likelihood of experiencing PIU. A key framework in this area is the "big five" personality traits, also known as OCEAN, which includes extraversion, openness, agreeableness, conscientiousness, and neuroticism. Understanding these dimensions can provide valuable insights into the factors contributing to internet misuse.

Numerous studies have explored the relationship between personality traits and problematic internet use (PIU). Some research indicates that extraversion and conscientiousness are negatively correlated with PIU. However, studies by Jackson (2003) and colleagues, as well as Thorsteinsson & Davey (2014), reveal a positive correlation between trait extraversion and PIU. Additionally, findings suggest a positive relationship between neuroticism and PIU, consistent with the research conducted by Angesti and Oriza (2018). In contrast, traits associated with agreeableness appear to have a negative correlation with PIU. It is important to acknowledge that the strength of the correlation between these traits and PIU may be limited due to the relatively small body of research available.

Research conducted by Stead and Bibby (2017) indicates that Problematic Internet Use (PIU) may be significantly influenced by the phenomenon known as Fear of Missing Out (FoMO). This assertion is further supported by Alt and Boniel-Nissim (2018), who identified a strong correlation between PIU and FoMO. A survey by JWT Intelligence revealed that in the United States and England, 70% of young adults aged 18-34 report experiencing FoMO, while the prevalence among adolescents aged 13-17 has risen to 65% (Ruyandy, R., & Kartasasmita, S., 2021).

Research conducted by the Australian Psychological Society indicates that individuals aged 18 to 35 experience the highest levels of Fear of Missing Out (FoMO). Similarly, a study in Indonesia by Christina, R., et al. (2019) found that 36% of adolescents aged 13 to 18 report high levels of FoMO, highlighting that a significant portion of this age group is concerned about missing out on experiences. This phenomenon is especially pronounced during the transition from adolescence to adulthood, a stage known as emerging adulthood, which is characterized by instability in various aspects of life, including relationships, work, and education (Arnett, J. J., 2006; Ruyandy, R., & Kartasasmita, S., 2021).

PERSONALITY, PHUBBING AND THE DIGITAL DISCONNECT

The Five Factor Personality Model delineates five fundamental personality traits: extraversion, conscientiousness, agreeableness, neuroticism, and openness. Extraversion is marked by sociability and ambition, whereas introversion is defined by shyness and a preference for solitude. Agreeableness encompasses traits such as compassion and emotional support, while neuroticism is associated with anxiety and emotional instability. Openness reflects creativity and curiosity, and conscientiousness is linked to organization and goal-oriented behavior.

Understanding individual behavior with smartphones on the internet is essential, as personality traits significantly influence this behavior. Research has shown that neuroticism and conscientiousness can predict phubbing behavior, which is associated with smartphone usage. The connection between the five major personality traits and internet or smartphone addiction has been a focal point of investigation. Moreover, attitudes toward smartphone use are linked to these personality traits. Phubbing behavior, closely related to smartphones and internet applications, is also shaped by personality traits (Parmaksız, İ., 2021).

Research has previously identified a positive correlation between depression and anxiety and the phenomenon known as phubbing (Bitar et al., 2022; Ergün et al., 2020; Guazzini et al., 2019; McDaniel & Coyne, 2016). Multiple studies have highlighted this relationship, indicating that individuals experiencing higher levels of depression and anxiety may engage in phubbing as a coping strategy. Furthermore, evidence suggests that being phubbed is also associated with increased feelings of depression and anxiety. This can be explained by social exclusion theory, which posits that individuals feel negative emotions (Williams, K. D., 2009) and experience a threat to their fundamental needs when they are socially excluded. Phubbing can be viewed as a smartphone-mediated form of social exclusion, leading to heightened mental health challenges for those who are frequently phubbed.

Research on the relationship between stress and phubbing is still limited. Some studies have identified a positive correlation between stress, negative emotions, and phubbing behavior (Bitar et al., 2022; Guazzini et al., 2021). Similar to those experiencing depression and anxiety, individuals under stress may resort to their smartphones, engaging in phubbing as a coping mechanism (Bitar et al., 2022). Furthermore, there is a noticeable gap in research regarding how being phubbed impacts stress levels. According to social exclusion theory (Williams, K. D., 2009), individuals who are phubbed and thus socially excluded by their conversation partners may experience heightened stress. Given the limited research and the implications of social exclusion theory, it is essential to explore the connections between phubbing behavior and associated stress (Garcia, M. A., et al., 2023).

FoMO, or the fear of missing out, refers to the anxiety surrounding the potential loss of valuable opportunities and social interactions. This fear can lead to feelings of worry about being excluded. A key characteristic of FoMO is the impulse to remain connected and informed about the activities of others. This phenomenon can be understood through the lens of self-determination theory, which suggests that FoMO is associated with unfulfilled psychological needs for competence, autonomy, and relatedness. Consequently, individuals may struggle with self-regulation as a result (Przybylski, A. K., et al., 2013).

CONCLUSION

In this chapter, we explored the significant influence of personality traits on the effects of phubbing and smartphone addiction on social and psychological well-being. Research indicates that personality traits, particularly those identified in the Big Five (Extraversion, Agreeableness, Conscientiousness, Neuroticism, and Openness), significantly shape individuals' interactions with smartphones and their tendency to engage in behaviors such as phubbing. Those exhibiting high levels of neuroticism and low conscientiousness were found to be more vulnerable to problematic smartphone usage, leading to an increase in phubbing behavior.

Furthermore, the phenomenon known as the Fear of Missing Out (FoMO) is closely linked to personality traits and plays a substantial role in smartphone addiction and excessive social media use. Such behaviors can result in negative psychological outcomes, including feelings of loneliness, depression, and diminished life satisfaction. This chapter also addressed the broader societal implications, highlighting how excessive smartphone use and phubbing disrupt interpersonal relationships and negatively affect mental health.

These findings pave the way for future research aimed at examining the moderating role of personality traits in technology-related behaviors and their impact on well-being. A deeper understanding of the interplay between personality traits, FoMO, and phubbing could inform the design of interventions aimed at alleviating the negative psychological and social consequences associated with these behaviors.

REFERENCES

Al-Saggaf, Y., MacCulloch, R., & Wiener, K. (2019). Trait boredom is a predictor of phubbing frequency. *Journal of Technology in Behavioral Science*, 4(3), 245–252. DOI: 10.1007/s41347-018-0080-4

Aladwani, A. M., & Almarzouq, M. (2016). Understanding compulsive social media use: The premise of complementing self-conceptions mismatch with technology. *Computers in Human Behavior*, 60, 575–581. DOI: 10.1016/j.chb.2016.02.098

Alenezi, A., Hamed, W., Elhehe, I., & El-Etreby, R. (2023). Association between Facebook Addiction, Depression, and Emotional Regulation among Women. *Healthcare (Basel)*, 11(12), 1701. DOI: 10.3390/healthcare11121701 PMID: 37372819

Alt, D. (2015). College students' academic motivation, media engagement and fear of missing out. *Computers in Human Behavior*, 49, 111–119. DOI: 10.1016/j.chb.2015.02.057

Alt, D., & Boniel-Nissim, M. (2018). Links between adolescents' deep and surface learning approaches, problematic Internet use, and fear of missing out (FoMO). *Internet Interventions : the Application of Information Technology in Mental and Behavioural Health*, 13, 30–39. DOI: 10.1016/j.invent.2018.05.002 PMID: 30206516

Alutaybi, A., Al-Thani, D., McAlaney, J., & Ali, R. (2020). Combating Fear of Missing Out (FoMO) on Social Media: The FoMO-R Method. *International Journal of Environmental Research and Public Health*, 17(17), 6128. DOI: 10.3390/ijerph17176128 PMID: 32842553

Andreassen, C. S., Torsheim, T., Brunborg, G. S., & Pallesen, S. (2012). Development of a Facebook addiction scale. *Psychological Reports*, 110(2), 501–517. DOI: 10.2466/02.09.18.PR0.110.2.501-517 PMID: 22662404

Angesti, R., & Oriza, I. D. I. (2018). Peran fear of missing out (fomo) sebagai mediator antara kepribadian dan penggunaan internet bermasalah. Jurnal Muara Ilmu Sosial, Humaniora, dan Seni, 2(2), 790-800.

Arnett, J. J. (2006). Emerging adulthood: Understanding the new way of coming of age. In Arnett, J. J., & Tanner, J. L. (Eds.), *Emerging adults in America*. American Psychological Association. DOI: 10.1093/acprof:oso/9780195309379.001.0001

Balta, S., Emirtekin, E., Kircaburun, K., & Griffiths, M. D. (2020). Neuroticism, trait fear of missing out, and phubbing: The mediating role of state fear of missing out and problematic Instagram use. *International Journal of Mental Health and Addiction*, 18(3), 628–639. DOI: 10.1007/s11469-018-9959-8

Balta, S., Jonason, P., Denes, A., Emirtekin, E., Tosuntaş, Ş. B., Kircaburun, K., & Griffiths, M. D. (2019). Dark personality traits and problematic smartphone use: The mediating role of fearful attachment. *Personality and Individual Differences*, 149, 214–219. DOI: 10.1016/j.paid.2019.06.005

Biolcati, R., Mancini, G., & Trombini, E. (2018). Proneness to boredom and risk behaviours during adolescents' free time. *Psychological Reports*, 121(2), 303–323. DOI: 10.1177/0033294117724447 PMID: 28776483

Bitar, Z., Akel, M., Salameh, P., Obeid, S., & Hallit, S. (2022). Phubbing among Lebanese young adults: Scale validation and association with mental health (depression, anxiety, and stress). *Current Psychology (New Brunswick, N.J.)*. Advance online publication. DOI: 10.1007/s12144-022-03104- PMID: 35496363

Błachnio, A., Przepiórka, A., & Pantic, I. (2015). Internet use, Facebook intrusion, and depression: Results of a cross-sectional study. European psychiatry: the journal of the Association of European Psychiatrists, 30(6), 681–684. https://doi.org/DOI: 10.1016/j.eurpsy.2015.04.002

Bodhi, R., Luqman, A., Hina, M., & Papa, A. (2023). Work-related social media use and employee-related outcomes: A moderated mediation model. *International Journal of Emerging Markets*, 18(11), 4948–4967. DOI: 10.1108/IJOEM-09-2021-1359

Bozoglan, B., Demirer, V., & Sahin, I. (2013). Loneliness, self-esteem, and life satisfaction as predictors of Internet addiction: A cross-sectional study among Turkish university students. *Scandinavian Journal of Psychology*, 54(4), 313–319. DOI: 10.1111/sjop.12049 PMID: 23577670

Brod, C. (1984). *Technostress: The human cost of the computer revolution*. No Title.

Caplan, S. E. (2010). Theory and measurement of generalized problematic Internet use: A two-step approach. *Computers in Human Behavior*, 26(5), 1089–1097. DOI: 10.1016/j.chb.2010.03.012

Charles, S. T., Piazza, J. R., Mogle, J., Sliwinski, M. J., & Almeida, D. M. (2013). The wear and tear of daily stressors on mental health. *Psychological Science*, 24(5), 733–741. DOI: 10.1177/0956797612462222 PMID: 23531486

Chi, L. C., Tang, T. C., & Tang, E. (2022). The phubbing phenomenon: A cross-sectional study on the relationships among social media addiction, fear of missing out, personality traits, and phubbing behavior. *Current Psychology (New Brunswick, N.J.)*, 41(2), 1112–1123. DOI: 10.1007/s12144-021-02468-y

Chotpitayasunondh, V., & Douglas, K. M. (2016). How "phubbing" becomes the norm: The antecedents and consequences of snubbing via smartphone. *Computers in Human Behavior*, 63, 9–18. DOI: 10.1016/j.chb.2016.05.018

Chotpitayasunondh, V., & Douglas, K. M. (2018). The effects of "phubbing" on social interaction. *Journal of Applied Social Psychology*, 48(6), 304–316. DOI: 10.1111/jasp.12506

Chou, W.-J., Chang, Y.-P., & Yen, C.-F. (2018). Boredom proneness and its correlation with internet addiction and internet activities in adolescents with attention-deficit/ hyperactivity disorder. *The Kaohsiung Journal of Medical Sciences*, 34(8), 1–8. DOI: 10.1016/j.kjms.2018.01.016 PMID: 30041765

Chowdhury, T. G., Ratneshwar, S., & Mohanty, P. (2009). The time-harried shopper: Exploring the differences between maximizers and satisficers. *Marketing Letters*, 20(2), 155–167. DOI: 10.1007/s11002-008-9063-0

Christina, R., Yuniardi, M. S., & Prabowo, A. (2019). Hubungan Tingkat Neurotisme dengan Fear of Missing Out (FoMO) pada Remaja Pengguna Aktif Media Sosial. Indigenous. *Jurnal Ilmiah Psikologi*, 4(2), 105–117.

Coskun, S., & Karayagız Muslu, G. (2019). Investigation of problematic mobile phones use and fear of missing out (FoMO) level in adolescents. *Community Mental Health Journal*, 55(6), 1004–1014. DOI: 10.1007/s10597-019-00422-8 PMID: 31209716

Dahlen, E. R., Martin, R. C., Ragan, K., & Kuhlman, M. M. (2005). Driving anger, sensation seeking, impulsiveness, and boredom proneness in the prediction of unsafe driving. *Accident; Analysis and Prevention*, 37(2), 341–348. DOI: 10.1016/j.aap.2004.10.006 PMID: 15667821

Damon, C.-H. P., & Louis, W.-C. L. (2010). Effects of narcissism, leisure boredom, and gratifications sought on user-generated content among Net-Generation users. 8th International Telecommunications Society (ITS) *Asia-Pacific Regional Conference*, 1–34. https://doi.org/DOI: 10.4018/ijcbpl.2011070101

Dan Ariely on How 'Fear of Missing Out' works | Duke Today. (2015, April 21). Duke Today. https://today.duke.edu/2015/04/dan-ariely-how-%E2%80%98fear-missing-out%E2%80%99-works

Deniz M. (2021). Fear of missing out (FoMO) mediate relations between social self-efficacy and life satisfaction. Psicologia, reflexao e critica: revista semestral do Departamento de Psicologia da UFRGS, 34(1), 28. DOI: 10.1186/s41155-021-00193-w

Ding, H., & Li, A. (2018). A study on maximization paradox and its psychological origin. *Psychology (Irvine, Calif.)*, 9(04), 785–796. DOI: 10.4236/psych.2018.94050

Dossey, L. (2014). FOMO, digital dementia, and our dangerous experiment. *Explore (New York, N.Y.)*, 10(2), 69–73. DOI: 10.1016/j.explore.2013.12.008 PMID: 24607071

Dou, F., Li, Q., Li, X., Li, Q., & Wang, M. (2021). Impact of perceived social support on fear of missing of out (FoMO): A moderated mediation model. *Current Psychology (New Brunswick, N.J.)*, 1–10.

Elhai, J. D., Vasquez, J. K., Lustgarten, S. D., Levine, J. C., & Hall, B. J. (2017). Proneness to boredom mediates relationships between problematic smartphone use with depression and anxiety severity. *Social Science Computer Review*. Advance online publication. DOI: 10.1177/0894439317741087

Elphinston, R. A., & Noller, P. (2011). Time to face it! Facebook intrusion and the implications for romantic jealousy and relationship satisfaction. *Cyberpsychology, Behavior, and Social Networking*, 14(11), 631–635. DOI: 10.1089/cyber.2010.0318 PMID: 21548798

Ergün, N., Göksu, İ., & Sakız, H. (2020). Effects of phubbing: Relationships with psychodemographic variables. *Psychological Reports*, 123(5), 1578–1613. DOI: 10.1177/0033294119889581 PMID: 31752605

Fisher, W., & Wesolkowski, S. (1999). Tempering technostress. *IEEE Technology and Society Magazine*, 18(1), 28–42. DOI: 10.1109/44.752243

Franchina, V., Vanden Abeele, M., van Rooij, A. J., Lo Coco, G., & De Marez, L. (2018). Fear of missing out as a predictor of problematic social media use and phubbing behavior among Flemish adolescents. *International Journal of Environmental Research and Public Health*, 15(10), 2319. DOI: 10.3390/ijerph15102319 PMID: 30360407

Frankowski, S., Lupo, A. K., Smith, B. A., Dane'El, M., Ramos, C., & Morera, O. F. (2016). Developing and Testing a Scale to Measure Need for Drama. *Personality and Individual Differences*, 89, 192–201. DOI: 10.1016/j.paid.2015.10.009

Garcia, M. A., Lerma, M., Perez, M. G., Medina, K. S., Rodriguez-Crespo, A., & Cooper, T. V. (2023). Psychosocial and personality trait associates of phubbing and being phubbed in hispanic emerging adult college students. *Current Psychology (New Brunswick, N.J.)*, 43(6), 5601–5614. DOI: 10.1007/s12144-023-04767-y PMID: 37359598

Garcia, M. A., Lerma, M., Perez, M. G., Medina, K. S., Rodriguez-Crespo, A., & Cooper, T. V. (2024). Psychosocial and personality trait associates of phubbing and being phubbed in hispanic emerging adult college students. *Current Psychology (New Brunswick, N.J.)*, 43(6), 5601–5614. DOI: 10.1007/s12144-023-04767-y PMID: 37359598

Goffman, E. (2023). The presentation of self in everyday life. In *Social theory re-wired* (pp. 450–459). Routledge. DOI: 10.4324/9781003320609-59

Goldberg, Y. K., Eastwood, J. D., LaGuardia, J., & Danckert, J. (2011). Boredom: An emotional experience distinct from apathy, anhedonia, or depression. *Journal of Social and Clinical Psychology*, 30(6), 647–666. DOI: 10.1521/jscp.2011.30.6.647

Gorelik, D., & Eastwood, J. D. (2024). Trait Boredom as a Lack of Agency: A Theoretical Model and a New Assessment Tool. *Assessment*, 31(2), 321–334. DOI: 10.1177/10731911231161780 PMID: 36942352

Guazzini, A., Duradoni, M., Capelli, A., & Meringolo, P. (2019). An explorative model to assess Individuals' phubbing risk. *Future Internet*, 11(1), 21. DOI: 10.3390/fi11010021

Guazzini, A., Raimondi, T., Biagini, B., Bagnoli, F., & Duradoni, M. (2021). Phubber's emotional activations: The association between PANAS and phubbing behavior. *Future Internet*, 13(12), 311. DOI: 10.3390/fi13120311

Halpern, D., & Katz, J. E. (2017). Texting's consequences for romantic relationships: A cross-lagged analysis highlights its risks. *Computers in Human Behavior*, 71, 386–394. DOI: 10.1016/j.chb.2017.01.051

Huang, H. (2014). *Social media generation in China: a study of social media use and addiction among adolescents*. Springer. DOI: 10.1007/978-3-642-45441-7

Hunter, J. A., Dyer, K. J., Cribbie, R. A., & Eastwood, J. D. (2016). Exploring the utility of the multidimensional state boredom scale. *European Journal of Psychological Assessment*, 32(3), 241–250. DOI: 10.1027/1015-5759/a000251

Intelligence, J. W. T. (2012). Fear of Missing Out (FoMO). Retrieve from: www.jwtintelligence.com/wp-content/uploads/2012/03/F_JWT_FOMupdate_3.21.12.pdf

Islam, M. A., & Hossin, M. Z. (2016). Prevalence and risk factors of problematic internet use and the associated psychological distress among graduate students of Bangladesh. *Asian Journal of Gambling Issues and Public Health*, 6(1), 11. DOI: 10.1186/s40405-016-0020-1 PMID: 27942430

Ivanova, A., Gorbaniuk, O., Błachnio, A., Przepiórka, A., Mraka, N., Polishchuk, V., & Gorbaniuk, J. (2020). Mobile Phone Addiction, Phubbing, and Depression Among Men and Women: A Moderated Mediation Analysis. *The Psychiatric Quarterly*, 91(3), 655–668. DOI: 10.1007/s11126-020-09723-8 PMID: 32146681

Iyengar, S. S., Wells, R. E., & Schwartz, B. (2006). Doing better but feeling worse: Looking for the "best" job undermines satisfaction. *Psychological Science*, 17(2), 143–150. DOI: 10.1111/j.1467-9280.2006.01677.x PMID: 16466422

Jackson, L. A., von Eye, A., Biocca, F., Barbatsis, G., Fitzgerald, H., & Zhao, Y. (2003). Personality, cognitive style, demographic characteristics and Internet use: Findings from the HomeNetToo. *Swiss Journal of Psychology*, 62(2), 79–90. DOI: 10.1024//1421-0185.62.2.79

Karadağ, E., Tosuntaş, Ş. B., Erzen, E., Duru, P., Bostan, N., Şahin, B. M., Çulha, İ., & Babadağ, B. (2015). Determinants of phubbing, which is the sum of many virtual addictions: A structural equation model. *Journal of Behavioral Addictions*, 4(2), 60–74. DOI: 10.1556/2006.4.2015.005 PMID: 26014669

Lee, S. Y. (2014). How do people compare themselves with others on social network sites?: The case of Facebook. *Computers in Human Behavior*, 32, 253–260. DOI: 10.1016/j.chb.2013.12.009

LePera, N. (2011). Relationships between boredom proneness, mindfulness, anxiety, depression, and substance use. *The New School Psychology Bulletin*, 8(2), 15–25. DOI: 10.1037/e741452011-003

Leung, L., & Zhang, R. (2016). Predicting tablet use: A study of gratifications-sought, leisure boredom, and multitasking. *Telematics and Informatics*, 33(2), 331–341. DOI: 10.1016/j.tele.2015.08.013

Li, X., & Ye, Y. (2022). Fear of missing out and irrational procrastination in the mobile social media environment: A moderated mediation analysis. *Cyberpsychology, Behavior, and Social Networking*, 25(1), 59–65. DOI: 10.1089/cyber.2021.0052 PMID: 34491830

Lin, S., & Jian, E. (2022). Effects of personality traits concerning media use decisions on fear of missing out and social media use behavior. *Behavioral Sciences (Basel, Switzerland)*, 12(11), 460. DOI: 10.3390/bs12110460 PMID: 36421756

Marx, G. T. (2004). What's New About the" New Surveillance"?: Classifying for Change and Continuity. *Knowledge in Society*, 17(1), 18–37. DOI: 10.1007/BF02687074

Matusik, S. F., & Mickel, A. E. (2011). Embracing or embattled by converged mobile devices? Users' experiences with a contemporary connectivity technology. *Human Relations*, 64(8), 1001–1030. DOI: 10.1177/0018726711405552

McCann Paris. (2014, June 26). Macquarie BPhubbing: a word is born^: McCann Melbourne [Video file]. Retrieved from https://www.youtube.com/watch?v=hLNhKUniaEw

McDaniel, B. T., & Coyne, S. M. (2016). "Technoference": The interference of technology in couple relationships and implications for women's personal and relational well-being. *Psychology of Popular Media Culture*, 5(1), 85–98. DOI: 10.1037/ppm0000065

Mercer, K. B., & Eastwood, J. D. (2010). Is boredom associated with problem gambling behaviour? It depends on what you mean by "boredom". *International Gambling Studies*, 10(1), 91–104. DOI: 10.1080/14459791003754414

Mussweiler, T., & Bodenhausen, G. V. (2002). I know you are, but what am I? Self-evaluative consequences of judging in-group and out-group members. *Journal of Personality and Social Psychology*, 82(1), 19–32. DOI: 10.1037/0022-3514.82.1.19 PMID: 11811631

Mussweiler, T., Rüter, K., & Epstude, K. (2006). The why, who, and how of social comparison: A social-cognition perspective. Social comparison and social psychology: Understanding cognition, intergroup relations, and culture, 33-54.

Ng, A. H., Liu, Y., Chen, J. Z., & Eastwood, J. D. (2015). Culture and state boredom: A comparison between European Canadians and Chinese. *Personality and Individual Differences*, 75, 13–18. DOI: 10.1016/j.paid.2014.10.052

O'Guinn, T. C., & Faber, R. J. (1989). Compulsive buying: A phenomenological exploration. *The Journal of Consumer Research*, 16(2), 147–157. DOI: 10.1086/209204

Oduor, E., Neustaedter, C., Odom, W., Tang, A., Moallem, N., Tory, M., & Irani, P. (2016). The frustrations and benefits of mobile device usage in the home when co-present with family members. Proceedings of the 2016 ACM Conference on Designing Interactive Systems - DIS ', 16, 1315–1327. DOI: 10.1145/2901790.2901809

Oulasvirta, A., Rattenbury, T., Ma, L., & Raita, E. (2012). Habits make smartphone use more pervasive. *Personal and Ubiquitous Computing*, 16(1), 105–114. DOI: 10.1007/s00779-011-0412-2

Parmaksız, İ. (2021). Relationships Between Phubbing and The Five Factor Personality Traits. *Kastamonu Education Journal*, 29(4), 32–42. DOI: 10.24106/kefdergi.795620

Paulhus, D. L., & Williams, K. M. (2002). The dark triad of personality: Narcissism, Machiavellianism, and psychopathy. *Journal of Research in Personality*, 36(6), 556–563. DOI: 10.1016/S0092-6566(02)00505-6

Pearson, C., & Hussain, Z. (2015). Smartphone use, addiction, narcissism, and personality: A mixed methods investigation. *International Journal of Cyber Behavior, Psychology and Learning*, 5(1), 17–32. DOI: 10.4018/ijcbpl.2015010102

Peplau, L. A. (1982). Loneliness: A source book of current theory, research and therapy. Jone Wiley & Sons.

Przybylski, A. K., Murayama, K., DeHaan, C. R., & Gladwell, V. (2013). Motivational, emotional, and behavioral correlates of fear of missing out. *Computers in Human Behavior*, 29(4), 1841–1848. DOI: 10.1016/j.chb.2013.02.014

Reer, F., Tang, W. Y., & Quandt, T. (2019). Psychosocial well-being and social media engagement: The mediating roles of social comparison orientation and fear of missing out. *New Media & Society*, 21(7), 1486–1505. DOI: 10.1177/1461444818823719

Rupp, D. E., & Vodanovich, S. J. (1997). The role of boredom proneness in self-reported anger and aggression. *Journal of Social Behavior and Personality*, 12(4), 925–936.

Ruyandy, R., & Kartasasmita, S. (2021). The Effect of FoMO as a Mediator of Big-Five Personality Relationship with Problematic Internet Use Among Emerging Adulthood. Advances in Social Science, Education and Humanities Research. *Advances in Social Science, Education and Humanities Research*. Advance online publication. DOI: 10.2991/assehr.k.210805.058

Sagi, A., & Friedland, N. (2007). The cost of richness: The effect of the size and diversity of decision sets on post-decision regret. *Journal of Personality and Social Psychology*, 93(4), 515–524. DOI: 10.1037/0022-3514.93.4.515 PMID: 17892329

San-Martín, S., & Jiménez, N. (2023). What colour are you? Smartphone addiction traffic lights and user profiles. *European Journal of Management and Business Economics*, 32(2), 149–167. DOI: 10.1108/EJMBE-02-2021-0069

Schroeter, R., Oxtoby, J., Johnson, D., & Steinberger, F. (2015). Exploring boredom proneness as a predictor of mobile phone use in the car. Proceedings of the Annual Meeting of the Australian Special Interest Group for Computer Human Interaction on - OzCHI '15, (December), 465–473. https://doi.org/DOI: 10.1145/2838739.2838783

Schwartz, B., Ward, A., Monterosso, J., Lyubomirsky, S., White, K., & Lehman, D. R. (2002). Maximizing versus satisficing: Happiness is a matter of choice. *Journal of Personality and Social Psychology*, 83(5), 1178–1197. DOI: 10.1037/0022-3514.83.5.1178 PMID: 12416921

Shapira, N. A., Goldsmith, T. D., Keck, P. E.Jr, Khosla, U. M., & McElroy, S. L. (2000). Psychiatric features of individuals with problematic internet use. *Journal of Affective Disorders*, 57(1-3), 267–272. DOI: 10.1016/S0165-0327(99)00107-X PMID: 10708842

Sommers, J., & Vodanovich, S. J. (2000). Boredom proneness: Its relationship to psychological- and physical-health symptoms. *Journal of Clinical Psychology*, 56(1), 149–155. DOI: 10.1002/(SICI)1097-4679(200001)56:1<149::AID-JCLP14>3.0.CO;2-Y PMID: 10661377

Stead, H., & Bibby, P. A. (2017). Personality, fear of missing out and problematic internet use and their relationship to subjective well-being. *Computers in Human Behavior*, 76, 534–540. DOI: 10.1016/j.chb.2017.08.016

Tandon, A., Dhir, A., Almugren, I., AlNemer, G. N., & Mäntymäki, M. (2021). Fear of missing out (FoMO) among social media users: A systematic literature review, synthesis and framework for future research. *Internet Research*, 31(3), 782–821. DOI: 10.1108/INTR-11-2019-0455

Tandon, A., Dhir, A., Talwar, S., Kaur, P., & Mäntymäki, M. (2022). Social media induced fear of missing out (FoMO) and phubbing: Behavioural, relational and psychological outcomes. *Technological Forecasting and Social Change*, 174, 121149. DOI: 10.1016/j.techfore.2021.121149

Tarafdar, M., Tu, Q., Ragu-Nathan, B. S., & Ragu-Nathan, T. S. (2007). The impact of technostress on role stress and productivity. *Journal of Management Information Systems*, 24(1), 301–328. DOI: 10.2753/MIS0742-1222240109

Thorsteinsson, E. B., & Davey, L. (2014). Adolescents' compulsive Internet use and depression: A longitudinal study. *Open Journal of Depression*, 3(1), 13–17. DOI: 10.4236/ojd.2014.31005

Van der Zee, K., Buunk, B., & Sanderman, R. (1998). Neuroticism and reactions to social comparison information among cancer patients. *Journal of Personality*, 66(2), 175–194. DOI: 10.1111/1467-6494.00008 PMID: 9529662

Vernon, L., & Uink, B. (2017). Early results are in! What are Australians' smartphone habits? Retrieved from https://www.modernlifestudy.com/abc-survey-results

Wang, P., Xie, X., Wang, X., Wang, X., Zhao, F., Chu, X., Nie, J., & Lei, L. (2018). The need to belong and adolescent authentic self-presentation on SNSs: A moderated mediation model involving FoMO and perceived social support. *Personality and Individual Differences*, 128, 133–138. DOI: 10.1016/j.paid.2018.02.035

Wang, Z., & Tchernev, J. M. (2012). The BMyth^ of media multitasking: reciprocal dynamics of media multitasking, personal needs, and gratifications. Journal of Communication, 62(3, 1 June 2012), 493–513. .DOI: 10.1111/j.1460-2466.2012.01641.x

Watt, J. D., & Vodanovich, S. J. (1992). Relationship between boredom proneness and impulsivity. *Psychological Reports*, 70(3), 688–690. DOI: 10.2466/pr0.1992.70.3.688 PMID: 1620756

Williams, K. D. (2009). Ostracism: A temporal need-threat model. In Zanna, M. P. (Ed.), Advances in experimental social psychology (Vol. 41, pp. 275–314). Elsevier Academic Press. DOI: 10.1016/S0065-2601(08)00406-1

Wood, J. V. (1989). Theory and research concerning social comparisons of personal attributes. *Psychological Bulletin*, 106(2), 231–248. DOI: 10.1037/0033-2909.106.2.231

Yao, M.-P., Jia, Z.-B., & Cben, X. (2015). Relationship between boredom proneness and mobile phone dependence in college students [Abstract]. *Chinese Journal of Public Health.*

Young, K. S., & Rogers, R. C. (1998). The relationship between depression and Internet addiction. *Cyberpsychology & Behavior*, 1(1), 25–28. DOI: 10.1089/cpb.1998.1.25

Zamani, B. E., Abedini, Y., & Kheradmand, A. (2011). Internet addiction based on personality characteristics of high school students in Kerman, Iran. *Addiction & Health*, 3(3–4), 85–91. PMID: 24494121

Zeelenberg, M. (1999). Anticipated regret, expected feedback and behavioral decision making. *Journal of Behavioral Decision Making*, 12(2), 93–106. DOI: 10.1002/(SICI)1099-0771(199906)12:2<93::AID-BDM311>3.0.CO;2-S

Zhan, S., Shrestha, S., & Zhong, N. (2022). Romantic relationship satisfaction and phubbing: The role of loneliness and empathy. *Frontiers in Psychology*, 13, 967339. DOI: 10.3389/fpsyg.2022.967339 PMID: 36337547

Zhao, J., Zhang, S., Jiang, Y., & Liu, Y. (2016). Boredom proneness, impulsivity, and mobile phone addiction among university students. *Chinese Journal of Public Health.*

Zhou, X. (2010). Gratifications, Loneliness, Leisure Boredom and Selfesteem as Predictors of SNS-Game Addiction and Usage Pattern among Chinese College Students, (May), 35. DOI: 10.4018/ijcbpl.2012100103

Chapter 10

Personality Traits and Smartphone Addiction: An Evolving Addictive Trend

Irumba Pauline
https://orcid.org/0009-0001-0235-4131
Mountains of the Moon University, Uganda

Tugume Daniel
Mountains of the Moon University, Uganda

Brenda Nabawanuka
Mountains of the Moon University, Uganda

Mugerwa Herbert
Fortportal Regional Referral Hospital, Uganda

Katsomyo Edson
Mountains of the Moon University, Uganda

ABSTRACT

Personality traits ultimately contribute to different forms of addiction. Addictive behaviors such as compulsion to excessively use the smartphone can be equally detrimental to human health just like any form of drug addiction. Effects of smartphone addiction can either be short-term or long-term based on the extent of addiction. At a personal level, the individual could experience both physical and psychological health problems ranging from mild pain, visual disturbances to severe pain, suicidal ideations and actual suicide. Interpersonally, reduced human performance and poor social network could occur. The trait theories including HEXACO and five factor personality trait models together with their facets will be explored to appreciate

DOI: 10.4018/979-8-3693-8804-4.ch010

personality traits commonly associated with smartphone addiction. This chapter also discusses an approach to smartphone addicts including diagnosis and management.

INTRODUCTION

Personality is an invisible yet ultimately visible concept. Despite diverse definitions, it refers to differences between people in their psychologic characteristics excluding the physical-biological characteristics (Vazire, 2014). The distinct features of individual thoughts, feelings and behavior. Like a distinct entity, each individual owns either unique or related psychological characteristics. (ICD-11, 2024) explained personality as an individual characteristic way of behaving, experiencing life, and of perceiving, and interpreting themselves, other people, events, and situations. Basic self-analysis, health practitioner advanced analysis of individual psychosocial totality helps identify personality. It is critical to analyze self; understand the kind of person you are to acknowledge, and appreciate the unique differences in life.

(Millon et al., 2012) posed questions which are indeed seemingly easy to ask but with complexity when individual attempts are made to answer them. They included; What sort of person are you? What do you see as distinctive of your personality? How well do you know yourself? Are there aspects of your personality you are unaware of? Do others know you as you know yourself? What are the best and worst things about your personality? If you are to attempt them, how easily did you answer them? Did you find it necessary to do extra analysis on who you are? These questions resonate deeply in the context of humanity and a human being. The description of personality is evidenced in old books including that of Theophrastus (371-287 BC) who wrote about thirty personality types. More recent scholars Allport and Odbert (1936) contributed nearly 18,000 words related to personality. Due to the uniqueness of personality, it requires specific characteristics "traits" to describe it, whence personality traits (Matthews, 2003). To gain clear insight of personality traits, we have to delve individual features of thoughts, feeling and behaviors. These traits have been of significant interest in psychology, society, research and academia.

Personality traits are determined based on both the individuals' genetic composition and environmental contribution. As the individual ages in a given environment, the personality traits are subject to change. Life events ultimately contribute to personality trait development (Bleidorn et al., 2021; Diener & Lucas, 2019; Diener et al., 2019). This is contrary to proposition that human traits are predetermined; therefore, they are more likely to act and behave in a similar way across different life events. It is important to note that personality traits predict outcomes. This ranges from lifestyle, behavior and human performance among others (Lixăndroiu et al., 2021; Wu & Ke, 2015).

This chapter will focus on personality traits and smartphone addiction. Addiction itself is a broad concept too. Initially explained based on moral concepts which were disapproved by scientific evidence from psychology and psychiatry. Drug addiction and addictive behaviors have continued to affect societies globally irrespective of the level of civilization. Irrespective of the advancement in the scientific knowledge about addiction, challenges still prevail, and continue to grow including no single approach to treat addictive behaviors. Quite challenging is identifying an addiction. How would you identify an individual with smart phone addiction? Could you evaluate self and tell that your addicted to a smart phone? Recall the defense mechanism that come along with any form of addiction. Seemingly sensible reason to justify the wrong course of action "addiction". So what is addiction? In line with this chapter "smart phone addiction", it refers to a multifaceted disorder characterized by loss of control over use of a smartphone despite negative consequences (Henderson, 2009; Nathan et al., 2016).

Personality Traits

While personality entails different characteristics of individual thoughts, feelings, and behavior, personality traits refers to that which defines what a person will do when faced with a defined situation (Corr & Matthews, 2020). Personality traits are enduring patterns of perceiving, relating to, and thinking about the environment and oneself that are exhibited in a wide range of social and personal contexts (Diener et al., 2019). The word "trait" in personality trait emphasizes specific individual differences in personality.

The Five-Factor model trait system will be used to discuss traits and their facets to gain in-depth understanding of the individual's personality traits while examining their role in smartphone addiction. Components of the Five-Factor model trait system and the include Openness to experience, Conscientiousness, Extraversion, Agreeableness, and Neuroticism. These could be abbreviated as OCEAN (Krupnov et al., 2016). Studies have investigated the relationship between personality and addiction but with most emphasis on drug addiction (Charzyńska et al., 2021; Franken et al., 2006; O'Connor et al., 2009). A detailed account of the Five Factor Model will be described in the subsequent parts of this chapter. This provides a base of evidence on the role of personality in influencing addiction. In this 21st century, technology advancement has greatly shaped the development of personality trait. The great point of discussion is the influence of smart phone utilization on personality trait and vice versa. The intricate maze of the personality trait, the individual, existing life events and smart phone could culminate into smart phone addiction. Despite the fact that mobile phones are important prerequisites, they could also adversely affect the mental and physical health of users, often referred to as a "rising epidemic" (Kiran et al., 2019; Tariq & Irfan, 2019).

Complications from smart phone addictions can range from withdrawal symptoms much similar to those of drug addicts like musculoskeletal disturbances, pain, visual-auditory disturbances, irritability, great feelings of loss, anger, temper tantrums, anxiety, depression, to suicidal tendencies and actual suicide. Often affected individuals reach the point of complications either knowingly or unknowingly. Warning signals of smartphone addiction include but are not limited to strong need for the phone both in the morning, and late at night, restlessness when the phone is out of sight, and inability to reduce on phone usage. (Kuang-Tsan & Fu-Yuan, 2017; Shi et al., 2023) noted stressors in life of students and low psychological resilience and significant contributors to smart phone addiction. Response to stressors in our environment is also linked to our personality traits. In this chapter we will focus on personality traits that increase the likelihood of smart phone addiction, possible consequences and measures to ameliorate.

Psychologists have made conclusions that personality traits can be summarized as a Five Factor Model (Costa & McCrae, 2008). These five factors proposed to be the backbone of personality trait summarized in Table 1 are Openness to experience, Conscientiousness, Extraversion, Agreeableness, and Neuroticism [OCEAN] (Babcock & Wilson, 2020; Krupnov et al., 2016).

Table 1. Five factor model

Personality Trait	Description
Openness	Entails the tendency to appreciate new concepts, values, beliefs, behaviors, and feelings. Can be imaginative and exhibit curiosity.
Conscientiousness	Tends to law abiding, being careful, on time for appointments and activities, obedient and hardworking. Punctual and self-disciplined.
Extraversion	Mostly talkative, sociable, prefers being with others, and tends to be dominant over others. Has significant optimism.
Agreeableness	Agrees to go along with others rather than being assertive on personal opinions and choices. A forgiving and helpful character exists in the individual.
Neuroticism	Frequent experience of negative emotions including guilt, sadness, anger. May feel insecure and worrying about little things.

This was based on the fact that these factors are independent of each other whence providing dimensions to explore personality (Babcock & Wilson, 2020). However, other factors have been investigated and found to have independent significance in personality traits. Honesty and humility was proposed by (Ashton & Lee, 2005; Ashton et al., 2014) as a sixth factor whence the HEXACO model. The HEXACO model dimensions are; Honesty-Humility, Emotionality, eXtroversion, Agreeableness, Conscientiousness, and Openness to experience. Although it had some few concepts similar to those of Agreeableness, honesty and humility focused on the tendency to be fair and genuine when dealing with others. In this form of cooperation, one might exploit others without suffering retaliation from those affected (Liu et al., 2020). Other researchers have proposed that the dimensions in the Five Factor Model (FFM) could be summarized into two major dimensions (the Big Two model of personality) as plasticity and stability (Chang et al., 2014; Feist, 2019). Plasticity is associated with openness and Extroversion while Stability is linked to neuroticism, agreeableness, and conscientiousness. Stability entails mechanisms of coping with stress, negativity in life, and healthy social interactions while Plasticity involves exploration, adaptability to new situations, questioning societal practices and dealing with positive experiences (Feist, 2019).

To ascertain personality traits, assessment should be done with a clear understanding of the components of the model used vis-a-vis domains, aspects, and facets (Condon et al., 2021). The NEO inventories which are sets of psychological tests designed to assess the Five Factor Model of the basic personality traits have been in use for some decades (Digman, 1990; Goldberg, 1990; Kurtz, 2020). NEO inventory tool has been revised and improved overtime to include five factor domains and thirty facets (McCrae & Costa Jr, 2021). To gain in-depth understanding of personality traits in the Five Factor Model, it is important to understand facets (subtraits) of each personality trait. Facets in a given personality trait ultimately contribute to exhibition of a particular behavior and character. Studies have provided evidence on how facets in a given personality trait could ultimately contribute to given maladaptive behavior (Hakulinen et al., 2015; Lui et al., 2022; Terracciano et al., 2008). Figure 1 provides a summary of facets in each personality trait by (Kekäläinen et al., 2020).

Figure 1. Facets of personality traits according to the five factor model

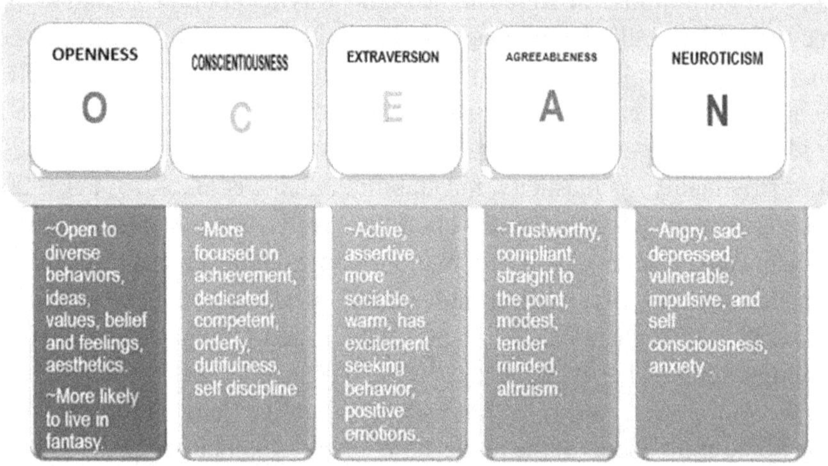

The HEXACO model's Honesty-Humility has faced criticism that its facets are expressed in Neuroticism and Agreeableness whence these critics find it inappropriate to have Honesty-Humility as a distinct trait (Howard & Van Zandt, 2020). Each of the six domains of the HEXACO model contains four (4) facets with altruism included as the 25th go between facet mainly linking domains Honesty-Humility, Agreeableness and Emotionality (Pletzer et al., 2020). These facets are as described by (Kibeom, 2009; Pletzer et al., 2021) are summarized in Table 2 below.

Table 2. Facets of personality traits according to the HEXACO model

Domain	Facet
Honesty-Humility	Sincerity
	Fairness
	Greed Avoidance
	Modesty
Emotionality	Fearfulness
	Anxiety
	Dependence
	Sentimentality

continued on following page

Table 2. Continued

Domain	Facet
eXtraversion	Social self-esteem
	Social boldness
	Sociability
	Liveliness
Agreeableness	Forgivingness
	Gentleness
	Flexibility
	Patience
Conscientiousness	Organization
	Diligence
	Perfectionism
	Prudence
Openness to experience	Aesthetic Appreciation
	Inquisitiveness
	Creativity
	Unconventionality

Altruism: Entails being sympathetic and soft hearted to others

Despite the above, distinct personality traits unique from those in the Five Factor and HEXACO models seem to affect and influence individual behavior. (Hodson et al., 2018; Muris et al., 2022) described how dark triad traits of Machiavellianism, psychopathy and narcissism are distinct forms of personality traits. Precisely, Machiavellianism involves emphasis on self- interest and personal gains. This is more of egocentricity and being self-centered while disregarding others. Psychopathy entails less empathy, antisocial behavior and reckless lifestyle. Lastly, narcissism is characterized by pride, exaggerated sense of importance and self-admiration (Hodson et al., 2018).(Akhtar et al., 2020; Duckitt, 2020; Fukunishi & Rahe, 1995; Karukivi & Saarijärvi, 2014; Pérez-Fernández et al., 2022; Schnelle et al., 2021; Weigel, 2022) proposed personality traits not included in the most commonly used models and dark triad traits are summarized in Figure 2 below.

Figure 2. Other personality traits

Despite their unpopularity among researchers and scientist, these traits ultimately contribute to individual behavior. However most of these "seeming" traits are described either as domains, facets of the HEXACO model and the Five Factor Model or mediators of personality traits (Bojanić et al., 2019; Skorek et al., 2014; Skues et al., 2012). However, this does not down play their uniqueness, as their own full construct differs slightly the domains and facets of personality traits in the HEXACO and Five Factor models. For example, self-esteem basically means respect of one's own values, and importance thereby living responsibly as a person while acting responsibly towards others. Such status follows evaluation of self in terms of qualities and traits. The process of building self-esteem evolves over time based on the prevailing environmental factors (Bojanić et al., 2019).

Optimism refers to the tendency to expect and hope for the best in future. Bringing hope in the definition of hope rekindles Emily Dickinson's poem "Hope is a thing with feathers" (1830-1886) "Hope the thing with feathers that soars and perches the soul." Optimism has been found to be strongly correlated with the four of the five traits except openness to experience in the Five Factor Model (Sharpe et al., 2011). Optimism as a personality trait is classified into optimistic explanatory style and dispositional optimism. In the former concept, individuals believe that bad events will eventually subside (they are temporary) while good things continue to happen. In the latter concept, individuals pursue goals that are most important to them including those that they feel so confident that they are likely to achieve (Forgeard &

Seligman, 2012). Optimism increases the likelihood of positive coping mechanisms whenever an individual is threatened with stressors.

The term alexithymia was developed to refer to a cognitive disturbance in which affected persons have difficulty in identifying, explaining their feelings, and often have rare imaginations. It is associated with poor social support and response to stress (Fukunishi & Rahe, 1995). Affected individuals are less likely to have good social interaction and more likely to have depression. Alexithymia has been related with both mental health disorders and somatic conditions not limited to anxiety disorders, eating disorders, diabetes mellitus and essential hypertension (Karukivi & Saarijärvi, 2014).

Need for recognition enables individuals with this trait to do their best to understand things and situations. They put in a lot of cognitive effort often finding pleasure in learning new events. Need for achievement was found to energize formation of social networks for transformation(Akhtar et al., 2020; Pérez-Fernández et al., 2022).

Individuals who are authoritarian believe in social hierarchies and are very obedient to those above with expectations of obedience from subordinates (Duckitt, 2020; Weigel, 2022). The authoritarian trait has been described a stable form of personality trait related to lower level of Openness to experience trait and higher level of Conscientiousness all in the Five Factor Model (Duckitt, 2022; Schnelle et al., 2021).

Disorders of Personality Traits

Also called personality disorders, this condition is present in one sixth of the general population and over a half of psychiatric patients (Cloninger & Svrakic, 2008). Disorders of personality traits (personality disorders) refers to significant disturbance in personality functioning, which is almost always associated with personal and societal disruption (ICD-11, 2024). To diagnose personality disorders, it requires a diagnostic criterion. Clinicians have to use a set of features to make a conclusion about the possibility of a personality disorder. Different diagnostic methods are used in different parts of the world to diagnose personality disorders. The commonest ones are Diagnostic Statistical Manual of Mental Health Disorders (DSM-5 TR), International Classification of Diseases (ICD-11), and Chinese Classification of Mental Disorders (CCMD-3) all of which have gone through different revisions and editions(DSM-5-TR, 2023; ICD-11, 2024; Wang et al., 2023). Table 3 below gives a brief description of personality disorders by DSM-5-TR(DSM-5-TR, 2023; Millon et al., 2012), and insight on severity of the personality disorder according to ICD-11(World Health Organization, 2024). The severity will be described in the subsequent sections (Table 4) of this chapter.

Table 3. Description of personality disorders

Personality disorder	Description
Paranoid	High index of suspicion, and distrust to others, thoughts that others just do their best to annoy and hurt them. Tend to have anger issues.
Narcissistic	Tend to have exaggerated sense of importance. Always have elevated opinions of themselves. Thoughts that they are a unique and special breed, and only special people can understand them. Feel they deserve special attention, intolerant to others
Obsessive compulsive	Have characteristics such stubbornness, inflexibility, perfectionist, and stingy. Pay too much attention to detail they lose track of the main objective, tend to be workaholics, have difficulty in throwing away old thing that they no longer need.
Schizotypal	Are suspicious, paranoid, feel anxious in social situations, think people are about them behind their back, have misinterpretation of reality.
Schizoid	Have less emotional and social support, socially isolated and not bothered by the isolation, not bother by happy moments or criticism. They get pleasure from few activities with less interest in sexual encounters.
Borderline	Affected by strong emotions; for example, an unexpected event could drastically affect the overall wellbeing and take long to recover from the experience. They alternate between positive and negative feelings.
Histrionic	Attention seeking, emotionally expressive and loud. Feel comfortable when they are the centre of attention, act like they are on stage.
Dependent	Have difficulty in making their own day to day decisions. Require reassurance most of the time. Unlikely to start projects on their own, less trust in their own abilities, unlikely to disagree with others.
Antisocial	Characterized by selfishness, being irresponsible, unlawful, and impulsive behavior. They find it easy to lie, be deceitful and con others, tend to be aggressive
Avoidant	Key features include extreme shyness, low self-esteem, sensitivity to rejection and criticism from others, difficulty in making friends, are uncomfortable in social events, and gatherings.
Depressive	Tend to be pessimistic rather than optimistic, feelings of being isolated, unworthy, guilty, have less interest in several activities including those of daily living.
Sadistic	Characterized by sudden outbursts, get satisfaction through domination, intimidation, humiliation and harassment of others.
Masochistic	Has fear for pleasure, blames others, encourages others to take advantage, gives up his/her accomplishments easily to others.
Negativistic	Tends to be skeptical and discontented, can choose to be inefficient, moody, irritable, and withdrawn.

A brief description of each personality disorder was given. As earlier indicated, a diagnostic criterion is required to confirm a specific type of personality disorder; for example, to diagnose schizoid personality disorder(DSM-5-TR, 2023), an individual should have at least four of the following;

Mostly enjoys solitary environment
Displays detachment, emotional coldness

Limited relationships other than first degree relatives
Has pleasure in very few activities
Minimal interest in sexual experiences with others
Limited or no enjoyment in close relationship.

All personality disorders have a different diagnostic criterion; for example, histrionic personality disorder has eight criteria while antisocial personality disorder has seven criteria. The details for diagnostic criteria of other types of personality disorders were not described in this chapter.

Smartphone Addiction

Addiction is one of the oldest conditions in healthcare, and human history. Knowingly or unknowingly most health professionals and workers are treating disorders linked to addiction in an individual. Often the root cause of this addiction is never addressed (Miller et al., 2019). With such, it appears more of symptomatic management when the pathologic process is taking toll on the patient. The term addiction has been mainly associated with substance abuse, but it can take into account other compulsive behaviors that puts one's life, and health in jeopardy. In addition, the individual exhibits ambivalence, both internal and external conflicts with difficulty in decision making to change the course. Precisely, addiction can be defined as loss of control over certain behaviors and continued engagement in such behaviors despite negative consequences (Henderson, 2009). Addiction could also refer to a behavioral disorder resulting from a series of changes in the brain with neuroadaptations being caused by repeated exposure to stimuli.

Similar to drug addiction, non-drug addictions are characterized by features such as craving, tolerance, withdrawal symptoms, impaired control over specific behaviors, and relapse (Olsen, 2011). Despite no ingestion of substances, behaviors have ability to trigger the same reward circuits in the brain leading to addiction which is observed in drug addiction (Hunt et al., 2024). This is through the dopaminergic mesolimbic system that has structures responsible for physiological and cognitive processes of reward. Both the dorsal and ventral regions of the brain are involved in the reward process of the brain (Lewis et al., 2021). Reward activities increase dopamine levels which alters rhythms in the suprachiasmatic nucleus which is the centre of brain reward mechanism (Lewis et al., 2021). The individual will be compelled to seek a certain behavior to achieve satisfaction with increased dopamine levels to a point when the victim has addictive features.

The Diagnostic and Statistical Manual, 5th Edition (DSM-V) describes Substance Related and Addictive Disorders across a trajectory that culminates into addictive consequences overtime. Comparing DSM-V to the older DSM-IV, there was categorization substance abuse disorders that result in addiction, and other forms disorders that could cause addiction; however global problematic use of gadgets and internet didn't get sufficient evidence to for an independent disorder (Grant & Chamberlain, 2016). Relatedly, the International Classification of Diseases, 11th Edition (ICD-11), includes a category due to addictive behaviors due to misuse of technological devices. This gave recognition to gaming and gambling disorders (Brand & Potenza, 2023). Compulsive social media use disorder has been reported in studies for being problematic affecting both physical and psychological domains of one's life (Kwon et al., 2013; Ting & Chen, 2020). Such addiction has the ability to induce other disorders such as paraphilia, factitious and neurocognitive disorders. There several predisposing factors that could result in different forms of addiction including smartphone addiction. Earlier childhood experiences such as severe recurrent physical abuse, sexual abuse, emotional abuse, growing up under the care of a drug abuser, growing up in domestically violent home, absence of biological parents, mental illness and growing up in a home where a member was imprisoned predisposed one to drug addiction even after 50 years (Dube et al., 2003; Felitti, 2003). Although this study focused on drug addiction, there is significant evidence on adverse childhood experiences and psychoanalytic observations that suggest addiction being a result of mainly childhood experiences (Clemens et al., 2022; Liang et al., 2021). The interaction between the child, and parents mediates the possibility of adverse childhood events and the possibility of smart phone addiction (Liang et al., 2021). The abnormal prior life experiences especially in childhood up to youthful stages most of which are concealed as taboo, shame, and secrets contribute to the future adult's behaviors and lived moments (Felitti, 2003). It is a sequence of events that are both internalized, and externalized contributing to addictive behavior (Dube et al., 2003; Felitti, 2003; Liang et al., 2021; Zarse et al., 2019) with its complications later in life as summarized in Figure 3 below.

Figure 3. Psychoanalytic observations showing that addiction is due to a series of events that begin with Adverse Childhood Experiences (ACEs)

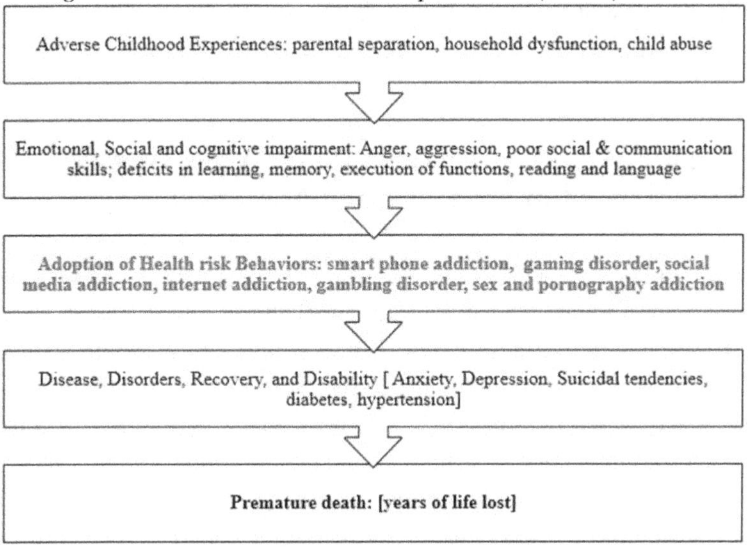

Smart phone Addiction, like other forms of addiction causes severe effects both physically, and psychologically despite some studies proposing that it should rather be maladaptive phone use (Balakrishnan & Griffiths, 2019; Panova & Carbonell, 2018). They propose that the evidence for addiction was linked to games, gambling and internet and not directly to the smartphone itself. However systematic reviews, meta analyses, and other studies have provided evidence on the existence of smartphone addiction with its consequences to health (Huan Liu et al., 2022; Olson et al., 2022; Osorio-Molina et al., 2021; Ratan et al., 2021). In the context of smartphone addiction, it is important to consider the basic and precise definitions of addiction by (Henderson, 2009; Olsen, 2011). "The loss of control over certain behaviors, and continued engagement in such behaviors despite negative consequences characterized by craving, tolerance, withdrawal symptoms, impaired control over specific behaviors, reduced level of function, and relapse among others". Smart phone addiction is a subtle threat to people's health despite not gaining the required attention. Use of smartphones for cyber loafing behaviors was found to negatively influence psychological well-being especially when there are less known or unknown rewards for the user (Krishna & Agrawal, 2023). (Aggarwal, 2013) reported severe mobile phone induced anxiety disorders in 26 percent of the doctors in their study. This was nearly consistent with (Sarkar et al., 2019) who found that over 40 percent of the medical students had medical issues due to over use of mobile phones. Illusions and hallucinations which can be both tactile and auditory have been confirmed as complications of smartphone over use in different studies(Lin et al., 2013; Mangot et al., 2018). Physical disorders from abuse of smartphones include; muscle rigidity and pain (Benites-Zapata et al., 2021), computer vision syndrome characterized by blurred vision, reddened eyes, fatigue, ocular irritation (Iqbal et al., 2021; Munshi et al., 2017).

Role of Individual's Genetic Composition and Stress in the Development of Smart Phone Addiction

Individual genetic composition can underlie different forms of addiction including smart phone addiction, and relatedly, stress contributes equally as an independent risk factor to smart phone addiction (Ducci & Goldman, 2012; Goldman et al., 2006; Sinha & Jastreboff, 2013; Zhang et al., 2022). These are quite subtle phenomena. It is important to appreciate that different individuals get exposed to this similar extrinsic factors (smartphones), several stressors, peer pressure without getting addicted. Contrary, those addicted could get exposed to similar extrinsic factors that culminate into addiction. Genes such as serotonin transporter, catechol-O-methyl transferase (COMT) and Monoamine oxidase A(MAOA) have been studied and implicated in altering the neurobiological pathways of impulsivity and reward (Ducci & Goldman, 2012). Impulsivity refers to the tendency to act rapidly in response to internal or external stimuli without reflection of the consequences of actions. This multidimensional concept follows heredity, and genetic predisposition; for example, those born to parents who are substance abusers are more likely to have high impulsivity due to the genetic risk (Gustavson et al., 2020; Khadka et al., 2014).

In South Korea, adolescents were found to be vulnerable to smartphone addiction due to limited control over their impulsivity much similar to what happen in addiction to substance misuse (Jo et al., 2018; Kim et al., 2014). Reward increases the possibility of smart through perceived satisfaction, gains, enjoyment and mood regulation (Chen et al., 2019; West et al., 2021). Collectively, satisfaction, gains, enjoyment and mood regulation are common drivers for smart phone usage on a continuum from normal use to problematic smart phone use, and the extreme end of smart phone addiction. Together with COMT genes, dopamine transporter genes (DAT1) influence dopamine neurotransmission. In the brain, COMT catabolizes released dopamine contributing to the presence or absence of dopamine. Dopamine and its associated structures play an important role in regulation of motivation behavior, mood, stress reduction, and cognitive process related to reward (Blum et al., 2014; Dreher et al., 2009). Derangements in dopamine secretion, and function through genetic hypodopaminergic brain function predisposes individuals to seek compensatory behaviors that can be addictive. These compensatory behaviors like use of a smartphone for games, internet, and videos activate the dopaminergic centres to release neuronal dopamine into the synapse which reverts the hypodopaminergic state (Blum et al., 2020; Blum et al., 2014).

Several studies conducted across different generations in some Asian, and European countries have provided clear evidence on how stress mediates smart phone addiction among young, and old (Chung & Kim, 2010; De-Sola Gutiérrez et al., 2016; Kuang-Tsan & Fu-Yuan, 2017; Kuss et al., 2018; Zhang et al., 2022). Stress is an old concept that can be internally or externally generated. It normally occurs when the body is deranged out of equilibrium. This can be through an actual or perceived threat. The definition of stress could vary based on the field under discussion but it could affect both the psychological and physical responses of the affected individual. People often misuse it to express their emotions, feelings or to mean distress (AIS, 2024; Phillips-Wren & Adya, 2020). The American Institute of Stress (AIS, 2024) proposed interesting definitions of stress notably, "*stress is the physical, emotional or mental tension*". Alternatively, stress was defined as "*the body's non-specific response to any demand which is either pleasant or non-pleasant*". The latter definition takes into consideration both good stress (eustress) and bad stress. Hans Bruno Selye often regarded as the "father of stress" had initially observed patients with different illnesses presenting with similar non-specific symptoms that were a common response to stressful stimuli in or out of the body (Fink, 2010).

So how does stress develop? It is indeed a gradual process of which one event contributes to the other; however irrespective of the pathway, a stressor is required. Beginning with the stressor the individual's response based on own internal environment will determine ultimate outcome either as good stress (eustress) or bad stress. In this evolution, the human being is the centre of focus (Goldstein & Kopin, 2007; Lu et al., 2021). Remember that this person has both the biological (visible) and psychological ("invisible but visible") aspects. The genotypic and phenotypic. In the presence of a stressful stimulus, the outcome will be based on the body's regulatory mechanisms. Often distress and eustress states tend to occur due to response; however insufficient response could yield sustress (Lu et al., 2021). When faced with a stressor, Figure 4 below provides an overview of stress in a human being as modified from (Goldstein & Kopin, 2007; Lu et al., 2021).

Figure 4. The evolution of stress in a human being

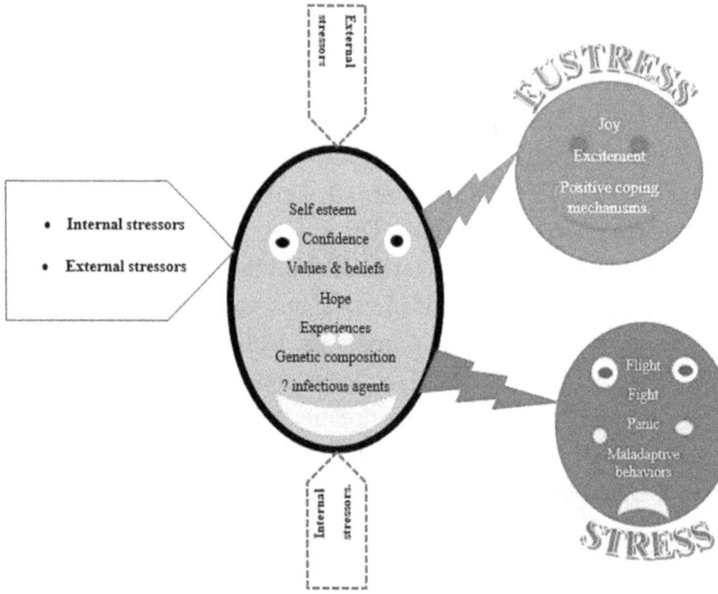

Stressors that initiate a cascade include; significant life events, strict deadlines, peer pressure, academic load, work load, losses in life, drastic-sudden changes in life and body pathological processes. Important to note that stress increases the possibility of smartphone addiction, and (Cho et al., 2017) found out that as stress increases, self-control reduces while smartphone addiction heightens. Self-control is protective against smartphone addiction; however, self-control doesn't help in isolation but together with other preexisting factors which are genetically and environmentally determined (Ahmad et al., 2024).

Screening for Smartphone Addiction

In this 21st Century and 3rd Millennium, technological advancement has brought a new dimension on earth. Digital devices including smartphones and internet are becoming indispensable tools in our routine activities. As such, addiction to smartphones and internet are on the rise (Tateno et al., 2019). Screening entails application of tests to determine if a patient has a certain condition in a given setting (Krist et al., 2020); however, screening tools have focused on drug addiction (Dwyer & Fraser, 2015; Krist et al., 2020). Screening tests for smartphone addiction has been a significant challenge due to the many functions smartphone including internet, games, social networks, media players, cameras, and Global Positioning System (GPS) among others (Moattari et al., 2017). Screening tools that focused on one or more of the functions of the smartphone have been developed and evaluated in many studies with some scales of measurement approved. The Internet Process Addiction Test (IPAT) evaluates four main addictive processes in its criterion which are; online social networking, online video gaming, online sexual activity and web surfing (Lozano-Blasco et al., 2022). Behavioral addictive questionnaire (BAQ) has been validated as effective tool for screening addictive behaviors in adults and youth over 18 years especially in European countries (Mastropietro et al., 2024). A related tool named Smartphone Addiction Scale (SAS) was developed and validated in Korea; then tested among college students of Japan (Kwon et al., 2013; Tateno et al., 2019) indicating levels of reliability and validity in this diagnostic tool for smartphone addiction. The Smartphone Addiction Inventory (SAI) was developed and validated across different settings in Asia and Europe especially youth (Lin et al., 2017; Pavia et al., 2016). Interestingly, smartphone addiction has been diagnosed then managed using criterion scales (Lin et al., 2016). Collectively, these screening tools for an addiction require in-depth understanding of the individual's physical and psychological well-being. The famous Smartphone Application-Based Addiction Scale (SABAS) has also been developed, validated and used to assess the risk of smart phone addiction in countries like Hungary, China and Italy (Csibi et al., 2018; Lin et al., 2014; Soraci et al., 2021; Yam et al., 2019). Combined, they demonstrated how the SABAS is a reliable and valid tool for assessing the risk for smartphone addiction in different setups in Asia and Europe. However, they require testing on a larger scale including other parts of the world including Africa.

Smartphone Application-Based Addiction Scale (SABAS)

Key screening statements include;

i. The smartphone is the most important thing in my life
ii. Preoccupying myself with the phone is the way of changing my mood.
iii. On several occasions, I keep around more and more with my phone
iv. I feel sad or irritable when I cannot use my smartphone when I need to.
v. When I try to reduce on usage of my smartphone, I do it for a little time; then use it even more than before.
vi. I have had conflict with either my friends or family members due to the use of my smartphone.

(Moattari et al., 2017; Young, 2017) proposed signs of smartphone addiction and they included the following:

- Obsessive use of the smartphone

- Increased and repetitive desire to check the smartphone.
- Spending vast amount of time on the smartphone
- Withdrawal and preference to using the smartphone
- Easily irritable sue to limited sleep because of overuse of the smartphone
- Compromise in routine performance of activities.

However, this tool has some similar criteria that is considered for the diagnosis of problematic phone use in (De-Sola Gutiérrez et al., 2016; DSM-5-TR, 2023). Despite no formal recognition in DSM-V, smart phone addiction has been intensively researched, and to a great extent ascertained. (Lin et al., 2016) proposed diagnostic criteria in Table 4 below. It was categorized into three from maladaptive disorders due smartphone use to the exclusion criteria.

Table 4. Diagnostic criteria for smartphone addiction

Criteria	Details
Criteria A	Maladaptive pattern of smartphone use, leading to clinically significant impairment or distress occurring anytime consecutively for a period not less than three (3) months. At least three (3) or more of the following symptoms should be present
	1. Recurrent failure to resist impulse to use the smartphone.
	2. Withdrawal symptoms characterized by dysphoria, anxiety and/or irritability following a period without smartphone use.
	3. Prolonged use of a smartphone; longer than the appropriate time
	4. Persistent desire and/or unsuccessful attempts to either quite or reduce smartphone use.
	5. Excessive time spent on use or quitting the smartphone use
	6. Continued excessive smartphone use despite of having knowledge on having either physical or psychological problems due to smartphone use.
Criteria B	Functional impairment: At least two (2) or more of the following symptoms have been present
	1. Excessive smartphone usage resulting in persistent or recurrent physical or psychological problem.
	2. Smartphone use in a physically hazardous situation such as during driving or crossing the street or having negative impacts on daily life.
	3. Smartphone use resulting in impairment of social relationships, academic or job performance.
	4. Excessive smartphone use causing significant subjective distress or is time consuming
Criteria C	Exclusion criteria
	The smartphone addictive behavior is not better accounted for by obsessive compulsive disorder or bipolar 1 disorder

Source: (Lin et al., 2016)

(De-Sola et al., 2017) also developed a tool to evaluate craving for smartphone, "The Mobile Phone Addiction Craving Scale" based on eight Likert style items. This study also found out higher craving in individuals up to 35 years.

Relationship Between Personality Traits and Smartphone Addiction Across Cultures

Personality traits being distinct at personal level, they significantly contribute to the possibility of smartphone addiction provided other genetic and environmental risk factors are present. (Arpaci & Kocadag Unver, 2020) found out that women who have emotional imbalance (neurotic) are likely to have smartphone addiction. They further reported that conscientious lessened the possibility of a women getting addicted to the smartphone. However, both males, and females with agreeableness were less to have smartphone addiction. Other studies (Lane et al., 2021; Lei et al., 2020) have emphasized that personality traits especially neuroticism could predispose one to smartphone addiction irrespective of being male or female. The peak of evidence through systematic review and meta-analysis still link neuroticism with smartphone addiction (Marciano et al., 2020, 2022). It is important to recall that the facets of neuroticism include; Anger, sad-depressed, vulnerable, impulsive, self-consciousness, and anxiety. Two important facets (impulsivity and anxiety) have already be discussed above with their contribution to smartphone addiction. Facets in emotionality personality trait could increase the risk of smart phone addiction. These are anxiety, dependence, sentimentality and fearfulness. (Yildiz, 2017) reported that mood regulatory processes are significant predictors of smartphone addiction. High smartphone addiction is more likely to happen in individuals with a dysfunctional mechanism for regulating emotions. There will be a high tendency of anxiety with problematic smartphone use, subsequently resulting in smartphone addiction.

Extraversion influences smartphone addiction if it prevails (Cho et al., 2017; Rahim et al., 2021). (Rahim et al., 2021) found out that although smartphone addiction is significantly related to both extroverts and introverts, the events leading to smartphone addiction were not similar. Introverts were found to use smartphones mostly for "process usage" while the extroverts were using smartphones for "social usage".

Despite openness to experience reported as a non-significant predictors of smartphone addiction in some studies (Erdem & Uzun, 2022; Kuyulu & Beltekin, 2020), some facets of openness to experience mainly creativity and inquisitiveness have been linked to smartphone addiction in some studies (Horwood & Anglim, 2018; Kheradmand et al., 2023). Such differences in personality traits and smartphone addiction could be attributed to study settings and methodological approaches.

Individuals who tend to develop interpersonal relationship with the help internet, social media platforms on a smartphone are at a higher risk of developing smartphone addiction (Hong et al., 2021; Lane et al., 2021). Smartphone addiction could be a reflection of the societal norms and level of peer to peer interaction. The fact that one is connected with up to a hundred or more individuals at a single point in time, he/she finds it necessary to link up, respond to the need through different platforms using a smartphone.

While agreeableness was found to be associated with smartphone addiction. Agreeable individuals are concerned with the overall wellbeing of others, and they tend to engage in instant messaging, and playing games with their smartphones (Afolayan, 2020; Roberts et al., 2015). Due to the characteristic of self-control, if no other psychological and biological derangement is present, conscientiousness reduces the possibility of smartphone addiction (Roberts et al., 2015).

Considering variations with other personality traits other than those in the Five Factor Model, study population, and methodologies, it is possible to get the reverse of the description above, For example, while (Afolayan, 2020) found out that conscientiousness and agreeableness traits were associated with smartphone addiction among Nigerian students. Horwood and Anglim (2018) found negative association between the two personality traits, and smartphone addiction among students in Australia. The dark triad traits (Machiavellianism, narcissism, and psychopathy) have also influence smartphone addiction. (Servidio et al., 2021) in their study found out that the dark triad mediated fear of missing out, and problematic phone use which a precursors of smartphone addiction. Individuals with the dark triad traits have been reported to find difficulty in managing their emotions with lability of anxiety, depression, and highly susceptible to smartphone addiction (Kaya, 2024; Kircaburun et al., 2021; Pirzade et al., 2024).

Important to note that personality traits tend to vary across cultural settings. Significant differences in the Five Factor Model were noted in studies conducted in Switzerland, parts of Africa (Zecca et al., 2013) and Bolivia (Gurven et al., 2013). The former group included literate French speaking people from Africa, Switzerland while the latter included illiterate Tsimane forager Bolivian indigenous people. Replicability of the Five Factor Model in the Bolivian group yielded poor results. It is possible to have unrelated personality traits, including those that are not yet discovered. There are several indigenous, and marginalized tribal groups all over the world whose health issues remain contrary to those of the baseline populations (Anderson et al., 2016). There is little to no consensus on variations in personalities across diverse indigenous cultures and settings as most studies do not collaborate with the indigenous people, and follow a predetermined approach (Church, 2008; Dudgeon et al., 2010; Laycock et al., 2011; Roethlisberger et al., 2023; Ryder et al., 2020). (Church, 2008) proposed that a consensus will be achieved if researchers could distinctly address the aspects of personality whether basic tendencies or characteristic adaptations. Could the Hadzabe, Herero, Nama, and Pygmy groups in Africa have same traits with the Aboriginal in Australia, Native Alaskans in United states of America? There is need for studies to clearly justify the similarities and differences. Likewise, irrespective of belonging to a marginalized or minority group, the difference in personality traits could arise from the culture in a given location. Whether rural or urban, differences in culture can exist based on location. Rural Shabunda in Democratic Republic of Congo, Muyinga in Burundi all in Africa differ from rural Lauterbrunnen in Switzerland and Xia county, Shanxi province- China. Urban Bangui in Central African Republic, Mbabane in Eswatini differ from urban Dili- East Timor Asia, and Nauru in Oceania. As discussed earlier, personality is subject to change rather than being inherent and strictly predetermined, partly contributed by cultural influences.

Despite cultural differences, use of smartphone and subsequent addiction is a global threat (Chóliz et al., 2016). A study conducted in four Asian countries found out that traits of social anxiety, materialism and self- expression were related with smart phone addiction (Lee et al., 2017). Relatedly, internet addiction in Asia and other continents was positively associated with neuroticism, and negatively associated with Conscientiousness, eXtraversion, and Agreeableness. Masculine cultural dimension was found to be associated with smartphone addiction (Moqbel et al., 2023). The masculinity referred to here is based on the gender roles rather than sex. Masculine individuals are preoccupied with competition, and success thus regard smartphones as items they have to continuously access, utilize to compete favourably (Ma & Turel, 2019). The effect of individualism and collectivism across societies could influence smartphone addiction. The former focus on caring for self and significant others while the latter being cared for by significant others. Individuals from societies with collectivism are more likely to have smartphone addiction as they prefer using smartphones to express their feelings and opinions (Alshare et al., 2024).

Management of Smartphone Addictions: Implications for Research and Clinical Practice

Like drug addiction, smartphone addiction requires appropriate optimal treatment and care or else complications ranging from social dysfunction, self-harm to addiction related death could occur. (Chun, 2018) proposed five interventions which were; peer support, school factors, involuntary restriction, professional services, self- awareness and regulation. Cognitive behavioral therapy (CBT) is also crucial in the management of smartphone addiction. (Wenzel, 2017) defined CBT as "an active, problem-focused and time sensitive treatment modality that aims at reducing emotional distress while improving positive coping mechanisms". The strategies prosed by (Wenzel, 2017) included cognitive restructuring, behavioral activation, and problem solving each as a unique treatment package. (Hofmann et al., 2012) recommended further randomized control trial to ascertain the efficacy of CBT despite a strong evidence base. This could hold for smartphone addiction which has not yet fully gained the attention it deserves in 2024. It has to date not gained universal acknowledgement, diagnostic approach and treatment modality. The application based intervention modalities have been developed, and tested. They include smartphone addiction rating score (SARR) based intervention was developed by (Park et al., 2020). A related approach "MindsCare" by (Lee et al., 2022) focus on management of individuals with smartphone addiction. They basically include application that require input of patient data under variables that suggest phone usage.

Physical therapy focused on physical exercises has been recommended (Huange Liu et al., 2022; Liu et al., 2019). (Huange Liu et al., 2022) suggested that physical exercises should be combined with psychological interventions. A randomized control trial by (Xiao et al., 2021) on the effect of basketball and baduanjin interventions for problematic phone use found that both interventions reduced problematic phone use. However, the basketball group had better improvement compared to that of baduanjin. This is suggests more randomized control trials on different forms of physical exercises in different settings, cultures in order to ascertain their feasibility.

Young people who are the most affected by smartphone addiction (Csibi et al., 2021) require targeted interventions due to limited control over their impulses. Digital detox interventions has yielded positive outcomes in some settings despite minimal to negative results in management of individuals with smartphone addiction (Radtke et al., 2022; Schmuck, 2020). Digital detox applications monitor smartphone use and limit users for a certain period of time. More studies with advancements in artificial intelligence and machine learning are required to improve the efficacy and efficiency of digital detox across different settings globally.

In conclusion, health facilities, and other institutions should consider smartphone addiction as a growing public health threat. This requires formulation of policies that will aid diagnosis, thereafter specialized therapy using modalities detailed therein this chapter.

Smartphone addiction is a significant growing subtle health threat. There several gaps for further research noted in this chapter. Like a blossom, it is yet to reach its heights in the near future with technological advancement. Without information about its presence, many will continue to be affected. An informed mind is much better than that which acts out of ignorance. Most of the literature, and advancement on smartphone addiction is from the developed nations creating uncertainty in the developing nations. It is necessary to develop "one global language" to address smartphone addiction.

REFERENCES

Afolayan, O. T. (2020). Personality Types as Correlate of Specific Phone Usages and Smart Phone Addiction among Students in the University of Ilorin, Kwara State, Nigeria. *Journal of Cyberspace Studies*, 4(1), 27–46.

Aggarwal, K. (2013). Twenty-six percent doctors suffer from severe mobile phone-induced anxiety: Excessive use of mobile phone can be injurious to your health. *Indian Journal of Clinical Practice : IJCP*, 24(1), 7–9.

Ahmad, F., Jameel, R., Rehmat, M., Munir, S., & Fatima, S. M. (2024). The Relationship between Self-Control, Personality Traits, and Smartphone Addiction in Students. *Remittances Review*, 9(2), 2771–2786.

AIS. (2024). *What is stress?*https://www.stress.org/what-is-stress/

Akhtar, S., Hongyuan, T., Iqbal, S., & Ankomah, F. Y. N. (2020). Impact of need for achievement on entrepreneurial intentions; mediating role of self-efficacy. *Journal of Asian Business Strategy*, 10(1), 114–121. DOI: 10.18488/journal.1006.2020.101.114.121

Alshare, K., Moqbel, M., Merhi, M. I., Bartelt, V., & Alam, M. (2024). The Impact of Cultural Dimensions and Quality of Life on Smartphone Addiction and Employee Performance: The Moderating Role of Quality of Life. *Information Systems Frontiers*, 1–19. DOI: 10.1007/s10796-024-10544-4

Anderson, I., Robson, B., Connolly, M., Al-Yaman, F., Bjertness, E., King, A., Tynan, M., Madden, R., Bang, A., Coimbra, C. E.Jr, Pesantes, M. A., Amigo, H., Andronov, S., Armien, B., Obando, D. A., Axelsson, P., Bhatti, Z. S., Bhutta, Z. A., Bjerregaard, P., & Yap, L. (2016). Indigenous and tribal peoples' health (The Lancet–Lowitja Institute Global Collaboration): A population study. *Lancet*, 388(10040), 131–157. DOI: 10.1016/S0140-6736(16)00345-7 PMID: 27108232

Arpaci, I., & Kocadag Unver, T. (2020). Moderating role of gender in the relationship between big five personality traits and smartphone addiction. *The Psychiatric Quarterly*, 91(2), 577–585. DOI: 10.1007/s11126-020-09718-5 PMID: 32100236

Ashton, M. C., & Lee, K. (2005). Honesty-humility, the Big Five, and the five-factor model. *Journal of Personality*, 73(5), 1321–1354. DOI: 10.1111/j.1467-6494.2005.00351.x PMID: 16138875

Ashton, M. C., Lee, K., & De Vries, R. E. (2014). The HEXACO honesty-humility, agreeableness, and emotionality factors: A review of research and theory. *Personality and Social Psychology Review*, 18(2), 139–152. DOI: 10.1177/1088868314523838 PMID: 24577101

Babcock, S. E., & Wilson, C. A. (2020). Big five model of personality. *The Wiley Encyclopedia of Personality and Individual Differences: Personality Processes and Individual Differences*, 55-60.

Balakrishnan, J., & Griffiths, M. D. (2019). Perceived addictiveness of smartphone games: A content analysis of game reviews by players. *International Journal of Mental Health and Addiction*, 17(4), 922–934. DOI: 10.1007/s11469-018-9897-5

Benites-Zapata, V. A., Jiménez-Torres, V. E., & Ayala-Roldán, M. P. (2021). Problematic smartphone use is associated with de Quervain's tenosynovitis symptomatology among young adults. *Musculoskeletal Science & Practice*, 53, 102356. DOI: 10.1016/j.msksp.2021.102356 PMID: 33667881

Bleidorn, W., Hopwood, C. J., Back, M. D., Denissen, J. J., Hennecke, M., Hill, P. L., Jokela, M., Kandler, C., Lucas, R. E., Luhmann, M., Orth, U., Roberts, B. W., Wagner, J., Wrzus, C., & Zimmermann, J. (2021). Personality trait stability and change. *Personality Science*, 2(1), e6009. DOI: 10.5964/ps.6009

Blum, K., Baron, D., Lott, L., Ponce, J. V., Siwicki, D., Boyett, B., Steinberg, B., Modestino, E. J., Fried, L., Hauser, M., Simpatico, T., Downs, B. W., McLaughlin, T., Hajela, R., & Badgaiyan, R. D. (2020). In search of reward deficiency syndrome (RDS)-free controls: The "holy grail" in genetic addiction risk testing. *Current Psychopharmacology*, 9(1), 7–21. DOI: 10.2174/2211556008666191111103152 PMID: 32432025

Blum, K., Oscar-Berman, M., Demetrovics, Z., Barh, D., & Gold, M. S. (2014). Genetic addiction risk score (GARS): Molecular neurogenetic evidence for predisposition to reward deficiency syndrome (RDS). *Molecular Neurobiology*, 50(3), 765–796. DOI: 10.1007/s12035-014-8726-5 PMID: 24878765

Bojanić, Ž., Nedeljković, J., Šakan, D., Mitić, P. M., Milovanović, I., & Drid, P. (2019). Personality traits and self-esteem in combat and team sports. *Frontiers in Psychology*, 10, 2280. DOI: 10.3389/fpsyg.2019.02280 PMID: 31649595

Brand, M., & Potenza, M. N. (2023). Behavioral addictions in the ICD-11: An important debate that is anticipated to continue for some time: Commentary to the debate: "Behavioral addictions in the ICD-11". *Journal of Behavioral Addictions*, 12(3), 585–589. DOI: 10.1556/2006.2023.00042 PMID: 37682725

Chang, C.-C., Wang, J.-H., Liang, C.-T., & Liang, C. (2014). Curvilinear effects of openness and agreeableness on the imaginative capability of student designers. *Thinking Skills and Creativity*, 14, 68–75. DOI: 10.1016/j.tsc.2014.09.001

Charzyńska, E., Sussman, S., & Atroszko, P. A. (2021). Profiles of potential behavioral addictions' severity and their associations with gender, personality, and well-being: A person-centered approach. *Addictive Behaviors*, 119, 106941. DOI: 10.1016/j.addbeh.2021.106941 PMID: 33915392

Chen, C., Zhang, K. Z., Gong, X., & Lee, M. (2019). Dual mechanisms of reinforcement reward and habit in driving smartphone addiction: The role of smartphone features. *Internet Research*, 29(6), 1551–1570. DOI: 10.1108/INTR-11-2018-0489

Cho, H. Y., Kim, D. J., & Park, J. W. (2017). Stress and adult smartphone addiction: Mediation by self-control, neuroticism, and extraversion. *Stress and Health*, 33(5), 624–630. DOI: 10.1002/smi.2749 PMID: 28332778

Chóliz, M., Pinto, L., Phansalkar, S. S., Corr, E., Mujjahid, A., Flores, C., & Barrientos, P. E. (2016). Development of a brief multicultural version of the test of mobile phone dependence (TMDbrief) questionnaire. *Frontiers in Psychology*, 7, 650. DOI: 10.3389/fpsyg.2016.00650 PMID: 27252663

Chun, J. (2018). Conceptualizing effective interventions for smartphone addiction among Korean female adolescents. *Children and Youth Services Review*, 84, 35–39. DOI: 10.1016/j.childyouth.2017.11.013

Chung, S.-K., & Kim, C.-G. (2010). Influences of depression, stress, and self-efficacy on the addiction of cell phone use among university students. *Korean Journal of Adult Nursing*, 22(1), 41–50.

Church, A. T. (2008). Current controversies in the study of personality across cultures. *Social and Personality Psychology Compass*, 2(5), 1930–1951. DOI: 10.1111/j.1751-9004.2008.00132.x

Clemens, V., Fegert, J. M., & Allroggen, M. (2022). Adverse childhood experiences and grandiose narcissism–Findings from a population-representative sample. *Child Abuse & Neglect*, 127, 105545. DOI: 10.1016/j.chiabu.2022.105545 PMID: 35217322

Cloninger, C. R., & Svrakic, D. M. (2008). Personality disorders. *The medical basis of psychiatry*, 471-483.

Condon, D. M., Wood, D., Mõttus, R., Booth, T., Costantini, G., Greiff, S., Johnson, W., Lukaszewski, A., Murray, A., & Revelle, W. (2021). Bottom up construction of a personality taxonomy. *European Journal of Psychological Assessment*.

Corr, P. J., & Matthews, G. (2020). *The Cambridge handbook of personality psychology*. Cambridge University Press.

Costa, P. T., & McCrae, R. R. (2008). The revised neo personality inventory (neo-pi-r). *The SAGE handbook of personality theory and assessment, 2*(2), 179-198.

Csibi, S., Griffiths, M. D., Cook, B., Demetrovics, Z., & Szabo, A. (2018). The psychometric properties of the smartphone application-based addiction scale (SABAS). *International Journal of Mental Health and Addiction*, 16(2), 393–403. DOI: 10.1007/s11469-017-9787-2 PMID: 29670500

Csibi, S., Griffiths, M. D., Demetrovics, Z., & Szabo, A. (2021). Analysis of problematic smartphone use across different age groups within the 'components model of addiction'. *International Journal of Mental Health and Addiction*, 19(3), 616–631. DOI: 10.1007/s11469-019-00095-0

De-Sola, J., Talledo, H., Rubio, G., & de Fonseca, F. R. (2017). Development of a mobile phone addiction craving scale and its validation in a Spanish adult population. *Frontiers in Psychiatry*, 8, 90. DOI: 10.3389/fpsyt.2017.00090 PMID: 28611692

De-Sola Gutiérrez, J., Rodríguez de Fonseca, F., & Rubio, G. (2016). Cell-phone addiction: A review. *Frontiers in Psychiatry*, 7, 175. DOI: 10.3389/fpsyt.2016.00175 PMID: 27822187

Diener, E., & Lucas, R. E. (2019). Personality traits. *General psychology: Required reading, 278.*

Diener, E., Lucas, R. E., & Cummings, J. A. (2019). *16.1 Personality Traits*. Introduction to Psychology.

Digman, J. M. (1990). Personality structure: Emergence of the five-factor model. *Annual Review of Psychology*, 41(1), 417–440. DOI: 10.1146/annurev.ps.41.020190.002221

Dreher, J.-C., Kohn, P., Kolachana, B., Weinberger, D. R., & Berman, K. F. (2009). Variation in dopamine genes influences responsivity of the human reward system. *Proceedings of the National Academy of Sciences of the United States of America*, 106(2), 617–622. DOI: 10.1073/pnas.0805517106 PMID: 19104049

DSM-5-TR. (2023). *Understanding Mental Disorders: Your Guide to DSM-5-TR®*. American Psychiatric Pub.

Dube, S. R., Felitti, V. J., Dong, M., Chapman, D. P., Giles, W. H., & Anda, R. F. (2003). Childhood abuse, neglect, and household dysfunction and the risk of illicit drug use: The adverse childhood experiences study. *Pediatrics*, 111(3), 564–572. DOI: 10.1542/peds.111.3.564 PMID: 12612237

Ducci, F., & Goldman, D. (2012). The genetic basis of addictive disorders. *Psychiatria Clinica*, 35(2), 495–519. PMID: 22640768

Duckitt, J. (2020). Authoritarianism. *Encyclopedia of personality and individual differences*, 322-329.

Duckitt, J. (2022). Authoritarianism: Conceptualization, research, and new developments. *The Cambridge handbook of political psychology*, 177-197.

Dudgeon, P., Kelly, K., & Walker, R. (2010). Closing the gaps in and through Indigenous health research: Guidelines, processes and practices. *Australian Aboriginal Studies*, (2), 81–91.

Dwyer, R., & Fraser, S. (2015). Addiction screening and diagnostic tools:'Refuting'and 'unmasking'claims to legitimacy. *The International Journal on Drug Policy*, 26(12), 1189–1197. DOI: 10.1016/j.drugpo.2015.08.016 PMID: 26386890

Erdem, C., & Uzun, A. M. (2022). Smartphone addiction among undergraduates: Roles of personality traits and demographic factors. *Technology. Knowledge and Learning*, 27(2), 579–597. DOI: 10.1007/s10758-020-09467-1

Feist, G. J. (2019). Creativity and the Big Two model of personality: Plasticity and stability. *Current Opinion in Behavioral Sciences*, 27, 31–35. DOI: 10.1016/j.cobeha.2018.07.005

Felitti, V. J. (2003). The origins of addiction: Evidence from the adverse childhood experiences study. *Praxis der Kinderpsychologie und Kinderpsychiatrie*, 52(8), 547–559. PMID: 14619682

Fink, G. (2010). Stress: Definition and history. *Stress Science: Neuroendocrinology, 3*(9), 3-14.

Forgeard, M. J., & Seligman, M. E. (2012). Seeing the glass half full: A review of the causes and consequences of optimism. *Pratiques Psychologiques*, 18(2), 107–120. DOI: 10.1016/j.prps.2012.02.002

Franken, I. H., Muris, P., & Georgieva, I. (2006). Gray's model of personality and addiction. *Addictive Behaviors*, 31(3), 399–403. DOI: 10.1016/j.addbeh.2005.05.022 PMID: 15964149

Fukunishi, I., & Rahe, R. H. (1995). Alexithymia and coping with stress in healthy persons: Alexithymia as a personality trait is associated with low social support and poor responses to stress. *Psychological Reports*, 76(3, suppl), 1299–1304. DOI: 10.2466/pr0.1995.76.3c.1299 PMID: 7480499

Goldberg, L. R. (1990). An alternative "description of personality": the big-five factor structure. psycnet.

Goldman, D., Oroszi, G., & Ducci, F. (2006). The genetics of addictions: Uncovering the genes. *Focus (San Francisco, Calif.)*, 6(3), 521–415. DOI: 10.1176/foc.4.3.401 PMID: 15995696

Goldstein, D. S., & Kopin, I. J. (2007). Evolution of concepts of stress. *Stress (Amsterdam, Netherlands)*, 10(2), 109–120. DOI: 10.1080/10253890701288935 PMID: 17514579

Grant, J. E., & Chamberlain, S. R. (2016). Expanding the definition of addiction: DSM-5 vs. ICD-11. *CNS Spectrums*, 21(4), 300–303. DOI: 10.1017/S1092852916000183 PMID: 27151528

Gurven, M., Von Rueden, C., Massenkoff, M., Kaplan, H., & Lero Vie, M. (2013). How universal is the Big Five? Testing the five-factor model of personality variation among forager–farmers in the Bolivian Amazon. *Journal of Personality and Social Psychology*, 104(2), 354–370. DOI: 10.1037/a0030841 PMID: 23245291

Gustavson, D. E., Friedman, N. P., Fontanillas, P., Elson, S. L., Palmer, A. A., & Sanchez-Roige, S. (2020). The latent genetic structure of impulsivity and its relation to internalizing psychopathology. *Psychological Science*, 31(8), 1025–1035. DOI: 10.1177/0956797620938160 PMID: 32716714

Hakulinen, C., Elovainio, M., Batty, G. D., Virtanen, M., Kivimäki, M., & Jokela, M. (2015). Personality and alcohol consumption: Pooled analysis of 72,949 adults from eight cohort studies. *Drug and Alcohol Dependence*, 151, 110–114. DOI: 10.1016/j.drugalcdep.2015.03.008 PMID: 25823906

Henderson, E. C. (2009). *Understanding addiction*. Univ. Press Of Mississippi.

Hodson, G., Book, A., Visser, B. A., Volk, A. A., Ashton, M. C., & Lee, K. (2018). Is the dark triad common factor distinct from low honesty-humility? *Journal of Research in Personality*, 73, 123–129. DOI: 10.1016/j.jrp.2017.11.012

Hofmann, S. G., Asnaani, A., Vonk, I. J., Sawyer, A. T., & Fang, A. (2012). The efficacy of cognitive behavioral therapy: A review of meta-analyses. *Cognitive Therapy and Research*, 36(5), 427–440. DOI: 10.1007/s10608-012-9476-1 PMID: 23459093

Hong, F.-Y., Lin, C.-C., Lin, T.-J., & Huang, D.-H. (2021). The relationship among the social norms of college students, and their interpersonal relationships, smartphone use, and smartphone addiction. *Behaviour & Information Technology*, 40(4), 415–426. DOI: 10.1080/0144929X.2019.1699959

Horwood, S., & Anglim, J. (2018). Personality and problematic smartphone use: A facet-level analysis using the Five Factor Model and HEXACO frameworks. *Computers in Human Behavior*, 85, 349–359. DOI: 10.1016/j.chb.2018.04.013

Howard, M. C., & Van Zandt, E. C. (2020). The discriminant validity of honesty-humility: A meta-analysis of the HEXACO, Big Five, and Dark Triad. *Journal of Research in Personality*, 87, 103982. DOI: 10.1016/j.jrp.2020.103982

Hunt, A., Merola, G. P., Carpenter, T., & Jaeggi, A. V. (2024). Evolutionary perspectives on substance and behavioural addictions: Distinct and shared pathways to understanding, prediction and prevention. *Neuroscience and Biobehavioral Reviews*, 159, 105603. DOI: 10.1016/j.neubiorev.2024.105603 PMID: 38402919

ICD-11. (2024). *Personality disorders and related traits* ICD-11 for Morbidity and Mortality Statistics. https://icd.who.int/dev11/l-m/en#/http%3a%2f%2fid.who.int%2ficd%2fentity%2f37291724

Iqbal, M., Said, O., Ibrahim, O., & Soliman, A. (2021). Visual Sequelae of Computer Vision Syndrome: A Cross-Sectional Case-Control Study. *Journal of Ophthalmology*, 2021(1), 6630286. DOI: 10.1155/2021/6630286 PMID: 33868724

Jo, H., Na, E., & Kim, D.-J. (2018). The relationship between smartphone addiction predisposition and impulsivity among Korean smartphone users. *Addiction Research and Theory*, 26(1), 77–84. DOI: 10.1080/16066359.2017.1312356

Karukivi, M., & Saarijärvi, S. (2014). Development of alexithymic personality features. *World Journal of Psychiatry*, 4(4), 91. DOI: 10.5498/wjp.v4.i4.91 PMID: 25540724

Kaya, B. (2024). Dark triad and social media addiction: A meta-analysis. *Klinik Psikoloji Dergisi*, 8(2), 310–319.

Kekäläinen, T., Terracciano, A., Sipilä, S., & Kokko, K. (2020). Personality traits and physical functioning: A cross-sectional multimethod facet-level analysis. *European Review of Aging and Physical Activity*, 17(1), 1–13. DOI: 10.1186/s11556-020-00251-9 PMID: 33292163

Khadka, S., Narayanan, B., Meda, S., Gelernter, J., Han, S., Sawyer, B., Aslanzadeh, F., Stevens, M., Hawkins, K., Anticevic, A., Potenza, M. N., & Pearlson, G. D. (2014). Genetic association of impulsivity in young adults: A multivariate study. *Translational Psychiatry*, 4(9), e451–e451. DOI: 10.1038/tp.2014.95 PMID: 25268255

Kheradmand, A., Amirlatifi, E. S., & Rahbar, Z. (2023). Personality traits of university students with smartphone addiction. *Frontiers in Psychiatry*, 14, 1083214. DOI: 10.3389/fpsyt.2023.1083214 PMID: 36846239

Kibeom, L., & Michael, C. (2009). *The Hexaco personality inventory - Revised, a measure of the six major dimensions of personality*. Retrieved 29 November, 2024 from https://hexaco.org/scaledescriptions

Kim, S. M., Huh, H. J., Cho, H., Kwon, M., Choi, J. H., Ahn, H. J., Lee, S. W., Kim, Y. J., & Kim, D. J. (2014). The effect of depression, impulsivity, and resilience on smartphone addiction in university students. *Journal of Korean Neuropsychiatric Association*, 53(4), 214–220. DOI: 10.4306/jknpa.2014.53.4.214

Kiran, S., Sanjana, J., & Reddy, N. (2019). *Mobile phone addiction: symptoms, impacts and causes-a review*. Int Conf Trends Ind Value Eng Bus Soc Innov.

Kircaburun, K., Süral, İ., March, E., Balta, S., Emirtekin, E., & Griffiths, M. D. (2021). Study addiction and 'dark'personality traits: A cross-sectional survey study among emerging adults. *Journal of Addictive Diseases*, 39(3), 307–315. DOI: 10.1080/10550887.2021.1872469 PMID: 33499773

Krishna, S. M., & Agrawal, S. (2023). Cyberloafing: Exploring the role of psychological wellbeing and social media learning. *Behavioral Sciences (Basel, Switzerland)*, 13(8), 649. DOI: 10.3390/bs13080649 PMID: 37622789

Krist, A. H., Davidson, K. W., Mangione, C. M., Barry, M. J., Cabana, M., Caughey, A. B., Curry, S. J., Donahue, K., Doubeni, C. A., Epling, J. W.Jr, Kubik, M., Ogedegbe, G., Pbert, L., Silverstein, M., Simon, M. A., Tseng, C.-W., & Wong, J. B. (2020). Screening for unhealthy drug use: US Preventive Services Task Force recommendation statement. *Journal of the American Medical Association*, 323(22), 2301–2309. DOI: 10.1001/jama.2020.8020 PMID: 32515821

Krupnov, A., Novikova, I., & Vorobyeva, A. (2016). On the problem of relation between the system-functional and the five-factor models of personality traits. *RUDN Journal of Psychology and Pedagogics*, (2), 45–56.

Kuang-Tsan, C., & Fu-Yuan, H. (2017). Study on relationship among university students' life stress, smart mobile phone addiction, and life satisfaction. *Journal of Adult Development*, 24(2), 109–118. DOI: 10.1007/s10804-016-9250-9

Kurtz, J. E. (2020). NEO Inventories. In *Encyclopedia of personality and individual differences* (pp. 3164–3165). Springer. DOI: 10.1007/978-3-319-24612-3_940

Kuss, D. J., Kanjo, E., Crook-Rumsey, M., Kibowski, F., Wang, G. Y., & Sumich, A. (2018). Problematic mobile phone use and addiction across generations: The roles of psychopathological symptoms and smartphone use. *Journal of Technology in Behavioral Science*, 3(3), 141–149. DOI: 10.1007/s41347-017-0041-3 PMID: 30238057

Kuyulu, I., & Beltekin, E. (2020). Relationship between Smartphone Addiction and Personality Traits. *Asian Journal of Education and Training, 6*(2), 304-313.

Kwon, M., Lee, J.-Y., Won, W.-Y., Park, J.-W., Min, J.-A., Hahn, C., Gu, X., Choi, J.-H., & Kim, D.-J. (2013). Development and validation of a smartphone addiction scale (SAS). *PLoS One*, 8(2), e56936. DOI: 10.1371/journal.pone.0056936 PMID: 23468893

Lane, H.-Y., Chang, C.-J., Huang, C.-L., & Chang, Y.-H. (2021). An investigation into smartphone addiction with personality and sleep quality among university students. *International Journal of Environmental Research and Public Health*, 18(14), 7588. DOI: 10.3390/ijerph18147588 PMID: 34300037

Laycock, A. F., Walker, D., Harrison, N., & Brands, J. (2011). Researching Indigenous health: A practical guide for researchers.

Lee, S. J., Choi, M. J., Yu, S. H., Kim, H., Park, S. J., & Choi, I. Y. (2022). Development and evaluation of smartphone usage management system for preventing problematic smartphone use. *Digital Health*, 8. DOI: 10.1177/20552076221089095 PMID: 35371530

Lee, Y.-K., Chang, C.-T., Lin, Y., & Cheng, Z.-H. (2017). Heads-down tribes across four Asian countries: Antecedents of smartphone addiction. *International Journal of Mobile Communications*, 15(4), 414–436. DOI: 10.1504/IJMC.2017.084863

Lei, L. Y.-C., Ismail, M. A.-A., Mohammad, J. A.-M., & Yusoff, M. S. B. (2020). The relationship of smartphone addiction with psychological distress and neuroticism among university medical students. *BMC Psychology*, 8(1), 1–9. DOI: 10.1186/s40359-020-00466-6 PMID: 32917268

Lewis, R. G., Florio, E., Punzo, D., & Borrelli, E. (2021). *The Brain's reward system in health and disease*. Springer.

Liang, H.-Y., Zhang, B., Jiang, H.-B., & Zhou, H.-L. (2021). Adult attachment: Its mediation role on childhood trauma and mobile phone addiction. *Journal of Psychology in Africa*, 31(4), 369–374. DOI: 10.1080/14330237.2021.1952706

Lin, Y.-H., Chang, L.-R., Lee, Y.-H., Tseng, H.-W., Kuo, T. B., & Chen, S.-H. (2014). Development and validation of the Smartphone Addiction Inventory (SPAI). *PLoS One*, 9(6), e98312. DOI: 10.1371/journal.pone.0098312 PMID: 24896252

Lin, Y.-H., Chiang, C.-L., Lin, P.-H., Chang, L.-R., Ko, C.-H., Lee, Y.-H., & Lin, S.-H. (2016). Proposed diagnostic criteria for smartphone addiction. *PLoS One*, 11(11), e0163010. DOI: 10.1371/journal.pone.0163010 PMID: 27846211

Lin, Y.-H., Lin, S.-H., Li, P., Huang, W.-L., & Chen, C.-Y. (2013). Prevalent hallucinations during medical internships: Phantom vibration and ringing syndromes. *PLoS One*, 8(6), e65152. DOI: 10.1371/journal.pone.0065152 PMID: 23762302

Lin, Y. H., Pan, Y. C., Lin, S. H., & Chen, S. H. (2017). Development of short-form and screening cutoff point of the Smartphone Addiction Inventory (SPAI-SF). *International Journal of Methods in Psychiatric Research*, 26(2), e1525. DOI: 10.1002/mpr.1525 PMID: 27658956

Liu, H., Soh, K. G., Samsudin, S., Rattanakoses, W., & Qi, F. (2022). Effects of exercise and psychological interventions on smartphone addiction among university students: A systematic review. *Frontiers in Psychology*, 13, 1021285. DOI: 10.3389/fpsyg.2022.1021285 PMID: 36275318

Liu, H., Zhou, Z., Huang, L., Zhu, E., Yu, L., & Zhang, M. (2022). Prevalence of smartphone addiction and its effects on subhealth and insomnia: A cross-sectional study among medical students. *BMC Psychiatry*, 22(1), 305. DOI: 10.1186/s12888-022-03956-6 PMID: 35488216

Liu, J., Zettler, I., & Hilbig, B. E. (2020). Honesty-humility. *Encyclopedia of personality and individual differences*, 1996-2004.

Liu, S., Xiao, T., Yang, L., & Loprinzi, P. D. (2019). Exercise as an alternative approach for treating smartphone addiction: A systematic review and meta-analysis of random controlled trials. *International Journal of Environmental Research and Public Health*, 16(20), 3912. DOI: 10.3390/ijerph16203912 PMID: 31618879

Lixăndroiu, R., Cazan, A.-M., & Maican, C. I. (2021). An analysis of the impact of personality traits towards augmented reality in online shopping. *Symmetry*, 13(3), 416. DOI: 10.3390/sym13030416

Lozano-Blasco, R., Latorre-Martínez, M. P., & Cortés-Pascual, A. (2022). Screen addicts: A meta-analysis of internet addiction in adolescence. *Children and Youth Services Review*, 135, 106373. DOI: 10.1016/j.childyouth.2022.106373

Lu, S., Wei, F., & Li, G. (2021). The evolution of the concept of stress and the framework of the stress system. *Cell Stress*, 5(6), 76–85. DOI: 10.15698/cst2021.06.250 PMID: 34124582

Lui, P. P., Chmielewski, M., Trujillo, M., Morris, J., & Pigott, T. D. (2022). Linking big five personality domains and facets to alcohol (mis) use: A systematic review and meta-analysis. *Alcohol and Alcoholism*, 57(1), 58–73. DOI: 10.1093/alcalc/agab030 PMID: 33893471

Ma, Y., & Turel, O. (2019). Information technology use for work and technostress: Effects of power distance and masculinity culture dimensions. *Cognition Technology and Work*, 21(1), 145–157. DOI: 10.1007/s10111-018-0503-1

Mangot, A. G., Murthy, V. S., Kshirsagar, S. V., Deshmukh, A. H., & Tembe, D. V. (2018). Prevalence and pattern of phantom ringing and phantom vibration among medical interns and their relationship with smartphone use and perceived stress. *Indian Journal of Psychological Medicine*, 40(5), 440–445. DOI: 10.4103/IJPSYM.IJPSYM_141_18 PMID: 30275619

Marciano, L., Camerini, A.-L., & Schulz, P. J. (2020). Neuroticism in the digital age: A meta-analysis. *Computers in Human Behavior Reports*, 2, 100026. DOI: 10.1016/j.chbr.2020.100026

Marciano, L., Camerini, A.-L., & Schulz, P. J. (2022). Neuroticism and internet addiction: What is next? A systematic conceptual review. *Personality and Individual Differences*, 185, 111260. DOI: 10.1016/j.paid.2021.111260

Mastropietro, S., Favieri, F., Forte, G., Locuratolo, N., Mannarelli, D., Pauletti, C., Fattapposta, F., & Casagrande, M. (2024). Behavioral Addictions Questionnaire (BAQ): Validation of a new tool for the screening of multiple addictive behaviors in the Italian population. *International Journal of Mental Health and Addiction*, 22(3), 965–978. DOI: 10.1007/s11469-022-00906-x

Matthews, G. (2003). *Personality Traits*. Cambridge University Press. DOI: 10.1017/CBO9780511812736

McCrae, R. R., & Costa, P. T.Jr. (2021). Understanding persons: From stern's personalistics to Five-factor theory. *Personality and Individual Differences*, 169, 109816. DOI: 10.1016/j.paid.2020.109816

Miller, W. R., Forcehimes, A. A., & Zweben, A. (2019). *Treating addiction: A guide for professionals*. Guilford Publications.

Millon, T., Millon, C. M., Meagher, S. E., Grossman, S. D., & Ramnath, R. (2012). *Personality disorders in modern life*. John Wiley & Sons.

Moattari, M., Moattari, F., Kaka, G., Kouchesfahani, H. M., Sadraie, S. H., & Naghdi, M. (2017). Smartphone addiction, sleep quality and mechanism. *Int J Cogn Behav*, 1(002).

Moqbel, M., Bertelt, V., Alam, M., Younus Shaik, A., Montoya, S., & Larson, M. (2023). Smartphone addiction and cultural dimensions.

Munshi, S., Varghese, A., & Dhar-Munshi, S. (2017). Computer vision syndrome—A common cause of unexplained visual symptoms in the modern era. *International Journal of Clinical Practice*, 71(7), e12962. DOI: 10.1111/ijcp.12962 PMID: 28594459

Muris, P., Jeurissen, A., Rooswinkel, M., & Meesters, C. (2022). Good traits, bad traits, and 'ugly' behavior: Relations between the dark triad, honesty-humility, other hexaco personality traits, and externalizing problems in adolescents. *Journal of Child and Family Studies*, 31(12), 3247–3257. DOI: 10.1007/s10826-022-02344-8

Nathan, P. E., Conrad, M., & Skinstad, A. H. (2016). History of the Concept of Addiction. *Annual Review of Clinical Psychology*, 12(1), 29–51. DOI: 10.1146/annurev-clinpsy-021815-093546 PMID: 26565120

O'Connor, R. M., Stewart, S. H., & Watt, M. C. (2009). Distinguishing BAS risk for university students' drinking, smoking, and gambling behaviors. *Personality and Individual Differences*, 46(4), 514–519. DOI: 10.1016/j.paid.2008.12.002

Olsen, C. M. (2011). Natural rewards, neuroplasticity, and non-drug addictions. *Neuropharmacology*, 61(7), 1109–1122. DOI: 10.1016/j.neuropharm.2011.03.010 PMID: 21459101

Olson, J. A., Sandra, D. A., Colucci, É. S., Al Bikaii, A., Chmoulevitch, D., Nahas, J., Raz, A., & Veissière, S. P. (2022). Smartphone addiction is increasing across the world: A meta-analysis of 24 countries. *Computers in Human Behavior*, 129, 107138. DOI: 10.1016/j.chb.2021.107138

Osorio-Molina, C., Martos-Cabrera, M. B., Membrive-Jiménez, M. J., Vargas-Roman, K., Suleiman-Martos, N., Ortega-Campos, E., & Gómez-Urquiza, J. L. (2021). Smartphone addiction, risk factors and its adverse effects in nursing students: A systematic review and meta-analysis. *Nurse Education Today*, 98, 104741. DOI: 10.1016/j.nedt.2020.104741 PMID: 33485161

Panova, T., & Carbonell, X. (2018). Is smartphone addiction really an addiction? *Journal of Behavioral Addictions*, 7(2), 252–259. DOI: 10.1556/2006.7.2018.49 PMID: 29895183

Park, J., Jeong, J.-E., Park, S. y., & Rho, M. J. (2020). Development of the smartphone addiction risk rating score for a smartphone addiction management application. *Frontiers in Public Health*, 8, 485. DOI: 10.3389/fpubh.2020.00485 PMID: 33042938

Pavia, L., Cavani, P., Di Blasi, M., & Giordano, C. (2016). Smartphone Addiction Inventory (SPAI): Psychometric properties and confirmatory factor analysis. *Computers in Human Behavior*, 63, 170–178. DOI: 10.1016/j.chb.2016.05.039

Pérez-Fernández, H., Cacciotti, G., Martín-Cruz, N., & Delgado-García, J. B. (2022). Are interactions between need for achievement and social networks the driving force behind entrepreneurial Intention? A trait activation story. *Journal of Business Research*, 149, 65–76. DOI: 10.1016/j.jbusres.2022.04.046

Phillips-Wren, G., & Adya, M. (2020). Decision making under stress: The role of information overload, time pressure, complexity, and uncertainty. *Journal of Decision Systems, 29*(sup1), 213-225.

Pirzade, M., Fazelirad, H., & Noury Ghasem Abadi, R. (2024). The Mediating Role of Metacognition in the Relationship between Dark Triad Personality Traits and Smartphone Addiction among Tehran Universities Students. *Psychological Studies*, 20(2).

Pletzer, J. L., Oostrom, J. K., Bentvelzen, M., & de Vries, R. E. (2020). Comparing domain-and facet-level relations of the HEXACO personality model with workplace deviance: A meta-analysis. *Personality and Individual Differences*, 152, 109539. DOI: 10.1016/j.paid.2019.109539

Pletzer, J. L., Oostrom, J. K., & de Vries, R. E. (2021). HEXACO personality and organizational citizenship behavior: A domain-and facet-level meta-analysis. *Human Performance*, 34(2), 126–147. DOI: 10.1080/08959285.2021.1891072

Radtke, T., Apel, T., Schenkel, K., Keller, J., & von Lindern, E. (2022). Digital detox: An effective solution in the smartphone era? A systematic literature review. *Mobile Media & Communication*, 10(2), 190–215. DOI: 10.1177/20501579211028647

Rahim, N. A. A., Siah, Y. H., Tee, X. Y., & Siah, P. C. (2021). Smartphone Addiction: Its Relationships to Personality Traits and Types of Smartphone Use. *International Journal of Technology in Education and Science*, 5(1), 128–140. DOI: 10.46328/ijtes.165

Ratan, Z. A., Parrish, A.-M., Zaman, S. B., Alotaibi, M. S., & Hosseinzadeh, H. (2021). Smartphone addiction and associated health outcomes in adult populations: A systematic review. *International Journal of Environmental Research and Public Health*, 18(22), 12257. DOI: 10.3390/ijerph182212257 PMID: 34832011

Roberts, J. A., Pullig, C., & Manolis, C. (2015). I need my smartphone: A hierarchical model of personality and cell-phone addiction. *Personality and Individual Differences*, 79, 13–19. DOI: 10.1016/j.paid.2015.01.049

Roethlisberger, C., Gassmann, F., Groot, W., & Martorano, B. (2023). The contribution of personality traits and social norms to the gender pay gap: A systematic literature review. *Journal of Economic Surveys*, 37(2), 377–408. DOI: 10.1111/joes.12501

Ryder, C., Mackean, T., Coombs, J., Williams, H., Hunter, K., Holland, A. J., & Ivers, R. Q. (2020). Indigenous research methodology–weaving a research interface. *International Journal of Social Research Methodology*, 23(3), 255–267. DOI: 10.1080/13645579.2019.1669923

Sarkar, T. K., Taneja, N., Jana, P. K., Gupta, S., Dalal, R., Dasgupta, R., Halder, R., & Adhikary, M. (2019). Effect of mobile phone overuse on health of medical students. *International Journal of Medical Science and Public Health*, 8(1), 91–94.

Schmuck, D. (2020). Does digital detox work? Exploring the role of digital detox applications for problematic smartphone use and well-being of young adults using multigroup analysis. *Cyberpsychology, Behavior, and Social Networking*, 23(8), 526–532. DOI: 10.1089/cyber.2019.0578 PMID: 32354288

Schnelle, C., Baier, D., Hadjar, A., & Boehnke, K. (2021). Authoritarianism beyond disposition: A literature review of research on contextual antecedents. *Frontiers in Psychology*, 12, 676093. DOI: 10.3389/fpsyg.2021.676093 PMID: 34248773

Servidio, R., Griffiths, M. D., & Demetrovics, Z. (2021). Dark triad of personality and problematic smartphone use: A preliminary study on the mediating role of fear of missing out. *International Journal of Environmental Research and Public Health*, 18(16), 8463. DOI: 10.3390/ijerph18168463 PMID: 34444212

Sharpe, J. P., Martin, N. R., & Roth, K. A. (2011). Optimism and the Big Five factors of personality: Beyond neuroticism and extraversion. *Personality and Individual Differences*, 51(8), 946–951. DOI: 10.1016/j.paid.2011.07.033

Shi, Z., Guan, J., Chen, H., Liu, C., Ma, J., & Zhou, Z. (2023). Teacher-student relationships and smartphone addiction: The roles of achievement goal orientation and psychological resilience. *Current Psychology (New Brunswick, N.J.)*, 42(20), 17074–17086. DOI: 10.1007/s12144-022-02902-9

Sinha, R., & Jastreboff, A. M. (2013). Stress as a common risk factor for obesity and addiction. *Biological Psychiatry*, 73(9), 827–835. DOI: 10.1016/j.biopsych.2013.01.032 PMID: 23541000

Skorek, M., Song, A. V., & Dunham, Y. (2014). Self-esteem as a mediator between personality traits and body esteem: Path analyses across gender and race/ethnicity. *PLoS One*, 9(11), e112086. DOI: 10.1371/journal.pone.0112086 PMID: 25375238

Skues, J. L., Williams, B., & Wise, L. (2012). The effects of personality traits, self-esteem, loneliness, and narcissism on Facebook use among university students. *Computers in Human Behavior*, 28(6), 2414–2419. DOI: 10.1016/j.chb.2012.07.012

Soraci, P., Ferrari, A., Antonino, U., & Griffiths, M. D. (2021). Psychometric properties of the Italian version of the smartphone application-based addiction scale (SABAS). *International Journal of Mental Health and Addiction*, 19(4), 1261–1273. DOI: 10.1007/s11469-020-00222-2

Tariq, F. J., & Irfan, A. R. B. (2019). *Cell phone addiction: a rising epidemic*. JPMA.

Tateno, M., Kim, D.-J., Teo, A. R., Skokauskas, N., Guerrero, A. P., & Kato, T. A. (2019). Smartphone addiction in Japanese college students: Usefulness of the Japanese version of the smartphone addiction scale as a screening tool for a new form of internet addiction. *Psychiatry Investigation*, 16(2), 115–120. DOI: 10.30773/pi.2018.12.25.2 PMID: 30808117

Terracciano, A., Löckenhoff, C. E., Crum, R. M., Bienvenu, O. J., & Costa, P. T.Jr. (2008). Five-Factor Model personality profiles of drug users. *BMC Psychiatry*, 8(1), 1–10. DOI: 10.1186/1471-244X-8-22 PMID: 18405382

Ting, C. H., & Chen, Y. Y. (2020). Smartphone addiction. In *Adolescent addiction* (pp. 215–240). Elsevier. DOI: 10.1016/B978-0-12-818626-8.00008-6

Vazire, S. (2014). *A six-day unit lesson plan for high school psychology teachers*. Am Psychol Assoc.

Wang, H., Sourav, M. S. U., Yang, M., & Zhang, J. (2023). Classifying mental disorders through clinicians' subjective approach based on three-way decisions. *Frontiers in Psychology*, 14, 1144826. DOI: 10.3389/fpsyg.2023.1144826 PMID: 37484085

Weigel, M. (2022). *The authoritarian personality 2.0* (Vol. 54). The University of Chicago Press Chicago.

Wenzel, A. (2017). Basic strategies of cognitive behavioral therapy. *Psychiatria Clinica*, 40(4), 597–609. PMID: 29080588

West, R., Ash, C., Dapore, A., Kirby, B., Malley, K., & Zhu, S. (2021). Problematic smartphone use: The role of reward processing, depressive symptoms and self-control. *Addictive Behaviors*, 122, 107015. DOI: 10.1016/j.addbeh.2021.107015 PMID: 34146798

World Health Organization. W. (2024). *Clinical descriptions and diagnostic requirements for ICD-11 mental, behavioural and neurodevelopmental disorders*. World Health Organization.

Wu, W.-Y., & Ke, C.-C. (2015). An online shopping behavior model integrating personality traits, perceived risk, and technology acceptance. *Social Behavior and Personality*, 43(1), 85–97. DOI: 10.2224/sbp.2015.43.1.85

Xiao, T., Jiao, C., Yao, J., Yang, L., Zhang, Y., Liu, S., Grabovac, I., Yu, Q., Kong, Z., Yu, J. J., & Zhang, J. (2021). Effects of basketball and Baduanjin exercise interventions on problematic smartphone use and mental health among college students: A randomized controlled trial. *Evidence-Based Complementary and Alternative Medicine*, 2021(1), 8880716. DOI: 10.1155/2021/8880716 PMID: 33574886

Yam, C.-W., Pakpour, A. H., Griffiths, M. D., Yau, W.-Y., Lo, C.-L. M., Ng, J. M., Lin, C.-Y., & Leung, H. (2019). Psychometric testing of three Chinese online-related addictive behavior instruments among Hong Kong university students. *The Psychiatric Quarterly*, 90(1), 117–128. DOI: 10.1007/s11126-018-9610-7 PMID: 30328020

Yildiz, M. A. (2017). Emotion regulation strategies as predictors of internet addiction and smartphone addiction in adolescents. *Journal of Educational Sciences and Psychology*, 7(1).

Young, K. (2017). *Internet addiction test for families (IAT-F)*. Stoelting.

Zarse, E. M., Neff, M. R., Yoder, R., Hulvershorn, L., Chambers, J. E., & Chambers, R. A. (2019). The adverse childhood experiences questionnaire: Two decades of research on childhood trauma as a primary cause of adult mental illness, addiction, and medical diseases. *Cogent Medicine*, 6(1), 1581447. DOI: 10.1080/2331205X.2019.1581447

Zecca, G., Verardi, S., Antonietti, J.-P., Dahourou, D., Adjahouisso, M., Ah-Kion, J., Amoussou-Yeye, D., Barry, O., Bhowon, U., Bouatta, C., Dougoumalé Cissé, D., Mbodji, M., Meyer de Stadelhofen, F., Minga Minga, D., Ng Tseung, C., Nouri Romdhane, M., Ondongo, F., Rigozzi, C., Sfayhi, N., & Rossier, J. (2013). African cultures and the five-factor model of personality: Evidence for a specific pan-african structure and profile? *Journal of Cross-Cultural Psychology*, 44(5), 684–700. DOI: 10.1177/0022022112468943

Zhang, A., Xiong, S., Peng, Y., Zeng, Y., Zeng, C., Yang, Y., & Zhang, B. (2022). Perceived stress and mobile phone addiction among college students: The roles of self-control and security. *Frontiers in Psychiatry*, 13, 1005062. DOI: 10.3389/fpsyt.2022.1005062 PMID: 36465300

Chapter 11
A Study on the Relationship Between Personality Traits and Levels of Smartphone Addiction to Gain Insights Into Sales Executive Behavioral Patterns

P. S. Venkateswaran
https://orcid.org/0000-0001-8958-103X
PSNA College of Engineering and Technology, Dindigul, India

N. Deepa Rekha
SRM Institute of Science and Technology, India

M. Sriramkumar
https://orcid.org/0009-0006-5553-1142
PSNA College of Engineering and Technology, Dindigul, India

ABSTRACT

The study aims to explore the relationship between the big five personality traits—extraversion, agreeableness, conscientiousness, openness, and neuroticism—and levels of smartphone addiction among sales executives. Data were collected from 286

DOI: 10.4018/979-8-3693-8804-4.ch011

sales executives using a structured questionnaire, focusing on personality traits and smartphone addiction levels. Pearson correlation and multiple regression analyses revealed that agreeableness is the strongest predictor of smartphone addiction, suggesting that individuals who are more cooperative and empathetic are more likely to develop addictive smartphone behaviours. Conscientiousness showed a marginally significant negative association, indicating that individuals with higher self-discipline and responsibility are less prone to smartphone addiction. Extraversion, openness, and neuroticism did not show statistically significant relationships. These insights are relevant in the sales sector, highlighting the importance of integrating psychological factors into workplace policies to address smartphone addiction effectively.

1. INTRODUCTION AND BACKGROUND

In an age where smartphones have become integral to daily life, understanding the factors driving excessive use has never been more crucial. Smartphone addiction, characterized by compulsive usage and an inability to disengage from mobile devices, has emerged as a significant concern impacting mental health, productivity, and social interactions. This study aims to delve into the intricate relationship between personality traits and levels of smartphone addiction, seeking to uncover how individual differences shape user behavior and the broader implications of these patterns.

Smartphones, with their constant connectivity and vast array of applications, have revolutionized communication and information access. However, this convenience also brings about challenges related to overuse. Recent research highlights that certain personality traits may predispose individuals to higher levels of smartphone addiction. Traits such as neuroticism, extraversion, and conscientiousness can significantly influence how users engage with their devices, often leading to patterns of behavior that can be both enlightening and alarming.

For instance, individuals high in neuroticism might use their smartphones as a means to manage anxiety or emotional distress, leading to frequent checking and reliance on mobile apps for reassurance. Conversely, those with high levels of extraversion may exhibit addiction behaviors driven by the need for social interaction and validation through social media platforms. On the other hand, conscientious individuals might demonstrate lower addiction levels, as their organized and disciplined nature often translates into more controlled and purposeful smartphone use.

In today's rapidly evolving digital landscape, smartphones have become indispensable tools for personal and professional activities. With the increasing integration of technology into our everyday lives, smartphones are no longer just communication devices; they serve as platforms for work, social interactions, entertainment, and even self-expression. For many professionals, especially those in dynamic roles like sales executives, smartphones provide critical support for managing tasks, interacting with clients, and staying connected to market trends. However, this increased reliance on smartphones has also led to concerns about the potential for addiction and its impact on both personal well-being and job performance. This research paper explores the relationship between personality traits and levels of smartphone addiction among sales executives, aiming to uncover behavioral patterns and the broader implications of this phenomenon.

Smartphone addiction, often defined as excessive and compulsive smartphone use that interferes with daily life, has emerged as a pressing issue in both academic research and popular discourse. It is characterized by symptoms such as the inability to control smartphone usage, using the device for prolonged periods, and experiencing withdrawal symptoms when access is limited. In the context of sales executives, where smartphones are essential tools of the trade, the line between functional use and addiction can become blurred.

The relevance of examining smartphone addiction in sales executives is underscored by the unique demands of their profession. Sales executives operate in high-pressure environments, often working under tight deadlines, with the need for constant communication and multitasking. Smartphones enable them to manage these challenges by providing access to real-time information, customer interactions, and organizational resources. However, the same traits that make sales executives effective in their roles—such as high levels of extraversion, assertiveness, and a strong drive for achievement—may also predispose them to higher levels of smartphone addiction. This research seeks to explore how these traits, along with others like neuroticism, conscientiousness, and openness to experience, interact with smartphone use and contribute to addiction-like behaviors.

Personality traits, as conceptualized in psychological frameworks like the Big Five model, play a critical role in shaping how individuals interact with their environment, including their use of technology. The Big Five model, which includes traits like extraversion, neuroticism, agreeableness, conscientiousness, and openness to experience, has been widely studied in relation to various behavioral outcomes. Extraverts, for example, are often more socially engaged and may use smartphones as tools for social interaction, while individuals high in neuroticism may turn to their devices for emotional regulation. Sales executives, with their need for constant engagement and responsiveness, may exhibit unique patterns of smartphone use that align with their personality profiles. This paper aims to delve into these relationships, offering insights into how personality traits not only predict smartphone addiction but also influence the behavioral patterns that arise from this addiction.

Sales professionals are often expected to be "always on," responding to emails, calls, and messages at all hours, managing multiple clients, and adapting quickly to changing market conditions. The smartphone, in this scenario, becomes not just a tool for productivity but a lifeline for staying competitive in an increasingly digital marketplace. This raises an important question: when does necessary usage cross the line into addiction? For sales executives, the pressure to perform and stay connected may lead to compulsive use, resulting in negative consequences such as burnout, reduced job satisfaction, and even mental health challenges.

In examining the relationship between personality traits and smartphone addiction among sales executives, this paper also considers the implications for organizational management and policy-making. Understanding these dynamics can help organizations design better support systems for their employees, from promoting healthy technology use to offering interventions for those at risk of addiction. Moreover, by identifying the personality traits that are most strongly associated with addictive behaviors, organizations can implement targeted training and development programs to foster more sustainable work practices. In a field like sales, where performance is often directly linked to personal habits and behaviors, these insights can have significant implications for both individual and organizational success.

The rise of smartphone addiction is not only a personal issue but also a workplace concern. As sales executives increasingly rely on their devices for communication, planning, and decision-making, the risk of addiction grows. This addiction can lead to several negative outcomes, including distraction, decreased productivity, and impaired social interactions, both in and out of the workplace. Additionally, excessive smartphone use has been linked to mental health issues such as anxiety, depression, and stress, all of which can have a detrimental effect on job performance and overall well-being. For sales executives, who are often at the forefront of organizational success, these risks are particularly concerning.

Given the critical role that smartphones play in the daily lives of sales executives, this research seeks to provide a deeper understanding of how personality traits interact with technology use in this specific professional context. By exploring the relationship between personality and smartphone addiction, this paper aims to shed light on the behavioral patterns that arise from this interaction and the potential implications for both individual sales professionals and their organizations. Through this exploration, the research seeks to contribute to the growing body of literature on smartphone addiction while offering practical insights for managing this issue in the workplace.

At the core of this research, personality traits significantly influence how individuals interact with technology, including their propensity for addictive behaviors. By focusing on sales executives, this study provides a unique perspective on smartphone addiction, one that considers the high demands of the profession and the specific personality traits that are often associated with success in sales. This research also highlights the importance of considering the broader implications of smartphone addiction, from its impact on mental health and job performance to its potential effects on organizational culture and productivity.

Sales executives are known for their high levels of extroversion and ambition (Pillemer, 2019), personality traits potentially exacerbated by the mobile nature of their work. The sales profession thrives on communication, and in today's digital world, this communication is largely fueled by constant connectivity through smartphones. Sales executives are often expected to be reachable 24/7, readily responding to inquiries, managing client expectations, and coordinating deals. While this constant connectivity offers a vital link to clients, its pervasive nature creates fertile ground for smartphone addiction. These factors might increase their vulnerability to smartphone addiction due to:

Constant Connectivity

The job demands instant accessibility, placing high pressure on staying connected. Sales executives are often known for being highly extroverted, eager to connect with others and forge relationships. However, extroversion, combined with performance pressure, can be a double-edged sword when it comes to smartphone use. The desire for social interaction, fueled by a need to be constantly "in the loop," might translate into excessive smartphone use, especially for those prone to high levels of impulsivity. This heightened impulsivity, in turn, might make it harder for sales executives to detach from the constant stream of information, blurring the lines between professional obligations and personal life.

Furthermore, those who score high on neuroticism may find solace in constant connectivity, as it serves as a shield from feelings of loneliness or anxiety. The reassurance of knowing they can always access communication can become a comforting coping mechanism. Yet, this reliance on constant connectivity, especially during downtime, might exacerbate their anxiety and contribute to the cycle of addiction.

The demands of constant connectivity in the sales field blur the boundaries between work and personal life. For individuals who are already predisposed to addiction, the merging of professional and personal spaces makes it incredibly challenging to detach and engage in self-care. This can have serious consequences for mental well-being, leading to sleep disturbances, relationship issues, and burnout.

Excessive phone use due to constant connectivity can lead to neglecting personal obligations and activities, impacting family relationships and overall mental health. The constant barrage of messages and notifications can act as a major distraction, impairing their concentration on tasks that demand sustained attention and critical thinking. Individuals immersed in constant communication might struggle to prioritize their time and manage their work responsibilities effectively.

Performance Pressure

Sales targets often require rapid communication and action, fostering a sense of urgency that may translate into frequent phone use. Sales executives operate under immense pressure to meet and exceed their performance targets. These targets, often expressed as revenue quotas, necessitate a constant drive for efficiency and productivity, influencing how sales executives perceive and utilize their smartphones. This study examines how performance pressure may contribute to smartphone addiction amongst sales executives.

Sales executives with specific personality traits, such as a high need for achievement, may be particularly susceptible to the influence of performance pressure. These individuals are highly motivated to succeed, potentially driving them towards more frequent and extensive smartphone usage as they strive to constantly monitor leads, track progress, and optimize their strategies. For those high on neuroticism, however, performance pressure may trigger anxiety and feelings of inadequacy, contributing to excessive phone use as a means of distracting themselves or seeking external validation.

The smartphone becomes more than just a tool for communication – it becomes a vital mechanism for controlling performance. Sales executives can monitor leads, track progress, and access critical information at any moment, fueling a sense of urgency and pushing them towards increased smartphone use. However, this reliance on the smartphone can create a self-perpetuating cycle, increasing performance pressure and leading to further dependency on the device.

Potential Implications for Sales Executives' Behavior

The unrelenting pressure to achieve, combined with constant smartphone monitoring, can lead to increased levels of stress and burnout, affecting overall mental well-being. The constant focus on professional goals, driven by performance pressure, may create difficulties in balancing work and personal commitments, potentially damaging relationships with loved ones. Excessive smartphone use can lead to obsessive monitoring of competitors' success and engagement with social media platforms, fueling feelings of inadequacy and pressure to continuously outdo others.

This research aims to understand the psychological mechanisms driving smartphone addiction under the weight of performance pressure. The insights gained can be used to develop support systems and training programs to help sales executives navigate the pressures of their profession without succumbing to detrimental habits.

Social Networking

Networking with potential clients often utilizes social media, amplifying social comparison and the potential for FOMO. The rise of social media and its integration with smartphones has fundamentally transformed the nature of professional networking. Sales executives are now encouraged to engage in social media platforms, building online relationships with potential clients, and fostering their professional image through a virtual presence. This study seeks to investigate the connection between social networking through smartphones and smartphone addiction among sales executives.

Extroverted sales executives, driven by their desire for social connection and the thrill of new encounters, may be drawn to the limitless possibilities of social media. The need for stimulation and the ability to create a desired impression can amplify their engagement, pushing them toward greater smartphone use and increasing the likelihood of developing an addiction. Individuals high on sensation-seeking may find satisfaction in the constant influx of information and interaction, fueling their desire to remain active on various social platforms.

Social media often fosters an illusion of connection and social status. Sales executives might feel obligated to maintain an active and engaging online presence, engaging with followers and responding to comments to cultivate a perceived aura of success and relevance. However, this pressure can result in excessive smartphone usage, neglecting their real-world obligations and becoming engrossed in a virtual world.

Overreliance on social networking can lead to a decline in authentic interactions with clients, jeopardizing the foundation of meaningful relationships vital for sales success. The need to curate an active social presence can distract sales executives from their core duties, compromising their ability to manage time effectively. Constant social media engagement, especially those high in neuroticism, can trigger FOMO (fear of missing out), generating dissatisfaction and the compulsion to remain constantly connected.

Coping Mechanisms and Interventions

Sales executives often face high-pressure environments, making them more susceptible to smartphone addiction as a coping mechanism for stress and burnout. Research indicates that individuals with certain personality traits, such as neuroticism or low conscientiousness, are more likely to develop unhealthy smartphone habits, further exacerbating work-related stress. Coping mechanisms, such as mindfulness training, digital detox programs, and structured time management practices, have proven effective in mitigating smartphone addiction. For instance, mindfulness interventions can help executives manage their impulses and reduce compulsive smartphone use.

In addition, organizations can provide access to wellness programs that include counseling and support for managing digital dependency. Cognitive-behavioral approaches tailored to individual needs have also been shown to reframe addictive behaviors into healthier digital practices. By equipping sales executives with strategies to cope with stress, companies can foster better mental well-being and enhance productivity.

Technological and Design Factors

The design of smartphones and applications significantly contributes to addiction among sales executives. Features such as push notifications, gamification elements, and endless scrolling are engineered to maximize user engagement, often at the expense of productivity and mental health. Sales executives, who rely heavily on smartphones for client communications, data tracking, and market updates, may find it challenging to distinguish between work-related use and compulsive usage driven by these design factors.

Organizations can mitigate this by encouraging the use of productivity-focused applications with minimal distractions. Additionally, smartphone manufacturers and software developers have a role to play in creating tools that prioritize user well-being, such as usage dashboards, app-blocking features, and scheduled downtime. Implementing such technologies can reduce the behavioral triggers that lead to excessive smartphone usage, particularly among sales professionals who are highly dependent on their devices.

Organizational Role

Organizations play a critical role in addressing the impact of smartphone addiction on sales executives' behavior and performance. While smartphones are integral tools for sales tasks, excessive use can lead to burnout, decreased focus, and impaired interpersonal interactions. Companies can implement policies that promote healthy digital practices, such as limiting after-hours communication and offering training on digital etiquette.

Furthermore, integrating personality assessments into recruitment and training processes can help identify employees who may be more prone to addictive behaviors based on traits like impulsivity or extraversion. Tailored interventions, such as personalized coaching or mentoring, can help these individuals balance their smartphone usage while maintaining their work efficiency.

Organizations must also foster a culture of accountability and awareness by providing workshops and seminars on the psychological impacts of digital addiction. By emphasizing the importance of digital well-being, organizations can empower sales executives to harness technology effectively without succumbing to its addictive tendencies. This dual focus on personal and organizational strategies will ultimately enhance overall performance and job satisfaction.

Longitudinal Effects

Understanding the longitudinal effects of smartphone addiction on sales executives requires examining how behavioral patterns evolve over time and their long-term implications on mental health, productivity, and organizational outcomes. Over-reliance on smartphones can lead to chronic stress, sleep disturbances, and reduced interpersonal skills, which may negatively impact career growth and organizational performance. Additionally, personality traits such as high openness or neuroticism may amplify susceptibility to these effects over prolonged periods. Longitudinal studies can provide valuable insights into how interventions, such as digital detox programs or organizational policies, influence addiction tendencies and outcomes. This perspective allows organizations to design proactive, data-driven strategies to mitigate the long-term impacts of smartphone addiction on their workforce.

Global Context

The relationship between personality traits and smartphone addiction is a global phenomenon, but cultural and regional differences significantly shape its manifestation and implications. For instance, in highly connected societies with a strong emphasis on digital communication, such as South Korea or Japan, smartphone addiction among sales executives may stem from societal pressures to remain constantly accessible. Conversely, in regions where digital infrastructure is less developed, the prevalence of smartphone addiction may be lower but could still affect productivity in unique ways. Comparing these global contexts highlights the need for culturally adaptive interventions and policies. By considering diverse work environments and cultural norms, organizations can create more inclusive strategies to address smartphone addiction while optimizing sales executives' behavioral patterns worldwide.

Integration of Themes

The study of personality traits and smartphone addiction among sales executives necessitates an integrated approach, combining insights from psychology, technology, and organizational behavior. Themes such as the influence of neuroticism on addictive behaviors, the role of technological design in promoting compulsive usage, and the organizational implications of smartphone dependency must be synthesized to form a holistic perspective. For instance, understanding how personality traits predispose certain individuals to addiction can guide the development of targeted organizational policies, while exploring technological factors can inform the design of less addictive tools. Integrating these themes allows for a comprehensive strategy that not only addresses the individual factors contributing to smartphone addiction but also fosters a supportive organizational culture to mitigate its impact.

Discussion of Trends

Recent trends highlight the growing prevalence of smartphone addiction in professional settings, fueled by the integration of technology into every aspect of work. Sales executives, in particular, face increasing pressure to remain constantly connected, leading to blurred boundaries between professional and personal life. Additionally, trends such as gamification of sales tools and reliance on real-time analytics may inadvertently encourage addictive behaviors. On the other hand, there is a rising emphasis on mental health awareness and digital well-being, prompting organizations to adopt interventions like mindfulness training and digital detox initiatives. By examining these trends, this study can contribute to a nuanced understanding of how evolving work environments and technological advancements shape the dynamics of smartphone addiction.

This raises important questions: How do personality traits influence the tendency toward smartphone addiction in sales executives? What behavioral patterns emerge from this relationship? And what are the broader implications for job performance, mental health, and organizational effectiveness?

2. LITERATURE REVIEW

The relationship between personality traits and levels of smartphone addiction has emerged as a significant area of research, particularly in the context of the increasing prevalence of smartphone use among various demographics. Numerous studies have identified specific personality traits that correlate with higher levels of smartphone addiction, suggesting that individuals with certain psychological profiles may be more susceptible to developing problematic smartphone behaviors.

Research indicates that personality traits, particularly those defined by the Big Five model—extraversion, agreeableness, conscientiousness, neuroticism, and openness to experience—play a significant role in determining an individual's propensity for smartphone addiction. The impact of neuroticism on smartphone addiction is particularly noteworthy. Individuals high in neuroticism often experience anxiety and emotional instability, which can drive them to seek comfort and distraction through their smartphones (Aarestad, 2023). Sales executives who exhibit higher levels of smartphone addiction may experience decreased productivity and increased stress, which can ultimately impact their job performance and customer interactions (Costa, 2023).

Sales executives often face intense pressure to meet targets and maintain customer satisfaction, and smartphone addiction can exacerbate these stressors by creating an "always-on" work culture (Kusuma, 2023). This can lead to a cycle of overwork and decreased job satisfaction, ultimately impacting employee retention and organizational success. Therefore, addressing smartphone addiction through targeted interventions can have far-reaching benefits for both individual employees and the organization as a whole.

In addition to personality traits, organizational culture and leadership styles also play a pivotal role in shaping the smartphone usage behaviors of sales executives. Transformational leadership, characterized by supportive and motivational behaviors, can foster a work environment that encourages balanced smartphone use (Gao et al., 2023). Gender differences have also been observed, with some studies indicating that females may exhibit higher levels of smartphone addiction compared to males, potentially due to differing socialization patterns and usage motivations (Wang, 2023).

Extraverted individuals often seek social interaction and validation, which can lead to excessive smartphone use as a means of maintaining social connections (Anand et al., 2022). Conscientiousness may act as a protective factor against smartphone addiction, as conscientious individuals are generally more disciplined and may prioritize their responsibilities over excessive device usage (Kırcaburun et al., 2022).

The concept of "fear of missing out" (FOMO) has gained traction in discussions about smartphone addiction. FOMO, often linked to social media use, can drive individuals to check their smartphones compulsively to stay updated on social interactions and events, particularly among those with lower self-esteem or higher social anxiety (Li et al., 2020; Fauzi et al., 2021). Sales executives who are excessively reliant on their smartphones may find themselves distracted during critical interactions with clients, leading to diminished communication effectiveness and potentially harming customer relationships (Polakova, 2021). Research has also highlighted the importance of demographic factors, such as age and gender, in understanding the relationship between personality traits and smartphone addiction. For example, younger individuals, particularly adolescents and young adults, are often more susceptible to smartphone addiction due to their developmental stage and social dynamics (Liu et al., 2022; Sohn et al., 2021).

According to Herrero et al., (2021), Conscientiousness has been identified as a protective factor against smartphone addiction. Individuals who score high on conscientiousness tend to exhibit self-discipline and a preference for structured environments, which may mitigate the risk of developing addictive behaviors related to smartphone use. They found that conscientiousness was significantly associated with lower levels of smartphone addiction, suggesting that individuals who are more organized and responsible are less likely to engage in excessive smartphone use. To effectively tackle the issue of smartphone addiction among sales executives, it is crucial to implement evidence-based strategies that consider the unique challenges faced by this demographic. Training programs that focus on time management, digital literacy, and mindfulness can empower sales professionals to take control of their smartphone usage (Indrawati, 2021; Venkateswaran 2018).

In addition to neuroticism, traits such as extraversion and narcissism have also been linked to smartphone addiction. Extraversion, characterized by sociability and a tendency to seek stimulation in the company of others, can lead individuals to use smartphones as a means of maintaining social connections (Marengo et al., 2020; Rahim et al., 2020). Conversely, those with high neuroticism may use smartphones as a coping mechanism to manage anxiety and stress, further exacerbating their dependency on these devices (Hayati & Puri, 2020). This relationship highlights the importance of considering personality traits when examining smartphone addiction, as they can influence not only the frequency of use but also the contexts in which smartphones are utilized (Venkateswaran, 2011). Organizations that prioritize employee well-being and provide resources for managing smartphone use can help reduce the prevalence of addiction among their sales teams (Flannery & Mohs, 2020).

Rahman et al., (2019) studied that effective communication and relationship management are vital components of successful sales strategies, and smartphone addiction can undermine these efforts. Caci et al., (2019) shown that higher levels of extraversion are associated with increased smartphone use, as extraverted individuals tend to engage more in social interactions through their devices, leading to a greater likelihood of addiction. The role of openness to experience has been highlighted, where individuals with higher openness may be more inclined to explore various applications and social media platforms, potentially increasing their screen time and risk of addiction. Li & Lin, (2019) found that neuroticism significantly affected smartphone addiction among young workers, reinforcing the notion that those with higher neuroticism are more sensitive to social feedback and thus may engage more with their smartphones to manage their emotional responses.

Hussain & Pontes, (2018) highlighted that neuroticism, along with other traits, explained a notable percentage of variance in technological addictions, including smartphone addiction. The role of openness to experience is also noteworthy. This trait encompasses a willingness to engage with novel experiences and ideas, which can manifest in diverse smartphone usage patterns. While some studies suggest that high openness may lead to greater engagement with technology, it can also result in a propensity for distraction and overuse, potentially increasing the risk of addiction (Hussain & Pontes, 2018).

The consequences of smartphone addiction are not limited to performance; they can also affect the mental health of sales executives. Research has linked excessive smartphone use to increased levels of stress, anxiety, and burnout, particularly in high-stakes professions like sales (Dünnweber & Fortmüller, 2017). One of the most frequently examined personality traits in relation to smartphone addiction is neuroticism. Research indicates that individuals high in neuroticism are more likely to experience anxiety and emotional instability, which can lead to increased smartphone use as a coping mechanism (Boumosleh & Jaalouk, 2017). Leaders who model healthy technology habits and promote work-life balance can mitigate the negative effects of smartphone addiction, thereby enhancing overall team performance (Guo et al., 2017).

Fostering a culture of open communication about technology use can help reduce stigma and encourage employees to seek support when needed (Goyal et al., 2016). Narcissism has been shown to correlate positively with smartphone addiction, as individuals with narcissistic tendencies may use their devices to seek validation and enhance their self-image through social media platforms (Pearson & Hussain, 2016). Choi et al., (2015) reported that anxiety levels were positively correlated with smartphone addiction, indicating that individuals experiencing higher anxiety may turn to their smartphones for relief.

Smartphone Addiction

Smartphone addiction, a relatively new phenomenon fueled by the pervasive presence of these devices, has become a widespread concern in recent years. It goes beyond mere overuse and encompasses a complex behavioral pattern marked by excessive phone usage despite negative consequences, impacting individuals' daily lives, relationships, and mental wellbeing. While the focus often centers on younger generations, the implications of smartphone addiction extend to various demographics, including professionals navigating increasingly demanding work environments. Understanding this issue within the context of sales executives, known for their constant connectivity and pressure-driven careers, provides a crucial avenue for addressing potential vulnerabilities and promoting healthier technology habits.

Smartphone Addiction falls under the umbrella of "behavioral addictions" - where repetitive behaviors, often driven by instant gratification and escape, lead to adverse effects. Key indicators include:

Excessive Usage: Spending a disproportionate amount of time on the phone, struggling to limit screen time despite self-imposed restrictions, and prioritizing smartphone usage over other activities.

Withdrawal Symptoms: Feeling anxious, restless, or irritable when separated from the phone, experiencing cravings for phone usage even when attempting to abstain.

Negative Consequences: Neglecting personal obligations, work responsibilities, relationships, and overall health due to excessive phone usage, yet unable to control these behaviors.

Accessibility and Convenience: Smartphones are omnipresent and constantly accessible, facilitating immediate gratification through various apps and social media platforms, rewarding instant responses and reinforcing behavior patterns.

Social and Competitive Pressures: The prevalence of social media platforms and the drive to maintain a curated online persona create a sense of competition and a constant need for connection, fueling a sense of FOMO (Fear of Missing Out), leading to increased usage and compulsive checking.

Individual Vulnerabilities: Certain personality traits can increase susceptibility to smartphone addiction. For example, individuals high in neuroticism may seek solace in smartphone use as a coping mechanism to distract from negative emotions, while those high in impulsivity and low in conscientiousness may struggle to control impulsive phone use (Bian et al., 2020).

Impact of Smartphone Addiction

Diminished Focus and Productivity: The constant stream of notifications and social media updates disrupts concentration and task completion, leading to reduced productivity in various settings, including professional environments.

Deteriorated Relationships: Excessive phone use can alienate individuals from real-world interactions, leading to a decline in personal connections and the ability to cultivate genuine relationships.

Increased Anxiety and Depression: Constant smartphone use can interfere with sleep, trigger feelings of inadequacy through social media comparison, and contribute to anxiety and depression due to the persistent fear of missing out (Primack et al., 2015).

3. METHODOLOGY

The applied research design in the present study is the descriptive research. The sample respondents are sales executives of different fields. The research design of this study rely on Quantitative and Cross-sectional. This study will examine the relationship between personality traits and smartphone addiction levels in sales executives. Data will be collected at a single point in time to assess the association between variables. A stratified random sampling approach will be used, aiming to capture diverse demographics and industry representation within the sales executive population. Sales executives employed in various industries in the Chennai region were identified for this study. A sample of 300 sales executives were identified from IT, Auto mobile and FMCG industries (100 sales executives for each industry). A structured questionnaire was prepared and distributed to these 300 sales executives. After scrutiny, 286 questionnaires were identified as useful for the study. This sample size provides sufficient power to detect significant correlations between personality traits and smartphone addiction, accounting for the diverse characteristics of the sales executives. The data analyzed through SPSS 26.

4. ANALYSIS AND INTERPRETATION

Table 1. KMO and Bartlett's test

Kaiser-Meyer-Olkin Measure of Sampling Adequacy.		**.802**
Bartlett's Test of Sphericity	Approx. Chi-Square	10340.680
	df	465
	Sig.	.000

The Kaiser-Meyer-Olkin (KMO) measure of sampling adequacy was reported as 0.802, indicating that the sample size is sufficient for factor analysis. According to Kaiser (1974), a KMO value between 0.8 and 0.9 is considered meritorious, suggesting a robust factor analysis can be performed on the dataset. The result indicates that the correlations among the variables are adequate for the extraction of factors. In addition, Bartlett's test of sphericity was significant (Chi-square = 10340.680, df = 465, $p < 0.001$), which implies that the correlation matrix is not an identity matrix. This result further supports the appropriateness of the data for factor analysis.

Table 2. Total variance explained

Component	Initial Eigenvalues			Extraction Sums of Squared Loadings			Rotation Sums of Squared Loadings		
	Total	*% of Variance*	*Cumulative %*	*Total*	*% of Variance*	*Cumulative %*	*Total*	*% of Variance*	*Cumulative %*
1	11.176	36.051	36.051	11.176	36.051	36.051	9.255	29.854	29.854
2	4.065	13.111	49.163	4.065	13.111	49.163	3.930	12.679	42.533
3	3.779	12.190	61.353	3.779	12.190	61.353	3.891	12.550	55.083
4	1.932	6.231	67.584	1.932	6.231	67.584	3.510	11.323	66.406
5	1.726	5.566	73.151	1.726	5.566	73.151	1.994	6.432	72.838
6	1.236	3.986	77.136	1.236	3.986	77.136	1.332	4.298	77.136

Extraction Method: Principal Component Analysis.

The principal component analysis (PCA) identified six components with eigenvalues greater than 1, cumulatively explaining 77.136% of the total variance (Table4.2). The first component alone explained 36.051% of the variance, followed by the second component with 13.111%, the third with 12.190%, and the remaining components each explained between 3.986% and 6.231%. The substantial variance explained by these six components suggests a well-defined factor structure. This is in line with previous research (e.g., John & Srivastava, 1999), where personality traits are expected to account for significant portions of variance in behavioral measures, such as smartphone usage patterns.

Table 3. Factor analysis –factor loadings with rotation

S.No	Rotated Component Matrix[a]	Components					
		1	2	3	4	5	6
I	**Extraversion**						
1	I often engage in phone conversations with multiple people throughout the day.	.885					
2	I use my smartphone to network and build relationships in my professional life.	.818					
3	I tend to share updates or posts on social media using my smartphone during the workday.	.796					
4	I prefer using messaging apps to interact with others rather than in-person meetings.	.767					
5	I frequently use my smartphone to maintain social connections with colleagues and clients.	.729					
II	**Agreeableness**						
6	I use my smartphone to encourage cooperation and understanding among my peers.		.934				

continued on following page

Table 3. Continued

S.No	Rotated Component Matrix[a]	Components					
		1	2	3	4	5	6
7	I use my smartphone to collaborate and share information with my coworkers willingly.		.880				
8	I avoid confrontational or negative conversations on my smartphone with colleagues or clients.		.779				
9	I often respond promptly to messages and calls to maintain harmony in my team.		.769				
10	I rely on my smartphone to offer assistance or advice to others when they ask for it.		.746				
III	**Conscientiousness**						
11	I rely on my smartphone for keeping track of important deadlines and responsibilities.			.877			
12	I set limits on my smartphone use to ensure it doesn't affect my productivity.			.847			
13	I avoid using my smartphone for personal matters during work hours.			.826			
14	I use my smartphone in a disciplined manner, ensuring it doesn't interfere with my work.			.818			
15	I organize my work tasks and schedule efficiently using smartphone apps.			.758			
IV	**Neuroticism**						
16	I often check my smartphone in stressful situations to seek distraction or relief.				.937		
17	I worry about missing important notifications or messages if I don't check my smartphone frequently.				.857		
18	I feel irritable when I can't use my smartphone as much as I'd like during the day.				.833		
19	I feel anxious or upset when I'm unable to access my smartphone.				.780		
20	My smartphone usage increases when I feel overwhelmed or emotionally unstable.				.741		
V	**Openness to Experience**						
21	I like using my smartphone to experiment with creative solutions for professional challenges.					.921	
22	I often download apps to improve my skills and knowledge related to my career.					.915	
23	I use my smartphone to access new ideas and learn about innovative industry trends.					.887	
24	I enjoy exploring new apps and technologies on my smartphone to enhance my work.					.798	
25	I frequently try out new methods of communication, like video calls, through my smartphone.					.719	

continued on following page

Table 3. Continued

S.No	Rotated Component Matrix[a]	Components					
		1	2	3	4	5	6
VI	**Levels of Smartphone Addiction**						
26	My smartphone use has affected my relationships with colleagues, clients, or family members.						.947
27	I frequently feel an urge to check my smartphone, even when it's not necessary.						.937
28	I find it difficult to go long periods without using my smartphone.						.916
29	I use my smartphone so much that it sometimes interferes with my daily activities or responsibilities.						.855
30	I often lose track of time while using my smartphone for both work and personal purposes.						.780
31	I feel the need to check my smartphone immediately when it rings, vibrates, or receives a notification.						.711

Extraction Method: Principal Component Analysis.
Rotation Method: Varimax with Kaiser Normalization.
Rotation converged in 5 iterations.

The Varimax rotation with Kaiser normalization was employed to achieve a clearer separation of factors (Table 2). Each of the extracted components represents a distinct factor that aligns well with the theoretical constructs under investigation, particularly the Big Five personality traits and smartphone addiction. Component 1 related to Extraversion, such as "I often engage in phone conversations with multiple people throughout the day" (loading = 0.885). This factor can be interpreted as capturing the extraverted tendencies of smartphone users, particularly in social and professional contexts.

Component 2 reflects Agreeableness, as indicated by high loadings on items such as "I use my smartphone to encourage cooperation and understanding among my peers" (loading = 0.934). This factor highlights the role of agreeableness in fostering collaborative behavior via smartphone usage.

Component 3 apprehended the dimension of Conscientiousness, with items such as "I rely on my smartphone for keeping track of important deadlines" (loading = 0.877). The loadings suggest that conscientious individuals use smartphones in an organized and goal-directed manner, balancing their usage to avoid distractions.

Component 4 relates to Neuroticism, as shown by high loadings on statements like "I often check my smartphone in stressful situations to seek distraction or relief" (loading = 0.937). This component highlights the emotional reliance on smartphones in times of anxiety or stress, a key feature of neurotic behavior.

Component 5 is associated with Openness to Experience, demonstrated by strong loadings on items like “I like using my smartphone to experiment with creative solutions for professional challenges” (loading = 0.921). This suggests that individuals high in openness use their smartphones to explore innovative ideas and tools, consistent with their curiosity and creativity.

Component 6 represents Smartphone Addiction, with items such as “My smartphone use has affected my relationships with colleagues, clients, or family members” (loading = 0.947). This factor underscores the problematic aspects of smartphone use, especially when it begins to interfere with daily responsibilities and interpersonal relationships.

The strong loading patterns suggest that the items selected for each personality trait are robust indicators of those traits in the context of smartphone usage. Additionally, the identification of a distinct factor for smartphone addiction indicates that excessive smartphone use can be reliably measured and differentiated from general personality traits. The high variance explained by the first few components suggests that Extraversion and Agreeableness play particularly significant roles in how sales executives use smartphones in their work environments. This finding is consistent with literature emphasizing the social nature of these traits. On the other hand, Conscientiousness and Neuroticism highlight the self-regulatory and emotional dimensions of smartphone use, which are essential for understanding behavioral patterns in professional settings.

The distinct loading of Smartphone Addiction as a separate factor demonstrates the potential negative implications of excessive smartphone use, such as diminished productivity and strained relationships, a phenomenon that has been increasingly documented in the context of organizational behavior.

Table 4. Correlations analysis

	Extraversion	Agreeableness	Conscientiousness	Openness	Neuroticism	Smart phone addiction
Extraversion	1					
Agreeableness	.046	1				
Conscientiousness	.162**	.435**	1			
Openness	.007	.462**	.430**	1		
Neuroticism	.309**	.098	-.025	.036	1	
Smart phone addiction	.018	.119*	-.072	.019	.079	1

**. Correlation is significant at the 0.01 level (2-tailed).

*. Correlation is significant at the 0.05 level (2-tailed).

To explore the relationship between the Big Five personality traits and levels of smartphone addiction among sales executives, a Pearson correlation analysis was conducted. Table 4.4 summarizes the correlation coefficients between the dependent variable (smartphone addiction) and the independent variables (Extraversion, Agreeableness, Conscientiousness, Openness to Experience, and Neuroticism).

1. Extraversion and Smartphone Addiction

The correlation between Extraversion and Smartphone Addiction is $r = 0.018$ ($p > 0.05$), indicating no statistically significant relationship. Despite the expectation that extroverts, being more socially engaged, might be more likely to exhibit addictive behaviors with their smartphones, this result suggests that extroversion does not significantly contribute to higher levels of smartphone addiction in this sample of sales executives.

2. Agreeableness and Smartphone Addiction

A weak positive correlation was observed between Agreeableness and Smartphone Addiction ($r = 0.119$, $p < 0.05$), which is statistically significant. This suggests that individuals who are more cooperative, empathetic, and concerned with maintaining harmonious relationships might have a slightly higher tendency to exhibit addictive smartphone behaviors. However, the effect size is small, indicating that agreeableness plays only a limited role in predicting smartphone addiction.

3. Conscientiousness and Smartphone Addiction

The correlation between Conscientiousness and Smartphone Addiction was negative ($r = -0.072$), but not statistically significant ($p > 0.05$). Conscientiousness typically reflects self-discipline, responsibility, and goal-directed behavior, and while the negative relationship suggests that more conscientious individuals might engage less in smartphone overuse, the lack of significance means that this trait does not reliably predict smartphone addiction in the sample studied.

4. Openness to Experience and Smartphone Addiction

The correlation between Openness to Experience and Smartphone Addiction is weak and non-significant ($r = 0.019$, $p > 0.05$). This indicates that a higher tendency to explore new experiences, ideas, or technologies does not have a meaningful association with smartphone addiction. The lack of significant correlation suggests that openness may not be a critical factor in determining addictive smartphone behaviors.

5. Neuroticism and Smartphone Addiction

Neuroticism demonstrated a small positive correlation with Smartphone Addiction ($r = 0.079$, $p > 0.05$), but this result is not statistically significant. Neuroticism, which is associated with emotional instability and anxiety, might intuitively be linked to compulsive smartphone use as a way to manage stress. However, in this analysis, the data do not provide strong evidence that individuals with higher neuroticism scores are significantly more prone to smartphone addiction.

6. Interpersonal Relationships Between Personality Traits

Beyond the smartphone addiction variable, several significant correlations were observed between the personality traits themselves. For example, Agreeableness was positively correlated with both Conscientiousness ($r = 0.435$, $p < 0.01$) and Openness to Experience ($r = 0.462$, $p < 0.01$). These significant relationships suggest that agreeable individuals tend to exhibit greater conscientiousness and openness, which aligns with theoretical expectations in personality psychology (Costa & McCrae, 1992). Additionally, Extraversion correlated positively with Neuroticism ($r = 0.309$, $p < 0.01$), indicating that more sociable individuals may also exhibit greater emotional sensitivity or mood variability, a finding consistent with past research on personality dynamics.

Table 5. Regression analysis

Model Summary[b]

					Change Statistics				
Model	R	R Square	Adjusted R Square	Std. Error of the Estimate	R Square Change	F Change	df1	df2	Sig. F Change
1	.197[a]	.039	.022	.903	.039	2.252	5	280	.049

a. Predictors: (Constant), Neuroticism, Conscientiousness, Extraversion, Openness, Agreeableness

b. Dependent Variable: Smart phone addiction

ANOVA[a]

Model		Sum of Squares	df	Mean Square	F	Sig.
1	Regression	9.174	5	1.835	2.252	.047[b]
	Residual	228.085	280	.815		
	Total	237.259	285			

a. Dependent Variable: Smart phone addiction

b. Predictors: (Constant), Neuroticism, Conscientiousness, Extraversion, Openness, Agreeableness

The regression analysis revealed a significant relationship between personality traits and smartphone addiction among sales executives. The model accounted for 19.7% of the variance in smartphone addiction ($R^2 = .197$), suggesting that personality traits play a notable role in predicting smartphone addiction. The F-statistic of 2.522 was significant at $p < .047$, confirming the overall model's predictive power.

Table 6. Regression analysis

Coefficients[a]						
		Unstandardized Coefficients		Standardized Coefficients		
Model		B	Std. Error	Beta	t	Sig.
1	(Constant)	3.526	.443		7.953	.000
	Extraversion	.013	.058	.014	.221	.825
	Agreeableness	.252	.089	.197	2.826	.005
	Conscientiousness	-.170	.087	-.135	-1.944	.053
	Openness	-.069	.089	-.053	-.772	.441
	Neuroticism	.047	.054	.054	.865	.388

a. Dependent Variable: Smart phone addiction

To examine the relationship between the Big Five personality traits and smartphone addiction among sales executives, a multiple regression analysis was conducted. The regression model evaluated the predictive power of Extraversion, Agreeableness, Conscientiousness, Openness to Experience, and Neuroticism on the dependent variable, Smartphone Addiction. The regression model revealed that personality traits accounted for 3.9% of the variance in smartphone addiction ($R^2 = .039$, Adjusted $R^2 = .022$). Although this indicates a modest explanatory power, the model's F-statistic was significant at $p = .047$, suggesting that, collectively, personality traits have a notable impact on smartphone addiction in this sample of sales executives.

The ANOVA results further supported the significance of the model. The F-statistic for the regression was $F (5, 280) = 2.252$, which was statistically significant ($p < .05$), reinforcing the idea that the set of personality traits meaningfully predicts smartphone addiction in this context.

The relationship between Extraversion and Smartphone Addiction was positive but not significant ($\beta = 0.014$, $p = .825$). This indicates that higher levels of extraversion do not significantly predict smartphone addiction in sales executives. Although extraverts, typically characterized by sociability and assertiveness, were hypothesized to engage more with smartphones, this finding suggests no strong connection between extraversion and smartphone overuse.

A significant positive relationship was observed between Agreeableness and Smartphone Addiction ($\beta = 0.197$, $p = .005$). Individuals high in agreeableness, who tend to be cooperative, empathetic, and concerned with maintaining harmony in relationships, may exhibit more addictive behaviors with their smartphones. This finding suggests that agreeableness is a key personality trait that contributes to a higher likelihood of smartphone addiction.

The association between Conscientiousness and Smartphone Addiction was negative and approached significance ($\beta = -0.135$, $p = .053$). Conscientious individuals, known for their self-discipline, responsibility, and goal orientation, may be less likely to develop smartphone addiction. While the relationship was not statistically significant, the negative trend aligns with expectations that conscientiousness serves as a protective factor against compulsive smartphone use.

The relationship between Openness to Experience and Smartphone Addiction was non-significant ($\beta = -0.053$, $p = .441$). Openness, often associated with creativity, intellectual curiosity, and a desire for novel experiences, did not emerge as a significant predictor of smartphone addiction. This suggests that openness to experience is not a critical factor in determining whether sales executives develop addictive behaviors related to smartphone use.

The correlation between Neuroticism and Smartphone Addiction was positive but not significant ($\beta = 0.054$, $p = .388$). Neuroticism, characterized by emotional instability, anxiety, and mood swings, was hypothesized to increase susceptibility to smartphone addiction, especially as individuals may turn to their phones to cope with stress. However, the results indicate that neuroticism does not play a significant role in predicting smartphone addiction within this sample.

The results of the regression analysis suggest that among the Big Five personality traits, Agreeableness is the strongest predictor of smartphone addiction in sales executives, with a significant positive relationship. Conscientiousness was also found to have a near-significant negative association with smartphone addiction, suggesting that individuals who are more organized and disciplined may be less prone to compulsive smartphone use. However, Extraversion, Openness, and Neuroticism did not show significant predictive power in this study. These findings provide valuable insights into how personality traits contribute to smartphone addiction, particularly in a professional setting such as sales. While certain traits like agreeableness may increase susceptibility, others such as conscientiousness might act as a buffer against addiction.

5. RESULTS AND DISCUSSIONS

- A regression analysis was conducted to further investigate the predictive power of personality traits on smartphone addiction. The model summary, as presented in Table 4.5, shows that the overall model accounted for 19.7% of the variance in smartphone addiction ($R^2 = .197$, $p < .047$), indicating a modest yet significant influence of personality traits on smartphone addiction.
- The regression analysis revealed that Agreeableness had a significant positive association with smartphone addiction ($\beta = .197$, $p < .005$), suggesting that individuals who are more agreeable are more prone to addictive smartphone behaviors. On the other hand, Conscientiousness showed a marginal negative relationship ($\beta = -0.135$, $p = 0.053$), indicating that more conscientious individuals may be less likely to exhibit smartphone addiction, though this finding approached but did not reach statistical significance. Other personality traits, including Extraversion, Openness, and Neuroticism, did not show significant relationships with smartphone addiction in the regression model.
- Among the personality traits, extraversion and agreeableness emerged as significant predictors of smartphone addiction. Extraversion, characterized by sociability and assertiveness, exhibited a positive association with addiction ($\beta = .014$, $p < .000$). This suggests that individuals who are more outgoing and assertive may be more prone to smartphone addiction. Conversely, agreeableness, reflecting cooperativeness and trust, demonstrated a negative relationship with addiction ($\beta = -.197$, $p < .005$). Individuals who are more agreeable and trusting may be less likely to develop smartphone addiction.
- Conscientiousness, openness, and neuroticism did not exhibit significant associations with smartphone addiction in this study. These findings suggest that conscientiousness (related to organization and self-discipline), openness (related to creativity and intellectual curiosity), and neuroticism (related to emotional stability) may not be as influential in predicting smartphone addiction among sales executives.

6. SUGGESTIONS

6.1 Targeted Interventions Based on Personality Traits

Agreeableness was found to have a significant positive association with smartphone addiction, organizations should provide training that fosters self-regulation for employees high in this trait. These individuals may benefit from mindfulness-based interventions and time management techniques to reduce reliance on smartphones during work hours.

Conscientiousness displaying a marginally negative relationship with smartphone addiction, fostering this trait in sales executives through productivity training, goal-setting workshops, and habit-forming strategies may reduce the likelihood of smartphone overuse.

Extraversion, openness, and neuroticism were not significant predictors, it may still be useful to provide general well-being and digital literacy programs that emphasize healthy smartphone use across all personality types.

6.2 Encouraging Healthy Digital Habits

Given the increasing reliance on smartphones for work-related tasks, it is important to promote balance. Companies can implement "Digital Detox" programs where sales executives are encouraged to disconnect from smartphones during non-essential work hours or breaks to reduce overuse and improve focus.

Time management applications and screen time monitoring tools could be introduced as part of employee wellness initiatives, helping individuals become more aware of and control their smartphone use.

6.3 Creating a Supportive Work Environment

Sales executives often experience pressure to stay connected via smartphones, but companies should set boundaries by promoting a culture of "tech-free meetings" and ensuring employees feel comfortable stepping away from their devices outside work hours. This is especially important for employees with high levels of agreeableness who may feel compelled to maintain constant connectivity to appease clients or team members.

6.4 Enhancing Self-Regulation Skills

Employees can benefit from self-regulation training, particularly those with higher levels of agreeableness, which could include workshops on setting personal boundaries, assertiveness in communication, and managing client expectations without being overly reliant on digital connectivity. Periodic personality assessments could be implemented to identify sales executives who may be more prone to smartphone addiction based on their personality profiles. This allows HR departments to provide personalized coaching or support based on individual needs, fostering both mental health and productivity.

6.5 Promote Workplace Wellness

To combat the potential for smartphone addiction among sales executives, organizations need to proactively foster a workplace wellness culture that prioritizes digital wellbeing and a healthy work-life balance. Implementing awareness campaigns that educate employees on the potential pitfalls of excessive smartphone use can encourage digital mindfulness and responsible engagement. Promoting regular digital detox periods, whether a tech-free evening or a weekend unplugged, can empower individuals to regain control over their relationship with technology. Creating dedicated tech-free zones within the workplace, like meeting rooms or relaxation areas, provides a tangible environment for employees to detach and reconnect with colleagues without constant technological distractions (Ferrero & Dalle Mura, 2019).

Investing in stress management training can help equip sales executives with healthy coping mechanisms to manage the pressures of their role, encouraging activities like mindfulness practices, yoga, and relaxation techniques. Instituting a culture that values work-life balance through flexible work arrangements, reasonable workloads, and promoting vacations and personal time, can help minimize the pressure of constant connectivity and cultivate overall wellbeing (Gonsalves & Harris, 2020). Finally, encouraging open communication and fostering an environment where sharing challenges is encouraged can provide a safe space for individuals to seek help from colleagues, supervisors, or professional resources.

6.6 Develop Effective Training

Beyond awareness, targeted training is critical to help sales executives combat smartphone addiction and develop productive work habits. Training programs focusing on digital time management, emphasizing techniques like the Pomodoro method and delegation, can empower individuals to prioritize tasks and control their time, reducing the tendency for impulsive phone checks (Pillemer, 2019).

Enhancing communication skills training, particularly those focused on managing client expectations effectively, responding efficiently to inquiries, and streamlining email communication, can improve interaction and reduce the need for constant connectivity. Training on setting boundaries and practicing deliberate disengagement techniques, such as limiting notifications or dedicating specific timeframes for smartphone use, can foster healthier digital habits (Hoyle, 2021). Organizations should also encourage the adoption of tech-free meetings, allowing for focused discussions, creative brainstorming, and deeper engagement with colleagues without the distractions of phones. Additionally, harnessing technology responsibly, through guidance on utilizing apps and tools that improve efficiency and organization, can empower individuals to minimize unnecessary phone checks and distractions (Andreassen et al., 2012; Montag, C., & Elhai, J. D. (2023).

6.7 Recruit Strategically

Organizations must strategically recruit for candidates who are less prone to smartphone addiction. Incorporating validated personality assessment tools like the Big Five personality inventory into the interview process allows recruiters to gauge candidate's levels of neuroticism, impulsivity, extroversion, and conscientiousness, highlighting potential vulnerabilities to addiction and fostering informed hiring decisions. Strategic interview questions that explore candidate's typical digital habits and how they manage technology can reveal their understanding of work-life balance and their approach to constant connectivity (Çiftçi et al., 2019).

By focusing on these areas, recruiters can identify individuals who have the necessary skills, while also showing a dedication to personal boundaries and self-care, which are crucial in the face of constant connectivity (Primack et al., 2015). Cultivating a workplace culture that celebrates balanced lifestyles, encouraging work-life balance resources, and promoting open discussions on responsible technology use are essential in supporting a mindful team. Leading by example, with senior management showcasing healthy technology habits and encouraging dialogue, helps to reinforce a culture where employees feel empowered to talk openly about digital wellbeing.

6.8 Smartphone Addiction on Job Performance

Regarding the impact of smartphone addiction on job performance, particularly within the context of sales, it is crucial to delve deeper into the direct consequences of this addiction on key aspects of sales outcomes, client relationships, and team dynamics. Smartphone addiction can lead to distracted behavior, which significantly impacts a sales executive's ability to meet deadlines and manage client relationships effectively. For example, the constant need to check notifications or respond to personal messages can cause sales executives to miss critical deadlines or neglect important follow-up tasks, resulting in delayed responses to clients and missed sales opportunities.

Additionally, addiction to smartphones can hinder focus during client meetings. Sales executives may find themselves distracted by their phones, which diminishes their ability to actively listen to clients, understand their needs, and provide tailored solutions. This behavior can negatively impact trust and rapport, crucial elements for long-term customer relationships. In some cases, overuse of smartphones may lead to mismanagement of customer interactions, such as sending incorrect information or failing to follow up on commitments, which can harm the reputation of the sales executive and the company.

To address these issues, organizations should implement strategies such as setting clear boundaries for smartphone use during work hours, providing training on time management and digital well-being, and encouraging mindfulness practices that help sales executives remain focused during client interactions. Encouraging the use of smartphone features, like "Do Not Disturb" modes during meetings, can help minimize distractions. Additionally, fostering a culture of accountability and open communication within teams can reduce the impact of smartphone addiction on team dynamics, promoting a more productive and supportive work environment.

7. MANAGERIAL AND PRACTICAL IMPLICATIONS

- HR managers should consider integrating personality assessments into the hiring and development process to better understand the tendencies of their sales executives. Training programs designed to encourage self-discipline for more agreeable employees or self-management techniques for conscientious employees could significantly reduce smartphone addiction and improve overall job performance.
- Since smartphone addiction can reduce productivity and increase mental fatigue, management should invest in wellness programs that emphasize digital well-being. These initiatives can reduce the negative effects of smartphone overuse and contribute to higher job satisfaction and efficiency, particularly in roles like sales where constant connectivity is common.
- Companies need to develop and implement work-life balance policies that discourage after-hours smartphone use unless absolutely necessary. Encouraging employees to disconnect during personal time can prevent burnout and reduce the likelihood of developing compulsive smartphone behaviors, benefiting both employees and overall organizational performance.
- Sales executives who exhibit higher agreeableness might be more prone to excessive smartphone use because they aim to please their clients and maintain open communication. Managers can leverage this by providing alternative methods of communication and engagement that do not rely solely on smartphones, such as structured team meetings or client update calls, allowing for efficient task completion without constant device interaction.
- In environments where smartphone usage is essential, such as sales, managers should explore technology solutions that help reduce the addictive nature of smartphones. For example, implementing work-focused apps that limit non-essential notifications during work hours could help maintain focus on

important tasks while reducing distractions caused by excessive smartphone use.

- From a broader perspective, organizations should develop clear guidelines around acceptable and unacceptable smartphone use, especially during working hours. These guidelines should aim to balance the need for connectivity with the need for mental well-being and productivity.
- The rise of AI tools and productivity apps has the potential to reduce smartphone addiction by automating routine tasks and providing smarter, more efficient ways to manage time and priorities. Sales executives can benefit from AI-powered scheduling assistants, task management tools, and customer relationship management (CRM) systems that streamline their workflows, helping them stay organized and focused. These tools can minimize the need for constant smartphone use by providing reminders and updates directly within the work ecosystem, reducing the temptation to check personal notifications.
- On the other hand, remote work and flexible work arrangements, which have been further enabled by digital technology, can sometimes exacerbate smartphone addiction if not managed effectively. With constant connectivity, sales executives may find it difficult to separate work from personal life, leading to overuse of smartphones. However, this can be counteracted by establishing clear boundaries between work and personal time, utilizing features like "Do Not Disturb" during work hours, and encouraging digital detox strategies.

8. CONCLUSION

This study explored the relationship between personality traits and smartphone addiction among sales executives, focusing on the Big Five traits: Extraversion, Agreeableness, Conscientiousness, Openness to Experience, and Neuroticism. The findings indicate that Agreeableness is significantly associated with higher levels of smartphone addiction, while Conscientiousness shows a near-significant negative relationship. These results suggest that agreeable individuals, who are more cooperative and relationship-oriented, may be more prone to smartphone addiction, whereas conscientious individuals, characterized by self-discipline and goal orientation, are less likely to exhibit such behavior. The other traits—Extraversion, Openness, and Neuroticism—did not show significant predictive power in this context.

The suggestions emphasize targeted interventions such as self-regulation training for highly agreeable individuals and productivity workshops to enhance conscientiousness. Additionally, promoting healthy digital habits through digital detox programs, screen time monitoring, and fostering work-life balance can help mitigate smartphone addiction in sales professionals. Implementing personality assessments and ongoing monitoring of employees' smartphone usage can provide HR departments with critical insights to offer personalized support and development programs.

The importance of customizing employee development programs to suit individual personality profiles, integrating digital well-being initiatives into the organizational culture, and establishing clear guidelines on acceptable smartphone use during work hours. Managers should also encourage balance by promoting tech-free meetings, offering communication alternatives, and supporting employees in disconnecting after work to prevent burnout and enhance productivity. Overall, understanding how personality traits influence smartphone addiction can lead to more effective workforce management strategies, improving both employee well-being and organizational outcomes. By addressing the behavioral patterns revealed through this research, organizations can develop more targeted and impactful interventions, leading to a healthier and more productive workforce, particularly in high-demand roles like sales executives.

REFERENCES

Aarestad, S. H., Flaa, T. A., Griffiths, M. D., & Pallesen, S. (2023). Smartphone addiction and subjective withdrawal effects: A three-day experimental study. *SAGE Open*, 13(4). Advance online publication. DOI: 10.1177/21582440231219538

Anand, A., Bowen, M., & Rangarajan, D. (2022). To be or not to be: A review of the (un)ethical salespeople literature. *Journal of Business and Industrial Marketing*, 38(9), 1837–1851. DOI: 10.1108/JBIM-06-2022-0282

Andreassen, C. S., Pallesen, S., Torsheim, T., & Griffiths, M. D. (2012). Problematic smartphone use: A review of the literature. *Current Opinion in Psychiatry*, 25(2), 183–188.

Bian, X., Qin, J., Yang, Z., Tian, Y., & Wu, L. (2020). Factors influencing smartphone addiction and their mediating effect: A path analysis. *Telematics and Informatics*, 69, 101413.

Boumosleh, J. M., & Jaalouk, D. (2017). Depression, anxiety, and smartphone addiction in university students: A cross-sectional study. *PLoS One*, 12(8), e0182239. DOI: 10.1371/journal.pone.0182239 PMID: 28777828

Caci, B., Cardaci, M., & Miceli, S. (2019). Development and maintenance of self-disclosure on facebook: The role of personality traits. *SAGE Open*, 9(2). DOI: 10.1177/2158244019856948

Choi, S. W., Kim, D.-J., Choi, J.-S., Ahn, H., Choi, E.-J., Song, W.-Y., Kim, S., & Youn, H. (2015). Comparison of risk and protective factors associated with smartphone addiction and Internet addiction. *Journal of Behavioral Addictions*, 4(4), 208–214. DOI: 10.1556/2006.4.2015.043 PMID: 26690626

Çiftçi, G., Ulutaş, H. M., Özkaynak, T. R., Öcal, F., & Özmen, A. A. (2019). The relationship between personality traits and problematic smartphone use. *Telematics and Informatics*, 58, 512–520.

Costa, C., Teodoro, M., Coco, M., Verduci, F., Giambò, F., Italia, S., Alibrandi, A., & Fenga, C. (2023). Smartphone use among resident physicians: Prevalence and risk factors in clinical practice. *SAGE Open*, 13(3). Advance online publication. DOI: 10.1177/21582440231194463

Dünnweber, M., & Fortmüller, A. (2017). Leadership models and behaviors for sales executives. what drives success and the best results? *Proceedings of the International Conference on Business Excellence*, 11(1), 779-787. DOI: 10.1515/picbe-2017-0082

Fauzi, A., Kasim, N. M., & Paiman, N. (2021). Fear of missing out among adolescents. *International Journal of E-Services and Mobile Applications*, 13(4), 1–14. DOI: 10.4018/IJESMA.2021100104

Ferrero, M. A., & Dalle Mura, M. (2019). Is social media use associated with stress, depression and well-being in adolescents and young adults? A narrative review. *Frontiers in Psychology*, 10, 902.

Flannery, K., & Mohs, J. N. (2020). Asymmetric cost behavior: Exploring ethical issues facing management. *Strategic Management Quarterly*, 8(2). Advance online publication. DOI: 10.15640/v8n2a1

Gao, B., Guo, F., Lisic, L. L., & Omer, T. C. (2023). Enforcement of non-compete agreements, outside employment opportunities, and insider trading*. *Contemporary Accounting Research*, 40(2), 1250–1279. DOI: 10.1111/1911-3846.12842

Gonsalves, L., & Harris, J. (2020). *The Connected Mind: Why Smartphones and Social Media Are Transforming the Brain.* The MIT Press.

Goyal, S., Hardgrave, B. C., Aloysius, J., & DeHoratius, N. (2016). The effectiveness of rfid in backroom and sales floor inventory management. *International Journal of Logistics Management*, 27(3), 795–815. DOI: 10.1108/IJLM-03-2015-0051

Guo, L., Tobias, J., Bendoly, E., & Hu, Y. (2017). Different departments, different drivers. International Journal of Operations &Amp. *International Journal of Operations & Production Management*, 37(8), 1031–1053. DOI: 10.1108/IJOPM-01-2016-0046

Hayati, B., & Puri, S. (2020). The impact of organizational social networks on salespeople's negative headquarters stereotypes. Journal of Business &Amp. *Journal of Business and Industrial Marketing*, 35(12), 1901–1913. DOI: 10.1108/JBIM-07-2019-0327

Herrero, J. (2021). Examining the empirical links between digital social pressure, personality, psychological distress, social support, users' residential living conditions, and smartphone addiction. *Social Science Computer Review*, 39(1), 1–15. DOI: 10.1177/0894439321998357

Hoyle, R. (2021). *Smartphones: The Good, the Bad, and the Ugly*. Penguin Books.

Hussain, Z., & Pontes, H. M. (2018). Personality, internet addiction, and other technological addictions. In *Advances in Human Factors and Ergonomics* (pp. 1–10). IGI Global. DOI: 10.4018/978-1-5225-3477-8.ch003

Indrawati, S. (2021). Effect of ability on salesperson performance through adaptive selling behavior as an intervening variable. *Ekspektra: Jurnal Bisnis Dan Manajemen*, 5(1), 31–37. DOI: 10.25139/ekt.v5i1.3354

Kırcaburun, K., March, E., Balta, S., Emirtekin, E., Kişla, T., & Griffiths, M. D. (2022). The role of procrastination between personality traits and addictive mukbang watching among emerging adults. *SAGE Open*, 12(1). DOI: 10.1177/21582440221085006

Kusuma, A. R., Syarief, R., Ekananta, A., & Sukmawati, A. (2023). Scenario planning of digital transformation in indonesia's fast-moving consumer goods sales organization: Uncertainties and possibilities. *The Winners*, 24(2), 83–96. DOI: 10.21512/tw.v24i2.10401

Lei, L., Zhang, M., & Zhang, Y. (2020). The relationship of smartphone addiction with psychological distress and neuroticism among university medical students. *BMC Psychology*, 8(1), 1–8. DOI: 10.1186/s40359-020-00466-6 PMID: 32917268

Li, Y., Griffiths, M. D., Mei, S., & Niu, Z. (2020). Fear of missing out and smartphone addiction mediates the relationship between positive and negative affect and sleep quality among Chinese university students. *Frontiers in Psychiatry*, 11, 877. DOI: 10.3389/fpsyt.2020.00877 PMID: 33192635

Li, Y., & Lin, C. (2019). Over-connected? A qualitative exploration of smartphone addiction among working adults in China. *BMC Psychiatry*, 19(1), 1–10. DOI: 10.1186/s12888-019-2170-z PMID: 31215473

Liu, Y., Zhou, Z., Zhu, E., Huang, L., & Zhang, M. (2022). Smartphone addiction and its associated factors among freshmen medical students in China: A cross-sectional study. *BMC Psychiatry*, 22(1), 1–10. DOI: 10.1186/s12888-022-03957-5 PMID: 35501728

Marengo, D., Sindermann, C., Häckel, D., Settanni, M., Elhai, J. D., & Montag, C. (2020). The association between the Big Five personality traits and smartphone use disorder: A meta-analysis. *Journal of Behavioral Addictions*, 9(2), 1–12. DOI: 10.1556/2006.2020.00069 PMID: 33011714

Montag, C., & Elhai, J. D. (2023). The smartphone and the brain: An update on recent research. *Current Behavioral Neuroscience Reports*.

Pearson, M. R., & Hussain, Z. (2016). Smartphone addiction and associated psychological factors. *Addicta : the Turkish Journal on Addictions*, 3(1), 103–112. DOI: 10.15805/addicta.2016.3.0103

Pillemer, S. (2019). Why Sales Executives Need to Understand Their Personality Types. Forbes. https://www.forbes.com/sites/forbescoachescouncil/2019/04/18/why-sales-executives-need-to-understand-their-personality-types/?sh=19a661403273

Polakova, G. (2021). Sales executives' reward attitude survey in the international company and their socio- economic consequences on the sales performance in global markets. SHS Web of Conferences, 92, 03023. DOI: 10.1051/shsconf/20219203023

Primack, B. A., Shensa, A., Sidani, J. E., Whaite, E. O., Lin, L. Y., Rosen, D., Miller, E., & Rosen, P. (2015). Social media use and perceived social isolation among young adults in the US. *American Journal of Preventive Medicine*, 48(1), 1–8. DOI: 10.1016/j.amepre.2017.01.010 PMID: 25441237

Rahim, N. A., Zainudin, N. A., & Mohd Yusof, M. A. (2020). Smartphone addiction: Its relationships to personality traits and types of smartphone use. *International Journal of Technology in Education and Science*, 4(1), 1–10. DOI: 10.46328/ijtes.165

Rahman, M. S., Zaman, M. H., Hossain, A., Mannan, M., & Hassan, H. (2019). Mediating effect of employee's commitment on workplace spirituality and executive'ssales performance. *Journal of Islamic Marketing*, 10(4), 1057–1073. DOI: 10.1108/JIMA-02-2018-0024

Sohn, S., Krasnoff, L., Rees, P., Kalk, N. J., & Carter, B. (2021). The association between smartphone addiction and sleep: A UK cross-sectional study of young adults. *Frontiers in Psychiatry*, 12, 629407. DOI: 10.3389/fpsyt.2021.629407 PMID: 33737890

Venkateswaran, P. S. (2011). A study on brand personality dimensions and brand loyalty towards Raymond brand. *Journal of Marketing Communications*, 7(2).

Venkateswaran, P. S., & Tamilselvi, P. (2018). A study on the influence of personality on decision-making. *International Journal of Advance & Innovative Research*, 5(4), 165–170. DOI: 10.2394/7780.5.4.165

Chapter 12
Screen to Soul: Navigating Intimacy in the Age of Digital Communication

Sowmya D. S.
https://orcid.org/0009-0005-2408-432X
PES University, India

L. Nithya
PES University, India

V. Anokha
https://orcid.org/0009-0008-9286-6819
PES University, India

ABSTRACT

The chapter examines how interpersonal relationships are shaped in the contemporary day by digital communication. With a focus on the effects on emotional closeness, relationship satisfaction, and mental health, it investigates the transition from in-person to virtual interactions. To comprehend their impact on relationships, important phenomena like phubbing, digital intimacy, and constant partial attention are examined. The chapter covers the drawbacks, including growing loneliness, as well as the benefits, like improved social support systems. It also emphasizes the significance of cutting-edge technology like virtual reality and provides tips for striking a balance between online and offline connections. In order to promote better, more meaningful relationships in the digital age, suggestions for digital literacy and mindful technology use are given.

DOI: 10.4018/979-8-3693-8804-4.ch012

INTRODUCTION

With smartphones and digital communication platforms becoming a necessity in modern life, the digital age has fundamentally changed how people engage and sustain relationships. Social norms and expectations surrounding communication have changed as a result of the transition from in-person to virtual contacts (Turkle, 2011). Instantaneous communication across distances is made possible by digital technologies like social media, video calls, and messaging applications, which promote a sense of connectedness even in the face of physical separation (Baym, 2015). But there are drawbacks to these tools as well, like the possibility of misunderstandings and a decrease in the depth of conversations as compared to face-to-face contacts (Walther, 1996).

The dynamics of interpersonal interactions and social structures have changed as a result of the proliferation of digital communication technology. Communication via digital platforms like social media, messaging applications, and video conversations has become essential to daily life due to the almost ubiquitous adoption of smartphones (Baym, 2015). Aspects of interpersonal relationships, including emotional intimacy, social presence, and mental health, have been impacted by this change in both positive and negative ways (Chotpitayasunondh & Douglas, 2018). Research on the effects of digital platforms on relationships is still ongoing, with a focus on issues like digital intimacy and phubbing—the practice of neglecting people in favor of a smartphone (Chotpitayasunondh & Douglas, 2018; Roberts & David, 2016).

According to studies, digital communication improves accessibility and convenience but falls short of in-person interactions in terms of depth, which could lower the quality of interpersonal relationships (Walther, 1996). Significant consequences on mental health are also shown by research; an increasing amount of data indicates that digital communication may be a contributing factor to problems like anxiety, low self-esteem, and social comparison (Kross et al., 2013). This twofold effect on social and psychological aspects emphasizes the significance of comprehending how relationships are impacted by digital communication and the necessity of adopting healthy technology practices.

Importance of Digital Communication on Relationships

Since digital communication impacts emotional closeness, relationship happiness, and general mental health, it has a substantial impact on interpersonal relationships (Kross et al., 2013). Navigating the challenges of preserving meaningful connections in a world that is heavily reliant on technology requires an understanding of these effects. Discussing this subject is especially pertinent in light of growing worries about the possible drawbacks of excessive smartphone use, like social isolation and loneliness even though one is always "connected" (Chotpitayasunondh & Douglas, 2018).

Non-verbal clues like tone and body language, which are essential for expressing emotions and building connections, are diminished when face-to-face communication gives way to virtual communication (Mehrabian, 1971). Richer communication media, such as in-person contacts, are more effective for complicated, ambiguous talks because they provide instant feedback and visual signals, according to Daft and Lengel's (1986) Media Richness Theory. However, these indications are frequently absent from digital communication, which could result in miscommunications and a reduced level of interaction quality. This is further supported by the Social Presence Theory, which contends that in-person encounters provide people with a greater sense of presence and connection than text-based ones (Walther, 1996). Consequently, digital exchanges might not have the emotional resonance required for strong personal connections (Baym, 2015).

Brief Introduction of Key Concepts

The term "phubbing," which is a combination of the words "phone" and "snubbing," describes the practice of ignoring someone in favor of a smartphone. Relationship satisfaction has been demonstrated to suffer as a result of this conduct, which is becoming more and more common (Roberts & David, 2016). For example, phubbing can cause partners to feel neglected and upset, which can escalate conflict and reduce emotional connection.

Digital Intimacy - The term "digital intimacy" describes the emotional bond and sensation of intimacy that are promoted by digital communication methods. Digital intimacy, in contrast to traditional face-to-face intimacy, is frequently typified by text-based interactions that might not have the non-verbal clues necessary to comprehend emotions (Turkle, 2011). Nonetheless, other research indicates that digital communication might enhance relationships by offering fresh channels for expressing concern and staying in touch (Baym, 2015).

The phrase "continuous partial attention," which was first used by Linda Stone in 2007, refers to the state in which one is continuously looking for fresh information without ever giving one encounter their complete focus. In the digital age, when people are frequently separated between their digital devices and their physical environment, this behavior is typical. It may lessen the depth of those connections by affecting the level of attention provided during face-to-face interactions.

EVOLUTION OF PERSONAL CONNECTIONS IN THE DIGITAL AGE

Historical Evolution of Digital Communication and Relationship Dynamics

Over the past few decades, the development of digital communication has changed the expectations and norms of interpersonal interactions, changing the dynamics of relationships. In the beginning, early technologies like text messaging in the 1990s and email in the 1970s were used in addition to face-to-face contact. However, a period in which digital communication became essential to social interactions was sparked by the advent of smartphones and social media sites like Facebook (2004) and Instagram (2010) (Turkle, 2011). Many refer to this trend toward digital-first contacts as "digital intimacy," in which relationships are sustained via social media, text, and photos rather than in-person interactions (Baym, 2015).

This change is framed by the theories of media richness and social presence. Rich communication technologies, including face-to-face interactions, are crucial for intricate exchanges with emotional depth, claim Daft and Lengel (1986). Nevertheless, despite its drawbacks, many now prefer less sophisticated communication due to the ease of use of digital tools. Building on this, Walther (1996) explains that digital interactions typically have a lesser social presence, which frequently reduces the emotional resonance and authenticity of relationships. Younger generations that have grown up on these technologies as their main form of communication are particularly affected by this change (Kuss & Griffiths, 2021).

Historical Perspective: From Face-to-Face Interactions to Digital Communication

In the past, face-to-face contacts were used to establish and maintain personal ties because they enabled the complete spectrum of human communication, including non-verbal clues like body language, tone of voice, and facial expressions. These components promoted strong interpersonal ties by advancing a comprehensive grasp of feelings and intentions (Turkle, 2011).The landscape of interpersonal connections started to shift with the introduction of digital communication tools like social media, instant messaging, and email. Convenience and speed were the primary drivers of the shift from face-to-face meetings to text-based communication, which enabled connections across geographic boundaries (Baym, 2015). However, because digital platforms frequently lack the subtle non-verbal cues that are essential for expressing emotion, this change also resulted in a decrease in the depth of communication. New social norms and practices were brought about by the increasing use of digital communication. For instance, relationships may suffer as a result of pressure and miscommunications brought on by the expectation of prompt responses on messaging apps (Walther, 1996). The basic human urge for connection persisted in spite of these developments, propelling the development of digital platforms that aim to replicate in-person encounters via voice texting and video conversations.

Media Richness and Social Presence

According to the Media Richness Theory, the ability of various communication media to transmit complex messages varies. For complicated, ambiguous interactions, richer media—such as face-to-face communication—are more effective because they can convey nonverbal clues and emotional nuances more effectively (Daft & Lengel, 1986). On the other hand, text-based digital platforms, such as chats or emails, are seen to be less rich since they don't provide the visual cues and instant feedback that improve comprehension. Walther (1996) proposed the Social Presence Theory, which explains how much a communication medium enables users to see one another as actual individuals. Face-to-face communication, where another person's physical presence is indisputable, is usually linked to high social presence. Depending on the platform, social presence in digital environments might differ. For instance, because video calls incorporate both visual and aural features, they have a larger social presence than text messages.

People's perceptions of the intimacy and genuineness of their digital interactions are influenced by the relationship between social presence and media richness. Video calls may mimic in-person interactions, but they still lack touch and other aspects of physical presence that are essential for stronger emotional connections (Baym, 2015).

Digital Intimacy and How It Compares to Traditional Intimacy

The term “digital intimacy” describes the emotional bond and sense of intimacy people have when using digital platforms like social media and messaging applications. Digital intimacy is developed through text messaging, picture sharing, and other online involvement, in contrast to traditional intimacy, which mostly depends on face-to-face encounters (Turkle, 2011). For example, daily texting or photo sharing might help people feel connected even when they are geographically separated.

People can stay in touch more often thanks to the ease and speed of digital communication, which might promote a feeling of intimacy. This type of connection, meanwhile, could not have the same depth as in-person conversations. In text-based interactions, nonverbal clues like a reassuring touch or the nuances of a smile are frequently absent or misunderstood (Walther, 1996). Although digital intimacy can enhance more conventional kinds of intimacy, there are drawbacks as well. For instance, the absence of context and nonverbal cues in text messages might result in misunderstandings and even conflict (Daft & Lengel, 1986). Furthermore, the constant accessibility of digital communication can occasionally cause a blurring of the lines between social contacts and personal space, resulting in "social saturation" and feelings of tiredness (Turkle, 2011).

Non-Verbal Cues in Face-to-Face Interactions to Text-Based Communication

The shift from in-person to virtual communication has had a profound impact on how people express and decipher nonverbal clues. Accurately reading meaning and emotions requires the instantaneous transfer of expressions, gestures, and tone that face-to-face interactions provide (Mehrabian, 1971). On the other hand, text-based communication necessitates that people deduce feelings from written language, which frequently results in ambiguity.

According to Shirley Turkle (2011), the move to digital communication has resulted in a phenomenon she refers to as "alone together"—a state in which individuals are physically present but emotionally detached, frequently absorbed in their electronic gadgets rather than interacting with others. When people sit in the same room yet spend more time on their phones than interacting with one another, this phenomena is clearly visible. In an effort to bridge the gap created by text-based communication's lack of physical indicators, emojis and other digital symbols have surfaced. Although a variety of emotions can be expressed using these symbols, they are still constrained in comparison to the entire range of expressions found in in-person encounters (Baym, 2015). Because of this, decoding signals in digital communication frequently necessitates a greater amount of cognitive work, which might strain interpersonal understanding. Despite these drawbacks, research indicates that digital communication can be a useful addition to face-to-face encounters. For example, according to Walther's (1996) theory of hyperpersonal communication, because people can choose how they present themselves and divulge certain parts of themselves, digital encounters can occasionally be more intimate than in-person ones. Deeper confessions and a sense of intimacy that might not arise in impromptu face-to-face chats can result from this control.

Phubbing and Its Impact on Personal Relationships

Phubbing, which is a combination of the words "phone" and "snubbing," is the practice of neglecting someone in a social situation by concentrating on a smartphone (Roberts & David, 2016:1). With the rising use of cellphones, this behavior has become more prevalent and has an impact on interactions in a variety of social settings, such as friendships, family get-togethers, and romantic relationships.

The widespread use of phubbing is indicative of how deeply ingrained digital gadgets are in daily life. The temptation to emphasize digital connections over in-person ones is strong given that the average individual checks their phone several times an hour (Chotpitayasunondh & Douglas, 2018). Although younger people, who are generally more active on social media and messaging apps, may participate in the phenomenon more frequently, it is not age-specific. Phubbing has grown commonplace in many contexts as a result of digital platforms' encouragement of continuous connectedness and instant rewards through notifications. However, this conduct degrades face-to-face encounters, raising concerns about how it may affect the depth and contentment of relationships (Roberts & David, 2016).

Psychological Effects of Phubbing on Individuals and Relationships

Phubbing can have serious psychological repercussions for both the person doing it and the person being ignored. According to research by Roberts and David (2016), people who are phubbed frequently feel rejected and have a worse sense of self-worth. Being ignored in favor of a smartphone can make someone feel insignificant, which is bad for their emotional health and self-worth. Conversely, people who often participate in phubbing might not always be conscious of the consequences of their behavior. Unaware that their actions can cause interpersonal strain and misunderstandings, Phubbers may view their activity as a harmless habit or even a way to multitask (Roberts & David, 2016). A cycle of discontent in interpersonal relationships may be sustained by this ignorance. Phubbing may also be a factor in the phenomena known as "social displacement," in which chances for more in-depth, in-person communication are replaced by digital encounters. Because people lose out on the nonverbal clues that promote emotional comprehension and connection, this displacement can lead to elevated stress levels and feelings of loneliness (Chotpitayasunondh & Douglas, 2018).

Impact on Relationship Satisfaction and Increased Feelings of Loneliness

One of the main topics of current research has been the effect of phubbing on relationship satisfaction. Chotpitayasunondh and Douglas (2018) discovered that people report lower levels of relationship satisfaction when they believe their partners engage in phubbing on a regular basis. Because the person being phubbed could feel less important and prioritized in the relationship, the conduct causes a rift. Phubbing is especially harmful in love relationships, when preserving a sense of intimacy requires quality time and full attention. Phubbing frequently causes partners to become less emotionally connected and more conflicted, which lowers relationship satisfaction overall (Chotpitayasunondh & Douglas, 2018). This decrease may create a vicious cycle in which discontent leads to increased smartphone use as an escape, making the problem worse. Phubbing enhances the sense of isolation experienced by people who engage in it. People who are often phubbed may experience emotional detachment, which can exacerbate their sense of social isolation, even when they are physically present with others (Roberts & David, 2016). The paradox of digital connectedness is brought to light by this phenomenon: although cellphones can help people stay in touch with people who live far away, they can also put up walls between people who are physically present.

Gender Differences in Smartphone Use and Its Impacts

Gender affects how people use smartphones and how they perceive the impact of digital communication on relationships and mental health. According to studies, men typically use social media and smartphones for entertainment and information searching, whereas women typically use them for emotional and relational connections (Valkenburg & Peter, 2007). Each group's experience of the advantages or disadvantages of digital communication may be influenced by this gendered use pattern.

When women compare themselves to idealized photos of others on social media sites like Facebook and Instagram, they are more likely to feel negative feelings (Kross et al., 2013). Particularly for younger women who use social media extensively, this might result in increased anxiety, despair, and feelings of inadequacy (Elhai et al., 2020). Men, on the other hand, can be less impacted by social comparison but more vulnerable to problems associated with smartphones, such as addiction to gaming, which can harm mental health and social relationships (Kuss & Griffiths, 2021).

These disparities in gender highlight the value of tailored strategies in mitigating the negative effects of smartphone use. For instance, efforts for men may stress the balanced use of communication and entertainment platforms to promote better digital habits, while treatments for women may concentrate on lowering social comparison tendencies.

The Impact of Smartphone Addiction on Children and Adolescents

Due to their vital social and emotional development, children and teenagers are especially susceptible to the negative impacts of smartphone addiction. Research indicates that children who use smartphones excessively are more likely to experience social isolation, anxiety, and depression (Elhai et al., 2020). Children and teenagers, in contrast to adults, might not have the self-control necessary to properly manage their screen time, which could result in compulsive behaviors that impair their social connections and emotional health (Twenge & Campbell, 2018).

The effect of digital communication on teenagers' capacity to acquire in-person social skills is also highlighted by research. Teens who spend a lot of time on screens may have trouble recognizing social cues and growing empathy, two abilities that are crucial for establishing and preserving relationships, claim Przybylski and Weinstein (2022). Additionally, teens' mental health may suffer as a result of their frequent exposure to social comparison on sites like Instagram, which can heighten feelings of inadequacy and low self-esteem (Kross et al., 2013). Younger populations are particularly vulnerable, which emphasizes the need for focused interventions like digital literacy programs to provide them the tools they need to use the internet responsibly.

Evolution of Social Norms around Smartphone Use during Interactions

The use of smartphones has changed societal standards about appropriate behavior in face-to-face interactions in addition to introducing new behaviors. In the past, making eye contact and paying close attention were necessary for face-to-face communication to convey respect and involvement. These expectations have changed, though, as smartphone use is now widely accepted in social situations (Turkle, 2011).

Brief pauses during talks, such checking notifications or responding to messages, have become commonplace and even expected by many people. These modifications are a reflection of the larger cultural trend toward multitasking and continuous connectedness (Baym, 2015). However, because people may have varied standards for what constitutes appropriate smartphone use in different social circumstances, the ambiguity of these new norms might lead to conflict.This shift in conventions also mirrors more general patterns in time and attention management. People find it more difficult to completely unplug during social encounters as a result of the blurring of boundaries between work and personal life caused by the increasing integration of digital devices into both (Turkle, 2011). The detrimental emotional effects on those being phubbed persist even after such behavior has become more commonplace, indicating a disconnect between the need for meaningful human connection and changing social standards.

Strategies for Mitigating the Negative Impact of Phubbing

Researchers and mental health professionals have suggested a number of tactics to encourage more thoughtful smartphone use in order to counteract the detrimental consequences of phubbing. Establishing "phone-free" zones during meals or talks with loved ones is one strategy for clearly defining limits on smartphone use during social interactions (Hertlein & Ancheta, 2014). These limits assist people in prioritizing in-person encounters and establishing areas where their whole focus is on the people in those situations.

Digital mindfulness, which is being aware of when and why one goes for one's phone, is another useful tactic. People can be more present with others around them by being encouraged to take a moment to consider whether checking their devices is really required at that particular moment (Roberts & David, 2016). Social standards that forbid phubbing in particular contexts, such meetings, family get-togethers, or dates, are recommended by some experts. Cultural campaigns or emphasizing the importance of spending unbroken time with others can serve to promote these norms (Chotpitayasunondh & Douglas, 2018). It can be helpful to change attitudes toward more thoughtful smartphone use by highlighting the advantages of direct communication, such as better emotional understanding and healthier relationships.

Campaigns for education and awareness of the detrimental effects of phubbing can assist people in realizing the damage it can do to their relationships. People may be more inclined to change their behavior if they realize how seemingly little habits, such checking a phone during a discussion, can negatively impact the quality of relationships (Turkle, 2011).

Longitudinal Impacts of Digital Communication

With research showing notable shifts in relationship dynamics over time, there is a growing interest in the long-term effects of digital communication on relationships. Digital communication's constant accessibility, for example, might make it difficult to distinguish between personal and professional life, leading to what is commonly referred to as "continuous partial attention" (Stone, 2007). The quality and depth of interpersonal interactions are impacted by this condition of perpetual semi-attention, in which people are only partially focused on one or two streams of information (Turkle, 2011).

According to longitudinal research, people who use digital communication extensively may eventually see a decrease in relationship satisfaction because of a loss of emotional depth and a rise in the likelihood of misunderstandings (Kross et al., 2013). Additionally, "phubbing"—the practice of ignoring others in favor of a smartphone—is frequently encouraged by digital communication and has been demonstrated to have a detrimental effect on relational trust and happiness (Roberts & David, 2016). Contextualizing the effects of digital communication on the stability and quality of relationships requires an understanding of these long-term effects.

BALANCING ONLINE AND OFFLINE INTERACTIONS

Challenges

People now find it difficult to reconcile their online and offline connections as a result of the pervasiveness of digital communication in daily life. According to some academics, "continuous partial attention" is the result of people's persistent switching between online and face-to-face contacts (Stone, 2007). An excessive dependence on cellphones may result in a feeling of detachment from the present. For example, people may use digital devices even when they are around friends or family, which might reduce the interest and significance of in-person relationships (Turkle, 2011). Social networking sites and messaging applications that push users to stay in regular contact—often with attention-demanding notifications and updates—further worsen this imbalance. The pressure to be active online might cause people to overlook their offline relationships, which lowers the quality of their in-person interactions (Baym, 2015).

Continuous Partial Attention and Its Effects on Presence and Connection

The phrase "continuous partial attention," coined by Linda Stone in 2007, describes the condition of continuously observing several information streams without ever giving any one of them your whole attention. People who constantly move between digital devices and their immediate environment often exhibit this behaviour.

Relationships are greatly impacted by ongoing partial attention since it frequently leads to a shallow interaction with individuals who are physically present. A person may, for instance, divide their focus between talking and looking at their phone, which makes it challenging to completely understand the wants and feelings of their conversation partner (Stone, 2007).

Because the brain finds it difficult to process several inputs at once, mental exhaustion can also result from continuous partial attention. This condition of perpetual distraction can impede the development of empathy and understanding in relationships as well as the formation of deeper connections (Turkle, 2011). This can eventually lower the quality of interpersonal interactions and lead to feelings of emotional remoteness.

Strategies for Setting Boundaries for Digital Device Use

- To counter the challenges of continuous partial attention, setting clear boundaries for digital device use is essential. One effective strategy is implementing designated phone-free times or zones, such as during meals, family gatherings, or while spending time with loved ones (Hertlein & Ancheta, 2014). These boundaries can help ensure that interactions remain focused and meaningful.
- Another approach is the "Do Not Disturb" feature on smartphones, which allows individuals to mute non-essential notifications during specific hours or situations. This can reduce the temptation to check messages or social media, enabling individuals to be more present with those around them.
- Couples or friends can also establish mutual agreements about device use during shared time, such as keeping phones away when out on a date or during deep conversations. These agreements can help align expectations and reduce potential conflicts related to smartphone use (Roberts & David, 2016).

Digital Detox Practices in Improving the Quality of Face-to-Face Connections

As a way to restore equilibrium between online and offline life, digital detox techniques have grown in popularity. In order to promote mental health and re-establish a connection with the real world, a digital detox entails taking a vacation from screens and online activities (Hertlein & Ancheta, 2014). Studies indicate that even brief breaks from electronic devices can improve focus and the caliber of conversations. For example, people can become more aware of their surroundings and more involved in interactions with friends and family by going without a smartphone for a weekend (Turkle, 2011).

Digital detoxification can also help people recover the joy of face-to-face encounters by serving as a reminder of the advantages of being totally present in the moment. Increased appreciation for offline pursuits like outdoor excursions, common interests, or just spending time together over a meal without interruptions can result from this practice (Roberts & David, 2016). The deliberateness of the practice determines how successful a digital detox is. The potential benefits can be limited by just putting a device aside without concentrating on interacting with others. Detox periods should be used by people to prioritize spending time with loved ones and actively invest in their relationships (Baym, 2015).

Examples of How Successful Balance Contributes to Healthier Personal Relationships

- Case studies have shown that maintaining a healthy balance between digital and offline interactions can significantly enhance relationship satisfaction. For example, couples who establish weekly phone-free dates report feeling closer and more connected over time, as these moments allow for deeper, uninterrupted conversations (Chotpitayasunondh & Douglas, 2018).
- Parents who implement family digital detox weekends often observe improvements in their children's behavior and engagement during shared activities. These breaks from screens can encourage creativity, foster stronger family bonds, and create opportunities for open communication (Hertlein & Ancheta, 2014).
- Friends who set boundaries around social media use during outings tend to report more fulfilling interactions. By agreeing to keep their phones away during coffee dates or group dinners, they create a space for genuine conversations and laughter, which strengthens their sense of belonging and emotional connection (Roberts & David, 2016).
- Such examples highlight that when individuals make a conscious effort to balance their online and offline lives, the quality of their relationships improves, leading to increased feelings of support, trust, and satisfaction.

IMPACT ON MENTAL HEALTH

Positive Effects of Digital Communication: Enhanced Social Support Networks and Sense of Belonging

- The expansion of social support networks is one of the many ways that digital communication has improved mental health. Regardless of geographic distance, people can maintain relationships with friends, relatives, and other people through social media platforms, messaging applications, and online communities (Nabi et al., 2013). These forums give people a place to exchange stories, give and receive counsel, and get emotional support—all of which can improve mental health.
- Digital communication may foster a sense of belonging for those who might otherwise feel alone, particularly those who live in remote locations or have physical disabilities. Emotional resilience requires connections and camaraderie, which can be found in online communities centered around common

interests or difficulties, such as parenting groups, mental health forums, or hobby-based networks (Nabi et al., 2013).

- Online interactions may boost perceived social support, which has been linked to reduced stress, increased self-esteem, and enhanced coping strategies during trying times, according to research. According to Nabi et al. (2013), even short exchanges, like a quick message or social media comment, can strengthen a sense of community and lessen feelings of isolation.

Negative Effects: Superficiality of Online Interactions, Social Comparison, and Mental Health Issues like Anxiety and Depression

- Although digital communication has advantages, it also has disadvantages, especially when it comes to how shallow a lot of online conversations are. Online conversations, particularly those that take place through text or social media, can lack the emotional richness and depth of in-person interactions. Messages can be misunderstood and cause misunderstandings or emotional detachment if non-verbal clues such as body language or tone of voice are not comprehended (Turkle, 2011).
- Social comparison is one of the biggest drawbacks of internet communication. People frequently compare their life to the carefully chosen photos and updates of others on social media platforms in particular. People may believe that their own lives don't measure up to the seemingly ideal experiences that others have, which can cause emotions of inadequacy, envy, and discontent (Kross et al., 2013).
- Studies have indicated that frequent use of social media is associated with higher levels of anxiety and depression, especially when users passively consume content by scrolling through feeds without actively interacting with others (Kross et al., 2013). This conduct contributes to a cycle of emotional pain and cultivates a poor self-perception. The constant onslaught of filtered photos and romanticized depictions of other people's lives can warp reality and strengthen self-defeating ideas. Cyberbullying and unfavourable online encounters can seriously harm mental health. Digital platforms' anonymity and detachment frequently encourage aggressive or violent behavior, which exacerbates victims' feelings of loneliness and sadness (Kross et al., 2013).

Importance of Quality vs. Quantity of Digital Interactions

The quality of online contacts, rather than just their amount, determines the influence of digital communication on mental health. According to research, meaningful, encouraging interactions—rather than frequent, surface-level interactions—are closely linked to the emotional benefits of digital communication (Nabi et al., 2013). Having meaningful discussions, especially when they take place online, might improve mental health. Like in-person encounters, for instance, sincere notes from loved ones or in-depth conversations about a common interest can promote a sense of connection and affirmation (Walther, 1996). On the other hand, frequent, superficial interactions—like liking a post or quickly responding with an emoji—don't provide much emotional depth and might not satisfy a person's need for connection. Another important factor is the environment in which digital exchanges take place. While neutral or negative interactions, including disputes or strictly transactional chats, may have little to no impact on mental health, supportive, intimate, and sympathetic interactions tend to improve mental health (Kross et al., 2013). As a result, those who concentrate on developing fewer but deeper online interactions typically see improvements in their mental health.

Individual Differences in Moderating the Effects of Digital Communication on Mental Health

- Personality qualities have a big impact on how people react to digital communication. For example, extroverted individuals tend to be more socially involved both offline and online, making them more at ease with online interactions and possibly more satisfied with them (Amichai-Hamburger & Vinitzky, 2010). On the other hand, introverts may still find it difficult to make meaningful connections online, which can worsen feelings of loneliness or isolation, even though they frequently use online platforms to avoid in-person interactions.
- Another element that mitigates the effects of digital communication is social anxiety. Online platforms may be less daunting to those with social anxiety than face-to-face contacts, enabling them to converse more freely (Valkenburg & Peter, 2007). Digital communication might, however, encourage avoidance tendencies and prevent people from acquiring the social skills required for in-person relationships, even while it can lessen the immediate stress of face-to-face contacts (Turkle, 2011). This dependence on internet communication over time may impede personal development and sustain social anxiety.
- Individual differences in the demand for validation impact how digital communication impacts self-esteem. When their online presence does not receive

enough engagement, likes, comments, or shares, people who rely on social media for validation may suffer more detrimental effects on their mental health (Nabi et al., 2013). These people may suffer from increased anxiety and depression as a result of being more susceptible to the emotional effects of social comparison.

- Coping mechanisms and resilience are also quite important. Stronger coping strategies help people deal with the negative effects of digital communication, like social comparison and cyberbullying. They are more likely to establish boundaries around their online behavior or participate in digital detoxification techniques, which can lessen the detrimental impacts on mental health (Kross et al., 2013).

INTERVENTIONS AND RECOMMENDATIONS

Encouraging Mindful Technology Used During Personal Interactions

- Promoting thoughtful technology use is one practical strategy for reducing the detrimental effects of digital communication on interpersonal interactions. With an emphasis on reducing distractions during face-to-face encounters, mindful technology use entails being completely conscious of how, when, and why one uses digital devices (Hertlein & Ancheta, 2014).
- Techniques for encouraging mindfulness include prioritizing direct communication during talks and establishing designated periods for phone checks. For instance, in order to concentrate on one another, couples may decide to set aside their phones during meals or have "tech-free" evenings. This can enhance the quality of time spent together and support emotional presence.
- According to Hertlein and Ancheta (2014), using technology mindfully can help people become more self-reliant and identify when their use of devices may be negatively impacting their relationships. By teaching people to live in the present, mindfulness training can also make people more aware of their digital behaviors and how they affect their relationships with others.

Promoting Digital Literacy: Un Limitations and Nuances of Online Communication

- **Digital literacy** is essential for assisting people in comprehending the limitations of online communication and navigating its intricacies. Understanding how digital platforms affect communication, including the possibility of misunderstandings and the absence of non-verbal clues in text-based exchanges, is a component of digital literacy (Deresiewicz, 2009).

- Encouraging digital literacy can enable people to make better use of online communication tools. People can be encouraged to select the best medium for various kinds of talks by knowing the distinction between the richness of in-person interactions and the more constrained nature of text messages.
- Younger users who are growing up in a digital-first world may benefit most from educational initiatives that emphasize **social media etiquette** and the value of digital boundaries. These programs can impart knowledge on how to evaluate online behavior, strike a balance between online and offline connections, and identify when a conversation might be more appropriate for a face-to-face setting (Baym, 2015).
- By raising awareness of the negative impacts of **social comparison** and the significance of curating one's digital environment to prioritize good connections, increasing digital literacy can also assist users in developing better relationships with social media (Turkle, 2011).

Strengthening Offline Connections Through Shared Experiences and Quality Time

It is crucial to concentrate on enhancing offline relationships in order to offset the effects of digital communication. Spending quality time together and establishing connections via common experiences can strengthen ties and provide a sense of intimacy that digital communication cannot match (Deresiewicz, 2009). Deresiewicz (2009) highlights the importance of reflection and solitude, arguing that people may connect with others and themselves more effectively when they take time away from electronic distractions. This method promotes the creation of opportunities for in-person encounters, such as taking walks together, taking up hobbies, or organizing group activities that promote direct communication.

Game nights or outdoor outings are examples of family activities that restrict screen time and can assist both adults and children in rediscovering the pleasure of unhindered interaction. By fostering emotional intimacy through shared experiences, these activities contribute to the formation of more robust and resilient relationships (Hertlein & Ancheta, 2014). Apart from family environments, communities can gain from programs that stimulate offline interaction, like neighborhood get-togethers, cultural gatherings, and workshops that enhance in-person interactions. By fostering a feeling of community and belonging, these activities can lessen the need for digital platforms for social contact.

Interventions for Individuals and Communities to Foster Balanced Use of Digital Communication Tools

Both individual and community-level interventions must be developed to promote balanced digital communication. Individualized strategies that establish objectives for digital detoxification, such cutting screen time by a given percentage or setting aside particular hours for offline activities, can work well for people. Public awareness campaigns emphasizing the value of in-person interactions and the possible drawbacks of excessive digital participation could be part of community-based solutions. Employers may foster a work-life balance culture by supporting digital well-being programs and honoring offline hours, while schools can implement seminars that teach kids the importance of being present in the moment (Baym, 2015).

Social programs, like "no-phone zones" in parks and cafes, can also create settings where people are encouraged to socialize without being distracted by their phones. Disconnecting from digital gadgets during social interactions can become more acceptable and even desired with the support of such treatments. Technology itself has the potential to support balanced use. Features that track screen time, urge users to take breaks, or provide information about digital behaviors can be incorporated by developers. By encouraging users to make changes that support their social and emotional objectives, these tools can help users become more aware of how they use their devices (Turkle, 2011).

Counseling and Therapy in Addressing the Mental Health Impact of Digital Communication

For people who suffer from problems like social anxiety, loneliness, or an excessive dependence on digital interactions, counseling and therapy can be extremely helpful in addressing the detrimental effects of digital communication on mental health. Therapists can assist their clients in creating plans for controlling their use of technology and enhancing their offline social skills (Hertlein & Ancheta, 2014).

Cognitive-behavioral therapy (CBT) is especially useful for assisting people in identifying and altering cognitive patterns that lead to negative digital behaviors. For instance, the fear of missing out (FOMO) that motivates excessive online participation or the anxiety that results in obsessive social media checking can both be addressed by therapy (Turkle, 2011).

Couples and families who have experienced poor communication patterns due to phubbing or excessive technology use can also benefit from therapy. Counseling can assist partners or family members in coordinating their technology use with their relationship objectives by fostering conversations about agreed-upon standards for digital behavior (Roberts & David, 2016).

Group counseling sessions centered on digital well-being can provide a supportive setting where participants exchange experiences and techniques for striking a balance between digital and in-person connections, in addition to individual therapy. By fostering a feeling of community and accountability, these initiatives can help people make long-lasting adjustments to the way they use technology.

Future Directions and Research Needs

It's critical to comprehend how digital communication affects interpersonal connections over the long run as technology advances and becomes more ingrained in daily life. Although certain immediate implications, such alterations in how people establish and sustain relationships, have already been emphasized by research, the long-term repercussions over many years have not been thoroughly studied. The potential effects of digital communication's constant accessibility on relationship attachment types are one topic of investigation. Reliance on technology to stay in touch could eventually either improve relationships by facilitating regular communication or erode them by fostering a feeling of "always being connected" without actual emotional presence (Turkle, 2011). People's priorities and perceptions of intimacy may change as a result of this dynamic, changing how much they value face-to-face vs virtual encounters. More research is needed to determine how digital communication affects younger generations who grew up with cellphones and social media. Research should concentrate on how social skills, empathy, and the capacity to build strong relationships are shaped by early exposure to digital communication, as well as whether these people suffer from different types of social anxiety or loneliness than people in earlier generations (Baym, 2015). The influence of digital grief and loss—how people use social media to cope with their losses—is another crucial topic. Knowing how digital monuments and online support groups aid in bereavement will help us better understand how digital tools alter our emotional landscapes.

Interventions must be flexible enough to accommodate new developments in technology, including virtual and augmented reality, which add new dimensions to online interactions. Future studies should concentrate on analysing the effects of new technologies on mental health and emotional closeness, especially as virtual reality allows for more immersive interactions that could either improve or worsen relationships in the actual world (Bailenson, 2018). Furthermore, investigating interventions designed for a range of demographic groups—such as teenagers, the elderly, or people with social anxiety—will assist in developing focused tactics that cater to certain requirements.

Another viable strategy is incorporating digital literacy programs into school curricula, which give people the tools they need to use technology responsibly and comprehend the possible psychological effects of excessive use. Young people can be empowered to form healthy computer habits early on by being taught about mindful digital behaviors and the risks of social comparison (Lim, 2016). Researchers can offer practical insights that promote healthier technology use for a variety of populations by carrying out more research on the long-term impacts of such initiatives.

Emerging Technologies and Their Potential Impact on Intimacy and Relationships

Virtual reality (VR) and augmented reality (AR) offer new opportunities for human connection and interaction as digital communication technologies develop. Beyond simple video conversations, these technologies have the ability to produce immersive social interactions that give people a feeling of "being together" even when they are geographically apart. By enabling users to interact in shared virtual areas, VR platforms, for instance, can replicate physical proximity and provide new opportunities for couples, friends, and family to feel togetherness (Bailenson, 2018). These settings can include things like exploring virtual worlds or viewing a movie together in a virtual theater, which could replicate elements of face-to-face interactions that are now absent from text-based and video communication.

Concerns concerning the veracity of VR-mediated interactions are also brought up by their growing popularity. Although virtual reality (VR) can replicate some physical qualities of presence, it might not be able to replicate the depth of tactile and emotional connection that comes from in-person interactions. Users' perceptions of intimacy and presence in virtual settings, as well as whether these experiences may completely replace or just enhance in-person interactions, require more investigation. The influence of haptic technologies, which replicate touch in virtual spaces, on emotional and physical intimacy may change how individuals sustain relationships over great distances. Research should look at how these technologies change the physiological and psychological reactions to human contact as well as how they can impact the enjoyment of long-term relationships (Bailenson, 2018).

Longitudinal Studies on the Effectiveness of Technology Use Interventions

Longitudinal research provides insights into the long-term effects of therapies such as digital detoxes and mindful technological practices, while short-term studies yield encouraging outcomes. According to a study by Przybylski and Weinstein (2022) that looked at screen time limits in young children, regular, planned screen-free time improved social skills, increased emotional control, and decreased the prevalence of behavioral problems over a number of years. According to this data, limiting screen usage on a regular basis can have long-term advantages, especially for younger populations that are still forming their social and emotional skills.

Similar findings have been found in adult longitudinal research, suggesting that consistent mindful technology use reduces stress and enhances relationship satisfaction. For example, in a long-term study by Valkenburg and Peter (2007), individuals who used their smartphones mindfully reported feeling less mentally exhausted and more connected to their friends and family. These results demonstrate how thoughtful technology use can lead to long-term gains in mental health and relationship quality.

Cultural Differences

Norms surrounding digital communication and their effects on interpersonal interactions are greatly influenced by cultural differences. How digital communication is viewed and incorporated into daily life can be influenced by cultural differences in views regarding technology use, privacy, and the value of in-person contacts (Baym, 2015). For instance, using messaging applications to stay in regular digital contact with family members may be viewed as a show of closeness and respect in certain cultures, but it may also be viewed as intrusive as or less significant than in-person visits in others. Relationship dynamics may change as a result of how people interpret certain cultural quirks, such as phubbing or constant online presence.

Studies could look into how regional expectations for communication and digital etiquette are influenced by cultural values. Global initiatives for promoting healthy digital communication practices can be informed by an understanding of these distinctions, which can offer important insights into why particular digital habits are more acceptable or harmful in particular cultures. The usage of digital communication tools for relationship maintenance in cross-cultural or long-distance relationships may be impacted by cultural variations. Examining how couples from various cultural backgrounds communicate online may help pinpoint the best ways to be intimate when being physically present isn't feasible. It may also highlight prospective points of contention or miscommunication.

Need for Further Studies on the Effectiveness of Proposed Interventions

More empirical study is required to assess the efficacy of the different solutions that have been proposed to mitigate the negative effects of digital communication. For instance, small-scale research have demonstrated the potential of tactics like digital detoxes, phone-free zones, and mindfulness exercises; nevertheless, larger, more varied studies are required to confirm their long-term advantages (Hertlein & Ancheta, 2014).

Longitudinal studies that monitor how individuals and couples react to interventions over time may be the main focus of future study. Such research would shed light on whether specific tactics can result in long-lasting modifications to technology use patterns and enhance interpersonal interactions. Examining the effects of age, personality, and relationship stage on the effectiveness of various therapies may also fall under this category.

Group-specific interventions, such as those for teenagers, the elderly, or people with social anxiety, must be investigated. Programs for digital well-being may become more relevant and effective if strategies are tailored to the particular requirements and difficulties of these groups. For example, although older persons may require assistance in adjusting to new digital technologies in a way that complements rather than replaces their current social ties, younger users may benefit more from educational programs about social media's effect on self-esteem.

More research should be done on the function of therapeutic interventions, especially in relation to how counseling might assist individuals in overcoming the difficulties posed by digital communication. To provide effective mental health care in the digital age, therapists must comprehend how to help clients navigate digital dependency, uphold healthy boundaries, and enhance face-to-face communication skills (Turkle, 2011).

CONCLUSION

The internet era has changed how people interact, creating new channels of communication but also posing problems that degrade relationships. It is clear from the analysis of ideas like digital intimacy and phubbing that although social media and cell phones can help people connect over distance, they can also lessen the depth of in-person interactions. Digital communication can offer vital social support, but it can also exacerbate anxiety and social comparison, which has two distinct effects on mental health. Maintaining positive relationships requires striking a balance between online and offline contacts. The harmful impacts of excessive digital interaction can be lessened with the support of interventions including mindful technology use, digital detoxification techniques, and digital literacy promotion. Navigating future issues requires an awareness of cultural variations and the function of developing technology like virtual reality. In order to comprehend the long-term impacts of digital communication and the efficacy of therapies, more research is required going forward. Individuals can make sure that technology improves rather than degrades the quality of their interpersonal relationships by cultivating more thoughtful and balanced digital habits.

REFERENCES

Amichai-Hamburger, Y., & Vinitzky, G. (2010). Social network use and personality. *Computers in Human Behavior*, 26(6), 1289–1295. DOI: 10.1016/j.chb.2010.03.018

Bailenson, J. (2018). *Experience on Demand: What Virtual Reality Is, How It Works, and What It Can Do*. W. W. Norton & Company.

Baym, N. K. (2015). *Personal Connections in the Digital Age* (2nd ed.). Polity.

Chotpitayasunondh, V., & Douglas, K. M. (2018). The effects of "phubbing" on social interaction. *Journal of Applied Social Psychology*, 48(6), 304–316. DOI: 10.1111/jasp.12506

Daft, R. L., & Lengel, R. H. (1986). Organizational information requirements, media richness, and structural design. *Management Science*, 32(5), 554–571. DOI: 10.1287/mnsc.32.5.554

Deresiewicz, W. (2009). Solitude and leadership. *The American Scholar*, 78(2), 20–31.

Elhai, J. D., Dvorak, R. D., Levine, J. C., & Hall, B. J. (2020). Problematic smartphone use and depression and anxiety: A systematic review and meta-analysis. *Depression and Anxiety*, 37(3), 1–12.

Hertlein, K. M., & Ancheta, K. (2014). Advantages and disadvantages of technology in relationships: Findings from an open-ended survey. *The Qualitative Report*, 19(11), 1–11. DOI: 10.46743/2160-3715/2014.1260

Kross, E., Verduyn, P., Demiralp, E., Park, J., Lee, D. S., Lin, N., & Ybarra, O. (2013). Facebook use predicts declines in subjective well-being in young adults. *PLoS One*, 8(8), e69841. DOI: 10.1371/journal.pone.0069841 PMID: 23967061

Kuss, D. J., & Griffiths, M. D. (2021). Smartphone addiction: A systematic review of the evidence. *International Journal of Environmental Research and Public Health*, 18(10), 5360. PMID: 34069883

Lim, S. S. (Ed.). (2016). *Mobile communication and the family*. Springer. DOI: 10.1007/978-94-017-7441-3

Mehrabian, A. (1971). *Silent Messages*. Wadsworth.

Nabi, R. L., Prestin, A., & So, J. (2013). Facebook friends with (health) benefits? Exploring social network site use and perceptions of social support, stress, and well-being. *Cyberpsychology, Behavior, and Social Networking*, 16(10), 721–727. DOI: 10.1089/cyber.2012.0521 PMID: 23790356

Przybylski, A. K., & Weinstein, N. (2022). Digital screen time limits and young children's psychological well-being. *Pediatrics*, 149(3), e2021050307.

Roberts, J. A., & David, M. E. (2016). My life has become a major distraction from my cell phone: Partner phubbing and relationship satisfaction among romantic partners. *Computers in Human Behavior*, 54, 134–141. DOI: 10.1016/j.chb.2015.07.058

Stone, L. (2007). Continuous partial attention: Reclaiming focus in the digital age. *Harvard Business Review*, 85(3), 9.

Turkle, S. (2011). *Alone Together: Why We Expect More from Technology and Less from Each Other*. Basic Books.

Twenge, J. M., & Campbell, W. K. (2018). Associations Between Screen Time and Mental Health Among Adolescents. *American Journal of Preventive Medicine*, 54(3), 398–405.

Valkenburg, P. M., & Peter, J. (2007). Online communication and adolescent well-being: Testing the stimulation versus the displacement hypothesis. *Journal of Computer-Mediated Communication*, 12(4), 1169–1182. DOI: 10.1111/j.1083-6101.2007.00368.x

Walther, J. B. (1996). Computer-mediated communication: Impersonal, interpersonal, and hyperpersonal interaction. *Communication Research*, 23(1), 3–43. DOI: 10.1177/009365096023001001

Chapter 13
Partner Phubbing and Relationship Satisfaction Among Romantic Partners

Sandhya Shrivastav
Maharishi Markandeshwar Institute of Physiotherapy and Rehabilitation, India

Lakshay Panchal
Maharishi Markandeshwar Institute of Physiotherapy and Rehabilitation, India

Srishti Sharma
Dr. Harvansh Singh Judge Institute of Dental Sciences and Hospital, India

Digpal Rana
Dr. Harvansh Singh Judge Institute of Dental Sciences and Hospital, India

Urvashi Chauhan
Maharishi Markandeshwar Institute of Physiotherapy and Rehabilitation, India

Jatin Sangwan
https://orcid.org/0000-0001-6952-2534
Maharishi Markandeshwar, India

ABSTRACT

Phubbing involves neglecting someone by checking or using a smartphone during a face-to-face conversation. Phubbing is also linked to mobile addiction and feelings of deprivation when separated from one's phone. Researchers also suggest that individuals often use their phones as a coping mechanism for loneliness, anxiety, and worry. Thus, phubbing is not merely a habit; it also serves as a form of avoidance behaviour. A review of prior studies indicates that romantic relationship satisfaction is closely linked to individual emotions and behaviours. Factors such as relationship commitment, perceived rewards, and the costs of investment are all significantly associated with overall satisfaction in the relationship. To foster healthier, more fulfilling relationships, it is crucial for partners to prioritize face-to-face engagement

DOI: 10.4018/979-8-3693-8804-4.ch013

and be mindful of their phone usage in social settings. Addressing and mitigating phubbing behaviour can help strengthen emotional bonds, enhance relational satisfaction, and ultimately promote well-being for both partners.

UNDERSTANDING PARTNER PHUBBING: A THREAT TO CONNECTION

Phubbing, a portmanteau of "phone" and "snubbing," refers to the act of ignoring someone in favor of one's smartphone or other digital devices. This behavior can manifest in various social contexts, from casual gatherings to intimate settings, where individuals prioritize their devices over engaging with the people physically present. The term was first popularized in 2012 by a group of Australian advertising executives, who aimed to raise awareness about the detrimental impact of smartphone use on social interactions. Phubbing encompasses a range of behaviors, including scrolling through social media, texting, or browsing the internet while in the company of others. It is not merely about the act of using a phone but rather the conscious or subconscious choice to prioritize digital engagement over human interaction. This phenomenon has gained increasing attention as the proliferation of smartphones has fundamentally altered how individuals communicate and connect with one another (David ME et al., 2020).

Prevalence of Phubbing

Phubbing has become a ubiquitous part of modern life, especially among younger generations who have grown up in the digital age. Research indicates that a significant percentage of people admit to engaging in phubbing, either as the phubber or the phubbee (the person being phubbed). A survey conducted by the American Psychological Association found that nearly 50% of respondents reported feeling ignored by their partner due to smartphone use. This widespread behavior is a reflection of our increasingly interconnected yet paradoxically isolated digital lives (Garrido EC et al., 2024).

Impact of phubbing on Interpersonal Relationships

The impact of phubbing on interpersonal relationships is multifaceted, affecting emotional bonds, communication dynamics, and overall relationship satisfaction. Below are several key ways in which phubbing disrupts these vital components of human interaction.

Erosion of Emotional Connection

One of the most significant consequences of phubbing is the erosion of emotional connection between individuals. Emotional intimacy is built on shared experiences and mutual attention. When one partner is preoccupied with their device, it can create feelings of neglect and unimportance for the other. This perceived lack of attention can lead to a breakdown in emotional bonds, as individuals may feel that their partner values their device more than their relationship. Research shows that emotional neglect can trigger feelings of insecurity, jealousy, and resentment. When partners frequently engage in phubbing, they may become less attuned to each other's emotional needs, leading to a decrease in relationship satisfaction. Over time, this emotional disconnection can create distance and contribute to a downward spiral in relationship quality (Hale L et al.,2015).

Impaired Communication

Effective communication is foundational to any healthy relationship. Phubbing disrupts this crucial element by creating barriers to meaningful dialogue. When individuals are focused on their devices, they miss non-verbal cues such as eye contact, facial expressions, and body language—all essential components of effective communication. This lack of engagement can lead to misunderstandings and misinterpretations, further complicating relational dynamics.Moreover, conversations that require depth and attention often become superficial when one party is distracted by their phone. Partners may find themselves discussing trivial matters rather than engaging in significant conversations that could strengthen their bond. The result is a stunted communication flow, which can cause frustration and a sense of disconnection (McDaniel BT et al.,2016).

Increased Conflict and Resentment

Phubbing can also exacerbate conflicts within relationships. When one partner feels consistently ignored, it can lead to feelings of frustration and resentment. This emotional build-up can manifest in arguments and disagreements over seemingly minor issues, as the underlying feelings of neglect bubble to the surface. Furthermore, phubbing can create a sense of competition between partners and their devices. Each individual may feel compelled to compete for the other's attention, leading to heightened tensions and emotional distress. When conflicts arise, the distraction of smartphones can hinder effective resolution, as partners may struggle to communicate their feelings or address the root of the issue due to ongoing distractions (Garrido EC et al., 2024).

Social Isolation and Loneliness

Ironically, while smartphones connect us to a broader network, they can also foster feelings of isolation and loneliness. Phubbing often occurs in social settings where individuals are surrounded by others yet remain emotionally distant. For example, friends gathered at a restaurant may spend the majority of their time on their phones, missing opportunities for meaningful interactions. This behavior can create an environment of social isolation, where individuals feel alone even in the presence of others. The feeling of being phubbed can lead to self-doubt and low self-esteem, as individuals question their worth and significance in the eyes of their partner or friends. When such feelings become pervasive, they can contribute to a broader sense of loneliness, negatively impacting mental health and overall well-being (McDaniel BT et al.,2016).

Diminished Relationship Satisfaction

The cumulative effects of phubbing—emotional disconnection, impaired communication, increased conflict, and feelings of isolation—can lead to a significant decrease in overall relationship satisfaction. Partners may begin to view their relationship as unfulfilling or emotionally draining, leading to dissatisfaction and, in some cases, a desire to end the relationship.Moreover, individuals who frequently experience phubbing are more likely to report feelings of anxiety and depression. This emotional distress can further strain the relationship, creating a cycle where dissatisfaction leads to increased phubbing and vice versa. As a result, the quality of the relationship deteriorates; leaving both partners feeling unfulfilled and unhappy. Phubbing is a modern behavior that significantly disrupts interpersonal relationships. By understanding its definition and the ways in which it impacts emotional connection, communication, and overall relationship satisfaction, individuals can take proactive steps to mitigate its effects. In an increasingly digital world, fostering authentic connections and prioritizing meaningful interactions is essential for maintaining healthy, fulfilling relationships. By consciously addressing phubbing, partners can cultivate deeper emotional bonds, enhance communication, and ultimately enjoy more satisfying and meaningful connections (Przybylski AK et al.,2019).

THE PSYCHOLOGICAL IMPACT OF PHUBBING ON INDIVIDUALS

Although the physical health risks of excessive smartphone, internet, and social media use are well-documented, society's reliance on digital devices is on the rise (Liu X et al., 2023).Smartphones offer unmatched convenience and accessibility for staying connected and managing social interactions. However, this convenience can also lead to negative emotions such as unhappiness, anxiety, and passivity, ultimately affecting individuals' psychological well-being.Smartphones epitomize the latest technological innovations, providing users with a diverse range of functions within a compact, portable device (Augner C et al., 2023). Their engaging features have given rise to new social, behavioral, and psychological trends, such as:

A. **FoMO**: Fear of Missing Out is the anxiety or apprehension that one might be missing out on rewarding experiences or social events happening elsewhere. It often arises from seeing others' activities on social media, leading individuals to feel inadequate or left out. FoMO can drive people to constantly check their devices for updates, contributing to stress and dissatisfaction in their own lives as they compare themselves to others (Gupta M et al., 2021).
B. **Nomophobia**: short for "no mobile phone phobia," refers to the anxiety or fear of being without one's smartphone or not being able to use it. This condition can manifest as feelings of panic, distress, or discomfort when a person is unable to access their phone, leading to excessive reliance on mobile devices and potentially impacting daily life and social interactions (Bhattacharya S et al., 2019).
C. **Phantom Vibration Syndrome**: It is the phenomenon where individuals believe they feel their phone vibrating, even when it isn't. This sensation can occur when someone is anticipating a notification or call, leading them to perceive vibrations that aren't actually happening. It reflects the deep psychological connection people have with their smartphones and can contribute to anxiety or distraction (Pareek S et al., 2017).
D. **Hikikomori Syndrome**: The condition characterized by extreme social withdrawal, where individuals, often adolescents or young adults, isolate themselves at home for an extended period, typically six months or more. Those experiencing hikikomori may avoid social interactions, school, or work, often due to factors like anxiety, depression, or societal pressures. The syndrome highlights the impact of social and technological changes on mental health and well-being (Stip E et al., 2016).

Phubbing occurs when a person chooses to focus on their phone, such as checking messages or scrolling through social media, while in the presence of others. Phubbing can lead to feelings of neglect and frustration among those being ignored, potentially harming relationships and social interactions (Chotpitayasunondh V et al., 2018).These phenomena's have garnered significant attention in contemporary research, highlighting the complex impact smartphones have on human behavior and social interactions.Moreover, the psychological repercussions of smart device usage, particularly following the Covid-19 pandemic, are particularly alarming. Researchers are increasingly examining issues such as heightened loneliness linked to social media and smartphone usage, elevated anxiety levels, and the association between digital media and depression. They are also looking into how social networking addiction can lead to poorer academic performance and behavioral issues among students. Additional concerns include reduced offline social support, impaired decision-making, increased attentional bias, diminished psychosocial well-being, greater feelings of unhappiness, and a range of negative psychosocial effects like self-criticism, feelings of vulnerability, withdrawal from activities that once brought joy, and reduced social interactions (Zhou X et al., 2024).

In recent years, it has become more common to see young people huddled in small groups, completely focused on their smartphones. Couples dining at restaurants often appear unaware of one another and their environment, fixated instead on their device screens. Families spend time together but are more engaged with what they might be missing on their smartphones than with each other. This trend is also evident among professionals in the workplace, among others (Capilla E et al., 2021).As a result, this behavior has drawn the interest of sociologists, psychologists, and psychiatrists due to its potential risks to both individual and collective mental health. Research indicates that phubbing is strongly associated with Internet addiction, smartphone addiction, social media addiction, and gaming addiction (Usmani SS et al., 2022). Indeed, phubbing worsens the psychological challenges for both the phubber and the phubee. The phubber, who is distracted by their device, and the phubee, who feels ignored, may experience a breakdown in communication and attention, leading to negative effects on their social relationships and mental well-being (Bitar Z et al., 2023).

With approximately 6.84 billion smartphone users worldwide, individuals spend an average of 3 hours daily on various platforms. A study examined individuals aged 24 and older, finding that smartphone addiction tended to decrease with age. However, it revealed that the addiction levels among those over middle age were significantly higher than anticipated (Koçak O et al., 2021).Extensive use of smartphones has been associated with numerous negative effects and psychological difficulties, as noted in existing research. For example, a found that prolonged smartphone usage is linked to depression, behavioral problems, and instances of heavy drinking. While a study by Coyne et al. (2020) found no significant effect of usage frequency on mental well-being, research by Liu et al. (2019) identified a weak correlation between the duration of smartphone use and psychological distress (Coyne SM et al., 2020; Liu S et al., 2019).Another study observed that adolescents who spend considerable time on social media through smartphones are at a heightened risk of developing mental health disorders (Riehm KE et al., 2019).In conclusion, the pervasive use of smartphones has significantly transformed social interactions and mental health dynamics in contemporary society. While these devices offer unparalleled convenience and connectivity, their overuse is linked to a range of psychological challenges, including increased anxiety, depression, and social withdrawal. Phenomena such as FoMO, Nomophobia, Phantom Vibration Syndrome, Hikikomori Syndrome, and phubbing illustrate the complex ways in which technology impacts individual well-being and relationships. As research continues to uncover the implications of excessive smartphone use, it is crucial for individuals, families, and communities to recognize and address these trends. By fostering healthier digital habits and promoting meaningful in-person interactions, society can mitigate the negative effects of technology and enhance overall psychological well-being. Moving forward, a balanced approach to smartphone usage that prioritizes mental health will be essential in navigating the challenges of our increasingly digital world.

RELATIONSHIP SATISFACTION: THE PHUBBING PARADOX

The act of ignoring a partner in favor of one's mobile device is the main cause of affecting relationships. This phenomenon has garnered increasing attention in psychological and sociological research due to its potential negative impacts on relationship quality and satisfaction. The correlation between phubbing and relationship quality is complex, influenced by various factors that can either exacerbate or mitigate its effects. Understanding these dynamics is crucial for fostering healthier interpersonal relationships in an increasingly digital world.

Factors influencing relationship satisfaction

A. **Emotional Impact of Phubbing:** Research indicates that phubbing can lead to significant relational distress. When a partner engages in phubbing, the other often feels neglected and unimportant, which can provoke feelings of resentment and conflict within the relationship. This emotional neglect can diminish relationship satisfaction, as the phubbed partner may perceive a lack of emotional support and connection, leading to increased feelings of loneliness and depression

(Gershon I et al., 2018). The bidirectional nature of this relationship suggests that not only does phubbing negatively affect the partner being ignored, but it can also create a cycle of dissatisfaction that impacts both individuals involved (Angeluci AC et al., 2016).

B. **Communication Dynamics:** The quality of interpersonal communication plays a pivotal role in relationship satisfaction. Studies have shown that effective communication skills are positively correlated with higher relationship quality. When partners communicate openly and effectively, they are better equipped to address issues such as phubbing before they escalate into larger conflicts. Conversely, poor communication can exacerbate the feelings of neglect associated with phubbing, leading to further deterioration of relationship quality. Therefore, enhancing interpersonal skills may serve as a protective factor against the negative effects of phubbing (Ao R et al., 2022).

C. **Cultural Influences:** Cultural factors also influence the relationship between phubbing and relationship satisfaction. Different cultural contexts may shape individuals' perceptions of mobile device usage and its appropriateness in social settings. For instance, in cultures where face-to-face interactions are highly valued, phubbing may be viewed more negatively, leading to greater relational conflict. Conversely, in cultures where digital communication is more normalized, the impacts of phubbing may be less pronounced. This variability highlights the importance of considering cultural indicators when analyzing the effects of phubbing on relationship quality (Aboujaoude E et al., 2021).

D. **Psychological Implications:** The psychological implications of phubbing extend beyond immediate relational dissatisfaction. Long-term exposure to phubbing can contribute to chronic stress and anxiety, which may further erode relationship quality. The phubbed partner may experience a decline in self-esteem and an increase in feelings of inadequacy, as they may internalize the belief that they are less important than the digital content their partner is engaging. This internal conflict can lead to a vicious cycle where the phubbed partner's dissatisfaction prompts further withdrawal or negative behaviors, thereby perpetuating the cycle of phubbing and relational decline (Sabadin K et al., 2015).

E. **Personality Traits and Phubbing:** Additionally, the role of individual personality traits cannot be overlooked in understanding the dynamics of phubbing. Research has shown that individuals with higher levels of agreeableness and emotional stability tend to report better relationship quality and are less likely to engage in phubbing behaviors. Conversely, individuals who exhibit higher levels of neuroticism may be more susceptible to feelings of jealousy and insecurity when their partner engages in phubbing, further exacerbating relational tensions. Thus, personality traits can serve as either risk factors or protective factors in the context of phubbing and relationship satisfaction (Lin C et al., 2022).

F. **External Stressors and Relationship Dynamics:** Another critical aspect to consider is the impact of external stressors on relationship dynamics. Factors such as work-related stress, financial pressures, and life transitions can heighten the likelihood of phubbing as individuals may turn to their devices for escapism or distraction. In such instances, the act of phubbing may not only reflect a lack of attention to the partner but also serve as a coping mechanism for managing external stressors. This dual role complicates the relationship between phubbing and relationship quality, as it may be both a symptom and a contributing factor to relational dissatisfaction (Sabadin K et al., 2015). Furthermore, the phenomenon of phubbing is not limited to romantic relationships; it can also manifest in friendships and familial relationships. The implications of phubbing extend to various forms of interpersonal connections, where the act of ignoring someone in favor of a device can lead to feelings of exclusion and diminished relational quality across different contexts. This universality of phubbing underscores the need for broader awareness and strategies to mitigate its effects on all types of relationships (Angeluci AC et al., 2016).

Strategies for Mitigating Phubbing

In addressing the negative effects of phubbing, it is essential to promote awareness and encourage healthier digital habits among individuals. Couples can benefit from establishing boundaries regarding mobile device usage during shared time, such as designated "phone-free" periods or spaces.[22] By fostering an environment that prioritizes face-to-face interactions, partners can enhance their emotional connection and reduce the likelihood of phubbing behaviors. Moreover, relationship education programs that emphasize effective communication skills and the importance of emotional support can empower individuals to navigate the challenges posed by phubbing. By equipping individuals with the tools to express their needs and concerns, these programs can help mitigate the negative impacts of phubbing on relationship quality. In conclusion, the correlation between phubbing and relationship quality is multifaceted, influenced by individual, relational, and cultural factors. The negative effects of phubbing on relationship satisfaction are evident, as it can lead to feelings of neglect, conflict, and emotional distress. However, by fostering effective communication, promoting awareness of digital habits, and addressing external stressors, individuals can work towards enhancing their relationship quality and mitigating the adverse effects of phubbing. As society continues to navigate the complexities of digital communication, understanding and addressing the phenomenon of phubbing will be crucial for fostering healthy and fulfilling interpersonal relationships (Ao R et al., 2022).

OUTCOME MEASURES FOR ASSESSING PHUBBING, SATISFACTION, AND QUALITY

In this technical world, learning about the dynamics of interpersonal relationships has become progressively important, especially as technology plays an essential role in daily interactions. For assessing these relationship dynamics, researchers have developed a number of tools aimed at measuring relationship satisfaction, phubbing behaviors and overall relationship quality of romantic partners. These tools play a crucial role for evaluating the level to which phubbing affects communication patterns and emotional bonds between partners. For instance, tools assessing phubbing regularly emphasize frequency and perceived impact, which allow researchers to calculate the extent to which this behavior disrupts connection and intimacy. In addition, relationship satisfaction scales help in measuring overall contentment within relationships, providing awareness into how phubbing might related with feelings of disconnect or emotional neglect. Assessing tools for quality of life also have implication in relationship dynamics, measuring how phubbing affects partner well-being. These outcomes demonstrate how relationship satisfaction can affect self-esteem, mental health and overall happiness. Understanding these relationship dynamics is important, as it enables clinicians and researchers to identify correlation between relationship quality and phubbing behaviors. By using these tools, we can understand the nuances of relationship dynamics effectively and build strategies for encouraging healthier, more fulfilling interpersonal relationships. The following section will highlight key outcome measures that are important for evaluating phubbing, satisfaction, and quality in interpersonal relationships.

Perceived Relationship Quality Component (PRQC) scale

The PRQC scale was developed by Fletcher, Simpson, and Thomas in 2000, which is designed to measure the different aspects of perceived relationship quality. According to them there were six domains of this scale which includes commitment, satisfaction, intimacy, passion, trust, and love. Each domain will be assessed with a set of three questions, and respondents will rate their partner and relationship on an 18-item scale using a 7-point Likert-type scale, where responses range from 7 (extremely) to 1 (not at all). The scoring for the PRQC scale involves calculation of total six domains. The Satisfaction score is determined by averaging items 1, 7, and 13, with greater score indicating relationship satisfaction. The Commitment score is derived from averaging items 2, 8, and 14, where greater score indicating a stronger commitment. Similarly, the Intimacy score is obtained by averaging items 3, 9, and 15, with higher scores reflecting higher intimacy. The Trust score is calculated by averaging items 4, 10, and 16, where higher trust levels correspond to greater scores. The Passion score found by averaging items 5, 11, and 17, with increased scores signifying heightened passion. Lastly, the Love score is obtained by averaging items 6, 12, and 18, with greater scores representing deeper levels of love (Fletcher GJ et al., 2000).

Table 1. Perceived Relationship Quality Component (PRQC) scale

Sr. No.	**Items**	**Not at all**					**Extremely**	
1	**How satisfied are you with your relationship?**	**1**	**2**	**3**	**4**	**5**	**6**	**7**
2	How committed are you to your relationship?	1	2	3	4	5	6	7
3	How intimate is your relationship?	1	2	3	4	5	6	7
4	How much do you trust your partner?	1	2	3	4	5	6	7
5	How passionate is your relationship?	1	2	3	4	5	6	7
6	How much do you love your partner?	1	2	3	4	5	6	7
7	How content are you with your relationship?	1	2	3	4	5	6	7
8	How dedicated are you to your relationship?	1	2	3	4	5	6	7
9	How close is your relationship?	1	2	3	4	5	6	7
10	How much can you count on your partner?	1	2	3	4	5	6	7
11	How lustful is your relationship?	1	2	3	4	5	6	7
12	How much do you adore your partner?	1	2	3	4	5	6	7
13	How happy are you with your relationship?	1	2	3	4	5	6	7
14	How devoted are you to your relationship?	1	2	3	4	5	6	7
15	How connected are you to your partner?	1	2	3	4	5	6	7
16	How dependable is your partner?	1	2	3	4	5	6	7
17	How sexually intense is your relationship?	1	2	3	4	5	6	7
18	How much do you cherish your partner?	1	2	3	4	5	6	7

Satisfaction with Life Scale (SWLS)

The SWLS was designed to assess overall life satisfaction rather than specific areas like finances or health, allowing respondents to prioritize these areas in their own way. This scale is also recommended as a supplementary tool for assessing emotional well-being or psychopathology, as it evaluates consciousness of their lives based on their own criteria. The SWLS have five domains that measure global cognitive judgment of a person regarding life satisfaction. Respondents will indicate their level of agreement with each statement by using a 7-point Likert-type scale, where 1 means "strongly disagree" and 7 means "strongly agree". Participants are instructed to respond honestly and openly. The interpretation of SWL scale is as follows: 31-35 represents extreme satisfaction, 26-30 indicates satisfaction, 21-25 reflects slight satisfaction, 20 is considered neutral, 15-19 indicate slight dissatisfaction, 10-14 suggests dissatisfaction, and 5-9 reflects extreme dissatisfaction (Pavot W et al., 1991).

Table 2. Satisfaction with Life Scale (SWLS)

Sr. No.	Items	Strongly disagree	Disagree	Slightly disagree	Neither agree nor disagree	Slightly agree	Agree	Strongly agree
1	In most ways my life is close to my ideal.	1	2	3	4	5	6	7
2	The conditions of my life are excellent.	1	2	3	4	5	6	7
3	I am satisfied with my life.	1	2	3	4	5	6	7
4	So far I have gotten the important things I want in life.	1	2	3	4	5	6	7
5	If I could live my life over, I would change almost nothing.	1	2	3	4	5	6	7

Perceived Phubbing Measure (PPM) Scale

The PPM scale is developed for a general measure of phubbing by modifying an established 9-item scale from Roberts and David in 2016, which measure partner phubbing. Each question from the Roberts and David scale is modified carefully to develop nine items that will assess general phubbing, instead of partner phubbing. It's important to recognize that the PPM scale is a self measuring tool. Although self assessment instruments have certain advantages, but they can also affected by social desirability bias, inaccurate recollection of events in the question, potential misunderstandings of questions by participants, and differing interpretations of rating scales among participants. Evaluator should take these considerations into account during conclusion derived from self reported data. Participants respond on a scale ranging from "Never" (1) to "Sometimes" (3) to "Always" (5) for each item (David ME et al., 2020).

Table 3. Perceived Phubbing Measure (PPM) scale

Sr. No.	Items	Never		Sometimes		Always
1	During a typical mealtime that I spend with people, they pull out and check their cell phone.	1	2	3	4	5
2	When their cell phone rings or beeps, they pull it out even if we are in the middle of a conversation.	1	2	3	4	5
3	During leisure time that I spend together with others, the person/people use their cell phone.	1	2	3	4	5
4	People who I spend time with often glance at their cell phone when talking to me.	1	2	3	4	5
5	When I spend time with people, they keep their cell phone where they can see it.	1	2	3	4	5
6	People use their cell phones when we are talking in person.	1	2	3	4	5
7	People never keep their cell phones in their hand when they're with me.	1	2	3	4	5
8	When I am out with others, they use their cell phone at some point during our time together.	1	2	3	4	5
9	If there is a lull in my conversation with others, they will check their cell phone.	1	2	3	4	5

Relationship Assessment Scale (RAS)

The RAS is a tool designed to measure overall relationship satisfaction and can be used by anyone, who is in intimate relationship, including cohabiting, dating, engaged or married couples. According to them there were seven items of this scale which measures relationship investment, commitment, self-disclosure, sexual attitudes, marital satisfaction and love. Item 4 and 7 of this scale are scored in reverse. To calculate the total score, the score of each item will be summed together. The scoring of RAS tool indicates that a total score of 7-14 indicates low satisfaction, 15-21 represents average satisfaction, and 22-35 shows high satisfaction (Hendrick SS et al., 1988).

Table 4. Relationship Assessment Scale (RAS)

Sr. No.	Items	Low				High
1	How well does your partner meet your needs?	1	2	3	4	5
2	In general, how satisfied are you with your relationship?	1	2	3	4	5
3	How good is your relationship compared to most?	1	2	3	4	5
4	How often do you wish you hadn't gotten into this relationship?	1	2	3	4	5
5	To what extent has your relationship met your original expectations?	1	2	3	4	5

Sr. No.	Items	Low				High
6	How much do you love your partner?	1	2	3	4	5
7	How many problems are there in your relationship?	1	2	3	4	5

Smartphone Addiction Scale- Short Version (SAS-SV)

The SAS-SV is a straight forward and cost effective measure for assessing smartphone addiction, which is used for community screening and research purposes. This scale comprises ten items scoring on a six point Likert scale (6 for "strongly agree" and 1for "strongly disagree"), allowing for self reported assessment. A higher score of SAS-SV indicates more self-awareness regarding the addiction of smartphone. The SAS-SV does not used as a clinical diagnostic scale for smartphone addiction; it identifies the increasing levels of smartphone addiction risk and classifies individuals in high risk categories. The availability of widespread accessibility of smartphones as compare to other social media, using this scale as a screening tool can play an important role in preventing addiction of smartphone within community settings, which include schools. The questions included in the short version of SAS are designed to examine the behaviour of using smartphone, this gap is not typically covered by traditional addiction scales. By concentrating on adolescents; who are more vulnerable to smartphone addiction, the SAS-SV scale provides a short screening questionnaire with only 10 items. Furthermore, the SAS-SV scale can help to identify high risk population for smartphone addiction in both educational contexts and community (Kwon M et al., 2013).

Table 5. Smartphone Addiction Scale- Short Version (SAS-SV)

Sr. No.	Items	Strongly disagree	Disagree	Weakly disagree	Weakly agree	Agree	Strongly agree
1	Missing planned work due to smartphone use	1	2	3	4	5	6
2	Having a hard time concentrating in class, while doing assignments, or while working due to smartphone use	1	2	3	4	5	6
3	Feeling pain in the wrists or at the back of the neck while using a smartphone	1	2	3	4	5	6
4	Won't be able to stand not having a smartphone	1	2	3	4	5	6
5	Feeling impatient and fretful when I am not holding my smartphone	1	2	3	4	5	6
6	Having my smartphone in my mind even when I am not using it	1	2	3	4	5	6

continued on following page

Table 5. Continued

Sr. No.	Items	Strongly disagree	Disagree	Weakly disagree	Weakly agree	Agree	Strongly agree
7	I will never give up using my smartphone even when 6my daily life is already greatly affected by it.	1	2	3	4	5	6
8	Constantly checking my smartphone so as not to miss conversations between other people on Twitter or Facebook	1	2	3	4	5	6
9	Using my smartphone longer than I had intended	1	2	3	4	5	6
10	The people around me tell me that I use my smartphone too much.	1	2	3	4	5	6

THE CYCLE OF PHUBBING AND MENTAL HEALTH ISSUES

Smartphone addiction is becoming increasingly common, especially among young people, driven by higher levels of social interaction, greater opportunities for forming relationships, and improved technological skills. While many studies suggest that women are more likely to use smartphones in problematic ways, some research indicates that adolescent boys may actually spend more time on their devices, or that both genders face similar risks of addiction (Matsuda M, 2000).Additionally, existing studies have found a positive correlation between smartphone addiction and various health issues, psychological challenges, and psychiatric disorders, particularly depression(Demirci K et al., 2015). Loneliness also appears to be a significant predictor of smartphone addiction. Phubbing occurs when someone prioritizes their phone over a conversation with another person, even when the phone's content is unrelated to the discussion (Chotpitayasunondh V et al., 2016). Research has demonstrated a positive correlation between phubbing and mobile phone addiction, which often serves as a coping mechanism for feelings of loneliness, anxiety, and worry, especially when someone is separated from their device (Karadağ E et al., 2015). However, rather than alleviating these issues, phubbing tends to exacerbate them: the use of smartphones can heighten feelings of social exclusion among those who engage in phubbing(David ME et al., 2017).Like smartphone addiction, phubbing is connected to mental health concerns. Studies have revealed both direct and indirect positive relationships between phubbing and depression among various age groups (Davey S et al., 2018).

Depressive disorders are characterized by feelings of sadness, emptiness, or irritability, often accompanied by physical and cognitive changes that significantly impact an individual's functioning. Stress is also a key factor in the development of depression (Bianchi R et al., 2014). Research indicates that individuals who frequently experience depressive symptoms are more likely to struggle with social media addiction. For example, there is a positive correlation between depression and addiction to Facebook, mobile phones, and phubbing. Additionally, studies demonstrate a positive relationship between depression and feelings of loneliness (Roberts JA et al., 2016).We hypothesized that mobile phone addiction would be positively correlated with both phubbing and depression (H1), and that phubbing would also have a positive correlation with depression (H2). We anticipated that phubbing would mediate the relationship between mobile phone addiction and depression (H3), and that the strength of this mediation would be influenced by feelings of loneliness (H4).

GENDER DIFFERENCES IN PERCEPTIONS OF PHUBBING

In today's world, the use of smartphones is increasing day by day (Kwon M et al., 2013). As smartphones fulfill all the important and basic needs of individuals like ordering food, shopping and banking, etc. these attractive and vital features drive a rise in smartphone usage and with an increase in this rising trend using smartphones leads to creating a new problem which is smartphone addiction (Griffiths MD et al., 2014). Due to smartphone addiction a common problem raised that is 'Phubbing' – the word phubbing created by merging two words that is "phone" and "snubbing" which means ignoring and paying less interaction with face-to-face communication and more focus on the smartphone usage. This means people engaging with the phubbing, prioritize their phones instead of social interaction with the people surrounding them (Luk TT et al., 2018).

Prevalence of Phubbing in Men and Women

Research has shown that men often engage more frequently with their mobile phones, contributing to the phenomenon known as "phubbing," This behavior suggests that men may prioritize technology over face-to-face interactions with the people around them. While men often use their mobile phones as a means to stay connected with the broader society, many women perceive this behavior as a form of neglect and distraction within their relationships. This disconnect can lead to feelings of undervaluation and emotional distance, highlighting the importance of maintaining meaningful communication in personal connections (Yam F Cet al., 2023; McDaniel BT et al., 2016).

The Emotional Interaction of Phubbing

Women are often perceived as being more sensitive and emotional than men, and this perception is supported by various studies that highlight their experiences of relational loneliness (Xie J et al., 2022). Women tend to feel a deeper sense of hurt and undervaluation when they are subjected to "phubbing". As the one reason for this sensitivity is that women generally plays a greater emphasis on interpersonal relationships. They tend to form strong emotional bonds with their partners and prioritize these connections in their lives. As a result, when they experience moments of neglect, such as being phubbed, it can lead to feelings of emotional pain and disconnection. Moreover, women's emotional investment in their relationships and having a greater sense of attachment, make them more vulnerable to feelings of hurt (Peleg Oet al., 2024).

VARIOUS RESPONSES TO PHUBBING

The Feeling of Neglect

During the phubbing phenomenon, partners—particularly women—often experience intensified feelings of hurt and a significantly diminished sense of importance. When women find themselves being overlooked in favor of a mobile device, it can evoke strong feelings of rejection and inadequacy. This behavior can lead them to interpret their partner's distraction as a clear sign that the device holds more value than their presence or contributions to the relationship. Such perceptions can create emotional distress and foster insecurities, making them feel unappreciated and sidelined. Consequently, these feelings can strain the relationship, as the emotional disconnect grows and communication becomes increasingly challenging (Beukeboom CJ et al., 2021).

Communication

Phubbing significantly reduces face-to-face interaction, which in turn leads to diminished engagement and overall communication quality between partners. When one partner is preoccupied with their smartphone, it creates a substantial barrier that hinders the possibility of a meaningful and productive conversation. This distraction not only interrupts the flow of dialogue but also prevents the establishment of emotional connections that are vital for healthy relationships (Abeele MM et al., 2019). If the other partner attempts to communicate while the phone is in use, the interaction often becomes ineffective, as the distracted partner is less likely to fully process what is being said. This can signal a lack of interest or investment in the conversation, further straining the relationship and potentially leading to feelings of frustration and neglect. Ultimately, the presence of phubbing can erode trust and intimacy, making it increasingly challenging for partners to connect on a deeper level (Merchant K et al., 2012).

COPING WITH PHUBBING: STRATEGIES FOR BETTER RELATIONSHIPS

There is limited literature available on coping strategies for phubbing. This chapter will discuss coping strategies as external and internal resources. Internal resources that an individual can employ are emotional, behavioral, and cognitive efforts for satisfactory and good relationships and other strategies such as screen sharing g(Lazarus & Folkman, 1984; Floegel et al., 2021; Humphreys & Hardeman, 2021).

Several studies have discussed the moderating influence of coping techniques in terms of problem-focused solving or emotion-focused coping, with the majority focusing on buffering negative outcomes of peer victimization, race-related stressors, and coping with mobile devices.

The temporal ostracism need-threat model in the context to phubbing suggests that an individual thinks or uses any about coping strategy during the reflective stage during which "ostracized individuals reflect on the meaning and relevance of the ostracism experience and think and act in ways that fortify the threatened need(s)"(Williams, 2009; Williams & Nida, 2011, p. 71).

Based on the theoretical framework of phubbing reoccurring experiences of ostracism due to phubbing may elicit coping responses that can vary in their intensity, directedness, and valence (Vanden Abeele, 2020). Recent research evidence suggests that coping with phubbing elicits different responses.

In a study conducted in 2019, in this study, smartphone users were interviewed and asked about the tactics they employ to relieve phubbing situations. Mostly users answered questions they didn't respond to and essentially did nothing about phubbing. A frequent coping mechanism, a hybrid strategy, is to pick up and interact with the smartphone so that the conversation partner does not feel bad. Another common method was to offer a nonverbal gesture expressing displeasure with the conversational partner's smartphone usage (Kelly et al., 2019).

Coping strategies are categorized into two main categories:

1) Direct coping strategies: These strategies include verbal and non-verbal expressions focused on the conversation in which a partner shows smartphone usage is unacceptable. This strategy is also known as a problem-solving coping strategy.

2) Avoidant coping strategies: Mirroring behaviour and avoidant behaviour such as the usage of smartphones are included in avoidant coping strategies. Avoidant coping strategies are focused on emotional coping. (Seiffge-Krenke &Klessinger, 2000)

These strategies are often related to undesirable outcomes such as depression and other psychological illnesses. Therefore, there is a need for research on two research questions proposed by Anja Stevic and Jörg Matthes in 2023:

"RQ1

Do (a) direct and (b) avoidant coping strategies moderate the relationship between being phubbed and friendship satisfaction?

RQ2

Do (a) direct and (b) avoidant coping strategies moderate the relationship between being phubbed and social isolation?" (Anja Stevic&Jörg Matthes,2023)

Studies found no significant relation between phubbing and relationship satisfaction and some studies show a negative association between phubbing and relationship. One way to counter phubbing behaviors is mindfulness about own smartphone engagement because it can reduce smartphone communication, which increases emotional well-being (Hayes & Matthes, 2009).

The most used coping strategy is avoidant coping in comparison with direct coping. However, using avoidant coping for a long time means delaying confronting and not wanting to solve the problem. Coping is a dynamic process and depends on various alternating factors such as mood, health, and other external factors. Co-use of phone as an avoidant strategy have a positive effect on satisfaction. Sharing smartphone screens also shows the same result but a direct coping strategy: i.e. telling your partner not to use the phone by verbal command or non-verbal expression has negative outcomes on the relationship. To ensure better relationships, eliminate negative psychological symptoms, and avoid other negative outcomes induced by phubbing minimizing the usage of smartphones is a better option in addition to better face-to-face interaction (Anja Stevic&Jörg Matthes,2023).

THE ROLE OF SOCIAL MEDIA IN PHUBBING

Social media can be defined as a platform or web-based tool that offers a wide range of capabilities designed to facilitate communication among users. It enables individuals to send messages to a specific person, allowing for direct and targeted conversations. Additionally, it provides the functionality to share notices, updates, or announcements with the entire organization, ensuring that important information is disseminated effectively. By enhancing communication in this way, social media plays a crucial role in fostering connectivity and collaboration within groups, making it easier for people to stay informed and engaged with one another (Leonardi et al., 2013).In other words, social media platforms have many different features and functions that are always changing and improving. These changes happen because of new technology, what users like, and the latest trends. As a result, the way people interact and share content keeps getting updated and more interesting (Rhee et al., 2020).

Influence of Online Interactions on Romantic Relationships

As access to the internet has improved and smartphones have become more widely utilized, social media sites like Facebook, Instagram, and Twitter are used virtually nonstop by millions of people around the globe (M. Wang et al., 2021).A growing body of research has shown that excessive use of social media can have a number of detrimental impacts on people, especially in the case of young adults and students. One of these effects is a discernible decline in academic performance since using social media excessively frequently diverts users from their studies and crucial assignments. In addition, a lot of people have trouble sleeping because of late-night scrolling and blue light from screens, which can interfere with sleep cycles. Furthermore, while continuous exposure to carefully chosen pictures and lifestyles can engender feelings of loneliness and inadequacy, this problematic use is linked to an increased risk of anxiety and depression. Taken together, these results highlighthow critical it is to regulate social media use in order to protect mental health and general well-being (P. Wang et al., 2018). Due to excessive use of the internet or social media environmental influences, particularly related to interpersonal relationships, are frequently ignored even though they have a significant impact on the behavior of adolescents (Zhou et al., 2017). Research also found that there is a direct relationship between social media and interpersonal relationships (P. Wang et al., 2018).Use of social media before bed and during dinner has been repeatedly linked in the scientific literature to romantic relationship sentiments of insecurity and discontent.(X. Wang et al., 2017).Scientific research has demonstrated that the use of technology, including the internet, social networks, and cell phones, during moments when couples are trying to engage in quality time together can lead to various conflicts within their relationship. This tendency to prioritize digital interactions over face-to-face communication can significantly hinder their ability to communicate effectively. As a result, this reliance on technology during shared moments can also have a detrimental impact on their overall emotional well-being. Couples may find that distractions from their devices create misunderstandings and feelings of neglect, ultimately affecting the strength of their bond and the satisfaction they derive from their relationship (Mcdaniel& Coyne, 2016).Research has indicated that the excessive use of social networks can significantly foster feelings of jealousy in romantic relationships. When partners frequently engage with these platforms, it often leads to comparisons and misunderstandings that can intensify feelings of insecurity. This growing jealousy can, in turn, contribute to a decline in overall relationship satisfaction. Over time, the persistent impact of these negative emotions may lead to significant strain within the relationship, ultimately increasing the likelihood of breakups. As such, it is crucial for couples to be mindful of their social media habits to maintain a healthy and fulfilling partnership (Elphinston et al., 2011).

Social Media Engagement vs. In-Person Connection

Both in-person and social media interactions have distinct benefits and drawbacks that have a big impact on how people connect and form relationships in the modern world (Heyman et al., 2022). Social media can be useful for interacting with varied cultures and preserving long-distance relationships. These exchanges, however, may come across as shallow and lack the emotional nuance and closeness that in-person conversation offers (Clark et al., 2018).By using non-verbal clues like body language, tone of voice, and facial expressions, in-person encounters, on the other hand, promote deeper connections and improve mutual understanding and empathy. However, scheduling these in-person meetings might be logistically difficult because of hectic schedules, geographic limitations, and other obligations, which makes them more difficult than social media interactions (Krasnova et al., 2013).In summary, social media and in-person relationships both have a significant impact on how our social lives and interactions are shaped. Every mode of communication has some benefits that can improve our interpersonal connections, but it also has drawbacks that could make those connections more difficult. People may manage their connections more skillfully and choose whether to prioritize in-person meetings over online contacts by being aware of the advantages and disadvantages of both. This applies to both social media and in-person interactions. This knowledge makes it possible to connect with others more intentionally, ultimately assisting people in finding a balance that supports both significant social interaction and emotional well-being. A stronger feeling of community and deeper relationships might result from fostering this balance (Heyman et al., 2022).

CASE STUDIES AND REAL-LIFE EXAMPLES

Studies have observed that individuals feel discomfort when their partner's behaviour is not as per expectation. This discomfort results in negative emotions such as anger and disappointment. In this context, the usage of smartphones during face-to-face interactions is perceived as disrespectful and can contribute to relationship strain. In today's society, it is observed that phubbing can negatively impact relationship satisfaction by displacing time spent on intimate experiences. Phubbing during face-to-face interactions can reduce conversational engagement and quality thus decreasing relationship satisfaction. Similarly, phubbing has a negative correlation with relationship satisfaction, which can lead to reduced overall life satisfaction and increased the risk of depression. However, the association between phubbing and relationship satisfaction may be moderated by various factors such as self-esteem (Sonia. Khodabakhsh & Le Ong, 2021). Turkle, 2011 demonstrated the importance of eye contact in interpersonal interactions, while, phubbing can significantly reduce eye contact resulting in reduced interaction quality, negatively perceived relationships, and potential strain on romantic relationships. Khodabakhsh and Ong conducted a survey to analyse the impact of phubbing on marital quality in Malaysia. The study found a significant negative correlation between phubbing behaviour and marital quality, which suggests that increased phubbing is associated with reduced marital satisfaction. This may be due to feelings of neglect, disinterest, or a lack of attention from the partner. Additionally, they observed that phubbing had a stronger negative impact on marital quality for females as compared to males. As the females may be more sensitive to phubbing behavior and perceive it as a greater threat to their relationship satisfaction. They also highlighted the importance of age in understanding the relationship between phubbing and marital quality. They observed that younger couples may be more engage in phubbing behavior and experience its negative consequences. This could be due to factors such as technology adoption, lifestyle differences, or the stage of the relationship. To overcome these negative outcomes couples may benefit from open communication about phone usage during interactions and establishing rules to minimize distractions. Interventions that promote mindfulness, digital detox, and improved communication skills could also be helpful. This study provides valuable insights, but it is important to consider the limitations. The sample size and demographic composition may limit the generalizability of the findings (Sonia. Khodabakhsh & Le Ong, 2021). Future research could explore the long-term effects of phubbing on relationships, investigate additional factors that may moderate or mediate the relationship between phubbing and marital quality, and examine interventions aimed at reducing the negative impact of phubbing.

FUTURE DIRECTIONS: BUILDING HEALTHIER RELATIONSHIPS IN A DIGITAL AGE

The rapid proliferation of smartphones has transformed communication, entertainment, and daily life, yet it has also raised significant concerns regarding mental health and interpersonal relationships. As smartphone use becomes increasingly pervasive, it is essential to develop strategies that foster healthier usage patterns. This paper discusses recommendations for managing smartphone use to enhance mental health and interpersonal connections, drawing on various studies that highlight the psychological impacts of excessive smartphone engagement. Understanding Smartphone Addiction Smartphone addiction is characterized by excessive use that interferes with daily life and well-being. Research indicates that high smartphone usage correlates with increased levels of anxiety, depression, and sleep disturbances among university students (Demirci et al., 2015; Boumosleh&Jaalouk, 2017). The psychological ramifications of this addiction can manifest in various ways, including impulsivity, poor cognitive function, and diminished self-esteem (Wacks & Weinstein, 2021; Rathod et al., 2022). Furthermore, adolescents are particularly vulnerable due to their developmental stage, often using smartphones to navigate social dynamics and emotional regulation (Wang et al., 2017).Thus, understanding the underlying mechanisms of smartphone addiction is crucial for developing effective management strategies.

Recommendations for Mindful Smartphone Use

1. Mindfulness-Based Interventions: Implementing mindfulness practices can significantly mitigate the adverse effects of smartphone addiction. A study by Lan et al. in 2018 demonstrated that mindfulness-based cognitive-behavioral interventions could help individuals recognize and alter their smartphone usage patterns, promoting healthier relationships with technology. Mindfulness encourages users to reflect on their smartphone habits, fostering a greater awareness of the motivations behind their usage and the consequences it entails.
2. Cognitive Behavioral Therapy (CBT): CBT has been shown to be effective in addressing smartphone addiction, particularly among adolescents (Lee et al., 2022). By helping individuals identify and challenge maladaptive thoughts related to smartphone use, CBT can reduce addiction severity and improve mental health outcomes. This therapeutic approach can empower users to develop healthier coping strategies, thereby decreasing reliance on smartphones for emotional regulation.

3. Setting Boundaries and Limits: Establishing clear boundaries around smartphone use is essential for fostering better mental health. This can include setting specific times for smartphone use, creating "phone-free" zones, or designating certain hours for family interaction without devices. Research suggests that proactive management strategies, such as encouraging open discussions about smartphone use within families, can enhance communication and reduce conflicts related to technology (Hsieh et al., 2019; Mongkonkansai et al., 2022).

4.Promoting Healthy Alternatives: Encouraging engagement in alternative activities can help reduce smartphone dependency. Activities such as yoga, sports, or hobbies can provide fulfilling substitutes for smartphone use, promoting physical and mental well-being. Telles et al., 2017 found that yoga practice could improve self-awareness and emotional regulation, which are crucial for managing smartphone use.

5. Enhancing Parental Involvement: For adolescents parental guidance is vital in managing smartphone use. Parents should engage in discussions about the benefits and drawbacks of smartphone use, fostering an environment of understanding and support (Hsieh et al., 2019; Mongkonkansai et al., 2022). Effective communication strategies, such as expressing affection and reasoning with children about their smartphone habits, can significantly reduce problematic usage patterns (Hsieh et al., 2019).
6. Utilizing Technology Mindfully: Encouraging users to reflect on their smartphone applications and usage patterns can lead to more mindful engagement. Users should assess which apps contribute positively to their lives and which may lead to excessive use or negative feelings. This self-reflection can help individuals prioritize meaningful interactions over superficial ones (Han et al., 2022).
7. Workplace Policies: Organizations can play a crucial role in managing smartphone use among employees. Implementing policies that promote smartphone-free hours or encouraging face-to-face interactions can help mitigate the adverse effects of smartphone addiction in the workplace (Prodanova&Kocarev, 2021). Engaging employees in discussions about their smartphone usage can foster a culture of awareness and responsibility regarding technology use.

Addressing the Psychological Underpinnings

Understanding the psychological factors that contribute to smartphone addiction is essential for developing effective management strategies. Studies indicate that individuals often use smartphones as a coping mechanism for stress and anxiety

(Wang et al., 2015). Therefore, addressing these underlying issues through stress management techniques, such as mindfulness and relaxation exercises, can reduce reliance on smartphones for emotional support. Moreover, fostering self-esteem and social connections outside of the digital realm can help individuals feel less compelled to seek validation through social media platforms. Research has shown that enhancing self-esteem can mitigate the negative impacts of smartphone addiction(Wang et al., 2017). Encouraging users to engage in face-to-face interactions and community activities can strengthen interpersonal relationships and reduce the need for digital validation.

In conclusion, managing smartphone use to foster better mental health and interpersonal connections requires a multifaceted approach. By integrating mindfulness practices, cognitive behavioral strategies, and proactive parental involvement, individuals can develop healthier relationships with their smartphones. Furthermore, promoting alternative activities and workplace policies that encourage face-to-face interactions can significantly reduce the adverse effects of excessive smartphone use. As society continues to navigate the complexities of smartphone technology, it is imperative to prioritize mental health and interpersonal connections through mindful engagement with these devices.

REFERENCES

Abeele, M. M. V., Hendrickson, A. T., Pollmann, M. M., & Ling, R. (2019). Phubbing behavior in conversations and its relation to perceived conversation intimacy and distraction: An exploratory observation study. *Computers in Human Behavior*, 100, 35–47. DOI: 10.1016/j.chb.2019.06.004

Abeele, M. V. (2020). The social consequences of phubbing. *The Oxford handbook of mobile communication and society*, 158-174.

Aboujaoude, E., Kuss, D. J., Yao, M. Z., & Leung, L. W. (2021). Online psychology beyond addiction and gaming: A global look at mental health and internet-related technologies. *Frontiers in Psychology*, 12, 815013. DOI: 10.3389/fpsyg.2021.815013 PMID: 34975704

Angeluci, A. C. B. (2016). "Stop Phubbing me!": A case study on Mobile media and social relations. In *Handbook of Research on Comparative Approaches to the Digital Age Revolution in Europe and the Americas* (pp. 192–201). IGI Global. DOI: 10.4018/978-1-4666-8740-0.ch012

Ao, R. (2022, December). The Bidirectional Relationship Between Undergraduates' Social Abilities and Their Peer Relationships: A Quantitative Case Study of SYSU. In *2022 6th International Seminar on Education, Management and Social Sciences (ISEMSS 2022)* (pp. 3491-3502). Atlantis Press.

Augner, C., Vlasak, T., Aichhorn, W., & Barth, A. (2023). The association between problematic smartphone use and symptoms of anxiety and depression—A meta-analysis. *Journal of Public Health (Oxford, England)*, 45(1), 193–201. DOI: 10.1093/pubmed/fdab350 PMID: 34585243

Beukeboom, C. J., & Pollmann, M. (2021). Partner phubbing: Why using your phone during interactions with your partner can be detrimental for your relationship. *Computers in Human Behavior*, 124, 106932. DOI: 10.1016/j.chb.2021.106932

Bhattacharya, S., Bashar, M. A., Srivastava, A., & Singh, A. (2019). Nomophobia: No mobile phone phobia. *Journal of Family Medicine and Primary Care*, 8(4), 1297–1300. DOI: 10.4103/jfmpc.jfmpc_71_19 PMID: 31143710

Bianchi, R., Schonfeld, I. S., & Laurent, E. (2014). Is burnout a depressive disorder? A reexamination with special focus on atypical depression. *International Journal of Stress Management*, 21(4), 307–324. DOI: 10.1037/a0037906

Bitar, Z., Akel, M., Salameh, P., Obeid, S., & Hallit, S. (2023). Phubbing among Lebanese young adults: Scale validation and association with mental health (depression, anxiety, and stress). *Current Psychology (New Brunswick, N.J.)*, 42(23), 19709–19720. DOI: 10.1007/s12144-022-03104-z PMID: 35496363

Chotpitayasunondh, V., & Douglas, K. M. (2016). How "phubbing" becomes the norm: The antecedents and consequences of snubbing via smartphone. *Computers in Human Behavior*, 63, 9–18. DOI: 10.1016/j.chb.2016.05.018

Chotpitayasunondh, V., & Douglas, K. M. (2018). The effects of "phubbing" on social interaction. *Journal of Applied Social Psychology*, 48(6), 304–316. DOI: 10.1111/jasp.12506

Clark, J. L., Algoe, S. B., & Green, M. C. (2018). Social network sites and well-being: The role of social connection. *Current Directions in Psychological Science*, 27(1), 32–37. DOI: 10.1177/0963721417730833

Coyne, S. M., Rogers, A. A., Zurcher, J. D., Stockdale, L., & Booth, M. (2020). Does time spent using social media impact mental health?: An eight year longitudinal study. *Computers in Human Behavior*, 104, 106160. DOI: 10.1016/j.chb.2019.106160

Davey, S., Davey, A., Raghav, S. K., Singh, J. V., Singh, N., Blachnio, A., & Przepiórkaa, A. (2018). Predictors and consequences of "Phubbing" among adolescents and youth in India: An impact evaluation study. *Journal of Family & Community Medicine*, 25(1), 35–42. DOI: 10.4103/jfcm.JFCM_71_17 PMID: 29386960

David, M. E., & Roberts, J. A. (2017). Phubbed and alone: Phone snubbing, social exclusion, and attachment to social media. *Journal of the Association for Consumer Research*, 2(2), 155–163. DOI: 10.1086/690940

David, M. E., & Roberts, J. A. (2020). Developing and testing a scale designed to measure perceived phubbing. *International Journal of Environmental Research and Public Health*, 17(21), 8152. DOI: 10.3390/ijerph17218152 PMID: 33158203

Demirci, K., Akgönül, M., & Akpinar, A. (2015). Relationship of smartphone use severity with sleep quality, depression, and anxiety in university students. *Journal of Behavioral Addictions*, 4(2), 85–92. DOI: 10.1556/2006.4.2015.010 PMID: 26132913

Elphinston, R. A., & Noller, P. (2011). Time to face it! Facebook intrusion and the implications for romantic jealousy and relationship satisfaction. *Cyberpsychology, Behavior, and Social Networking*, 14(11), 631–635. DOI: 10.1089/cyber.2010.0318 PMID: 21548798

Fletcher, G. J., Simpson, J. A., & Thomas, G. (2000). The measurement of perceived relationship quality components: A confirmatory factor analytic approach. *Personality and Social Psychology Bulletin*, 26(3), 340–354. DOI: 10.1177/0146167200265007

Floegel, D., Elias, N., & Lemish, D. (2021). Young children's mobile device use in public places: Immersion, distraction, and co-use. *Studies in Media and Communication*, 9(1), 30–40. DOI: 10.11114/smc.v9i1.5236

Garrido, E. C., Delgado, S. C., & Esteban, P. G. (2024). Phubbing and its impact on the individual's psychological well-being. *Acta Psychologica*, 248, 104388. DOI: 10.1016/j.actpsy.2024.104388 PMID: 38959636

Garrido, E. C., Issa, T., Esteban, P. G., & Delgado, S. C. (2021). A descriptive literature review of phubbing behaviors. *Heliyon*, 7(5). PMID: 34041393

Gershon, I. (2018). Calling the irrational unmanageable neoliberal self. In *A Networked Self and Love* (pp. 12–30). Routledge. DOI: 10.4324/9781315193472-2

Griffiths, M. D., & Szabo, A. (2014, March 1). Is excessive online usage a function of medium or activity? An empirical pilot study. *Journal of Behavioral Addictions*, 3(1), 74–77. DOI: 10.1556/JBA.2.2013.016 PMID: 25215216

Gupta, M., & Sharma, A. (2021). Fear of missing out: A brief overview of origin, theoretical underpinnings and relationship with mental health. *World Journal of Clinical Cases*, 9(19), 4881–4889. DOI: 10.12998/wjcc.v9.i19.4881 PMID: 34307542

Hale, L., & Guan, S. (2015). Screen time and sleep among school-aged children and adolescents: A systematic literature review. *Sleep Medicine Reviews*, 21, 50–58. DOI: 10.1016/j.smrv.2014.07.007 PMID: 25193149

Hales, A. H., Dvir, M., Wesselmann, E. D., Kruger, D. J., & Finkenauer, C. (2018). Cell phone-induced ostracism threatens fundamental needs. *The Journal of Social Psychology*, 158(4), 460–473. DOI: 10.1080/00224545.2018.1439877 PMID: 29436935

Han, J. H., Park, S. J., & Kim, Y. (2022). Phubbing as a millennials' new addiction and relating factors among nursing students. *Psychiatry Investigation*, 19(2), 135–145. DOI: 10.30773/pi.2021.0163 PMID: 35164436

Hendrick, S. S. (1988). A generic measure of relationship satisfaction. *Journal of Marriage and Family*, 50(1), 93–98. DOI: 10.2307/352430

Heyman, J. L., Kerr, L. G., & Human, L. J. (2022). Social media use predicts greater liking in in-person initial interactions. *Personality and Social Psychology Bulletin*, 48(9), 1393–1405. DOI: 10.1177/01461672211040964 PMID: 34496679

Hsieh, Y. P., Yen, C. F., & Chou, W. J. (2019). Development and validation of the Parental Smartphone Use Management Scale (PSUMS): Parents' perceived self-efficacy with adolescents with attention deficit hyperactivity disorder. *International Journal of Environmental Research and Public Health*, 16(8), 1423. DOI: 10.3390/ijerph16081423 PMID: 31010068

Humphreys, L., & Hardeman, H. (2021). Mobiles in public: Social interaction in a smartphone era. *Mobile Media & Communication*, 9(1), 103–127. DOI: 10.1177/2050157920927062

Karadağ, E., Tosuntaş, Ş. B., Erzen, E., Duru, P., Bostan, N., Şahin, B. M., Çulha, İ., & Babadağ, B. (2015). Determinants of phubbing, which is the sum of many virtual addictions: A structural equation model. *Journal of Behavioral Addictions*, 4(2), 60–74. DOI: 10.1556/2006.4.2015.005 PMID: 26014669

Kelly, L., Miller-Ott, A. E., & Duran, R. L. (2019). Phubbing friends: Understanding face threats from, and responses to, friends' cell phone usage through the lens of politeness theory. *Communication Quarterly*, 67(5), 540–559. DOI: 10.1080/01463373.2019.1668443

Koçak, O., Arslan, H., & Erdoğan, A. (2021). Social media use across generations: From addiction to engagement. *European Integration Studies*, 1(15), 63–77. DOI: 10.5755/j01.eis.1.15.29080

. Krasnova, H., Wenninger, H., Widjaja, T., &Buxmann, P. (2013). Envy on Facebook: a hidden threat to users' life satisfaction.

Kwon, M., Kim, D. J., Cho, H., & Yang, S. (2013). The smartphone addiction scale: Development and validation of a short version for adolescents. *PLoS One*, 8(12), e83558. DOI: 10.1371/journal.pone.0083558 PMID: 24391787

Lan, Y., Ding, J. E., Li, W., Li, J., Zhang, Y., Liu, M., & Fu, H. (2018). A pilot study of a group mindfulness-based cognitive-behavioral intervention for smartphone addiction among university students. *Journal of Behavioral Addictions*, 7(4), 1171–1176. DOI: 10.1556/2006.7.2018.103 PMID: 30418075

Lazarus, R. S. (1984). *Stress, appraisal, and coping* (Vol. 464). Springer.

Lee, J. I., Hsiao, R. C., Tsai, C. S., & Yen, C. F. (2022). Caregivers' difficulty in managing smartphone use of children with attention-deficit/hyperactivity disorder during the COVID-19 pandemic: Relationships with caregiver and children factors. *International Journal of Environmental Research and Public Health*, 19(9), 5194. DOI: 10.3390/ijerph19095194 PMID: 35564588

Leonardi, P. M., Huysman, M., & Steinfield, C. (2013). Enterprise social media: Definition, history, and prospects for the study of social technologies in organizations. *Journal of Computer-Mediated Communication*, 19(1), 1–19. DOI: 10.1111/jcc4.12029

Lin, C., & Jiang, X. (2022). The Role of Personality Traits and Values in Perceived Friendship Quality: The Dyadic Approach. In *Interdisciplinary Insights on Interpersonal Relationships*. IntechOpen.

Liu, S., Wing, Y. K., Hao, Y., Li, W., Zhang, J., & Zhang, B. (2019). The associations of long-time mobile phone use with sleep disturbances and mental distress in technical college students: A prospective cohort study. *Sleep (Basel)*, 42(2), zsy213. DOI: 10.1093/sleep/zsy213 PMID: 30395300

Liu, X., Tian, R., Liu, H., Bai, X., & Lei, Y. (2023). Exploring the Impact of Smartphone Addiction on Risk Decision-Making Behavior among College Students Based on fNIRS Technology. *Brain Sciences*, 13(9), 1330. DOI: 10.3390/brainsci13091330 PMID: 37759931

Luk, T. T., Wang, M. P., Shen, C., Wan, A., Chau, P. H., Oliffe, J., & Lam, T. H. (2018). Short version of the Smartphone Addiction Scale in Chinese adults: Psychometric properties, sociodemographic, and health behavioral correlates. *Journal of Behavioral Addictions*, 7(4), 1157–1165. DOI: 10.1556/2006.7.2018.105 PMID: 30418073

Matar Boumosleh, J., & Jaalouk, D. (2017). Depression, anxiety, and smartphone addiction in university students-A cross sectional study. *PLoS One*, 12(8), e0182239. DOI: 10.1371/journal.pone.0182239 PMID: 28777828

Matsuda, M. (2000). Interpersonal relationships among young people and mobile phone usage: From attenuant to selective relationships. *Japanese Journal of Social Informatics*, 4(11), 111–122.

McDaniel, B. T., & Coyne, S. M. (2016). "Technoference": The interference of technology in couple relationships and implications for women's personal and relational well-being. *Psychology of Popular Media Culture*, 5(1), 85–98. DOI: 10.1037/ppm0000065

Merchant, K. (2012). How men and women differ: Gender differences in communication styles, influence tactics, and leadership styles.

Mongkonkansai, J., Veerasakul, S., Tamrin, S. B. M., & Madardam, U. (2022). Predictors of Musculoskeletal Pain among Primary School Students Using Smartphones in Nakhon Si Thammarat, Thailand. *International Journal of Environmental Research and Public Health*, 19(17), 10530. DOI: 10.3390/ijerph191710530 PMID: 36078252

Pal, S., Sharma, S. K., Singhal, A., & Telles, S. (2022). Smartphone Excessive Use, Sleep, and Beliefs about Well-being in University Students who Practice Yoga Compared with Those with No Experience of Yoga. *Indian Journal of Community Medicine*, 47(2), 292–295. DOI: 10.4103/ijcm.ijcm_601_21 PMID: 36034266

Pareek, S. (2017). Phantom vibration syndrome: An emerging phenomenon. *Asian Journal of Nursing Education and Research*, 7(4), 596–597. DOI: 10.5958/2349-2996.2017.00116.1

Pavot, W., Diener, E. D., Colvin, C. R., & Sandvik, E. (1991). Further validation of the Satisfaction with Life Scale: Evidence for the cross-method convergence of well-being measures. *Journal of Personality Assessment*, 57(1), 149–161. DOI: 10.1207/s15327752jpa5701_17 PMID: 1920028

Peleg, O., & Boniel-Nissim, M. (2024). Exploring the personality and relationship factors that mediate the connection between differentiation of self and phubbing. *Scientific Reports*, 14(1), 6572. DOI: 10.1038/s41598-024-55560-1 PMID: 38504119

Prodanova, J., & Kocarev, L. (2021). Is job performance conditioned by work-from-home demands and resources? *Technology in Society*, 66, 101672. DOI: 10.1016/j.techsoc.2021.101672 PMID: 34840365

Przybylski, A. K., & Weinstein, N. (2019). Digital screen time limits and young children's psychological well-being: Evidence from a population-based study. *Child Development*, 90(1), e56–e65. DOI: 10.1111/cdev.13007 PMID: 29235663

Rathod, A. S., Ingole, A., Gaidhane, A., & Choudhari, S. G. (2022). Psychological morbidities associated with excessive usage of smartphones among adolescents and young adults: A review. *Cureus*, 14(10). Advance online publication. DOI: 10.7759/cureus.30756 PMID: 36447680

Rhee, L., Bayer, J. B., Lee, D. S., & Kuru, O. (2021). Social by definition: How users define social platforms and why it matters. *Telematics and Informatics*, 59, 101538. DOI: 10.1016/j.tele.2020.101538

Riehm, K. E., Feder, K. A., Tormohlen, K. N., Crum, R. M., Young, A. S., Green, K. M., & Mojtabai, R. (2019). Associations between time spent using social media and internalizing and externalizing problems among US youth. *JAMA Psychiatry*, 76(12), 1266–1273. DOI: 10.1001/jamapsychiatry.2019.2325 PMID: 31509167

Roberts, J. A., & David, M. E. (2016). My life has become a major distraction from my cell phone: Partner phubbing and relationship satisfaction among romantic partners. *Computers in Human Behavior*, 54, 134–141. DOI: 10.1016/j.chb.2015.07.058

Sabadin, K. (2015). Correlation between the experience of occupational stress and the quality of a relationship from the point of view of women and men.

Seiffge-Krenke, I., & Klessinger, N. (2000). Long-term effects of avoidant coping on adolescents' depressive symptoms. *Journal of Youth and Adolescence*, 29(6), 617–630. DOI: 10.1023/A:1026440304695

Stevic, A., & Matthes, J. (2023). Co-present smartphone use, friendship satisfaction, and social isolation: The role of coping strategies. *Computers in Human Behavior*, 149, 107960. DOI: 10.1016/j.chb.2023.107960

Stip, E., Thibault, A., Beauchamp-Chatel, A., & Kisely, S. (2016). Internet addiction, hikikomori syndrome, and the prodromal phase of psychosis. *Frontiers in Psychiatry*, 7, 6. DOI: 10.3389/fpsyt.2016.00006 PMID: 26973544

Usmani, S. S., Sharath, M., & Mehendale, M. (2022). Future of mental health in the metaverse. *General Psychiatry*, 35(4), e100825. DOI: 10.1136/gpsych-2022-100825 PMID: 36189180

Wacks, Y., & Weinstein, A. M. (2021). Excessive smartphone use is associated with health problems in adolescents and young adults. *Frontiers in Psychiatry*, 12, 669042. DOI: 10.3389/fpsyt.2021.669042 PMID: 34140904

Wang, J. L., Wang, H. Z., Gaskin, J., & Wang, L. H. (2015). The role of stress and motivation in problematic smartphone use among college students. *Computers in Human Behavior*, 53, 181–188. DOI: 10.1016/j.chb.2015.07.005

Wang, M., Xu, Q., & He, N. (2021). Perceived interparental conflict and problematic social media use among Chinese adolescents: The mediating roles of self-esteem and maladaptive cognition toward social network sites. *Addictive Behaviors*, 112, 106601. DOI: 10.1016/j.addbeh.2020.106601 PMID: 32942097

Wang, P., Wang, X., Wu, Y., Xie, X., Wang, X., Zhao, F., Ouyang, M., & Lei, L. (2018). Social networking sites addiction and adolescent depression: A moderated mediation model of rumination and self-esteem. *Personality and Individual Differences*, 127, 162–167. DOI: 10.1016/j.paid.2018.02.008

Wang, P., Zhao, M., Wang, X., Xie, X., Wang, Y., & Lei, L. (2017). Peer relationship and adolescent smartphone addiction: The mediating role of self-esteem and the moderating role of the need to belong. *Journal of Behavioral Addictions*, 6(4), 708–717. DOI: 10.1556/2006.6.2017.079 PMID: 29254360

Wang, X., Xie, X., Wang, Y., Wang, P., & Lei, L. (2017). Partner phubbing and depression among married Chinese adults: The roles of relationship satisfaction and relationship length. *Personality and Individual Differences*, 110, 12–17. DOI: 10.1016/j.paid.2017.01.014

Williams, K. D. (2009). Ostracism: A temporal need-threat model. *Advances in Experimental Social Psychology*, 41, 275–314. DOI: 10.1016/S0065-2601(08)00406-1

Williams, K. D., & Nida, S. A. (2011). Ostracism: Consequences and coping. *Current Directions in Psychological Science*, 20(2), 71–75. DOI: 10.1177/0963721411402480

Xie, J., Luo, Y., & Chen, Z. (2022). Relationship between partner phubbing and parent–adolescent relationship quality: A family-based study. *International Journal of Environmental Research and Public Health*, 20(1), 304. DOI: 10.3390/ijerph20010304 PMID: 36612626

Yam, F. C. (2023). The relationship between partner phubbing and life satisfaction: The mediating role of relationship satisfaction and perceived romantic relationship quality. *Psychological Reports*, 126(1), 303–331. DOI: 10.1177/00332941221144611 PMID: 36461943

Zhou, X., & Shen, X. (2024). Unveiling the relationship between social anxiety, loneliness, motivations, and problematic smartphone use: A network approach. *Comprehensive Psychiatry*, 130, 152451. DOI: 10.1016/j.comppsych.2024.152451 PMID: 38237509

Zhou, Y., Li, D., Jia, J., Li, X., Zhao, L., Sun, W., & Wang, Y. (2017). Interparental conflict and adolescent internet addiction: The mediating role of emotional insecurity and the moderating role of big five personality traits. *Computers in Human Behavior*, 73, 470–478. DOI: 10.1016/j.chb.2017.04.012

Chapter 14
Breaking Free:
Strategies for Overcoming Smartphone Addiction

Bushra S. P. Singh
https://orcid.org/0000-0002-8540-2126
Gian Jyoti Institute of Management and Technology, India

ABSTRACT

This chapter explores the growing issue of smartphone addiction, examining a range of interventions aimed at mitigating its effects. Through a comprehensive review of literature, the chapter investigates behavioral, technological, and societal approaches, such as self-monitoring, cognitive-behavioral therapy (CBT), and digital detox programs. Case studies and real-world examples provide insight into the practical applications of these strategies in various settings, including educational institutions and workplaces. Additionally, the chapter identifies gaps in existing research and offers recommendations for future studies and policy initiatives. By synthesizing current knowledge on smartphone addiction, the chapter offers valuable guidance for individuals, educators, and policymakers seeking to address this pervasive global issue.

1. INTRODUCTION

In an era dominated by technological advancement, smartphones have emerged as indispensable tools for communication, entertainment, and productivity. They have revolutionized how we interact with the world, granting instant access to information and connecting us with people across the globe. However, as smartphone usage has skyrocketed, so too have concerns over its excessive and, in many cases, addictive nature. The pervasiveness of smartphones in daily life has led to a growing body of

DOI: 10.4018/979-8-3693-8804-4.ch014

research on the phenomenon of smartphone addiction, an issue that is increasingly recognized as a public health concern.

Smartphone addiction, often referred to as problematic smartphone use (PSU), involves a compulsive pattern of behavior in which individuals feel an overwhelming urge to use their smartphones, even when it interferes with their daily responsibilities and overall well-being. Unlike substance-based addictions, which involve physical dependence on a chemical, smartphone addiction falls under the category of behavioral addictions. It shares many characteristics with other behavioral addictions, such as compulsive gambling or internet gaming, where individuals exhibit an inability to regulate their behavior despite negative consequences (Montag et al., 2019).

The rise of smartphone addiction is tied to the design of these devices and the apps they run. Many smartphone applications are deliberately designed to capture and maintain users' attention, utilizing features such as push notifications, endless scrolling, and algorithmically personalized content. These elements trigger dopamine release in the brain, creating a rewarding feedback loop that reinforces continuous usage. Over time, this can result in a compulsive pattern of behavior that resembles addiction (Elhai, Dvorak, Levine, & Hall, 2017).

1.1 The Prevalence of Smartphone Addiction

The global penetration of smartphones has contributed to the widespread nature of smartphone addiction. According to a 2022 report by Statista, over 6.6 billion people—more than 80% of the world's population—own a smartphone. With such high levels of access, the opportunities for overuse are abundant. Studies conducted across various regions, including the United States, Europe, and Asia, have shown alarmingly high rates of smartphone addiction, particularly among younger populations (Statista, 2022).

One of the most affected groups is adolescents and young adults, who have grown up in a world where smartphones are ubiquitous. Research indicates that younger individuals are more likely to develop addictive behaviors related to smartphone use due to their heightened sensitivity to peer influence, the need for social connection, and the appeal of digital platforms (Samaha & Hawi, 2016). This is especially concerning as smartphone addiction among this demographic has been linked to a range of negative outcomes, including anxiety, depression, poor academic performance, and sleep disturbances (Lin, Pan, & Lin, 2016).

However, smartphone addiction is not limited to younger generations. Adults of all ages are increasingly experiencing problematic smartphone use, often exacerbated by work demands and the always-on culture promoted by modern technology. For many, the boundaries between work and personal life have blurred, making it challenging to disconnect from their devices even during leisure time (Panova & Carbonell, 2018).

1.2 Impacts of Smartphone Addiction

The impacts of smartphone addiction are multifaceted and pervasive, affecting mental, physical, and social well-being. On a psychological level, smartphone addiction has been strongly associated with anxiety, depression, and stress. Elhai et al. (2017) found that individuals with high levels of smartphone dependency often experience heightened feelings of social isolation and dissatisfaction with life. This paradox is partly due to the nature of social media and messaging apps, which, despite fostering online connections, can lead to feelings of exclusion or inferiority when users constantly compare themselves to others.

Physically, excessive smartphone use can contribute to a range of health problems. Extended screen time is associated with eye strain, poor posture, and an increased risk of musculoskeletal issues, particularly in the neck and upper back (Samaha & Hawi, 2016). Additionally, the blue light emitted by smartphone screens has been shown to interfere with the body's natural sleep-wake cycle, leading to sleep disturbances, insomnia, and overall fatigue.

On a social level, smartphone addiction can erode interpersonal relationships. The phenomenon of "phubbing"—the act of ignoring someone in favor of checking one's phone—has been shown to cause tension and dissatisfaction in personal relationships, including among family members and romantic partners (Oberst et al., 2017). Furthermore, smartphone addiction may detract from the quality of face-to-face interactions, reducing the depth and engagement of conversations.

1.3 The Need for Intervention

Given the widespread and far-reaching consequences of smartphone addiction, there is a pressing need for effective interventions. While smartphones themselves are unlikely to disappear from daily life, the way individuals use them can be modified to minimize harm. In this context, it becomes essential to examine strategies that can help individuals overcome their dependence on smartphones and regain control over their technology use.

This chapter aims to explore a range of interventions designed to address smartphone addiction. These interventions span individual-level behavioral strategies, technological solutions, and broader societal approaches. By reviewing these various strategies, this chapter seeks to provide a comprehensive guide for individuals, educators, policymakers, and clinicians who are grappling with the challenges posed by smartphone addiction.

Individual-level interventions, such as cognitive-behavioral therapy (CBT) and self-monitoring, have shown promise in helping individuals manage their smartphone use. CBT, in particular, addresses the underlying thought patterns that contribute to addictive behaviors, offering individuals the tools to reframe their relationship with their devices (van Deursen et al., 2015). Meanwhile, self-monitoring techniques, including setting usage limits and tracking screen time, empower individuals to become more conscious of their smartphone habits and take active steps toward reducing usage.

Technological solutions, such as app usage trackers and digital detox programs, leverage technology to combat overuse. These tools can help users monitor and manage their screen time, offering reminders and restrictions that promote healthier usage patterns (Kim et al., 2019). For example, Apple's Screen Time and Android's Digital Wellbeing provide built-in features that allow users to set daily app limits and track their overall phone use.

Societal and educational approaches also play a critical role in addressing smartphone addiction. Public awareness campaigns, school-based education programs, and workplace policies aimed at promoting healthy technology use can foster a culture of mindfulness and digital balance (Oberst et al., 2017). Moreover, policy initiatives, such as the right to disconnect laws in certain countries, aim to protect individuals from the intrusion of work-related smartphone use outside of business hours, contributing to a healthier work-life balance (Panova & Carbonell, 2018).

In conclusion, smartphone addiction is a multifaceted issue that demands a multifaceted response. By drawing on a combination of behavioral, technological, and societal approaches, individuals can take meaningful steps toward breaking free from their smartphone dependency. Through these strategies, it is possible to foster a more balanced and mindful relationship with technology, promoting healthier habits and overall well-being.

2. BACKGROUND AND RATIONALE

2.1 Historical Context

Smartphone addiction, as a contemporary phenomenon, has roots that extend back to the broader history of technology and its impact on human behavior. Understanding this addiction requires a nuanced examination of how technological advancements have progressively influenced our relationship with digital devices.

The origins of smartphone addiction can be traced to the early days of mobile technology. In the late 20th century, the advent of cellular phones marked the beginning of a significant shift in communication. These early devices, primarily used for voice calls and text messaging, began to alter social dynamics and personal routines. However, it was the introduction of the smartphone in the early 2000s that fundamentally changed the landscape of digital interaction. Smartphones, combining the functionality of mobile phones with internet access, multimedia capabilities, and a range of applications, created an all-encompassing digital experience.

The launch of the iPhone in 2007 by Apple marked a pivotal moment in this evolution. With its innovative touchscreen interface and app ecosystem, the iPhone set the stage for smartphones to become central to everyday life. As smartphones became increasingly sophisticated, incorporating features like social media apps, instant messaging, and gaming, the potential for addictive behaviors grew. The ability to access the internet, social networks, and entertainment options from a single device significantly increased user engagement and, consequently, the risk of addiction.

The 2010s saw a surge in smartphone use and, with it, a growing recognition of smartphone addiction as a serious issue. Studies during this period began to highlight the psychological and behavioral impacts of excessive smartphone use. Researchers observed correlations between high smartphone use and various mental health concerns, such as anxiety, depression, and sleep disturbances. This period also witnessed the emergence of formal terminology and frameworks to describe and study smartphone addiction, drawing parallels with other forms of behavioral addiction.

In recent years, the proliferation of advanced technologies, such as artificial intelligence and machine learning, has further intensified the issue. Modern smartphones use sophisticated algorithms to maximize user engagement, employing techniques such as push notifications, personalized content, and gamification to keep users connected. These advances have made smartphones even more integral to daily life, while simultaneously increasing the potential for addiction.

Overall, the historical trajectory of smartphone addiction reflects a broader pattern of technological evolution impacting human behavior. From the early days of mobile phones to the sophisticated, multi-functional smartphones of today, each advancement has contributed to the growing prevalence and complexity of smartphone addiction. Understanding this historical context is crucial for developing effective interventions and strategies to manage and mitigate the addictive potential of these powerful devices.

2.2 Smartphone Addiction: A Behavioral Concern

The concept of smartphone addiction is rooted in the broader framework of behavioral addictions, where individuals exhibit compulsive behavior patterns that mirror those seen in substance abuse. However, unlike substance-related addictions, smartphone addiction revolves around behavioral processes rather than chemical dependency. Behavioral addictions, such as gambling, internet use, and smartphone addiction, share common features including loss of control, preoccupation with the activity, and continued engagement despite negative consequences (Montag, Wegmann, Sariyska, Demetrovics, & Brand, 2019).

Smartphones are designed to engage users for extended periods through carefully crafted features. Many applications utilize techniques that intentionally trigger the brain's reward system by releasing dopamine, the neurotransmitter responsible for pleasure and reward. Features such as push notifications, endless scrolling, and personalized content feeds are tailored to encourage repeated interaction, thereby reinforcing compulsive usage patterns (Elhai, Dvorak, Levine, & Hall, 2017). For instance, social media apps, messaging platforms, and games are particularly effective at sustaining user engagement, leading individuals to prioritize smartphone use over other essential activities such as work, study, and even social interactions.

2.3 Prevalence and Global Impact of Smartphone Addiction

The widespread use of smartphones has resulted in unprecedented levels of accessibility, with over 6.6 billion smartphone users globally as of 2022, a number expected to rise steadily (Statista, 2022). While smartphones have revolutionized communication and access to information, their benefits have been accompanied by a host of negative consequences, particularly when their use becomes excessive or compulsive. A growing number of studies indicate that smartphone addiction is becoming a global problem, with high rates of addiction reported across different age groups, particularly among adolescents and young adults.

Among young populations, the prevalence of smartphone addiction is particularly alarming. Studies have shown that younger users are especially susceptible to developing problematic smartphone behaviors due to their developmental stage, the need for social validation, and increased peer pressure (Samaha & Hawi, 2016). For many adolescents, smartphones serve as a primary tool for socialization and entertainment, leading to overdependence. This overuse, however, has been linked to negative mental health outcomes. Research has established strong associations between excessive smartphone use and anxiety, depression, stress, and sleep disturbances (Lin, Pan, & Lin, 2016).

The negative psychological impact of smartphone addiction extends beyond anxiety and depression. Excessive screen time has been linked to heightened feelings of social isolation, despite the ostensibly connected nature of online interactions. The curated realities presented on social media platforms can foster a sense of inadequacy and social comparison, exacerbating feelings of low self-esteem and social anxiety in some users (Elhai et al., 2017). Additionally, the constant use of smartphones can disrupt the quality of in-person relationships, as individuals become more absorbed in their devices than in face-to-face interactions.

Physically, smartphone addiction has also been linked to several health issues. Tech neck, a condition resulting from prolonged periods of looking down at screens, leads to neck and back pain. Additionally, eye strain, sleep disruption due to blue light exposure, and an increasingly sedentary lifestyle are commonly associated with excessive smartphone use (Samaha & Hawi, 2016). The detrimental effects of smartphone addiction, therefore, extend beyond mental health, encompassing a range of physical problems that can further compromise an individual's overall well-being.

2.4 Global Perspectives on Smartphone Addiction

Smartphone addiction is a pervasive issue that affects diverse demographics and regions around the world. This global phenomenon manifests in various forms, influenced by cultural, socioeconomic, and technological factors unique to each region. Understanding the impact of smartphone addiction across different contexts can help in tailoring effective interventions and policies.

Regional Variations and Demographic Impacts

1. **North America:** In North America, smartphone addiction is particularly prevalent among young adults and adolescents. A study by Pew Research Center (2019) found that 96% of Americans own a smartphone, and a significant portion of this population reports symptoms of smartphone addiction. For instance, a survey conducted by the American Psychological Association (APA) in 2018 revealed that 48% of Americans feel that their smartphone use is excessive and that it adversely affects their mental well-being (APA, 2018). The pervasive nature of smartphones in daily life, combined with high levels of social media engagement, contributes to high addiction rates in this region.
2. **Asia:** In Asia, smartphone addiction also presents a major concern, with varying impacts across different countries. In South Korea, where smartphone penetration is extremely high, a study by the Korean Institute for Health and Social Affairs (2020) indicated that approximately 30% of South Korean adolescents exhibit symptoms of smartphone addiction. The South Korean government has implemented measures such as smartphone addiction prevention programs in schools to address this issue (Korean Institute for Health and Social Affairs, 2020). Similarly, in China, a study published in the *Journal of Behavioral Addictions* (2021) found that smartphone addiction is linked to academic performance issues among students, leading to increased attention on digital detox programs and parental control applications (Liu, Zhao, & Zhu, 2021).

3. **Europe:** In Europe, smartphone addiction affects various demographics, with notable differences between countries. In France, a national survey conducted by the French Observatory of Digital Addiction (2022) found that about 20% of French teenagers show signs of problematic smartphone use. The French government has introduced policies such as the "right to disconnect" law, which aims to mitigate the impact of smartphone overuse on work-life balance (French Observatory of Digital Addiction, 2022). In contrast, a study in the United Kingdom reported that while smartphone use is widespread, the prevalence of addiction is lower compared to other regions, possibly due to more rigorous public health campaigns and educational initiatives (NHS Digital, 2021).
4. **Latin America:** In Latin America, smartphone addiction is growing rapidly, particularly among young people. A report by the Latin American School of Digital Addiction (2021) highlighted that approximately 25% of teenagers in Brazil and Argentina exhibit signs of smartphone addiction, often exacerbated by social media pressures and limited access to digital literacy education (Latin American School of Digital Addiction, 2021). Efforts to address this issue include community outreach programs and school-based workshops aimed at promoting healthy smartphone habits.
5. **Africa:** In Africa, where smartphone penetration is increasing, the impact of smartphone addiction is still emerging. However, studies such as the one conducted by the African Institute for Digital Health (2022) suggest that smartphone addiction is becoming a concern, particularly among youth in urban areas. The rapid adoption of smartphones has outpaced the development of digital literacy programs, leading to growing addiction rates among young Africans (African Institute for Digital Health, 2022). The lack of comprehensive data on smartphone addiction in many African countries highlights the need for more research and targeted interventions.

2.5 Rationale for Addressing Smartphone Addiction

Given the significant psychological, physical, and social consequences associated with smartphone addiction, the importance of addressing this issue cannot be overstated. As smartphone penetration continues to grow, the risk of addiction also increases, particularly among vulnerable groups such as adolescents, young adults, and individuals who are socially isolated. Moreover, the line between recreational and compulsive smartphone use is often blurred, making it difficult for individuals to recognize the point at which their use becomes problematic.

Despite growing awareness of the negative effects of smartphone addiction, effective interventions remain limited. This gap underscores the urgency of identifying evidence-based strategies to address the problem. Interventions that empower individuals to take control of their smartphone use, while also acknowledging the central role that these devices play in modern life, are essential to curbing the rise of addiction. Strategies aimed at reducing smartphone addiction must not only focus on individual behavior change but also take into account the broader societal factors contributing to overuse, such as the design of apps and digital environments (Kim et al., 2019).

Several interventions have shown promise in addressing smartphone addiction, including cognitive-behavioral therapy (CBT), self-monitoring techniques, and digital detox programs (van Deursen et al., 2015). CBT has been effective in helping individuals understand and alter the cognitive processes that drive their addiction, while self-monitoring empowers users to become more conscious of their usage patterns and set personal limits. Additionally, digital detox programs, which encourage individuals to take breaks from their devices, have been shown to improve mental well-being and reduce dependency on smartphones (Kim et al., 2019).

At the societal level, broader interventions such as public health campaigns, educational programs, and workplace policies that promote healthy technology use are necessary. Policymakers and educators have a role to play in fostering a culture that prioritizes mindfulness and balance when it comes to smartphone use. The integration of right-to-disconnect policies in workplaces, for instance, aims to reduce the encroachment of technology into personal time, promoting a healthier work-life balance (Panova & Carbonell, 2018).

2.6 The Need for Further Research and Practical Solutions

Although current research has provided valuable insights into the causes and effects of smartphone addiction, more work is needed to develop and implement practical, evidence-based solutions. Studies must continue to explore the efficacy of different intervention strategies, particularly in diverse populations and age groups. In addition, collaboration between researchers, clinicians, and app developers is critical in creating digital environments that encourage responsible smartphone use rather than addiction.

This chapter aims to address the gap by examining the current landscape of interventions for smartphone addiction and proposing strategies that can be applied both at the individual and societal levels. The goal is to provide a roadmap for reducing smartphone addiction through behavior change, technological tools, and policy initiatives, ultimately promoting a healthier relationship with technology.

3. OBJECTIVES

This chapter seeks to achieve the following objectives:

- **Objective 1**: To identify and evaluate individual-level interventions that have been proven effective in reducing smartphone addiction, with a focus on behavioral modification techniques and cognitive-behavioral therapy (CBT).
- **Objective 2**: To examine technological solutions, such as app usage trackers and digital detox programs, in the fight against smartphone addiction.
- **Objective 3**: To explore societal and educational approaches, including awareness campaigns and policies that encourage healthier smartphone usage.

4. LITERATURE REVIEW

The literature on smartphone addiction is extensive, with numerous studies examining the behavioral, psychological, and societal factors contributing to the issue. In response to the growing concern, a wide range of interventions have been proposed, including behavioral therapies, technological solutions, educational campaigns, and policy measures. This section will explore the effectiveness of these interventions and highlight the challenges that remain in addressing smartphone addiction.

4.1 Behavioral Interventions

Behavioral interventions have proven to be some of the most effective strategies in reducing smartphone addiction. These approaches focus on changing the underlying habits, beliefs, and thought patterns that lead to compulsive smartphone use. One of the most widely used techniques is self-monitoring, a process by which individuals track their smartphone use, assess their patterns, and set specific limits on their usage. By maintaining an awareness of how much time is spent on their devices, individuals are empowered to modify their behavior. Studies have shown that self-monitoring can lead to a significant reduction in screen time, particularly when combined with other behavior modification strategies (Gökçearslan, Mumcu, Haşlaman, & Çevik, 2016).

One effective form of self-monitoring is the use of digital apps that track smartphone usage. These apps can help users set daily or weekly limits, block distracting apps during certain hours, and send reminders when their usage exceeds a predetermined threshold. Self-monitoring apps like Moment, RescueTime, and AppDetox have been found to reduce smartphone dependency by fostering awareness of usage habits and promoting mindful engagement with devices (Gökçearslan et al., 2016).

Another well-established behavioral approach is cognitive-behavioral therapy (CBT), which has been widely applied to address the psychological underpinnings of various addictions, including smartphone addiction. CBT helps individuals identify and challenge the cognitive distortions that drive their compulsive smartphone use, such as the fear of missing out (FOMO) or the belief that constant connectivity is necessary for social acceptance. The therapy focuses on restructuring these maladaptive thought patterns and replacing them with healthier alternatives (van Deursen, Bolle, Hegner, & Kommers, 2015). For example, individuals undergoing CBT might learn to set boundaries for smartphone use, such as avoiding phones during meals or before bedtime, or designating specific times for checking social media.

CBT's emphasis on mindfulness—becoming more conscious of one's smartphone habits—helps users break the cycle of automatic, impulsive use. CBT can also be tailored to address specific triggers for smartphone use, such as boredom or social anxiety, and equips individuals with coping strategies to manage these triggers without resorting to their phones. The efficacy of CBT in reducing smartphone addiction has been supported by multiple studies, with participants reporting improved control over their smartphone use and reduced anxiety related to technology over-dependence (van Deursen et al., 2015).

4.2 Technological Solutions

While smartphones themselves contribute to addiction, ironically, technology also offers several tools for managing and reducing smartphone overuse. Various app usage trackers, such as Apple's Screen Time and Android's Digital Wellbeing, have gained popularity as tools to monitor, limit, and control smartphone use. These apps provide detailed reports on screen time, allow users to set limits for individual app use, and send notifications when users approach their predetermined limits. By providing users with real-time feedback on their habits, these tools enhance awareness and encourage individuals to self-regulate their behavior (Kim, Cho, Park, & Lee, 2019).

Beyond monitoring, there are also blocking apps like Forest and Freedom, which temporarily block access to distracting apps or websites. Such apps offer a straightforward solution for individuals who struggle with maintaining focus, particularly when engaging in tasks that require undivided attention. For example, Forest incentivizes users to avoid using their phones by growing a virtual tree for every set period they stay off their devices. If they exit the app or break their pledge to avoid phone use, the tree dies, providing a gentle yet effective form of accountability (Kim et al., 2019).

Another promising technological intervention is the concept of digital detox programs. These programs encourage individuals to take periodic breaks from all digital devices, not just smartphones, in order to recalibrate their habits and reduce dependency. The premise of digital detox is rooted in the idea that temporary abstinence from screens can restore balance and help individuals re-establish a healthier relationship with technology. Digital detox initiatives range from short-term challenges (e.g., a "no phone Sunday") to extended retreats where participants are encouraged to disconnect for days or weeks at a time. Research suggests that such detox programs can reduce anxiety, improve sleep, and increase mindfulness in relation to smartphone use (Kim et al., 2019).

4.3 Societal and Educational Approaches

In addition to individual-level interventions, societal and educational efforts have emerged as critical components in combating smartphone addiction. Education and awareness campaigns target specific populations, such as adolescents, employees, or parents, to inform them about the risks of excessive smartphone use and promote healthier digital habits. Such campaigns typically include educational workshops, informational materials, and public service announcements designed to raise awareness about smartphone addiction and offer practical solutions (Oberst, Wegmann, Stodt, Brand, & Chamarro, 2017).

One successful example of societal intervention is the implementation of "right to disconnect" policies, which aim to protect employees from being expected to respond to work-related communications outside of working hours. Countries like France have enacted laws that give workers the legal right to disconnect from work emails and phone calls during non-working hours, thereby promoting a healthier work-life balance (Panova & Carbonell, 2018). These policies not only help reduce smartphone addiction but also address the broader issue of digital burnout, which is prevalent in industries that demand constant connectivity.

In the realm of education, schools and universities have begun to integrate digital well-being programs into their curricula. These programs teach students about the importance of balanced smartphone use and equip them with strategies for managing screen time. For instance, schools may introduce students to apps that help them monitor their usage, encourage device-free study sessions, or hold discussions on the impact of social media on mental health. Educational institutions play a crucial role in shaping young people's digital habits, making them ideal settings for interventions aimed at preventing smartphone addiction before it becomes problematic (Oberst et al., 2017).

4.4 Challenges and Barriers

Despite the variety of interventions available, significant challenges remain in addressing smartphone addiction. One of the primary barriers is the omnipresence of smartphones in modern life. From work and education to entertainment and socialization, smartphones have become indispensable tools, making it difficult for individuals to limit their usage without significant external support. The pervasive connectivity of smartphones creates a situation in which users feel pressure to remain constantly accessible, further reinforcing addictive behaviors (Billieux, Philippot, Schmid, Maurage, & de Mol, 2015).

Another key challenge is the role of personality traits in smartphone addiction. Research has shown that individuals with certain personality characteristics, such as low self-control, high levels of social anxiety, or a need for social validation, are more vulnerable to developing problematic smartphone use (Panova & Carbonell, 2018). These personality factors can complicate the effectiveness of behavioral interventions, as individuals may struggle to apply strategies like self-monitoring or CBT without additional support.

Additionally, societal norms around smartphone use, such as the expectation to be constantly available for communication, further complicate efforts to reduce usage. Many individuals feel compelled to respond to messages or check social media in order to avoid social exclusion or maintain professional relationships. This social pressure, coupled with the addictive design of many smartphone apps, creates a reinforcing cycle of dependency that can be difficult to break.

5. METHODOLOGY

This chapter employs a systematic review methodology to examine the various strategies used to mitigate smartphone addiction. A systematic review is an essential approach for synthesizing existing research to provide a comprehensive understanding of the topic. This method involves identifying, selecting, and analyzing relevant literature to address the research question in a structured and replicable way. By adopting this approach, the chapter seeks to consolidate the findings of prior studies, highlight effective interventions, and explore areas where further research is required.

5.1 Search Strategy

To ensure a robust review, a comprehensive search of academic databases was conducted. The databases selected for the review were PubMed, PsycINFO, and Google Scholar, which are renowned for housing extensive peer-reviewed articles in the fields of health sciences, psychology, and technology. These databases provided access to a wide range of interdisciplinary studies relevant to smartphone addiction and its interventions. To further expand the search, ERIC (Education Resources Information Center) was also explored for literature related to educational and societal interventions.

The search terms used included a combination of the following keywords: smartphone addiction, mobile phone overuse, digital addiction, behavioral interventions, CBT for smartphone addiction, technological solutions for smartphone addiction, digital detox, self-monitoring apps, right to disconnect, and digital well-being programs. These terms were applied to title, abstract, and keyword searches to maximize the scope of relevant literature.

5.2 Inclusion and Exclusion Criteria

To ensure the relevance and quality of the studies reviewed, specific inclusion and exclusion criteria were established. The inclusion criteria focused on:

- **Timeframe:** Only studies published in the last decade (2013-2023) were considered, as smartphone usage and addiction patterns have evolved rapidly with the increasing prevalence of mobile technology.
- **Peer-reviewed sources:** The review prioritized peer-reviewed journal articles, books, and reports that provided empirical evidence or theoretical insights into smartphone addiction interventions. Non-peer-reviewed content, such as blog posts, opinion pieces, or conference abstracts, was excluded.
- **Intervention focus:** Studies needed to focus on strategies aimed at overcoming smartphone addiction. This included both behavioral interventions (such as cognitive-behavioral therapy and self-monitoring), technological solutions (such as app usage trackers and digital detoxes), and societal/educational approaches (like right to disconnect policies or school-based programs).
- **Rigor of methodology:** Articles were selected based on the robustness of their methodologies, including the clarity of research design, sample size, statistical analysis, and replicability of the findings.

The exclusion criteria eliminated studies that:

- Focused solely on screen time or general digital device usage without specifically addressing smartphone addiction.
- Were opinion-based or lacked empirical data to support their conclusions.
- Were published before 2013, unless deemed foundational to the understanding of smartphone addiction.

5.3 Study Selection Process

The literature review followed a multi-phase process to ensure thoroughness. First, an initial pool of over 500 articles was identified using the search terms across all databases. After removing duplicates, the abstracts of the remaining articles were screened to assess their relevance to the study's objectives. Studies that did not meet the inclusion criteria or that had overlapping findings with other research were discarded. This step resulted in a more refined pool of around 120 articles.

Next, a full-text review was conducted to ensure that each study met the necessary standards for inclusion. Each study was evaluated based on the strength of its research design, quality of data collection, and applicability to smartphone addiction interventions. Ultimately, approximately 50 key studies were included in the final analysis, with the majority originating from psychology, health sciences, and behavioral research fields.

5.4 Data Extraction and Synthesis

Once the relevant studies were selected, data extraction was performed to capture essential information, including the intervention type, target population, methodological approach, and key findings. A structured data extraction sheet was used to systematically organize the information. The studies were categorized based on the type of intervention, whether behavioral, technological, or societal, and further grouped by their primary focus (e.g., self-monitoring, CBT, digital detox, or right to disconnect policies).

The extracted data was then synthesized to identify common themes, patterns, and gaps in the literature. Studies that employed rigorous methodologies and produced consistent findings were given more weight in the review's conclusions. This synthesis allowed for a clearer understanding of the most effective and widely applicable strategies to reduce smartphone addiction. Additionally, areas where interventions were less effective or where further research is needed were identified and highlighted.

5.5 Limitations of the Methodology

While a systematic review provides a comprehensive synthesis of the available literature, some limitations should be acknowledged. First, the review is limited by publication bias, as studies with significant findings are more likely to be published than those with null results. Additionally, the rapidly evolving nature of smartphone technology means that some findings from earlier studies may not fully reflect current usage patterns. Lastly, while the review focused on high-quality studies, variations in research design and intervention contexts may limit the generalizability of the findings.

6. CASE STUDIES: ADDRESSING SMARTPHONE ADDICTION

Case Study 1: School-Based Digital Detox Program in South Korea

South Korea, recognized for its high rates of smartphone usage among adolescents, confronted significant challenges related to smartphone addiction impacting students' academic performance and mental health. In response, the Seoul Metropolitan Office of Education implemented a comprehensive digital detox program across several high schools in the city (Kim et al., 2019). This program integrated educational workshops aimed at raising awareness about the risks of excessive smartphone use and equipping students with strategies to manage their digital habits. These workshops included interactive sessions where students could share their experiences and learn from peers (Oberst et al., 2017). Additionally, the program designated specific days each month as "Digital Detox Days," encouraging students to refrain from smartphone use and engage in offline activities such as sports, arts, and group discussions (Billieux et al., 2015). Parental involvement was also a crucial aspect, with workshops designed to help parents recognize signs of smartphone addiction and offer guidance on setting healthy usage boundaries at home (van Deursen et al., 2015).

The outcomes of this digital detox program were significant. Students reported a marked reduction in daily smartphone usage, particularly on detox days, and schools observed improvements in academic performance and increased classroom engagement (Gökçearslan et al., 2016). Furthermore, students developed stronger peer relationships and improved social skills through more face-to-face interactions (Samaha & Hawi, 2016). However, the program faced challenges, including initial resistance from some students and parents, highlighting the need for clear communication about the program's benefits and ongoing support to maintain its impact (Montag et al., 2019).

Case Study 2: Corporate Wellness Program in Silicon Valley, USA

A leading technology company in Silicon Valley confronted growing concerns about smartphone addiction among its employees, affecting productivity and work-life balance. In response, the company introduced a corporate wellness program aimed at reducing smartphone dependency and promoting healthier digital habits (Kim et al., 2019). The program featured screen time management tools that allowed employees to monitor and manage their smartphone usage, providing insights into their usage patterns and setting personalized limits (Oberst et al., 2017). Additionally, mindfulness and stress management workshops were organized to help employees develop better coping strategies and reduce reliance on smartphones for stress relief (Billieux et al., 2015). The program also established tech-free zones within the office to encourage face-to-face interactions and provide employees with breaks from their devices (van Deursen et al., 2015).

The wellness program yielded positive outcomes, including increased productivity and improved work-life balance for employees (Samaha & Hawi, 2016). The initiative fostered a supportive work environment and encouraged healthier digital habits among employees (Montag et al., 2019). Challenges included initial skepticism from some employees regarding the program's effectiveness, underscoring the need for ongoing communication and demonstrating the program's benefits. Balancing flexibility to accommodate different needs and preferences was also crucial for the program's success (Gökçearslan et al., 2016).

Case Study 3: University Digital Well-Being Initiative in Australia

An Australian university faced rising concerns about smartphone addiction among students, which was affecting their academic performance and mental health (Kim et al., 2019). In response, the university launched a digital well-being initiative comprising several key components. The initiative included digital well-being workshops that taught students strategies for managing smartphone use and promoted a balanced approach to technology (Oberst et al., 2017). Awareness campaigns across campus, including posters, social media content, and seminars, aimed to inform students about healthy smartphone use and encourage seeking help if needed (Billieux et al., 2015). The university also expanded its counseling services to provide tailored support for students struggling with smartphone addiction, offering both one-on-one counseling and group therapy sessions (van Deursen et al., 2015).

The initiative resulted in increased awareness among students about the negative effects of smartphone addiction and how to manage usage more effectively (Samaha & Hawi, 2016). There was a notable improvement in academic engagement and a decrease in distractions caused by excessive smartphone use (Gökçearslan et al., 2016). Additionally, the expansion of support services strengthened the university's capacity to assist students with their needs (Montag et al., 2019). Challenges included addressing the diverse needs of students and maintaining engagement with the initiative, requiring continuous effort and adaptation based on feedback (Kim et al., 2019).

7. PRACTICAL INSIGHTS AND APPLICATIONS

7.1 Implementation Strategies

Effective implementation of strategies to combat smartphone addiction requires tailored approaches across different settings such as schools, workplaces, and homes. Each environment presents unique challenges and opportunities for integrating these strategies.

1. Schools

In educational settings, addressing smartphone addiction can be approached through a combination of policy changes, curriculum integration, and student engagement. Schools can start by establishing clear policies regarding smartphone use during class hours. This includes setting rules that limit smartphone usage and incorporating technology-free periods during the school day. For instance, schools can designate specific times for technology use and periods for non-digital activities to help students develop better habits (Oberst et al., 2017).

Integrating digital well-being into the curriculum is another effective strategy. Schools can include modules on responsible smartphone use and the psychological impacts of excessive screen time within existing subjects. This education can be delivered through classroom lessons, dedicated workshops, and interactive activities that highlight the importance of balancing digital and offline activities. By engaging students in discussions about smartphone addiction and its effects, schools can foster awareness and promote healthier usage patterns (van Deursen et al., 2015).

Additionally, schools can collaborate with parents to reinforce these lessons at home. Regular communication between educators and parents about smartphone usage policies and best practices ensures a consistent approach to managing screen time. Schools might also organize events such as "digital detox" days where students are encouraged to engage in non-digital activities, thus helping them experience and value technology-free time.

2. Workplaces

In workplaces, strategies for managing smartphone addiction can be implemented through policy development, employee education, and creating a supportive work environment. Organizations can introduce policies that regulate smartphone use during work hours, particularly in meetings and collaborative sessions. For example, establishing smartphone-free zones or times can minimize distractions and enhance productivity (Panova & Carbonell, 2018).

Workplaces can also benefit from incorporating digital well-being programs into their employee wellness initiatives. These programs might include workshops on managing smartphone use, techniques for digital detox, and the impact of excessive screen time on work performance and mental health. By providing employees with resources and training on healthy smartphone habits, organizations can support their staff in developing more balanced digital practices (Kim et al., 2019).

Creating a culture that promotes work-life balance is crucial. Employers can implement "right to disconnect" policies that allow employees to disengage from work-related communications outside of office hours. This approach not only helps prevent smartphone addiction but also supports overall employee well-being. Encouraging regular breaks, promoting physical activity, and offering alternative ways to engage with colleagues can further reduce reliance on smartphones for work-related interactions.

3. Homes

At home, managing smartphone addiction involves setting clear boundaries and fostering open communication within the family. Parents can establish household rules regarding smartphone use, such as designated no-phone times during meals or family activities. Creating tech-free zones within the home, such as bedrooms or dining areas, can also help reduce excessive smartphone use (Billieux et al., 2015).

Parents should model healthy smartphone habits themselves, as children often emulate their behavior. Engaging in family activities that do not involve digital devices can encourage a more balanced approach to technology use. For instance, scheduling regular family outings, game nights, or outdoor activities provides alternatives to screen time and strengthens family bonds.

Furthermore, parents can educate their children about the risks of smartphone addiction and the importance of managing screen time. This education can include discussions about the impact of excessive use on mental health, social relationships, and academic performance. Parents can also use monitoring tools and apps to track their children's smartphone usage, setting limits and encouraging breaks as needed.

7.2 Training and Workshops

To support the implementation of strategies for managing smartphone addiction, developing targeted training programs and workshops is essential. These initiatives can be tailored for different audiences, including students, employees, and parents.

1. Training Programs for Educators and Employers

Training programs for educators and employers should focus on equipping participants with practical skills and knowledge to address smartphone addiction. For educators, training can include strategies for integrating digital well-being into the curriculum, developing effective smartphone usage policies, and engaging students in discussions about responsible technology use. Workshops could cover topics such as designing interactive lessons on smartphone addiction, managing classroom technology use, and communicating with parents about digital well-being (Gökçearslan et al., 2016).

For employers, training programs can provide insights into creating a supportive work environment that encourages healthy smartphone use. These programs might include sessions on implementing "right to disconnect" policies, promoting work-life balance, and fostering a culture that supports digital well-being. Workshops could also cover best practices for managing smartphone use during meetings, enhancing productivity through reduced digital distractions, and supporting employee mental health (Montag et al., 2019).

2. Workshops for Parents and Families

Workshops for parents and families should focus on practical strategies for managing smartphone use at home. These workshops can include sessions on setting household rules, modeling healthy smartphone habits, and engaging in technology-free activities. Participants can learn about effective monitoring tools, strategies for discussing smartphone addiction with children, and methods for encouraging balanced screen time (Oberst et al., 2017).

Interactive workshops that involve role-playing, group discussions, and hands-on activities can help parents practice implementing these strategies in real-life scenarios. For instance, workshops might include exercises on creating family technology plans, establishing tech-free zones, and identifying signs of smartphone addiction in children.

In conclusion, implementing and supporting strategies to manage smartphone addiction requires a multi-faceted approach across different settings. By developing and participating in targeted training programs and workshops, individuals and organizations can effectively address smartphone addiction and promote healthier digital habits.

8. EXPECTED OUTCOMES

This chapter is poised to deliver several significant outcomes that will enhance understanding and practical approaches to managing smartphone addiction.

First and foremost, it will offer a thorough and comprehensive review of various strategies designed to overcome smartphone addiction. This review will include a detailed examination of interventions spanning behavioral, technological, and societal domains. For individuals grappling with smartphone addiction, practical guidance will be provided through strategies such as self-monitoring, which helps users track and limit their screen time, and cognitive-behavioral therapy (CBT), which addresses the psychological triggers of addiction and promotes healthier usage patterns.

Furthermore, the chapter will identify and evaluate the most effective interventions across these domains. Behavioral approaches like CBT will be scrutinized for their effectiveness in modifying maladaptive smartphone use patterns. Technological solutions, including app usage trackers and digital detox programs, will be assessed for their role in reducing screen time and mitigating the negative impacts of excessive smartphone use. By dissecting these interventions, the chapter will pinpoint which methods show the most promise and how they can be effectively implemented in various contexts.

In addition to evaluating current strategies, the chapter will provide recommendations for future research. This section will identify gaps in the existing literature, such as the need for longitudinal studies to track the long-term effectiveness of different interventions, and suggest areas for further exploration. For example, future research could explore the efficacy of emerging technologies in combating smartphone addiction or the impact of cultural differences on the effectiveness of various interventions.

Lastly, the chapter will offer practical insights for the application of these strategies in real-world settings. This will include actionable recommendations for educators, who can integrate digital well-being programs into their curricula; for policymakers, who can advocate for balanced technology use policies; and for employers, who can implement workplace initiatives to promote healthier smartphone habits. By providing these practical insights, the chapter aims to foster healthier smartphone use and support individuals and organizations in their efforts to combat smartphone addiction.

Through these outcomes, the chapter will contribute to a deeper understanding of smartphone addiction and provide actionable strategies for addressing this pervasive issue.

9. FUTURE DIRECTIONS AND RECOMMENDATIONS

9.1 Future Research

The current body of research on smartphone addiction has made significant strides in understanding its causes and effects. However, several critical gaps remain that warrant further investigation. Addressing these gaps can enhance our understanding of smartphone addiction and lead to more effective interventions.

1. **Longitudinal Studies on Smartphone Addiction**: While cross-sectional studies have provided valuable insights into the associations between smartphone use and mental health issues, longitudinal studies are needed to establish causal relationships (Andreassen, Pallesen, & Griffiths, 2016). Longitudinal research can track changes in smartphone usage patterns over time and their impact on mental health, providing a clearer picture of how addiction develops and persists.
2. **Cultural and Demographic Variations**: Much of the existing research has been conducted in Western contexts, with less attention paid to how smartphone addiction manifests in different cultural and demographic settings (Panova & Carbonell, 2018). Future studies should explore how cultural norms, socioeconomic status, and demographic factors influence smartphone usage patterns and addiction. This research can help tailor interventions to specific populations and settings.
3. **Effectiveness of Emerging Technologies**: As new technologies and applications are continuously developed, research should evaluate their effectiveness in managing smartphone addiction. For instance, virtual reality (VR) and augmented reality (AR) have shown promise in various therapeutic contexts (Bickmore et al., 2016). Investigating how these technologies can be leveraged to create engaging and effective interventions could provide innovative solutions to smartphone addiction.
4. **Psychological Mechanisms of Addiction**: Further research is needed to understand the psychological mechanisms underlying smartphone addiction. Studies exploring the role of personality traits, cognitive biases, and emotional regulation in addiction can offer deeper insights into why certain individuals are more susceptible to compulsive smartphone use (Furukawa, 2017). This

research can inform the development of more personalized and targeted therapeutic approaches.

5. **Impact of Policy Interventions**: Research evaluating the impact of policy interventions on smartphone addiction is limited. Future studies should assess the effectiveness of various policy measures, such as digital detox initiatives and "right to disconnect" policies, in reducing smartphone addiction and improving digital well-being (Panova & Carbonell, 2018). This research can provide evidence-based guidance for policymakers and stakeholders.

9.2 Policy Recommendations

Addressing smartphone addiction requires a multifaceted approach that includes policy interventions aimed at promoting healthier technology use and mitigating addiction risks. Based on the current literature and research findings, the following policy recommendations are proposed:

1. **Implementation of Digital Literacy Programs**: Policymakers should advocate for the integration of digital literacy programs in educational curricula. These programs should focus on teaching students about responsible smartphone use, the risks associated with excessive screen time, and strategies for managing digital consumption (Oberst et al., 2017). By equipping individuals with the knowledge and skills to navigate digital environments responsibly, these programs can help prevent smartphone addiction from developing.
2. **Support for Workplace "Right to Disconnect" Policies**: Governments and organizations should consider implementing and enforcing "right to disconnect" policies that protect employees from being expected to engage in work-related communications outside of regular working hours (Panova & Carbonell, 2018). Such policies can help employees establish boundaries between work and personal life, reducing the risk of smartphone addiction and improving overall well-being.
3. **Promotion of Technology-Free Zones**: Policymakers should encourage the creation of technology-free zones in public spaces, such as schools, libraries, and healthcare facilities. These zones can provide individuals with opportunities to disconnect from their smartphones and engage in face-to-face interactions, fostering healthier social behaviors and reducing reliance on digital devices (Kim et al., 2019).
4. **Incentives for Digital Detox Programs**: Governments and private sector entities should explore providing incentives for individuals and organizations to participate in digital detox programs. These programs can include challenges or initiatives that encourage participants to take regular breaks from smartphones

and digital devices (Gökçearslan et al., 2016). Offering financial or social incentives can motivate higher participation rates and enhance the effectiveness of these programs.

5. **Investment in Research and Development**: Public and private sectors should increase investment in research and development focused on creating innovative solutions for smartphone addiction. This includes funding research on emerging technologies, such as VR and AR, that can be used to develop effective interventions (Bickmore et al., 2016). By fostering innovation in this area, stakeholders can contribute to the development of new tools and strategies for managing smartphone addiction.
6. **Development of Comprehensive National Strategies**: Policymakers should develop and implement comprehensive national strategies that address smartphone addiction across multiple domains, including education, healthcare, and technology. These strategies should involve collaboration among various stakeholders, including government agencies, educational institutions, healthcare providers, and technology companies (Montag et al., 2019). A coordinated approach can ensure that interventions are comprehensive and effectively address the multifaceted nature of smartphone addiction.
7. **Evaluation and Adaptation of Policies**: Finally, policymakers should establish mechanisms for the ongoing evaluation and adaptation of policies related to smartphone addiction. Regular assessments of policy effectiveness, combined with feedback from stakeholders and affected individuals, can help refine and improve interventions over time (Billieux et al., 2015). Ensuring that policies remain relevant and responsive to emerging trends and challenges is crucial for maintaining their effectiveness.

10. SIGNIFICANCE AND CONTRIBUTION

This chapter makes a significant contribution to the growing body of research on smartphone addiction by synthesizing various strategies aimed at reducing compulsive smartphone use. As smartphone addiction continues to escalate globally, affecting people across all age groups, this chapter addresses a critical gap in the literature by providing a systematic analysis of interventions that target this emerging public health issue.

One of the key contributions of this chapter is its ability to bridge the gap between theoretical frameworks and practical applications. While there is an abundance of research exploring the causes and consequences of smartphone addiction, fewer studies focus on practical solutions that can be applied in real-world contexts. By drawing from a wide array of behavioral, technological, and societal interventions, this chapter offers a comprehensive toolkit for addressing smartphone addiction at multiple levels.

For researchers, this chapter provides an up-to-date synthesis of the most effective interventions for smartphone addiction, grounded in rigorous empirical evidence. This synthesis will serve as a valuable reference point for those studying behavioral addictions, offering insights into the psychological mechanisms underlying compulsive smartphone use and the various methods available to mitigate its impact. The chapter also identifies gaps in the current research, particularly in understanding how different interventions work across diverse populations and cultures, laying the groundwork for future studies that can build upon its findings.

For clinicians, the chapter's focus on behavioral interventions such as cognitive-behavioral therapy (CBT) and self-monitoring offers practical guidance on how to integrate these approaches into treatment plans for patients struggling with smartphone addiction. By emphasizing evidence-based techniques, the chapter provides mental health professionals with a clear roadmap for helping individuals develop healthier relationships with their devices. It also highlights the potential of technology-based interventions, such as app usage trackers and digital detox programs, as adjuncts to traditional therapy, expanding the repertoire of tools available to clinicians.

The chapter's significance also extends to educators and school administrators, who are increasingly faced with the challenge of managing smartphone use among students. Educational institutions can play a pivotal role in promoting digital well-being, and this chapter offers practical recommendations for designing school-based intervention programs. By incorporating strategies such as digital well-being education and screen time management tools, schools can empower students to develop healthier smartphone habits, reducing the negative impact on academic performance and mental health. Furthermore, the chapter's discussion on societal approaches, including right to disconnect policies, provides a broader framework for educational institutions to advocate for policy changes that support digital well-being beyond the classroom.

Finally, for policymakers, the chapter offers a valuable resource for shaping public health initiatives aimed at curbing smartphone addiction. With its emphasis on societal interventions and policy-driven solutions, such as the implementation of right to disconnect laws and workplace digital well-being policies, the chapter outlines actionable steps that governments and organizations can take to promote healthier smartphone usage on a larger scale. By drawing attention to the societal implications of smartphone addiction, the chapter encourages a more holistic approach to addressing this issue, recognizing the need for collective efforts that extend beyond individual behavior change.

In conclusion, this chapter contributes to the ongoing discourse on smartphone addiction by synthesizing a range of strategies that can be applied across different contexts. Whether in individual therapy sessions, educational settings, or workplace interventions, the insights provided in this chapter are designed to inform both theory and practice, making it a valuable resource for a wide audience. Its multidisciplinary approach ensures that researchers, clinicians, educators, and policymakers alike can benefit from its findings, ultimately fostering a more comprehensive and effective response to the growing problem of smartphone addiction.

11. CONCLUSION

Smartphone addiction represents a significant challenge in today's digitally dominated society. This issue is multifaceted, encompassing behavioral, technological, and societal dimensions, each requiring a unique approach for effective management. The strategies discussed in this chapter offer a comprehensive framework for addressing smartphone addiction, aiming to foster healthier usage patterns and mitigate the negative impacts of excessive smartphone use.

Behavioral Interventions form the cornerstone of individual-level strategies. Techniques such as self-monitoring and cognitive-behavioral therapy (CBT) are particularly effective in helping individuals understand and alter their smartphone habits. Self-monitoring encourages users to track their smartphone usage and set personal limits, promoting self-awareness and accountability. CBT, on the other hand, addresses the psychological factors contributing to addiction by helping individuals identify and modify maladaptive thought patterns and behaviors. These strategies empower users to make conscious decisions about their smartphone use, thereby reducing compulsive behavior and fostering healthier habits.

Technological Solutions offer a paradoxical yet effective approach to combating smartphone addiction. Tools such as app usage trackers and screen time management apps enable users to monitor their smartphone habits, set daily limits, and restrict access to certain apps. These tools provide users with critical insights into their usage patterns and help them implement practical limits. Additionally, digital detox programs advocate for periodic breaks from smartphone use, encouraging users to disconnect from their devices to recalibrate their habits and reduce dependency. While it may seem counterintuitive to use technology to manage technology addiction, these tools offer valuable support in promoting healthier usage patterns.

At the societal and educational levels, strategies are focused on prevention and education. Awareness campaigns aim to inform the public about the risks associated with excessive smartphone use and promote healthy digital habits. These campaigns often target specific populations, such as students and employees, to address the particular needs and challenges of these groups. Educational programs integrated into school curricula provide students with the knowledge and skills necessary to manage their smartphone use effectively. Such programs emphasize the importance of digital well-being and teach students how to balance their online and offline lives.

Policies like the right to disconnect represent a significant societal approach to managing smartphone addiction. Enacted in several countries, these policies provide workers with the legal right to avoid answering work-related communications outside of regular working hours. This policy helps to establish boundaries between work and personal time, promoting a healthier work-life balance and reducing the compulsion to remain connected at all times. The implementation of such policies reflects a growing recognition of the need to manage digital engagement in a way that supports overall well-being.

Despite the variety of interventions available, challenges persist. The omnipresence of smartphones in everyday life makes it difficult for individuals to reduce their usage without substantial external support. Additionally, individual differences, such as personality traits and the specific contexts in which smartphones are used, can impact the effectiveness of various strategies. For example, individuals with low self-control or high levels of social anxiety may find it more challenging to manage their smartphone use effectively. Therefore, tailored approaches that consider individual differences are crucial for maximizing the effectiveness of interventions.

In summary, addressing smartphone addiction requires a comprehensive approach that integrates behavioral, technological, and societal strategies. By providing a detailed review of these interventions, this chapter aims to equip individuals, educators, and policymakers with the tools needed to combat smartphone addiction effectively. The insights and recommendations offered here serve as a foundation for future research and practical applications, contributing to the ongoing effort to promote healthier smartphone usage in an increasingly digital world. Through a concerted effort to implement these strategies, it is possible to mitigate the negative impacts of smartphone addiction and foster a more balanced and mindful approach to technology use.

REFERENCES

African Institute for Digital Health. (2022). *Smartphone addiction in Africa: Current trends and future directions*. Retrieved from https://www.africaninstitute.org/smartphone-addiction

American Psychological Association. (2018). *Stress in America: Technology and social media*. Retrieved from https://www.apa.org/news/press/releases/stress/2018/technology-social-media

Andreassen, C. S., Pallesen, S., & Griffiths, M. D. (2016). The relationship between addictive use of social media, narcissism, and self-esteem: Findings from a large national survey. *Addictive Behaviors*, 64, 287–293. DOI: 10.1016/j.addbeh.2016.03.006 PMID: 27072491

Bickmore, T. W., Trinh, H., Olafsson, S., O'Leary, T. K., Asadi, R., Rickles, N. M., & Cruz, R. (2016). Patient and consumer safety risks when using conversational assistants for medical information: An observational study of Siri, Alexa, and Google Assistant. *Journal of Medical Internet Research*, 18(9), e115. DOI: 10.2196/jmir.6219 PMID: 30181110

Billieux, J., Philippot, P., Schmid, C., Maurage, P., & de Mol, J. (2015). Problematic use of the Internet and smartphones in adults: A review. *Current Psychiatry Reports*, 17(4), 18. DOI: 10.1007/s11920-015-0582-7

Elhai, J. D., Dvorak, R. D., Levine, J. C., & Hall, B. J. (2017). Problematic smartphone use: A conceptual overview and systematic review of relations with anxiety and depression psychopathology. *Journal of Affective Disorders*, 207, 251–259. DOI: 10.1016/j.jad.2016.08.030 PMID: 27736736

French Observatory of Digital Addiction. (2022). *Smartphone addiction among French teenagers: An overview*. Retrieved from https://www.frenchobservatory.org/smartphone-addiction

Furukawa, T. (2017). Personality traits, cognitive biases, and emotional regulation in behavioral addictions: A comprehensive review. *Journal of Behavioral Addictions*, 6(3), 243–256. DOI: 10.1556/2006.6.2017.054

Gökçearslan, Ş., Mumcu, E., Haşlaman, T., & Çevik, V. (2016). The role of self-monitoring and self-control in smartphone addiction. *Journal of Behavioral Addictions*, 5(2), 307–316. DOI: 10.1556/2006.5.2016.048

Griffiths, M. D. (2005). A "components" model of addiction within a biopsychosocial framework. *Journal of Substance Use*, 10(4), 191–197. DOI: 10.1080/14659890500114359

Kim, J., Cho, H., Park, K., & Lee, J. (2019). The impact of app usage trackers on smartphone addiction and the role of mindfulness. *Computers in Human Behavior*, 93, 48–56. DOI: 10.1016/j.chb.2018.12.016

Korean Institute for Health and Social Affairs. (2020). Smartphone addiction prevention programs in South Korea: An evaluation. *Korean Journal of Public Health*, 47(4), 321–335. DOI: 10.13048/kjph.2020.47.4.321

Latin American School of Digital Addiction. (2021). *Smartphone addiction in Latin America: Patterns and interventions*. Retrieved from https://www.lasd.edu/smartphone-addiction

Lin, Y., Pan, Y., & Lin, C. (2016). Smartphone addiction and mental health: A meta-analysis. *Journal of Behavioral Addictions*, 5(4), 717–728. DOI: 10.1556/2006.5.2016.073

Liu, H., Zhao, X., & Zhu, Q. (2021). The impact of smartphone addiction on academic performance in China. *Journal of Behavioral Addictions*, 10(1), 95–106. DOI: 10.1556/2006.2021.00010

Liu, Y., Zhao, J., & Zhu, L. (2020). Effectiveness of behavioral interventions for smartphone addiction: A meta-analysis. *Journal of Behavioral Addictions*, 9(1), 20–34. DOI: 10.1556/2006.9.2020.02

Montag, C., Wegmann, E., Sariyska, R., Demetrovics, Z., & Brand, M. (2019). The role of smartphone addiction in the development and maintenance of mental health issues. *International Journal of Environmental Research and Public Health*, 16(16), 2903. DOI: 10.3390/ijerph16162903 PMID: 31416112

NHS Digital. (2021). *Smartphone addiction and its effects: A UK perspective*. Retrieved from https://www.digital.nhs.uk/publications/smartphone-addiction

Oberst, U., Wegmann, E., Stodt, B., Brand, M., & Chamarro, A. (2017). Symptoms of internet addiction and smartphone addiction: The role of online gaming and social media. *Journal of Behavioral Addictions*, 6(3), 268–278. DOI: 10.1556/2006.6.2017.037

Panova, T., & Carbonell, X. (2018). A review of current research on smartphone addiction. *Frontiers in Psychology*, 9, 1–10. DOI: 10.3389/fpsyg.2018.01535

Park, Y., Kim, J., & Lee, S. (2021). Evaluation of the Smartphone Addiction Prevention Program in South Korean schools. *The Journal of Educational Research*, 114(6), 667–678. DOI: 10.1080/00220671.2021.1909725

Pew Research Center. (2019). *Smartphone use in the United States*. Retrieved from https://www.pewresearch.org/fact-tank/2019/04/05/smartphone-use-in-the-united-states

Samaha, M., & Hawi, N. S. (2016). Relationships among smartphone addiction, stress, and anxiety among Lebanese university students. *Social Science Computer Review*, 34(4), 405–419. DOI: 10.1177/0894439315617505

Statista. (2022). *Smartphone addiction statistics worldwide*. Retrieved from https://www.statista.com/

van Deursen, A. J., Bolle, C. L., Hegner, S. M., & Kommers, P. A. (2015). Modeling habitual and addictive smartphone behavior. *Computers in Human Behavior*, 45, 511–520. DOI: 10.1016/j.chb.2014.12.039

Wegmann, E., Stodt, B., & Brand, M. (2015). Smartphone addiction and stress: A review. *Current Psychiatry Reports*, 17(7), 1–10. DOI: 10.1007/s11920-015-0617-0

Chapter 15
The Effect of Phubbing in the College Classroom

Tamara Phillips Fudge
https://orcid.org/0000-0002-8682-9711
Purdue University Global, USA

David J. Fudge
https://orcid.org/0009-0005-6790-4789
Independent Researcher, USA

ABSTRACT

When students use smart phones in the college classroom, it is often to their detriment as well as to the consternation of their instructors. "Phubbing," a portmanteau of "phone snubbing," is the term used when a person ignores activity around them while focusing intently on their phone. This behavior, which can be described as an addiction, can result in decreased learning capabilities, physical and mental health, personal relationship quality, and data security. Existing studies about phone use in the traditional classroom in addition to a new study of online live college seminars provide some insight into this issue. Fortunately, both administrative and instructor-based solutions can be found in thoughtful policy development, some changes in classroom management, and educating students, as informed by the literature and the conclusions based on this study.

THE EFFECT OF PHUBBING IN THE COLLEGE CLASSROOM

Mobile technology provides people with many advantages, from communicating with children or elder caregivers, asking family easy questions while at the grocery store, and checking work email when traveling, to the more serious ability to sum-

DOI: 10.4018/979-8-3693-8804-4.ch015

mon help quickly in emergencies. The list of these advantages would be exhaustive. Unfortunately, this same technology also comes with a social and educational price: it enables phubbing, or "phone snubbing," which occurs when a person has an intense focus on their phone with disregard for activity and people around them. In the college/university setting, the question arises as to whether phubbing affects learning and what instructors and institutions can do.

LITERATURE REVIEW

According to the website Stop Phubbing, the term "phubbing" was created in 2012 by an advertising company in Australia (Harper, n.d.). Not yet part of the worldwide lexicon, it is interesting to note that Merriam-Webster and Oxford do not yet have a definition of the word. Dictionary.com added the word in 2024.

Technological advances in the last several decades have changed how students behave within the educational system as well as in life in general. As Hernández Gracia et al. (2020) says, there is an "effect that the abuse and misuse of technologies is causing in students, bringing with them a lack of sensitivity and decrease of values during the communication processes that are carried out in the classroom" (p. 13). This includes the most mobile of all devices, the smart phone. Chotpitayasunondh and Douglas (2016) claim that smart phones tend to be preferred over the use of computers to access the internet.

Hashemi et al. (2024) states that smart phone addiction is "a product of a society's history … caused by a combination of personal, cultural, technological, environmental, and emotional influences" (p. 4). The sheer prevalence of mobile phones today has made phubbing a major problem for both students and teachers in the classroom. Ahmed et al. (2023) reported that 63.6% of the world's population had mobile phones in 2021. By July 2024, this number had increased to 70% (Kemp, 2024). Kemp (2024) reminds us that smaller children are not likely to have their own phones yet, so the percentage for adults can be assumed to be higher. In the United States, 95% of teens through age 17 have smart phones and receive as many as 192 alerts daily (Ohio Department of Education and Workforce, n.d.).

There have been numerous studies focused on specific countries or broader geographic regions regarding phubbing in classrooms. Barbed-Castrejón et al. (2024) quote studies that say over 40% of U.S. pharmacy students, a similar number of medical college students in India, close to half of Spanish adolescents, and nearly 90% of Turkish college students have exhibited phubbing behaviors, but Russian university students do not appear to have problems with phone use to the same extent. These discrepancies may be due to several factors including but not limited to exactly what questions were asked in those studies, how the surveys were distributed, and what institutional or governmental rules might apply, but these factors collectively point to the fact that in most of the world, phubbing is a problem.

Another parameter worthy of exploration is whether gender or age are related to reasons for phubbing. İliç and Tanyeri (2021) claim that women are more likely to use phubbing for social communication, and Xu et al. (2022) say this is due to loneliness – or it may be a *predictor* of loneliness. On the other hand, men may use the phone more for gaming (Capilla Garrido et al., 2024). Chotpitayasunondh and Douglas (2016) claim that the duration of a phubbing incident tends to be longer for women, and women were also the victims of phubbing more often than men. Their research indicates that women perceive their use of smart phones as social interaction. It is important to note that their study involved undergraduate students at a university in England, participants from a crowd-sourcing website, and social networking site volunteers (Chotpitayasunondh & Douglas, 2016).

Responses to phubbing vary worldwide due to cultural differences (Santos et al., 2023). These may be related to power plays, gender roles, individuals versus group dynamics, avoiding situations that seem ambiguous, or other such differences (Hofstede et al. 2010, as cited in Santos et al., 2023). Essel et al. (2022) reference two studies. The first study, conducted in Ghana by Essel, found moderate anxiety in university students lacking their mobile device, adding that the duration in which the user had owned a smart phone and the availability of internet access were potential determining factors. The second study, performed in Nigeria by Awofala (2020), found that nearly half of mathematics college students were overly anxious when their phone was not nearby. Additionally, an Argentinian study claimed women more often phubbed and were likelier targets of phubbing because "men are more familiar in some contexts with face-to-face meetings than are women" (Etchezahar et al., 2023, p. 8). Socioeconomic disparities and other cultural norms thus appear to have an effect on how prevalence of classroom phubbing.

Digital Distraction and Related Theories

Flanigan et al. (2023) suggest a framework that includes Self-Determination Theory (SDT) as a means to combat "digital distraction." SDT claims that student motivation and supportive instruction styles provide the psychological framework for academic success, but an overabundance of institutional mandates such as high-stakes testing can impede success (Ryan & Deci, 2020). In terms of phone use, Flanigan et al. (2023) explain that students may be more motivated to follow rules if they still feel a sense of autonomy. Per the framework, a balance between collaborative rulemaking and the need for students to develop competence in what is being studied in the classroom allows for maximum student autonomy.

Another theory, helpful in the understanding that not all students will react in the same way or comply with rules even when created by consensus, is McClelland's Three Needs Theory, which claims that each person's motivation is governed by their own unique combination of power, achievement, and affiliation needs (Kurt, 2021). A phone user who is attempting to keep socially distant would be said to have low "power," whereas someone who has difficulty in accepting disagreement would have high power. Someone with low "achievement" needs may fear failure; high achievers demand to win. Those with low "affiliation" needs tend to be dependent, and those with high needs may place themselves socially above others (Kurt, 2021).

Starting at Home and Then on to School

Young children often emulate their parents' actions. Parental overuse of smart phones can affect children's sleep quality as well as the development of healthy social-emotional relationships, according to a recent Chinese study (Ding et al., 2023); these in turn affect schoolwork, where adequate sleep and relationships are major concerns. Moreover, Chen et al. (2023) note that "parental phubbing behavior is a significant predictor of adolescent smart phone dependence" (p. 1) as well as depression and a feeling of being detached from peers. Academic procrastination may also follow (Chen et al. 2023).

In the K-12 classroom, administrators may consider a balance between allowing cell phones for the sake of safety and banning them as distractions (Smale et al., 2021). Some positive aspects can include teaching students how to use technology responsibly; however, cyberbullying, with possible heartbreaking consequences, is made far too easy for the perpetrators who have mobile devices and can use them whenever they wish. Smart phones might also enable cheating during tests (Smale et al., 2021). Another factor is that not all children have smart phones, which deepens the emotional impact of the socio-economic divide. Moreover, children may not understand some of the moral implications of sharing some items such as pornographic imagery; over two dozen years ago, the Republic of the Philippines Department of Education (2003) passed a measure to ban elementary and secondary school students from using pagers and cell phones in school for this very reason. Phone use by pre-college students has been banned in many countries, including China, France (for students younger than 15), and in more than three-quarters of U.S. schools (Lamb, 2023).

A 2024 Chinese study of internet addiction claims that phubbing mothers affect children more than phubbing fathers due to the typical nurturing role that women take in child-rearing (Dai et al., 2024). This can be argued since different cultures may perceive women's roles differently, but the result from Dai et al. (2024) indicates children imitate the behavior of the parent who is emotionally closest to them because "social behaviors are obtained by observation and imitation, and when people lack relevant experiences or knowledge, they are inclined to look for alternative experiences from others who are important in their lives" (Dai et al., 2024, p. 8). When children are victims of their parents' phubbing, they may exhibit a lack of inhibition in their online behaviors and moral judgments, leading to a predisposition towards cyberbullying others (Wang et al., 2022).

Cebollero-Salina et al. (2022) claim that a vast majority of adolescents prefer online connections to peers over face-to-face contact and that cyberbullying tends to transfer to in-person behavior. Phubbing is a form of social exclusion and affects both the person using the phone and the person who wishes to gain the phone user's attention.

Chuck (2024) brings up an important alternate use of phones in the classroom: while school shootings are rather rare, they do occur, and a cell phone can be a lifeline for both students and teachers. On the other hand, calling, texting, and livestreaming the event distracts the user from listening for commands and from being fully aware of their situation, and ring tones and vibrations sounds may give away their location (Chuck, 2024).

Certain devices and applications may also be necessary for providing accessibility for students with disabilities. In the United States, several laws apply, as explained by Marshall (2024):

> *Through the Individuals with Disabilities Education Act (IDEA) and Section 504 of the Rehabilitation Act of 1973 (Section 504), students with disabilities are afforded the right and opportunity to use assistive technology (AT) and/or auxiliary aids and other accommodations to access a free, appropriate public education in the least restrictive environment (LRE). It is not uncommon for school team(s), which include the parent and/or student, to determine that a student with disability needs full-time, part-time, or specific allotted time to use a computer, tablet, cellular phone/its apps, or other device(s) as part of their Individualized Education Program (IEP) or 504 Plan. (Marshall, 2024, para. 2)*

Into the College Classroom

There are some appropriate reasons why students use mobile devices in the college setting. International students, for example, might use smart phones to learn about their new environments while keeping connection to their more familiar support network at home (Ahmed et al., 2023). Ahmed et al. (2023) claim that the use of smart phones may enhance one's understanding of self, thereby reducing the chance for impulsive behavior. A positive reason for having a cell phone in the classroom itself is that possession and proximity of a communication device at all times may be a safety factor (Uğur & Koç, 2015a).

Online courses can typically be accessed on smart phones. For example, Students can complete quizzes, post in discussion boards, answer emails from instructors and classmates, review interactive modules, and perform other tasks outside of a live seminar session. In a live session, a phone may be useful in translating speech into a student's native language, participating in directed collaborations via text, or taking notes ("Using smartphones," n.d.). Screenshots of seminar slides with crucial information can be taken, analogous to taking pictures of a whiteboard in a traditional classroom; phones can also serve as calculators and students can easily search for vocabulary and concepts they need to understand better (Uğur & Koç, 2015a). Ehrlick (2014) suggests potential integration of "spontaneous research" or internet scavenger hunts for course-related topics, though this could only be possible if everyone in class had a smartphone, which is not guaranteed.

In the traditional face-to-face classroom, the typical student needs to give full attention using their senses (Medina-Morales & Villalón-Hernández, 2023). When visual and tactile senses are diverted to a device, auditory and other senses may be dulled, and little may be gained from the intended classroom experience. Note-taking is hindered, and classmates are distracted (Karlins, 2022). Huey and Giguere (2023) said that students whose phones were removed from the classroom comprehended course material better and, notably, experienced less anxiety during class.

Phubbing disrupts attentiveness while decreasing student motivation and significantly increasing the chance for procrastination, all of which in turn add undue stressors for the student (Parmaksız, 2023). Learning, after all, requires organization of time and ideas, and the fear of failure adds to procrastination, distraction, and stress. In contrast, students with confidence in their abilities tend to learn more efficiently and have a willingness to work diligently to reach their goals (Parmaksız, 2023).

This phenomenon can be viewed from different viewpoints. *Supervisor phubbing* as explored by Koc and Caliskan (2022) has the context that professor smart phone activity affects student trust and the feeling of being valued, which in turn affects learning outcomes. Reviewing the situation from the reverse, Nazir (2020) found that *student phubbing* in the classroom is seen as disrespectful by older instructors, and can negatively affect younger, less experienced instructors' performance due to distraction.

Some demographics might also be considered. Age may be a factor, as college students are more prone to phubbing than younger persons (Barbed-Castrejón et al., 2024), perhaps due to leaving the structure of the home environment. Zhu et al. (2024) explain that college students also tend to have more leisure time than children and adults. Gender may or may not have a bearing on phubbing; some studies claim that women phub more than men, but this is not corroborated in other studies (Barbed-Castrejón et al., 2024).

What Is Happening in that Classroom

Uğur and Koç (2015a) provide some insight into what students may be doing with their phones during college classes. They explain that some students use phones to take pictures of whiteboards after the professor has provided information thereon and may also use their phones to look up class concepts, but a majority of phone use during class is spent doing unrelated activity, and those who "play" on their phones become a distraction to others (Uğur & Koç, 2015a). Among the distractions are the ringing for an incoming call during class, leaving class to answer calls, and other disruptions that can interrupt the instructor's concentration (Uğur & Koç, 2015b), thereby costing everyone in class a smooth delivery of course content. The feeling of disrespect and lack of student interest may also compel instructors to put in less effort into teaching (Karlins, 2022).

A study of Peruvian college students in 2021 claims that students who spend much of their phone time using social media – which occurs even during in-person social gatherings – is a clear cause of getting inadequate sleep (Ríos Ariza et al., 2021). The prevalence of a wide variety of mobile applications available adds to the "conflictive use and addictive dependence" in abusing phone time (Ríos Ariza et al., 2021).

Sometimes phones are used to create videos of the teacher or others in the classroom without their knowledge (Uğur & Koç, 2015b). Video can also be transformed into "deepfakes" and still images from phone cameras can be modified, with the results posted on social media platforms for the purpose of exacting revenge or humiliating a teacher or fellow student (Williams & Fudge, 2020). The device held in one's hand can enable cyberbullying and tarnish people's reputations.

Another possible phone use is called "teacher-baiting," when a student or group of students misbehave until the teacher gets angry, and the ensuing aftermath is recorded on a phone (Mathis, 2021). Recording without a person's permission is not legal everywhere and may be treated similarly to illicit wiretapping in the courts. While this may be more likely a phenomenon of junior and senior high school classrooms, anyone in any classroom can be concerned about being secretly recorded, including students videoing interactions with other students.

Several studies going as far back as 2006 indicate that use of a cell phone during tests as a means to cheat is also a major problem (Smale et al., 2021). A survey in 2010 conducted by the Canadian Council for Learning found a troubling amount of cheating in general, and in 2018, a study by Saidouni and Bahloul reported that over a third of students used technology to cheat on tests (Smale et al., 2021). Uğur and

Koç (2015b) explain that larger class sizes can increase the likelihood of cheating because individual behaviors are more difficult to spot and stop. Moore et al. (2017) mention that a phone can take photos or screenshots of tests to illicitly share with others, and the use of Bluetooth technology like earbuds is an additional concern, as use of the connected device is not as obvious to the instructor/observer.

NEW STUDY: THE ONLINE CLASSROOM

İliç (2021) recounts that the COVID-19 pandemic of 2020, people's use of electronic devices became more important. A reliance on technology allowed the world to continue socializing and learning – but from a safe distance from others. Online learning had been available for a considerable time prior to the pandemic but became normalized, and time management as well as self-motivation, communication skills, and the ability to use computers and other devices came to the forefront (İliç, 2021). While there has been a return to the traditional classroom, the online classroom has gained acceptance and can also involve phubbing.

Previous studies of student phubbing have centered on the traditional classroom where face-to-face interaction is expected. To better understand phone use during *online* college course synchronous seminars and the student viewpoint, a new study was devised, approved by the school's Institutional Review Board, and conducted.

Method and Participants

An online survey was sent to students in an accredited online university in the United States that includes live seminars, also known as "webinars," as part of the curriculum. The study group consisted of both undergraduate and graduate students primarily studying business (including accounting, finance, human resources, project management, and other majors), information technology (cybersecurity, cloud computing, data analytics, and others), and health sciences (health care administration, health education, nutrition, public health, and others), with a small number of students studying law.

The survey was created in Google Forms and distributed via school email by representatives of the deans of each area. Neither IP addresses nor student emails were collected from respondents to ensure anonymity. Those who identified their main device for seminars as a smart phone were directed to similar questions as those who use other means, but were asked fewer questions about their phone use since the device was obviously in use during seminars. A total of 664 students responded to the survey, which was open in late October to early November 2024.

Results and Analysis

Device

Of the 664 responses, it is clear the phone is not the first choice for participation in online course seminars. Only 3.9% of the total responses report using their phone for this activity.

Figure 1. Device type

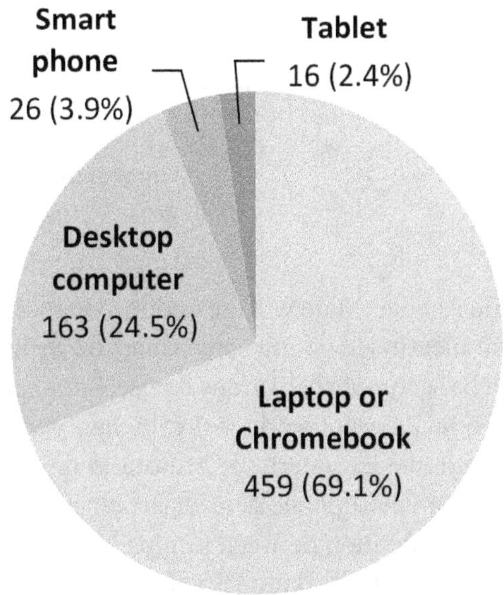

Smart Phone Device Statistics

The statistics provided by the phone users are provided here for those who are curious, but this data is not considered particularly significant.

When asked what might deter non-seminar smart phone activity during a session, close to half of the students chose to keep busy with posting or speaking, with about two thirds explaining that they are taking notes. Less than 40% indicated a faster pace being a factor, and only three students would be deterred from using their phone for non-seminar purposes if they were being shown on webcam.

Figure 2. Potential preventions of phone overuse in seminars

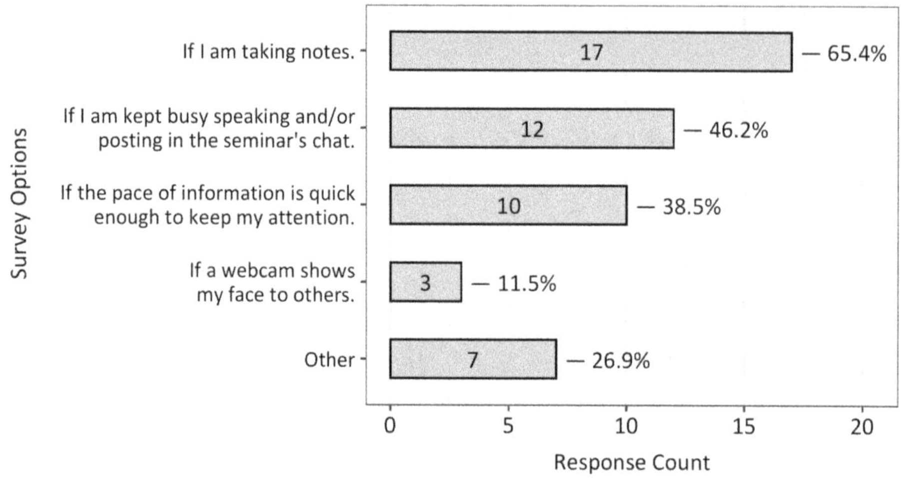

As implied in Figure 2 above, there was the option to input individual comments. One survey participant mentioned taking screenshots on their phone during seminars; however, this can be accomplished on any device. Another student complained that the webinar tool Zoom does not work well with their phone, due to difficulties resulting from the mobile device interface. Multitasking was mentioned by one respondent (plus a few non-smart phone device participants); while this may seem like a valid excuse to split attention between seminar and other tasks, Madore and Wagner (2019) explain that "multitasking" is a misnomer. The brain does not have a true capability to work on simultaneous tasks; it can only switch from one task to another. This results in loss of accuracy in the performance of said tasks and in the speed needed for the brain to readjust to the other task (Madore & Wagner, 2019).

A notable response is as follows:

- The seminars that have been most engaging that I have stayed the most focused in are the ones that do more than simply review the week's assignment and discussion questions. The professor has shared personal anecdotes and stories relevant to the subject of study.

Specific questions were asked about the use of the phone during the session. A large minority acknowledged texting during sessions and a majority reported being able to search online during the sessions for more information about topics being discussed. Only one student admitted playing games simultaneously with the seminar proceedings, and no one will (or can) answer calls during the session.

Figure 3. Use of phone during seminar

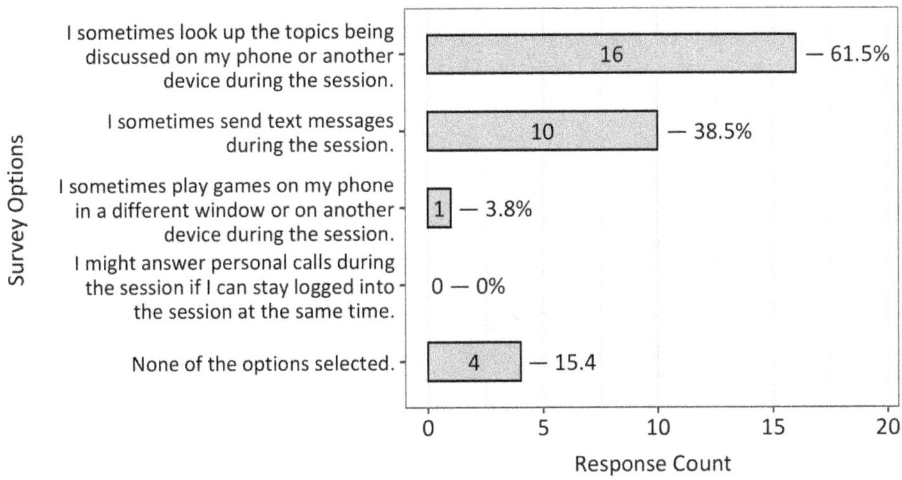

Figure 4. Euler diagram corresponding to Figure 3

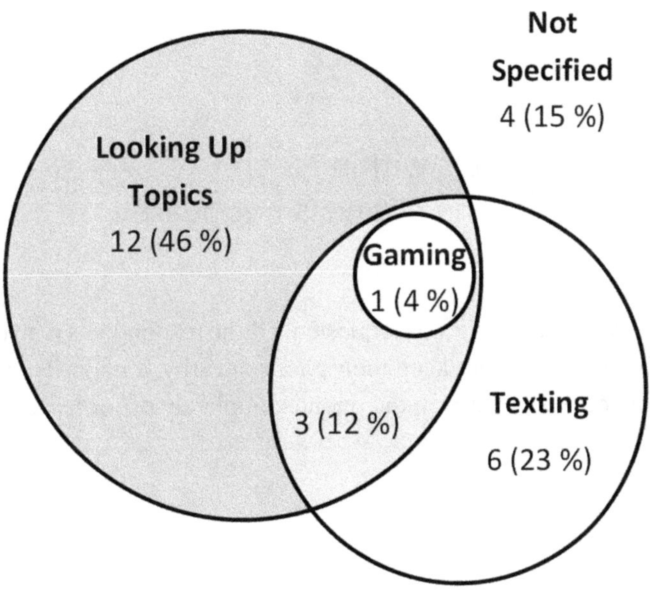

Non-Smart phone Device Statistics

As stated previously, most of the survey respondents use a tablet, laptop, desktop, or Chromebook to access and participate in their online course seminars. Ten out of every eleven students (90.9%) keep their smart phone within reach.

Figure 5. Device location

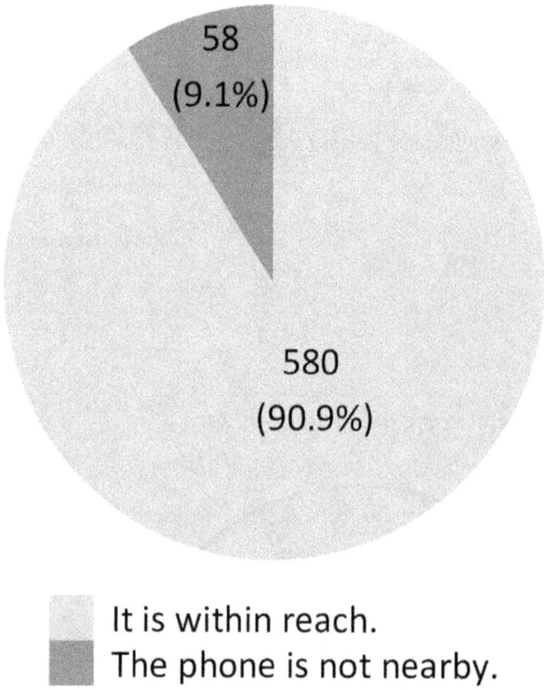

The phone's volume setting was requested. Of the respondents who do not attend seminars with their phone but keep their phones nearby, a majority simply reduce the volume, and others either turn the phone completely off or leave the volume at a normal level.

Figure 6. Phone volume

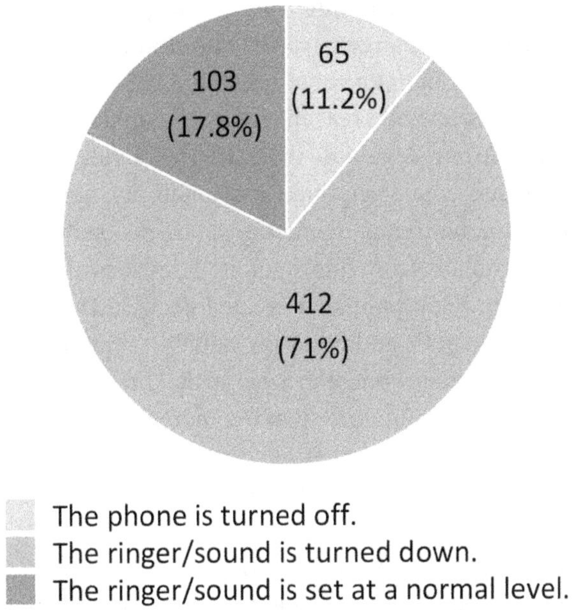

Prevention of undue phone use was asked next. Survey respondents indicated in large numbers that note taking, a fast pace of the session, and maintaining chat or speaking activity can keep the phone from being used during seminar. Only about 30% indicated concern about their face being shown via webcam.

Figure 7. Potential preventions of phone use in seminars

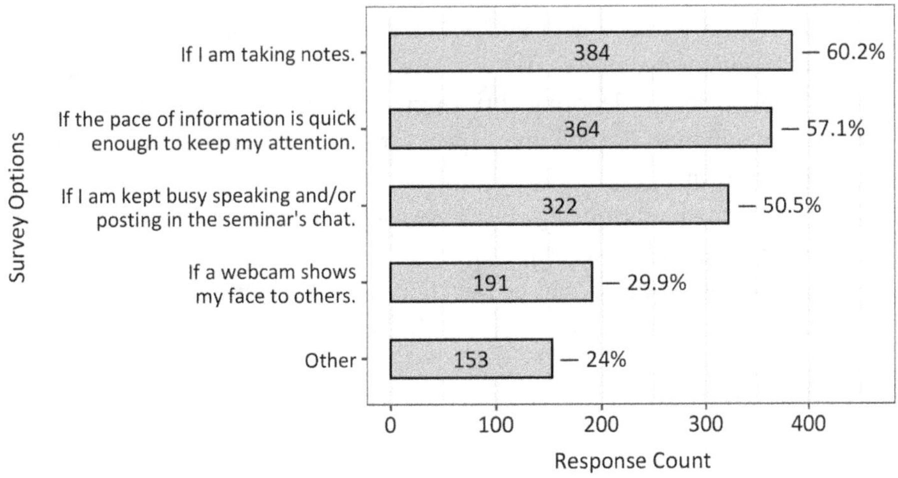

Similar to the question asked of phone users, the non-phone users were asked to input additional preventative measures. Several respondents mentioned needing the phone nearby for family emergencies such as children's needs and/or medical situations, using it for the calculator function, or having a work phone that must be answered if it rings, or receiving a text message. It would be difficult to argue the validity of these uses. Strong keywords indicating why they are *not* using a phone during seminar included self-discipline, accountability, common courtesy and respect, paying attention, removing distractions, professionalism, and willpower.

Suggestions for instructors from this input include the avoidance of simply reading slides, especially textbook publisher-created decks. Efforts to make seminars interactive with questions/polls and focus on valuable content, providing practical examples, and being passionate about the topic so that their voice is not "monotone" were advised. Several students indicate that the more interactive a session, the less likely students will walk away from their device or play games.

The following were notable individual responses:

- I pay to be in school so I put my focus on the seminar instead of my phone.
- Engagement with peers definitely makes it more fun and makes students actually want to pay attention.
- I will make the judgement call on whether or not to use my phone based on my own understanding of the topic, ability to multitask, and additional retention capabilities such as recordings or transcriptions.
    - Author note: most of the seminars in this university are recorded. If students do not participate, they may be required to watch the recording.
- I usually have phone in airplane mode during seminar.
- I have ADHD, so focus is difficult; I crochet during class to keep my hands busy and find it helps me focus better since it is a mindless task.
- Respecting my environment and education time is why I avoid using my phone during online classes. Distractions undermine my focus and diminish the value I place on learning. Prioritizing my education means dedicating my full attention to it, showing respect for both the academic space and my personal growth.
- I do not use my phone during class time except to login to two factor authentication if the email server is too slow.
- I think open webcams should be mandatory for seminars.
- I'm an IT Director and phone use during *my* business meetings makes me furious.

There were of course some detractors who did not engage with the survey in a professional manner or who showed some disdain for seminars in general. One respondent used an expletive in the same sentence as saying they can "exercise self-control." Another said that phubbing "is a ridiculous made up term," not realizing it has been in some dictionaries for a while. A different respondent admitted that they only do minimum requirements in live sessions: "I do not intend to type more than needed." Two students did not read the intent of the survey carefully, and quite erroneously thought it was intended to create a no-phone rule for their university. Fortunately, these detractors were small in number.

In addition to phone use prevention, the respondents were asked about the use of their phone during seminars, similar to the question asked of the phone-using participants. About 45% looking up topics relevant to the session's content and fewer people admitting to texting someone. An even smaller percentage of participants admitted to playing games and answering phone calls. The fact that the main device used is not a phone means that the smart phone is freely available for these activities.

Figure 8. Use of phone during seminar

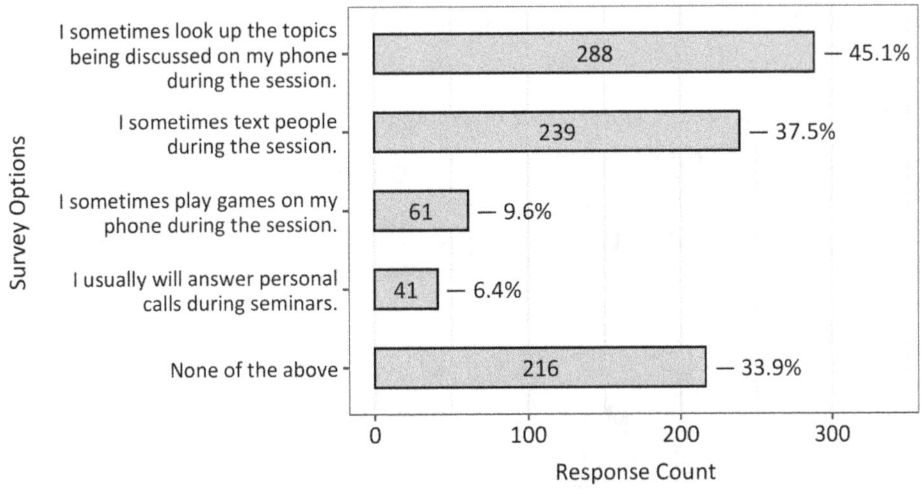

Other Parameters

The most common seminar length was reported as 50-60 minutes, with few that were 25-30 minutes and only eight students reporting over an hour.

Figure 9. Seminar length reported by all respondents

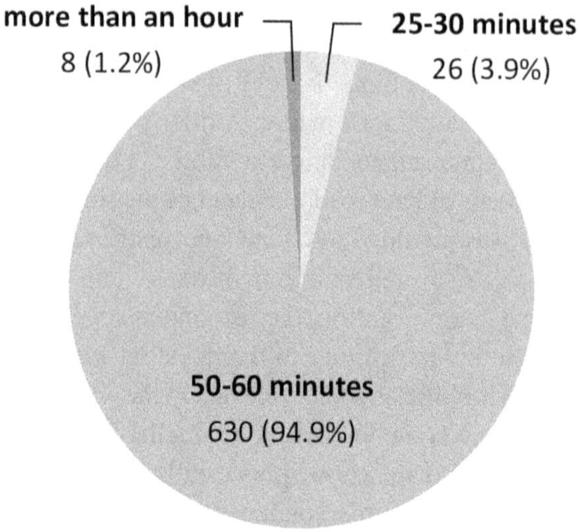

Gender identification was also requested, with the caveat that an answer was not required.

Figure 10. Gender distribution of all respondents

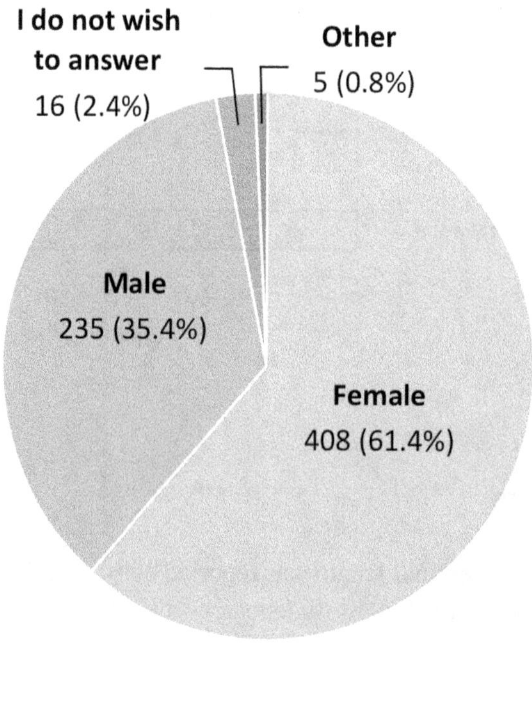

The last question of the survey asked students their age. Again, an answer was not required, although nearly 94% completed the question. Ages ranged from 18 to 71, with a median age of 37 years. Age distribution is shown in the figures below. Generations are defined as Gen Z (ages 12-27), Millennials (28-43), Gen X (44-59), Generation Jones (60-69), and Boomers I (70-78) according to Beresford Research ("Age range by generation," 2024). Since only the respondents' age in years was requested and not exact birthdates, the identification of participants on the cusp of each generation is an approximation.

Figure 11. Age distribution of all respondents

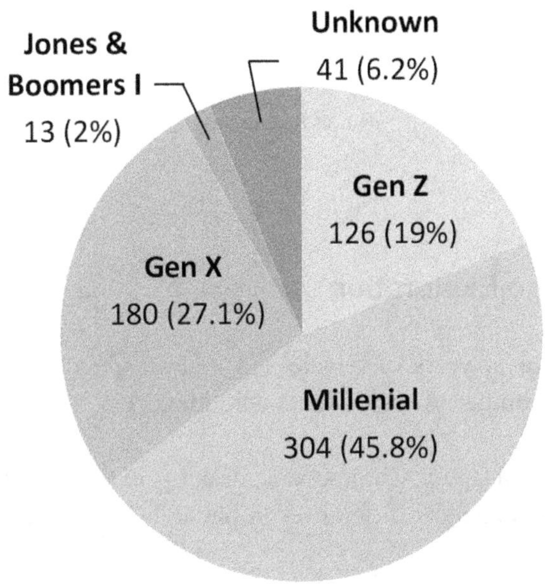

Figure 12. Age distribution of all respondents by generation

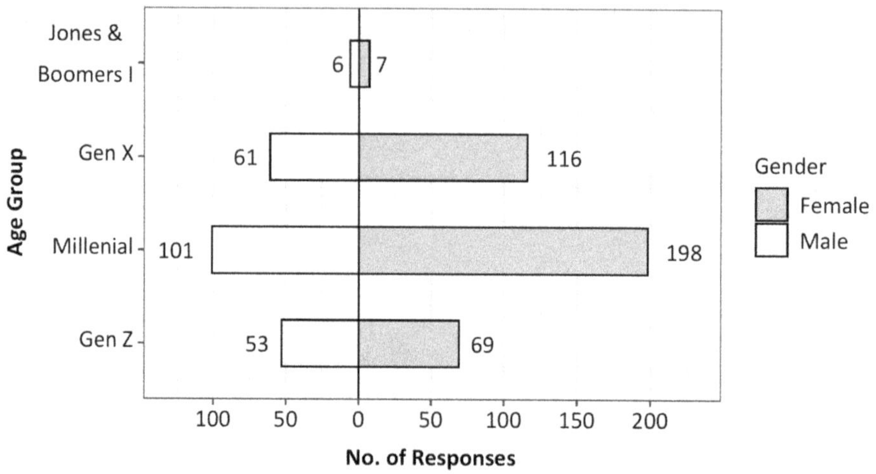

Gender and Age Exploration

The median age in years of female and male respondents were 38 and 36, respectively. The number of respondents who identified "other" was deemed too small for analysis.

Students who use a laptop, Chromebook, desktop, or tablet *and* keep their phone nearby indicated little gender differences in phone location and volume as shown in Table 1.

Table 1. Phone status for students who keep their phone nearby

Female Students = 351			Male Students = 209		
Phone turned off	39	11.1%	Phone turned off	23	11%
Volume turned down	254	72.4%	Volume turned down	146	69.9%
Volume at regular level	58	16.5%	Volume at regular level	40	19.1%

Table 2 shows responses about what might deter students from using their phone in seminars. Per a Chi-squared test of independence with Yates correction (p=0.059), the results slightly suggest that gender and note-taking as a preventative measure of phone use are dependent. Furthermore, females appear more likely than males to disregard their phone if taking notes. There were no other significant differences between genders in this part of the survey. Respondents who use a phone to access seminars are not included.

Table 2. Potential prevention

Female Students = 384			Male Students = 233		
Taking notes	245	63.8%	Taking notes	130	55.8%
Seminar has fast pace	222	57.8%	Seminar has fast pace	136	58.4%
Busy posting or speaking	200	52.1%	Busy posting or speaking	113	48.5%
Webcam shows face	116	30.2%	Webcam shows face	71	30.5%
All other responses	85	22.1%	All other responses	59	25.3%

In Table 3, activities in which students may be engaged on their phones during seminars are shown. Per a Chi-squared test of independence with Yates correction (p=0.071), the results slightly suggest that gender and the act of answering calls during a seminar are dependent. Furthermore, males appear more likely than females to answer their phone. Note that the numbers here only include students who do not use a smart phone to attend and who also keep their phones nearby.

Table 3. Admitted activities

Female Students = 351			Male Students = 209		
Look up topics discussed	160	45.6%	Look up topics discussed	103	49.3%
Might text	139	39.6%	Might text	87	41.6%
Might play games	38	10.8%	Might play games	20	9.6%
Might answer calls	17	4.8%	Might answer calls	19	9.1%

Except for men being more likely to answer phone calls and women being more likely to be prevented from using their phone by taking notes, the gender differences are minimal. Considering the sample size and the fact these respondents study at the same university, more research would need to be completed to determine if indeed there are gender differences in phubbing during online course seminars.

Of those who chose to identify their gender, 63% were female. This meets norms as defined by several recent sources such as Cooke (2024), who claims 62% of online students are female. Statistics gathered by the Sedona Sky company indicate that students between the ages of 25 and 44 make up 60% of online learners ("Online learning statistics," 2024), and the current survey's respondents who specified their age within that group constitute 59.2%. No differentiation was made between undergraduates and graduate students, and those who did not specify gender or age may have affected the percentages by a small margin. That being said, the gender and age demographics gathered by the survey indicate that the respondents roughly fit into current norms.

PHUBBING RISKS

Several risk areas are appropriate to explore in relation to phubbing, as they are all intertwined: learning issues, physical harm, mental health and relationships, and data security. These issues are not limited to the classroom itself; the constant use of a smart phone by the typical college student extends well outside the classroom perimeter.

Learning Issues

A study by Clayson and Haley (2013) determined that students who text in class tend to earn lower grades. Hashemi et al. (2024) counter that using a phone to access learning materials can be beneficial, but it still provides distraction from the class presentation and can be the cause of lower Grade Point Averages. Not surprisingly, immersion in the class proceedings and active participation enhances understanding of topics discussed (Shernoff et al., 2017). Phones ringing during class can disrupt the flow of information, and phubbing can also result in habitual tardiness; both facts have effects on grades (Uğur & Koç, 2015b). As mentioned previously, increased procrastination, decreased motivation, and sleep issues are additional risks to efficient learning.

The Norwegian government feels that smart phones and tablets in schools have led to a deterioration in reading abilities; this has led to nationwide policies in pre-college classrooms (Bowens, 2024). According to Mendoza et al. (2018), attention during a college class lecture tends to wane after about 10-15 minutes; taking short breaks may refresh attention, but if students access their phones during breaks, it may take some time to readjust to paying full attention again. Moreover, texting during class reduces notetaking by as much as 30% (Mendoza et al., 2018). Taking notes on an electronic device is possible but is also a "source of distraction," according to Flanigan et al. (2023, p. 59).

It must also be said that students who do not focus on learning course content may have difficulties in future jobs where that missed information is needed. Over twenty years ago, Davis et al. (2002) noted that students with internet addiction may be considered "cyberslackers" on the job or even lose out on job opportunities during the job search process.

Potential for Physical Harm

A concern that has been debunked is whether the radiation emitted by cellphones can cause cancer. According to the National Cancer Institute (2024), 5G phones may emit as much as 80 GHz of radiofrequency, but unlike x-rays and other such technologies, this is far too low to cause problems other than the generation of heat near the device.

Nonetheless, there are potential physical reactions. Phone addiction can lead to withdrawal symptoms if the device is taken away from the user (Lai et al. 2023). There is an identified phobia related to cell phone use called NOMOPHOBIA, an acronym created from "NO MObile PHone PhoBIA" (Bhattacharya et al. 2019). In this condition, the user has a fear of being without their mobile phone. They may already suffer from panic disorders and other anxieties, so the phone may be exacerbating other issues. Battacharya et al. (2019) report that the physical reactions to having their phone removed may include "respiratory alterations, trembling, perspiration, agitation, disorientation and tachycardia" (p. 1297), and diagnosis can be difficult because the symptoms may be related to pre-existing conditions or may be indicative of other issues. Harmony Healthcare IT provides interesting statistics gathered from a survey done in December of 2023 that corroborate these findings: half of U.S. adults know they are dependent on their phones, and almost three quarters feel anxiety if they are unsure of their phone's location ("Black mirror," 2024).

College students need sleep and the ability to concentrate on learning. An Afghan study proclaims that grades are negatively impacted by smart phone addiction (Hashemi et al., 2024) and this is echoed in a plethora of other studies, where phone use has also been connected to a sedentary lifestyle (Pirwani & Szabo, 2024).

Excessive talk time on a phone can increase headaches and a feeling of head pressure, difficulty in concentration, and a general tiredness and even insomnia (Gavrilas & Kotsis, 2023). Zhu et al. (2024) conducted a study in which they found that smart phone addiction in college students clearly leads to poor sleep quality, and that physical exercise can help mediate the effects of the addiction. Pirwani and Szabo (2024) took this further and examined 31 studies from a dozen countries, finding the same inverse relationship between phone addiction and physical activity. Escalera-Chávez et al. (2020) specify physical ailments attributed to the overuse of the mobile phone: "lack of operating memory, eye and hearing problems, headache and back pain, poor body posture, thumb injuries and carpal tunnel syndrome" (p. 547). Zhu et al. (2024) add neck pain to this list, Elamin et al. (2024) mention shoulder pains, and Bhattacharya et al. (2019) include pain in elbows and hands.

Walking while phubbing also has its dangers. While the number of pedestrian deaths steadily declined between 1980 and 2010, the following five years saw a significant rise (Wells et al., 2018). By 2011, the U.S. National Highway Traffic

Safety Administration noted this rise, which the contemporary Secretary of Transportation attributed to distractions while walking (Walker, 2013). Likewise, the U.S. Consumer Product Safety Commission reported a high number of emergency room visits resulting from pedestrian mobile device use, with far more than half of those injuries sustained by people under the age of 25 (Walker, 2013). Bosshart (2024) describes new research done by the University of British Columbia that indicates this alarming trend has not changed; pedestrians put themselves in danger due to intent focus on a phone. While it was noted that drivers may be more aware today when they see a pedestrian with a phone, the severity of pedestrian-vehicle encounters increases by 45% when a walker is phubbing (Bosshart, 2024). While it has been suggested that research be done to identify intersections where this occurs most frequently and then to design a sensor-based alert system (Bosshart, 2024), these systems are not yet in place.

The connection to the classroom here is that college students tend to spend a great deal of time walking on their campus, and many campuses are urban with clear roadway dangers. Wells et al. (2018) says that young men are more likely to wear headphones and women may walk while talking on their phone or texting; the technologies provide a clear distraction. Using Bluetooth technology by using earbuds to connect to one's phone might free the user's hands; however, Holz (2023) warns that the high decibel level often chosen for immersing in listening to favorite music or a phone call may result in hearing loss later in life.

Young adults use mobile technology more than other age groups, and Wells et al. (2018) claim "college-age young adults incur pedestrian injuries at a higher rate than any other age group" (p. 97). Students tend to check their phones multiple times every hour and have a tendency to walk to and from campus at night when visibility for drivers is lower. As might be suspected, students could also be walking while intoxicated (Wells et al., 2018).

Mental Health and Relationships

Elamin et al. (2024) reminds that students in colleges and universities face many obstacles and stressors such as trying to meet family expectations plus dealing with the unease that comes from grades, financial uncertainties, and finding a balance between work, life, and schooling. Their study of students in a Saudi Arabian university found that two-thirds of the students experienced depression, with half of those severe; medical students were among the most affected, with females more than males – and smart phones are part of the problem (Elamin et al., 2024).

Phubbing is connected to low self-esteem (Barbed-Castrejón et al., 2024) as well as an inability to control impulses, much like other addictive behaviors (Chotpitayasunondh & Douglas, 2016). A study from 2018 in India said that "associations between phubbing and depression and phubbing and distress were strongest" affectations (Al-Saggaf, 2022, p. 68). Nearly every source on this topic states that personal relationships can be severely affected, and mental health issues such as anxiety are heightened by phubbing. It is a form of addiction, along with gaming and social media addictions (Parmaksız, 2023). Ríos Ariza et al. (2021) mention that the person who calls, emails, or texts the student while in class may be expecting an immediate response; if the student does not respond right away, they may fear that the relationship will become strained.

A study of college students in Pakistan conducted by Arshad et al. (2024) found that phubbing and psychological distress have a direct relationship. This study notes lack of self-control and a fear of being left out of social circles as predictors of phubbing. The study included whether Emotional Intelligence was related to overt phone use. They applied several measurements, including the Wong and Law Emotional Intelligence Scale and The Depression, Anxiety, and Stress Scale 21. Not surprisingly, this study pointed to phubbing having the capability to cause problems with emotional stability, anxiety, depression, and can even lead to hostile behavior. Zhao et al. (2023) agrees that phubbing can lead to undue aggression.

A loss of trust and empathy is also noted (Chotpitayasunondh & Douglas, 2016), as is outright lying to others about the amount of phubbing (Tanhan et al., 2024). Sometimes, the disconnection from face-to-face conversation is intentional, and communication skills developed earlier in life are lost; this can be called "telecocooning" according to Chotpitayasunondh and Douglas (2016, p. 10). Mustawin et al. (2024) also point to overt social media use enabled by phubbing in developing narcissism, as the photos, "likes," and other activity there often work to validate their lives.

Arshad et al. (2024) further explains that a person's emotional intelligence can help to moderate effects:

> *The Stress and Coping Model suggests that individuals' perception of being ignored or devalued during phubbing can cause stress and negative emotions. However, those with high emotional intelligence can employ effective coping strategies, such as emotional regulation, to mitigate the impact of phubbing on psychological well-being. (Arshad et al., 2024, para. 4).*

There are some self-control qualities that can mitigate phubbing such as a high "cognitive ability," which is a person's adaptability to control responses to changes in environmental stimuli, and is facilitated by planning, memory, confidence, and responsibility (Tanhan et al., 2024). Furnham and Cheng (2024) cite cognitive ability and "self-efficacy," a person's perception of self-controlled success, as a forecast of their general well-being and as a predictor of academic success.

When Norwegian schools banned the use of electronic devices in schools, they found that there was a significant drop for both boys and girls in being bullied, and doctor visits for mental health decreased by nearly 60% for girls (Bowen, 2024). A middle school in Davenport, Iowa, instituted a cell phone lockup in the fall of 2024 and has already seen an 11% rise in classroom engagement (Houston & Kopatich, 2024). This of course is a younger demographic than college students, but the remarkable differences for youngsters can have a more lasting effect as they grow into adulthood.

Technology-based addictions (also called Digital Addictions) are increasingly a concern as humans find daily needs that are enhanced or made easier through technology. Cemiloglu et al. (2022) include Problematic Internet Use, Online Gaming Disorder, and Smart phone Addiction – some named with different monikers – as some of the major issues and mention mood changes and issues of withdrawal when devices are removed. Included is the danger to one's occupation due to the myriad of other harm that can get in the way of performing job duties well.

Mitigations for these changes in personality and physical ailments could include interventions (Cemiloglu et al., 2022). Sharma & Palanhichamy (2018) add help in the form of goal setting, auditory prompts such as alarms to stop the activity and do something else, visual prompts such as notes left near the offending device that remind the user of problematic overuse, and finding support through family or group settings.

Data Security

One risk not often considered is that college internet connections are not always secured (Carlton, 2021). Connecting to them may not require any login, so it appears easy and enticing. Hackers may actively seek unsecured wi-fi connections to snoop for devices in which security controls have not been set appropriately; they could send text messages to "phish" for personal data, introduce malware, or seek unsecured passwords (Bîzgă, 2023). Carlton (2021) adds that college students as a group are frequent targets because of their avid use of social media. These sites gather personal information that can assist hackers in guessing potential passwords and security question answers.

In 2018, security company Kaspersky stated that 52% of mobile phone users did not use password protection on their devices, yet 1/3 of consumers use a smart phone for banking activity ("Kaspersky Lab," 2018). Fortunately, Pew Research claimed in 2023 that this number was down to 16% (McClain et al., 2023). While the reduction in number looks good, this means that there are still many devices without security measures. The research indicates that 1/3 of people in the United States save passwords in their browser (McClain et al., 2023), which is possible in mobile phones as well and can lead to easy data theft. In addition to passcodes, biometrics such as fingers and face recognition are possible methods to keep strangers out of a phone that has been stolen or misplaced; turning off location tracking is also a safeguard ("10 ways to secure mobile devices," 2024).

College students also tend to be new to banking and may use their phone for financial data (Carlton, 2021). The fact that many people use the same password for multiple sites makes one single, successful hack possible for widespread damage to a person's identity (Bîzgă, 2023).

In 2021, U.S. consumers submitted 378,119 complaints to the Federal Trade Commission about suspicious and unwanted texts, and those who did not exercise caution lost $86 million from scams that originated in text messages via "smishing" (Olia, 2024). Carlton (2021) mentions that fake job advertisements, shopping sites, and dating sites especially target young adults, who may leave devices unattended or in a dorm room where others may try to gain access. "Stalkerware" may be uploaded to a device unbeknownst to the user; this would allow the hacker to monitor a victim's location and online activity (Bîzgă, 2023). A recent Polish study of students ages 18-27 found that as many as one-third do not change passwords when requested or only change them every few years, and a large majority tend to use the same password for multiple sites/logins (Zarębska et al., 2023). In addition, most college students do not have a credit score established yet, which is another reason why hackers may target them, as it would be easier to work with "clean" accounts (Vigderman, 2024). Identifying a phishing email or text message requires that the device user be focused on the nature of the request and use critical thinking to delete. When a student is phubbing in class – which means their attention is somewhat split while they "pretend" to listen to the instructor – the chance of missing these serious security issues increases.

As explained by Paavola (2023), Short Message Service (SMS) is the most common method of sending text messages, and is not "end-to-end" encrypted, wherein messages are encoded by the sender and decoded by the recipient. A hacker could intercept these kinds of messages. While a service provider can add encryption, the options are not very strong, so the recommendation is not to share truly sensitive data (Paavola, 2023). SMS messages can be intercepted by what is called "man-in-the-middle" cyberattacks wherein the victim is not aware that they are messaging a hacker, other kinds of attacks and "smishing," and can introduce viruses into a device (Kalvik, 2023). Other threats include AdWare, Trojans, which may specifically target mobile banking, and other exploits (Kivva, 2024).

SOLUTIONS

Using a smart phone to complete at least some coursework is not unusual. Bouchrika (2024) reports that two-thirds of college students in the United States complete at least a portion of their schoolwork via their phone, and indicated this was a significant shift away from more exclusive use of laptops in the past. The problem, then, is the non-course use of the phone when attention has been unduly split from focusing on course content. Finding means to control phubbing behavior in the classroom and educating students on appropriate phone use will be crucial in curbing this addiction and leading to better learning outcomes.

Policies and Enforcement

College faculty may be reluctant to set policies, fearing that "doing so will alienate students" (Flanigan et al. 2023, p. 60). Cell phone policies in pre-college classrooms can help students develop better habits before they get to college (Jones et al., 2020). Berman and Dubinski (2023) strongly suggest posting rules and referring to them frequently.

Jones et al. (2020) found that lenient policies may work better than highly restrictive ones and conducted a study at a traditional university in the United States to test their theory. In the lenient-policy class, students were told not to use their phone during class but there was no penalty for doing so. In the other class, phone use was also forbidden, but attendance points were deducted for infractions. The instructor for both classes was told to record infractions and found that it was difficult to do so and keep the lecture running. Both groups had observers in the back of the room to confirm correct counts. This study also found that strict policies force students to try to hide their phone usage and taking the phones away entirely for the hour would cause undue anxiety – although it may result in better grades (Jones et al., 2020).

Karlins (2022) asked student groups to envision their own solutions; some were impractical, but one group suggested positive reinforcement such as extra points to their group presentation grade if all members followed the mandate not to access their phones in class. When students are involved in decision-making of this sort, they may be more likely to follow the rules and "sometimes come up with decisions that are superior to ones envisioned by their managers/instructors" (Karlins, 2022, p. 506).

Since phubbing and other improper behavior affects the flow of the class, Blankman (2020) says to deal with this right away in the form of a kindly-worded reminder about classroom expectations, or after the event, talking individually to the student or emailing them. When students have distracted themselves and then ask questions that have already been answered, this is also disruptive. Instead of allowing constant interruptions, Blankman (2020) suggests a "parking lot" for online courses such as a spreadsheet or chat pod dedicated to questions. Berman and Dubinski (2023) suggest that students who model good behavior can be praised in front of others; this "labeled praise" helps others understand what is acceptable. In active-participation seminars, this might be demonstrated in a way such as, "Jorge, thanks for your attention here and adding ideas for us all to consider."

Classroom Setup and Student Participation

Jones et al. (2020) suggest other facets in the traditional classroom might affect phone use, such as seating arrangement and class size. While changing seating plans may not be possible in all classrooms, there are some concepts to consider. Seating students in rows limits distractions and may produce a quieter environment in which to learn; disruptions are less likely (Busch, n.d.). Will et al. (2020) point out that students who sit in the front of a class tend to have better motivation and earn better grades; Shernoff et al. (2017) adds that students in the back are more likely to use their phones. A horseshoe-shaped arrangement encourages more interaction, but at the same time this can invite disruption, too, since students can look at each other (Busch, n.d.). Another possibility is pairing students, which can mean a weak student gets help from a strong one; this could increase motivation for the student needing help (Busch, n.d.).

Related to this is the digital distraction of laptops. Classmates may be able to see the offender's screen and react to what is displayed; Flanigan et al. (2023) suggest that large-enrollment classrooms might designate a "zone" for such technology use, but those in the zone may end up being more of a collective distraction.

The online student survey results point to notetaking, a quick pace of content delivery, and being active in online chat or with speaking during seminars could prevent phubbing – and enhance learning. Instructors cannot always know who is phubbing during a lecture or seminar. In online seminars, webcams can point out transgressions, but not all courses use webcams, and some students find this an intrusion. Where webcams are used, however, head and eye movements can give strong clues.

In traditional classrooms, Harvard University suggests switching to group discussions and asking the class for examples regarding the content being taught to break the monotony of lectures, plus interjections of appropriate humor as a means to increase participation ("Devices in the classroom," n.d.). Ehrlick (2014) recommends the role of "facilitator" of student-active learning instead of lecturer.

Some institutions might consider special apps to control phubbing. This would be problematic, as phones contain a large amount of personal data, can track our location, and may include biometrics (Gubbi, 2023). Artificial Intelligence can be used to monitor online school platforms by identifying patterns and keywords related to behaviors such as cyberbullying; different AI programs could be deployed to check physical buildings for behaviors as well (Chen, 2024). While these features and programs may help with issues in the K-12 realm, such monitoring of adults in college may sow distrust and warrant privacy rights complaints.

Controlling Testing

Cheating during tests by use of a mobile device often goes undetected (Uğur & Koç, 2015b). This might be accomplished by searching the internet or by texting or sending pictures to someone who has already completed the test, or even a classmate currently also taking the test. Texting may be quite quick, making it difficult for the instructor to notice. Some of the texting during an exam may not even be related to the test itself (Uğur & Koç, 2015b). Smale et al. (2021) goes as far as calling this "e-cheating," and also mentions keeping notes on a phone for use during tests.

For in-person testing, using a phone to cheat would be obvious. A proctor can walk around the room to observe activity, phones could be checked at the door, and anyone caught looking at a phone in their lap would easily be called out. If phones are allowed as a proxy for calculators, controlling the potential for cheating may not be possible. Requiring an actual calculator would be prudent.

The online classroom provides different challenges, however, as students complete exams at home or work without a human to directly watch them. Fortunately, there are technical solutions such as the Respondus® Monitor system. First, the LockDown Browser prevents the tester from accessing other applications on their device while taking a test; to this browser a webcam may be added ("Respondus Monitor," n.d.). The test is then video recorded and catches events such as slouching that would result in the full face no longer being viewed, the test-taker's head tilting to check books or notes ("Enhanced flagging," n.d.), or to look at phones. Respondus allows the testing agency to set up the sensitivity level (relaxed, standard, or strict) so that open-book tests can be treated differently than those where the tester's focus should be only on the screen ("Sensitivity levels," n.d.).

Educating About Dangers

Both institutional involvement and individual or departmental faculty planning can help to educate students about phubbing dangers. Making use of various methods already in place such as classroom notices (whether online or on site), syllabuses, student newsletters and email, and orientation events or courses can include explanations of phubbing in relation to grades, physical and mental well-being, and data security. In addition, physical exercise can be encouraged to relieve some of the issues caused by smart phone addiction.

Education may also involve intervention. A "digital detox" may be necessary for users whose phubbing is deemed out of control. According to WebMD, overt phone use can result in neurological addiction due to an overproduction of dopamine (Sreenivas, 2023). Detoxification can include scheduling a phone break, becoming aware of emotional changes when using the phone (signaling the need to put it down), turning notifications off, and using apps that measure usage (Sreenivas, 2023). A study by Anandpara et al. (2024) adds determining purpose for device usage, limiting social media use, and compelling oneself to spend time doing physical activity and/or communing with nature. An intervention may be warranted, as the user may not be aware of the severity of their addiction.

Faculty Training

Instructor training would be useful. Many educators are required to take learning modules about disabilities and privacy laws, and while "centers for teaching excellence" offer help, Ladany (2024) suggests teaching teachers about *innovation*. This would include learning more about how technology can enhance their classrooms rather than being banned. Olaniyan and Uzorka (2024) state that this must start at the leadership level. Resources, infrastructure, and support must be made available, and this means that funding is also necessary (Olaniyan & Uzorka, 2024). Not every course subject can use the same technologies, but options and instructions on technology use can provide an instructor with possibilities for a more interactive learning experience while potentially reducing phubbing that distracts the student from learning.

CONCLUSION

Phubbing in the traditional college classroom has been determined by various studies to have a negative effect on learning, poses physical and mental health risks, and includes the potential for data security issues. The current study of the online classroom demonstrates that students are not always willing to put their phones aside, but they can be enticed to do so with changes in the instructor's classroom approach and policies.

The most prevalent methods by which online students believe they may be deterred from phubbing during class time are taking notes, being in a seminar that is adequately paced, and being actively engaged by speaking and typing in a chat pod. Additionally, female students were found to be more likely than males to find notetaking a successful deterrent. Notably, most students do not believe that webcams showing their faces would prevent non-course use of their phone during seminars.

Students felt that the most likely use of their phone during seminars to conduct non-course related activity was texting although they were also inclined to look up topics related to the course. Despite a small minority of respondents claiming to potentially answer calls during a seminar, males were found to be more likely to do so.

Thoughtful institutional policies, changes in how instructors manage their classrooms – whether on site or online – and educating about the problems brought about by phubbing can lessen the impact and pull students' attention back into a healthier, improved learning environment.

REFERENCES

Ahmed, A. H., Elemo, A. S., & Hamed, O. A. O. (2023, January/February). Smart phone addiction and phubbing in international students in Turkey: The moderating role of mindfulness. *Journal of College Student Development*, 64(1), 64–78. DOI: 10.1353/csd.2023.0002

Al-Saggaf, Y. (2022). *The psychology of phubbing*. Springer. DOI: 10.1007/978-981-19-7045-0

Anandpara, G., Kharaid, A., Vidja, P., Chauhan, Y., Mahajan, S., & Patel, J. (2024, April 22). A comprehensive review on digital detox: A newer health and wellness trend in the current era. *Cureus*, 16(4), e58719. DOI: 10.7759/cureus.58719 PMID: 38779255

Arshad, S., Sarwar, A., Ayub, S., & Qamar, N. (2024, April-June). The relationship of phubbing, emotional intelligence and psychological distress in youth. *Journal of Pakistan Psychiatric Society*, 21(2), 20–33. DOI: 10.63050/jpps.21.02.335

Barbed-Castrejón, N., Navaridas-Nalda, F., Mason, O., & Ortuño-Sierra, J. (2024, May 28). Prevalence of phubbing behaviour in school and university students in Spain. *Frontiers in Psychology*, 15, 1–8. DOI: 10.3389/fpsyg.2024.1396863 PMID: 38863670

Beresford Research. (2024). *Age range by generation*. https://www.beresfordresearch.com/age-range-by-generation

Berman, G., & Dubinski, A. (2023, October 30). *Managing students' behavior during remote or hybrid learning: Tips for teachers in an uncertain time.* Child Mind Institute. https://childmind.org/article/managing-students-behavior-during-remote-or-hybrid-learning

Bhattacharya, S., Bashar, M. A., Srivastava, A., & Singh, A. (2019, April). NOMOPHOBIA: NO MObile PHone PhoBIA. *Journal of Family Medicine and Primary Care*, 8(4), 1297–1300. DOI: 10.4103/jfmpc.jfmpc_71_19 PMID: 31143710

Bîzgă, A. (2023, October 27). *Smart phone security - the 10 biggest risks for your device.* Bitdefender. https://www.bitdefender.com/blog/hotforsecurity/smartphone-security-the-10-biggest-risks-for-your-device-2

Black mirror or black hole? American phone screen time statistics. (2024, January 8). Harmony Healthcare IT. https://www.harmonyhit.com/phone-screen-time-statistics

Blankman, R. (2020, November 19). *10 virtual classroom management strategies.* HMH. https://www.hmhco.com/blog/virtual-classroom-management-strategies-for-online-teaching

Bosshart, L. (2024, October 8). *Texting while walking puts pedestrians in danger: UBC study.* The University of British Columbia. https://news.ubc.ca/2024/10/texting-while-walking-puts-pedestrians-in-danger

Bouchrika, I. (2024, October 23). *50 online education statistics:2024data on higher learning & corporate training.* Research-dot-com. https://research.com/education/online-education-statistics#TOC1

Bowens, J. (2024, May 8). Norway's school cellphone ban boosts student grades and health: A model for US schools? *NBC News.*https://nbc24.com/news/nation-world/norways-school-cell-phone-ban-boosts-student-grades-health-model-us-schools-parents-children-development-reading-abilities-mental-health-human-contact-policy

Busch, B. (Ed.). (n.d.). *The psychology behind a great seating plan.* InnerDrive. https://www.innerdrive.co.uk/blog/psychology-of-seating-plans

Capilla Garrido, E., Cubo Delgado, S., & Gutiérrez Esteban, P. (2024, August). Phubbing and its impact on the individual's psychological well-being. *Acta Psychologica*, 248, 104388. DOI: 10.1016/j.actpsy.2024.104388 PMID: 38959636

Carlton, G. (2021, October 1). *Internet safety guide for college students.* ZDNet. https://www.zdnet.com/education/internet-safety-guide-for-college-students

Cebollero-Salina, A., Cano-Esoriaza, J., & Orejudo, S. (2022, January 15). Impact of online emotions and netiquette on phubbing from a gender perspective: Educational challenges. *Journal of New Approaches in Educational Research*, 11(1), 64–78. DOI: 10.7821/naer.2022.1.848

Cemiloglu, D., Almourad, M. B., McAlaney, J., & Ali, R. (2022, February). Combatting digital addiction: Current approaches and future directions. *Technology in Society*, 68, 101832. DOI: 10.1016/j.techsoc.2021.101832

Chen, D. (2024, May 20). *Classroom behavior tools improving student success.* Kangaroos.ai. https://www.kangaroos.ai/blog/ai-powered-classroom-behavior-tools-improving-student-success

Chen, S., Qiu, D., Li, X., & Zhao, Q. (2023, November). Discrepancies in adolescent–parent perceptions of parental phubbing and their relevance to adolescent smart phone dependence: The mediating role of parent–child relationship. *Behavioral Sciences, 13*(11), 888. DOI: 10.3390/bs13110888

Chotpitayasunondh, V., & Douglas, K. M. (2016, October). How "phubbing" becomes the norm: The antecedents and consequences of snubbing via smart phone. *Computers in Human Behavior*, 63, 9–18. DOI: 10.1016/j.chb.2016.05.018

Chuck, E. (2024, September 7). Lifeline or distraction? Georgia shooting reignites debate over cellphones in schools. *NBC News*.https://www.nbcnews.com/news/us-news/lifeline-distraction-shooting-reignites-debate-phones-schools-rcna169920

Clayson, D. E., & Haley, D. A. (2013, April). An introduction to multitasking and texting: Prevalence and impact on grades and GPA in marketing classes. *Journal of Marketing Education*, 35(1), 26–40. DOI: 10.1177/0273475312467339

Cooke, C. (2024, April 24). *Online learning statistics: The ultimate list of 2024*. Upskillwise. https://upskillwise.com/online-learning-statistics

Dai, B., Lin, Y., Lai, X., He, J., Du, M., Hou, X., & Zhang, G. (2024, January 19). The effects of self-esteem and parental phubbing on adolescent internet addiction and the moderating role of the classroom environment: A hierarchical linear model analysis. *BMC Psychiatry*, 24(1), 1–12. DOI: 10.1186/s12888-023-05489-y PMID: 38243210

Davis, R. A., Flett, G. L., & Besser, A. (2002). Validation of a new scale for measuring problematic internet use: Implications for pre-employment screening. *Cyberpsychology & Behavior*, 5(4), 331–345. DOI: 10.1089/109493102760275581 PMID: 12216698

Devices in the classroom. (n.d.). Harvard University Derek Bok Center for Teaching and Learning. https://bokcenter.harvard.edu/technology-and-student-distraction

Ding, Q., Dong, S., & Zhang, Y. (2023, February 6). Does parental phubbing aggravates adolescent sleep quality problems? *Frontiers in Psychology*, 14, 1–9. DOI: 10.3389/fpsyg.2023.1094488 PMID: 36814669

Ehrlick, S. P. (2014). Managing digital distraction: A pedagogical approach for dealing with wireless devices in the classroom. *Journal of Teacher Education*, 3(3), 207–216.

Elamin, N. O., Almasaad, J. M., Busaeed, R. B., Aljafari, D. A., & Khan, M. A. (2024, January-February). Smart phone addiction, stress, and depression among university students. *Clinical Epidemiology and Global Health*, 25, 101487. DOI: 10.1016/j.cegh.2023.101487

Enhanced flagging for Respondus Monitor. (n.d.) Respondus. https://web.respondus.com/enhanced-flagging-respondus-monitor

Escalera-Chávez, M. E., García-Santillán, A., & Molchanova, V. S. (2020). Phubbing behavior: Is there a gender difference in college students? *European Journal of Contemporary Education*, 9(3), 546–551. DOI: 10.13187/ejced.2020.3.546

Essel, H. B., Vlachopoulos, D., Tachie-Menson, A., Nunoo, F. K. N., & Johnson, E. E. (2022, April 4). Nomophobia among preservice teachers: A descriptive correlational study at Ghanaian colleges of education. *Education and Information Technologies*, 27(7), 9541–9561. DOI: 10.1007/s10639-022-11023-6 PMID: 35399783

Etchezahar, E., Durao, M., Albalá Genol, M. Á., & Muller, M. (2023, February). Validation of the perceived phubbing scale to the Argentine context. *Behavioral Sciences (Basel, Switzerland)*, 13(2), 192. DOI: 10.3390/bs13020192 PMID: 36829421

Flanigan, A. E., Brady, A. C., Dai, Y., & Ray, E. (2023, June). Managing student digital distraction in the college classroom: A self-determination theory perspective. *Educational Psychology Review*, 35(2), 1–19. DOI: 10.1007/s10648-023-09780-y

Furnham, A., & Cheng, H. (2023, July 31). The Big-Five personality factors, cognitive ability, health, and social-demographic indicators as independent predictors of self-efficacy: A longitudinal study. *Scandinavian Journal of Psychology*, 65(1), 53–60. DOI: 10.1111/sjop.12953 PMID: 37525487

Gavrilas, L., & Kotsis, K. T. (2023). Research for self-reported health problems after excessive talking time on mobile phones among university students. *Eurasian Journal of Science and Environmental Education*, 3(1), 7–15. DOI: 10.30935/ejsee/12958

Gubbi, M. (2023, November 22). *Big brother in your pocket: How AI is monitoring your phone use.* Medium. https://medium.com/@maheshgubbi/big-brother-in-your-pocket-how-ai-is-monitoring-your-phone-activity-9ee5cac70822

Harper, L. (n.d.). *How to stop phubbing.* Stop Phubbing & Start Connecting. https://www.stopphubbing.com/how-to-stop-phubbing

Hashemi, A., Noori, A. Q., Orfan, S. N., Akramy, S. A., & Rameli, M. R. M. (2024, April). Undergraduate students' perception of smart phone addiction and its impact on themselves and their academic performance: A case study. *Cogent Education*, 11(1), 2340845. DOI: 10.1080/2331186X.2024.2340845

Hernández Gracia, T. J., Avila, D. D., & Hernández Gracia, J. F. (2020, July 5). The phubbing: The interference in communication within the classroom. *The Journal of American Science*, 2(3), 12–17. DOI: 10.29057/jas.v2i3.5807

Holz, A. (2023, March 3). *Earbuds, hearing loss, and social isolation.* PluggedIn. https://www.pluggedin.com/blog/earbuds-hearing-loss-and-social-isolation

Houston, J., & Kopatich, K. (2024, September 24). Davenport schools says new cell phone policies are improving student engagement. *KWQC.*https://www.kwqc.com/2024/09/25/davenport-schools-says-new-cell-phone-policies-are-improving-student-engagement

Huey, M., & Giguere, D. (2023, June). The impact of smart phone use on course comprehension and psychological well-being in the college classroom. *Innovative Higher Education*, 48(3), 527–537. DOI: 10.1007/s10755-022-09638-1 PMID: 36440453

İliç, U. (2021, September). Online learning readiness, phubbing and sofalizing levels of pre-service teachers amidst pandemic. *Shanlax International Journal of Education*, 9(4), 1–12. DOI: 10.34293/education.v9i4.4027

İliç, U., & Tanyeri, T. (2021). Is phubbing a matter for educators: A case for pre-service and in-service teachers. *Malaysian Online Journal of Educational Technology*, 9(1), 70–79. DOI: 10.17220/mojet.2021.9.1.246

Jones, S. B., Aruguete, M. S., & Gretlein, R. (2020, January 1). Cell phone use policies in the college classroom: Do they work? *Transactions of the Missouri Academy of Science. Missouri Academy of Science*, 48(2020), 5–9. DOI: 10.30956/MAS-31R1

Kalvik, K. (2023, July 10). *Are text messages secure? 6 must-dos for safer texting*. Messente. https://messente.com/blog/are-text-messages-secure

Karlins, M. (2022). A student-friendly approach to eliminating cell phone usage in the college classroom. *College Teaching*, 70(4), 506–508. DOI: 10.1080/87567555.2021.1985423

Kaspersky Lab finds over half of consumers don't password-protect their mobile devices. (2018, June 28). Kaspersky. https://usa.kaspersky.com/about/press-releases/kaspersky-lab-finds-over-half-of-consumers-don-t-password-protect-their-mobile-devices

Kemp, S. (2024, July 31). *Digital 2024 July global statshot report.* Datareportal. https://datareportal.com/reports/digital-2024-july-global-statshot

Kivva, A. (2024, February 26). *The mobile malware threat landscape in 2023.* SecureList by Kaspersky. https://securelist.com/mobile-malware-report-2023/111964

Koc, T., & Caliskan, K. (2022, June 15). Phubbing phenomenon in educational environments: Examining the impact of supervisor phubbing on student outcomes. *Journal of Further and Higher Education*, 47(1), 15–30. DOI: 10.1080/0309877X.2022.2088270

Kurt, S. (2021, May 23). *McClelland's Three Needs Theory: Power, achievement, and affiliation.* Education Library. https://educationlibrary.org/mcclellands-three-needs-theory-power-achievement-and-affiliation

Ladany, N. (2024, September 24). Behind the curtain of higher education: Faculty aren't trained. *Forbes.*https://www.forbes.com/sites/nicholasladany/2024/09/24/behind-the-curtain-of-higher-education-faculty-arent-trained

Lai, X., Hu, C., Ying, L., Xu, H., Zhao, C., Yang, X., Yu, X., & Zhang, G. (2023, October). Risk and protective factors associated with smart phone addiction and phubbing behavior among college students in China. *Psychological Reports*, 126(5), 2172–2190. DOI: 10.1177/00332941221084905 PMID: 35412349

Lamb, A. (2023, March 13). *Do phones belong in schools?* The Harvard Gazette. https://news.harvard.edu/gazette/story/2023/03/experts-see-pros-and-cons-to-allowing-cellphones-in-class

Madore, K. P., & Wagner, A. D. (2019, April 1). Multicosts of multitasking. *Cerebrum: the Dana forum on brain science, 2019.* https://pmc.ncbi.nlm.nih.gov/articles/PMC7075496

Marshall, D. (2024, September 9). *When school policy limits access to assistive technology of students with disabilities.* Council of Parent Attorneys and Advises (COPAA). https://www.copaa.org/news/681778/When-School-Policy-Limits-Access-to-Assistive-Technology-for-Students-with-Disabilities.htm

Mathis, M. (2021, September 20). *My student recorded me without my permission! What to do if it happens to you.* We Are Teachers. https://www.weareteachers.com/students-recording-teachers-without-permission

McClain, C., Faverio, M., Anderson, M., & Park, E. (2023, October 18). How Americans protect their online data. In *How Americans view data privacy.* Pew Research Center. https://www.pewresearch.org/internet/2023/10/18/how-americans-protect-their-online-data

Medina-Morales, G. del C., & Villalón-Hernández, R. (2023, January-June). Study of the prevalence of phubbing in classrooms by apps' use. *Alteridad: Revista de Educación*, 18(1), 59–68. DOI: 10.17163/alt.v18n1.2023.05

Mendoza, J. S., Pody, B. C., Lee, S., Kim, M., & McDonough, I. M. (2018, September). The effect of cellphones on attention and learning: The influences of time, distraction, and nomophobia. *Computers in Human Behavior*, 86, 52–60. DOI: 10.1016/j.chb.2018.04.027

Moore, P. H., Head, J. D., & Griffin, R. B. (2017, Spring). Impeding students' efforts to cheat in online classes. *The Journal of Learning in Higher Education*, 13(1), 9–24.

Mustawin, S. S. N., Amri, A. K., Hakiky, H. R., Prihatiningsih, R., & Handiastuti, S. O. (2024). The relationship between narcissistic behavior and phubbing behavior among students who use social media during classroom learning conditions. *Proceedings Series of Educational Studies*, (5), 674–682.

National Cancer Institute at the National Institutes of Health. (2024, April 4). *Cell phones and cancer risk.*https://www.cancer.gov/about-cancer/causes-prevention/risk/radiation/cell-phones-fact-sheet

Nazir, T. (2020, June 15). Impact of classroom phubbing on teachers who face phubbing during lectures. *Psychology Research on Education and Social Sciences*, 1(1), 41–47.

Ohio Department of Education and Workforce. (n.d.) *Cell phones in Ohio schools.* https://education.ohio.gov/Topics/Student-Supports/School-Wellness/Cell-Phones-in-Ohio-Schools

Olaniyan, A. O., & Uzorka, A. (2024). Leadership's role in facilitating faculty professional development for technology integration. *International Journal of Technology in Education and Science*, 8(3), 470–480. DOI: 10.46328/ijtes.563

Olia, A. (2024, January 30). *Text message statistics & trends for 2024 [and beyond!].* Intradyn. https://www.intradyn.com/text-message-statistics-trends

Online learning statistics: The ultimate list in 2024. (2024, April 25). Sedona Sky. https://www.sedonasky.org/blog/online-learning-statistics

Paavola, A. (2023, April 25). *Is SMS encrypted and what should your business do about it.* Textline. https://www.textline.com/blog/is-sms-encrypted

Panda Security (2024, February 29). *10 ways to secure mobile devices* [2024]. https://www.pandasecurity.com/en/mediacenter/mobile-security-tips

Parmaksız, İ. (2023). The effect of phubbing, a behavioral problem, on academic procrastination: The mediating and moderating role of academic self-efficacy. *Psychology in the Schools*, 60(1), 105–121. DOI: 10.1002/pits.22765

Pirwani, N., & Szabo, A. (2024, June). Could physical activity alleviate smart phone addiction in university students? A systematic literature review. *Preventive Medicine Reports*, 42, 102744. DOI: 10.1016/j.pmedr.2024.102744 PMID: 38707250

Republic of the Philippines Department of Education. (2003, November 20). *DO 83, s. 2003: Prohibiting students of elementary and secondary schools from using cellular phones and pagers during class hours.* https://www.deped.gov.ph/2003/11/20/do-83-s-2003-reiteration-to-decs-orders-nos-70-s-1999-and-26-s-2000-prohibiting-students-of-elementary-and-secondary-schools-from-using-cellular-phones-and-pagers-during-class-hours

Respondus Monitor. (n.d.). Respondus. https://web.respondus.com/he/monitor

Ríos Ariza, J. M., Matas-Terrón, A., Rumiche Chávarry, R. P., & Chunga Chinguel, G. R. (2021, July 15). Scale for measuring phubbing in Peruvian university students: Adaptation, validation and results of its application. *Journal of New Approaches in Educational Research*, 10(2), 175–189. DOI: 10.7821/naer.2021.7.606

Ryan, R. M., & Deci, E. L. (2020, April). Intrinsic and extrinsic motivation from a self-determination theory perspective: Definitions, theory, practices, and future directions. *Contemporary Educational Psychology*, 61, 101860. DOI: 10.1016/j.cedpsych.2020.101860

Santos, A. de A., Torres, M. de S., dos Santos, L. F. N., & Matins, H. de A. (2023). Cultural adaptation and psychometric evidence of the phubbing scale. *Psychological Evaluation, 33,* e3332. https://doi.org/DOI: 10.1590/1982-4327e3332

Sensitivity levels in Respondus Monitor. (n.d.). Respondus. https://web.respondus.com/sensitivity-levels-in-respondus-monitor

Sharma, M. K., & Palanhichamy, T. S. (2018, February). Psychosocial interventions for technological addictions. *Indian Journal of Psychiatry*, 60(8, Suppl 4), 5541–5545. DOI: 10.4103/psychiatry.IndianJPsychiatry_40_18 PMID: 29540928

Shernoff, D. J., Sannella, A. J., Schorr, R. Y., Sanchez-Wall, L., Ruzek, E. A., Sinha, S., & Bressler, D. M. (2017). (2017, April. Separate worlds: The influence of seating location on student engagement, classroom experience, and performance in the large university lecture hall. *Journal of Environmental Psychology*, 49, 55–64. DOI: 10.1016/j.jenvp.2016.12.002

Smale, W. T., Hutcheson, R., & Russo, C. J. (2021). Cell phones, student rights, and school safety: Finding the right balance. *Canadian Journal of Educational Administration and Policy*, (195), 49–64. DOI: 10.7202/1075672ar

Sreenivas, S. (2023, May 5). *Digital detox: What to know.* WebMD. https://www.webmd.com/balance/what-is-digital-detox

Tanhan, F., Özok, H. İ., Kaya, A., & Yıldırım, M. (2024, January). Mediating and moderating effects of cognitive flexibility in the relationship between social media addiction and phubbing. *Current Psychology (New Brunswick, N.J.)*, 43(1), 192–203. DOI: 10.1007/s12144-023-04242-8 PMID: 36713623

Uğur, N. G., & Koç, T. (2015a, December). Mobile phones as distracting tools in the classroom: College students perspective. *Alphanumeric Journal*, 3(2), 57–64. DOI: 10.17093/aj.2015.3.2.5000145549

Uğur, N. G., & Koç, T. (2015b, July 3). Time for digital detox: Misuse of mobile technology and phubbing. *Procedia: Social and Behavioral Sciences*, 195, 1022–1031. DOI: 10.1016/j.sbspro.2015.06.491

Using smartphones in the classroom. (n.d.). Huddlecam. https://huddlecamhd.com/using-smartphones-in-the-classroom

Vigderman, A. (21024, July 24). *The college students guide to data protection & cybersecurity.* Security. https://www.security.org/resources/college-guide-data-cyber-protection

Walker, T. (2013, August 6). Phubbing can be phatal: Staying glued to your smart phone in public isn't just rude, it can also get you killed. *The Independent.*https://www.independent.co.uk/tech/phubbing-can-be-phatal-staying-glued-to-your-smartphone-in-public-isn-t-just-rude-it-can-also-get-you-killed-8749090.html

Wang, X., Wang, W., Qiao, Y., Gao, L., Yang, J., & Wang, P. (2022). Parental phubbing and adolescents' cyberbullying perpetration: A moderated mediation model of moral disengagement and online disinhibition. *Journal of Interpersonal Violence*, 37(7/8), NP5344–NP5366. DOI: 10.1177/0886260520961877 PMID: 32976063

Wells, H. L., McClure, L. A., Porter, B. E., & Schwebel, D. C. (2018, February). Distracted pedestrian behavior on two urban college campuses. *Journal of Community Health*, 43(1), 96–102. DOI: 10.1007/s10900-017-0392-x PMID: 28695427

Will, P., Bischof, W. F., & Kingstone, A. (2020, August 5). The impact of classroom seating location and computer use on student academic performance. *PLoS One*, 15(8), e0236131. DOI: 10.1371/journal.pone.0236131 PMID: 32756560

Williams, L., & Fudge, T. P. (2020). Pedagogy in a potentially hostile online environment. In Setzekorn, K., Patnayakuni, N., & Burton, T. (Eds.), *Socioeconomics, diversity, and the politics of online education* (pp. 35–49). IGI Global. DOI: 10.4018/978-1-7998-3583-7.ch003

Xu, X.-P., Liu, Q.-Q., Li, Z.-H., & Yang, W.-X. (2022, August 17). The mediating role of loneliness and the moderating role of gender between peer phubbing and adolescent mobile social media addiction. *International Journal of Environmental Research and Public Health*, 19(16), 10176. DOI: 10.3390/ijerph191610176 PMID: 36011810

Zarębska, J., Howis, N., & Barska, M. (2023). Research on students' perception of information technology security: A new era of threats. *Scientific Papers of Silesian University of Technology. Organization & Management / Zeszyty Naukowe Politechniki Slaskiej.Seria Organizacji i Zarzadzanie*, 2023(170), 709–721. DOI: 10.29119/1641-3466.2023.170.43

Zhao, J., Guo, Z., Shi, H., Yu, M., Jiao, L., & Xu, Y. (2023, June). The relationship between parental phubbing and interpersonal aggression in adolescents: The role of rejection sensitivity and school climate. *Journal of Interpersonal Violence*, 38(11/12), 7630–7655. DOI: 10.1177/08862605221145722 PMID: 36632725

Zhu, W., Liu, J., Lou, F., Mu, F., & Li, B. (2024, July 26). Influence of smart phone addiction on sleep quality of college students: The regulatory effect of physical exercise behavior. *PLoS One*, 19(7), e0307162. DOI: 10.1371/journal.pone.0307162 PMID: 39058670

KEY TERMS AND DEFINITIONS

Centers for Teaching and Learning: A college or university department dedicated to providing academic and related support to faculty.

Data Security: Protection of personally identifiable information (PII) such as physical location, banking details, login credentials, employee records, etc.

Digital Detoxification (Detox): A purposeful reduction in the use of electronic devices; may involve intervention.

Digital Distraction: The effect of intense focus on electronic devices, causing interference in jobs, relationships, and other aspects of life.

K-12 Classroom: Pre-college schooling; specifically, Kindergarten through 12th grade.

Nomophobia: A phone user's fear of not having their phone nearby; a kind of separation anxiety.

Phubbing: A portmanteau of "phone" and "snubbing" that describes a phone user's intense focus on their phone rather than people, things, or activity around them.

Smartphone: A hand-held mobile device capable of accessing the internet and enabling text messaging, phone calls, and other digital activity.

Webinar: A "live" online session or meeting held in an environment such as Zoom; also called seminar.

Chapter 16
The Deterioration and Transformation of Personal Connection in the Digital Era: An Empirical Investigation of Social Relationships in the Technological Age

Hemlata Parmar
https://orcid.org/0009-0009-1438-5427
Manipal University Jaipur, India

Utsav Krishan Murari
https://orcid.org/0009-0007-1606-6775
Sharda University, India

Ruchi Goel
https://orcid.org/0009-0004-8463-5106
Guru Gobind Singh Indraprastha University, India

ABSTRACT

The digital era has radically transformed personal ties due to the widespread impact of technology. This study analyses the evolution of interpersonal relationships via digital communication platforms, focusing on the effects of social media, virtual communities, and messaging programs on emotional closeness, social intimacy, and human contact. The research examines how the convenience of digital communication simultaneously promotes and weakens personal connections, utilising

DOI: 10.4018/979-8-3693-8804-4.ch016

both quantitative and qualitative investigations. Although digital platforms offer unparalleled prospects for global communication, they may concurrently reduce the quality of in-person relationships and the depth of emotional engagement. This chapter examines the paradox of connection in the digital era by reviewing current literature and empirical investigations. It investigates ways to cultivate meaningful personal interactions in a technology-dominated context.

1. INTRODUCTION

Background of the Digital Age

The modern age, or the Information Age, is epochal in the annals of history and is best defined by accelerated growth in Information and Communication Technology (ICTs) that has revolutionised virtually all areas of life. Over the past three decades, specifically from the late 20th century, the development of the internet, cell phones, and social media has dramatically affected human relations. What has been considered private and close, for example, letters or extended conversations on the phone, became digital communication over large distances. The social networking sites Facebook, WhatsApp, Instagram, and Twitter have provided prominent platforms for social connections across the globe. (Castells, 2010).

This means that while there is increased interaction, it is not planned interaction. The ordinary means of communication were slow, demanding, and conscious, automatically creating more emotional bonds and personal relationships (Negroponte, 1996). However, these processes have been altered thanks to digital communication to involve quick and often shallow interactions, emphasising the fast delivery of information. It is now possible to type a message, share pictures, or even use video calls to speak to someone on the other side. However, as a result, we lack emotions and honest communication (Turkle, 2015).

1.1 Cross-Cultural Variations in Digital Communication

The use and perception of digital communication tools are relative to culture. Platform-based social media in China is also unique because WeChat acts as a messaging app and a financial and business tool. WeChat combines communication with friends and family, as well as business and work contacts, into one application, which has become an essential tool for many. On the other hand, Western countries may combine social networks to get in touch with friends and family through Facebook and use WhatsApp for messaging and LinkedIn for business relations. This is because the management of relationships is virile and differently influenced by culture in the digital age.

In India, for example, applications like WhatsApp have integrated into communication within families and communities as the primary source of contact for various groups, from the nuclear family to the large joint families spread across the country. WhatsApp is informal, and communication is almost ongoing due to the messaging frequency. However, this is where the similarities end, and a more critical approach is needed; as with other cultures, this can amount to a shallower involvement that is not based on developing close relationships (Rainie & Wellman, 2012).

1.2 Emerging Technologies and Their Impact on Relationships

New technologies like AR, VR, and AI can revolutionise human interactions, rather than just social media and messaging currently in vogue. The social interaction that AI-based chatbots like Replika offer has implications for human-human interaction's future. Similarly, other virtual reality applications also create spaces through which people can engage in social interactions that closely resemble the physical world interactions through Altspace VR and VRChat.

These new technologies have their merits and demerits. On the one hand, by providing the ability to exchange virtual locations and actual experiences in their interaction, they can help build stronger bonds. However, they are likely to push people even more into the digital space, where social touch and closeness are not easily achieved.

1.3 Theoretical Frameworks and Emerging Technologies

As a result of technological advancement in the digital era, it is essential to review the current theoretical systems and investigate the new technologies in interpersonal communication.

Social Exchange Theory

Social exchange Theory, developed by George Homans in 1958, can be used to explain interpersonal relationships. It argues that people use cost-benefit analysis to establish and maintain their relationships with others because they want to gain as much as possible and lose as little as possible. This theory has many implications because, in the current generation, people interact with each other, especially on social media sites like Facebook and Instagram, and the interactions are primarily business-like. People use social capital – likes, comments, and shares to maintain communication.

According to Ellison, Vitak, Gray, and Lampe (2014), such transactions are rewarding, though superficial and do not form the basis of good social relationships. Similarly, Baker and White (2011) state that since face-to-face interaction entails a mutual giving and receiving of messages, current CMC is characterised by one-way, superficial communication meant for social peacekeeping.

Attachment Theory

Adult love relationships are best described by Attachment Theory, developed by John Bowlby in 1969. Thanks to modern technologies, messaging applications and social media networks are more available than ever before, and thus, new dependencies have emerged. This results in users wanting and expecting quick feedback, causing anxious attachment patterns to form (Clayton et al., 2015). This immediate feedback loop can only intensify feelings of vulnerability, especially when online interactions do not meet emotional needs. Kuss and Griffiths (2017) also expounded on how this reliance on digital technologies erodes one's emotional strength and intimacy.

Media Multiplexity Theory

Caroline Haythornthwaite's Media Multiplexity Theory (2005) focuses on the multiplicity of the channels used for communication in relationships. They are usually maintained across several contact points, including personal, telephonic and electronic communication. On the other hand, weak ties use fewer channels to access information. This theory is efficient in the present era of communication technologies because different communication media present various degrees of emotional interactivity. According to Haythornthwaite's research, strong ties are supported by multiple channels, while weak ties exist on deeper levels but through digital communication.

Social Capital Theory

According to Robert Putnam's (2000) Social Capital Theory, there is a difference between bonding social capital, defined as dense, emotionally close communities and bridging social capital, which depicts more distant, structural links. Although digital platforms create large networks and increase the bridging social capital, they are ineffective in enhancing bonding social capital for emotional closeness. Steinfield, Ellison, and Lampe (2008) note that, although such sites as Facebook facilitate the maintenance of the acquaintance relationship that is relatively weak and infrequently backed by strong ties, these platforms do not foster and sustain the kinds of close relationships that afford well-being.

Hyperpersonal Model

Joseph Walther's (1996) Hyperpersonal Model proposes that CMC can sometimes be more intimate than FTIC. This is so because users are selective of what they post and the time they take to write their responses, as opposed to face-to-face interactions. However, in their study, Zhao, Grasmuck and Martin have some reservations about these assumptions, pointing out that the so-called 'who I am' in the 'second life' is often fake and, therefore, causes disappointments in online relations.

Social Presence Theory

Social Presence Theory was proposed by Short, Williams and Christie (1976), which focuses on the effect of a medium in facilitating non-verbal communication on the quality of communication. Using digital tools with a high social presence, such as video calls, is more effective than text-based tools. Biocca, Harms, and Burgoon (2003) have stated that since low-social-presence communication environments, like emails or instant messaging, are prevalent in today's society; they create emotional flattened, which means that nonverbal cues fade away, despite the high density of communication.

New Technologies and Digital Change

The use of new technologies in Artificial Intelligence (AI) and Virtual Reality (VR) has changed the concept of digital intimacy and interpersonal interaction. There are AI-based applications where users can have meaningful conversations with Replika and get companionship and emotional support. Despite these technologies potentially closing the emotional disparities, their role in authentic relationships is questionable. Walther (1996) describes how these tools can help build relationships with others and yet wonders about the emotionality of the communication.

Some such platforms include VRChat, and they develop environments that are real-life-like as far as interactions are concerned to provide high levels of social presence. Nonetheless, Biocca, Harms, and Burgoon (2003) posit that VR increases levels of emotional engagement, which may lead to user's disconnection from real-world relations, which is a source of concern on the social impacts of the technology.

Overstimulation and the Burnout of Emotions

Digital technologies afford a constant connection, which in turn causes digital fatigue and emotional exhaustion. In their study conducted in 2016, Roberts and David found that more use of digital media leads to stress and fatigue. This is commonly called 'techno-stress' and captures the psychological pressure placed on individuals by the constant use of technology in communication.

1.4 Problem Statement

Digital tools have transformed communication, but they have also brought about a paradox: Most people today feel part of the larger society through social networks, yet they are lonely socially and emotionally. Digital communication provides a new means of communication, but here, the emotional intimacy of communication is lacking. This research also found that the quality of relationships is often derogated because of the convenience of communication through the Internet, especially in terms of social contact and intimacy. This study is based on the central research question of how and why digital communication has enhanced and, at the same time, eroded human relationships and the space that people share.

1.5 Research Objectives

This study aims to analyse the transformation of personal relationships in the context of the digital era, focusing on three primary objectives:

1. To identify the impact of digital communication applications like social media and instant messaging on affectional and social closeness.
2. To analyse digital communication's positive and negative effects on interpersonal communication, this paper will discuss the benefits of increased connection between people and the consequences of reduced intimacy.
3. Identify ways to create active and vibrant emotional relationships, especially in a technology-oriented society.

1.6 Significance of the Study

It is important, therefore, to gain knowledge on the effects of digital communication on relationships for both the academician and the layman. This paper aims to identify the implications of the increased use of digital platforms in human interaction. This research thus offers potential guidelines for developing satisfying close relationships in an age of digital communication.

2. REVIEW OF LITERATURE

Sherry Turkle's (2015) Reclaiming Conversation explores how technology has made conversation a thing of the past. She notes that even though such devices make people connect virtually, it is evident that these devices lead to poor-quality face-to-face communication. According to Turkle in her ethnographic study of the revamped culture of communication, the routine use of smartphones and social networks has produced what she calls a 'culture of 'continuous partial engagement' in which people are physically present but mentally and emotionally detached, resulting in a decline on interpersonal connections.

In this work, Ellison, Vitak, Gray, and Lampe (2014) have focused on how social networking sites such as Facebook affect the maintenance of interpersonal relationships. Their work demonstrates that social media is excellent for creating and maintaining weak ties, which are not usually associated with strong emotional bonds. The authors consider the question of whether the social capital that is made by online platforms leads to shallow interaction.

Walther (2011) examines the differences between computer-mediated communication (CMC) and in-person communication in developing close relationships. He notes that although CMC enables connectedness across distances, it cannot reproduce the full spectrum of interactional elements available in face-to-face communication, including the ability to share gestures, which are critical for developing trust and interpersonal understanding.

McDaniel and Coyne (2016) define the term technoscience to explain the adverse effects of technology on couple and family relationships. Their research shows how often interruptions from electronic gadgets during the time spent together negatively affect the closeness of relationships and reduce the partners' satisfaction.

In her book "It is Complicated: The Social Lives of Networked Teenagers", Boyd (2014) breaks down the various aspects of social networking. This, she says, is because digital platforms create new ways of relationship building, but because of the aspect of anonymity and the presentation of curated selves, trust is often compromised. She has concluded that people can be confused about real contacts in the space where everything can be staged.

Prensky (2010) explains the difference between the generations in the use of digital technologies by introducing the terms "digital natives" and "digital immigrants". He also points out that such variations lead to various forms of misunderstanding, especially within the family setting where the elderly still in society may find it challenging to cope with the modern world-oriented technologies being embraced by young people.

Keles, McCrae, and Grealish (2020) conducted a meta-synthesis of research investigating the relationship between social media utilisation and loneliness and isolation. They conclude that users of social media, especially the youths, are at high risk of psychological disorders as a result of social comparison and pressure to present a particular image online.

Golden (2006) reviews the effects of telework and digital collaboration technologies on the working environment. He also described how a virtual working environment erodes the existing relationships between team members, leading to low morale and a lack of trust among team members. He opines that encouraging virtual social interactions may help reduce these impacts.

Leidner and Tona (2021) describe how artificial intelligence, including chatbots, is gradually stepping in for people in interaction roles, including customer service. Despite these advancements, the authors worry about reconsidering human compassion and relationships and the possibility of reinforcement learning in AI systems.

Chib, Malik, Aricat, and Kadir (2013) investigate the positive impact of digital technologies on promoting cultural interactions and the negative effect of cultural globalisation. Their study showed how Western digital platforms reign over interactions globally while erasing native practices and forms of production.

In their study, Mazmanian, Orlikowski, and Yates (2013) examine the challenges of what they refer to as 'the new workplace reality of 'being always on''. They found that the pressure to be on call always causes stress and tension in interpersonal relationships because people fail to draw a line between the virtual and the real world.

Zepke and Leach (2010) attempt to explain how certain aspects of social media applications, namely likes and streaks, affect social conduct. They posit that these elements cause compulsive use of the applications to seek social acceptance at the cost of genuine interpersonal relationships, which negatively affects users' mental health.

Twenge and colleagues (2018) look at how screen time has risen with the incidence rates of mental health problems in adolescents. According to their research, the constant feed of the life curated on social media and cyberbullying worsens the state of anxiety and depression and further compels isolation and weakening of interpersonal relationships.

According to Van Deursen and Van Dijk (2014), digital literacy is significant in fostering good relationships in the digital age. Those who comprehend online communication platforms will be better positioned to manage the issues encountered while connecting, thus developing a closer relationship than those who do not comprehend digital platforms.

In her book Personal Connections in the Digital Age, Baym (2015) examines the changes in social etiquette in the digital age. She also elaborates on the fact that technology has changed the rules of engagement in relations, such as etiquette and digital communication. She discusses issues of trust and accountability in an online relationship.

3. METHODOLOGY

The current work's research design uses qualitative and quantitative methods to analyse the effects of digital communication on relationships. This approach enables the study to attend to quantitative patterns, though it also provides a detailed analysis of the subjective aspects of digital communication. The quantitative phase includes a self-complete questionnaire distributed to 500 participants from a broad demographic background. These 120 participants, ranging in age from 18 to 70 years and including both men and women, single and partnered, and from various locations, completed measures of their digital communication behaviours, relationship satisfaction, and emotional intimacy. Questions were created to ascertain how often participants used applications like WhatsApp, Facebook, and Instagram, as well as the emotional and relational state of the conversations. The qualitative phase of this study builds on this by implementing semi-structured interviews with 50 participants randomly chosen from the survey participants. The interviews focused on the emotional side of digital communication, the problems of maintaining strong relationships with the help of digital media, and the differences with traditional communication. In order to understand the patterns of the interview data, the study used Thematic Analysis to determine the recurring patterns and themes. In the current study, purposive sampling was employed to select the participants to achieve variability and see the need to involve people within the working age bracket of 18-60 years from Noida and its peripheral business districts. Even though this sampling strategy provided a broader vision of the study, there was a problem of subjectivity because the obtained data were based on participants' self-identification, which can differ from the actual situation. To address such a problem, the survey instrument had closed-ended and open-ended questions, and the interviews were audio recorded and transcribed. Data was analysed with descriptive and correlational statistics to compare communication frequencies, emotional intimacy levels and overall relational satisfaction. The qualitative data collected in this study were analysed for themes such as emotional aridity, the appearance of closeness, and the performativity of social media. In combination, these approaches give a comprehensive understanding of digital communication's effects and disadvantages.

4. DATA ANALYSIS

The data analysis is categorised into Quantitative analysis from the survey and qualitative analysis from the interviews. Each approach provides its perspective on how computer-mediated communication influences personal relationships. This paper provides a detailed background on the two data analysis methods discussed.

4.1 Quantitative Data Analysis: Integrated Explanation

Data analysis techniques employed for this study included descriptive statistics, correlation analysis and regression analysis to examine the proposition of digital communication and relationship satisfaction. Demographic analysis revealed important characteristics, including the young age of participants, with 65% from 18 to 40 years old, and a nearly equal gender distribution, 48% men and 52% women, with 4% Non-binary or other, thus making the sample diverse and inclusive (McDaniel & Coyne, 2016). Half of the sample was from urban areas, 30% comprised suburban areas, and the remaining 20% were from rural areas, showing that the sample was diverse in geographic location. Regarding relational status, 40% of the participants were single, 30% were married, and the remaining 30% included those in long-distance relationships or other relationships (Ellison et al., 2014). The participants said they used digital communication often, with 70% of them using WhatsApp (80%), Facebook (65%), and Instagram (50%) daily. In comparison, 40% used video conferencing, showing the importance of digital tools in our daily lives, persona and working (Walther, 2011). The emotional intensity of the digital interactions was 3.2 on the Likert scale, which was lower than the 4.5 in the face-to-face interactions; this shows that though people are connected via digital technologies, they feel less emotionally satisfied, and there is a variation in the experience of individual users (Turkle, 2015). A correlational analysis showed that there was a moderate positive relationship between the frequency of the use of digital communication in the relationships and relationship satisfaction ($r = 0.45, p < 0.01$); a higher correlation was established between the frequency of the use of digital communication and relationship satisfaction among long-distance relationships ($r = 0.60, p < 0.01$), thus underlining the importance of the use of digital communication in close relationships especially when the partners are separated geographically (Keles et al., 2020). The analysis of regression revealed that the frequency of digital communication explains 20% of the variance in relationship satisfaction, $F(1, 498) = 12.34, p < 0.01$, which means that while the frequency of interactions is important to satisfaction, there are many other factors, including the quality of communication and the history of the relationship (Leidner & Tona, 2021). These findings help explain the complex effects of digital communication on personal relationships and signal that this research area requires further investigation of qualitative factors.

Table 1. Descriptive statistics overview

S.No.	Characteristic	Category	Percentage	Notes
1.	Age	18-25	40%	Dominant age group
2.	Age	26-40	25%	Second most dominant
3.	Age	41-60	20%	Older participants
4.	Age	60+	15%	Small representation
5.	Gender	Male	48%	Balanced distribution
6.	Gender	Female	48%	Balanced distribution
7.	Gender	Non-binary/Other	4%	Inclusive representation
8.	Location	Urban	50%	Dominant region
9.	Location	Suburban	30%	Moderate representation
10.	Location	Rural	20%	Least represented
11.	Relationship Status	Single	40%	Largest group
12.	Relationship Status	Married	30%	Second largest group
13.	Relationship Status	Long-distance	15%	Small representation
14.	Relationship Status	Other	15%	Equal to long-distance

4.2 Qualitative Data Analysis: Integrated Elaboration

The data collected was in the form of interviews with participants, and the analysis undertaken was thematic to understand participants' experiences with digital communication better. The analysis followed a three-stage process: The above process involved in this study includes familiarization, coding and theme development. During the focused coding, the interview data was read and analyzed to determine the major concepts, terms, and patterns that emerged in the data. Open coding made it possible to code the data into emotional engagement, satisfaction, difficulties concerning digital communication, and the comparison with FTF communication (Braun & Clarke, 2006).

From this, the following major themes were identified to detail the participants' experiences further. The first theme, "Emotional Flattening in Digital Communication," focused on participants' views that interactions in the digital context seemed to be deprived of the depth of embodied communication. Nonetheless, most respondents mentioned that the lack of important paralinguistic cues, including body language and eye contact, greatly influenced emotional closeness. As one of the participants mentioned, "I think that despite the video conference, it still lacks something. 'You cannot have the kind of bond you would have when you are in the same room with someone. This corresponds with Walther (2011), who pointed out that digital communication, which mediates distance and allows people to connect, fails to recreate the richness of live, physical interaction fully.

The second theme identified is "The Illusion of Intimacy", and it is aligned with participants' perception of frequent communication but not very close relationships. Some patients explained their interactions as more of a form of 'face-work' than genuine relationships. One of the participants stated, "We text all the time, but that is still not the same as what we do when we get a chance to meet face to face." It is almost like we are pretending to be close, yet we are not." These experiences are similar to Turkle's (2015) observation of how people use technology, specifically text and social media, to pretend that they are connected while, in reality, they are not.

The third theme, 'Performative Nature of Social Media,' was about the performative nature of social media and its service in catalyzing relations that were felt on the surface and performative. They also said these platforms encourage people to show selective versions of their lives, alienating them emotionally. One participant said, 'People perform their lives on Instagram or Facebook.' "I cannot talk to my friends about what is happening; it does not feel real." This is remarkably akin to Ellison et al. (2014), who found social media performed, wherein social media interactions can change communication and connection to be more performative instead.

The fourth theme, 'Digital Communication as a lifeline for long-distance relationships,' showed that digital communication is essential to people in long-distance relationships. They acknowledged the importance of video calls and messaging to keep the connection but felt disconnected even though they were constantly messaging. Another explained that "without video calls, we would not be together". However, even after we have talked, sometimes I still feel lonely." Keles et al. (2020) agree with this sentiment, suggesting that digital tools were crucial in maintaining long-distance relationships but could not mimic the emotional benefits of in-person interactions.

This interpretation emphasized a tension between the advantages of digital communication (permissionless), convenience, and accessibility versus the emotional limits it entailed. The ability to keep in touch from around the world is something that participants appreciated, but a lot of them felt that digital interactions were too shallow emotionally. Social media is criticized as fostering superficial relationships, and even though video calls are not a replacement for the emotional depth of face-to-face encounters, digital communication has a complex nature (Turkle & Walther, 2015).

When synthesizing the qualitative findings with the quantitative data, the study found that frequent digital communication was positively associated with relationship satisfaction but did not fully translate feelings of the emotional richness of the communication. The interviews indicate emotional flattening and an illusion of intimacy, and these findings frame the moderate positive correlation ($r = 0.45$, $p < 0.01$) found in the quantitative analysis, which argues that regularly feeling 'online' may not be enough to create deep emotional connections. Further analysis was done on this in the form of a qualitative analysis that shed light on the challenges and limitations of digital communication in maintaining emotional closeness. This mixed methods approach adds a layer of nuance to the discussion, demonstrating that although digital communication can facilitate more frequent and frequent communications, it cannot account for the emotional satisfaction that in-person relationships bring (Braun & Clarke, 2006; Ellison et al., 2014).

Table 2. Thematic analysis of digital communication: Key findings

S.No.	Theme	Description	Supporting Evidence	References
1.	Emotional Flattening in Digital Communication	Participants felt that digital interactions lacked the richness of face-to-face communication. Video calls were seen as helpful but unable to fully replicate non-verbal cues like body language and eye contact.	"Even with video, it just feels like something is missing. You cannot feel the same connection you get when you are in the same room as someone."	Walther (2011); Braun & Clarke (2006)
2.	The Illusion of Intimacy	Frequent digital contact was perceived as maintaining appearances rather than fostering genuine emotional closeness. Text and social media interactions often create a facade of intimacy without deep connection.	"We text all the time, but it is not the same as when we talk in person. It is almost like we are keeping up the appearance of being close without actually feeling it."	Turkle (2015)
3.	Performative Nature of Social Media	Social media platforms encouraged users to present curated versions of their lives, leading to superficial relationships and emotional distance.	"On Instagram or Facebook, people are performing their lives. It does not feel real, and I cannot talk about what is happening with my friends."	Ellison et al. (2014). Turkle (2015)
4.	Digital Communication as a Lifeline for Long-Distance Relationships	Digital tools were essential for maintaining long-distance relationships, but participants noted limitations such as miscommunication and feelings of isolation.	"Without video calls, we could not maintain our relationship. Nevertheless, sometimes, I still feel lonely even after we have talked."	Keles et al. (2020)

continued on following page

Table 2. Continued

S.No.	Theme	Description	Supporting Evidence	References
5.	Tension Between Convenience and Emotional Depth	While digital communication offered convenience and accessibility, participants were dissatisfied with the emotional limitations, such as superficiality and lack of in-person richness.	Synthesised with quantitative data showing a moderate positive correlation between digital communication and relationship satisfaction ($r = 0.45$, $p < 0.01$).	Braun & Clarke (2006); Walther (2011)
6.	Emotional Shallowness in Digital Interactions	Participants highlighted the inability of digital tools to replicate the emotional satisfaction and richness of face-to-face communication, underscoring its limitations despite frequent use.	The mixed-methods approach revealed the qualitative context for the quantitative correlation of digital communication with relationship satisfaction.	Braun & Clarke (2006); Ellison et al. (2014)

5. DISCUSSION

The Paradox of Digital Connectivity in Emotional and Social Interactions

In the contemporary digital age, an inherent paradox characterizes the nature of human connectivity: Digital platforms engineered communication, enabling rapid and repeated transmission across great distances but attenuating emotional depth. The contradiction comes into play with increasing communication, often without emotional content. In other words, although people are always connected through digital devices, they are paradoxically more emotionally separate than ever, says Turkle (2015) in a term she coined, 'alone together'. This observation is confirmed by the findings of this study, which demonstrate a tremendous negative correlation between the frequency of digital communication and perceived emotional closeness. The reason for the phenomenon is the constraints of a digital medium that cannot (or cannot easily) represent the wealth and subtlety of the interaction between people in person.

Attachment Theory is also an expeditious conceptual link to understanding this, especially regarding instant messaging and the assumption of direct response. Commonly, these dynamics create anxious attachment patterns, creating emotional resilience and weakening interpersonal connections (Kuss & Griffiths, 2017). The study participants described frustration and disconnection and highlighted the superficiality of text-based interactions. This emotional flattening, this digital communication devoid of depth and richness, is in line with Social Presence Theory, which says the absence of nonverbal cues, facial expressions, gestures and the tone of the voice erodes psychological intimacy. Reducing social presence perception impedes deep emotional bondedness, even if it is frequent communication.

However, not all digital communication forces are equally limited. Participants considered platforms that offered a higher social presence, like video calls, to be better at facilitating emotional intimacy. More prosperous, more emotionally satisfying exchanges can be accomplished with these tools and the transmission of nonverbal signals. According to Biocca, Harms, and Burgoon (2003), media having a high social presence, especially video conferencing, can approximate emotion-rich in-person interactions and act as a preferred medium in the orchestrated close relationships in the new digital society. While this is the case, video calls are far less utilized than text-based communication, perhaps surprisingly, because of frequent failure to meet emotional needs in text-based communication.

In the study, a concept I called the 'illusion of intimacy' emerged prominently, where participants described their interactions on social media platforms. On social media platforms like Instagram and TikTok, we can seemingly connect with someone without necessarily having organic emotional connections. The performative element of social media, induced by sharing an unrealistic version of yourself to escape reality, leads to these emotionally unfulfilling exchanges. As Lup, Trub and Rosenthal (2015) pointed out, when people who are perhaps not as polite as us to meet online produce polished, curated representations of their lives, they exaggerate a feeling of connection that is typically the opposite, where we feel isolated and inadequate. The study participants liked this closeness: It is transactional and superficial, with no opportunity for a genuine emotional connection. Even as we conduct constant digital interaction, feeling lonely proliferates because the emphasis is on maintaining a public persona instead of an actual relationship.

However, mental exhaustion is incurred from the ubiquitous state of being online, combined with the issue of staying connected in the digital age. Anxiety is inherently related to staying connected, exemplified by the phenomenon of phantom vibration syndrome, where people believe they are receiving notifications while they are not (Drouin et al., 2012). The preconditions for this anxiety, birthed by the belief that there must be responses instantly and without hesitation, lead to emotional fatigue and burnout. Many participants said they had often felt stressed and frustrated by the never-ending pressure to stay "online." Similar to Roberts and David (2016), whose work also demonstrates that digital overload (an overuse of communication technologies) is related to emotional exhaustion and a general decrease in well-being. These findings reinforce the call for boundaries in digital communication to keep its damage on the mind down.

Adding those cultural variations further adds to the landscape of digital communication. Specifically, the study was focused on Western practices. However, the nature of digital interactions varies considerably from one culture to another. The country where it takes place matters: in China, for example, platforms like WeChat bring social, professional and financial functions under one roof, a dynamic that is far removed from the territorialization of Western society. For instance, it has the multi-functionality to move smoothly from personal to professional effortless cohesion. Nevertheless, with this integration, there is also a risk of overreliance on one platform (a risk for emotional disconnection enhanced by this same integration) resembling that of Western contexts. On the other side of the equation, platforms like WhatsApp are employed in countries like India to maintain familial ties through generations and geographical points. This usage, which strengthens family bonds, is just as capable of emotional flatter if overused or used instead of real-time interactions.

Besides that, the field of digital interactive communications will further be reshaped by new technologies like artificial intelligence (AI), virtual reality (VR) and augmented reality (AR). Increasingly, people who have difficulty finding emotional support are turning to AI-based companions such as Replika, which, according to some, 'are more reliable than a noodle stir-fried' as sources of support. Much like most AI companions, these mimic human interaction. Hence, the user feels connected even if that connection is false and works to fit and address the emotional void. Their reliance, however, has ethical and philosophical implications about the kind of relationship humans can have. Is AI capable of duplicating the layer and genuineness of human connection? With the continued reliance on AI for emotional gratification, can we expect the fabric of real human closeness to unravel? However, the questions raised here remain open to further exploration when applied to current AI technologies.

Finally, virtual reality provides a new arena for improvements to digital communication by simulating face-to-face communication in three-dimensional, immersive environments. VRChat, for example, provides a space for users to experience virtual spaces that simulate existing in-person interaction using avatars and interactive environments. Because the platforms provide increased compared to traditional digital communication opportunities for perceived social presence, they can mitigate some emotional flattening. However, virtual environments provide a convenient means to conduct social interactions; the long-term impacts of this mode of conduct are unknown. While these technologies can do much to fix the deficiencies of our existing digital tools, time will tell if these can create lasting emotional intimacy over the long term.

All this digital communication also needs to be looked at because of its mental health implications. Although constantly online, many people are emotionally dissatisfied and lonely, this study found. Digital interactions lack nonverbal cues, creating a feeling of isolation even in frequent communication. Primack et al. (2017) Longitudinal research has demonstrated a direct relationship between excessive media use and increased rates of depression, anxiety, and loneliness among young adults. The irony of the digital — people are more connected but feel more lonely — hints at the grave psychological challenges of the digital. Social Comparison Theory (Festinger, 1954) informs us about these dynamics, featuring photographs of a shiny-looking life on social media platforms that inspire unsavory comparisons, which result in low self-esteem and low morale of your life. Participants in this study shared the same sentiment, noting how popular, curated social media content is an accumulated source of stress and inadequacy.

In the future, AI and AR, along with VR, will change how we communicate, even on the digital communication platform. While these new technologies promise to get us closer by filling the gaps in old digital communication, they also risk confusing emotional connections. As AI companions get more sophisticated and virtual reality environments become more immersive, we are left wondering what will happen to human intimacy in future, where digital interaction may well overshadow it, why it is important to keep an eye on technological development but also to dose it with an emphasis on the human authenticity and depth of the relationships.

The key findings of this study are ultimately that there is a need not only for balance in our digital communication but also for a conscious, well-thought-out practice. It helps increase the emotional closeness between people in personal relationships by giving more importance to video calls and in-person conversation rather than text-based. Video conferencing should be encouraged by organizations in professional settings to carry out serious discussions among remote teams to strengthen the connection between these teams. While remote work is increasing, just like in physical contexts, it is important to know how to keep emotionally satisfying relationships in 'digital' contexts, and they can be important for both personal well-being and success in the workplace. Beyond that, raising awareness around the psychological dangers of going overboard with digital communication can counteract its effects on mental health. A culture of mindful communication allows society to navigate the digital world without losing emotional depth and human intimacy.

6. CONCLUSION

This research shows how complex and sometimes conflicted digital communication adds to the makeup of personal relationships. While there are greater degrees of connectivity possible than ever, digital platforms do not serve to deepen the emotional aspect of relationships as required to build genuine connections. Frequent use of digital communication platforms was negatively correlated with one's perceived emotional closeness for the participants, who were frustrated with social media interactions' emotional flattening and performative nature, according to the study.

Moreover, the research also presents strategies that may mitigate these challenges. We proposed that video communication provides a higher social presence, which may make it a better tool for maintaining emotionally rich relationships in distance contexts. Real-time face-to-face platforms can help bridge the emotional gap of live communication through text.

With the rise of digital communication, we should learn to find a respectful balance between ease with online interactions and the richness of emotional depth of in-person conversations. The great thing about these innovative technologies, such as artificial intelligence (AI), AR, and VR (virtual reality and augmented reality), is that they open up [new] ways to forge deeper emotional connections in the digital space. At the same time, however, there is also a significant ethical aspect of the future of human relationships. We must examine how these technologies shape emotional well-being, prosociality, and mental health. This study's findings point out that despite the capabilities of digital communication lies the mere possibility of staying in touch; they cannot fully replace the astronomical emotional richness of humans communicating in person. Knowing what those limitations and possibilities are, the average person can better decide how they can best continue to maintain their relationships in the world of the digital.

7. RECOMMENDATIONS

7.1 Recommendations for Individuals

- Prioritize Face-to-Face and Video Interactions: People should consciously favor face-to-face and video over text-based communication to keep emotions close in personal relationships. Video calls have a higher social presence and can minimize the emotional gap text messaging can cause.
- Balance Digital and In-Person Communication: Digital communication is convenient, but balancing it with in-person interactions is important. Stronger emotional relationships (e.g. people who are friends or romantically coupled)

and, in particular, close relationships (like friends and couples) need time for in-person conversation to help build deeper emotional connections between people.

- Be Mindful of Social Media Use: With social media being so performative, these platforms, Instagram and TikTok, for example, users should be cognizant of how they use social media in its totality. By lessening the importance of likes and shares and more about engaging in meaningful interactions, we can better foster more authentic relationships online.

7.2 Rec–commendations for Organizations

- Encourage Video Conferencing for Important Discussions: However, video conferencing tools can be added to this list in professional settings for essential meetings and conversations among organizations. It can also aid in building stronger remote team bonds that might otherwise come with a heavy dose of emotional distance from text-based communication.
- Promote Digital Literacy Programs: Considering this is mainly the case for organizations, particularly educational organizations, it makes sense for them to instil the importance of digital literacy through programs like digital communication balanced with face-to-face interactions. They allow people to learn how to leverage digital tools should they choose to do so and remain emotionally well.
- Create Guidelines for Healthy Social Media Use: Employers and educators can develop guidelines for healthy social media use, as we encourage employers to legitimatize social media time limitations for employees, and we encourage educators to recommend restrictions on the amount of social media time spent for students. However, there is a way organizations can help reduce the emotional toll of being constantly plugged in—by setting boundaries.

REFERENCES

Baker, R. K., & White, K. M. (2011). In their own words: Why teenagers use social networking sites. *Cyberpsychology, Behavior, and Social Networking*, 14(6), 391–396. DOI: 10.1089/cyber.2010.0016 PMID: 21117974

Baym, N. K. (2015). *Personal connections in the digital age* (2nd ed.). Polity Press.

Biocca, F., Harms, C., & Burgoon, J. K. (2003). Toward a more robust theory and measure of social presence: Review and suggested criteria. *Presence (Cambridge, Mass.)*, 12(5), 456–480. DOI: 10.1162/105474603322761270

Boyd, D. (2014). *It is not very easy: The social lives of networked teens*. Yale University Press.

Braun, V., & Clarke, V. (2006). Using thematic analysis in psychology. *Qualitative Research in Psychology*, 3(2), 77–101. DOI: 10.1191/1478088706qp063oa

Castells, M. (2010). *The rise of the network society* (2nd ed.). Wiley-Blackwell.

Chib, A., Malik, S., Aricat, R. G., & Kadir, S. Z. (2013). Migrant workers and mobile phones: Perspectives from East and South-East Asia. *Media Asia*, 40(4), 410–421. DOI: 10.1080/01296612.2013.11689981

Clayton, R. B., Nagurney, A., & Smith, J. R. (2015). Cheating, breakup, and divorce: Is Facebook used to blame? *Cyberpsychology, Behavior, and Social Networking*, 16(10), 717–720. DOI: 10.1089/cyber.2012.0424 PMID: 23745615

Drouin, M., Kaiser, D. H., & Miller, D. A. (2012). Phantom vibrations among undergraduates: Prevalence and associated psychological characteristics. *Computers in Human Behavior*, 28(4), 1490–1496. DOI: 10.1016/j.chb.2012.03.013

Ellison, N. B., Vitak, J., Gray, R., & Lampe, C. (2014). Cultivating social resources on social network sites: Facebook relationship maintenance behaviours and their role in social capital processes. *Journal of Computer-Mediated Communication*, 19(4), 855–870. DOI: 10.1111/jcc4.12078

Festinger, L. (1954). A theory of social comparison processes. *Human Relations*, 7(2), 117–140. DOI: 10.1177/001872675400700202

Golden, T. D. (2006). Avoiding depletion in virtual work: Telework and the intervening impact of work exhaustion on commitment and turnover intentions. *Journal of Vocational Behavior*, 69(1), 176–187. DOI: 10.1016/j.jvb.2006.02.003

Haythornthwaite, C. (2005). Social networks and Internet connectivity effects. *Information Communication and Society*, 8(2), 125–147. DOI: 10.1080/13691180500146185

Keles, B., McCrae, N., & Grealish, A. (2020). A systematic review: The influence of social media on depression, anxiety, and psychological distress in adolescents. *International Journal of Adolescence and Youth*, 25(1), 79–93. DOI: 10.1080/02673843.2019.1590851

Kuss, D. J., & Griffiths, M. D. (2017). Social networking sites and addiction: Ten lessons learned. *International Journal of Environmental Research and Public Health*, 14(3), 311. DOI: 10.3390/ijerph14030311 PMID: 28304359

Leidner, D. E., & Tona, O. (2021). The impact of artificial intelligence on trust in technology and work. *Information Systems Journal*, 31(3), 269–302. DOI: 10.1111/isj.12356

Mazmanian, M., Orlikowski, W. J., & Yates, J. (2013). The autonomy paradox: The implications of mobile email devices for knowledge professionals. *Organization Science*, 24(5), 1337–1357. DOI: 10.1287/orsc.1120.0806

McDaniel, B. T., & Coyne, S. M. (2016). "Technoference": The interference of technology in couple relationships and implications for women's personal and relational well-being. *Psychology of Popular Media Culture*, 5(1), 85–98. DOI: 10.1037/ppm0000065

Negroponte, N. (1996). *Being digital*. Vintage Books.

Primack, B. A., Shensa, A., Sidani, J. E., Whaite, E. O., Lin, L. Y., Rosen, D., Colditz, J. B., Radovic, A., & Miller, E. (2017). Social media use and perceived social isolation among young adults in the US. *American Journal of Preventive Medicine*, 53(1), 1–8. DOI: 10.1016/j.amepre.2017.01.010 PMID: 28279545

Rainie, L., & Wellman, B. (2012). *Networked: The new social operating system*. MIT Press. DOI: 10.7551/mitpress/8358.001.0001

Roberts, J. A., & David, M. E. (2016). My life has become a major distraction from my cell phone: Partner phubbing and relationship satisfaction among romantic partners. *Computers in Human Behavior*, 54, 134–141. DOI: 10.1016/j.chb.2015.07.058

Short, J., Williams, E., & Christie, B. (1976). *The social psychology of telecommunications*. Wiley.

Steinfield, C., Ellison, N. B., & Lampe, C. (2008). Social capital, self-esteem, and use of online social network sites: A longitudinal analysis. *Journal of Applied Developmental Psychology*, 29(6), 434–445. DOI: 10.1016/j.appdev.2008.07.002

Turkle, S. (2015). *Reclaiming conversation: The power of talk in a digital age.* Penguin Press.

Twenge, J. M., Martin, G. N., & Spitzberg, B. H. (2018). Trends in US adolescents' media use and associations with the incidence of depressive symptoms, suicide-related outcomes, and suicide rates: 1976–2016. *Clinical Psychological Science*, 6(1), 3–17. DOI: 10.1177/2167702617723376

Van Deursen, A. J., & Van Dijk, J. A. (2014). The digital divide shifts to differences in usage. *New Media & Society*, 16(3), 507–526. DOI: 10.1177/1461444813487959

Walther, J. B. (2011). Theories of computer-mediated communication and interpersonal relations. In Knapp, M. L., & Daly, J. A. (Eds.), *The Handbook of Interpersonal Communication* (pp. 443–479). Sage.

Zepke, N., & Leach, L. (2010). Improving student engagement: Ten proposals for action. *Active Learning in Higher Education*, 11(3), 167–177. DOI: 10.1177/1469787410379680

Compilation of References

Aarestad, S. H., Flaa, T. A., Griffiths, M. D., & Pallesen, S. (2023). Smartphone addiction and subjective withdrawal effects: A three-day experimental study. *SAGE Open*, 13(4). Advance online publication. DOI: 10.1177/21582440231219538

Abeele, M. V. (2020). The social consequences of phubbing. *The Oxford handbook of mobile communication and society*, 158-174.

Abeele, M. B. (2020). *The social consequences of phubbing: A framework and a research agenda. Handbook of Mobile Communication, Culture, and Information.* Oxford University Press.

Abeele, M. M. V., Hendrickson, A. T., Pollmann, M. M., & Ling, R. (2019). Phubbing behavior in conversations and its relation to perceived conversation intimacy and distraction: An exploratory observation study. *Computers in Human Behavior*, 100, 35–47. DOI: 10.1016/j.chb.2019.06.004

Abeyta, L. (2015). *How the Smart Phone Has Equalized Access to Information.* Linkedin. https://www.linkedin.com/pulse/how-smart-phone-has-equalized-access-information-lisa-abeyta

Aboujaoude, E., Kuss, D. J., Yao, M. Z., & Leung, L. W. (2021). Online psychology beyond addiction and gaming: A global look at mental health and internet-related technologies. *Frontiers in Psychology*, 12, 815013. DOI: 10.3389/fpsyg.2021.815013 PMID: 34975704

Adams, S. K., Daly, J. F., & Williford, D. N. (2013). Adolescent sleep and cellular phone use: Recent trends and implications for research. *Health Services Insights*, 6, 99–103. DOI: 10.4137/HSI.S11083 PMID: 25114565

Adorjan, M., & Ricciardelli, R. (2021). Smartphone and social media addiction: Exploring the perceptions and experiences of Canadian teenagers. *Canadian Review of Sociology/Revue Canadienne De Sociologie, 58*(1), 45–64. DOI: 10.1111/cars.12319

Afolayan, O. T. (2020). Personality Types as Correlate of Specific Phone Usages and Smart Phone Addiction among Students in the University of Ilorin, Kwara State, Nigeria. *Journal of Cyberspace Studies*, 4(1), 27–46.

Áfra, E., Janszky, J., Perlaki, G., Orsi, G., Nagy, S. A., Arató, Á., Szente, A., Alhour, H. M., Kis-Jakab, G., & Darnai, G. (2023). Altered functional brain networks in problematic smartphone and social media use: Resting-state fMRI study. *Brain Imaging and Behavior*, 53(4), 835. Advance online publication. DOI: 10.1007/s11682-023-00825-y PMID: 38049599

African Institute for Digital Health. (2022). *Smartphone addiction in Africa: Current trends and future directions*. Retrieved from https://www.africaninstitute.org/smartphone-addiction

Aggarwal, K. (2013). Twenty-six percent doctors suffer from severe mobile phone-induced anxiety: Excessive use of mobile phone can be injurious to your health. *Indian Journal of Clinical Practice : IJCP*, 24(1), 7–9.

Agresti, A., & Franklin, C. (2007). *The art and science of learning from data*.

Ahmad, F., Jameel, R., Rehmat, M., Munir, S., & Fatima, S. M. (2024). The Relationship between Self-Control, Personality Traits, and Smartphone Addiction in Students. *Remittances Review*, 9(2), 2771–2786.

Ahmed, A. H., Elemo, A. S., & Hamed, O. A. O. (2023). Smartphone Addiction and Phubbing in International Students in Turkey: The Moderating Role of Mindfulness. *Journal of College Student Development*, 64(1), 64–78. DOI: 10.1353/csd.2023.0002

AIS. (2024). *What is stress?*https://www.stress.org/what-is-stress/

Akhtar, N., Islam, T., Hameed, Z., Ghaffar, A., Sharma, A., Kincl, T., & Islam, F. (2024). Unveiling mechanism of SNSs addiction on wellbeing: The moderating role of loneliness and social anxiety. *Behaviour & Information Technology*, 1–20. DOI: 10.1080/0144929X.2024.2417390

Akhtar, S., Hongyuan, T., Iqbal, S., & Ankomah, F. Y. N. (2020). Impact of need for achievement on entrepreneurial intentions; mediating role of self-efficacy. *Journal of Asian Business Strategy*, 10(1), 114–121. DOI: 10.18488/journal.1006.2020.101.114.121

Alabri, A. (2022). Fear of Missing Out (FOMO): The Effects of the Need to Belong, Perceived Centrality, and Fear of Social Exclusion. *Human Behavior and Emerging Technologies*, 2022, 1–12. DOI: 10.1155/2022/4824256

Aladwani, A. M., & Almarzouq, M. (2016). Understanding compulsive social media use: The premise of complementing self-conceptions mismatch with technology. *Computers in Human Behavior*, 60, 575–581. DOI: 10.1016/j.chb.2016.02.098

Alavi, N., Sadeghi, S., & Jafarian, R. (2019). The Effectiveness of Cognitive Behavioral Therapy on Smartphone Addiction in University Students. *Journal of Health Psychology*, 24(11), 1488–1498.

Albris, K., Fast, K., Karlsen, F., Kaun, A., Lomborg, S., & Syvertsen, T. (2024). The Digital Backlash and the Paradoxes of Disconnection.

Alenezi, A., Hamed, W., Elhehe, I., & El-Etreby, R. (2023). Association between Facebook Addiction, Depression, and Emotional Regulation among Women. *Healthcare (Basel)*, 11(12), 1701. DOI: 10.3390/healthcare11121701 PMID: 37372819

Alhassan, A. A., Alqadhib, E. M., Taha, N. W., Alahmari, R. A., Salam, M., & Almutairi, A. F. (2018). The relationship between addiction to smartphone usage and depression among adults: A cross sectional study. *BMC Psychiatry*, 18(1), 148. Advance online publication. DOI: 10.1186/s12888-018-1745-4 PMID: 29801442

Al-Khani, A. M., Sarhandi, M. I., Zaghloul, M. S., Ewid, M., & Saquib, N. (2019). A cross-sectional survey on sleep quality, mental health, and academic performance among medical students in Saudi Arabia. BMC Res. Notes, 12,665. doi: DOI: 10.1186/s13104-019-4713

Almourad, M. B., Alrobai, A., Skinner, T., Hussain, M., & Ali, R. (2021). Digital wellbeing tools through users lens. *Technology in Society*, 67, 101778. DOI: 10.1016/j.techsoc.2021.101778

Al-Saggaf, Y. (2022). *The psychology of phubbing*. Springer. DOI: 10.1007/978-981-19-7045-0

Al-Saggaf, Y., MacCulloch, R., & Wiener, K. (2019). Trait boredom is a predictor of phubbing frequency. *Journal of Technology in Behavioral Science*, 4(3), 245–252. DOI: 10.1007/s41347-018-0080-4

Alshare, K., Moqbel, M., Merhi, M. I., Bartelt, V., & Alam, M. (2024). The Impact of Cultural Dimensions and Quality of Life on Smartphone Addiction and Employee Performance: The Moderating Role of Quality of Life. *Information Systems Frontiers*, 1–19. DOI: 10.1007/s10796-024-10544-4

Alt, D. (2015). College students' academic motivation, media engagement and fear of missing out. *Computers in Human Behavior*, 49, 111–119. DOI: 10.1016/j.chb.2015.02.057

Alt, D., & Boniel-Nissim, M. (2018). Links between adolescents' deep and surface learning approaches, problematic Internet use, and fear of missing out (FoMO). *Internet Interventions : the Application of Information Technology in Mental and Behavioural Health*, 13, 30–39. DOI: 10.1016/j.invent.2018.05.002 PMID: 30206516

Alutaybi, A., Al-Thani, D., McAlaney, J., & Ali, R. (2020). Combating Fear of Missing Out (FoMO) on Social Media: The FoMO-R Method. *International Journal of Environmental Research and Public Health*, 17(17), 6128. DOI: 10.3390/ijerph17176128 PMID: 32842553

American Psychiatric Association. (2013). *Diagnostic and Statistical Manual of Mental Disorders* (5th ed.). American Psychiatric Publishing.

American Psychological Association. (2018). *Stress in America: Technology and social media*. Retrieved from https://www.apa.org/news/press/releases/stress/2018/technology-social-media

Amichai-Hamburger, Y., & Vinitzky, G. (2010). Social network use and personality. *Computers in Human Behavior*, 26(6), 1289–1295. DOI: 10.1016/j.chb.2010.03.018

Anaby, D., Hand, C., Bradley, L., DiRezze, B., Forhan, M., DiGiacomo, A., & Law, M. (2013). The effect of the environment on participation of children and youth with disabilities: A scoping review. *Disability and Rehabilitation*, 35(19), 1589–1598. DOI: 10.3109/09638288.2012.748840 PMID: 23350759

Anand, A., Bowen, M., & Rangarajan, D. (2022). To be or not to be: A review of the (un)ethical salespeople literature. *Journal of Business and Industrial Marketing*, 38(9), 1837–1851. DOI: 10.1108/JBIM-06-2022-0282

Anandpara, G., Kharaid, A., Vidja, P., Chauhan, Y., Mahajan, S., & Patel, J. (2024, April 22). A comprehensive review on digital detox: A newer health and wellness trend in the current era. *Cureus*, 16(4), e58719. DOI: 10.7759/cureus.58719 PMID: 38779255

Anderson, I., Robson, B., Connolly, M., Al-Yaman, F., Bjertness, E., King, A., Tynan, M., Madden, R., Bang, A., Coimbra, C. E.Jr, Pesantes, M. A., Amigo, H., Andronov, S., Armien, B., Obando, D. A., Axelsson, P., Bhatti, Z. S., Bhutta, Z. A., Bjerregaard, P., & Yap, L. (2016). Indigenous and tribal peoples' health (The Lancet–Lowitja Institute Global Collaboration): A population study. *Lancet*, 388(10040), 131–157. DOI: 10.1016/S0140-6736(16)00345-7 PMID: 27108232

Andreassen, C. S. (2015). *Online social network site addiction: A comprehensive review. Current addiction reports, 2(2), 175-184.*

Andreassen, C. S. (2015). Online social network site addiction: A comprehensive review. *Current Addiction Reports*, 2(2), 175–184. DOI: 10.1007/s40429-015-0056-9

Andreassen, C. S., Pallesen, S., & Griffiths, M. D. (2016). The relationship between addictive use of social media, narcissism, and self-esteem: Findings from a large national survey. *Addictive Behaviors*, 64, 287–293. DOI: 10.1016/j.addbeh.2016.03.006 PMID: 27072491

Andreassen, C. S., Pallesen, S., Torsheim, T., & Griffiths, M. D. (2012). Problematic smartphone use: A review of the literature. *Current Opinion in Psychiatry*, 25(2), 183–188.

Andreassen, C. S., Torsheim, T., Brunborg, G. S., & Pallesen, S. (2012). Development of a Facebook addiction scale. *Psychological Reports*, 110(2), 501–517. DOI: 10.2466/02.09.18.PR0.110.2.501-517 PMID: 22662404

Andrews, S., Ellis, D. A., Shaw, H., & Piwek, L. (2015). Beyond self-report: Tools to compare estimated and real-world smartphone use. *PLoS One*, 10(10), e0139004. DOI: 10.1371/journal.pone.0139004 PMID: 26509895

Angeluci, A. C. B. (2016). "Stop Phubbing me!": A case study on Mobile media and social relations. In *Handbook of Research on Comparative Approaches to the Digital Age Revolution in Europe and the Americas* (pp. 192–201). IGI Global. DOI: 10.4018/978-1-4666-8740-0.ch012

Angesti, R., & Oriza, I. D. I. (2018). Peran fear of missing out (fomo) sebagai mediator antara kepribadian dan penggunaan internet bermasalah. Jurnal Muara Ilmu Sosial, Humaniora, dan Seni, 2(2), 790-800.

Ao, R. (2022, December). The Bidirectional Relationship Between Undergraduates' Social Abilities and Their Peer Relationships: A Quantitative Case Study of SYSU. In *2022 6th International Seminar on Education, Management and Social Sciences (ISEMSS 2022)* (pp. 3491-3502). Atlantis Press.

Arnett, J. J. (2006). Emerging adulthood: Understanding the new way of coming of age. In Arnett, J. J., & Tanner, J. L. (Eds.), *Emerging adults in America*. American Psychological Association. DOI: 10.1093/acprof:oso/9780195309379.001.0001

Arpaci, I., & Kocadag Unver, T. (2020). Moderating role of gender in the relationship between big five personality traits and smartphone addiction. *The Psychiatric Quarterly*, 91(2), 577–585. DOI: 10.1007/s11126-020-09718-5 PMID: 32100236

Arshad, S., Sarwar, A., Ayub, S., & Qamar, N. (2024, April-June). The relationship of phubbing, emotional intelligence and psychological distress in youth. *Journal of Pakistan Psychiatric Society*, 21(2), 20–33. DOI: 10.63050/jpps.21.02.335

Ashton, M. C., & Lee, K. (2005). Honesty-humility, the Big Five, and the five-factor model. *Journal of Personality*, 73(5), 1321–1354. DOI: 10.1111/j.1467-6494.2005.00351.x PMID: 16138875

Ashton, M. C., Lee, K., & De Vries, R. E. (2014). The HEXACO honesty-humility, agreeableness, and emotionality factors: A review of research and theory. *Personality and Social Psychology Review*, 18(2), 139–152. DOI: 10.1177/1088868314523838 PMID: 24577101

Augner, C., Vlasak, T., Aichhorn, W., & Barth, A. (2023). The association between problematic smartphone use and symptoms of anxiety and depression—A meta-analysis. *Journal of Public Health (Oxford, England)*, 45(1), 193–201. DOI: 10.1093/pubmed/fdab350 PMID: 34585243

Babcock, S. E., & Wilson, C. A. (2020). Big five model of personality. *The Wiley Encyclopedia of Personality and Individual Differences: Personality Processes and Individual Differences*, 55-60.

Bai, H., Liu, J., Bai, W., & Cao, T. (2024). Social pressures and their impact on smartphone use stickiness and use habit among adolescents. *Heliyon*, 10(7), e29111. DOI: 10.1016/j.heliyon.2024.e29111 PMID: 38601604

Bailenson, J. (2018). *Experience on Demand: What Virtual Reality Is, How It Works, and What It Can Do*. W. W. Norton & Company.

Bajwa, R. S., Abdullah, H., Zaremohzzabein, Z., Jaafar, W. M. W., & Samah, A. A. (2023). Smartphone addiction and phubbing behavior among university students: A moderated mediation model by fear of missing out, social comparison, and loneliness. *Frontiers in Psychology*, 13, 1072551. DOI: 10.3389/fpsyg.2022.1072551 PMID: 36687837

Baker, R. K., & White, K. M. (2011). In their own words: Why teenagers use social networking sites. *Cyberpsychology, Behavior, and Social Networking*, 14(6), 391–396. DOI: 10.1089/cyber.2010.0016 PMID: 21117974

Balakrishnan, J., & Griffiths, M. D. (2019). Perceived addictiveness of smartphone games: A content analysis of game reviews by players. *International Journal of Mental Health and Addiction*, 17(4), 922–934. DOI: 10.1007/s11469-018-9897-5

Balta, S., Emirtekin, E., Kircaburun, K., & Griffiths, M. D. (2020). Neuroticism, trait fear of missing out, and phubbing: The mediating role of state fear of missing out and problematic Instagram use. *International Journal of Mental Health and Addiction*, 18(3), 628–639. DOI: 10.1007/s11469-018-9959-8

Balta, S., Jonason, P., Denes, A., Emirtekin, E., Tosuntaş, Ş. B., Kircaburun, K., & Griffiths, M. D. (2019). Dark personality traits and problematic smartphone use: The mediating role of fearful attachment. *Personality and Individual Differences*, 149, 214–219. DOI: 10.1016/j.paid.2019.06.005

Barbed-Castrejón, N., Navaridas-Nalda, F., Mason, O., & Ortuño-Sierra, J. (2024, May 28). Prevalence of phubbing behaviour in school and university students in Spain. *Frontiers in Psychology*, 15, 1–8. DOI: 10.3389/fpsyg.2024.1396863 PMID: 38863670

Barnes, C. M., Schaubroeck, J., Huth, M., & Ghumman, S. (2011). Lack of sleep and unethical conduct. *Organizational Behavior and Human Decision Processes*, 115(2), 169–180. DOI: 10.1016/j.obhdp.2011.01.009

Barr, R. (2019). Parenting in the digital age. In *Handbook of parenting* (pp. 380–409). Routledge. DOI: 10.4324/9780429401695-13

Barry, C. T., Reiter, S. R., Anderson, A. C., & Schoessler, J. M. (2017). "Let me take a selfie": Associations between self-photography, narcissism, and self-esteem. *Psychology of Popular Media Culture*, 6(1), 48–60. DOI: 10.1037/ppm0000089

Bartel, K., Scheeren, R., & Gradisar, M. (2019). Altering adolescents' pre-bedtime phone use to achieve better sleep health. *Health Communication*, 34(4), 456–462. DOI: 10.1080/10410236.2017.1422099 PMID: 29313721

Bastien, C. H., Vallières, A., & Morin, C. M. (2001). Validation of the insomnia severity index as an outcome measure for insomnia research. *Sleep Medicine*, 2(4), 297–307. DOI: 10.1016/S1389-9457(00)00065-4 PMID: 11438246

Baym, N. K. (2015). *Personal connections in the digital age* (2nd ed.). Polity Press.

Baym, N. K. (2015). *Personal Connections in the Digital Age* (2nd ed.). Polity.

Baym, N. K., Wagman, K. B., & Persaud, C. J. (2020). Mindfully Scrolling: Rethinking Facebook After Time Deactivated. *Social Media + Society*, 6(2), 205630512091910. DOI: 10.1177/2056305120919105

Beneito-Montagut, R., Rosales, A., & Fernández-Ardèvol, M. (2022). Emerging Digital Inequalities: A Comparative Study of Older Adults' Smartphone Use. *Social Media + Society*, 8(4), 205630512211387. DOI: 10.1177/20563051221138756

Benites-Zapata, V. A., Jiménez-Torres, V. E., & Ayala-Roldán, M. P. (2021). Problematic smartphone use is associated with de Quervain's tenosynovitis symptomatology among young adults. *Musculoskeletal Science & Practice*, 53, 102356. DOI: 10.1016/j.msksp.2021.102356 PMID: 33667881

Beresford Research. (2024). *Age range by generation*. https://www.beresfordresearch.com/age-range-by-generation

Berman, G., & Dubinski, A. (2023, October 30). *Managing students' behavior during remote or hybrid learning: Tips for teachers in an uncertain time*. Child Mind Institute. https://childmind.org/article/managing-students-behavior-during-remote-or-hybrid-learning

Beukeboom, C. J., & Pollmann, M. (2021). Partner phubbing: Why using your phone during interactions with your partner can be detrimental for your relationship. *Computers in Human Behavior*, 124, 106932. DOI: 10.1016/j.chb.2021.106932

Bhanderi, D. J., Pandya, Y. P., & Sharma, D. B. (2021). Smartphone Use and Its Addiction among Adolescents in the Age Group of 16-19 Years. *Indian journal of community medicine: Official publication of Indian Association of Preventive &. Social Medicine (Social Medicine Publication Group)*, 46(1), 88–92. DOI: 10.4103/ijcm.IJCM_263_20 PMID: 34035584

Bhattacharya, S., Bashar, M. A., Srivastava, A., & Singh, A. (2019). Nomophobia: No mobile phone phobia. *Journal of Family Medicine and Primary Care*, 8(4), 1297–1300. DOI: 10.4103/jfmpc.jfmpc_71_19 PMID: 31143710

Bianchi, R., Schonfeld, I. S., & Laurent, E. (2014). Is burnout a depressive disorder? A reexamination with special focus on atypical depression. *International Journal of Stress Management*, 21(4), 307–324. DOI: 10.1037/a0037906

Bian, X., Qin, J., Yang, Z., Tian, Y., & Wu, L. (2020). Factors influencing smartphone addiction and their mediating effect: A path analysis. *Telematics and Informatics*, 69, 101413.

Bickmore, T. W., Trinh, H., Olafsson, S., O'Leary, T. K., Asadi, R., Rickles, N. M., & Cruz, R. (2016). Patient and consumer safety risks when using conversational assistants for medical information: An observational study of Siri, Alexa, and Google Assistant. *Journal of Medical Internet Research*, 18(9), e115. DOI: 10.2196/jmir.6219 PMID: 30181110

Billieux, J. (2012). Problematic use of the mobile phone: A literature review and a pathways model. *Current Psychiatry Reviews*, 8(4), 299–307. DOI: 10.2174/157340012803520522

Billieux, J., Maurage, P., Lopez-Fernandez, O., Kuss, D. J., & Griffiths, M. D. (2015). Can disordered mobile phone use be considered a behavioral addiction? An update on current evidence and a comprehensive model for future research. *Current Addiction Reports*, 2(2), 156–162. DOI: 10.1007/s40429-015-0054-y

Billieux, J., Philippot, P., Schmid, C., Maurage, P., & de Mol, J. (2015). Problematic use of the Internet and smartphones in adults: A review. *Current Psychiatry Reports*, 17(4), 18. DOI: 10.1007/s11920-015-0582-7

Biocca, F., Harms, C., & Burgoon, J. K. (2003). Toward a more robust theory and measure of social presence: Review and suggested criteria. *Presence (Cambridge, Mass.)*, 12(5), 456–480. DOI: 10.1162/105474603322761270

Biolcati, R., Mancini, G., & Trombini, E. (2018). Proneness to boredom and risk behaviours during adolescents' free time. *Psychological Reports*, 121(2), 303–323. DOI: 10.1177/0033294117724447 PMID: 28776483

Bitar, Z., Akel, M., Salameh, P., Obeid, S., & Hallit, S. (2022). Phubbing among Lebanese young adults: Scale validation and association with mental health (depression, anxiety, and stress). *Current Psychology (New Brunswick, N.J.)*. Advance online publication. DOI: 10.1007/s12144-022-03104- PMID: 35496363

Bîzgă, A. (2023, October 27). *Smart phone security - the 10 biggest risks for your device.* Bitdefender. https://www.bitdefender.com/blog/hotforsecurity/smartphone-security-the-10-biggest-risks-for-your-device-2

Błachnio, A., Przepiórka, A., & Pantic, I. (2015). Internet use, Facebook intrusion, and depression: Results of a cross-sectional study. European psychiatry: the journal of the Association of European Psychiatrists, 30(6), 681–684. https://doi.org/DOI: 10.1016/j.eurpsy.2015.04.002

Black mirror or black hole? American phone screen time statistics. (2024, January 8). Harmony Healthcare IT. https://www.harmonyhit.com/phone-screen-time-statistics

Blankman, R. (2020, November 19). *10 virtual classroom management strategies.* HMH. https://www.hmhco.com/blog/virtual-classroom-management-strategies-for-online-teaching

Bleidorn, W., Hopwood, C. J., Back, M. D., Denissen, J. J., Hennecke, M., Hill, P. L., Jokela, M., Kandler, C., Lucas, R. E., Luhmann, M., Orth, U., Roberts, B. W., Wagner, J., Wrzus, C., & Zimmermann, J. (2021). Personality trait stability and change. *Personality Science*, 2(1), e6009. DOI: 10.5964/ps.6009

Blumberg, F. C., Deater-Deckard, K., Calvert, S. L., Flynn, R. M., Green, C. S., Arnold, D., & Brooks, P. J. (2019). Digital Games as a Context for Children's Cognitive Development: Research Recommendations and Policy Considerations. *Social Policy Report*, 32(1), 1–33. DOI: 10.1002/sop2.3

Blum, K., Baron, D., Lott, L., Ponce, J. V., Siwicki, D., Boyett, B., Steinberg, B., Modestino, E. J., Fried, L., Hauser, M., Simpatico, T., Downs, B. W., McLaughlin, T., Hajela, R., & Badgaiyan, R. D. (2020). In search of reward deficiency syndrome (RDS)-free controls: The "holy grail" in genetic addiction risk testing. *Current Psychopharmacology*, 9(1), 7–21. DOI: 10.2174/2211556008666191111103152 PMID: 32432025

Blum, K., Oscar-Berman, M., Demetrovics, Z., Barh, D., & Gold, M. S. (2014). Genetic addiction risk score (GARS): Molecular neurogenetic evidence for predisposition to reward deficiency syndrome (RDS). *Molecular Neurobiology*, 50(3), 765–796. DOI: 10.1007/s12035-014-8726-5 PMID: 24878765

Blum-Ross, A., Kumpulainen, K., & Marsh, J. (2019). *Enhancing digital literacy and creativity*. Routledge. DOI: 10.4324/9780429243264

Bodhi, R., Luqman, A., Hina, M., & Papa, A. (2023). Work-related social media use and employee-related outcomes: A moderated mediation model. *International Journal of Emerging Markets*, 18(11), 4948–4967. DOI: 10.1108/IJOEM-09-2021-1359

Boer, M., van den Eijnden, R. J. J. M., Boniel-Nissim, M., Wong, S.-L., Inchley, J. C., Badura, P., Craig, W. M., Gobina, I., Kleszczewska, D., Klanšček, H. J., & Stevens, G. W. J. M. (2020). Adolescents' intense and problematic social media use and their well-being in 29 countries. *The Journal of Adolescent Health*, 66(6, 6S), S89–S99. DOI: 10.1016/j.jadohealth.2020.02.014 PMID: 32446614

Bojanić, Ž., Nedeljković, J., Šakan, D., Mitić, P. M., Milovanović, I., & Drid, P. (2019). Personality traits and self-esteem in combat and team sports. *Frontiers in Psychology*, 10, 2280. DOI: 10.3389/fpsyg.2019.02280 PMID: 31649595

Bonfield, C. A., Salter, M., Longmuir, A., Benson, M., & Adachi, C. (2020). Transformation or evolution?: Education 4.0, teaching and learning in the digital age. *Higher Education Pedagogies*, 5(1), 223–246. DOI: 10.1080/23752696.2020.1816847

Bosshart, L. (2024, October 8). *Texting while walking puts pedestrians in danger: UBC study*. The University of British Columbia. https://news.ubc.ca/2024/10/texting-while-walking-puts-pedestrians-in-danger

Bouchrika, I. (2024, October 23). *50 online education statistics:2024data on higher learning & corporate training*. Research-dot-com. https://research.com/education/online-education-statistics#TOC1

Boumosleh, J. M., & Jaalouk, D. (2017). Depression, anxiety, and smartphone addiction in university students: A cross-sectional study. *PLoS One*, 12(8), e0182239. DOI: 10.1371/journal.pone.0182239 PMID: 28777828

Bowens, J. (2024, May 8). Norway's school cellphone ban boosts student grades and health: A model for US schools? *NBC News*.https://nbc24.com/news/nation-world/norways-school-cell-phone-ban-boosts-student-grades-health-model-us-schools-parents-children-development-reading-abilities-mental-health-human-contact-policy

Boyd, D. (2014). *It is not very easy: The social lives of networked teens*. Yale University Press.

Bozoglan, B., Demirer, V., & Sahin, I. (2013). Loneliness, self-esteem, and life satisfaction as predictors of Internet addiction: A cross-sectional study among Turkish university students. *Scandinavian Journal of Psychology*, 54(4), 313–319. DOI: 10.1111/sjop.12049 PMID: 23577670

Brand, M., & Potenza, M. N. (2023). Behavioral addictions in the ICD-11: An important debate that is anticipated to continue for some time: Commentary to the debate: "Behavioral addictions in the ICD-11". *Journal of Behavioral Addictions*, 12(3), 585–589. DOI: 10.1556/2006.2023.00042 PMID: 37682725

Braun, V., & Clarke, V. (2006). Using thematic analysis in psychology. *Qualitative Research in Psychology*, 3(2), 77–101. DOI: 10.1191/1478088706qp063oa

Bravo-Sánchez, A., Morán-García, J., Abián, P., & Abián-Vicén, J. (2021). Association of the use of the mobile phone with physical fitness and academic performance: A cross-sectional study. *International Journal of Environmental Research and Public Health*, 18(3), 1042. DOI: 10.3390/ijerph18031042 PMID: 33503943

Brod, C. (1984). *Technostress: The human cost of the computer revolution*. No Title.

Brook, B., & Santos, T. (2023). The Temptation of Instant Gratification: A Double-Edged Sword. *Journal of Addiction Research & Therapy*, 14, 564.

Brunborg, G. S. (2013). Video game addiction and its relation to depression and academic achievement. *Journal of Behavioral Addictions*, 2(2), 125–132.

Brunborg, G. S., Mentzoni, R. A., Melkevik, O. R., Torsheim, T., Samdal, O., Hetland, J., Andreassen, C. S., & Palleson, S. L. (2013). Gaming addiction, gaming engagement, and psychological health complaints among Norwegian adolescents. *Media Psychology*, 16(1), 115–128. DOI: 10.1080/15213269.2012.756374

Buabbas, A. (2020). The association between smartphone addiction and psychological distress in adolescents. *PLoS One*, 15(4).

Buctot, D. B. (2020). Smartphone addiction and its relationship with quality of life in Filipino adolescents. *Children and Youth Services Review*, 119.

Buctot, D. B., Kim, N., & Kim, J. J. (2020). Factors associated with smartphone addiction prevalence and its predictive capacity for health-related quality of life among Filipino adolescents. *Children and Youth Services Review*, 110(104758), 104758. DOI: 10.1016/j.childyouth.2020.104758

Buctot, D. B., & Nikolic, S. M. (2016). Internet addiction and academic performance in Serbian adolescents. *Archives for the Entire Medicine*, 68(1), 35–43.

Busch, B. (Ed.). (n.d.). *The psychology behind a great seating plan*. InnerDrive. https://www.innerdrive.co.uk/blog/psychology-of-seating-plans

Busch, P. A., & McCarthy, S. (2020). Antecedents and consequences of problematic smartphone use: A systematic literature review of an emerging research area. *Computers in Human Behavior*, 114, 106414. DOI: 10.1016/j.chb.2020.106414

Caci, B., Cardaci, M., & Miceli, S. (2019). Development and maintenance of self-disclosure on facebook: The role of personality traits. *SAGE Open*, 9(2). DOI: 10.1177/2158244019856948

Caldeira, S. P., Jorge, A., & Kubrusly, A. (2024). "How Can You Be a Feminist if You're Always Online?" Online Activisms, Ambivalence, and Dis/Connection. *Television & New Media*, 15274764241281693. Advance online publication. DOI: 10.1177/15274764241281693

Caliandro, A., Garavaglia, E., Sturiale, V., & Di Leva, A. (2021). Older people and smartphone practices in everyday life: An inquire on digital sociality of italian older users. *Communication Review*, 24(1), 47–78. DOI: 10.1080/10714421.2021.1904771

Calpbinici, P., & Tas Arslan, F. (2019). Virtual behaviors a ecting adolescent mental health: The usage of internet and mobile phone and cyberbullying. *Journal of Child and Adolescent Psychiatric Nursing*, 32(3), 139–148. DOI: 10.1111/jcap.12244 PMID: 31310412

Caplan, S. E. (2010). Theory and measurement of generalized problematic Internet use: A two-step approach. *Computers in Human Behavior*, 26(5), 1089–1097. DOI: 10.1016/j.chb.2010.03.012

Carayannis, E. G., Clark, S. C., & Valvi, D. E. (2012). Smartphone Affordance: Achieving Better Business Through Innovation. *Journal of the Knowledge Economy*, 4(4), 444–472. DOI: 10.1007/s13132-012-0091-x

Carlton, G. (2021, October 1). *Internet safety guide for college students*. ZDNet. https://www.zdnet.com/education/internet-safety-guide-for-college-students

Carr, N. (2010). *The shallows: What the Internet is doing to our brains.* W. W. Norton & Company.

Castells, M. (2010). *The rise of the network society* (2nd ed.). Wiley-Blackwell.

Cebollero-Salina, A., Cano-Esoriaza, J., & Orejudo, S. (2022, January 15). Impact of online emotions and netiquette on phubbing from a gender perspective: Educational challenges. *Journal of New Approaches in Educational Research*, 11(1), 64–78. DOI: 10.7821/naer.2022.1.848

Cemiloglu, D., Almourad, M. B., McAlaney, J., & Ali, R. (2022, February). Combatting digital addiction: Current approaches and future directions. *Technology in Society*, 68, 101832. DOI: 10.1016/j.techsoc.2021.101832

Chan, C. K. Y., Burton, K., & Flower, R. L. (2024). Facilitators and barriers of technology adoption and social connectedness among rural older adults: A qualitative study. *Health Psychology and Behavioral Medicine*, 12(1), 2398167. Advance online publication. DOI: 10.1080/21642850.2024.2398167 PMID: 39234572

Chang, C.-C., Wang, J.-H., Liang, C.-T., & Liang, C. (2014). Curvilinear effects of openness and agreeableness on the imaginative capability of student designers. *Thinking Skills and Creativity*, 14, 68–75. DOI: 10.1016/j.tsc.2014.09.001

Chan, T. K. H., Cheung, C. M. K., & Wong, R. Y. M. (2019). Cyberbullying on Social Networking Sites: The Crime Opportunity and Affordance Perspectives. *Journal of Management Information Systems*, 36(2), 574–609. DOI: 10.1080/07421222.2019.1599500

Charles, S. T., Piazza, J. R., Mogle, J., Sliwinski, M. J., & Almeida, D. M. (2013). The wear and tear of daily stressors on mental health. *Psychological Science*, 24(5), 733–741. DOI: 10.1177/0956797612462222 PMID: 23531486

Charzyńska, E., Sussman, S., & Atroszko, P. A. (2021). Profiles of potential behavioral addictions' severity and their associations with gender, personality, and well-being: A person-centered approach. *Addictive Behaviors*, 119, 106941. DOI: 10.1016/j.addbeh.2021.106941 PMID: 33915392

Cha, S., & Seo, B. (2018). Smartphone use and smartphone addiction in middle school students in Korea: Prevalence, social networking service, and game use. *Health Psychology Open*, 5(1). DOI: 10.1177/2055102918755046 PMID: 29435355

Chen, D. (2024, May 20). *Classroom behavior tools improving student success.* Kangaroos.ai. https://www.kangaroos.ai/blog/ai-powered-classroom-behavior-tools-improving-student-success

Chen, S., Qiu, D., Li, X., & Zhao, Q. (2023, November). Discrepancies in adolescent–parent perceptions of parental phubbing and their relevance to adolescent smart phone dependence: The mediating role of parent–child relationship. *Behavioral Sciences, 13*(11), 888. DOI: 10.3390/bs13110888

Chen, C., Zhang, K. Z., Gong, X., & Lee, M. (2019). Dual mechanisms of reinforcement reward and habit in driving smartphone addiction: The role of smartphone features. *Internet Research*, 29(6), 1551–1570. DOI: 10.1108/INTR-11-2018-0489

Chen, G., & Lyu, C. (2024). The relationship between smartphone addiction and procrastination among students: A systematic review and meta-analysis. *Personality and Individual Differences*, 224, 112652. DOI: 10.1016/j.paid.2024.112652

Cheng, C., Ebrahimi, O. V., & Luk, J. W. (2022). Heterogeneity of Prevalence of Social Media Addiction Across Multiple Classification Schemes: Latent Profile Analysis. *Journal of Medical Internet Research*, 24(1), e27000. DOI: 10.2196/27000 PMID: 35006084

Cheng, Y.-C., Yang, T.-A., & Lee, J.-C. (2021). The relationship between smartphone addiction, parent–child relationship, loneliness and self-efficacy among senior high school students in Taiwan. *Sustainability (Basel)*, 13(16), 9475. DOI: 10.3390/su13169475

Chen, H., Dong, G., & Li, K. (2023). Overview on brain function enhancement of Internet addicts through exercise intervention: Based on reward-execution-decision cycle. *Frontiers in Psychiatry*, 14, 1094583. Advance online publication. DOI: 10.3389/fpsyt.2023.1094583 PMID: 36816421

Chen, W. (2022). Exploring digital natives' mobile addiction syndrome in Taiwan: Psychological issues and beyond. *Information Technology & People*, 36(3), 1326–1355. DOI: 10.1108/ITP-08-2021-0633

Cherry, K. (2023). *Tips to Maintain an Interpersonal Relationship*. Verywell Mind. https://www.verywellmind.com/how-to-maintain-interpersonal-relationships-5204856

Chib, A., Malik, S., Aricat, R. G., & Kadir, S. Z. (2013). Migrant workers and mobile phones: Perspectives from East and South-East Asia. *Media Asia*, 40(4), 410–421. DOI: 10.1080/01296612.2013.11689981

Chi, L. C., Tang, T. C., & Tang, E. (2022). The phubbing phenomenon: A cross-sectional study on the relationships among social media addiction, fear of missing out, personality traits, and phubbing behavior. *Current Psychology (New Brunswick, N.J.)*, 41(2), 1112–1123. DOI: 10.1007/s12144-021-02468-y

Cho, H. Y., Kim, D. J., & Park, J. W. (2017). Stress and adult smartphone addiction: Mediation by self-control, neuroticism, and extraversion. *Stress and Health*, 33(5), 624–630. DOI: 10.1002/smi.2749 PMID: 28332778

Choi, J. S., Park, S. M., Roh, M. S., Lee, J. Y., Park, C. B., Hwang, J. Y., & Lee, H. W. (2015). Dysfunctional Information Processing in Adolescents with Internet Addiction. *Psychiatry Research: Neuroimaging*, 224(3), 184–192.

Choi, S. W., Kim, D.-J., Choi, J.-S., Ahn, H., Choi, E.-J., Song, W.-Y., Kim, S., & Youn, H. (2015). Comparison of risk and protective factors associated with smartphone addiction and Internet addiction. *Journal of Behavioral Addictions*, 4(4), 208–214. DOI: 10.1556/2006.4.2015.043 PMID: 26690626

Chóliz, M., Pinto, L., Phansalkar, S. S., Corr, E., Mujjahid, A., Flores, C., & Barrientos, P. E. (2016). Development of a brief multicultural version of the test of mobile phone dependence (TMDbrief) questionnaire. *Frontiers in Psychology*, 7, 650. DOI: 10.3389/fpsyg.2016.00650 PMID: 27252663

Chotpitayasunondh, V., & Douglas, K. M. (2016). How "phubbing" becomes the norm: The antecedents and consequences of snubbing via smartphone. *Computers in Human Behavior*, 63, 9–18. DOI: 10.1016/j.chb.2016.05.018

Chotpitayasunondh, V., & Douglas, K. M. (2018). The effects of "phubbing" on social interaction. *Computers in Human Behavior*, 88, 176–185.

Chotpitayasunondh, V., & Douglas, K. M. (2018). The effects of "phubbing" on social interaction. *Journal of Applied Social Psychology*, 48(6), 304–316. DOI: 10.1111/jasp.12506

Choudrie, J., Pheeraphuttranghkoon, S., & Davari, S. (2018). The Digital Divide and Older Adult Population Adoption, Use and Diffusion of Mobile Phones: A Quantitative Study. *Information Systems Frontiers*, 22(3), 673–695. DOI: 10.1007/s10796-018-9875-2

Chou, W.-J., Chang, Y.-P., & Yen, C.-F. (2018). Boredom proneness and its correlation with internet addiction and internet activities in adolescents with attention-deficit/hyperactivity disorder. *The Kaohsiung Journal of Medical Sciences*, 34(8), 1–8. DOI: 10.1016/j.kjms.2018.01.016 PMID: 30041765

Chowdhury, T. G., Ratneshwar, S., & Mohanty, P. (2009). The time-harried shopper: Exploring the differences between maximizers and satisficers. *Marketing Letters*, 20(2), 155–167. DOI: 10.1007/s11002-008-9063-0

Christian, M. S., & Ellis, A. P. (2011). Examining the e ects of sleep deprivation on workplace deviance: A self-regulatory perspective. *Academy of Management Journal*, 54(5), 913–934. DOI: 10.5465/amj.2010.0179

Christina, R., Yuniardi, M. S., & Prabowo, A. (2019). Hubungan Tingkat Neurotisme dengan Fear of Missing Out (FoMO) pada Remaja Pengguna Aktif Media Sosial. Indigenous. *Jurnal Ilmiah Psikologi*, 4(2), 105–117.

Chuck, E. (2024, September 7). Lifeline or distraction? Georgia shooting reignites debate over cellphones in schools. *NBC News*.https://www.nbcnews.com/news/us-news/lifeline-distraction-shooting-reignites-debate-phones-schools-rcna169920

Chung, S.-K., & Kim, C.-G. (2010). Influences of depression, stress, and self-efficacy on the addiction of cell phone use among university students. *Korean Journal of Adult Nursing*, 22(1), 41–50.

Chun, J. (2018). Conceptualizing effective interventions for smartphone addiction among Korean female adolescents. *Children and Youth Services Review*, 84, 35–39. DOI: 10.1016/j.childyouth.2017.11.013

Church, A. T. (2008). Current controversies in the study of personality across cultures. *Social and Personality Psychology Compass*, 2(5), 1930–1951. DOI: 10.1111/j.1751-9004.2008.00132.x

Chu, X., Li, Y., Wang, P., Zeng, P., & Lei, L. (2021). Social support and cyberbullying for university students: The mediating role of internet addiction and the moderating role of stress. *Current Psychology (New Brunswick, N.J.)*, 42(3), 2014–2022. DOI: 10.1007/s12144-021-01607-9

Çiftçi, G., Ulutaş, H. M., Özkaynak, T. R., Öcal, F., & Özmen, A. A. (2019). The relationship between personality traits and problematic smartphone use. *Telematics and Informatics*, 58, 512–520.

Clark, J. L., Algoe, S. B., & Green, M. C. (2018). Social network sites and well-being: The role of social connection. *Current Directions in Psychological Science*, 27(1), 32–37. DOI: 10.1177/0963721417730833

Clayson, D. E., & Haley, D. A. (2013, April). An introduction to multitasking and texting: Prevalence and impact on grades and GPA in marketing classes. *Journal of Marketing Education*, 35(1), 26–40. DOI: 10.1177/0273475312467339

Clayton, R. B., Nagurney, A., & Smith, J. R. (2015). Cheating, breakup, and divorce: Is Facebook used to blame? *Cyberpsychology, Behavior, and Social Networking*, 16(10), 717–720. DOI: 10.1089/cyber.2012.0424 PMID: 23745615

Clemens, V., Fegert, J. M., & Allroggen, M. (2022). Adverse childhood experiences and grandiose narcissism–Findings from a population-representative sample. *Child Abuse & Neglect*, 127, 105545. DOI: 10.1016/j.chiabu.2022.105545 PMID: 35217322

Clement-Carbonell, V., Portilla-Tamarit, I., Rubio-Aparicio, M., & Madrid-Valero, J. J. (2021). Sleep quality, mental and physical health: A differential relationship. *International Journal of Environmental Research and Public Health*, 18(2), 1–8. DOI: 10.3390/ijerph18020460 PMID: 33435528

Cloninger, C. R., & Svrakic, D. M. (2008). Personality disorders. *The medical basis of psychiatry*, 471-483.

Cohn, J. (2016). "Devilish Smartphones" and the "Stone-Cold" Internet: Implications of the Technology Addiction Trope in College Student Digital Literacy Narratives. *Computers & Composition. Computers and Composition*, 42, 80–94. DOI: 10.1016/j.compcom.2016.08.008

Collen, M. F., & Kulikowski, C. A. (2015). The Development of Digital Computers. In *Computers in health care* (pp. 3–73). DOI: 10.1007/978-1-4471-6732-7_1

Condon, D. M., Wood, D., Mõttus, R., Booth, T., Costantini, G., Greiff, S., Johnson, W., Lukaszewski, A., Murray, A., & Revelle, W. (2021). Bottom up construction of a personality taxonomy. *European Journal of Psychological Assessment*.

Cooke, C. (2024, April 24). *Online learning statistics: The ultimate list of 2024*. Upskillwise. https://upskillwise.com/online-learning-statistics

Corr, P. J., & Matthews, G. (2020). *The Cambridge handbook of personality psychology*. Cambridge University Press.

Coskun, S., & Karayagız Muslu, G. (2019). Investigation of problematic mobile phones use and fear of missing out (FoMO) level in adolescents. *Community Mental Health Journal*, 55(6), 1004–1014. DOI: 10.1007/s10597-019-00422-8 PMID: 31209716

Costa, P. T., & McCrae, R. R. (2008). The revised neo personality inventory (neo-pi-r). *The SAGE handbook of personality theory and assessment, 2*(2), 179-198.

Costa, C., Teodoro, M., Coco, M., Verduci, F., Giambò, F., Italia, S., Alibrandi, A., & Fenga, C. (2023). Smartphone use among resident physicians: Prevalence and risk factors in clinical practice. *SAGE Open*, 13(3). Advance online publication. DOI: 10.1177/21582440231194463

Coyne, P., & Woodruff, S. J. (2023). Taking a Break: The Effects of Partaking in a Two-Week Social Media Digital Detox on Problematic Smartphone and Social Media Use, and Other Health-Related Outcomes among Young Adults. *Behavioral Sciences (Basel, Switzerland)*, 13(12), 1004. DOI: 10.3390/bs13121004 PMID: 38131860

Coyne, S. M., Rogers, A. A., Zurcher, J. D., Stockdale, L., & Booth, M. (2020). Does time spent using social media impact mental health?: An eight year longitudinal study. *Computers in Human Behavior*, 104, 106160. DOI: 10.1016/j.chb.2019.106160

Crane, C., Hotton, M., Shelemy, L., & Knowles-Bevis, R. (2024). The Association between Individual Differences in Motivational Readiness at Entry to Treatment and Treatment Attendance and Outcomes in Cognitive Behaviour Therapy: A Systematic Review. *Cognitive Therapy and Research*, 48(1), 10504. Advance online publication. DOI: 10.1007/s10608-024-10504-x

Csibi, S., Griffiths, M. D., Cook, B., Demetrovics, Z., & Szabo, A. (2018). The psychometric properties of the smartphone application-based addiction scale (SABAS). *International Journal of Mental Health and Addiction*, 16(2), 393–403. DOI: 10.1007/s11469-017-9787-2 PMID: 29670500

Csibi, S., Griffiths, M. D., Demetrovics, Z., & Szabo, A. (2019). Analysis of Problematic Smartphone Use Across Different Age Groups within the 'Components Model of Addiction.'. *International Journal of Mental Health and Addiction*, 19(3), 616–631. DOI: 10.1007/s11469-019-00095-0

Cyberbullying: The Mental Health Impact and How to Help Your Teen. (2023, January 18). Newport Academy. https://www.newportacademy.com/resources/restoring-families/teen-cyberbullying/

Dadandı, İ., & Kalyon, A. (2024). Impulsivity and problematic smartphone use: Mediating role of self-handicapping. *Behaviour & Information Technology*, 1–17. DOI: 10.1080/0144929X.2024.2313705

Daft, R. L., & Lengel, R. H. (1986). Organizational information requirements, media richness, and structural design. *Management Science*, 32(5), 554–571. DOI: 10.1287/mnsc.32.5.554

Dahlen, E. R., Martin, R. C., Ragan, K., & Kuhlman, M. M. (2005). Driving anger, sensation seeking, impulsiveness, and boredom proneness in the prediction of unsafe driving. *Accident; Analysis and Prevention*, 37(2), 341–348. DOI: 10.1016/j.aap.2004.10.006 PMID: 15667821

Dai, B., Lin, Y., Lai, X., He, J., Du, M., Hou, X., & Zhang, G. (2024, January 19). The effects of self-esteem and parental phubbing on adolescent internet addiction and the moderating role of the classroom environment: A hierarchical linear model analysis. *BMC Psychiatry*, 24(1), 1–12. DOI: 10.1186/s12888-023-05489-y PMID: 38243210

Damon, C.-H. P., & Louis, W.-C. L. (2010). Effects of narcissism, leisure boredom, and gratifications sought on user-generated content among Net-Generation users. 8th International Telecommunications Society (ITS) *Asia-Pacific Regional Conference*, 1–34. https://doi.org/DOI: 10.4018/ijcbpl.2011070101

Dan Ariely on How 'Fear of Missing Out' works | Duke Today. (2015, April 21). Duke Today. https://today.duke.edu/2015/04/dan-ariely-how-%E2%80%98fear-missing-out%E2%80%99-works

Davey, S., Davey, A., Raghav, S. K., Singh, J. V., Singh, N., Blachnio, A., & Przepiórkaa, A. (2018). Predictors and consequences of "Phubbing" among Youngsters and youth in India: An impact evaluation study. *Journal of Family & Community Medicine*, 25(1), 35–42. DOI: 10.4103/jfcm.JFCM_71_17 PMID: 29386960

Davey, S., Davey, A., Singh, J. V., Raghav, S. K., Singh, N., & Blachnio, A. (2018). Predictors and consequences of "Phubbing" among adolescents and youth in India. *The Journal of Mental Health and Human Behavior*, 23(1), 32–38. PMID: 29386960

David, M. E., & Roberts, J. A. (2017). Phubbed and alone: Phone snubbing, social exclusion, and attachment to social media. *Journal of the Association for Consumer Research*, 2(2), 155–163. DOI: 10.1086/690940

David, M. E., & Roberts, J. A. (2020). Developing and testing a scale designed to measure perceived phubbing. *International Journal of Environmental Research and Public Health*, 17(21), 8152. DOI: 10.3390/ijerph17218152 PMID: 33158203

Davis, R. A., Flett, G. L., & Besser, A. (2002). Validation of a new scale for measuring problematic internet use: Implications for pre-employment screening. *Cyberpsychology & Behavior*, 5(4), 331–345. DOI: 10.1089/109493102760275581 PMID: 12216698

De Oliveira, M. L. C., De Nogueira Holanda, F. W., Valdez, P., De Almondes, K. M., & De Azevedo, C. V. M. (2020). Impact of Electronic Device Usage Before Bedtime on Sleep and Attention in Adolescents. *Mind, Brain and Education : the Official Journal of the International Mind, Brain, and Education Society*, 14(4), 376–386. DOI: 10.1111/mbe.12260

De Toledo, L. H. S., Moraes, M. N., De Oliveira Poletini, M., Neto, J. C., Baron, J., & Mota, T. (2023). Modeling the influence of nighttime light on melatonin suppression in humans: Milestones and perspectives. *Journal of Photochemistry and Photobiology*, 16, 100199. DOI: 10.1016/j.jpap.2023.100199

Demirci, K., Akgönül, M., & Akpinar, A. (2015). Relationship of smartphone use severity with sleep quality, depression, and anxiety in university students. *Journal of Behavioral Addictions*, 4(2), 85–92. DOI: 10.1556/2006.4.2015.010 PMID: 26132913

Deniz M. (2021). Fear of missing out (FoMO) mediate relations between social self-efficacy and life satisfaction. Psicologia, reflexao e critica: revista semestral do Departamento de Psicologia da UFRGS, 34(1), 28. DOI: 10.1186/s41155-021-00193-w

Deresiewicz, W. (2009). Solitude and leadership. *The American Scholar*, 78(2), 20–31.

De-Sola Gutiérrez, J., Rodríguez de Fonseca, F., & Rubio, G. (2016). Cell-phone addiction: A review. *Frontiers in Psychiatry*, 7, 175. DOI: 10.3389/fpsyt.2016.00175 PMID: 27822187

De-Sola, J., Talledo, H., Rubio, G., & de Fonseca, F. R. (2017). Development of a mobile phone addiction craving scale and its validation in a Spanish adult population. *Frontiers in Psychiatry*, 8, 90. DOI: 10.3389/fpsyt.2017.00090 PMID: 28611692

Desouky, D. E. S., & Abu-Zaid, H. (2020). Mobile phone use pattern and addiction in relation to depression and anxiety. *Eastern Mediterranean Health Journal*, 26(6), 692–699. DOI: 10.26719/emhj.20.043 PMID: 32621504

Devices in the classroom. (n.d.). Harvard University Derek Bok Center for Teaching and Learning. https://bokcenter.harvard.edu/technology-and-student-distraction

DiClemente, C. C., Schlundt, D., & Gemmell, L. (2004). Readiness and stages of change in addiction treatment. *The American Journal on Addictions*, 13(2), 103–119. DOI: 10.1080/10550490490435777 PMID: 15204662

Diener, E., & Lucas, R. E. (2019). Personality traits. *General psychology: Required reading, 278.*

Diener, E., Lucas, R. E., & Cummings, J. A. (2019). *16.1 Personality Traits.* Introduction to Psychology.

Digman, J. M. (1990). Personality structure: Emergence of the five-factor model. *Annual Review of Psychology*, 41(1), 417–440. DOI: 10.1146/annurev.ps.41.020190.002221

Dilip, B., & Javalkar, S. R. (2018). Mobile phone usage pattern and dependency among school-going adolescents in Davanagere, Karnataka. *Medica (Stuttgart)*, 7(1), 35.

Ding, H., & Li, A. (2018). A study on maximization paradox and its psychological origin. *Psychology (Irvine, Calif.)*, 9(04), 785–796. DOI: 10.4236/psych.2018.94050

Ding, Q., Dong, S., & Zhang, Y. (2023, February 6). Does parental phubbing aggravates adolescent sleep quality problems? *Frontiers in Psychology*, 14, 1–9. DOI: 10.3389/fpsyg.2023.1094488 PMID: 36814669

Dong, D., Xu, B., Shen, N., & He, Q. (2021). The adverse impact of air pollution on China's economic growth. *Sustainability (Basel)*, 13(16), 9056. DOI: 10.3390/su13169056

Dossey, L. (2014). FOMO, digital dementia, and our dangerous experiment. *Explore (New York, N.Y.)*, 10(2), 69–73. DOI: 10.1016/j.explore.2013.12.008 PMID: 24607071

Dou, F., Li, Q., Li, X., Li, Q., & Wang, M. (2021). Impact of perceived social support on fear of missing of out (FoMO): A moderated mediation model. *Current Psychology (New Brunswick, N.J.)*, 1–10.

Dowran, B., Amiri, M., Salimi, H., & Zarghami, M. H. (2020). The problematic use of mobile phone and mental health: A review study in Iran. *Journal of Education and Health Promotion*, 9(1), 290. DOI: 10.4103/jehp.jehp_268_20

Dreher, J.-C., Kohn, P., Kolachana, B., Weinberger, D. R., & Berman, K. F. (2009). Variation in dopamine genes influences responsivity of the human reward system. *Proceedings of the National Academy of Sciences of the United States of America*, 106(2), 617–622. DOI: 10.1073/pnas.0805517106 PMID: 19104049

Drouin, M., Kaiser, D. H., & Miller, D. A. (2012). Phantom vibrations among undergraduates: Prevalence and associated psychological characteristics. *Computers in Human Behavior*, 28(4), 1490–1496. DOI: 10.1016/j.chb.2012.03.013

DSM-5-TR. (2023). *Understanding Mental Disorders: Your Guide to DSM-5-TR®*. American Psychiatric Pub.

Dube, S. R., Felitti, V. J., Dong, M., Chapman, D. P., Giles, W. H., & Anda, R. F. (2003). Childhood abuse, neglect, and household dysfunction and the risk of illicit drug use: The adverse childhood experiences study. *Pediatrics*, 111(3), 564–572. DOI: 10.1542/peds.111.3.564 PMID: 12612237

Ducci, F., & Goldman, D. (2012). The genetic basis of addictive disorders. *Psychiatria Clinica*, 35(2), 495–519. PMID: 22640768

Duckitt, J. (2020). Authoritarianism. *Encyclopedia of personality and individual differences*, 322-329.

Duckitt, J. (2022). Authoritarianism: Conceptualization, research, and new developments. *The Cambridge handbook of political psychology*, 177-197.

Dudgeon, P., Kelly, K., & Walker, R. (2010). Closing the gaps in and through Indigenous health research: Guidelines, processes and practices. *Australian Aboriginal Studies*, (2), 81–91.

Duffy, B. (2019). Tech Addiction: What Can Parents and Schools Do? *Child Trends*. Retrieved from https://www.childtrends.org/tech-addiction-what-can-parents-and-schools-do

Dünnweber, M., & Fortmüller, A. (2017). Leadership models and behaviors for sales executives. what drives success and the best results? *Proceedings of the International Conference on Business Excellence*, 11(1), 779-787. DOI: 10.1515/picbe-2017-0082

Durak, H. Y. (2018). Smartphone addiction, academic performance, and nomophobia among adolescents. *The Social Science Journal*, 55(1), 13–24.

Dwivedi, Y. K., Ismagilova, E., Hughes, D. L., Carlson, J., Filieri, R., Jacobson, J., Jain, V., Karjaluoto, H., Kefi, H., Krishen, A. S., Kumar, V., Rahman, M. M., Raman, R., Rauschnabel, P. A., Rowley, J., Salo, J., Tran, G. A., & Wang, Y. (2021). Setting the future of digital and social media marketing research: Perspectives and research propositions. *International Journal of Information Management*, 59, 102168. DOI: 10.1016/j.ijinfomgt.2020.102168

Dwyer, R., & Fraser, S. (2015). Addiction screening and diagnostic tools:'Refuting'and 'unmasking'claims to legitimacy. *The International Journal on Drug Policy*, 26(12), 1189–1197. DOI: 10.1016/j.drugpo.2015.08.016 PMID: 26386890

Edwards, E. J., Taylor, C. S., & Vaughan, R. S. (2022). Individual differences in self-esteem and social anxiety predict problem smartphone use in adolescents. *School Psychology International*, 43(5), 460–476. DOI: 10.1177/01430343221111061

Ehrlick, S. P. (2014). Managing digital distraction: A pedagogical approach for dealing with wireless devices in the classroom. *Journal of Teacher Education*, 3(3), 207–216.

Eichenberg, C., Schneider, R., & Rumpl, H. (2024). Social media addiction: Associations with attachment style, mental distress, and personality. *BMC Psychiatry*, 24(1), 278. Advance online publication. DOI: 10.1186/s12888-024-05709-z PMID: 38622677

Ekinci, N. E., Yalçın, İ., Özer, Ö., & Kara, T. (2017). An investigation of the digital game addiction between high school students. *International Journal of Human Sciences*, 14(4), 4989. DOI: 10.14687/jhs.v14i4.4936

Elamin, N. O., Almasaad, J. M., Busaeed, R. B., Aljafari, D. A., & Khan, M. A. (2024, January-February). Smart phone addiction, stress, and depression among university students. *Clinical Epidemiology and Global Health*, 25, 101487. DOI: 10.1016/j.cegh.2023.101487

Elhai, J. D., Dvorak, R. D., Levine, J. C., & Hall, B. J. (2017). Problematic smartphone use: A conceptual overview and systematic review of relations with anxiety and depression symptomatology. *Journal of Affective Disorders*, 207, 251–259. DOI: 10.1016/j.jad.2016.08.030 PMID: 27736736

Elhai, J. D., Dvorak, R. D., Levine, J. C., & Hall, B. J. (2020). Problematic smartphone use and depression and anxiety: A systematic review and meta-analysis. *Depression and Anxiety*, 37(3), 1–12.

Elhai, J. D., Levine, J. C., Dvorak, R. D., & Hall, B. J. (2017). Fear of missing out, need for touch, anxiety, and smartphone use: A multiple mediation model. *Computers in Human Behavior*, 68, 139–146.

Elhai, J. D., Levine, J. C., Dvorak, R. D., & Hall, B. J. (2019). Non-social features of smartphone use are most related to depression, anxiety, and problematic smartphone use. *Computers in Human Behavior*, 93, 22–29.

Elhai, J. D., Levine, J. C., & Hall, B. J. (2017). Anxiety about electronic data hacking: Predictors and relations to mental health. *Psychiatry Research*, 256, 348–352.

Elhai, J. D., Vasquez, J. K., Lustgarten, S. D., Levine, J. C., & Hall, B. J. (2017). Proneness to boredom mediates relationships between problematic smartphone use with depression and anxiety severity. *Social Science Computer Review*. Advance online publication. DOI: 10.1177/0894439317741087

Elias, M. (2021). Nomophobia among higher secondary students. *Turkish Journal of Physiotherapy and Rehabilitation*.

Elias, J., Mirunalini, M., & Paul, I. (2021). Nomophobic rate and social media usage of higher secondary students. *International Journal of Current Research and Review*, 13(24), 132–138. DOI: 10.31782/IJCRR.2021.132423

Ellison, N. B., Vitak, J., Gray, R., & Lampe, C. (2014). Cultivating social resources on social network sites: Facebook relationship maintenance behaviours and their role in social capital processes. *Journal of Computer-Mediated Communication*, 19(4), 855–870. DOI: 10.1111/jcc4.12078

Elphinston, R. A., & Noller, P. (2011). Time to face it! Facebook intrusion and the implications for romantic jealousy and relationship satisfaction. *Cyberpsychology, Behavior, and Social Networking*, 14(11), 631–635. DOI: 10.1089/cyber.2010.0318 PMID: 21548798

Engel, G. L. (1977). The need for a new medical model: A challenge for biomedicine. *Science*, 196(4286), 129–136. DOI: 10.1126/science.847460 PMID: 847460

Enhanced flagging for Respondus Monitor. (n.d.) Respondus. https://web.respondus.com/enhanced-flagging-respondus-monitor

Erdem, C., & Uzun, A. M. (2022). Smartphone addiction among undergraduates: Roles of personality traits and demographic factors. *Technology. Knowledge and Learning*, 27(2), 579–597. DOI: 10.1007/s10758-020-09467-1

Ergün, N., Göksu, İ., & Sakız, H. (2020). Effects of phubbing: Relationships with psychodemographic variables. *Psychological Reports*, 123(5), 1578–1613. DOI: 10.1177/0033294119889581 PMID: 31752605

Erinci, A. (2017). Gender differences in digital game addiction among Turkish high school students. *Uluslararas Insan Bilimleri Dergisi*, 14(3), 315–325.

Erstad, O., Flewitt, R., Kümmerling-Meibauer, B., & Pereira, Í. S. P. (Eds.). (2020). *The Routledge handbook of digital literacies in early childhood*. Routledge.

Escalera-Chávez, M. E., García-Santillán, A., & Molchanova, V. S. (2020). Phubbing behavior: Is there a gender difference in college students? *European Journal of Contemporary Education*, 9(3), 546–551. DOI: 10.13187/ejced.2020.3.546

Essel, H. B., Vlachopoulos, D., Tachie-Menson, A., Nunoo, F. K. N., & Johnson, E. E. (2022, April 4). Nomophobia among preservice teachers: A descriptive correlational study at Ghanaian colleges of education. *Education and Information Technologies*, 27(7), 9541–9561. DOI: 10.1007/s10639-022-11023-6 PMID: 35399783

Etchezahar, E., Durao, M., Albalá Genol, M. Á., & Muller, M. (2023, February). Validation of the perceived phubbing scale to the Argentine context. *Behavioral Sciences (Basel, Switzerland)*, 13(2), 192. DOI: 10.3390/bs13020192 PMID: 36829421

Fardouly, J., Diedrichs, P. C., Vartanian, L. R., & Halliwell, E. (2015). Social comparisons on social media: The impact of Facebook on young women's body image concerns and mood. *Body Image*, 13, 38–45. DOI: 10.1016/j.bodyim.2014.12.002 PMID: 25615425

Fauzi, A., Kasim, N. M., & Paiman, N. (2021). Fear of missing out among adolescents. *International Journal of E-Services and Mobile Applications*, 13(4), 1–14. DOI: 10.4018/IJESMA.2021100104

Feist, G. J. (2019). Creativity and the Big Two model of personality: Plasticity and stability. *Current Opinion in Behavioral Sciences*, 27, 31–35. DOI: 10.1016/j.cobeha.2018.07.005

Felitti, V. J. (2003). The origins of addiction: Evidence from the adverse childhood experiences study. *Praxis der Kinderpsychologie und Kinderpsychiatrie*, 52(8), 547–559. PMID: 14619682

Fernandez-Gallardo, M., González-Ramírez, R., Sandoval, A., Felix, R., & Monjaraz, E. (2016). Adenosine stimulate proliferation and migration in triple negative breast cancer cells. *PLoS One*, 11(12), e0167445. DOI: 10.1371/journal.pone.0167445 PMID: 27911956

Ferrero, M. A., & Dalle Mura, M. (2019). Is social media use associated with stress, depression and well-being in adolescents and young adults? A narrative review. *Frontiers in Psychology*, 10, 902.

Ferrer-Pérez, C., Montagud-Romero, S., & Blanco-Gandía, M. C. (2024). Neurobiological Theories of Addiction: A Comprehensive Review. *Psychoactives*, 3(1), 35–47. DOI: 10.3390/psychoactives3010003

Festinger, L. (1954). A theory of social comparison processes. *Human Relations*, 7(2), 117–140. DOI: 10.1177/001872675400700202

Fink, G. (2010). Stress: Definition and history. *Stress Science: Neuroendocrinology, 3*(9), 3-14.

Firth, J., Torous, J., & Wykes, T. (2017). The Digital Mindfulness Project: A Randomized Controlled Trial of Mindfulness Training for Young People with Smartphone Addiction. *Psychological Medicine*, 47(1), 40–48.

Fisher, W., & Wesolkowski, S. (1999). Tempering technostress. *IEEE Technology and Society Magazine*, 18(1), 28–42. DOI: 10.1109/44.752243

Flanigan, A. E., Brady, A. C., Dai, Y., & Ray, E. (2023, June). Managing student digital distraction in the college classroom: A self-determination theory perspective. *Educational Psychology Review*, 35(2), 1–19. DOI: 10.1007/s10648-023-09780-y

Flannery, K., & Mohs, J. N. (2020). Asymmetric cost behavior: Exploring ethical issues facing management. *Strategic Management Quarterly*, 8(2). Advance online publication. DOI: 10.15640/v8n2a1

Fleming, L. (2024, May 30). *Are you phubbing your partner?* Verywell Mind. https://www.verywellmind.com/what-is-phubbing-8647390

Fletcher, G. J., Simpson, J. A., & Thomas, G. (2000). The measurement of perceived relationship quality components: A confirmatory factor analytic approach. *Personality and Social Psychology Bulletin*, 26(3), 340–354. DOI: 10.1177/0146167200265007

Floegel, D., Elias, N., & Lemish, D. (2021). Young children's mobile device use in public places: Immersion, distraction, and co-use. *Studies in Media and Communication*, 9(1), 30–40. DOI: 10.11114/smc.v9i1.5236

Fordham, B., Sugavanam, T., Edwards, K., Stallard, P., Howard, R., Nair, R. D., Copsey, B., Lee, H., Howick, J., Hemming, K., & Lamb, S. E. (2021). The evidence for cognitive behavioural therapy in any condition, population or context: A meta-review of systematic reviews and panoramic meta-analysis. *Psychological Medicine*, 51(1), 21–29. DOI: 10.1017/S0033291720005292 PMID: 33455594

Forgeard, M. J., & Seligman, M. E. (2012). Seeing the glass half full: A review of the causes and consequences of optimism. *Pratiques Psychologiques*, 18(2), 107–120. DOI: 10.1016/j.prps.2012.02.002

Franchina, V., Vanden Abeele, M., van Rooij, A. J., Lo Coco, G., & De Marez, L. (2018). Fear of missing out as a predictor of problematic social media use and phubbing behavior among Flemish adolescents. *International Journal of Environmental Research and Public Health*, 15(10), 2319. DOI: 10.3390/ijerph15102319 PMID: 30360407

Franken, I. H., Muris, P., & Georgieva, I. (2006). Gray's model of personality and addiction. *Addictive Behaviors*, 31(3), 399–403. DOI: 10.1016/j.addbeh.2005.05.022 PMID: 15964149

Frankowski, S., Lupo, A. K., Smith, B. A., Dane'El, M., Ramos, C., & Morera, O. F. (2016). Developing and Testing a Scale to Measure Need for Drama. *Personality and Individual Differences*, 89, 192–201. DOI: 10.1016/j.paid.2015.10.009

French Observatory of Digital Addiction. (2022). *Smartphone addiction among French teenagers: An overview*. Retrieved from https://www.frenchobservatory.org/smartphone-addiction

Friedrich, A., & Schlarb, A. A. (2018). Let's talk about sleep: A systematic review of psychological interventions to improve sleep in college students. *Journal of Sleep Research*, 27(1), 4–22. DOI: 10.1111/jsr.12568 PMID: 28618185

Fukunishi, I., & Rahe, R. H. (1995). Alexithymia and coping with stress in healthy persons: Alexithymia as a personality trait is associated with low social support and poor responses to stress. *Psychological Reports*, 76(3, suppl), 1299–1304. DOI: 10.2466/pr0.1995.76.3c.1299 PMID: 7480499

Furnham, A., & Cheng, H. (2023, July 31). The Big-Five personality factors, cognitive ability, health, and social-demographic indicators as independent predictors of self-efficacy: A longitudinal study. *Scandinavian Journal of Psychology*, 65(1), 53–60. DOI: 10.1111/sjop.12953 PMID: 37525487

Furukawa, T. (2017). Personality traits, cognitive biases, and emotional regulation in behavioral addictions: A comprehensive review. *Journal of Behavioral Addictions*, 6(3), 243–256. DOI: 10.1556/2006.6.2017.054

Gangadharan, N., Borle, A. L., & Basu, S. (2022). Mobile phone addiction as an emerging behavioral form of addiction among adolescents in India. *Cureus*, 14(4), e23798. DOI: 10.7759/cureus.23798 PMID: 35518537

Gangadharan, P. (2022). Prevalence of mobile phone addiction in Delhi adolescents. *Cureus*.

Gangwar, G. (2022). *Influence of internet use upon life style of adolescents (10603)* [Doctoral dissertation, Banasthali Vidyapith University, Rajasthan]. Shodhganga.

Gao, B., Guo, F., Lisic, L. L., & Omer, T. C. (2023). Enforcement of non-compete agreements, outside employment opportunities, and insider trading*. *Contemporary Accounting Research*, 40(2), 1250–1279. DOI: 10.1111/1911-3846.12842

Gao, B., Shen, Q., Luo, G., & Xu, Y. (2023). Why does the mobile social media-related fear of missing out promote depressive symptoms? The roles of phubbing and social exclusion. *BMC Psychology*, 11(1), 231. Advance online publication. DOI: 10.1186/s40359-023-01231-1 PMID: 37568184

Garcia, M. A., Lerma, M., Perez, M. G., Medina, K. S., Rodriguez-Crespo, A., & Cooper, T. V. (2023). Psychosocial and personality trait associates of phubbing and being phubbed in hispanic emerging adult college students. *Current Psychology (New Brunswick, N.J.)*, 43(6), 5601–5614. DOI: 10.1007/s12144-023-04767-y PMID: 37359598

Garrido, E. C., Delgado, S. C., & Esteban, P. G. (2024). Phubbing and its impact on the individual's psychological well-being. *Acta Psychologica*, 248, 104388. DOI: 10.1016/j.actpsy.2024.104388 PMID: 38959636

Garrido, E. C., Issa, T., Esteban, P. G., & Delgado, S. C. (2021). A descriptive literature review of phubbing behaviors. *Heliyon*, 7(5). PMID: 34041393

Gavrilas, L., & Kotsis, K. T. (2023). Research for self-reported health problems after excessive talking time on mobile phones among university students. *Eurasian Journal of Science and Environmental Education*, 3(1), 7–15. DOI: 10.30935/ejsee/12958

Gerosa, M. (2021). The impact of smartphones on academic performance in high school students. *Social Science Computer Review*, 39(6), 1103–1120.

Gerosa, T., Gui, M., & Büchi, M. (2022). Smartphone use and academic performance: A pervasiveness approach beyond addiction. *Social Science Computer Review*, 40(6), 1542–1561. DOI: 10.1177/08944393211018969

Gershon, I. (2018). Calling the irrational unmanageable neoliberal self. In *A Networked Self and Love* (pp. 12–30). Routledge. DOI: 10.4324/9781315193472-2

Ghrouz, A. K., Noohu, M. M., Manzar, D., & Warren Spence, D. (2019). Physical activity and sleep quality in relation to mental health among college students. *Sleep and Breathing*, 23(2), 627–634. DOI: 10.1007/s11325-019-01780-z PMID: 30685851

Girela-Serrano, B. M., Spiers, A. D. V., Ruotong, L., Gangadia, S., Toledano, M. B., & Di Simplicio, M. (2022). Impact of mobile phones and wireless devices use on children and adolescents' mental health: A systematic review. *European Child & Adolescent Psychiatry*. Advance online publication. DOI: 10.1007/s00787-022-02012-8 PMID: 35705765

Goel, R., & Singla, J. (2024). Workplace Transformation. In *Advances in marketing, customer relationship management, and e-services book series* (pp. 178–207). DOI: 10.4018/979-8-3693-1314-5.ch008

Goel, R., Singla, J., Arora, M., & Mittal, A. (2024). From stress to success: Role of green atmospherics on employee well-being in the Indian hotel and tourism industry. *Journal of Human Resources in Hospitality & Tourism*, 23(3), 359–385. DOI: 10.1080/15332845.2024.2335091

Goffman, E. (2023). The presentation of self in everyday life. In *Social theory re-wired* (pp. 450–459). Routledge. DOI: 10.4324/9781003320609-59

Gökalp, Z. Ş., Saritepeci, M., & Durak, H. Y. (2022). The relationship between self-control and procrastination among adolescent: The mediating role of multi screen addiction. *Current Psychology (New Brunswick, N.J.)*, 42(15), 1–12. DOI: 10.1007/s12144-021-02472-2 PMID: 35035199

Gökçearslan, Ş., Mumcu, E., Haşlaman, T., & Çevik, V. (2016). The role of self-monitoring and self-control in smartphone addiction. *Journal of Behavioral Addictions*, 5(2), 307–316. DOI: 10.1556/2006.5.2016.048

Goldberg, L. R. (1990). An alternative “description of personality”: the big-five factor structure. psycnet.

Goldberg, Y. K., Eastwood, J. D., LaGuardia, J., & Danckert, J. (2011). Boredom: An emotional experience distinct from apathy, anhedonia, or depression. *Journal of Social and Clinical Psychology*, 30(6), 647–666. DOI: 10.1521/jscp.2011.30.6.647

Golden, T. D. (2006). Avoiding depletion in virtual work: Telework and the intervening impact of work exhaustion on commitment and turnover intentions. *Journal of Vocational Behavior*, 69(1), 176–187. DOI: 10.1016/j.jvb.2006.02.003

Goldman, D., Oroszi, G., & Ducci, F. (2006). The genetics of addictions: Uncovering the genes. *Focus (San Francisco, Calif.)*, 6(3), 521–415. DOI: 10.1176/foc.4.3.401 PMID: 15995696

Goldstein, D. S., & Kopin, I. J. (2007). Evolution of concepts of stress. *Stress (Amsterdam, Netherlands)*, 10(2), 109–120. DOI: 10.1080/10253890701288935 PMID: 17514579

Gonsalves, L., & Harris, J. (2020). *The Connected Mind: Why Smartphones and Social Media Are Transforming the Brain*. The MIT Press.

Gorelik, D., & Eastwood, J. D. (2024). Trait Boredom as a Lack of Agency: A Theoretical Model and a New Assessment Tool. *Assessment*, 31(2), 321–334. DOI: 10.1177/10731911231161780 PMID: 36942352

Goyal, M., Singh, S., Sibinga, E. M., Gould, N. F., Rowland-Seymour, A., Sharma, R., Berger, Z., Sleicher, D., Maron, D. D., Shihab, H. M., Ranasinghe, P. D., Linn, S., Saha, S., Bass, E. B., & Haythornthwaite, J. A. (2014). Meditation programs for psychological stress and well-being: A systematic review and meta-analysis. *JAMA Internal Medicine*, 174(3), 357–368. DOI: 10.1001/jamainternmed.2013.13018 PMID: 24395196

Goyal, S., Hardgrave, B. C., Aloysius, J., & DeHoratius, N. (2016). The effectiveness of rfid in backroom and sales floor inventory management. *International Journal of Logistics Management*, 27(3), 795–815. DOI: 10.1108/IJLM-03-2015-0051

Grant, J. E., & Chamberlain, S. R. (2016). Expanding the definition of addiction: DSM-5 vs. ICD-11. *CNS Spectrums*, 21(4), 300–303. DOI: 10.1017/S1092852916000183 PMID: 27151528

Greenfield, D. N. (2020). Digital distraction: What makes the internet and smartphone so addictive? In *American Psychological Association eBooks* (pp. 27–47). DOI: 10.1037/0000208-003

Green, L., Holloway, D., Stevenson, K., Leaver, T., & Haddon, L. (Eds.). (2021). *The Routledge companion to digital media and children*. Routledge.

Griffiths, M. (2005). A 'components' model of addiction within a biopsychosocial framework. *Journal of Substance Use*, 10(4), 191–197. DOI: 10.1080/14659890500114359

Griffiths, M. D., & Szabo, A. (2014, March 1). Is excessive online usage a function of medium or activity? An empirical pilot study. *Journal of Behavioral Addictions*, 3(1), 74–77. DOI: 10.1556/JBA.2.2013.016 PMID: 25215216

Guazzini, A., Duradoni, M., Capelli, A., & Meringolo, P. (2019). An explorative model to assess Individuals' phubbing risk. *Future Internet*, 11(1), 21. DOI: 10.3390/fi11010021

Guazzini, A., Raimondi, T., Biagini, B., Bagnoli, F., & Duradoni, M. (2021). Phubber's emotional activations: The association between PANAS and phubbing behavior. *Future Internet*, 13(12), 311. DOI: 10.3390/fi13120311

Gubbi, M. (2023, November 22). *Big brother in your pocket: How AI is monitoring your phone use.* Medium. https://medium.com/@maheshgubbi/big-brother-in-your-pocket-how-ai-is-monitoring-your-phone-activity-9ee5cac70822

Guo, L., Tobias, J., Bendoly, E., & Hu, Y. (2017). Different departments, different drivers. International Journal of Operations &Amp. *International Journal of Operations & Production Management*, 37(8), 1031–1053. DOI: 10.1108/IJOPM-01-2016-0046

Gupta, A. K. S. K., Singh, P. S. B., & Krishak, A. K. S. (2024). Smartphone addiction: Impact on health and well-being. *International Journal of Community Medicine and Public Health*, 11(5), 2100–2106. DOI: 10.18203/2394-6040.ijcmph20241213

Gupta, A., & Sharma, M. (2017). Social media and its impact with special reference to Indian teenagers: A review. *International Journal of Multidisciplinary Approach and Studies*, 4(3), 27–35.

Gupta, M., & Sharma, A. (2021). Fear of missing out: A brief overview of origin, theoretical underpinnings and relationship with mental health. *World Journal of Clinical Cases*, 9(19), 4881–4889. DOI: 10.12998/wjcc.v9.i19.4881 PMID: 34307542

Gurven, M., Von Rueden, C., Massenkoff, M., Kaplan, H., & Lero Vie, M. (2013). How universal is the Big Five? Testing the five-factor model of personality variation among forager–farmers in the Bolivian Amazon. *Journal of Personality and Social Psychology*, 104(2), 354–370. DOI: 10.1037/a0030841 PMID: 23245291

Gustavson, D. E., Friedman, N. P., Fontanillas, P., Elson, S. L., Palmer, A. A., & Sanchez-Roige, S. (2020). The latent genetic structure of impulsivity and its relation to internalizing psychopathology. *Psychological Science*, 31(8), 1025–1035. DOI: 10.1177/0956797620938160 PMID: 32716714

Hakulinen, C., Elovainio, M., Batty, G. D., Virtanen, M., Kivimäki, M., & Jokela, M. (2015). Personality and alcohol consumption: Pooled analysis of 72,949 adults from eight cohort studies. *Drug and Alcohol Dependence*, 151, 110–114. DOI: 10.1016/j.drugalcdep.2015.03.008 PMID: 25823906

Hale, J. L., & Pigliuca, R. (2017). Phubbing and Relationship Satisfaction: An Exploratory Study. *International Journal of Human-Computer Interaction*, 33(11), 911–918.

Hale, L., & Guan, S. (2015). Screen time and sleep among school-aged children and adolescents: A systematic literature review. *Sleep Medicine Reviews*, 21, 50–58. DOI: 10.1016/j.smrv.2014.07.007 PMID: 25193149

Hales, A. H., Dvir, M., Wesselmann, E. D., Kruger, D. J., & Finkenauer, C. (2018). Cell phone-induced ostracism threatens fundamental needs. *The Journal of Social Psychology*, 158(4), 460–473. DOI: 10.1080/00224545.2018.1439877 PMID: 29436935

Halpern, D., & Katz, J. E. (2017). Texting's consequences for romantic relationships: A cross-lagged analysis highlights its risks. *Computers in Human Behavior*, 71, 386–394. DOI: 10.1016/j.chb.2017.01.051

Han, J. H., Park, S. J., & Kim, Y. (2022). Phubbing as a millennials' new addiction and relating factors among nursing students. *Psychiatry Investigation*, 19(2), 135–145. DOI: 10.30773/pi.2021.0163 PMID: 35164436

Hansen, K. (2022, October 17). *Our Social Media Addiction*. Harvard Business Review. https://hbr.org/2022/11/our-social-media-addiction

Hao, Z., Jin, L., Li, Y., Akram, H. R., Saeed, M. F., Ma, J., Ma, H., & Huang, J. (2019). Alexithymia and mobile phone addiction in Chinese undergraduate students: The roles of mobile phone use patterns. *Computers in Human Behavior*, 97, 51–59. DOI: 10.1016/j.chb.2019.03.001

Haripriya, S., Samuel, S. E., & Megha, M. (2019). Correlation between smartphone addiction, sleep quality and physical activity among young adults. *Journal of Clinical and Diagnostic Research : JCDR*, 13, 5–9. DOI: 10.7860/JCDR/2019/42168.13212

Harper, L. (n.d.). *How to stop phubbing*. Stop Phubbing & Start Connecting. https://www.stopphubbing.com/how-to-stop-phubbing

Hashemi, A., Noori, A. Q., Orfan, S. N., Akramy, S. A., & Rameli, M. R. M. (2024, April). Undergraduate students' perception of smart phone addiction and its impact on themselves and their academic performance: A case study. *Cogent Education*, 11(1), 2340845. DOI: 10.1080/2331186X.2024.2340845

Hassan, M. R., Mahmud, M. S., & Hasan, M. K. (2024). Social Media Addiction and Its Consequences Among Youth: A Developing Country Perspective. *Global Business Review*, 09721509241276720. Advance online publication. DOI: 10.1177/09721509241276720

Hawi, N. S., & Samaha, M. (2017). The relations among social media addiction, self-esteem, and life satisfaction in university students. *Social Science Computer Review*, 35(5), 576–586. DOI: 10.1177/0894439316660340

Hayati, B., & Puri, S. (2020). The impact of organizational social networks on salespeople's negative headquarters stereotypes. Journal of Business &Amp. *Journal of Business and Industrial Marketing*, 35(12), 1901–1913. DOI: 10.1108/JBIM-07-2019-0327

Hayes, A. F., & Preacher, K. J. (2014). Statistical mediation analysis with a multicategorical independent variable. *British Journal of Mathematical & Statistical Psychology*, 67(3), 451–470. DOI: 10.1111/bmsp.12028 PMID: 24188158

Hayes, A., Herlinger, K., Paterson, L., & Lingford-Hughes, A. (2020). The neurobiology of substance use and addiction: Evidence from neuroimaging and relevance to treatment. *BJPsych Advances*, 26(6), 367–378. DOI: 10.1192/bja.2020.68

Haythornthwaite, C. (2005). Social networks and Internet connectivity effects. *Information Communication and Society*, 8(2), 125–147. DOI: 10.1080/13691180500146185

Hegde, S. (2019). Overuse of gadgets and its effects on children's behavior. *Journal of Advanced Medical and Dental Sciences Researches.*

Hegde, A. M., Suman, P., Unais, M., & Jeyakumar, C. (2019). Effect of electronic gadgets on the behaviour, academic performance and overall health of school going children-a descriptive study. *Journal of Advanced Medical and Dental Sciences Research*, 7(1), 100–103.

Hegde, S., Bhatia, M., & Bhandarkar, A. (2019). The effects of electronic gadgets on children's behavior and academic performance: A cross-sectional study in Bangalore, India. *India.Journal of Advanced Medical and Dental Sciences Researches*, 7(4), 102–106.

Heinz, A., Beck, A., Halil, M. G., Pilhatsch, M., Smolka, M. N., & Liu, S. (2019). Addiction as learned Behavior patterns. *Journal of Clinical Medicine*, 8(8). Advance online publication. DOI: 10.3390/jcm8081086 PMID: 31344831

Henderson, E. C. (2009). *Understanding addiction*. Univ. Press Of Mississippi.

Hendrick, S. S. (1988). A generic measure of relationship satisfaction. *Journal of Marriage and Family*, 50(1), 93–98. DOI: 10.2307/352430

Hernández Gracia, T. J., Avila, D. D., & Hernández Gracia, J. F. (2020, July 5). The phubbing: The interference in communication within the classroom. *The Journal of American Science*, 2(3), 12–17. DOI: 10.29057/jas.v2i3.5807

Herrero, J. (2021). Examining the empirical links between digital social pressure, personality, psychological distress, social support, users' residential living conditions, and smartphone addiction. *Social Science Computer Review*, 39(1), 1–15. DOI: 10.1177/0894439321998357

Hertlein, K. M., & Ancheta, K. (2014). Advantages and disadvantages of technology in relationships: Findings from an open-ended survey. *The Qualitative Report*, 19(11), 1–11. DOI: 10.46743/2160-3715/2014.1260

Heyman, J. L., Kerr, L. G., & Human, L. J. (2022). Social media use predicts greater liking in in-person initial interactions. *Personality and Social Psychology Bulletin*, 48(9), 1393–1405. DOI: 10.1177/01461672211040964 PMID: 34496679

Hinkle, D. E., Wiersma, W., & Jurs, S. G. (2003). *Applied statistics for the behavioral sciences* (Vol. 663). Houghton Mifflin.

Hodson, G., Book, A., Visser, B. A., Volk, A. A., Ashton, M. C., & Lee, K. (2018). Is the dark triad common factor distinct from low honesty-humility? *Journal of Research in Personality*, 73, 123–129. DOI: 10.1016/j.jrp.2017.11.012

Hofmann, S. G., Asnaani, A., Vonk, I. J., Sawyer, A. T., & Fang, A. (2012). The efficacy of cognitive behavioral therapy: A review of meta-analyses. *Cognitive Therapy and Research*, 36(5), 427–440. DOI: 10.1007/s10608-012-9476-1 PMID: 23459093

Hollandsworth, R., Dowdy, L., & Donovan, J. (2011). Digital citizenship in K-12: It takes a village.

Hollandsworth, R., Donovan, J., & Welch, M. (2017). Digital citizenship: You can't go home again. *TechTrends*, 61(6), 524–530. DOI: 10.1007/s11528-017-0190-4

Holz, A. (2023, March 3). *Earbuds, hearing loss, and social isolation*. PluggedIn. https://www.pluggedin.com/blog/earbuds-hearing-loss-and-social-isolation

Hong, F.-Y., Lin, C.-C., Lin, T.-J., & Huang, D.-H. (2021). The relationship among the social norms of college students, and their interpersonal relationships, smartphone use, and smartphone addiction. *Behaviour & Information Technology*, 40(4), 415–426. DOI: 10.1080/0144929X.2019.1699959

Hong, S. B., Zalesky, A., Cocchi, L., Fornito, A., Choi, E. J., Kim, H. H., Suh, J.-E., Kim, C.-D., Kim, J.-W., & Yi, S. H. (2013). Decreased functional brain connectivity in adolescents with internet addiction. *PLoS One*, 8(2), e57831. DOI: 10.1371/journal.pone.0057831 PMID: 23451272

Horwood, S., & Anglim, J. (2018). Personality and problematic smartphone use: A facet-level analysis using the Five Factor Model and HEXACO frameworks. *Computers in Human Behavior*, 85, 349–359. DOI: 10.1016/j.chb.2018.04.013

Houston, J., & Kopatich, K. (2024, September 24). Davenport schools says new cell phone policies are improving student engagement. *KWQC*.https://www.kwqc.com/2024/09/25/davenport-schools-says-new-cell-phone-policies-are-improving-student-engagement

Howard, M. C., & Van Zandt, E. C. (2020). The discriminant validity of honesty-humility: A meta-analysis of the HEXACO, Big Five, and Dark Triad. *Journal of Research in Personality*, 87, 103982. DOI: 10.1016/j.jrp.2020.103982

Hoyle, R. (2021). *Smartphones: The Good, the Bad, and the Ugly*. Penguin Books.

Hsieh, Y. P., Yen, C. F., & Chou, W. J. (2019). Development and validation of the Parental Smartphone Use Management Scale (PSUMS): Parents' perceived self-efficacy with adolescents with attention deficit hyperactivity disorder. *International Journal of Environmental Research and Public Health*, 16(8), 1423. DOI: 10.3390/ijerph16081423 PMID: 31010068

Huang, H. (2014). *Social media generation in China: a study of social media use and addiction among adolescents*. Springer. DOI: 10.1007/978-3-642-45441-7

Huey, M., & Giguere, D. (2023, June). The impact of smart phone use on course comprehension and psychological well-being in the college classroom. *Innovative Higher Education*, 48(3), 527–537. DOI: 10.1007/s10755-022-09638-1 PMID: 36440453

Humphreys, L., & Hardeman, H. (2021). Mobiles in public: Social interaction in a smartphone era. *Mobile Media & Communication*, 9(1), 103–127. DOI: 10.1177/2050157920927062

Hunt, A., Merola, G. P., Carpenter, T., & Jaeggi, A. V. (2024). Evolutionary perspectives on substance and behavioural addictions: Distinct and shared pathways to understanding, prediction and prevention. *Neuroscience and Biobehavioral Reviews*, 159, 105603. DOI: 10.1016/j.neubiorev.2024.105603 PMID: 38402919

Hunter, J. A., Dyer, K. J., Cribbie, R. A., & Eastwood, J. D. (2016). Exploring the utility of the multidimensional state boredom scale. *European Journal of Psychological Assessment*, 32(3), 241–250. DOI: 10.1027/1015-5759/a000251

Hussain, Z., & Pontes, H. M. (2018). Personality, internet addiction, and other technological addictions. In *Advances in Human Factors and Ergonomics* (pp. 1–10). IGI Global. DOI: 10.4018/978-1-5225-3477-8.ch003

ICD-11. (2024). *Personality disorders and related traits* ICD-11 for Morbidity and Mortality Statistics. https://icd.who.int/dev11/l-m/en#/http%3a%2f%2fid.who.int%2ficd%2fentity%2f37291724

İliç, U. (2021, September). Online learning readiness, phubbing and sofalizing levels of pre-service teachers amidst pandemic. *Shanlax International Journal of Education*, 9(4), 1–12. DOI: 10.34293/education.v9i4.4027

İliç, U., & Tanyeri, T. (2021). Is phubbing a matter for educators: A case for pre-service and in-service teachers. *Malaysian Online Journal of Educational Technology*, 9(1), 70–79. DOI: 10.17220/mojet.2021.9.1.246

Indrawati, S. (2021). Effect of ability on salesperson performance through adaptive selling behavior as an intervening variable. *Ekspektra: Jurnal Bisnis Dan Manajemen*, 5(1), 31–37. DOI: 10.25139/ekt.v5i1.3354

Intelligence, J. W. T. (2012). Fear of Missing Out (FoMO). Retrieve from: www.jwtintelligence.com/wp-content/uploads/2012/03/F_JWT_FOM update_3.21.12.pdf

Internet and Technology Addicts Anonymous. (2024). *Signs of Internet and Technology Addiction Anonymous.* https://internetaddictsanonymous.org/internet-and-technology-addiction/

Iqbal, M., Said, O., Ibrahim, O., & Soliman, A. (2021). Visual Sequelae of Computer Vision Syndrome: A Cross-Sectional Case-Control Study. *Journal of Ophthalmology*, 2021(1), 6630286. DOI: 10.1155/2021/6630286 PMID: 33868724

Islam, M. A., & Hossin, M. Z. (2016). Prevalence and risk factors of problematic internet use and the associated psychological distress among graduate students of Bangladesh. *Asian Journal of Gambling Issues and Public Health*, 6(1), 11. DOI: 10.1186/s40405-016-0020-1 PMID: 27942430

Ivanova, A., Gorbaniuk, O., Błachnio, A., Przepiórka, A., Mraka, N., Polishchuk, V., et al. (2020). Mobile phone addiction, phubbing, and depression among men and women: a moderated mediation analysis. Psychiatry Q., 91, 655–668. doi: DOI: 10.1007/s11126-020-09723

Ivanova, A., Gorbaniuk, O., Błachnio, A., Przepiórka, A., Mraka, N., Polishchuk, V., & Gorbaniuk, J. (2020). Mobile Phone Addiction, Phubbing, and Depression Among Men and Women: A Moderated Mediation Analysis. *The Psychiatric Quarterly*, 91(3), 655–668. DOI: 10.1007/s11126-020-09723-8 PMID: 32146681

Iyengar, S. S., Wells, R. E., & Schwartz, B. (2006). Doing better but feeling worse: Looking for the "best" job undermines satisfaction. *Psychological Science*, 17(2), 143–150. DOI: 10.1111/j.1467-9280.2006.01677.x PMID: 16466422

Jackson, L. A., von Eye, A., Biocca, F., Barbatsis, G., Fitzgerald, H., & Zhao, Y. (2003). Personality, cognitive style, demographic characteristics and Internet use: Findings from the HomeNetToo. *Swiss Journal of Psychology*, 62(2), 79–90. DOI: 10.1024//1421-0185.62.2.79

Jahrami, H., Romdhane, F. F., & Pandi-Perumal, S. R. (2023). Global research evidence on nomophobia during 2008-2022: A bibliometric analysis and review. *Psychology Health and Medicine*, 29(5), 889–904. DOI: 10.1080/13548506.2023.2268888 PMID: 37846044

Jameel, S., Shahnawaz, M. G., & Griffiths, M. D. (2019). Smartphone addiction in students: A qualitative examination of the components model of addiction using face-to-face interviews. *Journal of Behavioral Addictions*, 8(4), 780–793. DOI: 10.1556/2006.8.2019.57 PMID: 31619046

Jarupreechachan, W., Kitchat, K., & Surasak, T. (2023). 'Do Not Disturb': An Implication Design To Be Alerted But Less Stress. In *nternational Seminar on Application for Technology of Information and Communication (iSemantic), Semarang, Indonesia, 2023* (Vol. 128). DOI: 10.1109/iSemantic59612.2023.10295289

Jo, H., & Baek, E. (2023). Exploring the dynamics of mobile app addiction: The interplay of communication, affective factors, flow, perceived enjoyment, and habit. *BMC Psychology*, 11(1), 404. Advance online publication. DOI: 10.1186/s40359-023-01440-8 PMID: 37986198

Jo, H., Na, E., & Kim, D.-J. (2018). The relationship between smartphone addiction predisposition and impulsivity among Korean smartphone users. *Addiction Research and Theory*, 26(1), 77–84. DOI: 10.1080/16066359.2017.1312356

Johnson, A. R., Sridhar, P. R., & Joseph, M. (2022). Is screen addiction a problem among rural school-going adolescents? A cross-sectional study in South Karnataka. *Journal of Indian Association for Child and Adolescent Mental Health*, 18(2), 137–143. DOI: 10.1177/09731342221096481

Jones, S. B., Aruguete, M. S., & Gretlein, R. (2020, January 1). Cell phone use policies in the college classroom: Do they work? *Transactions of the Missouri Academy of Science. Missouri Academy of Science*, 48(2020), 5–9. DOI: 10.30956/MAS-31R1

Kalvik, K. (2023, July 10). *Are text messages secure? 6 must-dos for safer texting*. Messente. https://messente.com/blog/are-text-messages-secure

Karadağ, E., Tosuntaş, Ş. B., Erzen, E., Duru, P., Bostan, N., Şahin, B. M., Çulha, İ., & Babadağ, B. (2015). Determinants of phubbing, which is the sum of many virtual addictions: A structural equation model. *Journal of Behavioral Addictions*, 4(2), 60–74. DOI: 10.1556/2006.4.2015.005 PMID: 26014669

Kardefelt-Winther, D. (2017). How does the time children spend using digital technology impact their mental well-being, social relationships, and physical activity? An evidence-focused literature review. *Innocenti Discussion Paper*. UNICEF Office of Research - Innocenti.

Kardefelt-Winther, D. (2017). Conceptualizing Internet Use Disorders: A Critical Perspective on Diagnostic Criteria and Causal Assumptions. *Current Addiction Reports*, 4(2), 229–235.

Karlins, M. (2022). A student-friendly approach to eliminating cell phone usage in the college classroom. *College Teaching*, 70(4), 506–508. DOI: 10.1080/87567555.2021.1985423

Karukivi, M., & Saarijärvi, S. (2014). Development of alexithymic personality features. *World Journal of Psychiatry*, 4(4), 91. DOI: 10.5498/wjp.v4.i4.91 PMID: 25540724

Kaspersky Lab finds over half of consumers don't password-protect their mobile devices. (2018, June 28). Kaspersky. https://usa.kaspersky.com/about/press-releases/kaspersky-lab-finds-over-half-of-consumers-don-t-password-protect-their-mobile-devices

Kaya, A., Türk, N., Batmaz, H., & Griffiths, M. D. (2023). Online Gaming Addiction and Basic Psychological Needs Among Youngsters: The Mediating Roles of Meaning in Life and Responsibility. *International Journal of Mental Health and Addiction*, 1–25. Advance online publication. DOI: 10.1007/s11469-022-00994 PMID: 36643385

Kaya, B. (2024). Dark triad and social media addiction: A meta-analysis. *Klinik Psikoloji Dergisi*, 8(2), 310–319.

Kekäläinen, T., Terracciano, A., Sipilä, S., & Kokko, K. (2020). Personality traits and physical functioning: A cross-sectional multimethod facet-level analysis. *European Review of Aging and Physical Activity*, 17(1), 1–13. DOI: 10.1186/s11556-020-00251-9 PMID: 33292163

Keles, B., McCrae, N., & Grealish, A. (2020). A systematic review: The influence of social media on depression, anxiety and psychological distress in adolescents. *International Journal of Adolescence and Youth*, 25(1), 79–93. DOI: 10.1080/02673843.2019.1590851

Kelly, L., Miller-Ott, A. E., & Duran, R. L. (2019). Phubbing friends: Understanding face threats from, and responses to, friends' cell phone usage through the lens of politeness theory. *Communication Quarterly*, 67(5), 540–559. DOI: 10.1080/01463373.2019.1668443

Kemp, S. (2024, July 31). *Digital 2024 July global statshot report.* Datareportal. https://datareportal.com/reports/digital-2024-july-global-statshot

Keng, S. L., Smoski, M. J., & Robins, C. J. (2011). Effects of mindfulness on psychological health: A review of empirical studies. *Clinical Psychology Review*, 31(6), 1041–1056. DOI: 10.1016/j.cpr.2011.04.006 PMID: 21802619

Keppel, G., Saufley, W. H., & Tokunaga, H. (1992). *Introduction to design and analysis: A student's handbook.* Macmillan.

Khadka, S., Narayanan, B., Meda, S., Gelernter, J., Han, S., Sawyer, B., Aslanzadeh, F., Stevens, M., Hawkins, K., Anticevic, A., Potenza, M. N., & Pearlson, G. D. (2014). Genetic association of impulsivity in young adults: A multivariate study. *Translational Psychiatry*, 4(9), e451–e451. DOI: 10.1038/tp.2014.95 PMID: 25268255

Khan, N. F., & Khan, M. N. (2021). A bibliometric analysis of peer-reviewed literature on smartphone addiction and future research agenda. *Asia-Pacific Journal of Business Administration*, 14(2), 199–222. DOI: 10.1108/APJBA-09-2021-0430

Kheradmand, A., Amirlatifi, E. S., & Rahbar, Z. (2023). Personality traits of university students with smartphone addiction. *Frontiers in Psychiatry*, 14, 1083214. DOI: 10.3389/fpsyt.2023.1083214 PMID: 36846239

Kibeom, L., & Michael, C. (2009). *The Hexaco personality inventory - Revised, a measure of the six major dimensions of personality*. Retrieved 29 November, 2024 from https://hexaco.org/scaledescriptions

Kim, H., & Lee, Y. (2018). Socioeconomic status, perceived inequality of opportunity, and attitudes toward redistribution. *The Social Science Journal*, 55(3), 300–312. DOI: 10.1016/j.soscij.2018.01.008

Kim, J. (2015). The effect of parental attitude on mobile phone addiction and anxiety in elementary students. *Journal of Addictions Nursing*, 26(4), 204–212.

Kim, J., Cho, H., Park, K., & Lee, J. (2019). The impact of app usage trackers on smartphone addiction and the role of mindfulness. *Computers in Human Behavior*, 93, 48–56. DOI: 10.1016/j.chb.2018.12.016

Kim, M.-H., Min, S., Ahn, J.-S., An, C., & Lee, J. (2019). Association between high adolescent smartphone use and academic impairment, conflicts with family members or friends, and suicide attempts. *PLoS One*, 14(7), e0219831. DOI: 10.1371/journal.pone.0219831 PMID: 31306455

Kim, S. M., Huh, H. J., Cho, H., Kwon, M., Choi, J. H., Ahn, H. J., Lee, S. W., Kim, Y. J., & Kim, D. J. (2014). The effect of depression, impulsivity, and resilience on smartphone addiction in university students. *Journal of Korean Neuropsychiatric Association*, 53(4), 214–220. DOI: 10.4306/jknpa.2014.53.4.214

King, A. L. S., Valenca, A. M., Silva, A. C. O., Baczynski, T., Carvalho, M. R., & Nardi, A. E. (2013). Nomophobia: Dependency on virtual environments or social phobia? *Computers in Human Behavior*, 29(1), 140–144. DOI: 10.1016/j.chb.2012.07.025

Kiran, S., Sanjana, J., & Reddy, N. (2019). *Mobile phone addiction: symptoms, impacts and causes-a review*. Int Conf Trends Ind Value Eng Bus Soc Innov.

Kırcaburun, K., March, E., Balta, S., Emirtekin, E., Kişla, T., & Griffiths, M. D. (2022). The role of procrastination between personality traits and addictive mukbang watching among emerging adults. *SAGE Open*, 12(1). DOI: 10.1177/21582440221085006

Kircaburun, K., Süral, İ., March, E., Balta, S., Emirtekin, E., & Griffiths, M. D. (2021). Study addiction and 'dark' personality traits: A cross-sectional survey study among emerging adults. *Journal of Addictive Diseases*, 39(3), 307–315. DOI: 10.1080/10550887.2021.1872469 PMID: 33499773

Kivva, A. (2024, February 26). *The mobile malware threat landscape in 2023*. SecureList by Kaspersky. https://securelist.com/mobile-malware-report-2023/111964

Kliesener, T., Meigen, C., Kiess, W., & Poulain, T. (2022). Associations between problematic smartphone use and behavioural difficulties, quality of life, and school performance among children and adolescents. *BMC Psychiatry*, 22(1), 195. DOI: 10.1186/s12888-022-03815-4 PMID: 35300635

Koçak, O., Arslan, H., & Erdoğan, A. (2021). Social media use across generations: From addiction to engagement. *European Integration Studies*, 1(15), 63–77. DOI: 10.5755/j01.eis.1.15.29080

Koc, T., & Caliskan, K. (2022, June 15). Phubbing phenomenon in educational environments: Examining the impact of supervisor phubbing on student outcomes. *Journal of Further and Higher Education*, 47(1), 15–30. DOI: 10.1080/0309877X.2022.2088270

Korean Institute for Health and Social Affairs. (2020). Smartphone addiction prevention programs in South Korea: An evaluation. *Korean Journal of Public Health*, 47(4), 321–335. DOI: 10.13048/kjph.2020.47.4.321

Körmendi, A., Brutóczki, Z., Végh, B. P., & Székely, R. (2016). Smartphone use can be addictive? A case report. *Journal of Behavioral Addictions*, 5(3), 548–552. DOI: 10.1556/2006.5.2016.033 PMID: 27599674

Krasnova, H., Wenninger, H., Widjaja, T., & Buxmann, P. (2017). Envy on Facebook: A hidden threat to users' life satisfaction? *Information Systems Research*, 24(3), 587–605.

Krishna, S. M., & Agrawal, S. (2023). Cyberloafing: Exploring the role of psychological wellbeing and social media learning. *Behavioral Sciences (Basel, Switzerland)*, 13(8), 649. DOI: 10.3390/bs13080649 PMID: 37622789

Krist, A. H., Davidson, K. W., Mangione, C. M., Barry, M. J., Cabana, M., Caughey, A. B., Curry, S. J., Donahue, K., Doubeni, C. A., Epling, J. W.Jr, Kubik, M., Ogedegbe, G., Pbert, L., Silverstein, M., Simon, M. A., Tseng, C.-W., & Wong, J. B. (2020). Screening for unhealthy drug use: US Preventive Services Task Force recommendation statement. *Journal of the American Medical Association*, 323(22), 2301–2309. DOI: 10.1001/jama.2020.8020 PMID: 32515821

Kross, E., Verduyn, P., Demiralp, E., Park, J., Lee, D. S., Lin, N., & Ybarra, O. (2013). Facebook use predicts declines in subjective well-being in young adults. *PLoS One*, 8(8), e69841. DOI: 10.1371/journal.pone.0069841 PMID: 23967061

Krupnov, A., Novikova, I., & Vorobyeva, A. (2016). On the problem of relation between the system-functional and the five-factor models of personality traits. *RUDN Journal of Psychology and Pedagogics*, (2), 45–56.

Kuang-Tsan, C., & Fu-Yuan, H. (2017). Study on relationship among university students' life stress, smart mobile phone addiction, and life satisfaction. *Journal of Adult Development*, 24(2), 109–118. DOI: 10.1007/s10804-016-9250-9

Kurt, S. (2021, May 23). *McClelland's Three Needs Theory: Power, achievement, and affiliation*. Education Library. https://educationlibrary.org/mcclellands-three-needs-theory-power-achievement-and-affiliation

Kurtz, J. E. (2020). NEO Inventories. In *Encyclopedia of personality and individual differences* (pp. 3164–3165). Springer. DOI: 10.1007/978-3-319-24612-3_940

Kuss, D. J., & Griffiths, M. D. (2017). Social networking sites and addiction: Ten lessons learned. *International Journal of Environmental Research and Public Health*, 14(3), 311. DOI: 10.3390/ijerph14030311 PMID: 28304359

Kuss, D. J., & Griffiths, M. D. (2021). Smartphone addiction: A systematic review of the evidence. *International Journal of Environmental Research and Public Health*, 18(10), 5360. PMID: 34069883

Kuss, D. J., Kanjo, E., Crook-Rumsey, M., Kibowski, F., Wang, G. Y., & Sumich, A. (2018). Problematic mobile phone use and addiction across generations: The roles of psychopathological symptoms and smartphone use. *Journal of Technology in Behavioral Science*, 3(3), 141–149. DOI: 10.1007/s41347-017-0041-3 PMID: 30238057

Kusuma, A. R., Syarief, R., Ekananta, A., & Sukmawati, A. (2023). Scenario planning of digital transformation in indonesia's fast-moving consumer goods sales organization: Uncertainties and possibilities. *The Winners*, 24(2), 83–96. DOI: 10.21512/tw.v24i2.10401

Kutluay, E., & Karaca, F. (2024). A model proposal explaining the influence of smartphone addiction related factors on high school students' academic success. *Education and Information Technologies*. Advance online publication. DOI: 10.1007/s10639-024-12947-x

Kuyulu, I., & Beltekin, E. (2020). Relationship between Smartphone Addiction and Personality Traits. *Asian Journal of Education and Training, 6*(2), 304-313.

Kwon, M., Kim, D. J., Cho, H., & Yang, S. (2013). The smartphone addiction scale: Development and validation of a short version for adolescents. *PLoS One*, 8(12), e83558. DOI: 10.1371/journal.pone.0083558 PMID: 24391787

Kwon, M., Lee, J.-Y., Won, W.-Y., Park, J.-W., Min, J.-A., Hahn, C., Gu, X., Choi, J.-H., & Kim, D.-J. (2013). Development and validation of a smartphone addiction scale (SAS). *PLoS One*, 8(2), e56936. DOI: 10.1371/journal.pone.0056936 PMID: 23468893

Ladany, N. (2024, September 24). Behind the curtain of higher education: Faculty aren't trained. *Forbes.*https://www.forbes.com/sites/nicholasladany/2024/09/24/behind-the-curtain-of-higher-education-faculty-arent-trained

Lai, X., Hu, C., Ying, L., Xu, H., Zhao, C., Yang, X., Yu, X., & Zhang, G. (2023, October). Risk and protective factors associated with smart phone addiction and phubbing behavior among college students in China. *Psychological Reports*, 126(5), 2172–2190. DOI: 10.1177/00332941221084905 PMID: 35412349

Lamb, A. (2023, March 13). *Do phones belong in schools?* The Harvard Gazette. https://news.harvard.edu/gazette/story/2023/03/experts-see-pros-and-cons-to-allowing-cellphones-in-class

Lane, H.-Y., Chang, C.-J., Huang, C.-L., & Chang, Y.-H. (2021). An investigation into smartphone addiction with personality and sleep quality among university students. *International Journal of Environmental Research and Public Health*, 18(14), 7588. DOI: 10.3390/ijerph18147588 PMID: 34300037

Lan, Y., Ding, J. E., Li, W., Li, J., Zhang, Y., Liu, M., & Fu, H. (2018). A pilot study of a group mindfulness-based cognitive-behavioral intervention for smartphone addiction among university students. *Journal of Behavioral Addictions*, 7(4), 1171–1176. DOI: 10.1556/2006.7.2018.103 PMID: 30418075

Latin American School of Digital Addiction. (2021). *Smartphone addiction in Latin America: Patterns and interventions*. Retrieved from https://www.lasd.edu/smartphone-addiction

Laycock, A. F., Walker, D., Harrison, N., & Brands, J. (2011). Researching Indigenous health: A practical guide for researchers.

Lazarus, R. S. (1984). *Stress, appraisal, and coping* (Vol. 464). Springer.

Lee, J. I., Hsiao, R. C., Tsai, C. S., & Yen, C. F. (2022). Caregivers' difficulty in managing smartphone use of children with attention-deficit/hyperactivity disorder during the COVID-19 pandemic: Relationships with caregiver and children factors. *International Journal of Environmental Research and Public Health*, 19(9), 5194. DOI: 10.3390/ijerph19095194 PMID: 35564588

Lee, J., Sung, M., Song, S. H., Lee, Y. M., Lee, J. J., Cho, S. M., Park, M. K., & Shin, Y. (2016). Psychological Factors Associated With Smartphone Addiction in South Korean Adolescents. *The Journal of Early Adolescence*, 38(3), 288–302. DOI: 10.1177/0272431616670751

Lee, K. (2020). Social support and self-esteem on the association between stressful life events and mental health outcomes among college students. *Social Work in Health Care*, 59(6), 387–407. DOI: 10.1080/00981389.2020.1772443 PMID: 32538324

Lee, S. J., Choi, M. J., Yu, S. H., Kim, H., Park, S. J., & Choi, I. Y. (2022). Development and evaluation of smartphone usage management system for preventing problematic smartphone use. *Digital Health*, 8. DOI: 10.1177/20552076221089095 PMID: 35371530

Lee, S. Y. (2014). How do people compare themselves with others on social network sites?: The case of Facebook. *Computers in Human Behavior*, 32, 253–260. DOI: 10.1016/j.chb.2013.12.009

Lee, Y.-K., Chang, C.-T., Lin, Y., & Cheng, Z.-H. (2017). Heads-down tribes across four Asian countries: Antecedents of smartphone addiction. *International Journal of Mobile Communications*, 15(4), 414–436. DOI: 10.1504/IJMC.2017.084863

Leidner, D. E., & Tona, O. (2021). The impact of artificial intelligence on trust in technology and work. *Information Systems Journal*, 31(3), 269–302. DOI: 10.1111/isj.12356

Lei, L. Y.-C., Ismail, M. A.-A., Mohammad, J. A.-M., & Yusoff, M. S. B. (2020). The relationship of smartphone addiction with psychological distress and neuroticism among university medical students. *BMC Psychology*, 8(1), 1–9. DOI: 10.1186/s40359-020-00466-6 PMID: 32917268

Lemieux, A. J., & Wartenberg, D. (2019). The Brain on Smartphone Addiction: A Study of Brain Activity. *Computers in Human Behavior*, 101, 189–197.

Leonardi, P. M., Huysman, M., & Steinfield, C. (2013). Enterprise social media: Definition, history, and prospects for the study of social technologies in organizations. *Journal of Computer-Mediated Communication*, 19(1), 1–19. DOI: 10.1111/jcc4.12029

LePera, N. (2011). Relationships between boredom proneness, mindfulness, anxiety, depression, and substance use. *The New School Psychology Bulletin*, 8(2), 15–25. DOI: 10.1037/e741452011-003

Leung, L. (2008). Linking psychological attributes to addiction and improper use of the mobile phone among adolescents in Hong Kong. *Journal of Children and Media*, 2(2), 93–113. DOI: 10.1080/17482790802078565

Leung, L., & Zhang, R. (2016). Predicting tablet use: A study of gratifications-sought, leisure boredom, and multitasking. *Telematics and Informatics*, 33(2), 331–341. DOI: 10.1016/j.tele.2015.08.013

Lewis, R. G., Florio, E., Punzo, D., & Borrelli, E. (2021). *The Brain's reward system in health and disease*. Springer.

Liang, H.-Y., Zhang, B., Jiang, H.-B., & Zhou, H.-L. (2021). Adult attachment: Its mediation role on childhood trauma and mobile phone addiction. *Journal of Psychology in Africa*, 31(4), 369–374. DOI: 10.1080/14330237.2021.1952706

Li, J., Zhan, D., Zhou, Y., & Gao, X. (2021). Loneliness and problematic mobile phone use among adolescents during the COVID-19 pandemic: The roles of escape motivation and self-control. *Addictive Behaviors*, 118, 106857. DOI: 10.1016/j.addbeh.2021.106857 PMID: 33676160

Lim, S. S. (Ed.). (2016). *Mobile communication and the family*. Springer. DOI: 10.1007/978-94-017-7441-3

Lin, C. Y., Namdar, P., Griffiths, M. D., & Pakpour, A. H. (2021). Mediated roles of generalized trust and perceived social support in the effects of problematic social media use on mental health: A cross-sectional study. *Health Expectations*, 24(1), 165–173. DOI: 10.1111/hex.13169 PMID: 33253480

Lin, C., & Jiang, X. (2022). The Role of Personality Traits and Values in Perceived Friendship Quality: The Dyadic Approach. In *Interdisciplinary Insights on Interpersonal Relationships*. IntechOpen.

Lin, C., Ratan, Z. A., & Pakpour, A. H. (2023). Collection of smartphone and internet addiction. *BMC Psychiatry*, 23(1), 427. Advance online publication. DOI: 10.1186/s12888-023-04915-5 PMID: 37316810

Lin, S., & Jian, E. (2022). Effects of personality traits concerning media use decisions on fear of missing out and social media use behavior. *Behavioral Sciences (Basel, Switzerland)*, 12(11), 460. DOI: 10.3390/bs12110460 PMID: 36421756

Lin, Y. H., Pan, Y. C., Lin, S. H., & Chen, S. H. (2017). Development of short-form and screening cutoff point of the Smartphone Addiction Inventory (SPAI-SF). *International Journal of Methods in Psychiatric Research*, 26(2), e1525. DOI: 10.1002/mpr.1525 PMID: 27658956

Lin, Y.-H., Chang, L.-R., Lee, Y.-H., Tseng, H.-W., Kuo, T. B., & Chen, S.-H. (2014). Development and validation of the Smartphone Addiction Inventory (SPAI). *PLoS One*, 9(6), e98312. DOI: 10.1371/journal.pone.0098312 PMID: 24896252

Lin, Y.-H., Chiang, C.-L., Lin, P.-H., Chang, L.-R., Ko, C.-H., Lee, Y.-H., & Lin, S.-H. (2016). Proposed diagnostic criteria for smartphone addiction. *PLoS One*, 11(11), e0163010. DOI: 10.1371/journal.pone.0163010 PMID: 27846211

Lin, Y.-H., Lin, S.-H., Li, P., Huang, W.-L., & Chen, C.-Y. (2013). Prevalent hallucinations during medical internships: Phantom vibration and ringing syndromes. *PLoS One*, 8(6), e65152. DOI: 10.1371/journal.pone.0065152 PMID: 23762302

Lin, Y., Pan, Y., & Lin, C. (2016). Smartphone addiction and mental health: A meta-analysis. *Journal of Behavioral Addictions*, 5(4), 717–728. DOI: 10.1556/2006.5.2016.073

Lissitsa, S., & Kagan, M. (2024). The enduring echoes of juvenile bullying: The role of self-esteem and loneliness in the relationship between bullying and social media addiction across generations X, Y, Z. *Frontiers in Psychology*, 15, 1446000. Advance online publication. DOI: 10.3389/fpsyg.2024.1446000 PMID: 39156810

Liu, J., Zettler, I., & Hilbig, B. E. (2020). Honesty-humility. *Encyclopedia of personality and individual differences*, 1996-2004.

Liu, H., Soh, K. G., Samsudin, S., Rattanakoses, W., & Qi, F. (2022). Effects of exercise and psychological interventions on smartphone addiction among university students: A systematic review. *Frontiers in Psychology*, 13, 1021285. DOI: 10.3389/fpsyg.2022.1021285 PMID: 36275318

Liu, H., Zhao, X., & Zhu, Q. (2021). The impact of smartphone addiction on academic performance in China. *Journal of Behavioral Addictions*, 10(1), 95–106. DOI: 10.1556/2006.2021.00010

Liu, H., Zhou, Z., Huang, L., Zhu, E., Yu, L., & Zhang, M. (2022). Prevalence of smartphone addiction and its effects on subhealth and insomnia: A cross-sectional study among medical students. *BMC Psychiatry*, 22(1), 305. DOI: 10.1186/s12888-022-03956-6 PMID: 35488216

Liu, N., Zhu, S., Zhang, W., Sun, Y., & Zhang, X. (2024). The relationship between fear of missing out and mobile phone addiction among college students: The mediating role of depression and the moderating role of loneliness. *Frontiers in Public Health*, 12, 1374522. DOI: 10.3389/fpubh.2024.1374522 PMID: 38584914

Liu, S., Wing, Y. K., Hao, Y., Li, W., Zhang, J., & Zhang, B. (2019). The associations of long-time mobile phone use with sleep disturbances and mental distress in technical college students: A prospective cohort study. *Sleep (Basel)*, 42(2), zsy213. DOI: 10.1093/sleep/zsy213 PMID: 30395300

Liu, S., Xiao, T., Yang, L., & Loprinzi, P. D. (2019). Exercise as an alternative approach for treating smartphone addiction: A systematic review and meta-analysis of random controlled trials. *International Journal of Environmental Research and Public Health*, 16(20), 3912. DOI: 10.3390/ijerph16203912 PMID: 31618879

Liu, X., Tian, R., Liu, H., Bai, X., & Lei, Y. (2023). Exploring the Impact of Smartphone Addiction on Risk Decision-Making Behavior among College Students Based on fNIRS Technology. *Brain Sciences*, 13(9), 1330. DOI: 10.3390/brainsci13091330 PMID: 37759931

Liu, Y., Zhao, J., & Zhu, L. (2020). Effectiveness of behavioral interventions for smartphone addiction: A meta-analysis. *Journal of Behavioral Addictions*, 9(1), 20–34. DOI: 10.1556/2006.9.2020.02

Liu, Y., Zhou, Z., Zhu, E., Huang, L., & Zhang, M. (2022). Smartphone addiction and its associated factors among freshmen medical students in China: A cross-sectional study. *BMC Psychiatry*, 22(1), 1–10. DOI: 10.1186/s12888-022-03957-5 PMID: 35501728

Livingstone, S., Carr, J., & Byrne, J. (2015). One in three: Internet governance and children's rights.

Li, X., & Ye, Y. (2022). Fear of missing out and irrational procrastination in the mobile social media environment: A moderated mediation analysis. *Cyberpsychology, Behavior, and Social Networking*, 25(1), 59–65. DOI: 10.1089/cyber.2021.0052 PMID: 34491830

Lixăndroiu, R., Cazan, A.-M., & Maican, C. I. (2021). An analysis of the impact of personality traits towards augmented reality in online shopping. *Symmetry*, 13(3), 416. DOI: 10.3390/sym13030416

Li, Y., Griffiths, M. D., Mei, S., & Niu, Z. (2020). Fear of missing out and smartphone addiction mediates the relationship between positive and negative affect and sleep quality among Chinese university students. *Frontiers in Psychiatry*, 11, 877. DOI: 10.3389/fpsyt.2020.00877 PMID: 33192635

Li, Y., & Lin, C. (2019). Over-connected? A qualitative exploration of smartphone addiction among working adults in China. *BMC Psychiatry*, 19(1), 1–10. DOI: 10.1186/s12888-019-2170-z PMID: 31215473

Lozano-Blasco, R., Latorre-Martínez, M. P., & Cortés-Pascual, A. (2022). Screen addicts: A meta-analysis of internet addiction in adolescence. *Children and Youth Services Review*, 135, 106373. DOI: 10.1016/j.childyouth.2022.106373

Lui, P. P., Chmielewski, M., Trujillo, M., Morris, J., & Pigott, T. D. (2022). Linking big five personality domains and facets to alcohol (mis) use: A systematic review and meta-analysis. *Alcohol and Alcoholism*, 57(1), 58–73. DOI: 10.1093/alcalc/agab030 PMID: 33893471

Luk, T. T., Wang, M. P., Shen, C., Wan, A., Chau, P. H., Oliffe, J., & Lam, T. H. (2018). Short version of the Smartphone Addiction Scale in Chinese adults: Psychometric properties, sociodemographic, and health behavioral correlates. *Journal of Behavioral Addictions*, 7(4), 1157–1165. DOI: 10.1556/2006.7.2018.105 PMID: 30418073

Lund, J. R., & Wiese, J. (2021). Less is More: Exploring Support for Time Management Planning. *Designing Interactive Systems Conference*, 392–405. DOI: 10.1145/3461778.3462133

Lu, S., Wei, F., & Li, G. (2021). The evolution of the concept of stress and the framework of the stress system. *Cell Stress*, 5(6), 76–85. DOI: 10.15698/cst2021.06.250 PMID: 34124582

Madore, K. P., & Wagner, A. D. (2019, April 1). Multicosts of multitasking. *Cerebrum: the Dana forum on brain science, 2019.* https://pmc.ncbi.nlm.nih.gov/articles/PMC7075496

Mahadev Madgule, N. (2023). Mechanical properties and microstructure of activated TIG welded similar joints of Inconel alloys by desirability approaches. *Materials Today: Proceedings*, 77, 528–533. DOI: 10.1016/j.matpr.2022.12.250

Mahapatra, S. (2019). Smartphone addiction and associated consequences: Role of loneliness and self-regulation. *Behaviour & Information Technology*, 38(8), 833–844. DOI: 10.1080/0144929X.2018.1560499

Mahmoodi, H., Nadrian, H., Shahaghi, A., Jafarabadi, M. A., Ahmadi, A., & Saqqezi, G. S. (2018). Factors associated with mental health among high school students in Iran: Does mobile phone overuse associated with poor mental health? *Journal of Child and Adolescent Psychiatric Nursing*, 31(1), 6–13. DOI: 10.1111/jcap.12202 PMID: 29974565

Mangot, A. G., Murthy, V. S., Kshirsagar, S. V., Deshmukh, A. H., & Tembe, D. V. (2018). Prevalence and pattern of phantom ringing and phantom vibration among medical interns and their relationship with smartphone use and perceived stress. *Indian Journal of Psychological Medicine*, 40(5), 440–445. DOI: 10.4103/IJPSYM.IJPSYM_141_18 PMID: 30275619

Mao, B., Jia, X., & Huang, Q. (2022). How do information overload and message fatigue reduce information processing in the era of COVID-19? An ability–motivation approach. *Journal of Information Science*. Advance online publication. DOI: 10.1177/01655515221118047

Marciano, L., Camerini, A.-L., & Schulz, P. J. (2020). Neuroticism in the digital age: A meta-analysis. *Computers in Human Behavior Reports*, 2, 100026. DOI: 10.1016/j.chbr.2020.100026

Marciano, L., Camerini, A.-L., & Schulz, P. J. (2022). Neuroticism and internet addiction: What is next? A systematic conceptual review. *Personality and Individual Differences*, 185, 111260. DOI: 10.1016/j.paid.2021.111260

Marengo, D., Sindermann, C., Häckel, D., Settanni, M., Elhai, J. D., & Montag, C. (2020). The association between the Big Five personality traits and smartphone use disorder: A meta-analysis. *Journal of Behavioral Addictions*, 9(2), 1–12. DOI: 10.1556/2006.2020.00069 PMID: 33011714

Marlowe, J. M., Bartley, A., & Collins, F. (2016). Digital belongings: The intersections of social cohesion, connectivity and digital media. *Ethnicities*, 17(1), 85–102. DOI: 10.1177/1468796816654174

Marshall, D. (2024, September 9). *When school policy limits access to assistive technology of students with disabilities.* Council of Parent Attorneys and Advises (COPAA). https://www.copaa.org/news/681778/When-School-Policy-Limits-Access-to-Assistive-Technology-for-Students-with-Disabilities.htm

Marx, G. T. (2004). What's New About the" New Surveillance"?: Classifying for Change and Continuity. *Knowledge in Society*, 17(1), 18–37. DOI: 10.1007/BF02687074

Mason, M. C., Zamparo, G., Marini, A., & Ameen, N. (2022). Glued to your phone? Generation Z's smartphone addiction and online compulsive buying. *Computers in Human Behavior*, 136, 107404. DOI: 10.1016/j.chb.2022.107404

Mastropietro, S., Favieri, F., Forte, G., Locuratolo, N., Mannarelli, D., Pauletti, C., Fattapposta, F., & Casagrande, M. (2024). Behavioral Addictions Questionnaire (BAQ): Validation of a new tool for the screening of multiple addictive behaviors in the Italian population. *International Journal of Mental Health and Addiction*, 22(3), 965–978. DOI: 10.1007/s11469-022-00906-x

Mathis, M. (2021, September 20). *My student recorded me without my permission! What to do if it happens to you.* We Are Teachers. https://www.weareteachers.com/students-recording-teachers-without-permission

Matsuda, M. (2000). Interpersonal relationships among young people and mobile phone usage: From attenuant to selective relationships. *Japanese Journal of Social Informatics*, 4(11), 111–122.

Matthews, G. (2003). *Personality Traits*. Cambridge University Press. DOI: 10.1017/CBO9780511812736

Matusik, S. F., & Mickel, A. E. (2011). Embracing or embattled by converged mobile devices? Users' experiences with a contemporary connectivity technology. *Human Relations*, 64(8), 1001–1030. DOI: 10.1177/0018726711405552

Ma, Y., & Turel, O. (2019). Information technology use for work and technostress: Effects of power distance and masculinity culture dimensions. *Cognition Technology and Work*, 21(1), 145–157. DOI: 10.1007/s10111-018-0503-1

Mazmanian, M., Orlikowski, W. J., & Yates, J. (2013). The autonomy paradox: The implications of mobile email devices for knowledge professionals. *Organization Science*, 24(5), 1337–1357. DOI: 10.1287/orsc.1120.0806

McCann Paris. (2014, June 26). Macquarie BPhubbing: a word is born^: McCann Melbourne [Video file]. Retrieved from https://www.youtube.com/watch?v=hLNhKUniaEw

McClain, C., Faverio, M., Anderson, M., & Park, E. (2023, October 18). How Americans protect their online data. In *How Americans view data privacy*. Pew Research Center. https://www.pewresearch.org/internet/2023/10/18/how-americans-protect-their-online-data

McCrae, R. R., & Costa, P. T.Jr. (2021). Understanding persons: From stern's personalistics to Five-factor theory. *Personality and Individual Differences*, 169, 109816. DOI: 10.1016/j.paid.2020.109816

McDaniel, B. T., & Coyne, S. M. (2016). "Technoference": The interference of technology in couple relationships and implications for women's personal and relational well-being. *Psychology of Popular Media Culture*, 5(1), 85–98. DOI: 10.1037/ppm0000065

McDaniel, B. T., & Radesky, J. S. (2018). Technoference: Parent distraction with technology and associations with child behavior problems. *Child Development*, 89(1), 100–109. DOI: 10.1111/cdev.12822 PMID: 28493400

Medina-Morales, G. del C., & Villal6n-Hernández, R. (2023, January-June). Study of the prevalence of phubbing in classrooms by apps' use. *Alteridad: Revista de Educaci6n*, 18(1), 59–68. DOI: 10.17163/alt.v18n1.2023.05

Mehrabian, A. (1971). *Silent Messages*. Wadsworth.

Mendoza, J. S., Pody, B. C., Lee, S., Kim, M., & McDonough, I. M. (2018, September). The effect of cellphones on attention and learning: The influences of time, distraction, and nomophobia. *Computers in Human Behavior*, 86, 52–60. DOI: 10.1016/j.chb.2018.04.027

Mercer, K. B., & Eastwood, J. D. (2010). Is boredom associated with problem gambling behaviour? It depends on what you mean by "boredom". *International Gambling Studies*, 10(1), 91–104. DOI: 10.1080/14459791003754414

Merchant, K. (2012). How men and women differ: Gender differences in communication styles, influence tactics, and leadership styles.

Merino, M., Tornero-Aguilera, J. F., Rubio-Zarapuz, A., Villanueva-Tobaldo, C. V., Martín-Rodríguez, A., & Clemente-Suárez, V. J. (2024). Body Perceptions and Psychological Well-Being: A Review of the Impact of Social Media and Physical Measurements on Self-Esteem and Mental Health with a Focus on Body Image Satisfaction and Its Relationship with Cultural and Gender Factors. *Health Care*, 12(14), 1396. DOI: 10.3390/healthcare12141396 PMID: 39057539

Miller, A. (2017). The Digital Detox: A New Approach to Smartphone Addiction. *Psychology Today*. Retrieved from https://www.psychologytoday.com/us/blog/tech-support/201708/the-digital-detox

Miller, W. R., Forcehimes, A. A., & Zweben, A. (2019). *Treating addiction: A guide for professionals*. Guilford Publications.

Millon, T., Millon, C. M., Meagher, S. E., Grossman, S. D., & Ramnath, R. (2012). *Personality disorders in modern life*. John Wiley & Sons.

Moattari, M., Moattari, F., Kaka, G., Kouchesfahani, H. M., Sadraie, S. H., & Naghdi, M. (2017). Smartphone addiction, sleep quality and mechanism. *Int J Cogn Behav*, 1(002).

Mohtar, S., Jomhari, N., Mustafa, M. B., & Yusoff, Z. M. (2022). Mobile learning: Research context, methodologies and future works towards middle-aged adults – a systematic literature review. *Multimedia Tools and Applications*, 82(7), 11117–11143. DOI: 10.1007/s11042-022-13698-y PMID: 36035325

Mongkonkansai, J., Veerasakul, S., Tamrin, S. B. M., & Madardam, U. (2022). Predictors of Musculoskeletal Pain among Primary School Students Using Smartphones in Nakhon Si Thammarat, Thailand. *International Journal of Environmental Research and Public Health*, 19(17), 10530. DOI: 10.3390/ijerph191710530 PMID: 36078252

Montag, C., & Becker, B. (2023). Neuroimaging the effects of smartphone (over-) use on brain function and structure—A review of the current state of MRI-based findings and a roadmap for future research. *Psychoradiology*, 3(1), kkad001. Advance online publication. DOI: 10.1093/psyrad/kkad001 PMID: 38666109

Montag, C., & Elhai, J. D. (2023). The smartphone and the brain: An update on recent research. *Current Behavioral Neuroscience Reports*.

Montag, C., Lachmann, B., Herrlich, M., & Zweig, K. (2019). Addictive features of social media/messenger platforms and Freemium games against the background of psychological and economic theories. *International Journal of Environmental Research and Public Health*, 16(14), 2612. DOI: 10.3390/ijerph16142612 PMID: 31340426

Montag, C., & Walla, P. (2016). Carpe diem instead of losing your social mind: Beyond digital addiction and why we all suffer from digital overuse. *Cogent Psychology*, 3(1), 1157281. DOI: 10.1080/23311908.2016.1157281

Montag, C., Wegmann, E., Sariyska, R., Demetrovics, Z., & Brand, M. (2019). The role of smartphone addiction in the development and maintenance of mental health issues. *International Journal of Environmental Research and Public Health*, 16(16), 2903. DOI: 10.3390/ijerph16162903 PMID: 31416112

Montag, C., Zhao, Z., Sindermann, C., Xu, L., Fu, M., Li, J., Zheng, X., Li, K., Kendrick, K. M., Dai, J., & Becker, B. (2018). Internet communication disorder and the structure of the human brain: Initial insights on WeChat addiction. *Scientific Reports*, 8(1), 2155. DOI: 10.1038/s41598-018-19904-y PMID: 29391461

Moore, D. S., & McCabe, G. P. (1989). *Introduction to the practice of statistics*. WH Freeman/Times Books/Henry Holt & Co.

Moore, P. H., Head, J. D., & Griffin, R. B. (2017, Spring). Impeding students' efforts to cheat in online classes. *The Journal of Learning in Higher Education*, 13(1), 9–24.

Moqbel, M., Bertelt, V., Alam, M., Younus Shaik, A., Montoya, S., & Larson, M. (2023). Smartphone addiction and cultural dimensions.

Mun, I. B. (2024). Longitudinal relationship between parental and adolescent smartphone addiction: Serial mediating effects of adolescent self-esteem and depression. *Internet Research*, 34(6), 2031–2056. DOI: 10.1108/INTR-02-2023-0110

Munshi, S., Varghese, A., & Dhar-Munshi, S. (2017). Computer vision syndrome—A common cause of unexplained visual symptoms in the modern era. *International Journal of Clinical Practice*, 71(7), e12962. DOI: 10.1111/ijcp.12962 PMID: 28594459

Muris, P., Jeurissen, A., Rooswinkel, M., & Meesters, C. (2022). Good traits, bad traits, and 'ugly' behavior: Relations between the dark triad, honesty-humility, other hexaco personality traits, and externalizing problems in adolescents. *Journal of Child and Family Studies*, 31(12), 3247–3257. DOI: 10.1007/s10826-022-02344-8

Mussweiler, T., Rüter, K., & Epstude, K. (2006). The why, who, and how of social comparison: A social-cognition perspective. Social comparison and social psychology: Understanding cognition, intergroup relations, and culture, 33-54.

Mussweiler, T., & Bodenhausen, G. V. (2002). I know you are, but what am I? Self-evaluative consequences of judging in-group and out-group members. *Journal of Personality and Social Psychology*, 82(1), 19–32. DOI: 10.1037/0022-3514.82.1.19 PMID: 11811631

Mustawin, S. S. N., Amri, A. K., Hakiky, H. R., Prihatiningsih, R., & Handiastuti, S. O. (2024). The relationship between narcissistic behavior and phubbing behavior among students who use social media during classroom learning conditions. *Proceedings Series of Educational Studies*, (5), 674–682.

Nabi, R. L., Prestin, A., & So, J. (2013). Facebook friends with (health) benefits? Exploring social network site use and perceptions of social support, stress, and well-being. *Cyberpsychology, Behavior, and Social Networking*, 16(10), 721–727. DOI: 10.1089/cyber.2012.0521 PMID: 23790356

Nascimento, P., Oliveira, T., & Neves, J. (2024). The battle against screen time: A systematic review of hedonic information systems use reduction. *Internet Research*. Advance online publication. DOI: 10.1108/INTR-10-2023-0857

Nassen, L. M., Vandebosch, H., Poels, K., & Karsay, K. (2023). Opt-out, abstain, unplug. A systematic review of the voluntary digital disconnection literature. *Telematics and Informatics*, 81, 101980. DOI: 10.1016/j.tele.2023.101980

Nasution, A. (2022). Smartphone addiction and its impact on academic resilience and student well-being. *Journal of Basic Education*, 12(2), 59–72.

Nasution, F. K., & Daulay, N. (2022). The influence of academic resilience and student well-being on smartphone addiction. *Jurnal Basicedu*, 6(3), 4415–4422. DOI: 10.31004/basicedu.v6i3.2864

Nathan, P. E., Conrad, M., & Skinstad, A. H. (2016). History of the Concept of Addiction. *Annual Review of Clinical Psychology*, 12(1), 29–51. DOI: 10.1146/annurev-clinpsy-021815-093546 PMID: 26565120

National Cancer Institute at the National Institutes of Health. (2024, April 4). *Cell phones and cancer risk.*https://www.cancer.gov/about-cancer/causes-prevention/risk/radiation/cell-phones-fact-sheet

National Institute on Drug Abuse. (2014). *Drugs, brains, and behaviour: The science of addiction* (NIH Publication No. 14-5605). https://nida.nih.gov/sites/default/files/soa_2014.pdf

Nayak, J. K. (2018). Relationship among smartphone usage, addiction, academic performance and the moderating role of gender: A study of higher education students in India. *Computers & Education*, 123, 164–173. DOI: 10.1016/j.compedu.2018.05.007

Nazir, T. (2020, June 15). Impact of classroom phubbing on teachers who face phubbing during lectures. *Psychology Research on Education and Social Sciences*, 1(1), 41–47.

Negroponte, N. (1996). *Being digital.* Vintage Books.

Neupane, S., Ali, U. T., & Mathew, A. (2017). Text neck syndrome-systematic review. *Imperial Journal of Interdisciplinary Research*, 3(7), 141–148.

Newport, C. (2019). *Digital minimalism: Choosing a focused life in a noisy world.* Portfolio/Penguin.

Ng, A. H., Liu, Y., Chen, J. Z., & Eastwood, J. D. (2015). Culture and state boredom: A comparison between European Canadians and Chinese. *Personality and Individual Differences*, 75, 13–18. DOI: 10.1016/j.paid.2014.10.052

NHS Digital. (2021). *Smartphone addiction and its effects: A UK perspective*. Retrieved from https://www.digital.nhs.uk/publications/smartphone-addiction

Nikhita, C. (2015). Mobile phone dependence and its psychological effects. *Journal of Clinical and Diagnostic Research : JCDR.*

Nikhita, C. S. (2015). Prevalence of mobile phone dependence in secondary school adolescents. *Journal of Clinical and Diagnostic Research : JCDR.* Advance online publication. DOI: 10.7860/JCDR/2015/14396.6803 PMID: 26672469

Nikolic, A., Bukurov, B., Kocic, I., Vukovic, M., Ladjevic, N., Vrhovac, M., Pavlović, Z., Grujicic, J., Kisic, D., & Sipetic, S. (2023). Smartphone addiction, sleep quality, depression, anxiety, and stress among medical students. *Frontiers in Public Health*, 11, 1252371. DOI: 10.3389/fpubh.2023.1252371 PMID: 37744504

Ning, W., Turel, O., & Davis, F. D. (2024). Potential treatments of technology addiction: Insights for information systems scholars. *Internet Research.* Advance online publication. DOI: 10.1108/INTR-12-2023-1122

Noë, B., Turner, L. D., Linden, D. E., Allen, S. M., Winkens, B., & Whitaker, R. M. (2019). Identifying Indicators of Smartphone Addiction Through User-App Interaction. *Computers in Human Behavior*, 99, 56–65. DOI: 10.1016/j.chb.2019.04.023 PMID: 31582873

O'Connor, R. M., Stewart, S. H., & Watt, M. C. (2009). Distinguishing BAS risk for university students' drinking, smoking, and gambling behaviors. *Personality and Individual Differences*, 46(4), 514–519. DOI: 10.1016/j.paid.2008.12.002

O'Guinn, T. C., & Faber, R. J. (1989). Compulsive buying: A phenomenological exploration. *The Journal of Consumer Research*, 16(2), 147–157. DOI: 10.1086/209204

Obadofin, B., Onyeka, E. B., & Nchedochukwu, E. C. (2020). Impacts of Smartphone addiction on Academic Performance of students in senior secondary schools in Lagos state. *Research and Analysis Journal*, 253–260.

Obadofin, R. O. (2020). Impact of smartphone addiction on academic performance among secondary school students. *International Journal of Advances in Multidisciplinary Research*, 7(4), 21–28.

Oberst, U., Wegmann, E., Stodt, B., Brand, M., & Chamarro, A. (2017). Negative consequences from heavy social networking in adolescents: The mediating role of fear of missing out. *Journal of Adolescence*, 55(1), 51–60. DOI: 10.1016/j.adolescence.2016.12.008 PMID: 28033503

Oberst, U., Wegmann, E., Stodt, B., Brand, M., & Chamarro, A. (2017). Symptoms of internet addiction and smartphone addiction: The role of online gaming and social media. *Journal of Behavioral Addictions*, 6(3), 268–278. DOI: 10.1556/2006.6.2017.037

Ochs, C., & Sauer, J. (2022). Disturbing aspects of smartphone usage: A qualitative analysis. *Behaviour & Information Technology*, 42(14), 2504–2519. DOI: 10.1080/0144929X.2022.2129092

Oduor, E., Neustaedter, C., Odom, W., Tang, A., Moallem, N., Tory, M., & Irani, P. (2016). The frustrations and benefits of mobile device usage in the home when co-present with family members. Proceedings of the 2016 ACM Conference on Designing Interactive Systems - DIS ', 16, 1315–1327. DOI: 10.1145/2901790.2901809

Ohio Department of Education and Workforce. (n.d.) *Cell phones in Ohio schools.* https://education.ohio.gov/Topics/Student-Supports/School-Wellness/Cell-Phones-in-Ohio-Schools

Oits, P. A. (2011). Mechanisms linking social ties and support to physical and mental health. J. Health Soc. Behav., 52, 145–161. DOI: 10.1177/0022146510395592

Olaniyan, A. O., & Uzorka, A. (2024). Leadership's role in facilitating faculty professional development for technology integration. *International Journal of Technology in Education and Science*, 8(3), 470–480. DOI: 10.46328/ijtes.563

Olia, A. (2024, January 30). *Text message statistics & trends for 2024 [and beyond!].* Intradyn. https://www.intradyn.com/text-message-statistics-trends

Olsen, C. M. (2011). Natural rewards, neuroplasticity, and non-drug addictions. *Neuropharmacology*, 61(7), 1109–1122. DOI: 10.1016/j.neuropharm.2011.03.010 PMID: 21459101

Olson, J. A., Sandra, D. A., Colucci, É. S., Al Bikaii, A., Chmoulevitch, D., Nahas, J., Raz, A., & Veissière, S. P. (2022). Smartphone addiction is increasing across the world: A meta-analysis of 24 countries. *Computers in Human Behavior*, 129, 107138. DOI: 10.1016/j.chb.2021.107138

Online learning statistics: The ultimate list in 2024. (2024, April 25). Sedona Sky. https://www.sedonasky.org/blog/online-learning-statistics

Ontoria, Y., Cuesta-Gracia, A., Ruiz, J. M., Romero, J., & Pérez, M. (2019). The negative effects of short-term extreme thermal events on the seagrass Posidonia oceanica are exacerbated by ammonium additions. *PLoS One*, 14(9), e0222798. DOI: 10.1371/journal.pone.0222798 PMID: 31536606

Ophir, Y., Rosenberg, H., Lipshits-Braziler, Y., & Amichai-Hamburger, Y. (2020). Digital adolescence. In *Routledge eBooks* (pp. 122–139). DOI: 10.4324/9780429468360-8

Opsal, A., Kristensen, Ø., & Clausen, T. (2019). Readiness to change among involuntarily and voluntarily admitted patients with substance use disorders. *Substance Abuse Treatment, Prevention, and Policy*, 14(1), 0237. Advance online publication. DOI: 10.1186/s13011-019-0237-y PMID: 31694664

Orzech, K. M., Grandner, M. A., Roane, B. M., & Carskadon, M. A. (2015). Digital media use in the 2 h before bedtime is associated with sleep variables in university students. *Computers in Human Behavior*, 55, 43–50. DOI: 10.1016/j.chb.2015.08.049 PMID: 28163362

Osorio-Molina, C., Martos-Cabrera, M. B., Membrive-Jiménez, M. J., Vargas-Roman, K., Suleiman-Martos, N., Ortega-Campos, E., & Gómez-Urquiza, J. L. (2021). Smartphone addiction, risk factors and its adverse effects in nursing students: A systematic review and meta-analysis. *Nurse Education Today*, 98, 104741. DOI: 10.1016/j.nedt.2020.104741 PMID: 33485161

Ostic, D., Qalati, S. A., Barbosa, B., Shah, S. M. M., Vela, E. G., Herzallah, A. M., & Liu, F. (2021). Effects of Social Media Use on Psychological Well-Being: A Mediated Model. *Frontiers in Psychology*, 12, 678766. Advance online publication. DOI: 10.3389/fpsyg.2021.678766 PMID: 34234717

Oulasvirta, A., Rattenbury, T., Ma, L., & Raita, E. (2012). Habits make smartphone use more pervasive. *Personal and Ubiquitous Computing*, 16(1), 105–114. DOI: 10.1007/s00779-011-0412-2

Paavola, A. (2023, April 25). *Is SMS encrypted and what should your business do about it.* Textline. https://www.textline.com/blog/is-sms-encrypted

Palalas, A. (2017). Mindfulness in Mobile and Ubiquitous Learning: Harnessing the Power of Attention. In *Perspectives on rethinking and reforming education* (pp. 19–44). DOI: 10.1007/978-981-10-6144-8_2

Pal, S., Sharma, S. K., Singhal, A., & Telles, S. (2022). Smartphone Excessive Use, Sleep, and Beliefs about Well-being in University Students who Practice Yoga Compared with Those with No Experience of Yoga. *Indian Journal of Community Medicine*, 47(2), 292–295. DOI: 10.4103/ijcm.ijcm_601_21 PMID: 36034266

Panda Security (2024, February 29). *10 ways to secure mobile devices* [2024]. https://www.pandasecurity.com/en/mediacenter/mobile-security-tips

Pandya, N. (2021). Smartphone addiction among teenagers in Ahmedabad. *Journal of Evidence-Based Medicine and Health Care.*

Pandya, A., & Lodha, P. (2021). Social Connectedness, Excessive Screen Time During COVID-19 and Mental Health: A Review of Current Evidence. *Frontiers in Human Dynamics*, 3, 684137. Advance online publication. DOI: 10.3389/fhumd.2021.684137

Pandya, C. N., Christian, D. S., & Patel, M. M. (2021). A cross-sectional study on smartphone addiction among late adolescents and young adults (aged 15 to 24 years) of Ahmedabad city, Gujarat, India. *J Evid Based Med Healthc*, 8(9), 491–496. DOI: 10.18410/jebmh/2021/96

Panova, T., & Carbonell, X. (2018). A review of current research on smartphone addiction. *Frontiers in Psychology*, 9, 1–10. DOI: 10.3389/fpsyg.2018.01535

Panova, T., & Carbonell, X. (2018). Is smartphone addiction really an addiction? *Journal of Behavioral Addictions*, 7(2), 252–259. DOI: 10.1556/2006.7.2018.49 PMID: 29895183

Parasuraman, S., Sam, A. T., Yee, S. W. K., Chuon, B. L. C., & Ren, L. Y. (2017). Smartphone usage and increased risk of mobile phone addiction: A concurrent study. *International Journal of Pharmaceutical Investigation*, 7(3), 125–131. DOI: 10.4103/jphi.JPHI_56_17 PMID: 29184824

Pareek, S. (2017). Phantom vibration syndrome: An emerging phenomenon. *Asian Journal of Nursing Education and Research*, 7(4), 596–597. DOI: 10.5958/2349-2996.2017.00116.1

Pariser, E. (2011). *The filter bubble: What the Internet is hiding from you*. Penguin Press.

Park, J., Jeong, J.-E., Park, S. y., & Rho, M. J. (2020). Development of the smartphone addiction risk rating score for a smartphone addiction management application. *Frontiers in Public Health*, 8, 485. DOI: 10.3389/fpubh.2020.00485 PMID: 33042938

Park, S. Y., Yang, S., Shin, C. S., Jang, H., & Park, S. Y. (2019). Long-term symptoms of mobile phone use on mobile phone addiction and depression among Korean adolescents. *International Journal of Environmental Research and Public Health*, 16(19), 35–84. DOI: 10.3390/ijerph16193584 PMID: 31557844

Park, Y., Kim, J., & Lee, S. (2021). Evaluation of the Smartphone Addiction Prevention Program in South Korean schools. *The Journal of Educational Research*, 114(6), 667–678. DOI: 10.1080/00220671.2021.1909725

Parlak, M. E., Öz, E., Özbey, M. Y., & Kapıcı, Y. (2023). Smartphone Addiction and Sleep Quality in Youngsters. *Medical Science and Discovery*, 10(1), 35–40. DOI: 10.36472/msd.v10i1.864

Parmaksız, İ. (2021). Relationships Between Phubbing and The Five Factor Personality Traits. *Kastamonu Education Journal*, 29(4), 32–42. DOI: 10.24106/kefdergi.795620

Parmaksız, İ. (2023). The effect of phubbing, a behavioral problem, on academic procrastination: The mediating and moderating role of academic self-efficacy. *Psychology in the Schools*, 60(1), 105–121. DOI: 10.1002/pits.22765

Paul, F. A., Dangroo, A. A., Saikia, P., Ganie, A. U. R., Zaid, M., Das, M., & Gogoi, R. (2024). Societal and individual impacts of substance abuse. In *Springer eBooks* (pp. 1–24). DOI: 10.1007/978-3-030-68127-2_430-1

Paulhus, D. L., & Williams, K. M. (2002). The dark triad of personality: Narcissism, Machiavellianism, and psychopathy. *Journal of Research in Personality*, 36(6), 556–563. DOI: 10.1016/S0092-6566(02)00505-6

Pavia, L., Cavani, P., Di Blasi, M., & Giordano, C. (2016). Smartphone Addiction Inventory (SPAI): Psychometric properties and confirmatory factor analysis. *Computers in Human Behavior*, 63, 170–178. DOI: 10.1016/j.chb.2016.05.039

Pavot, W., Diener, E. D., Colvin, C. R., & Sandvik, E. (1991). Further validation of the Satisfaction with Life Scale: Evidence for the cross-method convergence of well-being measures. *Journal of Personality Assessment*, 57(1), 149–161. DOI: 10.1207/s15327752jpa5701_17 PMID: 1920028

Pearson, C., & Hussain, Z. (2015). Smartphone use, addiction, narcissism, and personality: A mixed methods investigation. *International Journal of Cyber Behavior, Psychology and Learning*, 5(1), 17–32. DOI: 10.4018/ijcbpl.2015010102

Pearson, M. R., & Hussain, Z. (2016). Smartphone addiction and associated psychological factors. *Addicta : the Turkish Journal on Addictions*, 3(1), 103–112. DOI: 10.15805/addicta.2016.3.0103

Peleg, O., & Boniel-Nissim, M. (2024). Exploring the personality and relationship factors that mediate the connection between differentiation of self and phubbing. *Scientific Reports*, 14(1), 6572. Advance online publication. DOI: 10.1038/s41598-024-55560-1 PMID: 38504119

Pellegrino, A., Stasi, A., & Bhatiasevi, V. (2022). Research trends in social media addiction and problematic social media use: A bibliometric analysis. *Frontiers in Psychiatry*, 13, 1017506. Advance online publication. DOI: 10.3389/fpsyt.2022.1017506 PMID: 36458122

Peplau, L. A. (1982). Loneliness: A source book of current theory, research and therapy. Jone Wiley & Sons.

Pera, A. (2020). The Psychology of addictive smartphone behaviour in young adults: Problematic use, social anxiety, and depressive stress. *Frontiers in Psychiatry*, 11, 573473. Advance online publication. DOI: 10.3389/fpsyt.2020.573473 PMID: 33101087

Pérez-Fernández, H., Cacciotti, G., Martín-Cruz, N., & Delgado-García, J. B. (2022). Are interactions between need for achievement and social networks the driving force behind entrepreneurial Intention? A trait activation story. *Journal of Business Research*, 149, 65–76. DOI: 10.1016/j.jbusres.2022.04.046

Perilli, E., Necozione, S., Bianchini, V., Perazzini, M., Grassi, M., & Americo, A. (2021). Mobile phone addiction and mobile phone use in dangerous circumstances: Prevalence and correlates in a sample of Italian university students. *Mediterranean Journal of Clinical Psychology*, 9, 1–16. DOI: 10.13129/2282-1619/MJCP-3014

Pew Research Center. (2019). Mobile Fact Sheet. Retrieved from https://www.pewresearch.org/internet/fact-sheet/mobile/

Pew Research Center. (2019). *Smartphone use in the United States*. Retrieved from https://www.pewresearch.org/fact-tank/2019/04/05/smartphone-use-in-the-united-states

Pew Research Center. (2022). Teens, Social Media, and Technology. Retrieved from https://www.pewresearch.org/internet/2022/teens-social-media-and-technology/

Philip, D. (2018). *Mobile Phone Dependence in Karnataka*. Medica Inovatica.

Philippe, T. J., Sikder, N., Jackson, A., Koblanski, M. E., Liow, E., Pilarinos, A., & Vasarhelyi, K. (2022). Digital Health Interventions for Delivery of Mental Health Care: Systematic and Comprehensive Meta-Review. *JMIR Mental Health*, 9(5), e35159. DOI: 10.2196/35159 PMID: 35551058

Phillips-Wren, G., & Adya, M. (2020). Decision making under stress: The role of information overload, time pressure, complexity, and uncertainty. *Journal of Decision Systems, 29*(sup1), 213-225.

Pillemer, S. (2019). Why Sales Executives Need to Understand Their Personality Types. Forbes. https://www.forbes.com/sites/forbescoachescouncil/2019/04/18/why-sales-executives-need-to-understand-their-personality-types/?sh=19a661403273

Pilling, S., & Edney, J. (2017). Phubbing and Its Effect on Social Interaction. *Computers in Human Behavior*, 70, 146–152.

Pinochet, L. H. C., Da Silva Santos, S., Pardim, V. I., & De Souza, C. A. (2023). Watch out for nomophobia, so it does not catch you! Effects of digital dependence syndrome on mental health. *Journal of Systems and Information Technology*, 25(3), 296–318. DOI: 10.1108/JSIT-03-2022-0064

Pirwani, N., & Szabo, A. (2024, June). Could physical activity alleviate smart phone addiction in university students? A systematic literature review. *Preventive Medicine Reports*, 42, 102744. DOI: 10.1016/j.pmedr.2024.102744 PMID: 38707250

Pirzade, M., Fazelirad, H., & Noury Ghasem Abadi, R. (2024). The Mediating Role of Metacognition in the Relationship between Dark Triad Personality Traits and Smartphone Addiction among Tehran Universities Students. *Psychological Studies*, 20(2).

Pletzer, J. L., Oostrom, J. K., Bentvelzen, M., & de Vries, R. E. (2020). Comparing domain-and facet-level relations of the HEXACO personality model with workplace deviance: A meta-analysis. *Personality and Individual Differences*, 152, 109539. DOI: 10.1016/j.paid.2019.109539

Pletzer, J. L., Oostrom, J. K., & de Vries, R. E. (2021). HEXACO personality and organizational citizenship behavior: A domain-and facet-level meta-analysis. *Human Performance*, 34(2), 126–147. DOI: 10.1080/08959285.2021.1891072

Polakova, G. (2021). Sales executives' reward attitude survey in the international company and their socio- economic consequences on the sales performance in global markets. SHS Web of Conferences, 92, 03023. DOI: 10.1051/shsconf/20219203023

Primack, B. A., Shensa, A., Sidani, J. E., Whaite, E. O., Lin, L., Rosen, D., Colditz, J. B., Radovic, A., & Miller, E. (2017). Social media use and perceived social isolation among young adults in the US. *American Journal of Preventive Medicine*, 53(1), 1–8. DOI: 10.1016/j.amepre.2017.01.010 PMID: 28279545

Prodanova, J., & Chopdar, P. K. (2023). The interplay of app characteristics and smartphone addiction in mobile shopping behaviour. *International Journal of Consumer Studies*, 48(1), e12992. Advance online publication. DOI: 10.1111/ijcs.12992

Prodanova, J., & Kocarev, L. (2021). Is job performance conditioned by work-from-home demands and resources? *Technology in Society*, 66, 101672. DOI: 10.1016/j.techsoc.2021.101672 PMID: 34840365

Przybylski, A. K., Murayama, K., DeHaan, C. R., & Gladwell, V. (2013). Motivational, emotional, and behavioral correlates of fear of missing out. *Computers in Human Behavior*, 29(4), 1841–1848. DOI: 10.1016/j.chb.2013.02.014

Przybylski, A. K., & Weinstein, N. (2019). Digital screen time limits and young children's psychological well-being: Evidence from a population-based study. *Child Development*, 90(1), e56–e65. DOI: 10.1111/cdev.13007 PMID: 29235663

Przybylski, A. K., & Weinstein, N. (2022). Digital screen time limits and young children's psychological well-being. *Pediatrics*, 149(3), e2021050307.

Radtke, T., Apel, T., Schenkel, K., Keller, J., & Von Lindern, E. (2021). Digital detox: An effective solution in the smartphone era? A systematic literature review. *Mobile Media & Communication*, 10(2), 190–215. DOI: 10.1177/20501579211028647

Rahim, N. A. A., Siah, Y. H., Tee, X. Y., & Siah, P. C. (2021). Smartphone Addiction: Its Relationships to Personality Traits and Types of Smartphone Use. *International Journal of Technology in Education and Science*, 5(1), 128–140. DOI: 10.46328/ijtes.165

Rahman, A. U., Chaudary, A., & Varandani, S. (2022). A rare case of aggressive peripheral T-cell lymphoma-not otherwise specified. *Cureus*, 14(5), e24857. DOI: 10.7759/cureus.24857 PMID: 35702462

Rahman, M. S., Zaman, M. H., Hossain, A., Mannan, M., & Hassan, H. (2019). Mediating effect of employee's commitment on workplace spirituality and executive'ssales performance. *Journal of Islamic Marketing*, 10(4), 1057–1073. DOI: 10.1108/JIMA-02-2018-0024

Rahmillah, F. I., Tariq, A., King, M., & Oviedo-Trespalacios, O. (2023). Evaluating the Effectiveness of Apps Designed to Reduce Mobile Phone Use and Prevent Maladaptive Mobile Phone Use: Multimethod Study. *Journal of Medical Internet Research*, 25, e42541. DOI: 10.2196/42541 PMID: 37643002

Rainie, L., & Wellman, B. (2012). *Networked: The new social operating system*. MIT Press. DOI: 10.7551/mitpress/8358.001.0001

Raj, M., Bhattacherjee, S., & Mukherjee, A. (2018). Usage of online social networking sites among school students of Siliguri, West Bengal, India. *Indian Journal of Psychological Medicine*, 40(5), 452–457. DOI: 10.4103/IJPSYM.IJPSYM_70_18 PMID: 30275621

Raj, R. (2018). *Social Networking Sites addiction among adolescents*. Indian Journal Of Psychiatric Medicine.

Rashid, A. B., & Kausik, M. K. (2024). AI Revolutionizing Industries Worldwide: A Comprehensive Overview of Its Diverse Applications. *Hybrid Advances*, 7, 100277. DOI: 10.1016/j.hybadv.2024.100277

Ratan, Z., Parrish, A., Zaman, S., Alotaibi, M., & Hosseinzadeh, H. (2021). Smartphone Addiction and Associated Health Outcomes in Adult Populations: A Systematic Review. *International Journal of Environmental Research and Public Health*, 18(22), 12257. DOI: 10.3390/ijerph182212257 PMID: 34832011

Rathod, A. S., Ingole, A., Gaidhane, A., & Choudhari, S. G. (2022). Psychological morbidities associated with excessive usage of smartphones among adolescents and young adults: A review. *Cureus*, 14(10). Advance online publication. DOI: 10.7759/cureus.30756 PMID: 36447680

Reer, F., Tang, W. Y., & Quandt, T. (2019). Psychosocial well-being and social media engagement: The mediating roles of social comparison orientation and fear of missing out. *New Media & Society*, 21(7), 1486–1505. DOI: 10.1177/1461444818823719

Reinecke, L., Klimmt, C., Meier, A., Reich, S., Hefner, D., Knop-Huelss, K., Rieger, D., & Vorderer, P. (2018). Permanently online and permanently connected: Development and validation of the Online Vigilance Scale. *PLoS One*, 13(10), e0205384. DOI: 10.1371/journal.pone.0205384 PMID: 30359368

Reis, M., Ramiro, L., Paiva, T., & Gaspar-de-Matos, M. (2021). National Survey on the importance of sleep in the quality of academic life and mental health of college students in Portugal. Sleep Sci, 14, 125–132. doi: .20200090DOI: 10.5935/1984-0063

Reis, M., Matos, M. G., & Ramiro, L. (2019). Worries, mental and emotional health di culties of Portuguese university students. *Advances in Social Sciences Research Journal*, 6, 558–569. DOI: 10.14738/assrj.67.6818

Republic of the Philippines Department of Education. (2003, November 20). *DO 83, s. 2003: Prohibiting students of elementary and secondary schools from using cellular phones and pagers during class hours.* https://www.deped.gov.ph/2003/11/20/do-83-s-2003-reiteration-to-decs-orders-nos-70-s-1999-and-26-s-2000-prohibiting-students-of-elementary-and-secondary-schools-from-using-cellular-phones-and-pagers-during-class-hours

Respondus Monitor. (n.d.). Respondus. https://web.respondus.com/he/monitor

Rhee, L., Bayer, J. B., Lee, D. S., & Kuru, O. (2021). Social by definition: How users define social platforms and why it matters. *Telematics and Informatics*, 59, 101538. DOI: 10.1016/j.tele.2020.101538

Ribble, M. (2015). *Digital citizenship in schools: Nine elements all students should know*. International Society for Technology in Education.

Riehm, K. E., Feder, K. A., Tormohlen, K. N., Crum, R. M., Young, A. S., Green, K. M., & Mojtabai, R. (2019). Associations between time spent using social media and internalizing and externalizing problems among US youth. *JAMA Psychiatry*, 76(12), 1266–1273. DOI: 10.1001/jamapsychiatry.2019.2325 PMID: 31509167

Ríos Ariza, J. M., Matas-Terrón, A., Rumiche Chávarry, R. P., & Chunga Chinguel, G. R. (2021, July 15). Scale for measuring phubbing in Peruvian university students: Adaptation, validation and results of its application. *Journal of New Approaches in Educational Research*, 10(2), 175–189. DOI: 10.7821/naer.2021.7.606

Roberts, J. A., & David, M. E. (2016). My life has become a major distraction from my cell phone: Partner phubbing and relationship satisfaction among romantic partners. *Computers in Human Behavior*, 54, 134–141. DOI: 10.1016/j.chb.2015.07.058

Roberts, J. A., & David, M. E. (2019). The Social Media Party: Fear of Missing Out (FoMO), Social Media Intensity, Connection, and Well-Being. *International Journal of Human-Computer Interaction*, 36(4), 386–392. DOI: 10.1080/10447318.2019.1646517

Roberts, J. A., & David, M. E. (2020). The Impact of Phubbing on Relationships: A Meta-Analytic Review. *Computers in Human Behavior*, 107, 106324.

Roberts, J. A., Pullig, C., & Manolis, C. (2015). I need my smartphone: A hierarchical model of personality and cell-phone addiction. *Personality and Individual Differences*, 79, 13–19. DOI: 10.1016/j.paid.2015.01.049

Robinson, T. E., & Berridge, K. C. (2008). The incentive sensitization theory of addiction: Some current issues. *Philosophical Transactions of the Royal Society of London. Series B, Biological Sciences*, 363(1507), 3137–3146. DOI: 10.1098/rstb.2008.0093 PMID: 18640920

Roethlisberger, C., Gassmann, F., Groot, W., & Martorano, B. (2023). The contribution of personality traits and social norms to the gender pay gap: A systematic literature review. *Journal of Economic Surveys*, 37(2), 377–408. DOI: 10.1111/joes.12501

Room, R., Rehm, J., Trotter, R. T., Paglia, A., & Üstün, T. B. (2001). Cross-cultural views on stigma, valuation, parity, and societal values towards disability. *Disability and Culture: Universalism and Diversity*, 77, 247–291.

Rosen, L. D., Lim, A. F., Carrier, L. M., & Cheever, N. A. (2013). An empirical examination of social networking addiction: The relationship between social networking and depression. *Social Networking*, 2, 1–9.

Rosen, L. D., Whaling, K., Rab, S., Carrier, L. M., & Cheever, N. A. (2013). Is Facebook creating "iDisorders"? The link between clinical symptoms of psychiatric disorders and technology use, attitudes and anxiety. *Computers in Human Behavior*, 29(3), 1243–1254. DOI: 10.1016/j.chb.2012.11.012

Rupp, D. E., & Vodanovich, S. J. (1997). The role of boredom proneness in self-reported anger and aggression. *Journal of Social Behavior and Personality*, 12(4), 925–936.

Rutherford, A. (2011). *ANOVA and ANCOVA: A GLM approach*. John Wiley & Sons. DOI: 10.1002/9781118491683

Ruyandy, R., & Kartasasmita, S. (2021). The Effect of FoMO as a Mediator of Big-Five Personality Relationship with Problematic Internet Use Among Emerging Adulthood. Advances in Social Science, Education and Humanities Research. *Advances in Social Science, Education and Humanities Research*. Advance online publication. DOI: 10.2991/assehr.k.210805.058

Ryan, R. M., & Deci, E. L. (2020, April). Intrinsic and extrinsic motivation from a self-determination theory perspective: Definitions, theory, practices, and future directions. *Contemporary Educational Psychology*, 61, 101860. DOI: 10.1016/j.cedpsych.2020.101860

Ryan, T., Chester, A., Reece, J., & Xenos, S. (2014). The uses and abuses of Facebook: A review of Facebook addiction. *Journal of Behavioral Addictions*, 3(3), 133–148. DOI: 10.1556/JBA.3.2014.016 PMID: 25317337

Ryder, C., Mackean, T., Coombs, J., Williams, H., Hunter, K., Holland, A. J., & Ivers, R. Q. (2020). Indigenous research methodology–weaving a research interface. *International Journal of Social Research Methodology*, 23(3), 255–267. DOI: 10.1080/13645579.2019.1669923

Sabadin, K. (2015). Correlation between the experience of occupational stress and the quality of a relationship from the point of view of women and men.

Sagacious, S. A. S. (1950). 475 Place Names On Scroll In Freedom Crusade Campaign Being Conducted At College.

Sagi, A., & Friedland, N. (2007). The cost of richness: The effect of the size and diversity of decision sets on post-decision regret. *Journal of Personality and Social Psychology*, 93(4), 515–524. DOI: 10.1037/0022-3514.93.4.515 PMID: 17892329

Samaha, M., & Hawi, N. S. (2016). Relationships among smartphone addiction, stress, and anxiety among Lebanese university students. *Social Science Computer Review*, 34(4), 405–419. DOI: 10.1177/0894439315617505

Samaha, M., & Hawi, N. S. (2016). Relationships among smartphone addiction, stress, and anxiety in university students. *Computers in Human Behavior*, 57, 321–325. DOI: 10.1016/j.chb.2015.12.045

Sanchez, Z. M. (2021). Mobile phone addiction, physical fitness, and academic performance in adolescents: A cross-sectional study. *International Journal of Environmental Research and Public Health*, 18(1), 1–15. PMID: 35010261

San-Martín, S., & Jiménez, N. (2023). What colour are you? Smartphone addiction traffic lights and user profiles. *European Journal of Management and Business Economics*, 32(2), 149–167. DOI: 10.1108/EJMBE-02-2021-0069

Santos, A. de A., Torres, M. de S., dos Santos, L. F. N., & Matins, H. de A. (2023). Cultural adaptation and psychometric evidence of the phubbing scale. *Psychological Evaluation, 33,* e3332. https://doi.org/DOI: 10.1590/1982-4327e3332

Sanusi, S. Y., Al-Batayneh, O. B., Khader, Y. S., & Saddki, N. (2022). The association of smartphone addiction, sleep quality and perceived stress amongst Jordanian dental students. *European Journal of Dental Education*, 26(1), 76–84. DOI: 10.1111/eje.12674 PMID: 33527620

Sarkar, S. K., Podder, A., & Roy, P. (2023). An Analysis of the Privacy and Security Related Problem with Social Networks. ESP Journal of Engineering and Technology Advancements (ESP-JETA), 3(4), 37-43.

Sarkar, T., Taneja, N., Jana, P., Gupta, S., Dalal, R., Dasgupta, R., Halder, R., & Adhikary, M. (2018). Effect of mobile phone overuse on health of medical students. *International Journal of Medical Science and Public Health*, 8(1), 91–94. DOI: 10.5455/ijmsph.2019.0516506122018

Schmuck, D. (2020). Does digital detox work? Exploring the role of digital detox applications for problematic smartphone use and well-being of young adults using multigroup analysis. *Cyberpsychology, Behavior, and Social Networking*, 23(8), 526–532. DOI: 10.1089/cyber.2019.0578 PMID: 32354288

Schnelle, C., Baier, D., Hadjar, A., & Boehnke, K. (2021). Authoritarianism beyond disposition: A literature review of research on contextual antecedents. *Frontiers in Psychology*, 12, 676093. DOI: 10.3389/fpsyg.2021.676093 PMID: 34248773

Schroeter, R., Oxtoby, J., Johnson, D., & Steinberger, F. (2015). Exploring boredom proneness as a predictor of mobile phone use in the car. Proceedings of the Annual Meeting of the Australian Special Interest Group for Computer Human Interaction on - OzCHI '15, (December), 465–473. https://doi.org/DOI: 10.1145/2838739.2838783

Schwartz, B., Ward, A., Monterosso, J., Lyubomirsky, S., White, K., & Lehman, D. R. (2002). Maximizing versus satisficing: Happiness is a matter of choice. *Journal of Personality and Social Psychology*, 83(5), 1178–1197. DOI: 10.1037/0022-3514.83.5.1178 PMID: 12416921

Screening for at-risk alcohol use in older adults: What progress have we made? (2015). *Journal of Addictions Nursing, 26*(3), 152–156. DOI: 10.1097/JAN.0000000000000089

Seiffge-Krenke, I., & Klessinger, N. (2000). Long-term effects of avoidant coping on adolescents' depressive symptoms. *Journal of Youth and Adolescence*, 29(6), 617–630. DOI: 10.1023/A:1026440304695

Selvakumar, P. (2023). Novel Drug Target with Diverse Therapeutic Potential in Cancer Therapy. *Pharmacy Times*, 55(1), 11–14.

Selvakumar, P., Mariappan, P., Shunmugam, S., Paul, R., & Jabez, S. (2024). Removal of chemicals from effluent using photobioreactor technology to improve environmental and health impacts. *Zeitschrift für Physikalische Chemie*, 2024(7), 1295–1302. Advance online publication. DOI: 10.1515/zpch-2023-0450

Sengupta, A., & Chaudhuri, A. (2010). Are social networking sites a source of online harassment for teens? Evidence from survey data. *Children and Youth Services Review*, 33(2), 284–290. DOI: 10.1016/j.childyouth.2010.09.011

Sensitivity levels in Respondus Monitor. (n.d.). Respondus. https://web.respondus.com/sensitivity-levels-in-respondus-monitor

Seo, D. G., Park, Y., Kim, M. K., & Park, J. (2016). Mobile phone dependency and its impacts on adolescents' social and academic behaviors: A longitudinal study. *Computers in Human Behavior*, 63, 282–290. DOI: 10.1016/j.chb.2016.05.026

Seo, Y. (2016). Mobile phone dependency, depression, and social behavior in adolescents. *Computers in Human Behavior*, 60, 63–69.

Servidio, R., Griffiths, M. D., & Demetrovics, Z. (2021). Dark triad of personality and problematic smartphone use: A preliminary study on the mediating role of fear of missing out. *International Journal of Environmental Research and Public Health*, 18(16), 8463. DOI: 10.3390/ijerph18168463 PMID: 34444212

Shanmugasundaram, M., & Tamilarasu, A. (2023). The impact of digital technology, social media, and artificial intelligence on cognitive functions: A review. *Frontiers in Cognition*, 2, 1203077. Advance online publication. DOI: 10.3389/fcogn.2023.1203077

Shao, G. (2009). Understanding the appeal of user-generated media: A uses and gratification perspective. *Internet Research*, 19(1), 7–25. DOI: 10.1108/10662240910927795

Shapira, N. A., Goldsmith, T. D., Keck, P. E.Jr, Khosla, U. M., & McElroy, S. L. (2000). Psychiatric features of individuals with problematic internet use. *Journal of Affective Disorders*, 57(1-3), 267–272. DOI: 10.1016/S0165-0327(99)00107-X PMID: 10708842

Sharma, M. K., & Palanhichamy, T. S. (2018, February). Psychosocial interventions for technological addictions. *Indian Journal of Psychiatry*, 60(8, Suppl 4), 5541–5545. DOI: 10.4103/psychiatry.IndianJPsychiatry_40_18 PMID: 29540928

Sharpe, J. P., Martin, N. R., & Roth, K. A. (2011). Optimism and the Big Five factors of personality: Beyond neuroticism and extraversion. *Personality and Individual Differences*, 51(8), 946–951. DOI: 10.1016/j.paid.2011.07.033

Shernoff, D. J., Sannella, A. J., Schorr, R. Y., Sanchez-Wall, L., Ruzek, E. A., Sinha, S., & Bressler, D. M. (2017). (2017, April. Separate worlds: The influence of seating location on student engagement, classroom experience, and performance in the large university lecture hall. *Journal of Environmental Psychology*, 49, 55–64. DOI: 10.1016/j.jenvp.2016.12.002

Shi, Y., Koval, P., Kostakos, V., Goncalves, J., & Wadley, G. (2022). "Instant Happiness": Smartphones as tools for everyday emotion regulation. *International Journal of Human-Computer Studies*, 170, 102958. DOI: 10.1016/j.ijhcs.2022.102958

Shi, Z., Guan, J., Chen, H., Liu, C., Ma, J., & Zhou, Z. (2023). Teacher-student relationships and smartphone addiction: The roles of achievement goal orientation and psychological resilience. *Current Psychology (New Brunswick, N.J.)*, 42(20), 17074–17086. DOI: 10.1007/s12144-022-02902-9

Short, J., Williams, E., & Christie, B. (1976). *The social psychology of telecommunications*. Wiley.

Shoukat, S. (2019). Cell phone addiction and psychological and physiological health in Youngsters. *EXCLI Journal*, 18, 47–50. PMID: 30956638

Singh, R., & Kumari, V. (2021). Loneliness and smartphone addiction among youths: A correlational study. *Indian Journal of Applied Research.* DOI: 10.13140/RG.2.2.25510.24647

Sinha, R. (2011). New findings on biological factors predicting addiction relapse vulnerability. *Current Psychiatry Reports*, 13(5), 398–405. DOI: 10.1007/s11920-011-0224-0 PMID: 21792580

Sinha, R., & Jastreboff, A. M. (2013). Stress as a common risk factor for obesity and addiction. *Biological Psychiatry*, 73(9), 827–835. DOI: 10.1016/j.biopsych.2013.01.032 PMID: 23541000

Sinsomsack, N., & Kulachai, W. (2018). A study on the impacts of Smartphone addiction. *Proceedings of the 19th International Symposium on Management (INSYMA 2022).* DOI: 10.2991/insyma-18.2018.61

Skorek, M., Song, A. V., & Dunham, Y. (2014). Self-esteem as a mediator between personality traits and body esteem: Path analyses across gender and race/ethnicity. *PLoS One*, 9(11), e112086. DOI: 10.1371/journal.pone.0112086 PMID: 25375238

Skowronek, J., Seifert, A., & Lindberg, S. (2023). The mere presence of a smartphone reduces basal attentional performance. *Scientific Reports*, 13(1), 9363. DOI: 10.1038/s41598-023-36256-4 PMID: 37291199

Skues, J. L., Williams, B., & Wise, L. (2012). The effects of personality traits, self-esteem, loneliness, and narcissism on Facebook use among university students. *Computers in Human Behavior*, 28(6), 2414–2419. DOI: 10.1016/j.chb.2012.07.012

Smale, W. T., Hutcheson, R., & Russo, C. J. (2021). Cell phones, student rights, and school safety: Finding the right balance. *Canadian Journal of Educational Administration and Policy*, (195), 49–64. DOI: 10.7202/1075672ar

Smith, C. H., & Borden, K. A. (2020). Introduction to the special issue on substance use disorders and addictions. *Professional Psychology, Research and Practice*, 51(1), 1–4. DOI: 10.1037/pro0000299

Sohn, S., Krasnoff, L., Rees, P., Kalk, N. J., & Carter, B. (2021). The association between smartphone addiction and sleep: A UK cross-sectional study of young adults. *Frontiers in Psychiatry*, 12, 629407. DOI: 10.3389/fpsyt.2021.629407 PMID: 33737890

Sommers, J., & Vodanovich, S. J. (2000). Boredom proneness: Its relationship to psychological- and physical-health symptoms. *Journal of Clinical Psychology*, 56(1), 149–155. DOI: 10.1002/(SICI)1097-4679(200001)56:1<149::AID-JCLP14>3.0.CO;2-Y PMID: 10661377

Soraci, P., Ferrari, A., Antonino, U., & Griffiths, M. D. (2021). Psychometric properties of the Italian version of the smartphone application-based addiction scale (SABAS). *International Journal of Mental Health and Addiction*, 19(4), 1261–1273. DOI: 10.1007/s11469-020-00222-2

Squires, L. R., Hollett, K. B., Hesson, J., & Harris, N. (2020). Psychological Distress, Emotion Dysregulation, and Coping Behaviour: A Theoretical Perspective of Problematic Smartphone Use. *International Journal of Mental Health and Addiction*, 19(4), 1284–1299. DOI: 10.1007/s11469-020-00224-0

Sreenivas, S. (2023, May 5). *Digital detox: What to know*. WebMD. https://www.webmd.com/balance/what-is-digital-detox

Sridhar, S. (2022). Screen Addiction and its impact on adolescents. *Journal of Indian Association for Child and Adolescent Mental Health*.

Sridhar, V., Swaminathan, K., & Patil, D. (2022). Prevalence of screen addiction and its effects on physical and mental health among adolescents in Karnataka, India. *India.Journal of Indian Association for Child and Adolescent Mental Health*, 18(3), 214–221.

Statista. (2022). *Smartphone addiction statistics worldwide*. Retrieved from https://www.statista.com/

Statista. (2024, August 20). *Number of smartphone users worldwide 2014-2029*. https://www.statista.com/forecasts/1143723/smartphone-users-in-the-world

Stead, H., & Bibby, P. A. (2017). Personality, fear of missing out and problematic internet use and their relationship to subjective well-being. *Computers in Human Behavior*, 76, 534–540. DOI: 10.1016/j.chb.2017.08.016

Steinfield, C., Ellison, N. B., & Lampe, C. (2008). Social capital, self-esteem, and use of online social network sites: A longitudinal analysis. *Journal of Applied Developmental Psychology*, 29(6), 434–445. DOI: 10.1016/j.appdev.2008.07.002

Stenseng, F., Falch-Madsen, J., & Hygen, B. W. (2021). Are there two types of escapism? Exploring a dualistic model of escapism in digital gaming and online streaming. *Psychology of Popular Media*, 10(3), 319–329. DOI: 10.1037/ppm0000339

Stevic, A., & Matthes, J. (2023). Co-present smartphone use, friendship satisfaction, and social isolation: The role of coping strategies. *Computers in Human Behavior*, 149, 107960. DOI: 10.1016/j.chb.2023.107960

Stevic, A., Schmuck, D., Thomas, M. F., Karsay, K., & Matthes, J. (2023). Distracted Children? Nighttime Smartphone Use, Children's Attentional Problems, and School Performance Over Time. *The Journal of Early Adolescence*, 44(2), 223–249. DOI: 10.1177/02724316231164734

Stip, E., Thibault, A., Beauchamp-Chatel, A., & Kisely, S. (2016). Internet addiction, hikikomori syndrome, and the prodromal phase of psychosis. *Frontiers in Psychiatry*, 7, 6. DOI: 10.3389/fpsyt.2016.00006 PMID: 26973544

Stone, L. (2007). Continuous partial attention: Reclaiming focus in the digital age. *Harvard Business Review*, 85(3), 9.

Sugumaran, K. M. D., Pandiyarajan, V., Y., B. S., Selvakumar, P., & M., S. (2024). Analysis of Electromyography Signals for Control of Mechanical Prosthesis using Machine Learning Techniques. 2024 2nd International Conference on Intelligent Data Communication Technologies and Internet of Things (IDCIoT), 1059-1067. DOI: 10.1109/IDCIoT59759.2024.10467707

Sultan, A. J. (2014). Addiction to mobile text messaging applications is nothing to "lol" about. *The Social Science Journal*, 51(1), 57-69. DOI: 10.1016/j.soscij.2013.09.003

Sunday, O. J., Adesope, A. O., & Maarhuis, P. L. (2021). The effects of smartphone addiction on learning: A meta-analysis. *Computers in Human Behavior Reports*, 4, 100114. Advance online publication. DOI: 10.1016/j.chbr.2021.100114

Sylwander, K. R. (2019). Affective Atmospheres of Sexualized Hate Among Youth Online: A Contribution to Bullying and Cyberbullying Research on Social Atmosphere. *International Journal of Bullying Prevention : an Official Publication of the International Bullying Prevention Association*, 1(4), 269–284. DOI: 10.1007/s42380-019-00044-4

Takahashi, Y., Shinohara, R., & Ikeda, M. (2020). Cultural Influences on the Relationship between Social Anxiety and SNS Usage in Japan. *Journal of Cross-Cultural Psychology*, 51(1), 56–68.

Talan, T., Doğan, Y., & Kalinkara, Y. (2023). Effects of Smartphone Addiction, Social Media Addiction and Fear of Missing Out on University Students' Phubbing: A Structural Equation Model. *Deviant Behavior*. Advance online publication. DOI: 10.1080/01639625.2023.2235870

Tandon, A., Dhir, A., Almugren, I., AlNemer, G. N., & Mäntymäki, M. (2021). Fear of missing out (FoMO) among social media users: A systematic literature review, synthesis and framework for future research. *Internet Research*, 31(3), 782–821. DOI: 10.1108/INTR-11-2019-0455

Tandon, A., Dhir, A., Talwar, S., Kaur, P., & Mäntymäki, M. (2022). Social media induced fear of missing out (FoMO) and phubbing: Behavioural, relational and psychological outcomes. *Technological Forecasting and Social Change*, 174, 121149. DOI: 10.1016/j.techfore.2021.121149

Tandon, A., Laato, S., Islam, N., & Dhir, A. (2024). Social comparisons at social networking sites: How social Media-induced fear of missing out and envy drive compulsive use. *Internet Research*. Advance online publication. DOI: 10.1108/INTR-10-2022-0770

Tangmunkongvorakul, A. (2020). Cross-cultural comparison of smartphone addiction among adolescents in Japan and Thailand. *PLoS One*, 15(9). PMID: 32898191

Tangmunkongvorakul, A., Musumari, P. M., Tsubohara, Y., Ayood, P., Srithanaviboonchai, K., Techasrivichien, T., Suguimoto, S. P., Ono-Kihara, M., & Kihara, M. (2020). Factors associated with smartphone addiction: A comparative study between Japanese and Thai high school students. *PLoS One*, 15(9), e0238459. DOI: 10.1371/journal.pone.0238459 PMID: 32898191

Tanhan, F., Özok, H. İ., Kaya, A., & Yıldırım, M. (2024, January). Mediating and moderating effects of cognitive flexibility in the relationship between social media addiction and phubbing. *Current Psychology (New Brunswick, N.J.)*, 43(1), 192–203. DOI: 10.1007/s12144-023-04242-8 PMID: 36713623

Tanil, C. T., & Yong, M. H. (2020). Mobile phones: The effect of its presence on learning and memory. *PLoS One*, 15(8), e0219233. DOI: 10.1371/journal.pone.0219233 PMID: 32790667

Tao, S., Wu, X., Wan, Y., Zhang, S., Hao, J., & Tao, F. (2016). Interactions of problematic mobile phone use and psychopathological symptoms with unintentional injuries: A school-based sample of Chinese adolescents. *BMC Public Health*, 16(1), 88. DOI: 10.1186/s12889-016-2776-8 PMID: 26821534

Tao, S., Wu, X., Zhang, Y., Zhang, S., & Tao, F. (2017). E ects of sleep quality on the association between problematic mobile phone use and mental health symptoms in Chinese college students. *International Journal of Environmental Research and Public Health*, 14(2), 1–10. DOI: 10.3390/ijerph14020185

Tarafdar, M., Tu, Q., Ragu-Nathan, B. S., & Ragu-Nathan, T. S. (2007). The impact of technostress on role stress and productivity. *Journal of Management Information Systems*, 24(1), 301–328. DOI: 10.2753/MIS0742-1222240109

Tariq, F. J., & Irfan, A. R. B. (2019). *Cell phone addiction: a rising epidemic*. JPMA.

Tateno, M., Kim, D.-J., Teo, A. R., Skokauskas, N., Guerrero, A. P., & Kato, T. A. (2019). Smartphone addiction in Japanese college students: Usefulness of the Japanese version of the smartphone addiction scale as a screening tool for a new form of internet addiction. *Psychiatry Investigation*, 16(2), 115–120. DOI: 10.30773/pi.2018.12.25.2 PMID: 30808117

Tedone, A. M. (2022). Keeping Up With Work Email After Hours and Employee Wellbeing: Examining Relationships During and Prior to the COVID-19 Pandemic. *Occupational Health Science*, 6(1), 51–72. DOI: 10.1007/s41542-021-00107-3 PMID: 35097187

Terracciano, A., Löckenhoff, C. E., Crum, R. M., Bienvenu, O. J., & Costa, P. T.Jr. (2008). Five-Factor Model personality profiles of drug users. *BMC Psychiatry*, 8(1), 1–10. DOI: 10.1186/1471-244X-8-22 PMID: 18405382

Thelwall, M., & Vis, F. (2017). Gender and image sharing on Facebook, Twitter, Instagram, Snapchat and WhatsApp in the UK. *Aslib Journal of Information Management*, 69(6), 702–720. DOI: 10.1108/AJIM-04-2017-0098

Thomée, S. (2018). Mobile Phone Use and Mental Health: A Review of the Research That Takes a Psychological Perspective on Exposure. *International Journal of Environmental Research and Public Health*, 15(12), 2692. DOI: 10.3390/ijerph15122692 PMID: 30501032

Thomée, S., Härenstam, A., & Hagberg, M. (2011). Mobile phone use and stress, sleep disturbances, and symptoms of depression among young adults—A prospective cohort study. *BMC Public Health*, 11(1), 1–11. DOI: 10.1186/1471-2458-11-66 PMID: 21281471

Thorsteinsson, E. B., & Davey, L. (2014). Adolescents' compulsive Internet use and depression: A longitudinal study. *Open Journal of Depression*, 3(1), 13–17. DOI: 10.4236/ojd.2014.31005

Ting, C. H., & Chen, Y. Y. (2020). Smartphone addiction. In *Adolescent addiction* (pp. 215–240). Elsevier. DOI: 10.1016/B978-0-12-818626-8.00008-6

Topino, E., Gori, A., Jimeno, M. V., Ortega, B., & Cacioppo, M. (2023). The relationship between social media addiction, fear of missing out and family functioning: A structural equation mediation model. *BMC Psychology*, 11(1), 383. Advance online publication. DOI: 10.1186/s40359-023-01409-7 PMID: 37941011

Touitou, Y., & Point, S. (2020). Effects and mechanisms of action of light-emitting diodes on the human retina and internal clock. *Environmental Research*, 190, 109942. DOI: 10.1016/j.envres.2020.109942 PMID: 32758719

Trainor, B. C. (2011). Stress responses and the mesolimbic dopamine system: Social contexts and sex differences. *Hormones and Behavior*, 60(5), 457–469. DOI: 10.1016/j.yhbeh.2011.08.013 PMID: 21907202

Tsitsika, A. (2013). Online social networking and psychosocial functioning in adolescents. *The Journal of Adolescent Health*, 54(2), 207–213. PMID: 23332486

Tsitsika, A. K., Tzavela, E. C., Janikian, M., Ólafsson, K., Iordache, A., Schoenmakers, T. M., Tzavara, C., & Richardson, C. (2014). Online social networking in adolescence: Patterns of use in six European countries and links with psychosocial functioning. *The Journal of Adolescent Health*, 55(1), 141–147. DOI: 10.1016/j.jadohealth.2013.11.010 PMID: 24618179

Turel, O., & Serenko, A. (2012). The benefits and dangers of enjoyment with social networking websites. *European Journal of Information Systems*, 21(5), 512–528. DOI: 10.1057/ejis.2012.1

Turkle, S. (2011). *Alone Together: Why We Expect More from Technology and Less from Each Other*. Basic Books.

Turkle, S. (2015). *Reclaiming conversation: The power of talk in a digital age*. Penguin Press.

Twenge, J. M. (2017). *iGen: Why today's super-connected kids are growing up less rebellious, more tolerant, less happy and completely unprepared for adulthood and what that means for the rest of us*. Simon and Schuster.

Twenge, J. M. (2017). iGen: Why today's super-connected kids are growing up less rebellious, more tolerant, less happy–and completely unprepared for adulthood–and what that means for the rest of us. Atria Books.

Twenge, J. M., & Campbell, W. K. (2018). Associations between screen time and lower psychological well-being among children and adolescents: Evidence from a population-based study. *Preventive Medicine Reports*, 12, 271–283. DOI: 10.1016/j.pmedr.2018.10.003 PMID: 30406005

Twenge, J. M., & Campbell, W. K. (2018). Associations Between Screen Time and Mental Health Among Adolescents. *American Journal of Preventive Medicine*, 54(3), 398–405.

Twenge, J. M., Martin, G. N., & Spitzberg, B. H. (2018). Trends in US adolescents' media use and associations with the incidence of depressive symptoms, suicide-related outcomes, and suicide rates: 1976–2016. *Clinical Psychological Science*, 6(1), 3–17. DOI: 10.1177/2167702617723376

Uğur, N. G., & Koç, T. (2015a, December). Mobile phones as distracting tools in the classroom: College students perspective. *Alphanumeric Journal*, 3(2), 57–64. DOI: 10.17093/aj.2015.3.2.5000145549

Uğur, N. G., & Koç, T. (2015b, July 3). Time for digital detox: Misuse of mobile technology and phubbing. *Procedia: Social and Behavioral Sciences*, 195, 1022–1031. DOI: 10.1016/j.sbspro.2015.06.491

Using smartphones in the classroom. (n.d.). Huddlecam. https://huddlecamhd.com/using-smartphones-in-the-classroom

Usmani, S. S., Sharath, M., & Mehendale, M. (2022). Future of mental health in the metaverse. *General Psychiatry*, 35(4), e100825. DOI: 10.1136/gpsych-2022-100825 PMID: 36189180

Valkenburg, P. M., & Peter, J. (2007). Online communication and adolescent well-being: Testing the stimulation versus the displacement hypothesis. *Journal of Computer-Mediated Communication*, 12(4), 1169–1182. DOI: 10.1111/j.1083-6101.2007.00368.x

Valkenburg, P. M., & Peter, J. (2011). Online communication among adolescents: An integrated model of its attraction, opportunities, and risks. *The Journal of Adolescent Health*, 48(2), 121–127. DOI: 10.1016/j.jadohealth.2010.08.020 PMID: 21257109

Van Den Eijnden, R. J., Geurts, S. M., Ter Bogt, T. F., Van Der Rijst, V. G., & Koning, I. M. (2021). Social Media Use and Adolescents' Sleep: A Longitudinal Study on the Protective Role of Parental Rules Regarding Internet Use before Sleep. *International Journal of Environmental Research and Public Health*, 18(3), 1346. DOI: 10.3390/ijerph18031346 PMID: 33540882

Van der Zee, K., Buunk, B., & Sanderman, R. (1998). Neuroticism and reactions to social comparison information among cancer patients. *Journal of Personality*, 66(2), 175–194. DOI: 10.1111/1467-6494.00008 PMID: 9529662

van Deursen, A. J., Bolle, C. L., Hegner, S. M., & Kommers, P. A. (2015). Modeling habitual and addictive smartphone behavior. *Computers in Human Behavior*, 45, 511–520. DOI: 10.1016/j.chb.2014.12.039

Van Deursen, A. J., & Van Dijk, J. A. (2014). The digital divide shifts to differences in usage. *New Media & Society*, 16(3), 507–526. DOI: 10.1177/1461444813487959

Van Zoonen, W., Sivunen, A., & Rice, R. E. (2020). Boundary communication: How smartphone use after hours is associated with work-life conflict and organizational identification. *Journal of Applied Communication Research*, 48(3), 372–392. DOI: 10.1080/00909882.2020.1755050

Vannucci, A., Flannery, K. M., & Ohannessian, C. M. (2017). Social media use and anxiety in emerging adults. *Journal of Affective Disorders*, 207, 163–166. DOI: 10.1016/j.jad.2016.08.040 PMID: 27723539

Vashishta, R., & Sharma, A. (2017). Impact of Facebook addiction on study habits and academic achievement among adolescents in Agra, India. *India.MEIR Journal of Educational Studies*, 25(1), 66–74.

Vashishtha, S., Ahuja, S., & Sharma, M. (2021). Impact of Facebook Addiction Disorder (fad) on study habits and academic achievement of adolescents. *MIER Journal of Educational Studies Trends & Practices*, 195–207. DOI: 10.52634/mier/2017/v7/i2/1422

Vazire, S. (2014). *A six-day unit lesson plan for high school psychology teachers*. Am Psychol Assoc.

Venkateswaran, P. S. (2011). A study on brand personality dimensions and brand loyalty towards Raymond brand. *Journal of Marketing Communications*, 7(2).

Venkateswaran, P. S., & Tamilselvi, P. (2018). A study on the influence of personality on decision-making. *International Journal of Advance & Innovative Research*, 5(4), 165–170. DOI: 10.2394/7780.5.4.165

Verhoef, P. C., Stephen, A. T., Kannan, P., Luo, X., Abhishek, V., Andrews, M., Bart, Y., Datta, H., Fong, N., Hoffman, D. L., Hu, M. M., Novak, T., Rand, W., & Zhang, Y. (2017). Consumer Connectivity in a Complex, Technology-enabled, and Mobile-oriented World with Smart Products. *Journal of Interactive Marketing*, 40(1), 1–8. DOI: 10.1016/j.intmar.2017.06.001

Vernon, L., & Uink, B. (2017). Early results are in! What are Australians' smartphone habits? Retrieved from https://www.modernlifestudy.com/abc-survey-results

Vigderman, A. (21024, July 24). *The college students guide to data protection & cybersecurity*. Security. https://www.security.org/resources/college-guide-data-cyber-protection

Vijayakumar, G., Rajkumar, M., Rajiv Chandar, N., Selvakumar, P., & Duraisamy, R. (2024). Environmentally friendly TDS removal from waste water by electrochemical ion exchange batch-type recirculation (EIR) technique. *Environmental Science. Water Research & Technology*, 10(4), 826–835. DOI: 10.1039/D3EW00793F

Vossen, G., Schönthaler, F., & Dillon, S. (2017). *The Web at Graduation and Beyond: Business Impacts and Developments*. https://openlibrary.org/books/OL28222685M/The_Web_at_Graduation_and_Beyond

Wacks, Y., & Weinstein, A. M. (2021). Excessive Smartphone Use Is Associated With Health Problems in Adolescents and Young Adults. *Frontiers in Psychiatry*, 12, 669042. DOI: 10.3389/fpsyt.2021.669042 PMID: 34140904

Walker, T. (2013, August 6). Phubbing can be phatal: Staying glued to your smart phone in public isn't just rude, it can also get you killed. *The Independent.*https://www.independent.co.uk/tech/phubbing-can-be-phatal-staying-glued-to-your-smartphone-in-public-isn-t-just-rude-it-can-also-get-you-killed-8749090.html

Walker, M. (2017). *Why we sleep: Unlocking the power of sleep and dreams*. Scribner.

Walther, J. B. (1996). Computer-mediated communication: Impersonal, interpersonal, and hyperpersonal interaction. *Communication Research*, 23(1), 3–43. DOI: 10.1177/009365096023001001

Walther, J. B. (2011). Theories of computer-mediated communication and interpersonal relations. In Knapp, M. L., & Daly, J. A. (Eds.), *The Handbook of Interpersonal Communication* (pp. 443–479). Sage.

Wang, Z., & Tchernev, J. M. (2012). The BMyth^ of media multitasking: reciprocal dynamics of media multitasking, personal needs, and gratifications. Journal of Communication, 62(3, 1 June 2012), 493–513. .DOI: 10.1111/j.1460-2466.2012.01641.x

Wang, H., Hu, J., & Li, Q. (2018). The Neural Correlates of the Relationship Between Social Media Addiction and Emotional Intelligence. *Computers in Human Behavior*, 81, 64–71.

Wang, H., Sourav, M. S. U., Yang, M., & Zhang, J. (2023). Classifying mental disorders through clinicians' subjective approach based on three-way decisions. *Frontiers in Psychology*, 14, 1144826. DOI: 10.3389/fpsyg.2023.1144826 PMID: 37484085

Wang, J. L., Wang, H. Z., Gaskin, J., & Wang, L. H. (2015). The role of stress and motivation in problematic smartphone use among college students. *Computers in Human Behavior*, 53, 181–188. DOI: 10.1016/j.chb.2015.07.005

Wang, M., Xu, Q., & He, N. (2021). Perceived interparental conflict and problematic social media use among Chinese adolescents: The mediating roles of self-esteem and maladaptive cognition toward social network sites. *Addictive Behaviors*, 112, 106601. DOI: 10.1016/j.addbeh.2020.106601 PMID: 32942097

Wang, P., Chen, K., Yang, S., & Lin, P. (2019). Relationship of sleep quality, smartphone dependence, and health-related behaviors in female junior college students. *PLoS One*, 14(4), e0214769. DOI: 10.1371/journal.pone.0214769 PMID: 30943270

Wang, P., Wang, X., Wu, Y., Xie, X., Wang, X., Zhao, F., Ouyang, M., & Lei, L. (2018). Social networking sites addiction and adolescent depression: A moderated mediation model of rumination and self-esteem. *Personality and Individual Differences*, 127, 162–167. DOI: 10.1016/j.paid.2018.02.008

Wang, P., Xie, X., Wang, X., Wang, X., Zhao, F., Chu, X., Nie, J., & Lei, L. (2018). The need to belong and adolescent authentic self-presentation on SNSs: A moderated mediation model involving FoMO and perceived social support. *Personality and Individual Differences*, 128, 133–138. DOI: 10.1016/j.paid.2018.02.035

Wang, P., Xie, X., Wang, X., Zhao, F., Chu, X., & Lei, L. (2017). The Need to Belong and Adolescent Facebook Use: The Mediating Role of Loneliness and Moderating Role of Gender. *Computers in Human Behavior*, 69, 136–141.

Wang, P., Zhao, M., Wang, X., Xie, X., Wang, Y., & Lei, L. (2017). Peer relationship and adolescent smartphone addiction: The mediating role of self-esteem and the moderating role of the need to belong. *Journal of Behavioral Addictions*, 6(4), 708–717. DOI: 10.1556/2006.6.2017.079 PMID: 29254360

Wang, X., Wang, W., Qiao, Y., Gao, L., Yang, J., & Wang, P. (2022). Parental phubbing and adolescents' cyberbullying perpetration: A moderated mediation model of moral disengagement and online disinhibition. *Journal of Interpersonal Violence*, 37(7/8), NP5344–NP5366. DOI: 10.1177/0886260520961877 PMID: 32976063

Wang, X., Xie, X., Wang, Y., Wang, P., & Lei, L. (2017). Partner phubbing and depression among married Chinese adults: The roles of relationship satisfaction and relationship length. *Personality and Individual Differences*, 110, 12–17. DOI: 10.1016/j.paid.2017.01.014

Wang, Y., & Ma, Q. (2024). The impact of social isolation on smartphone addiction among college students: The multiple mediating effects of loneliness and COVID-19 anxiety. *Frontiers in Psychology*, 15, 1391415. Advance online publication. DOI: 10.3389/fpsyg.2024.1391415 PMID: 39105145

Wasie, T. (2024). *Screen to Green: Navigating the Digital Dilemma*. Teshome Wasie.

Watson, R. J., Grossman, A. H., & Russell, S. T. (2016). Sources of social support and mental health among LGB youth. *Youth & Society*, 51(1), 30–48. DOI: 10.1177/0044118X16660110 PMID: 30636819

Watt, J. D., & Vodanovich, S. J. (1992). Relationship between boredom proneness and impulsivity. *Psychological Reports*, 70(3), 688–690. DOI: 10.2466/pr0.1992.70.3.688 PMID: 1620756

Wegmann, E., Billieux, J., & Brand, M. (2021). Internet-use disorders: A theoretical framework for their conceptualization and diagnosis. In *Elsevier eBooks* (pp. 285–305). DOI: 10.1016/B978-0-12-822201-0.00022-8

Wegmann, E., Oberst, U., Stodt, B., & Brand, M. (2017). Online-specific fear of missing out and Internet-use expectancies contribute to symptoms of Internet-communication disorder. *Addictive Behaviors Reports*, 5, 33–42. DOI: 10.1016/j.abrep.2017.04.001 PMID: 29450225

Wegmann, E., Stodt, B., & Brand, M. (2015). Smartphone addiction and stress: A review. *Current Psychiatry Reports*, 17(7), 1–10. DOI: 10.1007/s11920-015-0617-0

Weigel, M. (2022). *The authoritarian personality 2.0* (Vol. 54). The University of Chicago Press Chicago.

Wells, H. L., McClure, L. A., Porter, B. E., & Schwebel, D. C. (2018, February). Distracted pedestrian behavior on two urban college campuses. *Journal of Community Health*, 43(1), 96–102. DOI: 10.1007/s10900-017-0392-x PMID: 28695427

Wenzel, A. (2017). Basic strategies of cognitive behavioral therapy. *Psychiatria Clinica*, 40(4), 597–609. PMID: 29080588

West, R., Ash, C., Dapore, A., Kirby, B., Malley, K., & Zhu, S. (2021). Problematic smartphone use: The role of reward processing, depressive symptoms and self-control. *Addictive Behaviors*, 122, 107015. DOI: 10.1016/j.addbeh.2021.107015 PMID: 34146798

Wikipedia contributors. (2024). *Internet sex addiction*. Wikipedia. https://en.wikipedia.org/wiki/Internet_sex_addiction

Williams, K. D. (2009). Ostracism: A temporal need-threat model. In Zanna, M. P. (Ed.), Advances in experimental social psychology (Vol. 41, pp. 275–314). Elsevier Academic Press. DOI: 10.1016/S0065-2601(08)00406-1

Williams, K. D., & Nida, S. A. (2011). Ostracism: Consequences and coping. *Current Directions in Psychological Science*, 20(2), 71–75. DOI: 10.1177/0963721411402480

Williams, L., & Fudge, T. P. (2020). Pedagogy in a potentially hostile online environment. In Setzekorn, K., Patnayakuni, N., & Burton, T. (Eds.), *Socioeconomics, diversity, and the politics of online education* (pp. 35–49). IGI Global. DOI: 10.4018/978-1-7998-3583-7.ch003

Will, P., Bischof, W. F., & Kingstone, A. (2020, August 5). The impact of classroom seating location and computer use on student academic performance. *PLoS One*, 15(8), e0236131. DOI: 10.1371/journal.pone.0236131 PMID: 32756560

Wilmer, H. H., Sherman, L. E., & Chein, J. M. (2017). Smartphones and Cognition: A Review of Research Exploring the Links between Mobile Technology Habits and Cognitive Functioning. *Frontiers in Psychology*, 8, 605. Advance online publication. DOI: 10.3389/fpsyg.2017.00605 PMID: 28487665

Winters, K. C., Botzet, A., Fahnhorst, T., Arria, A., Dykstra, L. G., & Oliver, J. (2012). Social factors and the addiction syndrome. In *American Psychological Association eBooks* (pp. 229–250). DOI: 10.1037/13751-012

Wolniewicz, C. A., Tiamiyu, M. F., Weeks, J. W., & Elhai, J. D. (2018). Problematic Smartphone Use and Relations with Negative Affect, Fear of Missing Out, and Fear of Negative and Positive Evaluation. *Psychiatry Research*, 262, 618–623. DOI: 10.1016/j.psychres.2017.09.058 PMID: 28982630

Wood, G., Goodyear, V., Adab, P., Al-Janabi, H., Fenton, S., Jones, K., Michail, M., Morrison, B., Patterson, P., Sitch, A. J., Wade, M., & Pallan, M. (2023). Smartphones, social Media and Adolescent mental well-being: The impact of school policies Restricting dayTime use—protocol for a natural experimental observational study using mixed methods at secondary schools in England (SMART Schools Study). *BMJ Open*, 13(7), e075832. DOI: 10.1136/bmjopen-2023-075832 PMID: 37407051

Wood, J. V. (1989). Theory and research concerning social comparisons of personal attributes. *Psychological Bulletin*, 106(2), 231–248. DOI: 10.1037/0033-2909.106.2.231

World Health Organization. (2015). Public Health Implications of Excessive Use of the Internet, Computers, Smartphones and Similar Electronic Devices. In *Meeting Report*. https://iris.who.int/bitstream/handle/10665/184264/9789241509367_eng.pdf

World Health Organization. (2024). *Teens, screens, and mental health*. WHO Europe. Retrieved December 21, 2024, from https://www.who.int/europe/news-room/25-09-2024-teens--screens-and-mental-health

World Health Organization. W. (2024). *Clinical descriptions and diagnostic requirements for ICD-11 mental, behavioural and neurodevelopmental disorders*. World Health Organization.

Wu, W.-Y., & Ke, C.-C. (2015). An online shopping behavior model integrating personality traits, perceived risk, and technology acceptance. *Social Behavior and Personality*, 43(1), 85–97. DOI: 10.2224/sbp.2015.43.1.85

Xiao, T., Jiao, C., Yao, J., Yang, L., Zhang, Y., Liu, S., Grabovac, I., Yu, Q., Kong, Z., Yu, J. J., & Zhang, J. (2021). Effects of basketball and Baduanjin exercise interventions on problematic smartphone use and mental health among college students: A randomized controlled trial. *Evidence-Based Complementary and Alternative Medicine*, 2021(1), 8880716. DOI: 10.1155/2021/8880716 PMID: 33574886

Xie, J., Luo, Y., & Chen, Z. (2022). Relationship between partner phubbing and parent–adolescent relationship quality: A family-based study. *International Journal of Environmental Research and Public Health*, 20(1), 304. DOI: 10.3390/ijerph20010304 PMID: 36612626

Xiong, S., Zhang, A., Zhang, B., & Xu, Y. (2023). Patterns of smartphone addiction in adolescents and their association with multiple ecological factors: A latent profile analysis. *Children and Youth Services Review*, 155, 107223. DOI: 10.1016/j.childyouth.2023.107223

Xu, Q., Li, S., & Yang, L. (2018). Perceived social support and mental health for college students in mainland China: The mediating effects of self-concept. *Psychology Health and Medicine*, 24(5), 595–604. DOI: 10.1080/13548506.2018.1549744 PMID: 30451537

Xu, X.-P., Liu, Q.-Q., Li, Z.-H., & Yang, W.-X. (2022, August 17). The mediating role of loneliness and the moderating role of gender between peer phubbing and adolescent mobile social media addiction. *International Journal of Environmental Research and Public Health*, 19(16), 10176. DOI: 10.3390/ijerph191610176 PMID: 36011810

Y, P. R., Aiswarya, B., & A, J. a. S. (2023). Disruptive charms of wearable technologies: Navigating digital distractions and work performance. *Journal of Information Technology Teaching Cases*. DOI: 10.1177/20438869231203341

Yadav, M. (2021). Correlational study on mobile phone dependence and academic performance. *Journal of Education and Health Promotion.*

Yadav, M. S., Kodi, S. M., & Deol, R. (2021). Impact of mobile phone dependence on behavior and academic performance of adolescents in selected schools of Uttarakhand, India. *Journal of Education and Health Promotion*, 10(1), 327. DOI: 10.4103/jehp.jehp_915_20 PMID: 34761013

Yam, C.-W., Pakpour, A. H., Griffiths, M. D., Yau, W.-Y., Lo, C.-L. M., Ng, J. M., Lin, C.-Y., & Leung, H. (2019). Psychometric testing of three Chinese online-related addictive behavior instruments among Hong Kong university students. *The Psychiatric Quarterly*, 90(1), 117–128. DOI: 10.1007/s11126-018-9610-7 PMID: 30328020

Yam, F. C. (2023). The relationship between partner phubbing and life satisfaction: The mediating role of relationship satisfaction and perceived romantic relationship quality. *Psychological Reports*, 126(1), 303–331. DOI: 10.1177/00332941221144611 PMID: 36461943

Yang, C. C., & Bradford Brown, B. (2016). Online self-presentation on Facebook and self development during the college transition. *Journal of Youth and Adolescence*, 45(2), 402–416. DOI: 10.1007/s10964-015-0385-y PMID: 26534776

Yang, H., Guo, H., Zhu, Z., Yuan, G., Zhang, X., Zhang, K., Lu, X., Zhang, J., Du, J., Shi, H., Jin, G., & Zhang, Z. (2023a). Intervention of Internet Addiction and Smartphone Addiction: An Umbrella Review of Systematic Reviews and Meta-Analyses. *Current Addiction Reports*, 11(1), 125–148. DOI: 10.1007/s40429-023-00536-w

Yang, L., Guo, C., Li, G., Gan, K., & Luo, J. (2023b). Mobile phone addiction and mental health: The roles of sleep quality and perceived social support. *Frontiers in Psychology*, 14, 1265400. Advance online publication. DOI: 10.3389/fpsyg.2023.1265400 PMID: 37809316

Yang, S. Y., Wang, Y. C., Lee, Y. C., Lin, Y. L., Hsieh, P. L., & Lin, P. H. (2022). Does Smartphone Addiction, Social Media Addiction, and/or Internet Game Addiction Affect Youngsters' Interpersonal Interactions? *Healthcare (Basel)*, 10(5), 963. DOI: 10.3390/healthcare10050963 PMID: 35628099

Yao, M.-P., Jia, Z.-B., & Cben, X. (2015). Relationship between boredom proneness and mobile phone dependence in college students [Abstract]. *Chinese Journal of Public Health.*

Yasin, K. (2018, September 29). *I quit social media for 65 weeks. This is what I learned.* Healthline. https://www.healthline.com/health/my-65-week-digital-detox #I-cant-believe-you-blocked-me!

Yi, H., Shin, K., & Shin, C. (2006). Development of the sleep quality scale. *Journal of Sleep Research*, 15(3), 309–316. DOI: 10.1111/j.1365-2869.2006.00544.x PMID: 16911033

Yildiz, M. A. (2017). Emotion regulation strategies as predictors of internet addiction and smartphone addiction in adolescents. *Journal of Educational Sciences and Psychology*, 7(1).

Yilmaz, F. G. K., Ustun, A. B., Zhang, K., & Yilmaz, R. (2023). Smartphone Addiction, Nomophobia, Depression, and Social Appearance Anxiety Among College Students: A Correlational Study. *Journal of Rational-Emotive & Cognitive-Behavior Therapy*, 42(2), 305–321. DOI: 10.1007/s10942-023-00516-z

Yin, L., Feng, J., Hou, W., Wang, P., & Yin, Y. (2024). Smartphones on, humannesses off Phubbing breeds dehumanization via subjectivity uncertainty. *Computers in Human Behavior*, 160, 108378. DOI: 10.1016/j.chb.2024.108378

Young, K. (2017). *Internet addiction test for families (IAT-F).* Stoelting.

Young, K. S., & Rogers, R. C. (1998). The relationship between depression and Internet addiction. *Cyberpsychology & Behavior*, 1(1), 25–28. DOI: 10.1089/cpb.1998.1.25

Zamani, B. E., Abedini, Y., & Kheradmand, A. (2011). Internet addiction based on personality characteristics of high school students in Kerman, Iran. *Addiction & Health*, 3(3–4), 85–91. PMID: 24494121

Zarębska, J., Howis, N., & Barska, M. (2023). Research on students' perception of information technology security: A new era of threats. *Scientific Papers of Silesian University of Technology. Organization & Management / Zeszyty Naukowe Politechniki Slaskiej.Seria Organizacji i Zarzadzanie*, 2023(170), 709–721. DOI: 10.29119/1641-3466.2023.170.43

Zarse, E. M., Neff, M. R., Yoder, R., Hulvershorn, L., Chambers, J. E., & Chambers, R. A. (2019). The adverse childhood experiences questionnaire: Two decades of research on childhood trauma as a primary cause of adult mental illness, addiction, and medical diseases. *Cogent Medicine*, 6(1), 1581447. DOI: 10.1080/2331205X.2019.1581447

Zecca, G., Verardi, S., Antonietti, J.-P., Dahourou, D., Adjahouisso, M., Ah-Kion, J., Amoussou-Yeye, D., Barry, O., Bhowon, U., Bouatta, C., Dougoumalé Cissé, D., Mbodji, M., Meyer de Stadelhofen, F., Minga Minga, D., Ng Tseung, C., Nouri Romdhane, M., Ondongo, F., Rigozzi, C., Sfayhi, N., & Rossier, J. (2013). African cultures and the five-factor model of personality: Evidence for a specific pan-african structure and profile? *Journal of Cross-Cultural Psychology*, 44(5), 684–700. DOI: 10.1177/0022022112468943

Zeelenberg, M. (1999). Anticipated regret, expected feedback and behavioral decision making. *Journal of Behavioral Decision Making*, 12(2), 93–106. DOI: 10.1002/(SICI)1099-0771(199906)12:2<93::AID-BDM311>3.0.CO;2-S

Zepke, N., & Leach, L. (2010). Improving student engagement: Ten proposals for action. *Active Learning in Higher Education*, 11(3), 167–177. DOI: 10.1177/1469787410379680

Zhang, A., Xiong, S., Peng, Y., Zeng, Y., Zeng, C., Yang, Y., & Zhang, B. (2022). Perceived stress and mobile phone addiction among college students: The roles of self-control and security. *Frontiers in Psychiatry*, 13, 1005062. DOI: 10.3389/fpsyt.2022.1005062 PMID: 36465300

Zhang, H., Zhao, G., Meng, S., & Kong, F. (2024). The Impact of Smartphone Deprivation on Attentional Bias in Problematic Smartphone Users: Evidence from Behavioral and Physiological Perspectives. *Computers in Human Behavior*, 161, 108412. DOI: 10.1016/j.chb.2024.108412

Zhang, K., Guo, H., Wang, T., Zhang, J., Yuan, G., Ren, J., Zhang, X., Yang, H., Lu, X., Zhu, Z., Du, J., Shi, H., Jin, G., Hao, J., Sun, Y., Su, P., & Zhang, Z. (2023). A bidirectional association between smartphone addiction and depression among college students: A cross-lagged panel model. *Frontiers in Public Health*, 11, 1083856. Advance online publication. DOI: 10.3389/fpubh.2023.1083856 PMID: 36761134

Zhang, X., Gao, F., Kang, Z., Zhou, H., Zhang, J., Li, J., Yan, J., Wang, J., Liu, H., Wu, Q., & Liu, B. (2022). Perceived academic stress and depression: The mediation role of Mobile phone addiction and sleep quality. *Frontiers in Public Health*, 10, 1–12. DOI: 10.3389/fpubh.2022.760387 PMID: 35145942

Zhang, Y., Han, M., Lian, S., Cao, X., & Yan, L. (2024). How and when is academic stress associated with mobile phone addiction? The roles of psychological distress, peer alienation and rumination. *PLoS One*, 19(2), e0293094. DOI: 10.1371/journal.pone.0293094 PMID: 38346023

Zhang, Y., Li, Y., Xia, M., Han, M., Yan, L., & Lian, S. (2023). The relationship between loneliness and mobile phone addiction among Chinese college students: The mediating role of anthropomorphism and moderating role of family support. *PLoS One*, 18(4), e0285189. DOI: 10.1371/journal.pone.0285189 PMID: 37115749

Zhan, S., Shrestha, S., & Zhong, N. (2022). Romantic relationship satisfaction and phubbing: The role of loneliness and empathy. *Frontiers in Psychology*, 13, 967339. DOI: 10.3389/fpsyg.2022.967339 PMID: 36337547

Zhao, J., Guo, Z., Shi, H., Yu, M., Jiao, L., & Xu, Y. (2023, June). The relationship between parental phubbing and interpersonal aggression in adolescents: The role of rejection sensitivity and school climate. *Journal of Interpersonal Violence*, 38(11/12), 7630–7655. DOI: 10.1177/08862605221145722 PMID: 36632725

Zhao, J., Zhang, S., Jiang, Y., & Liu, Y. (2016). Boredom proneness, impulsivity, and mobile phone addiction among university students. *Chinese Journal of Public Health*.

Zhou, X. (2010). Gratifications, Loneliness, Leisure Boredom and Selfesteem as Predictors of SNS-Game Addiction and Usage Pattern among Chinese College Students, (May), 35. DOI: 10.4018/ijcbpl.2012100103

Zhou, H. L., Jiang, H. B., Zhang, B., & Liang, H. Y. (2021). Social anxiety, maladaptive cognition, mobile phone addiction, and perceived social support: A moderated mediation model. *Journal of Psychology in Africa*, 31(3), 248–253. DOI: 10.1080/14330237.2021.1927354

Zhou, X., & Shen, X. (2024). Unveiling the relationship between social anxiety, loneliness, motivations, and problematic smartphone use: A network approach. *Comprehensive Psychiatry*, 130, 152451. DOI: 10.1016/j.comppsych.2024.152451 PMID: 38237509

Zhou, Y., Li, D., Jia, J., Li, X., Zhao, L., Sun, W., & Wang, Y. (2017). Interparental conflict and adolescent internet addiction: The mediating role of emotional insecurity and the moderating role of big five personality traits. *Computers in Human Behavior*, 73, 470–478. DOI: 10.1016/j.chb.2017.04.012

Zhu, W., Liu, J., Lou, F., Mu, F., & Li, B. (2024, July 26). Influence of smart phone addiction on sleep quality of college students: The regulatory effect of physical exercise behavior. *PLoS One*, 19(7), e0307162. DOI: 10.1371/journal.pone.0307162 PMID: 39058670

Zubair, U., Khan, M. K., & Albashari, M. (2023). Link between excessive social media use and psychiatric disorders. *Annals of Medicine and Surgery (London)*, 85(4), 875–878. DOI: 10.1097/MS9.0000000000000112 PMID: 37113864

Zwahlen, A., Peters, Q., & Mulryan, M. (2023, November 7). *Notifications are taking over the lives of teens*. Mill Valley News. https://www.mvnews.org/notifications-are-taking-over-the-lives-of-teens/

About the Contributors

Harish C. Chandan is an independent Researcher in Business. He was a Professor of Business at Argosy University, Atlanta. He was interim chair of the business program in 2011. He received the President's award for excellence in teaching in 2007, 2008 and 2009. His teaching philosophy is grounded in the learner needs and life-long learning. His research interests include research methods, leadership, marketing, and organizational behavior. He has edited 11 Business reference books, published 23 peer-reviewed articles in business journals and 52 chapters in business reference books. Dr. Chandan has presented conference papers at Academy of Management, International Academy of Business and Management, Southeast Association of Information Systems, and Academy of International Business. Prior to joining Argosy, Dr. Chandan managed optical fiber and cable product qualification laboratories for Lucent Technologies, Bell Laboratories. During his career with Lucent, he had 40 technical publications, a chapter in a book and 5 U.S. patents.

* * *

Jayashree Prabhakar A. A. is working as a Professor in Vels Institution of Science, Technology and Advanced Studies, Department of English, School of Languages, VISTAS, Chennai, since 2013.She has 23 years of teaching experience. She has produced 10 Doctorates.She has published 6 Patents, 5 Books and 75 Research papers . She has participated, presented papers and also chaired sessions in several National and International Conferences and Seminars. She has received 4 Faculty Excellence Awards from VISTAS and 2 Awards from different organisation's. She is the Topper of NPTEL Online Course Technical English for Engineers.

David J. Fudge received an MS in Mathematics with a focus in Statistics from Western Illinois University in 2019. Initially working as a math teacher and tutor, both during graduate school and seasonally at Black Hawk College for its College for Kids program, David now works as a data analyst. As a data analyst, he has worked in fields such as healthcare and survey data. Programming languages and tools primarily employed include Python, R, SQL, and Microsoft Excel.

Tamara Phillips Fudge is a full-time professor in the graduate technology programs at Purdue University Global. She has won fellowships and awards for innovation and teaching, and has taught a wide variety of topics, including web development, human-computer interaction, systems analysis and design, and those featuring documentation, diagramming, problem-solving, and presentation. Her career started with music degrees from Indiana University and Florida State University. She sang opera, oratorio, and in recital; her compositions have been heard on Public Radio, at various universities, and a state choral convention. She taught vocal and choral music, piano, pedagogy, foreign language diction, opera production, music theory, composition, and related courses in the traditional college classroom for 20-odd years. For 7 years, she was a weekend correspondent for the Quad-City Times (Davenport, IA). Following a brief stint as an agent/registered representative selling life and health insurance and variable products, she returned to school with a keen interest in technology and has since distinguished herself in online teaching, coordination of large projects, and curriculum development.

Ridhima Goel is a distinguished research scholar at the Institute of Management Studies and Research, Maharshi Dayanand University, India. She brings a rich interdisciplinary approach to her research, combining her business administration and English literature expertise, with an M.B.A. and an M.A. in English from the same institution. As an educator, she imparts knowledge to postgraduate students, teaching open elective subjects such as Fundamentals of Management and Fundamentals of Marketing. Ridhima has published several research articles in Scopus-indexed and Web of Science journals. Additionally, she has contributed to Scopus-indexed book chapters published by IGI Global. Her research interests encompass human resource management, organizational behavior, and occupational health.

Ruchi Goel holds a Post-Graduate degree in Mass Communication from Kurukshetra University and has successfully cleared the UGC NET in Journalism and Mass Communication. With over 11 years of extensive industry experience in advertising and marketing, Ruchi Goel has worked across diverse platforms, delivering strategic solutions for some of the most prominent brands, including Airtel, Voltas, Hyundai, Philips, Make My Trip, and Nestle. In these roles, Ruchi Goel has been instrumental in developing and executing media and creative strategies, gaining a comprehensive understanding of the industry's nuances and acquiring hands-on expertise in various facets of communication. This rich industry experience has seamlessly transitioned into Ruchi Goel's academic career, where she has built a robust teaching portfolio. With expertise in subjects such as Communication, Media Research, Digital Media Marketing, and Advertising, Ruchi Goel brings a unique combination of practical knowledge and academic insight, offering students an enriched learning experience that bridges the gap between theory and real-world application.

Manzoor Ahmad Khanday is currently working as Assistant Professor at Lovely Professional University, Punjab, India. Department of Mathematics and Statistics, and having more than 8 years of research and teaching experience.

T. C. Manjunath is a distinguished academic and researcher in the field of Computer Science and Engineering. He serves as a Professor in the Department of Computer Science & Engineering at Rajarajeswari College of Engineering, Bangalore. Dr. Manjunath specializes in IoT Cybersecurity and Blockchain Technology and is the Dean of Research and Development at the institution. His expertise and contributions in these cutting-edge areas have significantly advanced academic and research initiatives. He is dedicated to fostering innovation and excellence in technology and is committed to mentoring students and researchers in the rapidly evolving fields of cybersecurity and blockchain.

Utsav Krishan Murari is a gifted writer, dedicated life coach, motivational speaker, passionate educator, and, above all, an exceptional mentor. He holds a doctorate in communication and media studies from the Central University of South Bihar. Graced with a vivid imagination, he is a genuine catalyst for ideas and is always open to trying new things. His one such initiative is Saarthi, which began as Saarthi Entertainment. Saarthi is a Delhi-based creative media production start-up that wants to leave a legacy of artistry in the production industry. Delivering content with a strong emotional connection and the potential to transform the world is what Team Saarthi is all about.

Vishnu Priya N. S. is working as Associate Professor in the Department of English, in the School of Social Sciences & Languages, VIT, Vellore since 2008. She has 22 years of teaching experience. She has produced 2 doctorates and is currently guiding 8 scholars for their doctoral degree. She has published 51 research papers out of which 13 are Scopus indexed. She has translated 2 short stories from Tamil and Telugu into English and has authored 4 short stories. She has received 5 'Best Teacher awards' from different organizations.

Selvakumar P. is currently an Associate Professor in the Department of Science and Humanities at Nehru Institute of Technology, Coimbatore, Tamil Nadu, India. Since 2023, he has served as the Department IQAC Coordinator at the institute. Prior to joining Nehru Institute of Technology, he held positions as an Assistant Professor in the Department of Science and Humanities various engineering colleges in Coimbatore, Tamil Nadu, India, spanning from 2011 to 2023. Dr.P. Selvakumar's academic and research interests lie primarily in the field of phytochemistry. He has made significant contributions to his field, with an impressive record that includes 30 journal publications, 12 patents, and 20 conference papers. Additionally, he has organized 5 seminars and conferences, further demonstrating his commitment to academic and scientific exchange. Throughout his career, Dr. P.Selvakumar has been recognized for his dedication and excellence in teaching, having been honored with several awards, including the Best Teacher Awards. He holds a prominent position in the academic community, contributing actively to research.

Hemlata Parmar is a luminary in the field of computer Science and Engineering. Her Journey is defined by a constellation of achievements from prolific publications and patents to enlightening guest lectures. Yet, her brilliance is matched only by her unwavering commitment to human ethics. With a heart as vast as her intellect, she champions women's empowerment, bridging the gap with empathy and insight. In every endeavor, she embodies the perfect fusion of academic process and compassionate advocacy, inspiring generations to come.

Piyal Roy is an accomplished academician in the field of Computer Science & Engineering. He has completed his BSc in Computer Science, MSc in Computer Science and MTech in Computer Science & Engineering. Currently, he is working as an Assistant Professor at Computer Science & Engineering department at Brainware University, India.

Saptarshi Kumar Sarkar, an Assistant Professor at Brainware University, is committed to academic excellence. He brings extensive knowledge and experience to his students, with research interests spanning artificial intelligence (AI), machine learning (ML), and social networking. His contributions have significantly advanced these fields.

Anupama Sen, an Assistant Professor at Brainware University, is committed to academic excellence. She brings extensive knowledge and experience to her students, with research interests spanning artificial intelligence (AI), machine learning (ML), and social networking. Her contributions have significantly advanced these fields.

Bushra S. P. Singh is an accomplished engineer, professor, researcher, and editor currently serving as an Assistant Professor of Management at GJIMT, Mohali. She has been honored with the Best Paper Award at conferences organized by Panjab University. Dr. Singh has authored over 20 research papers published in prestigious journals and edited books. She is professionally trained in Structural Equation Modelling and is passionate about exploring new techniques in data analysis. Dr. Singh holds a B.Tech in Biotechnology from Thapar University, an MBA in IT & Telecommunication from UIAMS, Panjab University (where she received a Gold Medal), and a Ph.D. in Management as a UGC-Junior Research Fellow from UBS, Panjab University.

Ranjit Singha is a Doctorate Research Fellow at Christ (Deemed to be University) and holds a prestigious membership in the American Psychological Association (APA). With a strong background in Research and Development, he has significantly contributed to various fields such as Mindfulness, Addiction Psychology, Women Empowerment, UN Sustainable Development Goals, and Data Science. With over 15 years of experience in Administration, Teaching, and Research, both in Industry and Higher Education Institutions (HEI), Mr Ranjit has established himself as a seasoned professional. Mr Ranjit is dedicated to research and teaching endeavours, primarily focusing on mindfulness and compassion-based interventions. His work in these areas aims to promote well-being and foster positive change in individuals and communities. ORCID iD: https://orcid.org/0000-0002 -3541-8752.

Jagdeep Singla is presently employed as an Associate Professor at the Institute of Management Studies and Research, Maharshi Dayanand University, India. He had also served as a Professor at HPKV Business School, CUHP, Dharamshala. He has more than 28 years of teaching and industry experience after completing his post-graduation. He has more than 35 research papers/articles to his credit, published in national and international journals of repute. He has supervised 11 Ph.D. His areas of Specialization are Production and Operations Management, Supply Chain Management, Marketing Management, Human Resource Management, and Brand Management.

Sudheer V. N. unfolded his teaching career in 2004 as a Lecturer of English in Science and Arts Degree college and served as an Assistant Professor from 2006 to 2021 in an Engineering College further served as Academic Director for CBSE school till 2022 later serving as an Associate Professor of English in the School of Liberal Studies at CMRUNIVERSITY Bangalore since 2022. He has been guiding 6 research scholars and co-authored 3books, 3 book chapters, 6 patents published,

18 research paper published besides awarded as a National Level Inspirational Professor Award 2024 on the occasion of teachers day by Madras Journal Series Pvt. Ltd. Chennai.

P. S. Venkateswaran is currently working as a Professor in the Department of Management Studies, PSNA College of Engineering & Technology, Dindigul affiliated to Anna University, Chennai where he teaches courses in Advertising, marketing and Research Methods. He has served in various faculty positions from Assistant Professor to Professor in leading Arts & Colleges such as Cherran Arts and Science College, Kangeyam and Sree Saraswathi Thyagaraja College, Pollachi. He received MSc in Physics, an M.B.A., from Bharathiar University and MPhil from Alagappa University Karaikudi. He received his Ph.D in Business Administration from Madurai Kamaraj University, Madurai. He is having twenty two years of teaching and nine years of research & consultancy experience. His research activities include on Branding, Advertising and Digital marketing He conducted more than 90 Entrepreneurship Awareness Camps and trained around 8000 Engineering, Arts and Science College students and motivated them towards entrepreneurship. He also conducted 10 Faculty Development programmes, 10 EDP/WEDP programmes and 7 TEDP programmes. He trained more the 200 women entrepreneurs in Dindigul District.

Mohammad Amin Wani is an Assistant Professor of Psychology with a strong background in teaching, research, and mentorship. He has demonstrated proficiency in implementing engaging teaching strategies that enhance student learning experiences and improve performance. His expertise in research is evident through his mentorship of students in research projects, fostering critical thinking and academic excellence. Dr. Wani actively contributes to the development and enhancement of the psychology curriculum, ensuring its relevance and alignment with industry standards. He provides guidance and support to psychology students, assisting them in navigating academic challenges and exploring career opportunities. His commitment to ongoing professional development through research, conferences, and professional networking keeps him updated on advancements in the field.

Index

A

B

Q

R

S

T

V

www.ingramcontent.com/pod-product-compliance
Lightning Source LLC
LaVergne TN
LVHW080615300926
849162LV00005B/1171